W9-BMH-025

THE AMBASSADORS

AN AUTHORITATIVE TEXT
THE AUTHOR ON THE NOVEL
CRITICISM

SECOND EDITION

W.W. NORTON & COMPANY, INC.
also publishes

THE NORTON ANTHOLOGY OF AMERICAN LITERATURE
edited by Nina Baym et al.

THE NORTON ANTHOLOGY OF CONTEMPORARY FICTION
edited by R. V. Cassill

THE NORTON ANTHOLOGY OF ENGLISH LITERATURE
edited by M. H. Abrams et al.

THE NORTON ANTHOLOGY OF LITERATURE BY WOMEN
edited by Sandra M. Gilbert and Susan Gubar

THE NORTON ANTHOLOGY OF MODERN POETRY
edited by Richard Ellmann and Robert O'Clair

THE NORTON ANTHOLOGY OF POETRY
edited by Alexander W. Allison et al.

THE NORTON ANTHOLOGY OF SHORT FICTION
edited by R. V. Cassill

THE NORTON ANTHOLOGY OF WORLD MASTERPIECES
edited by Maynard Mack et al.

THE NORTON FACSIMILE OF
THE FIRST FOLIO OF SHAKESPEARE
prepared by Charlton Hinman

THE NORTON INTRODUCTION TO LITERATURE
edited by Carl E. Bain, Jerome Beaty, and J. Paul Hunter

THE NORTON INTRODUCTION TO THE SHORT NOVEL
edited by Jerome Beaty

THE NORTON READER
edited by Arthur M. Eastman et al.

THE NORTON SAMPLER
edited by Thomas Cooley

HENRY JAMES

THE AMBASSADORS

AN AUTHORITATIVE TEXT
THE AUTHOR ON THE NOVEL
CRITICISM

SECOND EDITION

Edited by
S. P. ROSENBAUM
UNIVERSITY OF TORONTO

W • W • NORTON & COMPANY • *New York* • *London*

Copyright © 1994, 1964 by W. W. Norton & Company, Inc.

All rights reserved

Printed in the United States of America

Second Edition

The text of this book is composed in Electra
with the display set in Bernhard Modern.
Composition by PennSet, Inc.
Manufacturing by Courier.

Library of Congress Cataloging-in-Publication Data
James, Henry, 1843–1916.
The ambassadors : an authoritative text, the author on the novel, criticism / Henry
James; edited by S. P. Rosenbaum. 2nd ed.
p.   cm. (A Norton critical edition)
Includes bibliographical references.
1. Americans—France—Paris—Fiction. 2. James, Henry, 1843–1916.
Ambassadors. I. Rosenbaum, S. P. (Stanford Patrick), 1929–   . II. Title.
PS2116.A5   1994
813'.4—dc20   93-24724

ISBN 0-393-96314-4

W. W. Norton & Company, Inc., 500 Fifth Avenue, New York, N.Y. 10110
W. W. Norton & Company Ltd., 10 Coptic Street, London WC1A 1PU

1 2 3 4 5 6 7 8 9 0

Contents

Foreword

This revised and expanded Norton Critical Edition of the novel Henry James considered "frankly, quite the best, 'all round,' of all my productions" presents an emended and annotated reprint of the New York Edition text of 1909. It includes the author's preface to that edition as well as the most significant variants from the three earlier versions of *The Ambassadors* that were published in James's lifetime. The importance of these variants and the conditions under which the novel was written and revised—conditions leading to the continuing brouhaha over the order of chapters—are discussed in the editor's rewritten and updated essay on the editions and revisions of *The Ambassadors*. The annotations of the text have been made, as often as possible, by quoting or referring to places in James's other writings where he describes places, people, works, and even a character mentioned in the novel. A map of Strether's Paris has been added, and the original frontispieces to the New York Edition volumes of *The Ambassadors* have now been reproduced in their proper order for the first time, at the beginning of Book First and Book Seventh. The virtually unknown photograph of James preceding the text originally appeared with the fourth serialized installment of the novel. On the cover of this Norton Critical Edition is a reproduction of a painting by Emile Lambinet similar to the one evoked by the novel's hero on pp. 303–4.

The second part of this edition, "The Author on the Novel," contains James's notebook entries on the inspiration for the novel and all the important comments on *The Ambassadors* to be found in his published correspondence. Also included is approximately two-thirds of the long, remarkable preliminary statement of the novel that James composed for his publisher before writing *The Ambassadors*. This statement along with James's letters, notes, and preface constitute an extensive, varied, and illuminating commentary by James on his novel.

Two essays from the previous edition have been replaced by five new pieces in the third part of this edition, which now represents more than seventy years of criticism devoted to *The Ambassadors*. The criticism selected here ranges from evaluations, both favorable and unfavorable, of the novel as a whole through more limited analyses of point of view, style, and imagery to specific discussions of a symbol or the explication of a paragraph; more contemporary essays apply concepts of literary theory to the novel or consider the reading process involved in it. A chronology and an expanded bibliography including an extended list of additional criticism on *The Ambassadors* have also been added.

The first edition of this Norton Critical Edition was completed in 1963. At that time I expressed my gratitude to William M. Sale, Jr., and M. H. Abrams for general counsel, and to my wife Naomi Black for help in collating four editions of *The Ambassadors*. For this revised edition I am also obligated to Susan Dick for her helpful criticism, and to Carol Bemis for her editorial assistance. I am indebted as well to the collection of Lambinet photographs at the Witt Library of the Courtauldt Institute, University of London. And thirty years later I am profoundly grateful that I can still thank my wife for her unfailing advice, assistance, and love.

Toronto   S. P. Rosenbaum
August 1993

Photograph of Henry James accompanying the fourth installment of *The Ambassadors* in the *North American Review*, April 1903.

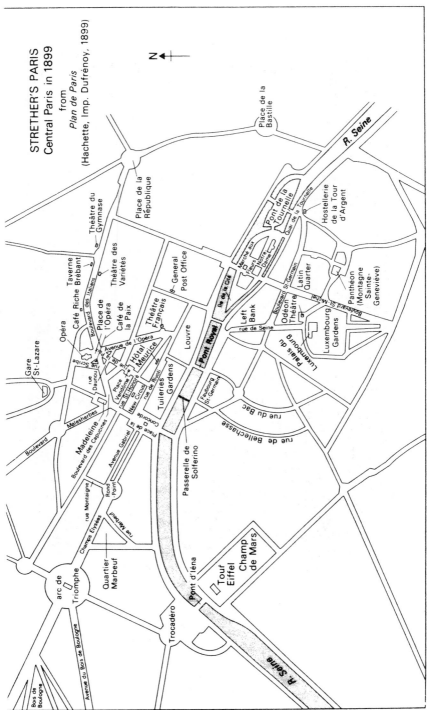

STRETHER'S PARIS
Central Paris in 1899
from
Plan de Paris
(Hachette, Imp. Dufrénoy, 1899)

Reproduced by permission of Alan W. Bellringer from his edition of *The Ambassadors* (London: Allen and Unwin, 1984).

The Text of
THE AMBASSADORS

Contents

Preface

Nothing is more easy than to state the subject of "The Ambassadors," which first appeared in twelve numbers of *The North American Review* (1903) and was published as a whole the same year. The situation involved is gathered up betimes, that is in the second chapter of Book Fifth, for the reader's benefit, into as few words as possible—planted or "sunk," stiffly and saliently, in the centre of the current, almost perhaps to the obstruction of traffic. Never can a composition of this sort have sprung straighter from a dropped grain of suggestion, and never can that grain, developed, overgrown and smothered, have yet lurked more in the mass as an independent particle. The whole case, in fine, is in Lambert Strether's irrepressible outbreak to little Bilham on the Sunday afternoon in Gloriani's garden, the candour with which he yields, for his young friend's enlightenment, to the charming admonition of that crisis. The idea of the tale resides indeed in the very fact that an hour of such unprecedented ease should have been felt by him *as* a crisis, and he is at pains to express it for us as neatly as we could desire. The remarks to which he thus gives utterance contain the essence of "The Ambassadors," his fingers close, before he has done, round the stem of the full-blown flower; which, after that fashion, he continues officiously to present to us. "Live all you can; it's a mistake not to. It doesn't so much matter what you do in particular so long as you have your life. If you haven't had that what *have* you had? I'm too old—too old at any rate for what I see. What one loses one loses; make no mistake about that. Still, we have the illusion of freedom; therefore don't, like me to-day, be without the memory of that illusion. I was either, at the right time, too stupid or too intelligent to have it, and now I'm a case of reaction against the mistake. Do what you like so long as you don't make it. For it *was* a mistake. Live, live!" Such is the gist of Strether's appeal to the impressed youth, whom he likes and whom he desires to befriend; the word "mistake" occurs several times, it will be seen, in the course of his remarks—which gives the measure of the signal warning he feels attached to his case. He has accordingly missed too much, though perhaps after all constitutionally qualified for a better part, and he wakes up to it in conditions that press the spring of a terrible question. *W*ould there yet perhaps be time for reparation?—reparation, that is, for the injury done his character; for the affront, he is quite ready to say, so stupidly put upon it and in which he has even himself had so clumsy a hand?

The answer to which is that he now at all events *sees;* so that the business of my tale and the march of my action, not to say the precious moral of everything, is just my demonstration of this process of vision.

Nothing can exceed the closeness with which the whole fits again into its germ.[1] That had been given me bodily, as usual, by the spoken word, for I was to take the image over exactly as I happened to have met it. A friend had repeated to me, with great appreciation, a thing or two said to him by a man of distinction, much his senior, and to which a sense akin to that of Strether's melancholy eloquence might be imputed—said as chance would have, and so easily might, in Paris, and in a charming old garden attached to a house of art, and on a Sunday afternoon of summer, many persons of great interest being present. The observation there listened to and gathered up had contained part of the "note" that I was to recognise on the spot as to my purpose—had contained in fact the greater part; the rest was in the place and the time and the scene they sketched: these constituents clustered and combined to give me further support, to give me what I may call the note absolute. There it stands, accordingly, full in the tideway; driven in, with hard taps, like some strong stake for the noose of a cable, the swirl of the current roundabout it. What amplified the hint to more than the bulk of hints in general was the gift with it of the old Paris garden, for in that token were sealed up values infinitely precious. There was of course the seal to break and each item of the packet to count over and handle and estimate; but somehow, in the light of the hint, all the elements of a situation of the sort most to my taste were there. I could even remember no occasion on which, so confronted, I had found it of a livelier interest to take stock, in this fashion, of suggested wealth. For I think, verily, that there are degrees of merit in subjects—in spite of the fact that to treat even one of the most ambiguous with due decency we must for the time, for the feverish and prejudiced hour, at least figure its merit and its dignity as *possibly* absolute. What it comes to, doubtless, is that even among the supremely good—since with such alone is it one's theory of one's honour to be concerned—there is an ideal *beauty* of goodness the invoked action of which is to raise the artistic faith to its maximum. Then truly, I hold, one's theme may be said to shine, and that of "The Ambassadors," I confess, wore this glow for me from beginning to end. Fortunately thus I am able to estimate this as, frankly, quite the best, "all round," of all my productions; any failure of that justification would have made such an extreme of complacency publicly fatuous.

I recall then in this connexion no moment of subjective inter-

---

1. For the original "germ," see James's notebook entry on pp. 373–76.

mittence, never one of those alarms as for a suspected hollow beneath one's feet, a felt ingratitude in the scheme adopted, under which confidence fails and opportunity seems but to mock. If the motive of "The Wings of the Dove," as I have noted, was to worry me at moments by a sealing-up of its face—though without prejudice to its again, of a sudden, fairly grimacing with expression—so in this other business I had absolute conviction and constant clearness to deal with; it had been a frank proposition, the whole bunch of data, installed on my premises like a monotony of fine weather. (The order of composition, in these things, I may mention, was reversed by the order of publication; the earlier written of the two books having appeared as the later.) Even under the weight of my hero's years I could feel my postulate firm; even under the strain of the difference between those of Madame de Vionnet and those of Chad Newsome, a difference liable to be denounced as shocking, I could still feel it serene. Nothing resisted, nothing betrayed, I seem to make out, in this full and sound sense of the matter; it shed from any side I could turn it to the same golden glow. I rejoiced in the promise of a hero so mature, who would give me thereby the more to bite into—since it's only into thickened motive and accumulated character, I think, that the painter of life bites more than a little. My poor friend should have accumulated character, certainly; or rather would be quite naturally and handsomely possessed of it, in the sense that he would have, and would always have felt he had, imagination galore, and that this yet wouldn't have wrecked him. It was immeasurable, the opportunity to "do" a man of imagination, for if *there* mightn't be a chance to "bite," where in the world might it be? This personage of course, so enriched, wouldn't give me, for his type, imagination in *predominance* or as his prime faculty, nor should I, in view of other matters, have found that convenient. So particular a luxury—some occasion, that is, for study of the high gift in *supreme* command of a case or of a career —would still doubtless come on the day I should be ready to pay for it; and till then might, as from far back, remain hung up well in view and just out of reach. The comparative case meanwhile would serve—it was only on the minor scale that I had treated myself even to comparative cases.

I was to hasten to add however that, happy stopgaps as the minor scale had thus yielded, the instance in hand should enjoy the advantage of the full range of the major; since most immediately to the point was the question of that *supplement* of situation logically involved in our gentleman's impulse to deliver himself in the Paris garden on the Sunday afternoon—or if not involved by strict logic then all ideally and enchantingly implied in it. (I say "ideally," because I need scarce mention that for development, for expression of

its maximum, my glimmering story was, at the earliest stage, to
have nipped the thread of connexion with the possibilities of the
actual reported speaker. *He* remains but the happiest of accidents;
his actualities, all too definite, precluded any range of possibilities;
it had only been his charming office to project upon that wide field
of the artist's vision—which hangs there ever in place like the white
sheet suspended for the figures of a child's magic-lantern—a more
fantastic and more moveable shadow.) No privilege of the teller of
tales and the handler of puppets is more delightful, or has more of
the suspense and the thrill of a game of difficulty breathlessly
played, than just this business of looking for the unseen and the
occult, in a scheme half-grasped, by the light or, so to speak, by the
clinging scent, of the gage already in hand. No dreadful old pursuit
of the hidden slave with bloodhounds and the rag of association can
ever, for "excitement," I judge, have bettered it at its best. For the
dramatist always, by the very law of his genius, believes not only in
a possible right issue from the rightly-conceived tight place; he
does much more than this—he believes, irresistibly, in the necessary, the precious "tightness" of the place (whatever the issue) on
the strength of any respectable hint. It being thus the respectable
hint that I had with such avidity picked up, what would be the
story to which it would most inevitably form the centre? It is part
of the charm attendant on such questions that the "story," with the
omens true, as I say, puts on from this stage the authenticity of
concrete existence. It then *is*, essentially—it begins to be, though
it may more or less obscurely lurk; so that the point is not in the
least what to make of it, but only, very delightfully and very damnably, where to put one's hand on it.

In which truth resides surely much of the interest of that admirable mixture for salutary application which we know as art. Art
deals with what we see, it must first contribute full-handed that
ingredient; it plucks its material, otherwise expressed, in the garden
of life—which material elsewhere grown is stale and uneatable. But
it has no sooner done this than it has to take account of a *process*—
from which only when it's the basest of the servants of man, incurring ignominious dismissal with no "character," does it, and
whether under some muddled pretext of morality or on any other,
pusillanimously edge away. The process, that of the expression, the
literal squeezing-out, of value is another affair—with which the
happy luck of mere finding has little to do. The joys of finding, at
this stage, are pretty well over; that quest of the subject as a whole
by "matching," as the ladies say at the shops, the big piece with
the snippet, having ended, we assume, with a capture. The subject
is found, and if the problem is then transferred to the ground of
what to do with it the field opens out for any amount of doing.

This is precisely the infusion that, as I submit, completes the strong mixture. It is on the other hand the part of the business that can least be likened to the chase with horn and hound. It's all a sedentary part—involves as much ciphering, of sorts, as would merit the highest salary paid to a chief accountant. Not, however, that the chief accountant hasn't *his* gleams of bliss; for the felicity, or at least the equilibrium, of the artist's state dwells less, surely, in the further delightful complications he can smuggle in than in those he succeeds in keeping out. He sows his seed at the risk of too thick a crop; wherefore yet again, like the gentlemen who audit ledgers, he must keep his head at any price. In consequence of all which, for the interest of the matter, I might seem here to have my choice of narrating my "hunt" for Lambert Strether, of describing the capture of the shadow projected by my friend's anecdote, or of reporting on the occurrences subsequent to that triumph. But I had probably best attempt a little to glance in each direction; since it comes to me again and again, over this licentious record, that one's bag of adventures, conceived or conceivable, has been only half-emptied by the mere telling of one's story. It depends so on what one means by that equivocal quantity. There is the story of one's hero, and then, thanks to the intimate connexion of things, the story of one's story itself. I blush to confess it, but if one's a dramatist one's a dramatist, and the latter imbroglio is liable on occasion to strike me as really the more objective of the two.

The philosophy imputed to him in that beautiful outbreak, the hour there, amid such happy provision, striking for him, would have been then, on behalf of my man of imagination, to be logically and, as the artless craft of comedy has it, "led up" to; the probable course to such a goal, the goal of so conscious a predicament, would have in short to be finely calculated. Where has he come from and why has he come, what is he doing (as we Anglo-Saxons, and we only, say, in our foredoomed clutch of exotic aids to expression) in that *galère*?[2] To answer these questions plausibly, to answer them as under cross-examination in the witness-box by counsel for the prosecution, in other words satisfactorily to account for Strether and for his "peculiar tone," was to possess myself of the entire fabric. At the same time the clue to its whereabouts would lie in a certain *principle* of probability: he wouldn't have indulged in his peculiar tone without a reason; it would take a felt predicament or a false position to give him so ironic an accent. One hadn't been noting "tones" all one's life without recognising when one heard it the voice of the false position. The dear man in the Paris garden was then admirably and unmistakeably *in* one

---

2. Difficult place (*lit.*, galley).

—which was no small point gained; what next accordingly concerned us was the determination of *this* identity. One could only
go by probabilities, but there was the advantage that the most
general of the probabilities were virtual certainties. Possessed of
our friend's nationality, to start with, there was a general probability in his narrower localism; which, for that matter, one had
really but to keep under the lens for an hour to see it give up its
secrets. He would have issued, our rueful worthy, from the very
heart of New England—at the heels of which matter of course a
perfect train of secrets tumbled for me into the light. They had to
be sifted and sorted, and I shall not reproduce the detail of that
process; but unmistakeably they were all there, and it was but a
question, auspiciously, of picking among them. What the "position" would infallibly be, and why, on his hands, it had turned
"false"—these inductive steps could only be as rapid as they were
distinct. I accounted for everything—and "everything" had by
this time become the most promising quantity—by the view that
he had come to Paris in some state of mind which was literally
undergoing, as a result of new and unexpected assaults and in-
fusions, a change almost from hour to hour. He had come with a
view that might have been figured by a clear green liquid, say, in a
neat glass phial; and the liquid, once poured into the open cup of
application, once exposed to the action of another air, had begun
to turn from green to red, or whatever, and might, for all he knew,
be on its way to purple, to black, to yellow. At the still wilder
extremes represented perhaps, for all he could say to the contrary,
by a variability so violent, he would at first, naturally, but have
gazed in surprise and alarm; whereby the *situation* clearly would
spring from the play of wildness and the development of extremes.
I saw in a moment that, should this development proceed both with
force and logic, my "story" would leave nothing to be desired.
There is always, of course, for the story-teller, the irresistible determinant and the incalculable advantage of his interest in the story
as such; it is ever, obviously, overwhelmingly, the prime and
precious thing (as other than this I have never been able to see it);
as to which what makes for it, with whatever headlong energy, may
be said to pale before the energy with which it simply makes for
itself. It rejoices, none the less, at its best, to seem to offer itself
in a light, to seem to know, and with the very last knowledge, what
it's about—liable as it yet is at moments to be caught by us with
its tongue in its cheek and absolutely no warrant but its splendid
impudence. Let us grant then that the impudence is always there
—there, so to speak, for grace and effect and *allure*; there, above
all, because the Story is just the spoiled child of art, and because,
as we are always disappointed when the pampered don't "play up,"

we like it, to that extent, to look all its character. It probably does so, in truth, even when we most flatter ourselves that we negotiate with it by treaty.

All of which, again, is but to say that the *steps*, for my fable, placed themselves with a prompt and, as it were, functional assurance—an air quite as of readiness to have dispensed with logic had I been in fact too stupid for my clue. Never, positively, none the less, as the links multiplied, had I felt less stupid than for the determination of poor Strether's errand and for the apprehension of his issue. These things continued to fall together, as by the neat action of their own weight and form, even while their commentator scratched his head about them; he easily sees now that they were always well in advance of him. As the case completed itself he had in fact, from a good way behind, to catch up with them, breathless and a little flurried, as he best could. *The* false position, for our belated man of the world—belated because he had endeavoured so long to escape being one, and now at last had really to face his doom—the false position for him, I say, was obviously to have presented himself at the gate of that boundless menagerie primed with a moral scheme of the most approved pattern which was yet framed to break down on any approach to vivid facts; that is to any at all liberal appreciation of them. There would have been of course the case of the Strether prepared, wherever presenting himself, only to judge and to feel meanly; but *he* would have moved for me, I confess, enveloped in no legend whatever. The actual man's note, from the first of our seeing it struck, is the note of discrimination, just as his drama is to become, under stress, the drama of discrimination. It would have been his blest imagination, we have seen, that had already helped him to discriminate; the element that was for so much of the pleasure of my cutting thick, as I have intimated, into his intellectual, into his moral substance. Yet here it was, at the same time, just here, that a shade for a moment fell across the scene.

There was the dreadful little old tradition, one of the platitudes of the human comedy, that people's moral scheme *does* break down in Paris; that nothing is more frequently observed; that hundreds of thousands of more or less hypocritical or more or less cynical persons annually visit the place for the sake of the probable catastrophe, and that I came late in the day to work myself up about it. There was in fine the *trivial* association, one of the vulgarest in the world; but which give me pause no longer, I think, simply because its vulgarity is so advertised. The revolution performed by Strether under the influence of the most interesting of great cities was to have nothing to do with any *bêtise*[3] of the

3. Foolishness.

imputably "tempted" state; he was to be thrown forward, rather, thrown quite with violence, upon his lifelong trick of intense reflexion: which friendly test indeed was to bring him out, through winding passages, through alternations of darkness and light, very much *in* Paris, but with the surrounding scene itself a minor matter, a mere symbol for more things than had been dreamt of in the philosophy of Woollett.[4] Another surrounding scene would have done as well for our show could it have represented a place in which Strether's errand was likely to lie and his crisis to await him. The *likely* place had the great merit of sparing me preparations; there would have been too many involved—not at all impossibilities, only rather worrying and delaying difficulties—in positing elsewhere Chad Newsome's interesting relation, his so interesting complexity of relations. Strether's appointed stage, in fine, could be but Chad's most luckily selected one. The young man had gone in, as they say, for circumjacent charm; and where he would have found it, by the turn of his mind, most "authentic," was where his earnest friend's analysis would most find *him*; as well as where, for that matter, the former's whole analytic faculty would be led such a wonderful dance.

"The Ambassadors" had been, all conveniently, "arranged for";[5] its first appearance was from month to month, in the *North American Review* during 1903, and I had been open from far back to any pleasant provocation for ingenuity that might reside in one's actively adopting—so as to make it, in its way, a small compositional law—recurrent breaks and resumptions. I had made up my mind here regularly to exploit and enjoy these often rather rude jolts—having found, as I believed, an admirable way to it; yet every question of form and pressure, I easily remember, paled in the light of the major propriety, recognised as soon as really weighed; that of employing but one centre and keeping it all within my hero's compass. The thing was to be so much this worthy's intimate adventure that even the projection of his consciousness upon it from beginning to end without intermission or deviation would probably still leave a part of its value for him, and *a fortiori*[6] for ourselves, unexpressed. I might, however, express every grain of it that there would be room for—on condition of contriving a splendid particular economy. Other persons in no small number were to people the scene, and each with his or her axe to grind, his or her situation to treat, his or her coherency not to fail of, his or her relation to my leading motive, in a word, to establish and carry on. But Strether's sense of these things, and Strether's only, should avail me for showing them; I should know them but through his

---

4. "There are more things in heaven and earth, Horatio, / Than are dreamt of in our philosophy." *Hamlet* 1. 5. 168–69.
5. For the story of these arrangements, see pp. 355–59.
6. All the more.

more or less groping knowledge of them, since his very gropings would figure among his most interesting motions, and a full observance of the rich rigour I speak of would give me more of the effect I should be most "after" than all other possible observances together. It would give me a large unity, and that in turn would crown me with the grace to which the enlightened story-teller will at any time, for his interest, sacrifice if need be all other graces whatever. I refer of course to the grace of intensity, which there are ways of signally achieving and ways of signally missing—as we see it, all round us, helplessly and woefully missed. Not that it isn't, on the other hand, a virtue eminently subject to appreciation—there being no strict, no absolute measure of it; so that one may hear it acclaimed where it has quite escaped one's perception, and see it unnoticed where one has gratefully hailed it. After all of which I am not sure, either, that the immense amusement of the whole cluster of difficulties so arrayed may not operate, for the fond fabulist, when judicious not less than fond, as his best of determinants. That charming principle is always there, at all events, to keep interest fresh: it is a principle, we remember, essentially ravenous, without scruple and without mercy, appeased with no cheap nor easy nourishment. It enjoys the costly sacrifice and rejoices thereby in the very odour of difficulty—even as ogres, with their "Fee-faw-fum!" rejoice in the smell of the blood of Englishmen.

Thus it was, at all events, that the ultimate, though after all so speedy, definition of my gentleman's job—his coming out, all solemnly appointed and deputed, to "save" Chad, and his then finding the young man so disobligingly and, at first, so bewilderingly not lost that a new issue altogether, in the connexion, prodigiously faces them, which has to be dealt with in a new light—promised as many calls on ingenuity and on the higher branches of the compositional art as one could possibly desire. Again and yet again, as, from book to book, I proceed with my survey, I find no source of interest equal to this verification after the fact, as I may call it, and the more in detail the better, of the scheme of consistency "gone in" for. As always—since the charm never fails—the retracing of the process from point to point brings back the old illusion. The old intentions bloom again and flower—in spite of all the blossoms they were to have dropped by the way. This is the charm, as I say, of adventure *transposed*—the thrilling ups and downs, the intricate ins and outs of the compositional problem, made after such a fashion admirably objective, becoming the question at issue and keeping the author's heart in his mouth. Such an element, for instance, as his intention that Mrs. Newsome, away off with her finger on the pulse of Massachusetts, should yet be no less intensely than circuitously present through the whole thing, should be no less felt as to be reckoned with than the most direct exhibition, the finest portrayal at first hand could make her, such a sign of artistic good faith, I say, once it's unmistakeably there, takes on again an actuality not too much impaired by the comparative dimness of the particular success. Cherished intention too inevitably acts and operates, in the book, about fifty times as little as I had fondly dreamt it might; but that scarce spoils for me the pleasure of recognising the fifty ways in which I had sought to provide for it. The mere charm of seeing such an idea constituent, in its degree; the fineness of the measures taken—a real extension, if successful, of the very terms and possibilities of representation and figuration—such things alone were, after this fashion, inspiring, such things alone were a gage of the probable success of that dissimulated calculation with which the whole effort was to square. But oh the cares begotten, none the less, of that same "judicious" sacrifice to a particular form of interest! One's work should have composition, because composition alone is positive beauty; but all the while—apart from one's inevitable consciousness too of the dire paucity of readers ever recognising or ever missing positive beauty—how, as to the cheap and easy, at every turn, how, as to immediacy and facility, and even as to the commoner vivacity, positive beauty might have to be sweated for and paid for! Once achieved and installed it may always be trusted to make the poor seeker feel he would have blushed to the roots of his hair for failing of it; yet, how, as its virtue can be essentially but the virtue of the whole, the wayside traps set in the interest of muddlement and pleading but the cause of the moment, of the particular bit in itself, have to be kicked out of the path! All the sophistications in life, for example, might have appeared to muster on behalf of the menace—the menace to a bright variety—involved in Strether's having all the subjective "say," as it were, to himself.

Had I, meanwhile, made him at once hero and historian, endowed him with the romantic privilege of the "first person"—the darkest abyss of romance this, inveterately, when enjoyed on the grand scale—variety, and many other queer matters as well, might have been smuggled in by a back door. Suffice it, to be brief, that the first person, in the long piece, is a form foredoomed to looseness, and that looseness, never much my affair, had never been so little so as on this particular occasion. All of which reflexions flocked to the standard from the moment—a very early one—the question of how to keep my form amusing while sticking so close to my central figure and constantly taking its pattern from him had to be faced. He arrives (arrives at Chester) as for the dreadful purpose of giving his creator "no end" to tell about him—before which rigorous mission the serenest of creators might well have quailed. I was far from the serenest; I was more than agitated enough to reflect that, grimly deprived of one alternative or one substitute for "telling," I must address myself tooth and nail to another. I couldn't, save by implication, make other persons tell *each other* about him —blest resource, blest necessity, of the drama, which reaches its effects of unity, all remarkably, by paths absolutely opposite to the paths of the novel: with other persons, save as they were primarily *his* persons (not he primarily but one of theirs), I had simply nothing to do. I had relations for him none the less, by the mercy of Providence, quite as much as if my exhibition *was* to be a muddle; if I could only by implication and a show of consequence make other persons tell each other about him, I could at least make him tell *them* whatever in the world he must; and could so, by the same token—which was a further luxury thrown in—see straight into the deep differences between what that could do for me, or at all events for *him*, and the large ease of "autobiography." It may be asked why, if one so keeps to one's hero, one shouldn't make a single mouthful of "method," shouldn't throw the reins on his neck and, letting them flap there as free as in "Gil Blas" or in "David Copperfield,"[7] equip him with the double privilege of subject and object—a course that has at least the merit of brushing away questions at a sweep. The answer to which is, I think, that one makes that surrender only if one is prepared *not* to make certain precious discriminations.

The "first person" then, so employed, is addressed by the author directly to ourselves, his possible readers, whom he has to reckon with, at the best, by our English tradition, so loosely and vaguely after all, so little respectfully, on so scant a presumption of exposure to criticism. Strether, on the other hand, encaged and provided for as "The Ambassadors" encages and provides, has to keep in view proprieties much stiffer and more salutary than any our straight and credulous gape are likely to bring home to him, has exhibitional conditions to meet, in a word, that forbid the terrible *fluidity* of self-revelation. I may seem not to better the case for my discrimination if I say that, for my first care, I had thus inevitably to set him up a confidant or two, to wave away with energy the custom of the seated mass of explanation after the fact, the inserted block of merely referential narrative, which flourishes so, to the shame of the modern impatience, on the serried page of Balzac, but which seems simply to appal our actual, our general weaker, digestion. "Harking back to make up" took at any rate more doing, as the phrase is, not only than the reader of to-day demands, but

---

7. In both René Lesage's *Gil Blas* (1715–35) and Charles Dickens's *David Copperfield* (1849–50) the central characters tell the stories of their own lives.

than he will tolerate at any price any call upon him either to understand or remotely to measure; and for the beauty of the thing
when done the current editorial mind in particular appears wholly
without sense. It is not, however, primarily for either of these
reasons, whatever their weight, that Strether's friend Waymarsh
is so keenly clutched at, on the threshold of the book, or that no
less a pounce is made on Maria Gostrey—without even the pretext,
either, of *her* being, in essence, Strether's friend. She is the reader's
friend much rather—in consequence of dispositions that make
him so eminently require one; and she acts in that capacity, and
really in that capacity alone, with exemplary devotion, from beginning to end of the book. She is an enrolled, a direct, aid to lucidity; she is in fine, to tear off her mask, the most unmitigated and
abandoned of *ficelles*.[8] Half the dramatist's art, as we well know
—since if we don't it's not the fault of the proofs that lie scattered
about us—is in the use of *ficelles*; by which I mean in a deep dissimulation of his dependence on them. Waymarsh only to a slighter
degree belongs, in the whole business, less to my subject than to my
treatment of it; the interesting proof, in these connexions, being
that one has but to take one's subject for the stuff of drama to
interweave with enthusiasm as many Gostreys as need be.

The material of "The Ambassadors," conforming in this respect exactly to that of "The Wings of the Dove," published just
before it, is taken absolutely for the stuff of drama; so that, availing
myself of the opportunity given me by this edition for some
prefatory remarks on the latter work, I had mainly to make on its
behalf the point of its scenic consistency. It disguises that virtue,
in the oddest way in the world, by just *looking*, as we turn its
pages, as little scenic as possible; but it sharply divides itself, just as
the composition before us does, into the parts that prepare, that
tend in fact to over-prepare, for scenes, and the parts, or otherwise
into the scenes, that justify and crown the preparation. It may
definitely be said, I think, that everything in it that is not scene
(not, I of course mean, complete and functional scene, treating *all*
the submitted matter, as by logical start, logical turn, and logical
finish) is discriminated preparation, is the fusion and synthesis
of picture. These alternations propose themselves all recogniseably,
I think, from an early stage, as the very form and figure of "The
Ambassadors"; so that, to repeat, such an agent as Miss Gostrey,
pre-engaged at a high salary, but waits in the draughty wing with
her shawl and her smelling-salts. Her function speaks at once for
itself, and by the time she has dined with Strether in London and
gone to a play with him her intervention as a *ficelle* is, I hold, ex-

8. Tricks or devices (*lit.*, strings or threads), from the idiom *ficelles du théâtre*, meaning stage
tricks.

pertly justified. Thanks to it we have treated scenically, and scenically alone, the whole lumpish question of Strether's "past," which has seen us more happily on the way than anything else could have done; we have strained to a high lucidity and vivacity (or at least we hope we have) certain indispensable facts; we have seen our two or three immediate friends all conveniently and profitably in "action"; to say nothing of our beginning to descry others, of a remoter intensity, getting into motion, even if a bit vaguely as yet, for our further enrichment. Let my first point be here that the scene in question, that in which the whole situation at Woollett and the complex forces that have propelled my hero to where this lively extractor of his value and distiller of his essence awaits him, is normal and entire, is really an excellent *standard* scene; copious, comprehensive, and accordingly never short, but with its office as definite as that of the hammer on the gong of the clock, the office of expressing *all that is in* the hour.

The *"ficelle"* character of the subordinate party is as artfully dissimulated, throughout, as may be, and to that extent that, with the seams or joints of Maria Gostrey's ostensible connectedness taken particular care of, duly smoothed over, that is, and anxiously kept from showing as "pieced on;" this figure doubtless achieves, after a fashion, something of the dignity of a prime idea: which circumstance but shows us afresh how many quite incalculable but none the less clear sources of enjoyment for the infatuated artist, how many copious springs of our never-to-be-slighted "fun" for the reader and critic susceptible of contagion, may sound their incidental plash as soon as an artistic process begins to enjoy free development. Exquisite—in illustration of this—the mere interest and amusement of such at once "creative" and critical questions as how and where and why to make Miss Gostrey's false connexion carry itself, under a due high polish, as a real one. Nowhere is it more of an artful expedient for mere consistency of form, to mention a case, than in the last "scene" of the book, where its function is to give or to add nothing whatever, but only to express as vividly as possible certain things quite other than itself and that are of the already fixed and appointed measure. Since, however, all art is *expression*, and is thereby vividness, one was to find the door open here to any amount of delightful dissimulation. These verily are the refinements and ecstasies of method—amid which, or certainly under the influence of any exhilarated demonstration of which, one must keep one's head and not lose one's way. To cultivate an adequate intelligence for them and to make that sense operative is positively to find a charm in any produced ambiguity of appearance that is not by the same stroke, and all helplessly, an ambiguity of sense. To project imaginatively, for my hero, a rela-

tion that has nothing to do with the matter (the matter of my subject) but has everything to do with the manner (the manner of my
presentation of the same) and yet to treat it, at close quarters and
for fully economic expression's possible sake, as if it were important and essential—to do that sort of thing and yet muddle
nothing may easily become, as one goes, a signally attaching proposition; even though it all remains but part and parcel, I hasten to
recognise, of the merely general and related question of expressional curiosity and expressional decency.

I am moved to add after so much insistence on the scenic side
of my labour that I have found the steps of re-perusal almost as
much waylaid here by quite another style of effort in the same
signal interest—or have in other words not failed to note how, even
so associated and so discriminated, the finest proprieties and
charms of the non-scenic may, under the right hand for them, still
keep their intelligibility and assert their office. Infinitely suggestive
such an observation as this last on the whole delightful head,
where representation is concerned, of possible variety, of effective
expressional change and contrast. One would like, at such an hour
as this, for critical licence, to go into the matter of the noted inevitable deviation (from too fond an original vision) that the exquisite treachery even of the straightest execution may ever be
trusted to inflict even on the most mature plan—the case being
that, though one's last reconsidered production always seems to
bristle with that particular evidence, "The Ambassadors" would
place a flood of such light at my service. I must attach to my final
remark here a different import; noting in the other connexion I
just glanced at that such passages as that of my hero's first encounter with Chad Newsome, absolute attestations of the non-
scenic form though they be, yet lay the firmest hand too—so far
at least as intention goes—on representational effect. To report at
all closely and completely of what "passes" on a given occasion is
inevitably to become more or less scenic; and yet in the instance I
allude to, *with* the conveyance, expressional curiosity and expressional decency are sought and arrived at under quite another law.
The true inwardness of this may be at bottom but that one of the
suffered treacheries has consisted precisely, for Chad's whole figure
and presence, of a direct presentability diminished and compromised—despoiled, that is, of its *proportional* advantage; so that,
in a word, the whole economy of his author's relation to him has
at important points to be redetermined. The book, however, critically viewed, is touchingly full of these disguised and repaired
losses, these insidious recoveries, these intensely redemptive consistencies. The pages in which Mamie Pocock gives her appointed
and, I can't but think, duly felt lift to the whole action by the so

inscrutably-applied side-stroke or short-cut of our just watching, and as quite at an angle of vision as yet untried, her single hour of suspense in the hotel salon, in our partaking of her concentrated study of the sense of matters bearing on her own case, all the bright warm Paris afternoon, from the balcony that overlooks the Tuileries garden—these are as marked an example of the representational virtue that insists here and there on being, for the charm of opposition and renewal, other than the scenic. It wouldn't take much to make me further argue that from an equal play of such oppositions the book gathers an intensity that fairly adds to the dramatic —though the latter is supposed to be the sum of all intensities; or that has at any rate nothing to fear from juxtaposition with it. I consciously fail to shrink in fact from that extravagance—I risk it, rather, for the sake of the moral involved; which is not that the particular production before us exhausts the interesting questions it raises, but that the Novel remains still, under the right persuasion, the most independent, most elastic, most prodigious of literary forms.[9]

HENRY JAMES.

9. For brief remarks on *The Ambassadors* in James's other prefaces, see Henry James, *Literary Criticism: French Writers, Other European Writers. The Prefaces to the New York Edition*, ed. Leon Edel and Mark Wilson (New York: Library of America, 1984), 1080, 1082, 1096, 1209, 1337.

The Luxembourg Gardens

The Ambassadors

Volume I

Book First

I

Strether's first question, when he reached the hotel, was about his friend; yet on his learning that Waymarsh was apparently not to arrive till evening he was not wholly disconcerted. A telegram from him bespeaking a room "only if not noisy," reply paid, was produced for the enquirer at the office, so that the understanding they should meet at Chester rather than at Liverpool[1] remained to that extent sound. The same secret principle, however, that had prompted Strether not absolutely to desire Waymarsh's presence at the dock, that had led him thus to postpone for a few hours his enjoyment of it, now operated to make him feel he could still wait without disappointment. They would dine together at the worst, and, with all respect to dear old Waymarsh—if not even, for that matter, to himself—there was little fear that in the sequel they shouldn't see enough of each other. The principle I have just mentioned as operating had been, with the most newly disembarked of the two men, wholly instinctive—the fruit of a sharp sense that, delightful as it would be to find himself looking, after so much separation, into his comrade's face, his business would be a trifle bungled should he simply arrange for this countenance to present itself to the nearing steamer as the first "note," of Europe. Mixed with everything was the apprehension, already, on Strether's part, that it would, at best, throughout, prove the note of Europe in quite a sufficient degree.

That note had been meanwhile—since the previous afternoon, thanks to this happier device—such a consciousness of personal freedom as he hadn't known for years; such a deep taste of change and of having above all for the moment nobody and nothing to consider, as promised already, if headlong hope were not too foolish,

---

1. Liverpool, the main seaport in central England, is located on the estuary of the Mersey about fifteen miles from the medieval town of Chester. In an essay on Chester written in 1872, James noted that "it is almost a misfortune perhaps that Chester lies so close to the threshold of England; for it is so rare and complete a specimen of an antique town that the later-coming wonders of its sisters in renown * * * suffer a trifle by comparison, and the tourist's appetite for the picturesque just loses its finer edge." Henry James, "Chester," *The Art of Travel*, ed. Morton Dauwen Zabel (Garden City, N.Y.: Doubleday, 1958), 103.

to colour his adventure with cool success. There were people on
the ship with whom he had easily consorted—so far as ease could
up to now be imputed to him—and who for the most part plunged
straight into the current that set from the landing-stage to London;
there were others who had invited him to a tryst at the inn and had
even invoked his aid for a "look round" at the beauties of Liverpool; but he had stolen away from every one alike, had kept no
appointment and renewed no acquaintance, had been indifferently
aware of the number of persons who esteemed themselves fortunate
in being, unlike himself, "met," and had even independently, un-
sociably, alone, without encounter or relapse and by mere quiet
evasion, given his afternoon and evening to the immediate and the
sensible. They formed a qualified draught of Europe, an afternoon
and an evening on the banks of the Mersey, but such as it was he
took his potion at least undiluted. He winced a little, truly, at the
thought that Waymarsh might be already at Chester; he reflected
that, should he have to describe himself there as having "got in"
so early, it would be difficult to make the interval look particularly
eager; but he was like a man who, elatedly finding in his pocket
more money than usual, handles it a while and idly and pleasantly
chinks it before addressing himself to the business of spending.
That he was prepared to be vague to Waymarsh about the hour
of the ship's touching, and that he both wanted extremely to see
him and enjoyed extremely the duration of delay—these things,
it is to be conceived, were early signs in him that his relation to his
actual errand might prove none of the simplest. He was burdened,
poor Strether—it had better be confessed at the outset—with the
oddity of a double consciousness. There was detachment in his zeal
and curiosity in his indifference.

After the young woman in the glass cage had held up to him
across her counter the pale-pink leaflet bearing his friend's name,
which she neatly pronounced, he turned away to find himself, in
the hall, facing a lady who met his eyes as with an intention suddenly determined, and whose features—not freshly young, not
markedly fine, but on happy terms with each other—came back to
him as from a recent vision. For a moment they stood confronted;
then the moment placed her: he had noticed her the day before,
noticed her at his previous inn, where—again in the hall—she had
been briefly engaged with some people of his own ship's company.
Nothing had actually passed between them, and he would as little
have been able to say what had been the sign of her face for him
on the first occasion as to name the ground of his present recognition. Recognition at any rate appeared to prevail on her own
side as well—which would only have added to the mystery. All she
now began by saying to him nevertheless was that, having chanced

to catch his enquiry, she was moved to ask, by his leave, if it were possibly a question of Mr. Waymarsh of Milrose Connecticut— Mr. Waymarsh the American lawyer.

"Oh yes," he replied, "my very well-known friend. He's to meet me here, coming up from Malvern,[2] and I supposed he'd already have arrived. But he doesn't come till later, and I'm relieved not to have kept him. Do you know him?" Strether wound up.

It wasn't till after he had spoken that he became aware of how much there had been in him of response; when the tone of her own rejoinder, as well as the play of something more in her face— something more, that is, than its apparently usual restless light— seemed to notify him. "I've met him at Milrose—where I used sometimes, a good while ago, to stay; I had friends there who were friends of his, and I've been at his house. I won't answer for it that he would know me," Strether's new acquaintance pursued; "but I should be delighted to see him. Perhaps," she added, "I shall—for I'm staying over." She paused while our friend took in these things, and it was as if a good deal of talk had already passed. They even vaguely smiled at it, and Strether presently observed that Mr. Waymarsh would, no doubt, be easily to be seen. This, however, appeared to affect the lady as if she might have advanced too far. She appeared to have no reserves about anything. "Oh," she said, "he won't care!"—and she immediately thereupon remarked that she believed Strether knew the Munsters; the Munsters being the people he had seen her with at Liverpool.

But he didn't, it happened, know the Munsters well enough to give the case much of a lift; so that they were left together as if over the mere laid table of conversation. Her qualification of the mentioned connexion had rather removed than placed a dish, and there seemed nothing else to serve. Their attitude remained, none the less, that of not forsaking the board; and the effect of this in turn was to give them the appearance of having accepted each other with an absence of preliminaries practically complete. They moved along the hall together, and Strether's companion threw off that the hotel had the advantage of a garden. He was aware by this time of his strange inconsequence: he had shirked the intimacies of the steamer and had muffled the shock of Waymarsh only to find himself forsaken, in this sudden case, both of avoidance and of caution. He passed, under this unsought protection and before he had so much as gone up to his room, into the garden of the hotel, and at the end of ten minutes had agreed to meet there again, as soon as he should have made himself tidy, the dispenser of such good assurances. He wanted to look at the town, and they would forthwith look together. It was almost as if she had been in

2. A town in the west of England noted for its medicinal baths.

possession and received him as a guest. Her acquaintance with the
place presented her in a manner as a hostess, and Strether had a
rueful glance for the lady in the glass cage. It was as if this personage had seen herself instantly superseded.

When in a quarter of an hour he came down, what his hostess
saw, what she might have taken in with a vision kindly adjusted,
was the lean, the slightly loose figure of a man of the middle
height and something more perhaps than the middle age—a man
of five-and-fifty, whose most immediate signs were a marked blood-
less brownness of face, a thick dark moustache, of characteristically
American cut, growing strong and falling low, a head of hair still
abundant but irregularly streaked with grey, and a nose of bold free
prominence, the even line, the high finish, as it might have been
called, of which, had a certain effect of mitigation. A perpetual
pair of glasses astride of this fine ridge, and a line, unusually deep
and drawn, the prolonged pen-stroke of time, accompanying the
curve of the moustache from nostril to chin, did something to complete the facial furniture that an attentive observer would have
seen catalogued, on the spot, in the vision of the other party to
Strether's appointment. She waited for him in the garden, the
other party, drawing on a pair of singularly fresh soft and elastic
light gloves and presenting herself with a superficial readiness which,
as he approached her over the small smooth lawn and in the watery
English sunshine, he might, with his rougher preparation, have
marked as the model for such an occasion. She had, this lady, a
perfect plain propriety, an expensive subdued suitability, that her
companion was not free to analyse, but that struck him, so that his
consciousness of it was instantly acute, as a quality quite new to
him. Before reaching her he stopped on the grass and went through
the form of feeling for something, possibly forgotten, in the light
overcoat he carried on his arm; yet the essence of the act was no
more than the impulse to gain time. Nothing could have been
odder than Strether's sense of himself as at that moment launched
in something of which the sense would be quite disconnected from
the sense of his past and which was literally beginning there and
then. It had begun in fact already upstairs and before the dressing-
glass that struck him as blocking further, so strangely, the dimness
of the window of his dull bedroom; begun with a sharper survey of
the elements of Appearance than he had for a long time been moved
to make. He had during those moments felt these elements to be
not so much to his hand as he should have liked, and then had
fallen back on the thought that they were precisely a matter as to
which help was supposed to come from what he was about to do.
He was about to go up to London, so that hat and necktie might
wait. What had come as straight to him as a ball in a well-played

game—and caught moreover not less neatly—was just the air, in the person of his friend, of having seen and chosen, the air of achieved possession of those vague qualities and quantities that collectively figured to him as the advantage snatched from lucky chances. Without pomp or circumstance, certainly, as her original address to him, equally with his own response, had been, he would have sketched to himself his impression of her as: "Well, she's more thoroughly civilized—!" If "More thoroughly than *whom?*" would not have been for him a sequel to this remark, that was just by reason of his deep consciousness of the bearing of his comparison.

The amusement, at all events, of a civilisation intenser was what —familiar compatriot as she was, with the full tone of the compatriot and the rattling link not with mystery but only with dear dyspeptic Waymarsh—she appeared distinctly to promise. His pause while he felt in his overcoat was positively the pause of confidence, and it enabled his eyes to make out as much of a case for her, in proportion, as her own made out for himself. She affected him as almost insolently young; but an easily carried five-and-thirty could still do that. She was, however, like himself, marked and wan; only it naturally couldn't have been known to him how much a spectator looking from one to the other might have discerned that they had in common. It wouldn't for such a spectator have been altogether insupposable that, each so finely brown and so sharply spare, each confessing so to dents of surface and aids to sight, to a disproportionate nose and a head delicately or grossly grizzled, they might have been brother and sister. On this ground indeed there would have been a residuum of difference; such a sister having surely known in respect to such a brother the extremity of separation, and such a brother now feeling in respect to such a sister the extremity of surprise. Surprise, it was true, was not on the other hand what the eyes of Strether's friend most showed him while she gave him, stroking her gloves smoother, the time he appreciated. They had taken hold of him straightway, measuring him up and down as if they knew how; as if he were human material they had already in some sort handled. Their possessor was in truth, it may be communicated, the mistress of a hundred cases or categories, receptacles of the mind, subdivisions for convenience, in which, from a full experience, she pigeon-holed her fellow mortals with a hand as free as that of a compositor scattering type. She was as equipped in this particular as Strether was the reverse, and it made an opposition between them which he might well have shrunk from submitting to if he had fully suspected it. So far as he did suspect it he was on the contrary, after a short shake of his consciousness, as pleasantly passive as might be. He really had a sort of sense of what she knew. He had quite the sense that she knew things he didn't, and though this was a concession that in general he found not easy to make to women, he made it now as good-humouredly as if it lifted a burden. His eyes were so quiet behind his eternal nippers that they might almost have been absent without changing his face, which took its expression mainly, and not least its stamp of sensibility, from other sources, surface and grain and form. He joined his guide in an instant, and then felt she had profited still better than he by his having been, for the moments just mentioned, so at the disposal of her intelligence. She knew even intimate things about him that he hadn't yet told her and perhaps never would. He wasn't unaware that he had told her rather remarkably many for the time, but these were not the real ones. Some of the real ones, however, precisely, were what she knew.

They were to pass again through the hall of the inn to get into the street, and it was here she presently checked him with a question. "Have you looked up my name?"

He could only stop with a laugh. "Have you looked up mine?"

"Oh dear, yes—as soon as you left me. I went to the office and asked. Hadn't *you* better do the same?"

He wondered. "Find out who you are?—after the uplifted young woman there has seen us thus scrape acquaintance!"

She laughed on her side now at the shade of alarm in his amusement. "Isn't it a reason the more? If what you're afraid of is the injury for me—my being seen to walk off with a gentleman who has to ask who I am—I assure you I don't in the least mind. Here, however," she continued, "is my card, and as I find there's something else again I have to say at the office, you can just study it during the moment I leave you."

She left him after he had taken from her the small pasteboard she had extracted from her pocket-book, and he had extracted another from his own, to exchange with it, before she came back. He read thus the simple designation "Maria Gostrey," to which was attached, in a corner of the card, with a number, the name of a street, presumably in Paris, without other appreciable identity than its foreignness. He put the card into his waistcoat pocket, keeping his own meanwhile in evidence; and as he leaned against the door-post he met with the smile of a straying thought what the expanse before the hotel offered to his view. It was positively droll to him that he should already have Maria Gostrey, whoever she was—of which he hadn't really the least idea—in a place of safe keeping. He had somehow an assurance that he should carefully preserve the little token he had just tucked in. He gazed with unseeing lingering eyes as he followed some of the implications of his act, asking himself if he really felt admonished to qualify it as disloyal. It was prompt, it was possibly even premature, and there was little doubt of the expression of face the sight of it would have produced in a certain person. But if it was "wrong"—why then he had better not have come out at all. At this, poor man, had he already—and even before meeting Waymarsh—arrived. He had believed he had a limit, but the limit had been transcended within thirty-six hours. By how long a space on the plane of manners, or even of morals, moreover, he felt still more sharply after Maria Gostrey had come back to him and with a gay decisive "So now—!" led him forth into the world. This counted, it struck him as he walked beside her with his overcoat on an arm, his umbrella under another and his personal pasteboard a little stiffly retained between forefinger and thumb, this struck him as really, in comparison, his introduction to things. It hadn't been "Europe" at Liverpool, no —not even in the dreadful delightful impressive streets the night before—to the extent his present companion made it so. She hadn't yet done that so much as when, after their walk had lasted a few minutes and he had had time to wonder if a couple of side-long glances from her meant that he had best have put on gloves, she almost pulled him up with an amused challenge. "But why— fondly as it's so easy to imagine your clinging to it—don't you put it away? Or if it's an inconvenience to you to carry it, one's often glad to have one's card back. The fortune one spends in them!"

Then he saw both that his way of marching with his own pre-pared tribute had affected her as a deviation in one of those direc-tions he couldn't yet measure, and that she supposed this emblem to be still the one he had received from her. He accordingly handed her the card as if in restitution, but as soon as she had it she felt the difference and, with her eyes on it, stopped short for apology. "I like," she observed, "your name."

"Oh," he answered, "you won't have heard of it!" Yet he had his reasons for not being sure but that she perhaps might.

Ah it was but too visible! She read it over again as one who had never seen it. " 'Mr. Lewis Lambert Strether' "—she sounded it almost as freely as for any stranger. She repeated however that she liked it—"particularly the Lewis Lambert. It's the name of a novel of Balzac's."[3]

---

3. Honoré de Balzac's *Louis Lambert* (1832–33) concerns a mystical thinker who while trying to write a treatise on the spiritual nature of the will falls first in love with one Mlle. de Villenois and then, just before his marriage, into a cataleptic fit. When Louis Lambert awakes, he has transcended both reality and sanity.

"Oh I know that!" said Strether.

"But the novel's an awfully bad one."

"I know that too," Strether smiled. To which he added with an irrelevance that was only superficial: "I come from Woollett Massachusetts." It made her for some reason—the irrelevance or whatever—laugh. Balzac had described many cities, but hadn't described Woollett Massachusetts. "You say that," she returned, "as if you wanted one immediately to know the worst."

"Oh I think it's a thing," he said, "that you must already have made out. I feel it so that I certainly must look it, speak it, and, as people say there, 'act' it. It sticks out of me, and you knew surely for yourself as soon as you looked at me."

"The worst, you mean?"

"Well, the fact of where I come from. There at any rate it *is*; so that you won't be able, if anything happens, to say I've not been straight with you."

"I see"—and Miss Gostrey looked really interested in the point he had made. "But what do you think of as happening?"

Though he wasn't shy—which was rather anomalous—Strether gazed about without meeting her eyes; a motion that was frequent with him in talk, yet of which his words often seemed not at all the effect. "Why that you should find me too hopeless." With which they walked on again together while she answered, as they went, that the most "hopeless" of her countryfolk were in general precisely those she liked best. All sorts of other pleasant small things— small things that were yet large for him—flowered in the air of the occasion; but the bearing of the occasion itself on matters still remote concerns us too closely to permit us to multiply our illustrations. Two or three, however, in truth, we should perhaps regret to lose. The tortuous wall—girdle, long since snapped, of the little swollen city, half held in place by careful civic hands—wanders in narrow file between parapets smoothed by peaceful generations, pausing here and there for a dismantled gate or a bridged gap, with rises and drops, steps up and steps down, queer twists, queer contacts, peeps into homely streets and under the brows of gables, views of cathedral tower and waterside fields, of huddled English town and ordered English country. Too deep almost for words was the delight of these things to Strether; yet as deeply mixed with it were certain images of his inward picture. He had trod this walk[4] in the far-off time, at twenty-five; but that, instead of spoiling it, only enriched it for present feeling and marked his renewal as a thing substantial enough to share. It was with Waymarsh he should have shared it, and he was now accordingly taking from

---

4. It was possible to walk around Chester on the medieval wall that enclosed the city.

him something that was his due. He looked repeatedly at his watch, and when he had done so for the fifth time Miss Gostrey took him up.

"You're doing something that you think not right."

It so touched the place that he quite changed colour and his laugh grew almost awkward. "Am I enjoying it as much as *that?*"

"You're not enjoying it, I think, so much as you ought."

"I see"—he appeared thoughtfully to agree. "Great is my privilege."

"Oh it's not your privilege! It has nothing to do with *me*. It has to do with yourself. Your failure's general."

"Ah there you are!" he laughed. "It's the failure of Woollett. *That's* general."

"The failure to enjoy," Miss Gostrey explained, "is what I mean."

"Precisely. Woollett isn't sure it ought to enjoy. If it were it would. But it hasn't, poor thing," Strether continued, "any one to show it how. It's not like me. I have somebody."

They had stopped, in the afternoon sunshine—constantly pausing, in their stroll, for the sharper sense of what they saw—and Strether rested on one of the high sides of the old stony groove of the little rampart. He leaned back on this support with his face to the tower of the cathedral, now admirably commanded by their station, the high red-brown mass, square and subordinately spired and crocketed, retouched and restored, but charming to his long-sealed eyes and with the first swallows of the year weaving their flight all round it. Miss Gostrey lingered near him, full of an air, to which she more and more justified her right, of understanding the effect of things. She quite concurred. "You've indeed somebody." And she added: "I wish you *would* let me show you how!"

"Oh I'm afraid of you!" he cheerfully pleaded.

She kept on him a moment, through her glasses and through his own, a certain pleasant pointedness. "Ah no, you're not! You're not in the least, thank goodness! If you had been we shouldn't so soon have found ourselves here together. I think," she comfortably concluded, "you trust me."

"I think I do!—but that's exactly what I'm afraid of. I shouldn't mind if I didn't. It's falling thus in twenty minutes so utterly into your hands. I dare say," Strether continued, "it's a sort of thing you're thoroughly familiar with; but nothing more extraordinary has ever happened to me."

She watched him with all her kindness. "That means simply that you've recognised me—which *is* rather beautiful and rare. You see what I am." As on this, however, he protested, with a good-humoured headshake, a resignation of any such claim, she had a moment of explanation. "If you'll only come on further as you *have* come you'll at any rate make out. My own fate has been too many for me, and I've succumbed to it. I'm a general guide—to 'Europe,' don't you know? I wait for people—I put them through. I pick them up—I set them down. I'm a sort of superior 'courier-maid.' I'm a companion at large. I take people, as I've told you, about. I never sought it—it has come to me. It has been my fate, and one's fate one accepts. It's a dreadful thing to have to say, in so wicked a world, but I verily believe that, such as you see me, there's nothing I don't know. I know all the shops and the prices—but I know worse things still. I bear on my back the huge load of our national consciousness, or, in other words—for it comes to that—of our nation itself. Of what is our nation composed but of the men and women individually on my shoulders? I don't do it, you know, for any particular advantage. I don't do it, for instance—some people do, you know—for money."

Strether could only listen and wonder and weigh his chance. "And yet, affected as you are then to so many of your clients, you can scarcely be said to do it for love." He waited a moment. "How do we reward you?"

She had her own hesitation, but "You don't!" she finally returned, setting him again in motion. They went on, but in a few minutes, though while still thinking over what she had said, he once more took out his watch; mechanically, unconsciously and as if made nervous by the mere exhilaration of what struck him as her strange and cynical wit. He looked at the hour without seeing it, and then, on something again said by his companion, had another pause. "You're really in terror of him."

He smiled a smile that he almost felt to be sickly. "Now you can see why I'm afraid of you."

"Because I've such illuminations? Why they're all for your help! It's what I told you," she added, "just now. You feel as if this were wrong."

He fell back once more, settling himself against the parapet as if to hear more about it. "Then get me out!"

Her face fairly brightened for the joy of the appeal, but, as if it were a question of immediate action, she visibly considered. "Out of waiting for him?—of seeing him at all?"

"Oh no—not that," said poor Strether, looking grave. "I've got to wait for him—and I want very much to see him. But out of the terror. You did put your finger on it a few minutes ago. It's general, but it avails itself of particular occasions. That's what it's doing for me now. I'm always considering something else; something else, I mean, than the thing of the moment. The obsession of the other thing is the terror. I'm considering at present for instance something else than *you*."

She listened with charming earnestness. "Oh you oughtn't to do that!"

"It's what I admit. Make it then impossible."

She continued to think. "Is it really an 'order' from you?—that I shall take the job? *Will* you give yourself up?"

Poor Strether heaved his sigh. "If I only could! But that's the deuce of it—that I never can. No—I can't."

She wasn't, however, discouraged. "But you want to at least?"

"Oh unspeakably!"

"Ah then, if you'll try!"—and she took over the job, as she had called it, on the spot. "Trust me!" she exclaimed; and the action of this, as they retraced their steps, was presently to make him pass his hand into her arm in the manner of a benign dependent paternal old person who wishes to be "nice" to a younger one. If he drew it out again indeed as they approached the inn this may have been because, after more talk had passed between them, the relation of age, or at least of experience—which, for that matter, had already played to and fro with some freedom—affected him as incurring a readjustment. It was at all events perhaps lucky that they arrived in sufficiently separate fashion within range of the hotel-door. The young lady they had left in the glass cage watched as if she had come to await them on the threshold. At her side stood a person equally interested, by his attitude, in their return, and the effect of the sight of whom was instantly to determine for Strether another of those responsive arrests that we have had so repeatedly to note. He left it to Miss Gostrey to name, with the fine full bravado, as it almost struck him, of her "Mr. Waymarsh!" what was to have been, what—he more than ever felt as his short stare of suspended welcome took things in—would have been, but for herself, his doom. It was already upon him even at that distance—Mr. Waymarsh was for *his* part joyless.

II

He had none the less to confess to this friend that evening that he knew almost nothing about her, and it was a deficiency that Waymarsh, even with his memory refreshed by contact, by her own prompt and lucid allusions and enquiries, by their having publicly partaken of dinner in her company, and by another stroll, to which she was not a stranger, out into the town to look at the cathedral by moonlight—it was a blank that the resident of Milrose, though admitting acquaintance with the Munsters, professed himself unable to fill. He had no recollection of Miss Gostrey, and two or three questions that she put to him about those members of his circle had, to Strether's observation, the same effect he himself had already more directly felt—the effect of appearing to place all knowledge, for the time, on this original woman's side. It interested

him indeed to mark the limits of any such relation for her with his
friend as there could possibly be a question of, and it particularly
struck him that they were to be marked altogether in Waymarsh's
quarter. This added to his own sense of having gone far with her—
gave him an early illustration of a much shorter course. There was
a certitude he immediately grasped—a conviction that Waymarsh
would quite fail, as it were, and on whatever degree of acquaintance,
to profit by her.

There had been after the first interchange among the three a
talk of some five minutes in the hall, and then the two men had
adjourned to the garden, Miss Gostrey for the time disappearing.
Strether in due course accompanied his friend to the room he had
bespoken and had, before going out, scrupulously visited; where at
the end of another half-hour he had no less discreetly left him. On
leaving him he repaired straight to his own room, but with the
prompt effect of feeling the compass of that chamber resented by
his condition. There he enjoyed at once the first consequence of
their reunion. A place was too small for him after it that had
seemed large enough before. He had awaited it with something
he would have been sorry, have been almost ashamed not to
recognise as emotion, yet with a tacit assumption at the same time
that emotion would in the event find itself relieved. The actual
oddity was that he was only more excited; and his excitement—
to which indeed he would have found it difficult instantly to give
a name—brought him once more downstairs and caused him for
some minutes vaguely to wander. He went once more to the garden;
he looked into the public room, found Miss Gostrey writing letters
and backed out; he roamed, fidgeted and wasted time; but he was to
have his more intimate session with his friend before the evening
closed.

It was late—not till Strether had spent an hour upstairs with him
—that this subject consented to betake himself to doubtful rest.
Dinner and the subsequent stroll by moonlight—a dream, on
Strether's part, of romantic effects rather prosaically merged in a
mere missing of thicker coats—had measurably intervened, and
this midnight conference was the result of Waymarsh's having
(when they were free, as he put it, of their fashionable friend)
found the smoking-room not quite what he wanted, and yet bed
what he wanted less. His most frequent form of words was that
he knew himself, and they were applied on this occasion to his
certainty of not sleeping. He knew himself well enough to know
that he should have a night of prowling unless he should succeed,
as a preliminary, in getting prodigiously tired. If the effort directed
to this end involved till a late hour the presence of Strether—
consisted, that is, in the detention of the latter for full discourse

—there was yet an impression of minor discipline involved for our friend in the picture Waymarsh made as he sat in trousers and shirt on the edge of his couch. With his long legs extended and his large back much bent, he nursed alternately, for an almost incredible time, his elbows and his beard. He struck his visitor as extremely, as almost wilfully uncomfortable; yet what had this been for Strether, from that first glimpse of him disconcerted in the porch of the hotel, but the predominant note? The discomfort was in a manner contagious, as well as also in a manner inconsequent and unfounded; the visitor felt that unless he should get used to it —or unless Waymarsh himself should—it would constitute a menace for his own prepared, his own already confirmed, consciousness of the agreeable. On their first going up together to the room Strether had selected for him Waymarsh had looked it over in silence and with a sigh that represented for his companion, if not the habit of disapprobation, at least the despair of felicity; and this look had recurred to Strether as the key of much he had since observed. "Europe," he had begun to gather from these things, had up to now rather failed of its message to him; he hadn't got into tune with it and had at the end of three months almost renounced any such expectation.

He really appeared at present to insist on that by just perching there with the gas in his eyes. This of itself somehow conveyed the futility of single rectifications in a multiform failure. He had a large handsome head and a large sallow seamed face—a striking significant physiognomic total, the upper range of which, the great political brow, the thick loose hair, the dark fuliginous eyes, recalled even to a generation whose standard had dreadfully deviated the impressive image, familiar by engravings and busts, of some great national worthy of the earlier part of the mid-century. He was of the personal type—and it was an element in the power and promise that in their early time Strether had found in him—of the American statesman, the statesman trained in "Congressional halls," of an elder day. The legend had been in later years that as the lower part of his face, which was weak, and slightly crooked, spoiled the likeness, this was the real reason for the growth of his beard, which might have seemed to spoil it for those not in the secret. He shook his mane; he fixed, with his admirable eyes, his auditor or his observer; he wore no glasses and had a way, partly formidable, yet also partly encouraging, as from a representative to a constituent, of looking very hard at those who approached him. He met you as if you had knocked and he had bidden you enter. Strether, who hadn't seen him for so long an interval, apprehended him now with a freshness of taste, and had perhaps never done him such ideal justice. The head was bigger, the eyes finer, than they need have been for the career; but that only meant, after all, that the career was itself expressive. What it expressed at midnight in the gas-glaring bedroom at Chester was that the subject of it had, at the end of years, barely escaped, by flight in time, a general nervous collapse. But this very proof of the full life, as the full life was understood at Milrose, would have made to Strether's imagination an element in which Waymarsh could have floated easily had he only consented to float. Alas nothing so little resembled floating as the rigour with which, on the edge of his bed, he hugged his posture of prolonged impermanence. It suggested to his comrade something that always, when kept up, worried him—a person established in a railway-coach with a forward inclination. It represented the angle at which poor Waymarsh was to sit through the ordeal of Europe.

Thanks to the stress of occupation, the strain of professions, the absorption and embarrassment of each, they had not, at home, during years before this sudden brief and almost bewildering reign of comparative ease, found so much as a day for a meeting; a fact that was in some degree an explanation of the sharpness with which most of his friend's features stood out to Strether. Those he had lost sight of since the early time came back to him; others that it was never possible to forget struck him now as sitting, clustered and expectant, like a somewhat defiant family-group, on the door-step of their residence. The room was narrow for its length, and the occupant of the bed thrust so far a pair of slippered feet that the visitor had almost to step over them in his recurrent rebounds from his chair to fidget back and forth. There were marks the friends made on things to talk about, and on things not to, and one of the latter in particular fell like the tap of chalk on the blackboard. Married at thirty, Waymarsh had not lived with his wife for fifteen years, and it came up vividly between them in the glare of the gas that Strether wasn't to ask about her. He knew they were still separate and that she lived at hotels, travelled in Europe, painted her face and wrote her husband abusive letters, of not one of which, to a certainty, that sufferer spared himself the perusal; but he respected without difficulty the cold twilight that had settled on this side of his companion's life. It was a province in which mystery reigned and as to which Waymarsh had never spoken the informing word. Strether, who wanted to do him the highest justice wherever he *could* do it, singularly admired him for the dignity of this reserve, and even counted it as one of the grounds —grounds all handled and numbered—for ranking him, in the range of their acquaintance, as a success. He *was* a success, Way-marsh, in spite of overwork, or prostration, of sensible shrinkage, of his wife's letters and of his not liking Europe. Strether would have reckoned his own career less futile had he been able to put into it anything so handsome as so much fine silence. One might one's self easily have left Mrs. Waymarsh; and one would assuredly have paid one's tribute to the ideal in covering with that attitude the derision of having been left by her. Her husband had held his tongue and had made a large income; and these were in especial the achievements as to which Strether envied him. Our friend had had indeed on his side too a subject for silence, which he fully appreciated; but it was a matter of a different sort, and the figure of the income he had arrived at had never been high enough to look any one in the face.

"I don't know as I quite see what you require it for. You don't appear sick to speak of." It was of Europe Waymarsh thus finally spoke.

"Well," said Strether, who fell as much as possible into step, "I guess I don't *feel* sick now that I've started. But I had pretty well run down before I did start."

Waymarsh raised his melancholy look. "Ain't you about up to your usual average?"

It was not quite pointedly sceptical, but it seemed somehow a plea for the purest veracity, and it thereby affected our friend as the very voice of Milrose. He had long since made a mental distinction—though never in truth daring to betray it—between the voice of Milrose and the voice even of Woollett. It was the former, he felt, that was most in the real tradition. There had been occasions in his past when the sound of it had reduced him to temporary confusion, and the present, for some reason, suddenly became such another. It was nevertheless no light matter that the very effect of his confusion should be to make him again prevaricate. "That description hardly does justice to a man to whom it has done such a lot of good to see *you*."

Waymarsh fixed on his washing-stand the silent detached stare with which Milrose in person, as it were, might have marked the unexpectedness of a compliment from Woollett; and Strether, for his part, felt once more like Woollett in person. "I mean," his friend presently continued, "that your appearance isn't as bad as I've seen it: it compares favourably with what it was when I last noticed it." On this appearance Waymarsh's eyes yet failed to rest; it was almost as if they obeyed an instinct of propriety, and the effect was still stronger when, always considering the basin and jug, he added: "You've filled out some since then."

"I'm afraid I have," Strether laughed: "one does fill out some with all one takes in, and I've taken in, I dare say, more than I've natural room for. I was dog-tired when I sailed." It had the oddest sound of cheerfulness.

"I was dog-tired," his companion returned, "when I arrived, and it's this wild hunt for rest that takes all the life out of me. The fact is, Strether—and it's a comfort to have you here at last to say it to; though I don't know, after all, that I've really waited; I've told it to people I've met in the cars—the fact is, such a country as this ain't my *kind* of country anyway. There ain't a country I've seen over here that *does* seem my kind. Oh I don't say but what there are plenty of pretty places and remarkable old things; but the trouble is that I don't seem to feel anywhere in tune. That's one of the reasons why I suppose I've gained so little. I haven't had the first sign of that lift I was led to expect." With this he broke out more earnestly. "Look here—I want to go back."

His eyes were all attached to Strether's now, for he was one of the men who fully face you when they talk of themselves. This enabled his friend to look at him hard and immediately to appear to the highest advantage in his eyes by doing so. "That's a genial thing to say to a fellow who has come out on purpose to meet you!"

Nothing could have been finer, on this, than Waymarsh's sombre glow. "*Have* you come out on purpose?"

"Well—very largely."

"I thought from the way you wrote there was something back of it."

Strether hesitated. "Back of my desire to be with you?"

"Back of your prostration."

Strether, with a smile made more dim by a certain consciousness, shook his head. "There are all the causes of it!"

"And no particular cause that seemed most to drive you?"

Our friend could at last conscientiously answer. "Yes. One. There *is* a matter that has had much to do with my coming out."

Waymarsh waited a little. "Too private to mention?"

"No, not too private—for *you*. Only rather complicated."

"Well," said Waymarsh, who had waited again, "I *may* lose my mind over here, but I don't know as I've done so yet."

"Oh you shall have the whole thing. But not tonight."

Waymarsh seemed to sit stiffer and to hold his elbows tighter. "Why not—if I can't sleep?"

"Because, my dear man, I *can*!"

"Then where's your prostration?"

"Just in that—that I can put in eight hours." And Strether brought it out that if Waymarsh didn't "gain" it was because he didn't go to bed: the result of which was, in its order, that, to do the latter justice, he permitted his friend to insist on his really getting settled. Strether, with a kind coercive hand for it, assisted him to this consummation, and again found his own part in their relation auspiciously enlarged by the smaller touches of lowering the lamp and seeing to a sufficiency of blanket. It somehow ministered for him to indulgence to feel Waymarsh, who looked unnaturally big and black in bed, as much tucked in as a patient in a hospital and, with his covering up to his chin, as much simplified by it. He hovered in vague pity, to be brief, while his companion challenged him out of the bedclothes. "Is she really after you? Is that what's behind?"

Strether felt an uneasiness at the direction taken by his companion's insight, but he played a little at uncertainty. "Behind my coming out?"

"Behind your prostration or whatever. It's generally felt, you know, that she follows you up pretty close."

Strether's candour was never very far off. "Oh it has occurred to you that I'm literally running away from Mrs. Newsome?"

"Well, I haven't *known* but what you are. You're a very attractive man, Strether. You've seen for yourself," said Waymarsh, "what that lady downstairs makes of it. Unless indeed," he rambled on with an effect between the ironic and the anxious, "it's you who are after *her*. Is Mrs. Newsome *over* here?" He spoke as with a droll dread of her.

It made his friend—though rather dimly—smile. "Dear no; she's safe, thank goodness—as I think I more and more feel—at home. She thought of coming, but she gave it up. I've come in a manner instead of her; and come to that extent—for you're right in your inference—on her business. So you see there *is* plenty of connexion."

Waymarsh continued to see at least all there was. "Involving accordingly the particular one I've referred to?"

Strether took another turn about the room, giving a twitch to his companion's blanket and finally gaining the door. His feeling was that of a nurse who had earned personal rest by having made everything straight. "Involving more things than I can think of breaking ground on now. But don't be afraid—you shall have them from me: you'll probably find yourself having quite as much of them as you can do with. I shall—if we keep together—very much depend on your impression of some of them."

Waymarsh's acknowledgement of this tribute was characteristically indirect. "You mean to say you don't believe we *will* keep together?"

"I only glance at the danger," Strether paternally said, "because when I hear you wail to go back I seem to see you open up such possibilities of folly."

Waymarsh took it—silent a little—like a large snubbed child. "What are you going to do with me?"

It was the very question Strether himself had put to Miss Gostrey, and he wondered if he had sounded like that. But *he* at least could be more definite. "I'm going to take you right down to London."

"Oh I've *been* down to London!" Waymarsh more softly moaned. "I've no use, Strether, for anything down there."

"Well," said Strether, good-humouredly, "I guess you've some use for *me*."

"So I've got to go?"

"Oh you've got to go further yet."

"Well," Waymarsh sighed, "do your damnedest! Only you *will* tell me before you lead me on all the way—?"

Our friend had again so lost himself, both for amusement and for contrition, in the wonder of whether he had made, in his own challenge that afternoon, such another figure, that he for an instant missed the thread. "Tell you—?"

"Why what you've got on hand."

Strether hesitated. "Why it's such a matter as that even if I positively wanted I shouldn't be able to keep it from you."

Waymarsh gloomily gazed. "What does that mean then but that your trip is just *for* her?"

"For Mrs. Newsome? Oh it certainly is, as I say. Very much."

"Then why do you also say it's for me?"

Strether, in impatience, violently played with his latch. "It's simple enough. It's for both of you."

Waymarsh at last turned over with a groan. "Well, *I* won't marry you!"

"Neither, when it comes to that—!" But the visitor had already laughed and escaped.

III

He had told Miss Gostrey he should probably take, for departure with Waymarsh, some afternoon train, and it thereupon in the morning appeared that this lady had made her own plan for an earlier one. She had breakfasted when Strether came into the coffee-room; but, Waymarsh not having yet emerged, he was in time to recall her to the terms of their understanding and to pronounce her discretion overdone. She was surely not to break away at the very moment she had created a want. He had met her as she rose from her little table in a window, where, with the morning papers beside her, she reminded him, as he let her know, of Major Pendennis breakfasting at his club[5]—a compliment of which she professed a deep appreciation; and he detained her as pleadingly as if he had already—and notably under pressure of the visions of

---

5. William Thackeray's *Pendennis* (1848–50) opens with Major Pendennis having his usual elaborately served breakfast at his club.

the night—learned to be unable to do without her. She must teach him at all events, before she went, to order breakfast as breakfast was ordered in Europe, and she must especially sustain him in the problem of ordering for Waymarsh. The latter had laid upon his friend, by desperate sounds through the door of his room, dreadful divined responsibilities in respect to beefsteak and oranges—responsibilities which Miss Gostrey took over with an alertness of action that matched her quick intelligence. She had before this weaned the expatriated from traditions compared with which the matutinal beefsteak was but the creature of an hour, and it was not for her, with some of her memories, to falter in the path; though she freely enough declared, on reflexion, that there was always in such cases a choice of opposed policies. "There are times when to give them their head, you know—!"

They had gone to wait together in the garden for the dressing of the meal, and Strether found her more suggestive than ever. "Well, what?"

"Is to bring about for them such a complexity of relations—unless indeed we call it a simplicity!—that the situation *has* to wind itself up. They want to go back."

"And you want them to go!" Strether gaily concluded.

"I always want them to go, and I send them as fast as I can."

"Oh I know—you take them to Liverpool."

"Any port will serve in a storm. I'm—with all my other functions—an agent for repatriation. I want to re-people our stricken country. What will become of it else? I want to discourage others."

The ordered English garden, in the freshness of the day, was delightful to Strether, who liked the sound, under his feet, of the tight fine gravel, packed with the chronic damp, and who had the idlest eye for the deep smoothness of turf and the clean curves of paths. "Other people?"

"Other countries. Other people—yes. I want to encourage our own."

Strether wondered. "Not to come? Why then do you 'meet' them? —since it doesn't appear to be to stop them?"

"Oh that they shouldn't come is as yet too much to ask. What I attend to is that they come quickly and return still more so. I meet them to help it to be over as soon as possible, and though I don't stop them I've my way of putting them through. That's my little system; and, if you want to know," said Maria Gostrey, "it's my real secret, my innermost mission and use. I only seem, you see, to beguile and approve; but I've thought it all out and I'm working all the while underground. I can't perhaps quite give you my formula, but I think that practically I succeed. I send you back spent. So you stay back. Passed through my hands—"

"We don't turn up again?" The further she went the further he always saw himself able to follow. "I don't want your formula —I feel quite enough, as I hinted yesterday, your abysses. Spent!" he echoed. "If that's how you're arranging so subtly to send me I thank you for the warning."

For a minute, amid the pleasantness—poetry in tariffed items, but all the more, for guests already convicted, a challenge to consumption—they smiled at each other in confirmed fellowship. "Do you call it subtly? It's a plain poor tale. Besides, you're a special case."

"Oh special cases—that's weak!" She was weak enough, further still, to defer her journey and agree to accompany the gentlemen on their own, might a separate carriage mark her independence; though it was in spite of this to befall after luncheon that she went off alone and that, with a tryst taken for a day of her company in London, they lingered another night. She had, during the morning —spent in a way that he was to remember later on as the very climax of his foretaste, as warm with presentiments, with what he would have called collapses—had all sorts of things out with Strether; and among them the fact that though there was never a moment of her life when she wasn't "due" somewhere, there was yet scarce a perfidy to others of which she wasn't capable for his sake. She explained moreover that wherever she happened to be she found a dropped thread to pick up, a ragged edge to repair, some familiar appetite in ambush, jumping out as she approached, yet appeasable with a temporary biscuit. It became, on her taking the risk of the deviation imposed on him by her insidious arrangement of his morning meal, a point of honour for her not to fail with Waymarsh of the larger success too; and her subsequent boast to Strether was that she had made their friend fare—and quite without his knowing what was the matter—as Major Pendennis would have fared at the Megatherium.[6] She had made him breakfast like a gentleman, and it was nothing, she forcibly asserted, to what she would yet make him do. She made him participate in the slow reiterated ramble with which, for Strether, the new day amply filled itself; and it was by her art that he somehow had the air, on the ramparts and in the Rows,[7] of carrying a point of his own.

The three strolled and stared and gossiped, or at least the two

---

6. In Thackeray's The Newcomes (1853–55), one of the Major's clubs is called the Megatherium.
7. "Next after its wall—possibly even before it—Chester values its Rows, an architectural idiosyncrasy which must be seen to be appreciated. They are a sort of gothic edition of the blessed arcades and porticoes of Italy, and consist, roughly speaking, of a running public passage tunnelled through the second story of the houses. ° ° ° The upper portion of the houses projects to the outer line of the gallery, where they are propped with pillars and posts and parapets. The shop-fronts face along the arcade and admit you to little caverns of traffic." Henry James, "Chester," The Art of Travel, 107.

did; the case really yielding for their comrade, if analysed, but the
element of stricken silence. This element indeed affected Strether as
charged with audible rumblings, but he was conscious of the care
of taking it explicitly as a sign of pleasant peace. He wouldn't appeal too much, for that provoked stiffness; yet he wouldn't be too
freely tacit, for that suggested giving up. Waymarsh himself ad-
hered to an ambiguous dumbness that might have represented
either the growth of a perception or the despair of one; and at
times and in places—where the low-browed galleries were darkest,
the opposite gables queerest, the solicitations of every kind densest
—the others caught him fixing hard some object of minor interest, fixing even at moments nothing discernible, as if he were
indulging it with a truce. When he met Strether's eye on such occasions he looked guilty and furtive, fell the next minute into some
attitude of retractation. Our friend couldn't show him the right
things for fear of provoking some total renouncement, and was
tempted even to show him the wrong in order to make him differ
with triumph. There were moments when he himself felt shy of
professing the full sweetness of the taste of leisure, and there were
others when he found himself feeling as if his passages of interchange with the lady at his side might fall upon the third member
of their party very much as Mr. Burchell, at Dr. Primrose's fireside, was influenced by the high flights of the visitors from London.[8]
The smallest things so arrested and amused him that he repeatedly
almost apologised—brought up afresh in explanation his plea of a
previous grind. He was aware at the same time that his grind had
been as nothing to Waymarsh's, and he repeatedly confessed that,
to cover his frivolity, he was doing his best for his previous virtue.
Do what he might, in any case, his previous virtue was still there,
and it seemed fairly to stare at him out of the windows of shops
that were not as the shops of Woollett, fairly to make him want
things that he shouldn't know what to do with. It was by the
oddest, the least admissible of laws demoralising him now; and the
way it boldly took was to make him want more wants. These first
walks in Europe were in fact a kind of finely lurid intimation of
what one might find at the end of that process. Had he come
back after long years, in something already so like the evening of

---

8. In Chapter XI of Oliver Goldsmith's *The Vicar of Wakefield* (1766), two London prostitutes
disguised as ladies of fashion visit the Vicar's family and carry on for the benefit of the
unsuspecting Primroses what is supposed to be a conversation of high society. Also present,
however, is Mr. Burchell—a wealthy and knowledgeable baronet in disguise—and he periodically punctuates the conversation with exclamations of "Fudge!" For a sample of this
conversation in *The Ambassadors*, see p. 306. (Shortly before writing *The Ambassadors*, James
had written an introduction to *The Vicar of Wakefield*, and in it he mentions both the
conversation and Burchell's reaction as among the novel's "felicities that have become familiar
and famous." Henry James, "The Vicar of Wakefield," *A Book of Modern Essays*, ed. Bruce
McCullough and Edwin Berry Burgum [New York: Century, 1926], 369.)

life, only to be exposed to it? It was at all events over the shop-windows that he made, with Waymarsh, most free; though it would have been easier had not the latter most sensibly yielded to the appeal of the merely useful trades. He pierced with his sombre detachment the plate-glass of ironmongers and saddlers, while Strether flaunted an affinity with the dealers in stamped letter-paper and in smart neckties. Strether was in fact recurrently shameless in the presence of the tailors, though it was just over the heads of the tailors that his countryman most loftily looked. This gave Miss Gostrey a grasped opportunity to back up Way-marsh at his expense. The weary lawyer—it was unmistakeable —had a conception of dress; but that, in view of some of the features of the effect produced, was just what made the danger of insistence on it. Strether wondered if he by this time thought Miss Gostrey less fashionable or Lambert Strether more so; and it appeared probable that most of the remarks exchanged between this latter pair about passers, figures, faces, personal types, exemplified in their degree the disposition to talk as "society" talked.

Was what was happening to himself then, was what already *had* happened, really that a woman of fashion was floating him into society and that an old friend deserted on the brink was watching the force of the current? When the woman of fashion permitted Strether—as she permitted him at the most—the purchase of a pair of gloves, the terms she made about it, the prohibition of neckties and other items till she should be able to guide him through the Burlington Arcade,[9] were such as to fall upon a sensitive ear as a challenge to just imputations. Miss Gostrey was such a woman of fashion as could make without a symptom of vulgar blinking an appointment for the Burlington Arcade. Mere discriminations about a pair of gloves could thus at any rate represent —always for such sensitive ears as were in question—possibilities of something that Strether could make a mark against only as the peril of apparent wantonness. He had quite the consciousness of his new friend, for their companion, that he might have had of a Jesuit in petticoats, a representative of the recruiting interests of the Catholic Church. The Catholic Church, for Waymarsh— that was to say the enemy, the monster of bulging eyes and far-reaching quivering groping tentacles—was exactly society, exactly the multiplication of shibboleths, exactly the discrimination of types and tones, exactly the wicked old Rows of Chester, rank with feudalism; exactly in short Europe.

There was light for observation, however, in an incident that occurred just before they turned back to luncheon. Waymarsh had been for a quarter of an hour exceptionally mute and distant,

9. An arcade of fashionable shops in London.

and something, or other—Strether was never to make out exactly
what—proved, as it were, too much for him after his comrades
had stood for three minutes taking in, while they leaned on an old
balustrade that guarded the edge of the Row, a particularly crooked
and huddled street-view. "He thinks us sophisticated, he thinks
us worldly, he thinks us wicked, he thinks us all sorts of queer
things," Strether reflected; for wondrous were the vague quantities
our friend had within a couple of short days acquired the habit of
conveniently and conclusively lumping together. There seemed
moreover a direct connexion between some such inference and a
sudden grim dash taken by Waymarsh to the opposite side. This
movement was startlingly sudden, and his companions at first supposed him to have espied, to be pursuing, the glimpse of an
acquaintance. They next made out, however, that an open door had
instantly received him, and they then recognised him as engulfed
in the establishment of a jeweller, behind whose glittering front he
was lost to view. The fact had somehow the note of a demonstration, and it left each of the others to show a face almost of fear.
But Miss Gostrey broke into a laugh. "What's the matter with
him?"

"Well," said Strether, "he can't stand it."

"But can't stand what?"

"Anything. Europe."

"Then how will that jeweller help him?"

Strether seemed to make it out, from their position, between the
interstices of arrayed watches, of close-hung dangling gewgaws.
"You'll see."

"Ah that's just what—if he buys anything—I'm afraid of:
that I shall see something rather dreadful."

Strether studied the finer appearances. "He may buy everything."

"Then don't you think we ought to follow him?"

"Not for worlds. Besides we can't. We're paralysed. We exchange
a long scared look, we publicly tremble. The thing is, you see, we
'realise.' He has struck for freedom."

She wondered but she laughed. "Ah what a price to pay! And
I was preparing some for him so cheap."

"No, no," Strether went on, frankly amused now; "don't call it
that: the kind of freedom you deal in is dear." Then as to justify
himself: "Am I not in my way trying it? It's this."

"Being here, you mean, with me?"

"Yes, and talking to you as I do. I've known you a few hours,
and I've known him all my life; so that if the ease I thus take with
you about him isn't magnificent"—and the thought of it held him
a moment—"why it's rather base."

"It's magnificent!" said Miss Gostrey to make an end of it. "And you should hear," she added, "the ease I take—and I above all intend to take—with Mr. Waymarsh."

Strether thought. "About *me*? Ah that's no equivalent. The equivalent would be Waymarsh's himself serving me up—his remorseless analysis of me. And he'll never do that"—he was sadly clear. "He'll never remorselessly analyse me." He quite held her with the authority of this. "He'll never say a word to you about me."

She took it in; she did it justice; yet after an instant her reason, her restless irony, disposed of it. "Of course he won't. For what do you take people, that they're able to say words about anything, able remorselessly to analyse? There are not many like you and me. It will be only because he's too stupid."

It stirred in her friend a sceptical echo which was at the same time the protest of the faith of years. "Waymarsh stupid?"

"Compared with you."

Strether had still his eyes on the jeweller's front, and he waited a moment to answer. "He's a success of a kind that I haven't approached."

"Do you mean he has made money?"

"He makes it—to my belief. And I," said Strether, "though with a back quite as bent, have never made anything. I'm a perfectly equipped failure."

He feared an instant she'd ask him if he meant he was poor; and he was glad she didn't, for he really didn't know to what the truth on this unpleasant point mightn't have prompted her. She only, however, confirmed his assertion. "Thank goodness you're a failure—it's why I so distinguish you! Anything else to-day is too hideous. Look about you—look at the successes. Would you *be* one, on your honour? Look, moreover," she continued, "at me."

For a little accordingly their eyes met. "I see," Strether returned. "You too are out of it."

"The superiority you discern in me," she concurred, "announces my futility. If you knew," she sighed, "the dreams of my youth! But our realities are what has brought us together. We're beaten brothers in arms."

He smiled at her kindly enough, but he shook his head. "It doesn't alter the fact that you're expensive. You've cost me already—!"

But he had hung fire. "Cost you what?"

"Well, my past—in one great lump. But no matter," he laughed: "I'll pay with my last penny."

Her attention had unfortunately now been engaged by their comrade's return, for Waymarsh met their view as he came out of his shop. "I hope he hasn't paid," she said, "with *his* last; though

I'm convinced he has been splendid, and has been so for you."

"Ah no—not that!"

"Then for me?"

"Quite as little." Waymarsh was by this time near enough to show signs his friend could read, though he seemed to look almost carefully at nothing in particular.

"Then for himself?"

"For nobody. For nothing. For freedom."

"But what has freedom to do with it?"

Strether's answer was indirect. "To be as good as you and me. But different."

She had had time to take in their companion's face; and with it, as such things were easy for her, she took in all. "Different—yes. But better!"

If Waymarsh was sombre he was also indeed almost sublime. He told them nothing, left his absence unexplained, and though they were convinced he had made some extraordinary purchase they were never to learn its nature. He only glowered grandly at the tops of the old gables. "It's the sacred rage," Strether had had further time to say; and this sacred rage was to become between them, for convenient comprehension, the description of one of his periodical necessities. It was Strether who eventually contended that it did make him better than they. But by that time Miss Gostrey was convinced that she didn't want to be better than Strether.

Book Second

I [IV][1]

Those occasions on which Strether was, in association with the exile from Milrose, to see the sacred rage glimmer through would doubtless have their due periodicity; but our friend had meanwhile to find names for many other matters. On no evening of his life perhaps, as he reflected, had he had to supply so many as on the third of his short stay in London; an evening spent by Miss Gostrey's side at one of the theatres, to which he had found himself transported, without his own hand raised, on the mere expression of a conscientious wonder. She knew her theatre, she knew her play, as she had triumphantly known, three days running, everything else, and the moment filled to the brim, for her companion, that apprehension of the interesting which, whether or no the interesting happened to filter through his guide, strained now to its limits his brief opportunity. Waymarsh hadn't come with them; he had

---

1. To facilitate references to the text in the critical essays and elsewhere, the chapter numbers in earlier editions of *The Ambassadors* have been added in brackets when they differ from the chapter numbers in the New York Edition.

seen plays enough, he signified, before Strether had joined him—
an affirmation that had its full force when his friend ascertained by
questions that he had seen two and a circus. Questions as to what he
had seen had on him indeed an effect only less favourable than
questions as to what he hadn't. He liked the former to be discriminated; but how could it be done, Strether asked of their constant counsellor, without discriminating the latter?

Miss Gostrey had dined with him at his hotel, face to face over
a small table on which the lighted candles had rose-coloured shades;
and the rose-coloured shades and the small table and the soft
fragrance of the lady—had anything to his mere sense ever been so
soft?—were so many touches in he scarce knew what positive high
picture. He had been to the theatre, even to the opera, in Boston,
with Mrs. Newsome, more than once acting as her only escort; but
there had been no little confronted dinner, no pink lights, no whiff
of vague sweetness, as a preliminary: one of the results of which
was that at present, mildly rueful, though with a sharpish accent,
he actually asked himself *why* there hadn't. There was much the
same difference in his impression of the noticed state of his companion, whose dress was "cut down," as he believed the term to be,
in respect to shoulders and bosom, in a manner quite other than
Mrs. Newsome's, and who wore round her throat a broad red velvet
band with an antique jewel—he was rather complacently sure it
was antique—attached to it in front. Mrs. Newsome's dress was
never in any degree "cut down," and she never wore round her
throat a broad red velvet band: if she had, moreover, would it ever
have served so to carry on and complicate, as he now almost felt,
his vision?

It would have been absurd of him to trace into ramifications the
effect of the ribbon from which Miss Gostrey's trinket depended,
had he not for the hour, at the best, been so given over to uncontrolled perceptions. What was it but an uncontrolled perception
that his friend's velvet band somehow added, in her appearance, to
the value of every other item—to that of her smile and of the way
she carried her head, to that of her complexion, of her lips, her
teeth, her eyes, her hair? What, certainly, had a man conscious of
a man's work in the world to do with red velvet bands? He wouldn't
for anything have so exposed himself as to tell Miss Gostrey how
much he liked hers, yet he *had* none the less not only caught himself in the act—frivolous, no doubt, idiotic, and above all unexpected—of liking it: he had in addition taken it as a starting-point
for fresh backward, fresh forward, fresh lateral flights. The manner
in which Mrs. Newsome's throat *was* encircled suddenly represented
for him, in an alien order, almost as many things as the manner in
which Miss Gostrey's was. Mrs. Newsome wore, at operatic hours,

a black silk dress—very handsome, he knew it was "handsome"—
and an ornament that his memory was able further to identify as a
ruche. He had his association indeed with the ruche, but it was
rather imperfectly romantic. He had once said to the wearer—and
it was as "free" a remark as he had ever made to her—that she
looked, with her ruff and other matters, like Queen Elizabeth; and
it had after this in truth been his fancy that, as a consequence of
that tenderness and an acceptance of the idea, the form of this special tribute to the "frill" had grown slightly more marked. The
connexion, as he sat there and let his imagination roam, was to
strike him as vaguely pathetic; but there it all was, and pathetic was
doubtless in the conditions the best thing it could possibly be. It
had assuredly existed at any rate; for it seemed now to come over
him that no gentleman of his age at Woollett could ever, to a lady
of Mrs. Newsome's, which was not much less than his, have em-
barked on such a simile.

All sorts of things in fact now seemed to come over him, comparatively few of which his chronicler can hope for space to mention. It came over him for instance that Miss Gostrey looked perhaps like Mary Stuart:[2] Lambert Strether had a candour of fancy
which could rest for an instant gratified in such an antithesis. It
came over him that never before—no, literally never—had a lady
dined with him at a public place before going to the play. The
publicity of the place was just, in the matter, for Strether, the rare
strange thing; it affected him almost as the achievement of privacy
might have affected a man of a different experience. He had married, in the far-away years, so young as to have missed the time
natural in Boston for taking girls to the Museum;[3] and it was
absolutely true of him that—even after the close of the period of
conscious detachment occupying the centre of his life, the grey
middle desert of the two deaths, that of his wife and that, ten years
later, of his boy—he had never taken any one anywhere. It came
over him in especial—though the monition had, as happened, already sounded, fitfully gleamed, in other forms—that the business
he had come out on hadn't yet been so brought home to him as
by the sight of the people about him. She gave him the impression,
his friend, at first, more straight than he got it for himself—gave it
simply by saying with off-hand illumination: "Oh yes, they're
types!"—but after he had taken it he made to the full his own use
of it; both while he kept silence for the four acts and while he
talked in the intervals. It was an evening, it was a world of types,
and this was a connexion above all in which the figures and faces in
the stalls were interchangeable with those on the stage.

2. Once Queen of France, Mary Stuart, Queen of Scots and a Catholic claimant to the English
throne, was executed for treason by Queen Elizabeth in 1587.
3. The Boston Museum of Fine Arts, founded in 1870.

He felt as if the play itself penetrated him with the naked elbow of his neighbour, a great stripped handsome red-haired lady who conversed with a gentleman on her other side in stray dissyllables which had for his ear, in the oddest way in the world, so much sound that he wondered they hadn't more sense; and he recognised by the same law, beyond the footlights, what he was pleased to take for the very flush of English life. He had distracted drops in which he couldn't have said if it were actors or auditors who were most true, and the upshot of which, each time, was the consciousness of new contacts. However he viewed his job it was "types" he should have to tackle. Those before him and around him were not as the types of Woollett, where, for that matter, it had begun to seem to him that there must only have been the male and the female. These made two exactly, even with the individual varieties. Here, on the other hand, apart from the personal and the sexual range—which might be greater or less—a series of strong stamps had been applied, as it were, from without; stamps that his observation played with as, before a glass case on a table, it might have passed from medal to medal and from copper to gold. It befell that in the drama precisely there was a bad woman in a yellow frock who made a pleasant weak good-looking young man in perpetual evening dress do the most dreadful things. Strether felt himself on the whole not afraid of the yellow frock, but he was vaguely anxious over a certain kindness into which he found himself drifting for its victim. He hadn't come out, he reminded himself, to be too kind, or indeed to be kind at all, to Chadwick Newsome. Would Chad also be in perpetual evening dress? He somehow rather hoped it—it seemed so to add to *this* young man's general amenability; though he wondered too if, to fight him with his own weapons, he himself (a thought almost startling) would have likewise to be. This young man furthermore would have been much more easy to handle—at least for *him*—than appeared probable in respect to Chad.

It came up for him with Miss Gostrey that there were things of which she would really perhaps after all have heard; and she admitted when a little pressed that she was never quite sure of what she heard as distinguished from things such as, on occasions like the present, she only extravagantly guessed. "I seem with this freedom, you see, to have guessed Mr. Chad. He's a young man on whose head high hopes are placed at Woollett; a young man a wicked woman has got hold of and whom his family over there have sent you out to rescue. You've accepted the mission of separating him from the wicked woman. Are you quite sure she's very bad for him?"

Something in his manner showed it as quite pulling him up. "Of course we are. Wouldn't *you* be?"

"Oh I don't know. One never does—does one?—beforehand. One can only judge on the facts. Yours are quite new to me; I'm really not in the least, as you see, in possession of them: so it will be awfully interesting to have them from you. If you're satisfied, that's all that's required. I mean if you're sure you *are* sure: sure it won't do."

"That he should lead such a life? Rather!"

"Oh but I don't know, you see, about his life; you've not told me about his life. She may be charming—his life!"

"Charming?"—Strether stared before him. "She's base, venal—out of the streets."

"I see. And *he*—?"

"Chad, wretched boy?"

"Of what type and temper is he?" she went on as Strether had lapsed.

"Well—the obstinate." It was as if for a moment he had been going to say more and had then controlled himself.

That was scarce what she wished. "Do you like him?"

This time he was prompt. "No. How *can* I?"

"Do you mean because of your being so saddled with him?"

"I'm thinking of his mother," said Strether after a moment. "He has darkened her admirable life." He spoke with austerity. "He has worried her half to death."

"Oh that's of course odious." She had a pause as if for renewed emphasis of this truth, but it ended on another note. "Is her life very admirable?"

"Extraordinarily."

There was so much in the tone that Miss Gostrey had to devote another pause to the appreciation of it. "And has he only *her*? I don't mean the bad woman in Paris," she quickly added—"for I assure you I shouldn't even at the best be disposed to allow him more than one. But has he only his mother?"

"He has also a sister, older than himself and married; and they're both remarkably fine women."

"Very handsome, you mean?"

This promptitude—almost, as he might have thought, this precipitation, gave him a brief drop; but he came up again. "Mrs. Newsome, I think, is handsome, though she's not of course, with a son of twenty-eight and a daughter of thirty, in her very first youth. She married, however, extremely young."

"And is wonderful," Miss Gostrey asked, "for her age?"

Strether seemed to feel with a certain disquiet the pressure of it. "I don't say she's wonderful. Or rather," he went on the next moment, "I do say it. It's exactly what she *is*—wonderful. But I wasn't thinking of her appearance," he explained—"striking as that doubtless is. I was thinking—well, of many other things." He seemed to look at these as if to mention some of them; then took, pulling himself up, another turn. "About Mrs. Pocock people may differ."

"Is that the daughter's name—'Pocock'?"

"That's the daughter's name," Strether sturdily confessed.

"And people may differ, you mean, about *her* beauty?"

"About everything."

"But *you* admire her?"

He gave his friend a glance as to show how he could bear this. "I'm perhaps a little afraid of her."

"Oh," said Miss Gostrey, "I see her from here! You may say then I see very fast and very far, but I've already shown you I do. The young man and the two ladies," she went on, "are at any rate all the family?"

"Quite all. His father has been dead ten years, and there's no brother, nor any other sister. They'd do," said Strether, "anything in the world for him."

"And you'd do anything in the world for *them*?"

He shifted again; she had made it perhaps just a shade too affirmative for his nerves. "Oh I don't know!"

"You'd do at any rate this, and the 'anything' they'd do is represented by their *making* you do it."

"Ah they couldn't have come—either of them. They're very busy people and Mrs. Newsome in particular has a large full life. She's moreover highly nervous—and not at all strong."

"You mean she's an American invalid?"

He carefully distinguished. "There's nothing she likes less than to be called one, but she would consent to be one of those things, I think," he laughed, "if it were the only way to be the other."

"Consent to be an American in order to be an invalid?"

"No," said Strether, "the other way round. She's at any rate delicate sensitive high-strung. She puts so much of herself into everything—"

Ah Maria knew these things! "That she has nothing left for anything else? Of course she hasn't. To whom do you say it? Highstrung? Don't I spend my life, for them, jamming down the pedal? I see moreover how it has told on you."

Strether took this more lightly. "Oh I jam down the pedal too!"

"Well," she lucidly returned, "we must from this moment bear on it together with all our might." And she forged ahead. "Have they money?"

But it was as if, while her energetic image still held him, her enquiry fell short. "Mrs. Newsome," he wished further to explain, "hasn't moreover your courage on the question of contact. If she had come it would have been to see the person herself."

"The woman? Ah but that's courage."

"No—it's exaltation, which is a very different thing. Courage," he, however, accommodatingly threw out, "is what *you* have."

She shook her head. "You say that only to patch me up—to cover the nudity of my want of exaltation. I've neither the one nor the other. I've mere battered indifference. I see that what you mean," Miss Gostrey pursued, "is that if your friend *had* come she would take great views, and the great views, to put it simply, would be too much for her."

Strether looked amused at her notion of the simple, but he adopted her formula. "Everything's too much for her."

"Ah then such a service as this of yours—"

"Is more for her than anything else? Yes—far more. But so long as it isn't too much for *me*—!"

"Her condition doesn't matter? Surely not; we leave her condition out; we take it, that is, for granted. I see it, her condition, as behind and beneath you; yet at the same time I see it as bearing you up."

"Oh it does bear me up!" Strether laughed.

"Well then as yours bears *me* nothing more's needed." With which she put again her question. "Has Mrs. Newsome money?"

This time he heeded. "Oh plenty. That's the root of the evil. There's money, to very large amounts, in the concern. Chad has had the free use of a great deal. But if he'll pull himself together and come home, all the same, he'll find his account in it."

She had listened with all her interest. "And I hope to goodness you'll find yours!"

"He'll take up his definite material reward," said Strether without acknowledgement of this. "He's at the parting of the ways. He can come into the business now—he can't come later."

"Is there a business?"

"Lord, yes—a big brave bouncing business. A roaring trade."

"A great shop?"

"Yes—a workshop; a great production, a great industry. The concern's a manufacture—and a manufacture that, if it's only properly looked after, may well be on the way to become a monopoly. It's a little thing they make—make better, it appears, than other people can, or than other people, at any rate, do. Mr. Newsome, being a man of ideas, at least in that particular line," Strether explained, "put them on it with great effect, and gave the place altogether, in his time, an immense lift."

"It's a place in itself?"

"Well, quite a number of buildings; almost a little industrial colony. But above all it's a thing. The article produced."

"And what *is* the article produced?"

Strether looked about him as in slight reluctance to say; then the curtain, which he saw about to rise, came to his aid. "I'll tell you next time." But when the next time came he only said he'd tell her later on—after they should have left the theatre; for she had immediately reverted to their topic, and even for himself the picture of the stage was now overlaid with another image. His postponements, however, made her wonder—wonder if the article referred to were anything bad. And she explained that she meant improper or ridiculous or wrong. But Strether, so far as that went, could satisfy her. "Unmentionable? Oh no, we constantly talk of it; we are quite familiar and brazen about it. Only, as a small, trivial, rather ridiculous object of the commonest domestic use, it's just wanting in—what shall I say? Well, dignity, or the least approach to distinction. Right here therefore, with everything about us so grand—!" In short he shrank.

"It's a false note?"

"Sadly. It's vulgar."

"But surely not vulgarer than this." Then on his wondering as she herself had done: "Than everything about us." She seemed a trifle irritated. "What do you take this for?"

"Why for—comparatively—divine!"

"This dreadful London theatre? It's impossible, if you really want to know."

"Oh then," laughed Strether, "I *don't* really want to know!"

It made between them a pause, which she, however, still fascinated by the mystery of the production at Woollett, presently broke. "'Rather ridiculous'? Clothes-pins? Saleratus? Shoe-polish?"

It brought him round. "No—you don't even 'burn.' I don't think, you know, you'll guess it."

"How then can I judge how vulgar it is?"

"You'll judge when I do tell you"—and he persuaded her to patience. But it may even now frankly be mentioned that he in the sequel never *was* to tell her. He actually never did so, and it moreover oddly occurred that by the law, within her, of the incalculable, her desire for the information dropped and her attitude to the question converted itself into a positive cultivation of ignorance. In ignorance she could humour her fancy, and that proved a useful freedom. She could treat the little nameless object as indeed unnameable—she could make their abstention enormously definite. There might indeed have been for Strether the portent of this in what she next said.

"Is it perhaps then because it's so bad—because your industry, as you call it, *is* so vulgar—that Mr. Chad won't come back? Does he feel the taint? Is he staying away not to be mixed up in it?"

"Oh," Strether laughed, "it wouldn't appear—would it?—that he feels 'taints'! He's glad enough of the money from it, and the money's his whole basis. There's appreciation in that—I mean as to the allowance his mother has hitherto made him. She has of course the resource of cutting this allowance off; but even then he has unfortunately, and on no small scale, his independent supply —money left him by his grandfather, her own father."

"Wouldn't the fact you mention then," Miss Gostrey asked, "make it just more easy for him to be particular? Isn't he conceivable as fastidious about the source—the apparent and public source—of his income?"

Strether was able quite good-humouredly to entertain the proposition. "The source of his grandfather's wealth—and thereby of his own share in it—was not particularly noble."

"And what source was it?"

Strether cast about. "Well—practices."

"In business? Infamies? He was an old swindler?"

"Oh," he said with more emphasis than spirit, "I shan't describe *him* nor narrate his exploits."

"Lord, what abysses! And the late Mr. Newsome then?"

"Well, what about him?"

"Was he like the grandfather?"

"No—he was on the other side of the house. And he was different."

Miss Gostrey kept it up. "Better?"

Her friend for a moment hung fire. "No."

Her comment on his hesitation was scarce the less marked for being mute. "Thank you. *Now* don't you see," she went on, "why the boy doesn't come home? He's drowning his shame."

"His shame? What shame?"

"What shame? *Comment donc?*⁴ *The* shame."

"But where and when," Strether asked, "is '*the* shame'—where is any shame—to-day? The men I speak of—they did as every one does; and (besides being ancient history) it was all a matter of appreciation."

She showed how she understood. "Mrs. Newsome has appreciated?"

"Ah I can't speak for *her!*"

"In the midst of such doings—and, as I understand you, profiting by them, she at least has remained exquisite?"

"Oh I can't talk of her!" Strether said.

"I thought she was just what you *could* talk of. You *don't* trust me," Miss Gostrey after a moment declared.

It had its effect. "Well, her money is spent, her life conceived

4. How's that?

and carried on with a large beneficence—"

"That's a kind of expiation of wrongs? Gracious," she added before he could speak, "how intensely you make me see her!"

"If you see her," Strether dropped, "it's all that's necessary."

She really seemed to have her. "I feel that. She *is*, in spite of everything, handsome."

This at least enlivened him. "What do you mean by everything?"

"Well, I mean *you*." With which she had one of her swift changes of ground. "You say the concern needs looking after; but doesn't Mrs. Newsome look after it?"

"So far as possible. She's wonderfully able, but it's not her affair, and her life's a good deal overcharged. She has many, many things."

"And you also?"

"Oh yes—I've many too, if you will."

"I see. But what I mean is," Miss Gostrey amended, "do you also look after the business?"

"Oh no, I don't touch the business."

"Only everything else?"

"Well, yes—some things."

"As for instance—?"

Strether obligingly thought. "Well, the Review."

"The Review?—you have a Review?"

"Certainly. Woollett has a Review—which Mrs. Newsome, for the most part, magnificently pays for and which I, not at all magnificently, edit. My name's on the cover," Strether pursued, "and I'm really rather disappointed and hurt that you seem never to have heard of it."

She neglected for a moment this grievance. "And what kind of a Review is it?"

His serenity was now completely restored. "Well, it's green."

"Do you mean in political colour as they say here—in thought?"

"No; I mean the cover's green—of the most lovely shade."

"And with Mrs. Newsome's name on it too?"

He waited a little. "Oh as for that you must judge if she peeps out. She's behind the whole thing; but she's of a delicacy and a discretion—!"

Miss Gostrey took it all. "I'm sure. She *would* be. I don't underrate her. She must be rather a swell."

"Oh yes, she's rather a swell!"

"A Woollett swell—*bon!* I like the idea of a Woollett swell. And you must be rather one too, to be so mixed up with her."

"Ah no," said Strether, "that's not the way it works."

But she had already taken him up. "The way it works—you needn't tell me!—is of course that you efface yourself."

"With my name on the cover?" he lucidly objected.

"Ah but you don't put it on for yourself."

"I beg your pardon—that's exactly what I do put it on for. It's exactly the thing that I'm reduced to doing for myself. It seems to rescue a little, you see, from the wreck of hopes and ambitions, the refuse-heap of disappointments and failures, my one presentable little scrap of an identity."

On this she looked at him as to say many things, but what she at last simply said was: "She likes to see it there. You're the bigger swell of the two," she immediately continued, "because you think you're not one. She thinks she *is* one. However," Miss Gostrey added, "she thinks you're one too. You're at all events the biggest she can get hold of." She embroidered, she abounded. "I don't say it to interfere between you, but on the day she gets hold of a bigger one—!" Strether had thrown back his head as in silent mirth over something that struck him in her audacity or felicity, and her flight meanwhile was already higher. "Therefore close with her—!"

"Close with her?" he asked as she seemed to hang poised.

"Before you lose your chance."

Their eyes met over it. "What do you mean by closing?"

"And what do I mean by your chance? I'll tell you when you tell me all the things *you* don't. Is it her *greatest* fad?" she briskly pursued.

"The Review?" He seemed to wonder how he could best describe it. This resulted however but in a sketch. "It's her tribute to the ideal."

"I see. You go in for tremendous things."

"We go in for the unpopular side—that is so far as we dare."

"And how far *do* you dare?"

"Well, she very far. I much less. I don't begin to have her faith. She provides," said Strether, "three fourths of that. And she provides, as I've confided to you, *all* the money."

It evoked somehow a vision of gold that held for a little Miss Gostrey's eyes, and she looked as if she heard the bright dollars shovelled in. "I hope then you make a good thing—"

"I *never* made a good thing!" he at once returned.

She just waited. "Don't you call it a good thing to be loved?"

"Oh we're not loved. We're not even hated. We're only just sweetly ignored."

She had another pause. "You don't trust me!" she once more repeated.

"Don't I when I lift the last veil?—tell you the very secret of the prison-house?"[5]

Again she met his eyes, but to the result that after an instant her

<hr />

5. "But that I am forbid / To tell the secrets of my prison-house, / I could a tale unfold whose lightest word / Would harrow up thy soul." The Ghost in *Hamlet* 1. 5. 13–16.

own turned away with impatience. "You don't sell? Oh I'm glad of *that!*" After which however, and before he could protest, she was off again. "She's just a *moral* swell."

He accepted gaily enough the definition. "Yes—I really think that describes her."

But it had for his friend the oddest connexion. "How does she do her hair?"

He laughed out. "Beautifully!"

"Ah that doesn't tell me. However, it doesn't matter—I know. It's tremendously neat—a real reproach; quite remarkably thick and without, as yet, a single strand of white. There!"

He blushed for her realism, but gaped at her truth. "You're the very deuce."

"What else *should* I be? It was as the very deuce I pounced on you. But don't let it trouble you, for everything but the very deuce —at our age—is a bore and a delusion, and even he himself, after all, but half a joy." With which, on a single sweep of her wing, she resumed. "You assist her to expiate—which is rather hard when you've yourself not sinned."

"It's she who hasn't sinned," Strether replied. "I've sinned the most."

"Ah," Miss Gostrey cynically laughed, "what a picture of *her!* Have you robbed the widow and the orphan?"

"I've sinned enough," said Strether.

"Enough for whom? Enough for what?"

"Well, to be where I am."

"Thank you!" They were disturbed at this moment by the passage between their knees and the back of the seats before them of a gentleman who had been absent during a part of the performance and who now returned for the close; but the interruption left Miss Gostrey time, before the subsequent hush, to express as a sharp finality her sense of the moral of all their talk. "I knew you had something up your sleeve!" This finality, however, left them in its turn, at the end of the play, as disposed to hang back as if they had still much to say; so that they easily agreed to let every one go before them—they found an interest in waiting. They made out from the lobby that the night had turned to rain; yet Miss Gostrey let her friend know that he wasn't to see her home. He was simply to put her, by herself, into a four-wheeler; she liked so in London, of wet nights after wild pleasures, thinking things over, on the return, in lonely four-wheelers. This was her great time, she intimated, for pulling herself together. The delays caused by the weather, the struggle for vehicles at the door, gave them occasion to subside on a divan at the back of the vestibule and just beyond the reach of the fresh damp gusts from the street. Here Strether's comrade resumed that free handling of the subject to which his own imagination of it already owed so much. "Does your young friend in Paris like you?"

It had almost, after the interval, startled him. "Oh I hope not! Why *should* he?"

"Why shouldn't he?" Miss Gostrey asked. "That you're coming down on him need have nothing to do with it."

"You see more in it," he presently returned, "than I."

"Of course I see *you* in it."

"Well then you see more in 'me'!"

"Than you see in yourself? Very likely. That's always one's right. What I was thinking of," she explained, "is the possible particular effect on him of his *milieu*."

"Oh his *milieu*—!" Strether really felt he could imagine it better now than three hours before.

"Do you mean it can only have been so lowering?"

"Why that's my very starting-point."

"Yes, but you start so far back. What do his letters say?"

"Nothing. He practically ignores us—or spares us. He doesn't write."

"I see. But there are all the same," she went on, "two quite distinct things that—given the wonderful place he's in—may have happened to him. One is that he may have got brutalised. The other is that he may have got refined."

Strether stared—this *was* a novelty. "Refined?"

"Oh," she said quietly, "there *are* refinements."

The way of it made him, after looking at her, break into a laugh. "*You* have them!"

"As one of the signs," she continued in the same tone, "they constitute perhaps the worst."

He thought it over and his gravity returned. "Is it a refinement not to answer his mother's letters?"

She appeared to have a scruple, but she brought it out. "Oh I should say the greatest of all."

"Well," said Strether, "*I'm* quite content to let it, as one of the signs, pass for the worst that I know he believes he can do what he likes with me."

This appeared to strike her. "How do you know it?"

"Oh I'm sure of it. I feel it in my bones."

"Feel he *can* do it?"

"Feel that he believes he can. It may come to the same thing!" Strether laughed.

She wouldn't, however, have this. "Nothing for you will ever come to the same thing as anything else." And she understood what she meant, it seemed, sufficiently to go straight on. "You say that if he does break he'll come in for things at home?"

"Quite positively. He'll come in for a particular chance—a chance that any properly constituted young man would jump at. The business has so developed that an opening scarcely apparent three years ago, but which his father's will took account of as in certain conditions possible and which, under that will, attaches to Chad's availing himself of it a large contingent advantage—this opening, the conditions having come about, now simply awaits him. His mother has kept it for him, holding out against strong pressure, till the last possible moment. It requires, naturally, as it carries with it a handsome 'part,' a large share in profits, his being on the spot and making a big effort for a big result. That's what I mean by his chance. If he misses it he comes in, as you say, for nothing. And to see that he doesn't miss it is, in a word, what I've come out for."

She let it all sink in. "What you've come out for then is simply to render him an immense service."

Well, poor Strether was willing to take it so. "Ah if you like."

"He stands, as they say, if you succeed with him, to gain—"

"Oh a lot of advantages." Strether had them clearly at his fingers' ends.

"By which you mean of course a lot of money."

"Well, not only. I'm acting with a sense for him of other things too. Consideration and comfort and security—the general safety of being anchored by a strong chain. He wants, as I see him, to be protected. Protected I mean from life."

"Ah voilà!"—her thought fitted with a click. "From life. What you *really* want to get him home for is to marry him."

"Well, that's about the size of it."

"Of course," she said, "it's rudimentary. But to any one in particular?"

He smiled at this, looking a little more conscious. "You get everything out."

For a moment again their eyes met. "You put everything in!"

He acknowledged the tribute by telling her. "To Mamie Pocock."

She wondered; then gravely, even exquisitely, as if to make the oddity also fit: "His own niece?"

"Oh you must yourself find a name for the relation. His brother-in-law's sister. Mrs. Jim's sister-in-law."

It seemed to have on Miss Gostrey a certain hardening effect. "And who in the world's Mrs. Jim?"

"Chad's sister—who was Sarah Newsome. She's married—didn't I mention it?—to Jim Pocock."

"Ah yes," she tacitly replied; but he had mentioned things—! Then, however, with all the sound it could have, "Who in the world's Jim Pocock?" she asked.

"Why Sally's husband. That's the only way we distinguish people at Woollett," he good-humouredly explained.

"And is it a great distinction—being Sally's husband?"

He considered. "I think there can be scarcely a greater—unless it may become one, in the future, to be Chad's wife."

"Then how do they distinguish *you*?"

"They *don't*—except, as I've told you, by the green cover."

Once more their eyes met on it, and she held him an instant. "The green cover won't—nor will *any* cover—avail you with *me*. You're of a depth of duplicity!" Still, she could in her own large grasp of the real condone it. "Is Mamie a great *parti*?"[6]

"Oh the greatest we have—our prettiest brightest girl."

Miss Gostrey seemed to fix the poor child. "I know what they *can* be. And with money?"

"Not perhaps with a great deal of that—but with so much of everything else that we don't miss it. We *don't* miss money much, you know," Strether added, "in general, in America, in pretty girls."

"No," she conceded; "but I know also what you do sometimes miss. And do you," she asked, "yourself admire her?"

It was a question, he indicated, that there might be several ways of taking; but he decided after an instant for the humorous. "Haven't I sufficiently showed you how I admire *any* pretty girl?"

Her interest in his problem was by this time such that it scarce left her freedom, and she kept close to the facts. "I supposed that at Woollett you wanted them—what shall I call it?—blameless. I mean your young men for your pretty girls."

"So did I!" Strether confessed. "But you strike there a curious fact—the fact that Woollett too accommodates itself to the spirit of the age and the increasing mildness of manners. Everything changes, and I hold that our situation precisely marks a date. We *should* prefer them blameless, but we have to make the best of them as we find them. Since the spirit of the age and the increasing mildness send them so much more to Paris—"

"You've to take them back as they come. When they *do* come. *Bon!*" Once more she embraced it all, but she had a moment of thought. "Poor Chad!"

"Ah," said Strether cheerfully, "Mamie will save him!"

She was looking away, still in her vision, and she spoke with impatience and almost as if he hadn't understood her. "*You'll* save him. That's who'll save him."

"Oh but with Mamie's aid. Unless indeed you mean," he added, "that I shall effect so much more with yours!"

It made her at last again look at him. "You'll do more—as you're

6. (Marital) match or catch.

so much better—than all of us put together."

"I think I'm only better since I've known *you!*" Strether bravely returned.

The depletion of the place, the shrinkage of the crowd and now comparatively quiet withdrawal of its last elements had already brought them nearer the door and put them in relation with a messenger of whom he bespoke Miss Gostrey's cab. But this left them a few minutes more, which she was clearly in no mood not to use. "You've spoken to me of what—by your success—Mr. Chad stands to gain. But you've not spoken to me of what you do."

"Oh I've nothing more to gain," said Strether very simply.

She took it as even quite too simple. "You mean you've got it all 'down'? You've been paid in advance?"

"Ah don't talk about payment!" he groaned.

Something in the tone of it pulled her up, but as their messenger still delayed she had another chance and she put it in another way. "What—by failure—do you stand to lose?"

He still, however, wouldn't have it. "Nothing!" he exclaimed, and on the messenger's at this instant reappearing he was able to sink the subject in their responsive advance. When, a few steps up the street, under a lamp, he had put her into her four-wheeler and she had asked him if the man had called for him no second conveyance, he replied before the door was closed. "You won't take me with you?"

"Not for the world."

"Then I shall walk."

"In the rain?"

"I like the rain," said Strether. "Good-night!"

She kept him a moment, while his hand was on the door, by not answering; after which she answered by repeating her question. "What do you stand to lose?"

Why the question now affected him as other he couldn't have said; he could only this time meet it otherwise. "Everything."

"So I thought. Then you shall succeed. And to that end I'm yours—"

"Ah, dear lady!" he kindly breathed.

"Till death!" said Maria Gostrey. "Good-night."

II [v]

Strether called, his second morning in Paris, on the bankers of the Rue Scribe[7] to whom his letter of credit was addressed, and he

7. In his first letter to the *Herald Tribune* in 1875 as their Parisian correspondent, James described as "the classic region" in which American tourists congregated the square mile on the right bank of the Seine that was bounded on the south by the Louvre and the Rue de Rivoli and on the north by the Rue Scribe, which was located just off the Place de l'Opéra; "the most sacred spot" in this region, according to James, was the corner of the Boulevard des Capucines. See *Parisian Sketches*, ed. Leon Edel and Ilse Dusoir Lind (New York: New York University Press, 1961), 6.

made this visit attended by Waymarsh, in whose company he had crossed from London two days before. They had hastened to the Rue Scribe on the morrow of their arrival, but Strether had not then found the letters the hope of which prompted this errand. He had had as yet none at all; hadn't expected them in London, but had counted on several in Paris, and, disconcerted now, had presently strolled back to the Boulevard with a sense of injury that he felt himself taking for as good a start as any other. It would serve, this spur to his spirit, he reflected, as, pausing at the top of the street, he looked up and down the great foreign avenue, it would serve to begin business with. His idea was to begin business immediately, and it did much for him the rest of his day that the beginning of business awaited him. He did little else till night but ask himself what he should do if he hadn't fortunately had so much to do; but he put himself the question in many different situations and connexions. What carried him hither and yon was an admirable theory that nothing he could do wouldn't be in some manner related to what he fundamentally had on hand, or *would* be—should he happen to have a scruple—wasted for it. He did happen to have a scruple—a scruple about taking no definite step till he should get letters; but this reasoning carried it off. A single day to feel his feet—he had felt them as yet only at Chester and in London—was, he could consider, none too much; and having, as he had often privately expressed it, Paris to reckon with, he threw these hours of freshness consciously into the reckoning. They made it continually greater, but that was what it had best be if it was to be anything at all, and he gave himself up till far into the evening, at the theatre and on the return, after the theatre, along the bright congested Boulevard, to feeling it grow. Waymarsh had accompanied him this time to the play, and the two men had walked together, as a first stage, from the Gymnase to the Café Riche,[8] into the crowded "terrace" of which establishment—the night, or rather the morning, for midnight had struck, being bland and populous —they had wedged themselves for refreshment. Waymarsh, as a result of some discussion with his friend, had made a marked virtue of his having now let himself go; and there had been elements of impression in their half-hour over their watered beer-glasses that gave him his occasion for conveying that he held this compromise with his stiffer self to have become extreme. He conveyed it—for it was still, after all, his stiffer self who gloomed out of the glare of the terrace—in solemn silence; and there was indeed a great deal of

8. The Théâtre du Gymnase was devoted primarily to the performance of comedies. The Café Riche, one of the best Parisian restaurants, was located in "the classic region."

critical silence, every way, between the companions, even till they gained the Place de l'Opéra, as to the character of their nocturnal progress.

This morning there *were* letters—letters which had reached London, apparently all together, the day of Strether's journey, and had taken their time to follow him; so that, after a controlled impulse to go into them in the reception-room of the bank, which, reminding him of the post-office at Woollett, affected him as the abutment of some transatlantic bridge, he slipped them into the pocket of his loose grey overcoat with a sense of the felicity of carrying them off. Waymarsh, who had had letters yesterday, had had them again to-day, and Waymarsh suggested in this particular no controlled impulses. The last one he was at all events likely to be observed to struggle with was clearly that of bringing to a premature close any visit to the Rue Scribe. Strether had left him there yesterday; he wanted to see the papers, and he had spent, by what his friend could make out, a succession of hours with the papers. He spoke of the establishment, with emphasis, as a post of superior observation; just as he spoke generally of his actual damnable doom as a device for hiding from him what was going on. Europe was best described, to his mind, as an elaborate engine for dissociating the confined American from that indispensable knowledge, and was accordingly only rendered bearable by these occasional stations of relief, traps for the arrest of wandering western airs. Strether, on his side, set himself to walk again—he had his relief in his pocket; and indeed, much as he had desired his budget, the growth of restlessness might have been marked in him from the moment he had assured himself of the superscription of most of the missives it contained. This restlessness became therefore his temporary law; he knew he should recognise as soon as see it the best place of all for settling down with his chief correspondent. He had for the next hour an accidental air of looking for it in the windows of shops; he came down the Rue de la Paix in the sun and, passing across the Tuileries[9] and the river, indulged more than once—as if on finding himself determined—in a sudden pause before the book-stalls of the opposite quay. In the garden of the Tuileries he had lingered, on two or three spots, to look; it was as if the wonderful Paris spring had stayed him as he roamed. The prompt Paris morning struck its cheerful notes—in a soft breeze and a sprinkled smell, in the light flit, over the garden-floor, of bareheaded girls with the buckled strap of oblong boxes, in the type of ancient thrifty persons basking betimes where terrace-walls were

9. The Rue de la Paix runs from the Place de l'Opéra toward the garden of the Tuileries, which adjoins the Louvre Museum. The palace of the Tuileries was burned in the uprising of 1871 and the ground was added to the garden, which became a favorite park for fashionable Parisians.

warm, in the blue-frocked brass-labelled officialism of humble rakers
and scrapers, in the deep references of a straight-pacing priest or
the sharp ones of a white-gaitered red-legged soldier. He watched
little brisk figures, figures whose movement was as the tick of the
great Paris clock, take their smooth diagonal from point to point;
the air had a taste as of something mixed with art, something that
presented nature as a white-capped master-chef. The palace was
gone, Strether remembered the palace; and when he gazed into the
irremediable void of its site the historic sense in him might have
been freely at play—the play under which in Paris indeed it so
often winces like a touched nerve. He filled out spaces with dim
symbols of scenes; he caught the gleam of white statues at the base
of which, with his letters out, he could tilt back a straw-bottomed
chair. But his drift was, for reasons, to the other side, and it floated
him unspent up the Rue de Seine and as far as the Luxembourg.[1]

In the Luxembourg Gardens he pulled up; here at last he found
his nook, and here, on a penny chair from which terraces, alleys,
vistas, fountains, little trees in green tubs, little women in white
caps and shrill little girls at play all sunnily "composed" together,
he passed an hour in which the cup of his impressions seemed truly
to overflow. But a week had elapsed since he quitted the ship, and
there were more things in his mind than so few days could account
for. More than once, during the time, he had regarded himself as admonished; but the admonition this morning was formidably sharp.
It took as it hadn't done yet the form of a question—the question
of what he was doing with such an extraordinary sense of escape.
This sense was sharpest after he had read his letters, but that was
also precisely why the question pressed. Four of the letters were
from Mrs. Newsome and none of them short; she had lost no time,
had followed on his heels while he moved, so expressing herself that
he now could measure the probable frequency with which he should
hear. They would arrive, it would seem, her communications, at the
rate of several a week; he should be able to count, it might even
prove, on more than one by each mail. If he had begun yesterday
with a small grievance he had therefore an opportunity to begin
to-day with its opposite. He read the letters successively and slowly,
putting others back into his pocket but keeping these for a long time
afterwards gathered in his lap. He held them there, lost in thought,
as if to prolong the presence of what they gave him; or as if at the

---

1. The Rue de Seine leads from the river south to the Luxembourg Gardens, the most popular
park on the left bank. In the first volume of his autobiography (1913), James describes a walk
similar to Strether's that he used to take as a boy in Paris, recalling that the Luxembourg
Gardens "formed the right, the sober social antithesis to the 'elegant' Tuileries." *A Small Boy
and Others: Autobiography*, ed. F. W. Dupee (New York: Criterion Books, 1956), 191–92.
James used a photograph of the Luxembourg Gardens as the frontispiece to the second volume
of the New York Edition of *The Ambassadors*. (See p. 16 for the photograph and pp. 368–
69 for a discussion of the photograph.)

least to assure them their part in the constitution of some lucidity. His friend wrote admirably, and her tone was even more in her style than in her voice—he might almost, for the hour, have had to come this distance to get its full carrying quality; yet the plenitude of his consciousness of difference consorted perfectly with the deepened intensity of the connexion. It was the difference, the difference of being just where he was and *as* he was, that formed the escape—this difference was so much greater than he had dreamed it would be; and what he finally sat there turning over was the strange logic of his finding himself so free. He felt it in a manner his duty to think out his state, to approve the process, and when he came in fact to trace the steps and add up the items they sufficiently accounted for the sum. He had never expected—that was the truth of it—again to find himself young, and all the years and other things it had taken to make him so were exactly his present arithmetic. He had to make sure of them to put his scruple to rest.

It all sprang at bottom from the beauty of Mrs. Newsome's desire that he should be worried with nothing that was not of the essence of his task; by insisting that he should thoroughly intermit and break she had so provided for his freedom that she would, as it were, have only herself to thank. Strether could not at this point indeed have completed his thought by the image of what she might have to thank herself *for*: the image, at best, of his own likeness— poor Lambert Strether washed up on the sunny strand by the waves of a single day, poor Lambert Strether thankful for breathing-time and stiffening himself while he gasped. There he was, and with nothing in his aspect or his posture to scandalise: it was only true that if he had seen Mrs. Newsome coming he would instinctively have jumped up to walk away a little. He would have come round and back to her bravely, but he would have had first to pull himself together. She abounded in news of the situation at home, proved to him how perfectly she was arranging for his absence, told him who would take up this and who take up that exactly where he had left it, gave him in fact chapter and verse for the moral that nothing would suffer. It filled for him, this tone of hers, all the air; yet it struck him at the same time as the hum of vain things. This latter effect was what he tried to justify—and with the success that, grave though the appearance, he at last lighted on a form that was happy. He arrived at it by the inevitable recognition of his having been a fortnight before one of the weariest of men. If ever a man had come off tired Lambert Strether was that man; and hadn't it been distinctly on the ground of his fatigue that his wonderful friend at home had so felt for him and so contrived? It seemed to him somehow at these instants that, could he only maintain with sufficient firmness his grasp of that truth, it might become in a manner his compass and his helm. What he wanted most was some idea that would simplify, and nothing would do this so much as the fact that he was done for and finished. If it had been in such a light that he had just detected in his cup the dregs of youth, that was a mere flaw of the surface of his scheme. He was so distinctly fagged-out that it must serve precisely as his convenience, and if he could but consistently be good for little enough he might do everything he wanted.

Everything he wanted was comprised moreover in a single boon —the common unattainable art of taking things as they came. He appeared to himself to have given his best years to an active appreciation of the way they didn't come; but perhaps—as they would seemingly here be things quite other—this long ache might at last drop to rest. He could easily see that from the moment he should accept the notion of his foredoomed collapse the last thing he would lack would be reasons and memories. Oh if he *should* do the sum no slate would hold the figures! The fact that he had failed, as he considered, in everything, in each relation and in half a dozen trades, as he liked luxuriously to put it, might have made, might still make, for an empty present; but it stood solidly for a crowded past. It had not been, so much achievement missed, a light yoke nor a short road. It was at present as if the backward picture had hung there, the long crooked course, grey in the shadow of his solitude. It had been a dreadful cheerful sociable solitude, a solitude of life or choice, of community; but though there had been people enough all round it there had been but three or four persons *in* it. Waymarsh was one of these, and the fact struck him just now as marking the record. Mrs. Newsome was another, and Miss Gostrey had of a sudden shown signs of becoming a third. Beyond, behind them was the pale figure of his real youth, which held against its breast the two presences paler than itself—the young wife he had early lost and the young son he had stupidly sacrificed. He had again and again made out for himself that he might have kept his little boy, his little dull boy who had died at school of rapid diphtheria, if he had not in those years so insanely given himself to merely missing the mother. It was the soreness of his remorse that the child had in all likelihood not really been dull—had been dull, as he had been banished and neglected, mainly because the father had been unwittingly selfish. This was doubtless but the secret habit of sorrow, which had slowly given way to time; yet there remained an ache sharp enough to make the spirit, at the sight now and again of some fair young man just growing up, wince with the thought of an opportunity lost. Had ever a man, he had finally fallen into the way of asking himself, lost so much and even done so much for so little? There had been particular reasons why all yesterday, beyond other days, he should have had in one ear this cold enquiry. His name on the green cover, where he had put it for Mrs. Newsome, expressed him doubtless just enough to make the world—the world as distinguished, both for more and for less, from Woollett—ask who he was. He had incurred the ridicule of having to have his explanation explained. He was Lambert Strether because he was on the cover, whereas it should have been, for anything like glory, that he was on the cover because he was Lambert Strether. He would have done anything for Mrs. Newsome, have been still more ridiculous—as he might, for that matter, have occasion to be yet; which came to saying that this acceptance of fate was all he had to show at fifty-five.

He judged the quantity as small because it *was* small, and all the more egregiously since it couldn't, as he saw the case, so much as thinkably have been larger. He hadn't had the gift of making the most of what he tried, and if he had tried and tried again—no one but himself knew how often—it appeared to have been that he might demonstrate what else, in default of that, *could* be made. Old ghosts of experiments came back to him, old drudgeries and delusions, and disgusts, old recoveries with their relapses, old fevers with their chills, broken moments of good faith, others of still better doubt; adventures, for the most part, of the sort qualified as lessons. The special spring that had constantly played for him the day before was the recognition—frequent enough to surprise him—of the promises to himself that he had after his other visit never kept. The reminiscence to-day most quickened for him was that of the vow taken in the course of the pilgrimage that, newly-married, with the War[2] just over, and helplessly young in spite of it, he had recklessly made with the creature who was so much younger still. It had been a bold dash, for which they had taken money set apart for necessities, but kept sacred at the moment in a hundred ways, and in none more so than by this private pledge of his own to treat the occasion as a relation formed with the higher culture and see that, as they said at Woollett, it should bear a good harvest. He had believed, sailing home again, that he had gained something great, and his theory—with an elaborate innocent plan of reading, digesting, coming back even, every few years—had then been to preserve, cherish and extend it. As such plans as these had come to nothing, however, in respect to acquisitions still more precious, it was doubtless little enough of a marvel that he should have lost account of that handful of seed. Buried for long years in dark corners at any rate these few germs had sprouted again under forty-eight hours of Paris. The process of yesterday had really been the process of feeling the general stirred life of connexions long since individ-

2. The American Civil War (1861–65).

ually dropped. Strether had become acquainted even on this ground with short gusts of speculation—sudden flights of fancy in Louvre galleries, hungry gazes through clear plates behind which lemon-coloured volumes[3] were as fresh as fruit on the tree.

There were instants at which he could ask whether, since there had been fundamentally so little question of his keeping anything, the fate after all decreed for him hadn't been only to *be* kept. Kept for something, in that event, that he didn't pretend, didn't possibly dare as yet to divine; something that made him hover and wonder and laugh and sigh, made him advance and retreat, feeling half ashamed of his impulse to plunge and more than half afraid of his impulse to wait. He remembered for instance how he had gone back in the sixties with lemon-coloured volumes in general on the brain as well as with a dozen—selected for his wife too—in his trunk; and nothing had at the moment shown more confidence than this invocation of the finer taste. They were still somewhere at home, the dozen—stale and soiled and never sent to the binder; but what had become of the sharp initiation they represented? They represented now the mere sallow paint on the door of the temple of taste that he had dreamed of raising up—a structure he had practically never carried further. Strether's present highest flights were perhaps those in which this particular lapse figured to him as a symbol, a symbol of his long grind and his want of odd moments, his want moreover of money, of opportunity, of positive dignity. That the memory of the vow of his youth should, in order to throb again, have had to wait for this last, as he felt it, of all his accidents —that was surely proof enough of how his conscience had been encumbered. If any further proof were needed it would have been to be found in the fact that, as he perfectly now saw, he had ceased even to measure his meagreness, a meagreness that sprawled, in this retrospect, vague and comprehensive, stretching back like some unmapped Hinterland from a rough coast-settlement. His conscience had been amusing itself for the forty-eight hours by forbidding him the purchase of a book; he held off from that, held off from everything; from the moment he didn't yet call on Chad he wouldn't for the world have taken any other step. On this evidence, however, of the way they actually affected him he glared at the lemon-coloured covers in confession of the subconsciousness that, all the same, in the great desert of the years, he must have had of them. The green covers at home comprised, by the law of their purpose, no tribute to letters; it was of a mere rich kernel of economics, politics, ethics that, glazed and, as Mrs. Newsome maintained rather against *his* view, pre-eminently pleasant to touch, they formed the specious shell. Without therefore any needed instinctive

3. French fiction was customarily published in yellow paper-backed editions.

knowledge of what was coming out, in Paris, on the bright high-
way, he struck himself at present as having more than once flushed
with a suspicion: he couldn't otherwise at present be feeling so
many fears confirmed. There were "movements" he was too late
for: weren't they, with the fun of them, already spent? There were
sequences he had missed and great gaps in the procession: he might
have been watching it all recede in a golden cloud of dust. If the
playhouse wasn't closed his seat had at least fallen to somebody else.
He had had an uneasy feeling the night before that if he was at the
theatre at all—though he indeed justified the theatre, in the specific sense, and with a grotesqueness to which his imagination did
all honour, as something he owed poor Waymarsh—he should have
been there with, and as might have been said, *for* Chad.

This suggested the question of whether he could properly have
taken him to such a play, and what effect—it was a point that
suddenly rose—his peculiar responsibility might be held in general
to have on his choice of entertainment. It had literally been present
to him at the Gymnase—where one was held moreover comparatively safe—that having his young friend at his side would have been
an odd feature of the work of redemption; and this quite in spite
of the fact that the picture presented might well, confronted with
Chad's own private stage, have seemed the pattern of propriety. He
clearly hadn't come out in the name of propriety but to visit unat-
tended equivocal performances; yet still less had he done so to
undermine his authority by sharing them with the graceless youth.
Was he to renounce all amusement for the sweet sake of that authority? and *would* such renouncement give him for Chad a moral
glamour? The little problem bristled the more by reason of poor
Strether's fairly open sense of the irony of things. Were there
then sides on which his predicament threatened to look rather droll
to him? Should he have to pretend to believe—either to himself or
the wretched boy—that there was anything that could make the
latter worse? Wasn't some such pretence on the other hand involved
in the assumption of possible processes that would make him better?
His greatest uneasiness seemed to peep at him out of the imminent
impression that almost any acceptance of Paris might give one's
authority away. It hung before him this morning, the vast bright
Babylon, like some huge iridescent object, a jewel brilliant and
hard, in which parts were not to be discriminated nor differences
comfortably marked. It twinkled and trembled and melted together,
and what seemed all surface one moment seemed all depth the
next. It was a place of which, unmistakeably, Chad was fond;
wherefore if he, Strether, should like it too much, what on earth,
with such a bond, would become of either of them? It all depended of course—which was a gleam of light—on how the "too

much" was measured; though indeed our friend fairly felt, while
he prolonged the meditation I describe, that for himself even already a certain measure had been reached. It will have been sufficiently seen that he was not a man to neglect any good chance for
reflexion. Was it at all possible for instance to like Paris enough
without liking it too much? He luckily however hadn't promised
Mrs. Newsome not to like it at all. He was ready to recognise at
this stage that such an engagement *would* have tied his hands. The
Luxembourg Gardens were incontestably just so adorable at this
hour by reason—in addition to their intrinsic charm—of his not
having taken it. The only engagement he had taken, when he
looked the thing in the face, was to do what he reasonably could.

It upset him a little none the less and after a while to find himself at last remembering on what current of association he had been
floated so far. Old imaginations of the Latin Quarter[4] had played
their part for him, and he had duly recalled having been with
this scene of rather ominous legend that, like so many young men
in fiction as well as in fact, Chad had begun. He was now quite out
of it, with his "home," as Strether figured the place, in the Boulevard Malesherbes;[5] which was perhaps why, repairing, not to fail of
justice either, to the elder neighbourhood, our friend had felt he
could allow for the element of the usual, the immemorial, without
courting perturbation. He was not at least in danger of seeing the
youth and the particular Person flaunt by together; and yet he was
in the very air of which—just to feel what the early natural note
must have been—he wished most to take counsel. It became at
once vivid to him that he had originally had, for a few days, an almost envious vision of the boy's romantic privilege. Melancholy
Mürger, with Francine and Musette and Rodolphe,[6] at home, in
the company of the tattered, one—if he not in his single self two
or three—of the unbound, the paper-covered dozen on the shelf;
and when Chad had written, five years ago, after a sojourn then
already prolonged to six months, that he had decided to go in for
economy and the real thing, Strether's fancy had quite fondly accompanied him in this migration, which was to convey him, as
they somewhat confusedly learned at Woollett, across the bridges

4. The district on the left bank of the Seine that includes the Sorbonne, the Luxembourg Gardens,
   and the centers of bohemian life.
5. One of the grander and more fashionable boulevards of the right bank; it leads from a square
   adjoining the Boulevard des Capucines to the outskirts of the old city, and was named after
   the liberal eighteenth-century statesman Lamoignon-Malesherbes, who was guillotined after
   defending Louis XVI at his trial during the French Revolution. In Old French the name may
   have originally meant poisonous plants.
6. Henry Murger's *Scènes de la vie de Bohème* (*Scenes of Bohemian Life*, 1848) depicts the lives
   of penniless students and artists such as Rodolphe the poet, Musette the gay mistress of painters,
   and Francine the consumptive mistress of a sculptor. (Murger's stories were turned into a play
   that became the basis for Puccini's opera *La Bohème*.)

and up the Montagne Sainte-Geneviève.[7] This was the region—
Chad had been quite distinct about it—in which the best French,
and many other things, were to be learned at least cost, and in
which all sorts of clever fellows, compatriots there for a purpose,
formed an awfully pleasant set. The clever fellows, the friendly
countrymen were mainly young painters, sculptors, architects, med-
ical students; but they were, Chad sagely opined, a much more
profitable lot to be with—even on the footing of not being quite
one of them—than the "terrible toughs" (Strether remembered
the edifying discrimination) of the American bars and banks
roundabout the Opéra. Chad had thrown out, in the communications following this one—for at that time he did once in a while
communicate—that several members of a band of earnest workers
under one of the great artists had taken him right in, making him
dine every night, almost for nothing, at their place, and even
pressing him not to neglect the hypothesis of there being as much
"in him" as in any of them. There had been literally a moment at
which it appeared there might be something in him; there had been
at any rate a moment at which he had written that he didn't know
but what a month or two more might see him enrolled in some
atelier. The season had been one at which Mrs. Newsome was
moved to gratitude for small mercies; it had broken on them all as a
blessing that their absentee *had* perhaps a conscience—that he was
sated in fine with idleness, was ambitious of variety. The exhibition
was doubtless as yet not brilliant, but Strether himself, even by that
time much enlisted and immersed, had determined, on the part of
the two ladies, a temperate approval and in fact, as he now recol-
lected, a certain austere enthusiasm.

But the very next thing that happened had been a dark drop of
the curtain. The son and brother had not browsed long on the
Montagne Sainte-Geneviève—his effective little use of the name of
which, like his allusion to the best French, appeared to have been
but one of the notes of his rough cunning. The light refreshment
of these vain appearances had not accordingly carried any of them
very far. On the other hand it had gained Chad time; it had given
him a chance, unchecked, to strike his roots, had paved the way for
initiations more direct and more deep. It was Strether's belief that
he had been comparatively innocent before this first migration, and
even that the first effects of the migration would not have been,
without some particular bad accident, to have been deplored. There
had been three months—he had sufficiently figured it out—in which
Chad had wanted to try. He *had* tried, though not very hard—he
had had his little hour of good faith. The weakness of this principle

7. On the side of the "Mountain of St. Geneviève"—a slight hill in the Latin Quarter—are the
remains of the abbey in which the patron saint of Paris is buried.

in him was that almost any accident attestedly bad enough was
stronger. Such had at any rate markedly been the case for the precipitation of a special series of impressions. They had proved, successively, these impressions—all of Musette and Francine, but
Musette and Francine vulgarised by the larger evolution of the type
—irresistibly sharp: he had "taken up," by what was at the time to
be shrinkingly gathered, as it was scantly mentioned, with one
ferociously "interested" little person after another. Strether had
read somewhere[8] of a Latin motto, a description of the hours, observed on a clock by a traveller in Spain; and he had been led to
apply it in thought to Chad's number one, number two, number
three. *Omnes vulnerant, ultima necat*—they had all morally
wounded, the last had morally killed. The last had been longest in
possession—in possession, that is, of whatever was left of the poor
boy's finer mortality. And it hadn't been she, it had been one of her
early predecessors, who had determined the second migration, the
expensive return and relapse, the exchange again, as was fairly to be
presumed, of the vaunted best French for some special variety of
the worst.

He pulled himself then at last together for his own progress back;
not with the feeling that he had taken his walk in vain. He prolonged it a little, in the immediate neighbourhood, after he had
quitted his chair; and the upshot of the whole morning for him was
that his campaign had begun. He had wanted to put himself in
relation, and he would be hanged if he were *not* in relation. He
was that at no moment so much as while, under the old arches of the
Odéon,[9] he lingered before the charming open-air array of literature classic and casual. He found the effect of tone and tint, in
the long charged tables and shelves, delicate and appetising; the
impression—substituting one kind of low-priced *consommation*[1]
for another—might have been that of one of the pleasant cafés that
overlapped, under an awning, to the pavement; but he edged along,
grazing the tables, with his hands firmly behind him. He wasn't
there to dip, to consume—he was there to reconstruct. He wasn't
there for his own profit—not, that is, the direct; he was there on
some chance of feeling the brush of the wing of the stray spirit of
youth. He felt it in fact, he had it beside him; the old arcade indeed, as his inner sense listened, gave out the faint sound, as from
far off, of the wild waving of wings. They were folded now over the

8. In the first English edition of *The Ambassadors*, the author of Strether's reading is identified
as "Théophile Gautier (see p. 350). The motto, actually given as *Vulnerant omnes, ultima
necat* ("All wound, the last kills"), appears in Chapter II of Gautier's *Voyage en Espagne*
(*Travels in Spain*, 1845), which James once described as "a masterpiece and model" (*French
Poets and Novelists* [London: 1878], 52).
9. Located near the Luxembourg Gardens, the Odéon was the most prominent French theater
after the Théâtre Français. It was devoted mainly to French classical drama.
1. Drink (on a menu).

breasts of buried generations; but a flutter or two lived again in the turned page of shock-headed slouch-hatted loiterers whose young intensity of type, in the direction of pale acuteness, deepened his vision, and even his appreciation, of racial differences, and whose manipulation of the uncut volume was too often, however, but a listening at closed doors. He reconstructed a possible groping Chad of three or four years before, a Chad who had, after all, simply— for that was the only way to see it—been too vulgar for his privilege. Surely it *was* a privilege to have been young and happy just there. Well, the best thing Strether knew of him was that he had had such a dream.

But his own actual business half an hour later was with a third floor on the Boulevard Malesherbes—so much as that was definite; and the fact of the enjoyment by the third-floor windows of a continuous balcony, to which he was helped by this knowledge, had perhaps something to do with his lingering for five minutes on the opposite side of the street. There were points as to which he had quite made up his mind, and one of these bore precisely on the wisdom of the abruptness to which events had finally committed him, a policy that he was pleased to find not at all shaken as he now looked at his watch and wondered. He *had* announced himself—six months before; had written out at least that Chad wasn't to be surprised should he see him some day turn up. Chad had thereupon, in a few words of rather carefully colourless answer, offered him a general welcome; and Strether, ruefully reflecting that he might have understood the warning as a hint to hospitality, a bid for an invitation, had fallen back upon silence as the corrective most to his own taste. He had asked Mrs. Newsome moreover not to announce him again; he had so distinct an opinion on his attacking his job, should he attack it at all, in his own way. Not the least of this lady's high merits for him was that he could absolutely rest on her word. She was the only woman he had known, even at Woollett, as to whom his conviction was positive that to lie was beyond her art. Sarah Pocock, for instance, her own daughter, though with social ideals, as they said, in some respects different—Sarah who *was*, in her way, æsthetic, had never refused to human commerce that mitigation of rigour; there were occasions when he had distinctly seen her apply it. Since, accordingly, at all events, he had had it from Mrs. Newsome that she had, at whatever cost to her more strenuous view, conformed, in the matter of preparing Chad, wholly to his restrictions, he now looked up at the fine continuous balcony with a safe sense that if the case had been bungled the mistake was at least his property. Was there perhaps just a suspicion of that in his present pause on the edge of the Boulevard and well in the pleasant light?

Many things came over him here, and one of them was that he should doubtless presently know whether he had been shallow or sharp. Another was that the balcony in question didn't somehow show as a convenience easy to surrender. Poor Strether had at this very moment to recognise the truth that wherever one paused in Paris the imagination reacted before one could stop it. This perpetual reaction put a price, if one would, on pauses; but it piled up consequences till there was scarce room to pick one's steps among them. What call had he, at such a juncture, for example, to like Chad's very house? High broad clear—he was expert enough to make out in a moment that it was admirably built—it fairly embarrassed our friend by the quality that, as he would have said, it "sprang" on him. He had struck off the fancy that it might, as a preliminary, be of service to him to be seen, by a happy accident, from the third-story windows, which took all the March sun, but of what service was it to find himself making out after a moment that the quality "sprung," the quality produced by measure and balance, the fine relation of part to part and space to space, was probably—aided by the presence of ornament as positive as it was discreet, and by the complexion of the stone, a cold fair grey, warmed and polished a little by life—neither more nor less than a case of distinction, such a case as he could only feel unexpectedly as a sort of delivered challenge? Meanwhile, however, the chance he had allowed for—the chance of being seen in time from the balcony—had become a fact. Two or three of the windows stood open to the violet air; and, before Strether had cut the knot by crossing, a young man had come out and looked about him, had lighted a cigarette and tossed the match over, and then, resting on the rail, had given himself up to watching the life below while he smoked. His arrival contributed, in its order, to keeping Strether in position; the result of which in turn was that Strether soon felt himself noticed. The young man began to look at him as in acknowledgement of his being himself in observation.

This was interesting so far as it went, but the interest was affected by the young man's not being Chad. Strether wondered at first if he were perhaps Chad altered, and then saw that this was asking too much of alteration. The young man was light bright and alert—with an air too pleasant to have been arrived at by patching. Strether had conceived Chad as patched, but not beyond recognition. He was in presence, he felt, of amendments enough as they stood; it was a sufficient amendment that the gentleman up there should be Chad's friend. He was young too then, the gentleman up there—he was very young; young enough apparently to be amused at an elderly watcher, to be curious even to see what the elderly watcher would do on finding himself watched. There was youth in that, there was youth in the surrender to the balcony, there was youth for Strether at this moment in everything but his own business; and Chad's thus pronounced association with youth had given the next instant an extraordinary quick lift to the issue. The balcony, the distinguished front, testified suddenly, for Strether's fancy, to something that was up and up; they placed the whole case materially, and as by an admirable image, on a level that he found himself at the end of another moment rejoicing to think he might reach. The young man looked at him still, he looked at the young man; and the issue, by a rapid process, was that this knowledge of a perched privacy appeared to him the last of luxuries. To him too the perched privacy was open, and he saw it now but in one light—that of the only domicile, the only fireside, in the great ironic city, on which he had the shadow of a claim. Miss Gostrey had a fireside; she had told him of it, and it was something that doubtless awaited him; but Miss Gostrey hadn't yet arrived—she mightn't arrive for days; and the sole attenuation of his excluded state was his vision of the small, the admittedly secondary hotel in the bye-street from the Rue de la Paix, in which her solicitude for his purse had placed him, which affected him somehow as all indoor chill, glass-roofed court and slippery staircase, and which, by the same token, expressed the presence of Waymarsh even at times when Waymarsh might have been certain to be round at the bank. It came to pass before he moved that Waymarsh, and Waymarsh alone, Waymarsh not only undiluted but positively strengthened, struck him as the present alternative to the young man in the balcony. When he did move it was fairly to escape that alternative. Taking his way over the street at last and passing through the porte-cochère[2] of the house was like consciously leaving Waymarsh out. However, he would tell him all about it.

Book Third

I [VI]

Strether told Waymarsh all about it that very evening, on their dining together at the hotel; which needn't have happened, he was all the while aware, hadn't he chosen to sacrifice to this occasion a rarer opportunity. The mention to his companion of the sacrifice was moreover exactly what introduced his recital—or, as he would have called it with more confidence in his interlocutor, his confession. His confession was that he had been captured and that one of the features of the affair had just failed to be his engaging himself on the spot to dinner. As by such a freedom Waymarsh would have lost him he had obeyed his scruple; and he had like-

2. A large gateway leading to a courtyard.

wise obeyed another scruple—which bore on the question of his himself bringing a guest.

Waymarsh looked gravely ardent, over the finished soup, at this array of scruples; Strether hadn't yet got quite used to being so unprepared for the consequences of the impression he produced. It was comparatively easy to explain, however, that he hadn't felt sure his guest would please. The person was a young man whose acquaintance he had made but that afternoon in the course of rather a hindered enquiry for another person—an enquiry his new friend had just prevented in fact from being vain. "Oh," said Strether, "I've all sorts of things to tell you!"—and he put it in a way that was a virtual hint to Waymarsh to help him to enjoy the telling. He waited for his fish, he drank of his wine, he wiped his long moustache, he leaned back in his chair, he took in the two English ladies who had just creaked past them and whom he would even have articulately greeted if they hadn't rather chilled the impulse; so that all he could do was—by way of doing something—to say "Merci, François!" out quite loud when his fish was brought. Everything was there that he wanted, everything that could make the moment an occasion, that would do beautifully—everything but what Waymarsh might give. The little waxed *salle-à-manger*[1] was sallow and sociable; François, dancing over it, all smiles, was a man and a brother; the high-shouldered patronne,[2] with her high-held, much-rubbed hands, seemed always assenting exuberantly to something unsaid; the Paris evening in short was, for Strether, in the very taste of the soup, in the goodness, as he was innocently pleased to think it, of the wine, in the pleasant coarse texture of the napkin and the crunch of the thick-crusted bread. These all were things congruous with his confession, and his confession was that he *had* —it would come out properly just there if Waymarsh would only take it properly—agreed to breakfast out, at twelve literally, the next day. He didn't quite know where; the delicacy of the case came straight up in the remembrance of his new friend's "We'll see; I'll take you somewhere!"—for it had required little more than that, after all, to let him right in. He was affected after a minute, face to face with his actual comrade, by the impulse to overcolour. There had already been things in respect to which he knew himself tempted by this perversity. If Waymarsh thought them bad he should at least have his reason for his discomfort; so Strether showed them as worse. Still, he was now, in his way, sincerely perplexed.

Chad had been absent from the Boulevard Malesherbes—was absent from Paris altogether; he had learned that from the concierge,[3] but had nevertheless gone up, and gone up—there were no

1. Dining room.
2. Proprietress.
3. Doorkeeper.

two ways about it—from an uncontrollable, a really, if one would, depraved curiosity. The concierge had mentioned to him that a friend of the tenant of the troisième[4] was for the time in possession; and this had been Strether's pretext for a further enquiry, an experiment carried on, under Chad's roof, without his knowledge. "I found his friend in fact there keeping the place warm, as he called it, for him; Chad himself being, as appears, in the south. He went a month ago to Cannes[5] and though his return begins to be looked for it can't be for some days. I might, you see, perfectly have waited a week; might have beaten a retreat as soon as I got this essential knowledge. But I beat no retreat; I did the opposite; I stayed, I dawdled, I trifled; above all I looked round. I saw, in fine; and—I don't know what to call it—I sniffed. It's a detail, but it's as if there were something—something very good—*to* sniff."

Waymarsh's face had shown his friend an attention apparently so remote that the latter was slightly surprised to find it at this point abreast with him. "Do you mean a smell? What of?"

"A charming scent. But I don't know."

Waymarsh gave an inferential grunt. "Does he live there with a woman?"

"I don't know."

Waymarsh waited an instant for more, then resumed. "Has he taken her off with him?"

"And will he bring her back?"—Strether fell into the enquiry. But he wound it up as before. "I don't know."

The way he wound it up, accompanied as this was with another drop back, another degustation of the Léoville,[6] another wipe of his moustache and another good word for François, seemed to produce in his companion a slight irritation. "Then what the devil *do* you know?"

"Well," said Strether almost gaily, "I guess I don't know anything!" His gaiety might have been a tribute to the fact that the state he had been reduced to did for him again what had been done by his talk of the matter with Miss Gostrey at the London theatre. It was somehow enlarging; and the air of that amplitude was now doubtless more or less—and all for Waymarsh to feel—in his further response. "That's what I found out from the young man."

"But I thought you said you found out nothing."

"Nothing but that—that I don't know anything."

"And what good does that do you?"

"It's just," said Strether, "what I've come to you to help me to discover. I mean anything about anything over here. I *felt* that, up there. It regularly rose before me in its might. The young man

4. Third (*i.e.*, the third floor after the ground floor, hence the fourth story).
5. A fashionable seaside town on the southern coast of France.
6. A red Bordeaux wine.

moreover—Chad's friend—as good as told me so."

"As good as told you you know nothing about anything?" Waymarsh appeared to look at some one who might have as good as told *him.* "How old is he?"

"Well, I guess not thirty."

"Yet you had to take that from him?"

"Oh I took a good deal more—since, as I tell you, I took an invitation to déjeuner."[7]

"And are you *going* to that unholy meal?"

"If you'll come with me. He wants you too, you know. I told him about you. He gave me his card," Strether pursued, "and his name's rather funny. It's John Little Bilham, and he says his two surnames are, on account of his being small, inevitably used together."

"Well," Waymarsh asked with due detachment from these details, "what's he doing up there?"

"His account of himself is that he's 'only a little artist-man.' That seemed to me perfectly to describe him. But he's yet in the phase of study; this, you know, is the great art-school—to pass a certain number of years in which he came over. And he's a great friend of Chad's, and occupying Chad's rooms just now because they're so pleasant. *He's* very pleasant and curious too," Strether added—"though he's not from Boston."

Waymarsh looked already rather sick of him. "Where *is* he from?"

Strether thought. "I don't know that, either. But he's 'notoriously,' as he put it himself, not from Boston."

"Well," Waymarsh moralised from dry depths, "every one can't notoriously *be* from Boston. Why," he continued, "is he curious?"

"Perhaps just for *that*—for one thing! But really," Strether added, "for everything. When you meet him you'll see."

"Oh I don't want to meet him," Waymarsh impatiently growled. "Why don't he go home?"

Strether hesitated. "Well, because he likes it over here."

This appeared in particular more than Waymarsh could bear. "He ought then to be ashamed of himself, and, as you admit that you think so too, why drag him in?"

Strether's reply again took time. "Perhaps I do think so myself —though I don't quite yet admit it. I'm not a bit sure—it's again one of the things I want to find out. I liked him, and *can* you like people—? But no matter." He pulled himself up. "There's no doubt I want you to come down on me and squash me."

Waymarsh helped himself to the next course, which, however, proving not the dish he had just noted as supplied to the English

7. Breakfast or lunch.

ladies, had the effect of causing his imagination temporarily to wander. But it presently broke out at a softer spot. "Have they got a handsome place up there?"

"Oh a charming place; full of beautiful and valuable things. I never saw such a place"—and Strether's thought went back to it. "For a little artist-man—!" He could in fact scarce express it.

But his companion, who appeared now to have a view, insisted. "Well?"

"Well, life can hold nothing better. Besides, they're things of which he's in charge."

"So that he does doorkeeper for your precious pair? Can life," Waymarsh enquired, "hold nothing better than *that?*" Then as Strether, silent, seemed even yet to wonder, "Doesn't he know what *she* is?" he went on.

"I don't know. I didn't ask him. I couldn't. It was impossible. You wouldn't either. Besides I didn't want to. No more would you." Strether in short explained it at a stroke. "You can't make out over here what people do know."

"Then what did you come over for?"

"Well, I suppose exactly to see for myself—without their aid."

"Then what do you want mine for?"

"Oh," Strether laughed, "you're not one of *them!* I do know what *you* know."

As, however, this last assertion caused Waymarsh again to look at him hard—such being the latter's doubt of its implications—he felt his justification lame. Which was still more the case when Waymarsh presently said: "Look here, Strether. Quit this."

Our friend smiled with a doubt of his own. "Do you mean my tone?"

"No—damn your tone. I mean your nosing round. Quit the whole job. Let them stew in their juice. You're being used for a thing you ain't fit for. People don't take a fine-tooth comb to groom a horse."

"Am I a fine-tooth comb?" Strether laughed. "It's something I never called myself!"

"It's what you are, all the same. You ain't so young as you were, but you've kept your teeth."

He acknowledged his friend's humour. "Take care I don't get them into *you!* You'd like them, my friends at home, Waymarsh," he declared; "you'd really particularly like them. And I know"—it was slightly irrelevant, but he gave it sudden and singular force— "I know they'd like you!"

"Oh don't work them off on *me!*" Waymarsh groaned.

Yet Strether still lingered with his hands in his pockets. "It's really quite as indispensable as I say that Chad should be got back."

"Indispensable to whom? To you?"

"Yes," Strether presently said.

"Because if you get him you also get Mrs. Newsome?"

Strether faced it. "Yes."

"And if you don't get him you don't get her?"

It might be merciless, but he continued not to flinch. "I think it might have some effect on our personal understanding. Chad's of real importance—or can easily become so if he will—to the business."

"And the business is of real importance to his mother's husband?"

"Well, I naturally want what my future wife wants. And the thing will be much better if we have our own man in it."

"If you have your own man in it, in other words," Waymarsh said, "you'll marry—you personally—more money. She's already rich, as I understand you, but she'll be richer still if the business can be made to boom on certain lines that you've laid down."

"I haven't laid them down," Strether promptly returned. "Mr. Newsome—who knew extraordinarily well what he was about—laid them down ten years ago."

Oh well, Waymarsh seemed to indicate with a shake of his mane, *that* didn't matter! "You're fierce for the boom anyway."

His friend weighed a moment in silence the justice of the charge. "I can scarcely be called fierce, I think, when I so freely take my chance of the possibility, the danger, of being influenced in a sense counter to Mrs. Newsome's own feelings."

Waymarsh gave this proposition a long hard look. "I see. You're afraid yourself of being squared. But you're a humbug," he added, "all the same."

"Oh!" Strether quickly protested.

"Yes, you ask me for protection—which makes you very interesting; and then you won't take it. You say you want to be squashed—"

"Ah but not so easily! Don't you see," Strether demanded, "where my interest, as already shown you, lies? It lies in my not being squared. If I'm squared where's my marriage? If I miss my errand I miss that; and if I miss that I miss everything—I'm nowhere."

Waymarsh—but all relentlessly—took this in. "What do I care where you are if you're spoiled?"

Their eyes met on it an instant. "Thank you awfully," Strether at last said. "But don't you think *her* judgement of that—?"

"Ought to content me? No."

It kept them again face to face, and the end of this was that Strether again laughed. "You do her injustice. You really *must* know her. Good-night."

He breakfasted with Mr. Bilham on the morrow, and, as inconsequently befell, with Waymarsh massively of the party. The latter announced, at the eleventh hour and much to his friend's surprise, that, damn it, he would as soon join him as do anything else; on which they proceeded together, strolling in a state of detachment practically luxurious for them to the Boulevard Malesherbes, a couple engaged that day with the sharp spell of Paris as confessedly, it might have been seen, as any couple among the daily thousands so compromised. They walked, wandered, wondered and, a little, lost themselves; Strether hadn't had for years so rich a consciousness of time—a bag of gold into which he constantly dipped for a handful. It was present to him that when the little business with Mr. Bilham should be over he would still have shining hours to use absolutely as he liked.[8] There was no great pulse of haste yet in this process of saving Chad; nor was that effect a bit more marked as he sat, half an hour later, with his legs under Chad's mahogany, with Mr. Bilham on one side, with a friend of Mr. Bilham's on the other, with Waymarsh stupendously opposite, and with the great hum of Paris coming up in softness, vagueness—for Strether himself indeed already positive sweetness—through the sunny windows toward which, the day before, his curiosity had raised its wings from below. The feeling strongest with him at that moment had borne fruit almost faster than he could taste it, and Strether literally felt at the present hour that there was a precipitation in his fate. He had known nothing and nobody as he stood in the street; but hadn't his view now taken a bound in the direction of every one and of every thing?

"What's he up to, what's he up to?"—something like that was at the back of his head all the while in respect to little Bilham; but meanwhile, till he should make out, every one and every thing were as good as represented for him by the combination of his host and the lady on his left. The lady on his left, the lady thus promptly and ingeniously invited to "meet" Mr. Strether and Mr. Waymarsh—it was the way she herself expressed her case—was a very marked person, a person who had much to do with our friend's asking himself if the occasion weren't in its essence the most baited, the most gilded of traps. Baited it could properly be called when the repast was of so wise a savour, and gilded surrounding objects seemed inevitably to need to be when Miss Barrace—which was the lady's name—looked at them with convex Parisian eyes and through a glass with a remarkably long tortoise-shell handle. Why Miss Barrace, mature meagre erect and eminently gay, highly adorned, perfectly familiar, freely contradictious and reminding him of some last-century portrait of a clever head without powder—why Miss

8. "How doth the little busy bee / Improve each shining hour." Isaac Watts, "Against Idleness and Mischief."

Barrace should have been in particular the note of a "trap" Strether couldn't on the spot have explained; he blinked in the light of a conviction that he should know later on, and know well—as it came over him, for that matter, with force, that he should need to. He wondered what he was to think exactly of either of his new friends; since the young man, Chad's intimate and deputy, had, in thus constituting the scene, practised so much more subtly than he had been prepared for, and since in especial Miss Barrace, surrounded clearly by every consideration, hadn't scrupled to figure as a familiar object. It was interesting to him to feel that he was in the presence of new measures, other standards, a different scale of relations, and that evidently here were a happy pair who didn't think of things at all as he and Waymarsh thought. Nothing was less to have been calculated in the business than that it should now be for him as if he and Waymarsh were comparatively quite at one.

The latter was magnificent—this at least was an assurance privately given him by Miss Barrace. "Oh your friend's a type, the grand old American—what shall one call it? The Hebrew prophet, Ezekiel, Jeremiah, who used when I was a little girl in the Rue Montaigne [9] to come to see my father and who was usually the American Minister to the Tuileries or some other court. I haven't seen one these ever so many years; the sight of it warms my poor old chilled heart; this specimen is wonderful; in the right quarter, you know, he'll have a *succès fou*." [1] Strether hadn't failed to ask what the right quarter might be, much as he required his presence of mind to meet such a change in their scheme. "Oh the artist-quarter and that kind of thing; *here* already, for instance, as you see." He had been on the point of echoing " 'Here'?—is *this* the artist-quarter?" but she had already disposed of the question with a wave of all her tortoise-shell and an easy "Bring him to *me!*" He knew on the spot how little he should be able to bring him, for the very air was by this time, to his sense, thick and hot with poor Waymarsh's judgement of it. He was in the trap still more than his companion and, unlike his companion, not making the best of it; which was precisely what doubtless gave him his admirable sombre glow. Little did Miss Barrace know that what was behind it was his grave estimate of her own laxity. The general assumption with which our two friends had arrived had been that of finding Mr. Bilham ready to conduct them to one or other of those resorts of the earnest, the æsthetic fraternity which were shown among the sights of Paris. In this character it would have justified them in a proper insistence on discharging their score. Waymarsh's only proviso at the last had been that nobody should pay for him; but he found himself, as the occasion developed, paid for on

9. The Avenue Montaigne leads from the Champs-Élysées to the right bank of the Seine.
1. Huge success.

a scale as to which Strether privately made out that he already nursed retribution. Strether was conscious across the table of what worked in him, conscious when they passed back to the small salon to which, the previous evening, he himself had made so rich a reference; conscious most of all as they stepped out to the balcony in which one would have had to be an ogre not to recognise the perfect place for easy aftertastes. These things were enhanced for Miss Barrace by a succession of excellent cigarettes—acknowledged, acclaimed, as a part of the wonderful supply left behind him by Chad—in an almost equal absorption of which Strether found himself blindly, almost wildly pushing forward. He might perish by the sword as well as by famine, and he knew that his having abetted the lady by an excess that was rare with him would count for little in the sum—as Waymarsh might so easily add it up—of her licence. Waymarsh had smoked of old, smoked hugely; but Waymarsh did nothing now, and that gave him his advantage over people who took things up lightly just when others had laid them heavily down. Strether had never smoked, and he felt as if he flaunted at his friend that this had been only because of a reason. The reason, it now began to appear even to himself, was that he had never had a lady to smoke with.

It was this lady's being there at all, however, that was the strange free thing; perhaps, since she *was* there, her smoking was the least of her freedoms. If Strether had been sure at each juncture of what—with Bilham in especial—she talked about, he might have traced others and winced at them and felt Waymarsh wince; but he was in fact so often at sea that his sense of the range of reference was merely general and that he on several different occasions guessed and interpreted only to doubt. He wondered what they meant, but there were things he scarce thought they could be supposed to mean, and "Oh no—not *that!*" was at the end of most of his ventures. This was the very beginning with him of a condition as to which, later on, it will be seen, he found cause to pull himself up; and he was to remember the moment duly as the first step in a process. The central fact of the place was neither more nor less, when analysed—and a pressure superficial sufficed—than the fundamental impropriety of Chad's situation, round about which they thus seemed cynically clustered. Accordingly, since they took it for granted, they took for granted all that was in connexion with it taken for granted at Woollett—matters as to which, verily, he had been reduced with Mrs. Newsome to the last intensity of silence. That was the consequence of their being too bad to be talked about, and was the accompaniment, by the same token, of a deep conception of their badness. It befell therefore that when poor Strether put it to himself that their badness was ultimately, or perhaps even insolently, what such a scene as the one before him was, so to speak, built upon, he could scarce shirk the dilemma of reading a roundabout echo of them into almost anything that came up. This, he was well aware, was a dreadful necessity; but such was the stern logic, he could only gather, of a relation to the irregular life.

It was the way the irregular life sat upon Bilham and Miss Barrace that was the insidious, the delicate marvel. He was eager to concede that their relation to it was all indirect, for anything else in him would have shown the grossness of bad manners; but the indirectness was none the less consonant—*that* was striking—with a grateful enjoyment of everything that was Chad's. They spoke of him repeatedly, invoking his good name and good nature, and the worst confusion of mind for Strether was that all their mention of him was of a kind to do him honour. They commended his munificence and approved his taste, and in doing so sat down, as it seemed to Strether, in the very soil out of which these things flowered. Our friend's final predicament was that he himself was sitting down, for the time, *with* them, and there was a supreme moment at which, compared with his collapse, Waymarsh's erectness affected him as really high. One thing was certain—he saw he must make up his mind. He must approach Chad, must wait for him, deal with him, master him, but he mustn't dispossess himself of the faculty of seeing things as they were. He must bring him to *him*—not go himself, as it were, so much of the way. He must at any rate be clearer as to what—should he continue to do that for convenience—he was still condoning. It was on the detail of this quantity—and what could the fact be but mystifying?—that Bilham and Miss Barrace threw so little light. So there they were.

II [VII]

When Miss Gostrey arrived, at the end of a week, she made him a sign; he went immediately to see her, and it wasn't till then that he could again close his grasp on the idea of a corrective. This idea however was luckily all before him again from the moment he crossed the threshold of the little entresol[1] of the Quartier Marbœuf[2] into which she had gathered, as she said, picking them up in a thousand flights and funny little passionate pounces, the makings of a final nest. He recognised in an instant that there really, there only, he should find the boon with the vision of which he had first mounted Chad's stairs. He might have been a little scared at the picture of how much more, in this place, he should know himself "in" hadn't his friend been on the spot to measure the amount to his appetite. Her compact and crowded little chambers,

1. Mezzanine.
2. In 1900 a modern and handsome section of Paris on the right bank between the Seine and the Champs-Élysées.

almost dusky, as they at first struck him, with accumulations, represented a supreme general adjustment to opportunities and conditions. Wherever he looked he saw an old ivory or an old brocade,
and he scarce knew where to sit for fear of a misappliance. The
life of the occupant struck him of a sudden as more charged with
possession even than Chad's or than Miss Barrace's; wide as his
glimpse had lately become of the empire of "things," what was before him still enlarged it; the lust of the eyes and the pride of life
had indeed thus their temple. It was the innermost nook of the
shrine—as brown as a pirate's cave. In the brownness were glints
of gold; patches of purple were in the gloom; objects all that caught,
through the muslin, with their high rarity, the light of the low
windows. Nothing was clear about them but that they were precious,
and they brushed his ignorance with their contempt as a flower,
in a liberty taken with him, might have been whisked under his
nose. But after a full look at his hostess he knew none the less
what most concerned him. The circle in which they stood together
was warm with life, and every question between them would live
there as nowhere else. A question came up as soon as they had
spoken, for his answer, with a laugh, was quickly: "Well, they've
got hold of me!" Much of their talk on this first occasion was his
development of that truth. He was extraordinarily glad to see her,
expressing to her frankly what she most showed him, that one might
live for years without a blessing unsuspected, but that to know it at
last for no more than three days was to need it or miss it for ever.
She was the blessing that had now become his need, and what
could prove it better than that without her he had lost himself?

"What do you mean?" she asked with an absence of alarm that,
correcting him as if he had mistaken the "period" of one of her
pieces, gave him afresh a sense of her easy movement through the
maze he had but begun to tread. "What in the name of all the
Pococks have you managed to do?"

"Why exactly the wrong thing. I've made a frantic friend of little
Bilham."

"Ah that sort of thing was of the essence of your case and to
have been allowed for from the first." And it was only after this
that, quite as a minor matter, she asked who in the world little
Bilham might be. When she learned that he was a friend of
Chad's and living for the time in Chad's rooms in Chad's absence,
quite as if acting in Chad's spirit and serving Chad's cause, she
showed, however, more interest. "Should you mind my seeing him?
Only once, you know," she added.

"Oh the oftener the better: he's amusing—he's original."

"He doesn't shock you?" Miss Gostrey threw out.

"Never in the world! We escape that with a perfection—! I feel it to be largely, no doubt, because I don't half-understand him; but our *modus vivendi*[3] isn't spoiled even by that. You must dine with me to meet him," Strether went on. "Then you'll see."

"Are you giving dinners?"

"Yes—there I am. That's what I mean."

All her kindness wondered. "That you're spending too much money?"

"Dear no—they seem to cost so little. But that I do it to *them.* I ought to hold off."

She thought again—she laughed. "The money you must be spending to think it cheap! But I must be out of it—to the naked eye."

He looked for a moment as if she were really failing him. "Then you won't meet them?" It was almost as if she had developed an unexpected personal prudence.

She hesitated. "Who are they—first?"

"Why little Bilham to begin with." He kept back for the moment Miss Barrace. "And Chad—when he comes—you must absolutely see."

"When then does he come?"

"When Bilham has had time to write him, and hear from him, about me. Bilham, however," he pursued, "will report favourably —favourably for Chad. That will make him not afraid to come. I want you the more therefore, you see, for my bluff."

"Oh you'll do yourself for your bluff." She was perfectly easy. "At the rate you've gone I'm quiet."

"Ah but I haven't," said Strether, "made one protest."

She turned it over. "Haven't you been seeing what there's to protest about?"

He let her, with this, however ruefully, have the whole truth. "I haven't yet found a single thing."

"Isn't there any one *with* him then?"

"Of the sort I came out about?" Strether took a moment. "How do I know? And what do I care?"

"Oh oh!"—and her laughter spread. He was struck in fact by the effect on her of his joke. He saw now how he meant it as a joke. *She* saw, however, still other things, though in an instant she had hidden them. "You've got at no facts at all?"

He tried to muster them. "Well, he has a lovely home."

"Ah that, in Paris," she quickly returned, "proves nothing. That is rather it *dis*proves nothing. They may very well, you see, the people your mission is concerned with, have done it *for* him."

"Exactly. And it was on the scene of their doings then that Waymarsh and I sat guzzling."

3. Mode of living.

"Oh if you forbore to guzzle here on scenes of doings," she replied, "you might easily die of starvation." With which she smiled at him. "You've worse before you."

"Ah I've *everything* before me. But on our hypothesis, you know, they must be wonderful."

"They *are!*" said Miss Gostrey. "You're not therefore, you see," she added, "wholly without facts. They've *been*, in effect, wonderful."

To have got at something comparatively definite appeared at last a little to help—a wave by which moreover, the next moment, recollection was washed. "My young man does admit furthermore that they're our friend's great interest."

"Is that the expression he uses?"

Strether more exactly recalled. "No—not quite."

"Something more vivid? Less?"

He had bent, with neared glasses, over a group of articles on a small stand; and at this he came up. "It was a mere allusion, but, on the lookout as I was, it struck me. 'Awful, you know, as Chad is'—those were Bilham's words."

" 'Awful, you know'—? Oh!"—and Miss Gostrey turned them over. She seemed, however, satisfied. "Well, what more do you want?"

He glanced once more at a bibelot or two, and everything sent him back. "But it *is* all the same as if they wished to let me have it between the eyes."

She wondered. "Quoi donc?"[4]

"Why what I speak of. The amenity. They can stun you with that as well as with anything else."

"Oh," she answered, "you'll come round! I must see them each," she went on, "for myself. I mean Mr. Bilham and Mr. Newsome— Mr. Bilham naturally first. Once only—once for each; that will do. But face to face—for half an hour. What's Mr. Chad," she immediately pursued, "doing at Cannes? Decent men don't go to Cannes with the—well, with the kind of ladies you mean."

"Don't they?" Strether asked with an interest in decent men that amused her.

"No; elsewhere, but not to Cannes. Cannes is different. Cannes is better. Cannes is best. I mean it's all people you know—when you do know them. And if *he* does, why that's different too. He must have gone alone. She can't be with him."

"I haven't," Strether confessed in his weakness, "the least idea." There seemed much in what she said, but he was able after a little to help her to a nearer impression. The meeting with little Bilham took place, by easy arrangement, in the great gallery of the Louvre;

4. What then?

and when, standing with his fellow visitor before one of the splendid Titians—the overwhelming portrait of the young man with the strangely-shaped glove and the blue-grey eyes[5]—he turned to see the third member of their party advance from the end of the waxed and gilded vista, he had a sense of having at last taken hold. He had agreed with Miss Gostrey—it dated even from Chester— for a morning at the Louvre, and he had embraced independently the same idea as thrown out by little Bilham, whom he had already accompanied to the museum of the Luxembourg.[6] The fusion of these schemes presented no difficulty, and it was to strike him again that in little Bilham's company contrarieties in general dropped.

"Oh he's all right—he's one of *us!*" Miss Gostrey, after the first exchange, soon found a chance to murmur to her companion; and Strether, as they proceeded and paused and while a quick unanimity between the two appeared to have phrased itself in half a dozen remarks—Strether knew that he knew almost immediately what she meant, and took it as still another sign that he had got his job in hand. This was the more grateful to him that he could think of the intelligence now serving him as an acquisition positively new. He wouldn't have known even the day before what she meant—that is if she meant, what he assumed, that they were intense Americans together. He had just worked round—and with a sharper turn of the screw than any yet—to the conception of an American intense as little Bilham was intense. The young man was his first specimen; the specimen had profoundly perplexed him; at present however there was light. It was by little Bilham's amazing serenity that he had at first been affected, but he had inevitably, in his circumspection, felt it as the trail of the serpent, the corruption, as he might conveniently have said, of Europe; whereas the promptness with which it came up for Miss Gostrey but as a special little form of the oldest thing they knew justified it at once to his own vision as well. He wanted to be able to like his specimen with a clear good conscience, and this fully permitted it. What had muddled him was precisely the small artist-man's way—it was so complete—of being more American than anybody. But it now for the time put Strether vastly at his ease to have this view of a new way.

The amiable youth then looked out, as it had first struck Strether, at a world in respect to which he hadn't a prejudice. The one our friend most instantly missed was the usual one in favour of an

---

5. There is a Titian portrait in the Louvre of a dark, young, prosperous, and very handsome man with an oddly gloved hand in the foreground; the picture is entitled "Portrait of a Man with Gloves" (1523–24).

6. In Strether's time the Luxembourg Museum (located in the Luxembourg Gardens) displayed mainly the works of contemporary artists while the paintings of the masters were to be found in the Louvre.

occupation accepted. Little Bilham had an occupation, but it was only an occupation declined; and it was by his general exemption from alarm, anxiety or remorse on this score that the impression of his serenity was made. He had come out to Paris to paint—to fathom, that is, at large, that mystery; but study had been fatal to him so far as anything *could* be fatal, and his productive power faltered in proportion as his knowledge grew. Strether had gathered from him that at the moment of his finding him in Chad's rooms he hadn't saved from his shipwreck a scrap of anything but his beautiful intelligence and his confirmed habit of Paris. He referred to these things with an equal fond familiarity, and it was sufficiently clear that, as an outfit, they still served him. They were charming to Strether through the hour spent at the Louvre, where indeed they figured for him as an unseparated part of the charged iridescent air, the glamour of the name, the splendour of the space, the colour of the masters. Yet they were present too wherever the young man led, and the day after the visit to the Louvre they hung, in a different walk, about the steps of our party. He had invited his companions to cross the river with him, offering to show them his own poor place; and his own poor place, which was very poor, gave to his idiosyncrasies, for Strether—the small sublime indifferences and independences that had struck the latter as fresh—an odd and engaging dignity. He lived at the end of an alley that went out of an old short cobbled street, a street that went in turn out of a new long smooth avenue—street and avenue and alley having, however, in common a sort of social shabbiness; and he introduced them to the rather cold and blank little studio which he had lent to a comrade for the term of his elegant absence. The comrade was another ingenuous compatriot, to whom he had wired that tea was to await them "regardless," and this reckless repast, and the second ingenuous compatriot, and the faraway makeshift life, with its jokes and its gaps, its delicate daubs and its three or four chairs, its overflow of taste and conviction and its lack of nearly all else—these things wove round the occasion a spell to which our hero unreservedly surrendered.

He liked the ingenuous compatriots—for two or three others soon gathered; he liked the delicate daubs and the free discriminations—involving references indeed, involving enthusiasms and execrations that made him, as they said, sit up; he liked above all the legend of good-humoured poverty, of mutual accommodation fairly raised to the romantic, that he soon read into the scene. The ingenuous compatriots showed a candour, he thought, surpassing even the candour of Woollett; they were red-haired and long-legged, they were quaint and queer and dear and droll; they made the place resound with the vernacular, which he had never known so marked as when figuring for the chosen language, he must suppose, of contemporary art. They twanged with a vengeance the æsthetic lyre—they drew from it wonderful airs. This aspect of their life had an admirable innocence; and he looked on occasion at Maria Gostrey to see to what extent that element reached her. She gave him however for the hour, as she had given him the previous day, no further sign than to show how she dealt with boys; meeting them with the air of old Parisian practice that she had for every one, for everything, in turn. Wonderful about the delicate daubs, masterful about the way to make tea, trustful about the legs of chairs and familiarly reminiscent of those, in the other time, the named, the numbered or the caricatured, who had flourished or failed, disappeared or arrived, she had accepted with the best grace her second course of little Bilham, and had said to Strether, the previous afternoon, on his leaving them, that, since her impression was to be renewed, she would reserve judgement till after the new evidence.

The new evidence was to come, as it proved, in a day or two. He soon had from Maria a message to the effect that an excellent box at the Français[7] had been lent her for the following night; it seeming on such occasions not the least of her merits that she was subject to such approaches. The sense of how she was always paying for something in advance was equalled on Strether's part only by the sense of how she was always being paid; all of which made for his consciousness, in the larger air, of a lively bustling traffic, the exchange of such values as were not for him to handle. She hated, he knew, at the French play, anything but a box—just as she hated at the English anything but a stall; and a box was what he was already in this phase girding himself to press upon her. But she had for that matter her community with little Bilham: she too always, on the great issues, showed as having known in time. It made her constantly beforehand with him and gave him mainly the chance to ask himself how on the day of their settlement their account would stand. He endeavoured even now to keep it a little straight by arranging that if he accepted her invitation she should dine with him first; but the upshot of this scruple was that at eight o'clock on the morrow he awaited her with Waymarsh under the pillared portico. She hadn't dined with him, and it was characteristic of their relation that she had made him embrace her refusal without in the least understanding it. She ever caused her rearrangements to affect him as her tenderest touches. It was on

7. The Théâtre de Comédie Française, the most important French theater, was described by James in 1872 as "not only the most amiable but the most characteristic of French institutions," a place that could offer "to an ingenious American * * * an aesthetic education." Henry James, "The Parisian Stage," *The Scenic Art*, ed. Allan Wade (New Brunswick, N.J.: Rutgers University Press, 1948), 3–4, 11.

that principle for instance that, giving him the opportunity to be amiable again to little Bilham, she had suggested his offering the young man a seat in their box. Strether had dispatched for this purpose a small blue missive to the Boulevard Malesherbes, but up to the moment of their passing into the theatre he had received no response to his message. He held, however, even after they had been for some time conveniently seated, that their friend, who knew his way about, would come in at his own right moment. His temporary absence moreover seemed, as never yet, to make the right moment for Miss Gostrey. Strether had been waiting till to-night to get back from her in some mirrored form her impressions and conclusions. She had elected, as they said, to see little Bilham once; but now she had seen him twice and had nevertheless not said more than a word.

Waymarsh meanwhile sat opposite him with their hostess between; and Miss Gostrey spoke of herself as an instructor of youth introducing her little charges to a work that was one of the glories of literature. The glory was happily unobjectionable, and the little charges were candid; for herself she had travelled that road and she merely waited on their innocence. But she referred in due time to their absent friend, whom it was clear they should have to give up. "He either won't have got your note," she said, "or you won't have got his: he has had some kind of hindrance, and, of course, for that matter, you know, a man never writes about coming to a box." She spoke as if, with her look, it might have been Waymarsh who had written to the youth, and the latter's face showed a mixture of austerity and anguish. She went on however as if to meet this. "He's far and away, you know, the best of them."

"The best of whom, ma'am?"

"Why of all the long procession—the boys, the girls, or the old men and old women as they sometimes really are; the hope, as one may say, of our country. They've all passed, year after year; but there has been no one in particular I've ever wanted to stop. I feel —don't *you?*—that I want to stop little Bilham; he's so exactly right as he is." She continued to talk to Waymarsh. "He's too delightful. If he'll only not spoil it! But they always *will*; they always do; they always have."

"I don't think Waymarsh knows," Strether said after a moment, "quite what it's open to Bilham to spoil."

"It can't be a good American," Waymarsh lucidly enough replied; "for it didn't strike me the young man had developed much in *that* shape."

"Ah," Miss Gostrey sighed, "the name of the good American is as easily given as taken away! What *is* it, to begin with, to *be* one, and what's the extraordinary hurry? Surely nothing that's so press-

ing was ever so little defined. It's such an order, really, that before
we cook you the dish we must at least have your receipt. Besides,
the poor chicks have time! What I've seen so often spoiled," she
pursued, "is the happy attitude itself, the state of faith and—what
shall I call it?—the sense of beauty. You're right about him"—she
now took in Strether; "little Bilham has them to a charm; we must
keep little Bilham along." Then she was all again for Waymarsh.
"The others have all wanted so dreadfully to do something, and
they've gone and done it in too many cases indeed. It leaves them
never the same afterwards; the charm's always somehow broken.
Now *he*, I think, you know, really won't. He won't do the least
dreadful little thing. We shall continue to enjoy him just as he is.
No—he's quite beautiful. He sees everything. He isn't a bit
ashamed. He has every scrap of the courage of it that one could ask.
Only think what he *might* do. One wants really—for fear of some
accident—to keep him in view. At this very moment perhaps what
mayn't he be up to? I've had my disappointments—the poor things
are never really safe; or only at least when you have them under your
eye. One can never completely trust them. One's uneasy, and I
think that's why I most miss him now."

She had wound up with a laugh of enjoyment over her embroidery of her idea—an enjoyment that her face communicated to
Strether, who almost wished none the less at this moment that she
would let poor Waymarsh alone. *He* knew more or less what she
meant; but the fact wasn't a reason for her not pretending to
Waymarsh that he didn't. It was craven of him perhaps, but he
would, for the high amenity of the occasion, have liked Waymarsh
not to be so sure of his wit. Her recognition of it gave him away
and, before she had done with him or with that article, would
give him worse. What was he, all the same, to do? He looked
across the box at his friend; their eyes met; something queer and
stiff, something that bore on the situation but that it was better
not to touch, passed in silence between them. Well, the effect of it
for Strether was an abrupt reaction, a final impatience of his own
tendency to temporise. Where was that taking him anyway? It
was one of the quiet instants that sometimes settle more matters
than the outbreaks dear to the historic muse. The only qualification
of the quietness was the synthetic "Oh hang it!" into which
Strether's share of the silence soundlessly flowered. It represented,
this mute ejaculation, a final impulse to burn his ships. These ships,
to the historic muse, may seem of course mere cockles, but when
he presently spoke to Miss Gostrey it was with the sense at least of
applying the torch. "Is it then a conspiracy?"

"Between the two young men? Well, I don't pretend to be a
seer or a prophetess," she presently replied; "but if I'm simply a

woman of sense he's working for you to-night. I don't quite know how—but it's in my bones." And she looked at him at last as if, little material as she yet gave him, he'd really understand. "For an opinion *that's* my opinion. He makes you out too well not to."

"Not to work for me to-night?" Strether wondered. "Then I hope he isn't doing anything very bad."

"They've got you," she portentously answered.

"Do you mean he *is*—?"

"They've got you," she merely repeated. Though she disclaimed the prophetic vision she was at this instant the nearest approach he had ever met to the priestess of the oracle. The light was in her eyes. "You must face it now."

He faced it on the spot. "They *had* arranged—?"

"Every move in the game. And they've been arranging ever since. He has had every day his little telegram from Cannes."

It made Strether open his eyes. "Do you *know* that?"

"I do better. I see it. This was, before I met him, what I wondered whether I *was* to see. But as soon as I met him I ceased to wonder, and our second meeting made me sure. I took him all in. He was acting—he is still—on his daily instructions."

"So that Chad has done the whole thing?"

"Oh no—not the whole. *We've* done some of it. You and I and 'Europe.' "

"Europe—yes," Strether mused.

"Dear old Paris," she seemed to explain. But there was more, and, with one of her turns, she risked it. "And dear old Waymarsh. You," she declared, "have been a good bit of it."

He sat massive. "A good bit of what, ma'am?"

"Why of the wonderful consciousness of our friend here. You've helped too in your way to float him to where he is."

"And where the devil *is* he?"

She passed it on with a laugh. "Where the devil, Strether, are you?"

He spoke as if he had just been thinking it out. "Well, quite already in Chad's hands, it would seem." And he had had with this another thought. "Will that be—just all through Bilham—the way he's going to work it? It would be, for him, you know, an idea. And Chad with an idea—!"

"Well?" she asked while the image held him.

"Well, is Chad—what shall I say?—monstrous?"

"Oh as much as you like! But the idea you speak of," she said, "won't have been his best. He'll have a better. It won't be all through little Bilham that he'll work it."

This already sounded almost like a hope destroyed. "Through whom else then?"

"That's what we shall see!" But quite as she spoke she turned, and Strether turned; for the door of the box had opened, with the click of the *ouvreuse*,[8] from the lobby, and a gentleman, a stranger to them, had come in with a quick step. The door closed behind him, and, though their faces showed him his mistake, his air, which was striking, was all good confidence. The curtain had just again arisen, and, in the hush of the general attention, Strether's challenge was tacit, as was also the greeting, with a quickly-deprecating hand and smile, of the unannounced visitor. He discreetly signed that he would wait, would stand, and these things and his face, one look from which she had caught, had suddenly worked for Miss Gostrey. She fitted to them all an answer for Strether's last question. The solid stranger was simply the answer —as she now, turning to her friend, indicated. She brought it straight out for him—it presented the intruder. "Why, through this gentleman!" The gentleman indeed, at the same time, though sounding for Strether a very short name, did practically as much to explain. Strether gasped the name back—then only had he seen. Miss Gostrey had said more than she knew. They were in presence of Chad himself.

Our friend was to go over it afterwards again and again—he was going over it much of the time that they were together, and they were together constantly for three or four days: the note had been so strongly struck during that first half-hour that everything happening since was comparatively a minor development. The fact was that his perception of the young man's identity—so absolutely checked for a minute—had been quite one of the sensations that count in life; he certainly had never known one that had acted, as he might have said, with more of a crowded rush. And the rush, though both vague and multitudinous, had lasted a long time, protected, as it were, yet at the same time aggravated, by the circumstance of its coinciding with a stretch of decorous silence. They couldn't talk without disturbing the spectators in the part of the balcony just below them; and it, for that matter, came to Strether —being a thing of the sort that did come to him—that these were the accidents of a high civilisation; the imposed tribute to propriety, the frequent exposure to conditions, usually brilliant, in which relief has to await its time. Relief was never quite near at hand for kings, queens, comedians and other such people, and though you might be yourself not exactly one of those, you could yet, in leading the life of high pressure, guess a little how they sometimes felt. It was truly the life of high pressure that Strether had seemed to feel himself lead while he sat there, close to Chad, during the long tension of the act. He was in presence of a fact that occupied

8. Theater attendant.

his whole mind, that occupied for the half-hour his senses themselves all together; but he couldn't without inconvenience show
anything—which moreover might count really as luck. What he
might have shown, had he shown at all, was exactly the kind of
emotion—the emotion of bewilderment—that he had proposed to
himself from the first, whatever should occur, to show least. The
phenomenon that had suddenly sat down there with him was a
phenomenon of change so complete that his imagination, which
had worked so beforehand, felt itself, in the connexion, without
margin or allowance. It had faced every contingency but that
Chad should not *be* Chad, and this was what it now had to face
with a mere strained smile and an uncomfortable flush.

He asked himself if, by any chance, before he should have in
some way to commit himself, he might feel his mind settled to the
new vision, might habituate it, so to speak, to the remarkable truth.
But oh it was too remarkable, the truth; for what could be more
remarkable than this sharp rupture of an identity? You could deal
with a man as himself—you couldn't deal with him as somebody
else. It was a small source of peace moreover to be reduced to
wondering how little he might know in such an event what a sum
he was setting you. He couldn't absolutely not know, for you
couldn't absolutely not let him. It was a *case* then simply, a strong
case, as people nowadays called such things, a case of transformation unsurpassed, and the hope was but in the general law that
strong cases were liable to control from without. Perhaps he,
Strether himself, was the only person after all aware of it. Even
Miss Gostrey, with all her science, wouldn't be, would she?—
and he had never seen any one less aware of anything than Waymarsh as he glowered at Chad. The social sightlessness of his old
friend's survey marked for him afresh, and almost in an humiliating
way, the inevitable limits of direct aid from this source. He was
not certain, however, of not drawing a shade of compensation from
the privilege, as yet untasted, of knowing more about something in
particular than Miss Gostrey did. His situation too was a case, for
that matter, and he was now so interested, quite so privately agog,
about it, that he had already an eye to the fun it would be to open
up to her afterwards. He derived during his half-hour no assistance
from her, and just this fact of her not meeting his eyes played a
little, it must be confessed, into his predicament.

He had introduced Chad, in the first minutes, under his breath,
and there was never the primness in her of the person unacquainted;
but she had none the less betrayed at first no vision but of the stage,
where she occasionally found a pretext for an appreciative moment
that she invited Waymarsh to share. The latter's faculty of participation had never had, all round, such an assault to meet; the pres-

sure on him being the sharper for this chosen attitude in her, as Strether judged it, of isolating, for their natural intercourse, Chad and himself. This intercourse was meanwhile restricted to a frank friendly look from the young man, something markedly like a smile, but falling far short of a grin, and to the vivacity of Strether's private speculation as to whether *he* carried himself like a fool. He didn't quite see how he could so feel as one without somehow showing as one. The worst of that question moreover was that he knew it as a symptom the sense of which annoyed him. "If I'm going to be odiously conscious of how I may strike the fellow," he reflected, "it was so little what I came out for that I may as well stop before I begin." This sage consideration too, distinctly, seemed to leave untouched the fact that he *was* going to be conscious. He was conscious of everything but of what would have served him.

He was to know afterwards, in the watches of the night, that nothing would have been more open to him than after a minute or two to propose to Chad to seek with him the refuge of the lobby. He hadn't only not proposed it, but had lacked even the presence of mind to see it as possible. He had stuck there like a schoolboy wishing not to miss a minute of the show; though for that portion of the show then presented he hadn't had an instant's real attention. He couldn't when the curtain fell have given the slightest account of what had happened. He had therefore, further, not at that moment acknowledged the amenity added by this acceptance of his awkwardness to Chad's general patience. Hadn't he none the less known at the very time—known it stupidly and without reaction—that the boy was accepting something? He was modestly benevolent, the boy—that was at least what he had been capable of the superiority of making out his chance to be; and one had one's self literally not had the gumption to get in ahead of him. If we should go into all that occupied our friend in the watches of the night we should have to mend our pen; but an instance or two may mark for us the vividness with which he could remember. He remembered the two absurdities that, if his presence of mind *had* failed, were the things that had had most to do with it. He had never in his life seen a young man come into a box at ten o'clock at night, and would, if challenged on the question in advance, have scarce been ready to pronounce as to different ways of doing so. But it was in spite of this definite to him that Chad had had a way that was wonderful: a fact carrying with it an implication that, as one might imagine it, he knew, he had learned, how.

Here already then were abounding results; he had on the spot and without the least trouble of intention taught Strether that even in so small a thing as that there were different ways. He had done in the same line still more than this; had by a mere shake or two of the head made his old friend observe that the change in him was perhaps more than anything else, for the eye, a matter of the marked streaks of grey, extraordinary at his age, in his thick black hair; as well as that this new feature was curiously becoming to him, did something for him, as characterisation, also even—of all things in the world—as refinement, that had been a good deal wanted. Strether felt, however, he would have had to confess, that it wouldn't have been easy just now, on this and other counts, in the presence of what had been supplied, to be quite clear as to what had been missed. A reflexion a candid critic might have made of old, for instance, was that it would have been happier for the son to look more like the mother; but this was a reflexion that at present would never occur. The ground had quite fallen away from it, yet no resemblance whatever to the mother had supervened. It would have been hard for a young man's face and air to disconnect themselves more completely than Chad's at this juncture from any discerned, from any imaginable aspect of a New England female parent. That of course was no more than had been on the cards; but it produced in Strether none the less one of those frequent phenomena of mental reference with which all judgement in him was actually beset.

Again and again as the days passed he had had a sense of the pertinence of communicating quickly with Woollett—communicating with a quickness with which telegraphy alone would rhyme; the fruit really of a fine fancy in him for keeping things straight, for the happy forestalment of error. No one could explain better when needful, nor put more conscience into an account or a report; which burden of conscience is perhaps exactly the reason why his heart always sank when the clouds of explanation gathered. His highest ingenuity was in keeping the sky of life clear of them. Whether or no he had a grand idea of the lucid, he held that nothing ever was in fact—for any one else—explained. One went through the vain motions, but it was mostly a waste of life. A personal relation was a relation only so long as people either perfectly understood or, better still, didn't care if they didn't. From the moment they cared if they didn't it was living by the sweat of one's brow; and the sweat of one's brow was just what one might buy one's self off from by keeping the ground free of the wild weed of delusion. It easily grew too fast, and the Atlantic cable now alone could race with it. That agency would each day have testified for him to something that was not what Woollett had argued. He was not at this moment absolutely sure that the effect of the morrow's—or rather of the night's—appreciation of the crisis wouldn't be to determine some brief missive. "Have at last seen him, but oh

dear!"—some temporary relief of that sort seemed to hover before
him. It hovered somehow as preparing them all—yet preparing
them for what? If he might do so more luminously and cheaply he
would tick out in four words: "Awfully old—grey hair." To this
particular item in Chad's appearance he constantly, during their
mute half-hour, reverted; as if so very much more than he could
have said had been involved in it. The most he could have said
would have been: "If he's going to make me feel young—!" which
indeed, however, carried with it quite enough. If Strether was to
feel young, that is, it would be because Chad was to feel old; and
an aged and hoary sinner had been no part of the scheme.

The question of Chadwick's true time of life was, doubtless,
what came up quickest after the adjournment of the two, when the
play was over, to a café in the Avenue de l'Opéra.[9] Miss Gostrey
had in due course been perfect for such a step; she had known
exactly what they wanted—to go straight somewhere and talk;
and Strether had even felt she had known what he wished to say
and that he was arranging immediately to begin. She hadn't pretended this, as she *had* pretended on the other hand, to have
divined Waymarsh's wish to extend to her an independent protection homeward; but Strether nevertheless found how, after he had
Chad opposite to him at a small table in the brilliant halls that his
companion straightway selected, sharply and easily discriminated
from others, it was quite, to his mind, as if she heard him speak;
as if, sitting up, a mile away, in the little apartment he knew, she
would listen hard enough to catch. He found too that he liked
that idea, and he wished that, by the same token, Mrs. Newsome
might have caught as well. For what had above all been determined
in him as a necessity of the first order was not to lose another hour,
nor a fraction of one; was to advance, to overwhelm, with a rush.
This was how he would anticipate—by a night-attack, as might be
—any forced maturity that a crammed consciousness of Paris was
likely to take upon itself to assert on behalf of the boy. He knew to
the full, on what he had just extracted from Miss Gostrey, Chad's
marks of alertness; but they were a reason the more for not dawdling.
If he was himself moreover to be treated as young he wouldn't at
all events be so treated before he should have struck out at least
once. His arms might be pinioned afterwards, but it would have
been left on record that he was fifty. The importance of this he
had indeed begun to feel before they left the theatre; it had become a wild unrest, urging him to seize his chance. He could
scarcely wait for it as they went; he was on the verge of the in-
decency of bringing up the question in the street; he fairly caught

9. A central avenue leading from the Théâtre Française to the Place de l'Opéra.

himself going on—so he afterwards invidiously named it—as if
there would be for him no second chance should the present be lost.
Not till, on the purple divan before the perfunctory *bock*,[1] he had
brought out the words themselves, was he sure, for that matter,
that the present would be saved.

Book Fourth

I [VIII]

"I've come, you know, to make you break with everything,
neither more nor less, and take you straight home; so you'll be so
good as immediately and favourably to consider it!"—Strether,
face to face with Chad after the play, had sounded these words almost breathlessly, and with an effect at first positively disconcerting
to himself alone. For Chad's receptive attitude was that of a person who had been gracefully quiet while the messenger at last
reaching him has run a mile through the dust. During some seconds
after he had spoken Strether felt as if *he* had made some such
exertion; he was not even certain that the perspiration wasn't on
his brow. It was the kind of consciousness for which he had to
thank the look that, while the strain lasted, the young man's eyes
gave him. They reflected—and the deuce of the thing was that they
reflected really with a sort of shyness of kindness—his momentarily
disordered state; which fact brought on in its turn for our friend
the dawn of a fear that Chad might simply "take it out"—take
everything out—in being sorry for him. Such a fear, any fear, was
unpleasant. But everything was unpleasant; it was odd how everything had suddenly turned so. This however was no reason for
letting the least thing go. Strether had the next minute proceeded
as roundly as if with an advantage to follow up. "Of course I'm a
busybody, if you want to fight the case to the death; but after all
mainly in the sense of having known you and having given you
such attention as you kindly permitted when you were in jackets
and knickerbockers. Yes—it was knickerbockers, I'm busybody
enough to remember that; and that you had, for your age—I speak
of the first far-away time—tremendously stout legs. Well, we want
you to break. Your mother's heart's passionately set upon it, but
she has above and beyond that excellent arguments and reasons.
I've not put them into her head—I needn't remind you how little
she's a person who needs that. But they exist—you must take it
from me as a friend both of hers and yours—for myself as well. I
didn't invent them, I didn't originally work them out; but I understand them, I think I can explain them—by which I mean make

1. Glass of beer.

you actively do them justice; and that's why you see me here. You
had better know the worst at once. It's a question of an immediate
rupture and an immediate return. I've been conceited enough to
dream I can sugar that pill. I take at any rate the greatest interest
in the question. I took it already before I left home; and I don't
mind telling you that, altered as you are, I take it still more now
that I've seen you. You're older and—I don't know what to call it!
—more of a handful; but you're by so much the more, I seem to
make out, to our purpose."

"Do I strike you as improved?" Strether was to recall that Chad
had at this point enquired.

He was likewise to recall—and it had to count for some time as
his greatest comfort—that it had been "given" him, as they said at
Woollett, to reply with some presence of mind: "I haven't the least
idea." He was really for a while to like thinking he had been
positively hard. On the point of conceding that Chad had improved
in appearance, but that to the question of appearance the remark
must be confined, he checked even that compromise and left his
reservation bare. Not only his moral, but also, as it were, his æsthetic
sense had a little to pay for this, Chad being unmistakeably—and
wasn't it a matter of the confounded grey hair again?—handsomer
than he had ever promised. That however fell in perfectly with what
Strether had said. They had no desire to keep down his proper expansion, and he wouldn't be less to their purpose for not looking,
as he had too often done of old, only bold and wild. There was
indeed a signal particular in which he would distinctly be more
so. Strether didn't, as he talked, absolutely follow himself; he
only knew he was clutching his thread and that he held it from
moment to moment a little tighter; his mere uninterruptedness during the few minutes helped him to do that. He had frequently, for
a month, turned over what he should say on this very occasion, and
he seemed at last to have said nothing he had thought of—everything was so totally different.

But in spite of all he had put the flag at the window. This was
what he had done, and there was a minute during which he affected
himself as having shaken it hard, flapped it with a mighty flutter,
straight in front of his companion's nose. It gave him really almost
the sense of having already acted his part. The momentary relief
—as if from the knowledge that nothing of *that* at least could be
undone—sprang from a particular cause, the cause that had flashed
into operation, in Miss Gostrey's box, with direct apprehension,
with amazed recognition, and that had been concerned since then
in every throb of his consciousness. What it came to was that
with an absolutely *new* quantity to deal with one simply couldn't
know. The new quantity was represented by the fact that Chad

had been made over. That was all; whatever it was it was everything. Strether had never seen the thing so done before—it was perhaps a speciality of Paris. If one had been present at the process one might little by little have mastered the result; but he was face to face, as matters stood, with the finished business. It had freely been noted for him that he might be received as a dog among skittles, but that was on the basis of the old quantity. He had originally thought of lines and tones as things to be taken, but these possibilities had now quite melted away. There was no computing at all what the young man before him would think or feel or say on any subject whatever. This intelligence Strether had afterwards, to account for his nervousness, reconstituted as he might, just as he had also reconstituted the promptness with which Chad had corrected his uncertainty. An extraordinarily short time had been required for the correction, and there had ceased to be anything negative in his companion's face and air as soon as it was made. "Your engagement to my mother has become then what they call here a *fait accompli?*"[1]—it had consisted, the determinant touch, in nothing more than that.

Well, that was enough, Strether had felt while his answer hung fire. He had felt at the same time, however, that nothing could less become him than that it should hang fire too long. "Yes," he said brightly, "it was on the happy settlement of the question that I started. You see therefore to what tune I'm in your family. Moreover," he added, "I've been supposing you'd suppose it."

"Oh I've been supposing it for a long time, and what you tell me helps me to understand that you should want to do something. To do something, I mean," said Chad, "to commemorate an event so—what do they call it?—so auspicious. I see you make out, and not unnaturally," he continued, "that bringing me home in triumph as a sort of wedding-present to Mother would commemorate it better than anything else. You want to make a bonfire in fact," he laughed, "and you pitch me on. Thank you, thank you!" he laughed again.

He was altogether easy about it, and this made Strether now see how at bottom, and in spite of the shade of shyness that really cost him nothing, he had from the first moment been easy about everything. The shade of shyness was mere good taste. People with manners formed could apparently have, as one of their best cards, the shade of shyness too. He had leaned a little forward to speak; his elbows were on the table; and the inscrutable new face that he had got somewhere and somehow was brought by the movement nearer to his critic's. There was a fascination for that critic in its not being, this ripe physiognomy, the face that, under observation at least, he

1. An accomplished deed.

had originally carried away from Woollett. Strether found a certain freedom on his own side in defining it as that of a man of the world —a formula that indeed seemed to come now in some degree to his relief; that of a man to whom things had happened and were variously known. In gleams, in glances, the past did perhaps peep out of it; but such lights were faint and instantly merged. Chad was brown and thick and strong, and of old Chad had been rough. Was all the difference therefore that he was actually smooth? Possibly; for that he *was* smooth was as marked as in the taste of a sauce or in the rub of a hand. The effect of it was general—it had retouched his features, drawn them with a cleaner line. It had cleared his eyes and settled his colour and polished his fine square teeth—the main ornament of his face; and at the same time that it had given him a form and a surface, almost a design, it had toned his voice, established his accent, encouraged his smile to more play and his other motions to less. He had formerly, with a great deal of action, expressed very little; and he now expressed whatever was necessary with almost none at all. It was as if in short he had really, copious perhaps but shapeless, been put into a firm mould and turned successfully out. The phenomenon—Strether kept eyeing it as a phenomenon, an eminent case—was marked enough to be touched by the finger. He finally put his hand across the table and laid it on Chad's arm. "If you'll promise me—here on the spot and giving me your word of honour—to break straight off, you'll make the future the real right thing for all of us alike. You'll ease off the strain of this decent but none the less acute suspense in which I've for so many days been waiting for you, and let me turn in to rest. I shall leave you with my blessing and go to bed in peace."

Chad again fell back at this and, his hands pocketed, settled himself a little; in which posture he looked, though he rather anxiously smiled, only the more earnest. Then Strether seemed to see that he was really nervous, and he took that as what he would have called a wholesome sign. The only mark of it hitherto had been his more than once taking off and putting on his wide-brimmed crush hat.[2] He had at this moment made the motion again to remove it, then had only pushed it back, so that it hung informally on his strong young grizzled crop. It was a touch that gave the note of the familiar—the intimate and the belated—to their quiet colloquy; and it was indeed by some such trivial aid that Strether became aware at the same moment of something else. The observation was at any rate determined in him by some light too fine to distinguish from so many others, but it was none the less sharply determined. Chad looked unmistakeably during these instants— well, as Strether put it to himself, all he was worth. Our friend had

2. A collapsible top hat.

a sudden apprehension of what that would on certain sides be. He saw him in a flash as the young man marked out by women; and for a concentrated minute the dignity, the comparative austerity, as he funnily fancied it, of this character affected him almost with awe. There was an experience on his interlocutor's part that looked out at him from under the displaced hat, and that looked out moreover by a force of its own, the deep fact of its quantity and quality, and not through Chad's intending bravado or swagger. That was then the way men marked out by women *were*—and also the men by whom the women were doubtless in turn sufficiently distinguished. It affected Strether for thirty seconds as a relevant truth; a truth which, however, the next minute, had fallen into its relation. "Can't you imagine there being some questions," Chad asked, "that a fellow—however much impressed by your charming way of stating things—would like to put to you first?"

"Oh yes—easily. I'm here to answer everything. I think I can even tell you things, of the greatest interest to you, that you won't know enough to ask me. We'll take as many days to it as you like. But I want," Strether wound up, "to go to bed now."

"Really?"

Chad had spoken in such surprise that he was amused. "Can't you believe it?—with what you put me through?"

The young man seemed to consider. "Oh I haven't put you through much—yet."

"Do you mean there's so much more to come?" Strether laughed. "All the more reason then that I should gird myself." And as if to mark what he felt he could by this time count on he was already on his feet.

Chad, still seated, stayed him, with a hand against him, as he passed between their table and the next. "Oh we shall get on!"

The tone was, as who should say, everything Strether could have desired; and quite as good the expression of face with which the speaker had looked up at him and kindly held him. All these things lacked was their not showing quite so much as the fruit of experience. Yes, experience was what Chad did play on him, if he didn't play any grossness of defiance. Of course experience was in a manner defiance; but it wasn't, at any rate—rather indeed quite the contrary!—grossness; which was so much gained. He fairly grew older, Strether thought, while he himself so reasoned. Then with his mature pat of his visitor's arm he also got up; and there had been enough of it all by this time to make the visitor feel that something *was* settled. Wasn't it settled that he had at least the testimony of Chad's own belief in a settlement? Strether found himself treating Chad's profession that they would get on as a sufficient basis for going to bed. He hadn't nevertheless after this gone to bed directly; for when they had again passed out together into the mild bright night a check had virtually sprung from nothing more than a small circumstance which might have acted only as confirming quiescence. There were people, expressive sound, projected light, still abroad, and after they had taken in for a moment, through everything, the great clear architectural street, they turned off in tacit union to the quarter of Strether's hotel. "Of course," Chad here abruptly began, "of course Mother's making things out with you about me has been natural—and of course also you've had a good deal to go upon. Still, you must have filled out."

He had stopped, leaving his friend to wonder a little what point he wished to make; and this it was that enabled Strether meanwhile to make one. "Oh we've never pretended to go into detail. We weren't in the least bound to *that*. It was 'filling out' enough to miss you as we did."

But Chad rather oddly insisted, though under the high lamp at their corner, where they paused, he had at first looked as if touched by Strether's allusion to the long sense, at home, of his absence. "What I mean is you must have imagined."

"Imagined what?"

"Well—horrors."

It affected Strether: horrors were so little—superficially at least —in this robust and reasoning image. But he was none the less there to be veracious. "Yes, I dare say we *have* imagined horrors. But where's the harm if we haven't been wrong?"

Chad raised his face to the lamp, and it was one of the moments at which he had, in his extraordinary way, most his air of designedly showing himself. It was as if at these instants he just presented himself, his identity so rounded off, his palpable presence and his massive young manhood, as such a link in the chain as might practically amount to a kind of demonstration. It was as if—and how but anomalously?—he couldn't after all help thinking sufficiently well of these things to let them go for what they were worth. What could there be in this for Strether but the hint of some self-respect, some sense of power, oddly perverted; something latent and beyond access, ominous and perhaps enviable? The intimation had the next thing, in a flash, taken on a name—a name on which our friend seized as he asked himself if he weren't perhaps really dealing with an irreducible young Pagan. This description—he quite jumped at it—had a sound that gratified his mental ear, so that of a sudden he had already adopted it. Pagan—yes, that was, wasn't it? what Chad *would* logically be. It was what he must be. It was what he was. The idea was a clue and, instead of darkening the prospect, projected a certain clearness. Strether made out in this quick ray that a Pagan was perhaps, at the pass they had come to, the thing most wanted at Woollett. They'd be able to do with one —a good one; he'd find an opening—yes; and Strether's imagination even now prefigured and accompanied the first appearance there of the rousing personage. He had only the slight discomfort of feeling, as the young man turned away from the lamp, that his thought had in the momentary silence possibly been guessed. "Well, I've no doubt," said Chad, "you've come near enough. The details, as you say, don't matter. It *has* been generally the case that I've let myself go. But I'm coming round—I'm not so bad now." With which they walked on again to Strether's hotel.

"Do you mean," the latter asked as they approached the door, "that there isn't any woman with you now?"

"But pray what has that to do with it?"

"Why it's the whole question."

"Of my going home?" Chad was clearly surprised. "Oh not much! Do you think that when I want to go any one will have any power—"

"To keep you"—Strether took him straight up—"from carrying out your wish? Well, our idea has been that somebody has hitherto —or a good many persons perhaps—kept you pretty well from 'wanting.' That's what—if you're in anybody's hands—may again happen. You don't answer my question"—he kept it up; "but if you aren't in anybody's hands so much the better. There's nothing then but what makes for your going."

Chad turned this over. "I don't answer your question?" He spoke quite without resenting it. "Well, such questions have always a rather exaggerated side. One doesn't know quite what you mean by being in women's 'hands.' It's all so vague. One is when one isn't. One isn't when one is. And then one can't quite give people away." He seemed kindly to explain. "I've *never* got stuck —so very hard; and, as against anything at any time really better, I don't think I've ever been afraid." There was something in it that held Strether to wonder, and this gave him time to go on. He broke out as with a more helpful thought. "Don't you know how I like Paris itself?"

The upshot was indeed to make our friend marvel. "Oh if *that's* all that's the matter with you—!" It was *he* who almost showed resentment.

Chad's smile of a truth more than met it. "But isn't that enough?"

Strether hesitated, but it came out. "Not enough for your mother!" Spoken, however, it sounded a trifle odd—the effect of which was that Chad broke into a laugh. Strether, at this, succumbed as well, though with extreme brevity. "Permit us to have still our theory. But if you *are* so free and so strong you're inexcusable. I'll write in the morning," he added with decision. "I'll say I've got you."

This appeared to open for Chad a new interest. "How often do you write?"

"Oh perpetually."

"And at great length?"

Strether had become a little impatient. "I hope it's not found too great."

"Oh I'm sure not. And you hear as often?"

Again Strether paused. "As often as I deserve."

"Mother writes," said Chad, "a lovely letter."

Strether, before the closed porte-cochère, fixed him a moment. "It's more, my boy, than *you* do! But our suppositions don't matter," he added, "if you're actually not entangled."

Chad's pride seemed none the less a little touched. "I never *was* that—let me insist. I always had my own way." With which he pursued: "And I have it at present."

"Then what are you here for? What has kept you," Strether asked, "if you *have* been able to leave?"

It made Chad, after a stare, throw himself back. "Do you think one's kept only by women?" His surprise and his verbal emphasis rang out so clear in the still street that Strether winced till he remembered the safety of their English speech. "Is that," the young man demanded, "what they think at Woollett?" At the good faith in the question Strether had changed colour, feeling that, as he would have said, he had put his foot in it. He had appeared stupidly to misrepresent what they thought at Woollett; but before he had time to rectify Chad again was upon him. "I must say then you show a low mind!"

It so fell in, unhappily for Strether, with that reflexion of his own prompted in him by the pleasant air of the Boulevard Malesherbes, that its disconcerting force was rather unfairly great. It was a dig that, administered by himself—and administered even to poor Mrs. Newsome—was no more than salutary; but administered by Chad—and quite logically—it came nearer drawing blood. They *hadn't* a low mind—nor any approach to one; yet incontestably they had worked, and with a certain smugness, on a basis that might be turned against them. Chad had at any rate pulled his visitor up; he had even pulled up his admirable mother; he had absolutely, by a turn of the wrist and a jerk of the far-flung noose, pulled up, in a bunch, Woollett browsing in its pride. There was no doubt Woollett *had* insisted on his coarseness; and what he at present stood there for in the sleeping street was, by his manner of striking the other note, to make of such insistence a preoccupation compromising to the insisters. It was exactly as if they had

imputed to him a vulgarity that he had by a mere gesture caused
to fall from him. The devil of the case was that Strether felt it, by
the same stroke, as falling straight upon himself. He had been
wondering a minute ago if the boy weren't a Pagan, and he found
himself wondering now if he weren't by chance a gentleman. It
didn't in the least, on the spot, spring up helpfully for him that a
person couldn't at the same time be both. There was nothing at
this moment in the air to challenge the combination; there was
everything to give it on the contrary something of a flourish. It
struck Strether into the bargain as doing something to meet the
most difficult of the questions; though perhaps indeed only by
substituting another. Wouldn't it be precisely by having learned to
be a gentleman that he had mastered the consequent trick of
looking so well that one could scarce speak to him straight? But
what in the world was the clue to such a prime producing cause?
There were too many clues then that Strether still lacked, and
these clues to clues were among them. What it accordingly
amounted to for him was that he had to take full in the face a fresh
attribution of ignorance. He had grown used by this time to reminders, especially from his own lips, of what he didn't know;
but he had borne them because in the first place they were private
and because in the second they practically conveyed a tribute. He
didn't know what was bad, and—as others didn't know how little
he knew it—he could put up with his state. But if he didn't know,
in so important a particular, what was good, Chad at least was now
aware he didn't; and that, for some reason, affected our friend
as curiously public. It was in fact an exposed condition that the
young man left him in long enough for him to feel its chill—till he
saw fit, in a word, generously again to cover him. This last was in
truth what Chad quite gracefully did. But he did it as with a
simple thought that met the whole of the case. "Oh I'm all right!"
It was what Strether had rather bewilderedly to go to bed on.

II [IX]

It really looked true moreover from the way Chad was to behave
after this. He was full of attentions to his mother's ambassador; in
spite of which, all the while, the latter's other relations rather remarkably contrived to assert themselves. Strether's sittings pen in
hand with Mrs. Newsome up in his own room were broken, yet
they were richer; and they were more than ever interspersed with
the hours in which he reported himself, in a different fashion, but
with scarce less earnestness and fulness, to Maria Gostrey. Now
that, as he would have expressed it, he had really something to talk
about he found himself, in respect to any oddity that might reside
for him in the double connexion, at once more aware and more indifferent. He had been fine to Mrs. Newsome about his useful

friend, but it had begun to haunt his imagination that Chad, taking up again for her benefit a pen too long disused, might possibly be finer. It wouldn't at all do, he saw, that anything should come up for him at Chad's hand but what specifically *was* to have come; the greatest divergence from which would be precisely the element of any lubrication of their intercourse by levity. It was accordingly to forestall such an accident that he frankly put before the young man the several facts, just as they had occurred, of his funny alliance. He spoke of these facts, pleasantly and obligingly, as "the whole story," and felt that he might qualify the alliance as funny if he remained sufficiently grave about it. He flattered himself that he even exaggerated the wild freedom of his original encounter with the wonderful lady; he was scrupulously definite about the absurd conditions in which they had made acquaintance—their having picked each other up almost in the street; and he had (finest inspiration of all!) a conception of carrying the war into the enemy's country by showing surprise at the enemy's ignorance.

He had always had a notion that this last was the grand style of fighting; the greater therefore the reason for it, as he couldn't remember that he had ever before fought in the grand style. Every one, according to this, knew Miss Gostrey: how came it Chad didn't know her? The difficulty, the impossibility, was really to escape it; Strether put on him, by what he took for granted, the burden of proof of the contrary. This tone was so far successful as that Chad quite appeared to recognise her as a person whose fame had reached him, but against his acquaintance with whom much mischance had worked. He made the point at the same time that his social relations, such as they could be called, were perhaps not to the extent Strether supposed with the rising flood of their compatriots. He hinted at his having more and more given way to a different principle of selection; the moral of which seemed to be that he went about little in the "colony." For the moment certainly he had quite another interest. It was deep, what he understood; and Strether, for himself, could only so observe it. He couldn't see as yet how deep. Might he not all too soon! For there was really too much of their question that Chad had already committed himself to liking. He liked, to begin with, his prospective stepfather; which was distinctly what had not been on the cards. His hating him was the untowardness for which Strether had been best prepared; he hadn't expected the boy's actual form to give him more to do than his imputed. It gave him more through suggesting that he must somehow make up to himself for not being sure he was sufficiently disagreeable. That had really been present to him as his only way to be sure he was sufficiently thorough. The point was that if Chad's tolerance of his thoroughness were insincere, were but the best of devices for gaining time, it none the less did treat everything as tacitly concluded.

That seemed at the end of ten days the upshot of the abundant, the recurrent talk through which Strether poured into him all it concerned him to know, put him in full possession of facts and figures. Never cutting these colloquies short by a minute, Chad behaved, looked and spoke as if he were rather heavily, perhaps even a trifle gloomily, but none the less fundamentally and comfortably free. He made no crude profession of eagerness to yield, but he asked the most intelligent questions, probed, at moments, abruptly, even deeper than his friend's layer of information, justified by these touches the native estimate of his latent stuff, and had in every way the air of trying to live, reflectively, into the square bright picture. He walked up and down in front of this production, sociably took Strether's arm at the points at which he stopped, surveyed it repeatedly from the right and from the left, inclined a critical head to either quarter, and, while he puffed a still more critical cigarette, animadverted to his companion on this passage and that. Strether sought relief—there were hours when he required it—in repeating himself; it was in truth not to be blinked that Chad had a way. The main question as yet was of what it was a way *to*. It made vulgar questions no more easy; but that was unimportant when all questions save those of his own asking had dropped. That he was free was answer enough, and it wasn't quite ridiculous that this freedom should end by presenting itself as what was difficult to move. His changed state, his lovely home, his beautiful things, his easy talk, his very appetite for Strether, insatiable and, when all was said, flattering—what were such marked matters all but the notes of his freedom? He had the effect of making a sacrifice of it just in these handsome forms to his visitor; which was mainly the reason the visitor was privately, for the time, a little out of countenance. Strether was at this period again and again thrown back on a felt need to remodel somehow his plan. He fairly caught himself shooting rueful glances, shy looks of pursuit, toward the embodied influence, the definite adversary, who had by a stroke of her own failed him and on a fond theory of whose palpable presence he had, under Mrs. Newsome's inspiration, altogether proceeded. He had once or twice, in secret, literally expressed the irritated wish that *she* would come out and find her.

He couldn't quite yet force it upon Woollett that such a career, such a perverted young life, showed after all a certain plausible side, *did* in the case before them flaunt something like an impunity for the social man; but he could at least treat himself to the statement that would prepare him for the sharpest echo. This echo—as distinct over there in the dry thin air as some shrill "heading" above a column of print—seemed to reach him even as he wrote. "He says there's no woman," he could hear Mrs. Newsome report, in capitals almost of newspaper size, to Mrs. Pocock; and he could focus in Mrs. Pocock the response of the reader of the journal. He could see in the younger lady's face the earnestness of her attention and catch the full scepticism of her but slightly delayed "What is there then?" Just so he could again as little miss the mother's clear decision: "There's plenty of disposition, no doubt, to pretend there isn't." Strether had, after posting his letter, the whole scene out; and it was a scene during which, coming and going, as befell, he kept his eye not least upon the daughter. He had his fine sense of the conviction Mrs. Pocock would take occasion to reaffirm—a conviction bearing, as he had from the first deeply divined it to bear, on Mr. Strether's essential inaptitude. She had looked him in his conscious eyes even before he sailed, and that she didn't believe *he* would find the woman had been written in her look. Hadn't she at the best but a scant faith in his ability to find women? It wasn't even as if he had found her mother—so much more, to her discrimination, had her mother performed the finding. Her mother had, in a case her private judgement of which remained educative of Mrs. Pocock's critical sense, found the man. The man owed his unchallenged state, in general, to the fact that Mrs. Newsome's discoveries were accepted at Woollett; but he knew in his bones, our friend did, how almost irresistibly Mrs. Pocock would now be moved to show what she thought of his own. Give *her* a free hand, would be the moral, and the woman would soon be found.

His impression of Miss Gostrey after her introduction to Chad was meanwhile an impression of a person almost unnaturally on her guard. He struck himself as at first unable to extract from her what he wished; though indeed *of* what he wished at this special juncture he would doubtless have contrived to make but a crude statement. It sifted and settled nothing to put to her, *tout bêtement*,[3] as she often said, "Do you like him, eh?"—thanks to his feeling it actually the least of his needs to heap up the evidence in the young man's favour. He repeatedly knocked at her door to let her have it afresh that Chad's case—whatever else of minor interest it might yield—was first and foremost a miracle almost monstrous. It was the alteration of the entire man, and was so signal an instance that nothing else, for the intelligent observer, could—*could* it?—signify. "It's a plot," he declared—"there's more in it than meets the eye." He gave the rein to his fancy. "It's a plant!"

His fancy seemed to please her. "Whose then?"

"Well, the party responsible is, I suppose, the fate that waits for one, the dark doom that rides. What I mean is that with such ele-

3. Very stupidly.

ments one can't count. I've but my poor individual, my modest human means. It isn't playing the game to turn on the uncanny. All one's energy goes to facing it, to tracking it. One wants, confound it, don't you see?" he confessed with a queer face—"one wants to enjoy anything so rare. Call it then life"—he puzzled it out—"call it poor dear old life simply that springs the surprise. Nothing alters the fact that the surprise is paralysing, or at any rate engrossing— all, practically, hang it, that one sees, that one *can* see."

Her silences were never barren, nor even dull. "Is that what you've written home?"

He tossed it off. "Oh dear, yes!"

She had another pause while, across her carpets, he had another walk. "If you don't look out you'll have them straight over."

"Oh but I've said he'll go back."

"And *will* he?" Miss Gostrey asked.

The special tone of it made him, pulling up, look at her long. "What's that but just the question I've spent treasures of patience and ingenuity in giving *you*, by the sight of him—after everything had led up—every facility to answer? What is it but just the thing I came here to-day to get out of you? Will he?"

"No—he won't," she said at last. "He's not free."

The air of it held him. "Then you've all the while known—?"

"I've known nothing but what I've seen; and I wonder," she declared with some impatience, "that you didn't see as much. It was enough to be with him there—"

"In the box? Yes," he rather blankly urged.

"Well—to feel sure."

"Sure of what?"

She got up from her chair, at this, with a nearer approach than she had ever yet shown to dismay at his dimness. She even, fairly pausing for it, spoke with a shade of pity. "Guess!"

It was a shade, fairly, that brought a flush into his face; so that for a moment, as they waited together, their difference was between them. "You mean that just your hour with him told you so much of his story? Very good; I'm not such a fool, on my side, as that I don't understand you, or as that I didn't in some degree understand *him*. That he has done what he liked most isn't, among any of us, a matter the least in dispute. There's equally little question at this time of day of what it is he does like most. But I'm not talking," he reasonably explained, "of any mere wretch he may still pick up. I'm talking of some person who in his present situation may have held her own, may really have counted."

"That's exactly what *I* am!" said Miss Gostrey. But she as quickly made her point. "I thought you thought—or that they think at Woollett—that that's what mere wretches necessarily do.

Mere wretches necessarily *don't!*" she declared with spirit. "There must, behind every appearance to the contrary, still be somebody—somebody who's not a mere wretch, since we accept the miracle. What else but such a somebody can such a miracle be?"

He took it in. "Because the fact itself *is* the woman?"

"A woman. Some woman or other. It's one of the things that *have* to be."

"But you mean then at least a good one."

"A good woman?" She threw up her arms with a laugh. "I should call her excellent!"

"Then why does he deny her?"

Miss Gostrey thought a moment. "Because she's too good to admit! Don't you see," she went on, "how she accounts for him?"

Strether clearly, more and more, did see; yet it made him also see other things. "But isn't what we want that he shall account for *her?*"

"Well, he does. What you have before you is his way. You must forgive him if it isn't quite outspoken. In Paris such debts are tacit."

Strether could imagine; but still—! "Even when the woman's good?"

Again she laughed out. "Yes, and even when the man is! There's always a caution in such cases," she more seriously explained—"for what it may seem to show. There's nothing that's taken as showing so much here as sudden unnatural goodness."

"Ah then you're speaking now," Strether said, "of people who are *not* nice."

"I delight," she replied, "in your classifications. But do you want me," she asked, "to give you in the matter, on this ground, the wisest advice I'm capable of? Don't consider her, don't judge her at all in herself. Consider her and judge her only in Chad."

He had the courage at least of his companion's logic. "Because then I shall like her?" He almost looked, with his quick imagination, as if he already did, though seeing at once also the full extent of how little it would suit his book. "But is that what I came out for?"

She had to confess indeed that it wasn't. But there was something else. "Don't make up your mind. There are all sorts of things. You haven't seen him all."

This on his side Strether recognised; but his acuteness none the less showed him the danger. "Yes, but if the more I see the better he seems?"

Well, she found something. "That may be—but his disavowal of her isn't, all the same, pure consideration. There's a hitch." She made it out. "It's the effort to sink her."

Strether winced at the image. "To 'sink'—?"

"Well, I mean there's a struggle, and a part of it is just what he hides. Take time—that's the only way not to make some mistake that you'll regret. Then you'll see. He does really want to shake her off."

Our friend had by this time so got into the vision that he almost gasped. "After all she has done for him?"

Miss Gostrey gave him a look which broke the next moment into a wonderful smile. "He's not so good as you think!"

They remained with him, these words, promising him, in their character of warning, considerable help; but the support he tried to draw from them found itself on each renewal of contact with Chad defeated by something else. What could it be, this disconcerting force, he asked himself, but the sense, constantly renewed, that Chad *was*—quite in fact insisted on being—as good as he thought? It seemed somehow as if he couldn't *but* be as good from the moment he wasn't as bad. There was a succession of days at all events when contact with him—and in its immediate effect, as if it could produce no other—elbowed out of Strether's consciousness everything but itself. Little Bilham once more pervaded the scene, but little Bilham became even in a higher degree than he had originally been one of the numerous forms of the inclusive relation; a consequence promoted, to our friend's sense, by two or three incidents with which we have yet to make acquaintance. Waymarsh himself, for the occasion, was drawn into the eddy; it absolutely, though but temporarily, swallowed him down, and there were days when Strether seemed to bump against him as a sinking swimmer might brush a submarine object. The fathomless medium held them—Chad's manner was the fathomless medium; and our friend felt as if they passed each other, in their deep immersion, with the round impersonal eye of silent fish. It was practically produced between them that Waymarsh was giving him then his chance; and the shade of discomfort that Strether drew from the allowance resembled not a little the embarrassment he had known at school, as a boy, when members of his family had been present at exhibitions. He could perform before strangers, but relatives were fatal, and it was now as if, comparatively, Waymarsh were a relative. He seemed to hear him say "Strike up then!" and to enjoy a foretaste of conscientious domestic criticism. He *had* struck up, so far as he actually could; Chad knew by this time in profusion what he wanted; and what vulgar violence did his fellow pilgrim expect of him when he had really emptied his mind? It went somehow to and fro that what poor Waymarsh meant was "I told you so—that you'd lose your immortal soul!" but it was also fairly explicit that Strether had his own challenge and that, since they must go to the bottom of things, he wasted no more virtue in watching Chad than Chad wasted in watching him. His dip for duty's sake—where was it worse than Waymarsh's own? For *he* needn't have stopped resisting and refusing, needn't have parleyed, at that rate, with the foe.

The strolls over Paris to see something or call somewhere were accordingly inevitable and natural, and the late sessions in the wondrous troisième, the lovely home, when men dropped in and the picture composed more suggestively through the haze of tobacco, of music more or less good and of talk more or less polyglot, were on a principle not to be distinguished from that of the mornings and the afternoons. Nothing, Strether had to recognise as he leaned back and smoked, could well less resemble a scene of violence than even the liveliest of these occasions. They were occasions of discussion, none the less, and Strether had never in his life heard so many opinions on so many subjects. There were opinions at Woollett, but only on three or four. The differences were there to match; if they were doubtless deep, though few, they were quiet—they were, as might be said, almost as shy as if people had been ashamed of them. People showed little diffidence about such things, on the other hand, in the Boulevard Malesherbes, and were so far from being ashamed of them—or indeed of anything else—that they often seemed to have invented them to avert those agreements that destroy the taste of talk. No one had ever done that at Woollett, though Strether could remember times when he himself had been tempted to it without quite knowing why. He saw why at present—he had but wanted to promote intercourse.

These, however, were but parenthetic memories; and the turn taken by his affair on the whole was positively that if his nerves were on the stretch it was because he missed violence. When he asked himself if none would then, in connexion with it, ever come at all, he might almost have passed as wondering how to provoke it. It would be too absurd if such a vision as *that* should have to be invoked for relief; it was already marked enough as absurd that he should actually have begun with flutters and dignities on the score of a single accepted meal. What sort of a brute had he expected Chad to be, anyway?—Strether had occasion to make the enquiry but was careful to make it in private. He could himself, comparatively recent as it was—it was truly but the fact of a few days since —focus his primal crudity; but he would on the approach of an observer, as if handling an illicit possession, have slipped the reminiscence out of sight. There were echoes of it still in Mrs. Newsome's letters, and there were moments when these echoes made him exclaim on her want of tact. He blushed of course, at once, still more for the explanation than for the ground of it: it came to him in time to save his manners that she couldn't at the best become tactful as quickly as he. Her tact had to reckon with the Atlantic Ocean, the General Post-Office and the extravagant curve of the globe.

Chad had one day offered tea at the Boulevard Malesherbes to a chosen few, a group again including the unobscured Miss Barrace; and Strether had on coming out walked away with the acquaintance whom in his letters to Mrs. Newsome he always spoke of as the little artist-man. He had had full occasion to mention him as the other party, so oddly, to the only close personal alliance observation had as yet detected in Chad's existence. Little Bilham's way this afternoon was not Strether's, but he had none the less kindly come with him, and it was somehow a part of his kindness that as it had sadly begun to rain they suddenly found themselves seated for conversation at a café in which they had taken refuge. He had passed no more crowded hour in Chad's society than the one just ended; he had talked with Miss Barrace, who had reproached him with not having come to see her, and he had above all hit on a happy thought for causing Waymarsh's tension to relax. Something might possibly be extracted for the latter from the idea of his success with that lady, whose quick apprehension of what might amuse her had given Strether a free hand. What had she meant if not to ask whether she couldn't help him with his splendid encumbrance, and mightn't the sacred rage at any rate be kept a little in abeyance by thus creating for his comrade's mind even in a world of irrelevance the possibility of a relation? What was it but a relation to be regarded as so decorative and, in especial, on the strength of it, to be whirled away, amid flounces and feathers, in a coupé lined, by what Strether could make out, with dark blue brocade? He himself had never been whirled away—never at least in a coupé and behind a footman; he had driven with Miss Gostrey in cabs, with Mrs. Pocock, a few times, in an open buggy, with Mrs. Newsome in a four-seated cart and, occasionally up at the mountains, on a buckboard; but his friend's actual adventure transcended his personal experience. He now showed his companion soon enough indeed how inadequate, as a general monitor, this last queer quantity could once more feel itself.

"What game under the sun is he playing?" He signified the next moment that his allusion was not to the fat gentleman immersed in dominoes on whom his eyes had begun by resting, but to their host of the previous hour, as to whom, there on the velvet bench, with a final collapse of all consistency, he treated himself to the comfort of indiscretion. "Where do you see him come out?"

Little Bilham, in meditation, looked at him with a kindness almost paternal. "Don't you like it over here?"

Strether laughed out—for the tone was indeed droll; he let himself go. "What has that to do with it? The only thing I've any business to like is to feel that I'm moving him. That's why I ask you whether you believe I *am*? Is the creature"—and he did his best to show that he simply wished to ascertain—"honest?"

His companion looked responsible, but looked it through a small dim smile. "What creature do you mean?"

It was on this that they did have for a little a mute interchange. "Is it untrue that he's free? How then," Strether asked wondering, "does he arrange his life?"

"Is the creature you mean Chad himself?" little Bilham said.

Strether here, with a rising hope, just thought, "We must take one of them at a time." But his coherence lapsed. "*Is* there some woman? Of whom he's really afraid of course I mean—or who does with him what she likes."

"It's awfully charming of you," Bilham presently remarked, "not to have asked me that before."

"Oh I'm not fit for my job!"

The exclamation had escaped our friend, but it made little Bilham more deliberate. "Chad's a rare case!" he luminously observed. "He's awfully changed," he added.

"Then you see it too?"

"The way he has improved? Oh yes—I think every one must see it. But I'm not sure," said little Bilham, "that I didn't like him about as well in his other state."

"Then this *is* really a new state altogether?"

"Well," the young man after a moment returned, "I'm not sure he was really meant by nature to be quite so good. It's like the new edition of an old book that one has been fond of—revised and amended, brought up to date, but not quite the thing one knew and loved. However that may be at all events," he pursued, "I don't think, you know, that he's really playing, as you call it, any game. I believe he really wants to go back and take up a career. He's capable of one, you know, that will improve and enlarge him still more. He won't then," little Bilham continued to remark, "be my pleasant well-rubbed old-fashioned volume at all. But of course I'm beastly immoral. I'm afraid it would be a funny world altogether—a world with things the way I like them. I ought, I dare say, to go home and go into business myself. Only I'd simply rather die—simply. And I've not the least difficulty in making up my mind not to, and in knowing exactly why, and in defending my ground against all comers. All the same," he wound up, "I assure you I don't say a word against it—for himself, I mean—to Chad. I seem to see it as much the best thing for him. You see he's not happy."

"Do I?"—Strether stared. "I've been supposing I see just the opposite—an extraordinary case of the equilibrium arrived at and assured."

"Oh there's a lot behind it."

"Ah there you are!" Strether exclaimed. "That's just what I want to get at. You speak of your familiar volume altered out of recognition. Well, who's the editor?"

Little Bilham looked before him a minute in silence. "He ought to get married. *That* would do it. And he wants to."

"Wants to marry her?"

Again little Bilham waited, and, with a sense that he had information, Strether scarce knew what was coming. "He wants to be free. He isn't used, you see," the young man explained in his lucid way, "to being so good."

Strether hesitated. "Then I may take it from you that he *is* good?"

His companion matched his pause, but making it up with a quiet fulness. "Do take it from me."

"Well then why isn't he free? He swears to me he is, but meanwhile does nothing—except of course that he's so kind to me—to prove it; and couldn't really act much otherwise if he weren't. My question to you just now was exactly on this queer impression of his diplomacy: as if instead of really giving ground his line were to keep me on here and set me a bad example."

As the half-hour meanwhile had ebbed Strether paid his score, and the waiter was presently in the act of counting out change. Our friend pushed back to him a fraction of it, with which, after an emphatic recognition, the personage in question retreated. "You give too much," little Bilham permitted himself benevolently to observe.

"Oh I always give too much!" Strether helplessly sighed. "But you don't," he went on as if to get quickly away from the contemplation of that doom, "answer my question. Why isn't he free?"

Little Bilham had got up as if the transaction with the waiter had been a signal, and had already edged out between the table and the divan. The effect of this was that a minute later they had quitted the place, the gratified waiter alert again at the open door. Strether had found himself deferring to his companion's abruptness as to a hint that he should be answered as soon as they were more isolated. This happened when after a few steps in the outer air they had turned the next corner. There our friend had kept it up. "Why isn't he free if he's good?"

Little Bilham looked him full in the face. "Because it's a virtuous attachment."

This had settled the question so effectually for the time—that is for the next few days—that it had given Strether almost a new lease of life. It must be added however that, thanks to his constant habit of shaking the bottle in which life handed him the wine of experience, he presently found the taste of the lees rising as usual into his draught. His imagination had in other words already dealt with his young friend's assertion; of which it had made something that sufficiently came out on the very next occasion of his seeing Maria Gostrey. This occasion moreover had been determined promptly by a new circumstance—a circumstance he was the last man to leave her for a day in ignorance of. "When I said to him last night," he immediately began, "that without some definite word from him now that will enable me to speak to them over there of our sailing—or at least of mine, giving them some sort of date—my responsibility becomes uncomfortable and my situation awkward; when I said that to him what do you think was his reply?" And then as she this time gave it up: "Why that he has two particular friends, two ladies, mother and daughter, about to arrive in Paris —coming back from an absence; and that he wants me so furiously to meet them, know them and like them, that I shall oblige him by kindly not bringing our business to a crisis till he has had a chance to see them again himself. Is that," Strether enquired, "the way he's going to try to get off? These are the people," he explained, "that he must have gone down to see before I arrived. They're the best friends he has in the world, and they take more interest than any one else in what concerns him. As I'm his next best he sees a thousand reasons why we should comfortably meet. He hasn't broached the question sooner because their return was uncertain —seemed in fact for the present impossible. But he more than intimates that—if you can believe it—their desire to make my acquaintance has had to do with their surmounting difficulties."

"They're dying to see you?" Miss Gostrey asked.

"Dying. Of course," said Strether, "they're the virtuous attachment." He had already told her about that—had seen her the day after his talk with little Bilham; and they had then threshed out together the bearing of the revelation. She had helped him to put into it the logic in which little Bilham had left it slightly deficient. Strether hadn't pressed him as to the object of the preference so unexpectedly described; feeling in the presence of it, with one of his irrepressible scruples, a delicacy from which he had in the quest of the quite other article worked himself sufficiently free. He had held off, as on a small principle of pride, from permitting his young friend to mention a name; wishing to make with this the great point that Chad's virtuous attachments were none of his business. He had wanted from the first not to think too much of his dignity, but that was no reason for not allowing it any little benefit that might turn up. He had often enough wondered to what degree his interference might pass for interested; so that there was no want of luxury in letting it be seen whenever he could that he didn't interfere. That had of course at the same time not deprived him of the further luxury of much private astonishment; which however he had reduced to some order before communicating his knowledge. When he had done this at last it was with the remark that, surprised as Miss Gostrey might, like himself, at first be, she would probably agree with him on reflexion that such an account of the matter did after all fit the confirmed appearances. Nothing certainly, on all the indications, could have been a greater change for him than a virtuous attachment, and since they had been in search of the "word" as the French called it, of that change, little Bilham's announcement—though so long and so oddly delayed—would serve as well as another. She had assured Strether in fact after a pause that the more she thought of it the more it did serve; and yet her assurance hadn't so weighed with him as that before they parted he hadn't ventured to challenge her sincerity. Didn't she believe the attachment *was* virtuous?—he had made sure of her again with the aid of that question. The tidings he brought her on this second occasion were moreover such as would help him to make surer still.

She showed at first none the less as only amused. "You say there are two? An attachment to them both then would, I suppose, almost necessarily be innocent."

Our friend took the point, but he had his clue. "Mayn't he be still in the stage of not quite knowing which of them, mother or daughter, he likes best?"

She gave it more thought. "Oh it must be the daughter—at his age."

"Possibly. Yet what do we know," Strether asked, "about hers? She may be old enough."

"Old enough for what?"

"Why to marry Chad. That may be, you know, what they want. And if Chad wants it too, and little Bilham wants it, and even *we*, at a pinch, could do with it—that is if she doesn't prevent repatriation—why it may be plain sailing yet."

It was always the case for him in these counsels that each of his remarks, as it came, seemed to drop into a deeper well. He had at all events to wait a moment to hear the slight splash of this one. "I don't see why if Mr. Newsome wants to marry the young lady he hasn't already done it or hasn't been prepared with some statement to you about it. And if he both wants to marry her and is on good terms with them why isn't he 'free'?"

Strether, responsively, wondered indeed. "Perhaps the girl herself doesn't like him."

"Then why does he speak of them to you as he does?"

Strether's mind echoed the question, but also again met it. "Perhaps it's with the mother he's on good terms."

"As against the daughter?"

"Well, if she's trying to persuade the daughter to consent to him, what could make him like the mother more? Only," Strether threw out, "why shouldn't the daughter consent to him?"

"Oh," said Miss Gostrey, "mayn't it be that every one else isn't quite so struck with him as you?"

"Doesn't regard him you mean as such an 'eligible' young man? *Is* that what I've come to?" he audibly and rather gravely sought to know. "However," he went on, "his marriage is what his mother most desires—that is if it will help. And oughtn't *any* marriage to help? They must want him"—he had already worked it out—"to be better off. Almost any girl he may marry will have a direct interest in his taking up his chances. It won't suit *her* at least that he shall miss them."

Miss Gostrey cast about. "No—you reason well! But of course on the other hand there's always dear old Woollett itself."

"Oh yes," he mused—"there's always dear old Woollett itself."

She waited a moment. "The young lady mayn't find herself able to swallow *that* quantity. She may think it's paying too much; she may weigh one thing against another."

Strether, ever restless in such debates, took a vague turn. "It will all depend on who she is. That of course—the proved ability to deal with dear old Woollett, since I'm sure she does deal with it—is what makes so strongly for Mamie."

"Mamie?"

He stopped short, at her tone, before her; then, though seeing that it represented not vagueness, but a momentary embarrassed fulness, let his exclamation come. "You surely haven't forgotten about Mamie!"

"No, I haven't forgotten about Mamie," she smiled. "There's no doubt whatever that there's ever so much to be said for her. Mamie's *my* girl!" she roundly declared.

Strether resumed for a minute his walk. "She's really perfectly lovely, you know. Far prettier than any girl I've seen over here yet."

"That's precisely on what I perhaps most build." And she mused a moment in her friend's way. "I should positively like to take her in hand!"

He humoured the fancy, though indeed finally to deprecate it. "Oh but don't, in your zeal, go over to her! I need you most and can't, you know, be left."

But she kept it up. "I wish they'd send her out to me!"

"If they knew you," he returned, "they would."

"Ah but don't they?—after all that, as I've understood you, you've told them about me?"

He had paused before her again, but he continued his course. "They *will*—before, as you say, I've done." Then he came out with the point he had wished after all most to make. "It seems to give away now his game. This is what he has been doing—keeping me along for. He has been waiting for them."

Miss Gostrey drew in her lips. "You see a good deal in it!"

"I doubt if I see as much as you. Do you pretend," he went on, "that you don't see—?"

"Well, what?"—she pressed him as he paused.

"Why that there must be a lot between them—and that it has been going on from the first; even from before I came."

She took a minute to answer. "Who are they then—if it's so grave?"

"It mayn't be grave—it may be gay. But at any rate it's marked. Only I don't know," Strether had to confess, "anything about them. Their name for instance was a thing that, after little Bilham's information, I found it a kind of refreshment not to feel obliged to follow up."

"Oh," she returned, "if you think you've got off—!"

Her laugh produced in him a momentary gloom. "I don't think I've got off. I only think I'm breathing for about five minutes. I dare say I *shall* have, at the best, still to get on." A look, over it all, passed between them, and the next minute he had come back to good humour. "I don't meanwhile take the smallest interest in their name."

"Nor in their nationality?—American, French, English, Polish?"

"I don't care the least little 'hang,'" he smiled, "for their nationality. It would be nice if they're Polish!"[4] he almost immediately added.

"Very nice indeed." The transition kept up her spirits. "So you see you do care."

He did this contention a modified justice. "I think I should if they *were* Polish. Yes," he thought—"there might be joy in *that*."

"Let us then hope for it." But she came after this nearer to the question. "If the girl's of the right age of course the mother can't be. I mean for the virtuous attachment. If the girl's twenty—and she can't be less—the mother must be at least forty. So it puts the mother out. *She's* too old for him."

Strether, arrested again, considered and demurred. "Do you think so? Do you think any one would be too old for him? *I'm* eighty, and I'm too young. But perhaps the girl," he continued, "*isn't* twenty. Perhaps she's only ten—but such a little dear that Chad finds himself counting her in as an attraction of the acquaintance. Perhaps she's only five. Perhaps the mother's but five-and-twenty—a charming young widow."

4. Unsuccessful revolts in conquered and partitioned Poland in 1830, 1846, and again in 1863 peopled Western Europe with thousands of exiles, many of them from the Polish upper class.

Miss Gostrey entertained the suggestion. "She *is* a widow then?"

"I haven't the least idea!" They once more, in spite of this vagueness, exchanged a look—a look that was perhaps the longest yet. It seemed in fact, the next thing, to require to explain itself; which it did as it could. "I only feel what I've told you—that he has some reason."

Miss Gostrey's imagination had taken its own flight. "Perhaps she's *not* a widow."

Strether seemed to accept the possibility with reserve. Still he accepted it. "Then that's why the attachment—if it's to her—is virtuous."

But she looked as if she scarce followed. "Why is it virtuous if —since she's free—there's nothing to impose on it any condition?"

He laughed at her question. "Oh I perhaps don't mean as virtuous as *that!* Your idea is that it can be virtuous—in any sense worthy of the name—only if she's *not* free? But what does it become then," he asked, "for *her?*"

"Ah that's another matter." He said nothing for a moment, and she soon went on. "I dare say you're right, at any rate, about Mr. Newsome's little plan. He *has* been trying you—has been reporting on you to these friends."

Strether meanwhile had had time to think more. "Then where's his straightness?"

"Well, as we say, it's struggling up, breaking out, asserting itself as it can. We can be on the side, you see, of his straightness. We can help him. But he has made out," said Miss Gostrey, "that you'll do."

"Do for what?"

"Why, for *them*—for *ces dames.*[5] He has watched you, studied you, liked you—and recognised that *they* must. It's a great compliment to you, my dear man; for I'm sure they're particular. You came out for a success. Well," she gaily declared, "you're having it!"

He took it from her with momentary patience and then turned abruptly away. It was always convenient to him that there were so many fine things in her room to look at. But the examination of two or three of them appeared soon to have determined a speech that had little to do with them. "You don't believe in it!"

"In what?"

"In the character of the attachment. In its innocence."

But she defended herself. "I don't pretend to know anything about it. Everything's possible. We must see."

"See?" he echoed with a groan. "Haven't we seen enough?"

"*I* haven't," she smiled.

"But do you suppose then little Bilham has lied?"

5. Those ladies.

"You must find out."

It made him almost turn pale. "Find out any *more?*"

He had dropped on a sofa for dismay; but she seemed, as she stood over him, to have the last word. "Wasn't what you came out for to find out *all?*"

Book Fifth

I [x]

The Sunday of the next week was a wonderful day, and Chad Newsome had let his friend know in advance that he had provided for it. There had already been a question of his taking him to see the great Gloriani, who was at home on Sunday afternoons and at whose house, for the most part, fewer bores were to be met than elsewhere; but the project, through some accident, had not had instant effect, and now revived in happier conditions. Chad had made the point that the celebrated sculptor had a queer old garden, for which the weather—spring at last frank and fair—was propitious; and two or three of his other allusions had confirmed for Strether the expectation of something special. He had by this time, for all introductions and adventures, let himself recklessly go, cherishing the sense that whatever the young man showed him he was showing at least himself. He could have wished indeed, so far as this went, that Chad were less of a mere cicerone; for he was not without the impression—now that the vision of his game, his plan, his deep diplomacy, did recurrently assert itself—of his taking refuge from the realities of their intercourse in profusely dispensing, as our friend mentally phrased it, *panem et circenses.*[1] Our friend continued to feel rather smothered in flowers, though he made in his other moments the almost angry inference that this was only because of his odious ascetic suspicion of any form of beauty. He periodically assured himself—for his reactions were sharp—that he shouldn't reach the truth of anything till he had at least got rid of that.

He had known beforehand that Madame de Vionnet and her daughter would probably be on view, an intimation to that effect having constituted the only reference again made by Chad to his good friends from the south. The effect of Strether's talk about them with Miss Gostrey had been quite to consecrate his reluctance to pry; something in the very air of Chad's silence—judged in the light of that talk—offered it to him as a reserve he could markedly match. It shrouded them about with he scarce knew what, a con-

---

1. According to the Roman satirist Juvenal (c. 100 A.D.), the only things that the once great Roman people now wanted was *panem et circenses*—"bread and circuses" (Tenth Satire 1. 81).

sideration, a distinction; he was in presence at any rate—so far as it placed him there—of ladies; and the one thing that was definite for him was that they themselves should be, to the extent of his responsibility, in presence of a gentleman. Was it because they were very beautiful, very clever, or even very good—was it for one of these reasons that Chad was, so to speak, nursing his effect? Did he wish to spring them, in the Woollett phrase, with a fuller force—to confound his critic, slight though as yet the criticism, with some form of merit exquisitely incalculable? The most the critic had at all events asked was whether the persons in question were French; and that enquiry had been but a proper comment on the sound of their name. "Yes. That is no!" had been Chad's reply; but he had immediately added that their English was the most charming in the world, so that if Strether were wanting an excuse for not getting on with them he wouldn't in the least find one. Never in fact had Strether—in the mood into which the place had quickly launched him—felt, for himself, less the need of an excuse. Those he might have found would have been, at the worst, all for the others, the people before him, in whose liberty to be as they were he was aware that he positively rejoiced. His fellow guests were multiplying, and these things, their liberty, their intensity, their variety, their conditions at large, were in fusion in the admirable medium of the scene.

The place itself was a great impression—a small pavilion, clear-faced and sequestered, an effect of polished parquet, of fine white panel and spare sallow gilt, of decoration delicate and rare, in the heart of the Faubourg Saint-Germain[2] and on the edge of a cluster of gardens attached to old noble houses. Far back from streets and unsuspected by crowds, reached by a long passage and a quiet court, it was as striking to the unprepared mind, he immediately saw, as a treasure dug up; giving him too, more than anything yet, the note of the range of the immeasurable town and sweeping away, as by a last brave brush, his usual landmarks and terms. It was in the garden, a spacious cherished remnant, out of which a dozen persons had already passed, that Chad's host presently met them; while the tall bird-haunted trees, all of a twitter with the spring and the weather, and the high party-walls, on the other side of which grave hôtels[3] stood off for privacy, spoke of survival, transmission, association, a strong indifferent persistent order. The day was so soft that the little party had practically adjourned to the open air, but the open air was in such conditions all a chamber of state. Strether had presently the sense of a great convent, a convent of

2. The section of Paris called the Faubourg Saint-Germain is located on the left bank; it was the aristocratic quarter of Paris and included as well many of the foreign embassies.
3. Mansions.

missions, famous for he scarce knew what, a nursery of young priests, of scattered shade, of straight alleys and chapel-bells, that spread its mass in one quarter; he had the sense of names in the air, of ghosts at the windows, of signs and tokens, a whole range of expression, all about him, too thick for prompt discrimination.

This assault of images became for a moment, in the address of the distinguished sculptor, almost formidable: Gloriani[4] showed him, in such perfect confidence, on Chad's introduction of him, a fine worn handsome face, a face that was like an open letter in a foreign tongue. With his genius in his eyes, his manners on his lips, his long career behind him and his honours and rewards all round, the great artist, in the course of a single sustained look and a few words of delight at receiving him, affected our friend as a dazzling prodigy of type. Strether had seen in museums—in the Luxembourg as well as, more reverently, later on, in the New York of the billionaires—the work of his hand; knowing too that after an earlier time in his native Rome he had migrated, in mid-career, to Paris, where, with a personal lustre almost violent, he shone in a constellation: all of which was more than enough to crown him, for his guest, with the light, with the romance, of glory. Strether, in contact with that element as he had never yet so intimately been, had the consciousness of opening to it, for the happy instant, all the windows of his mind, of letting this rather grey interior drink in for once the sun of a clime not marked in his old geography. He was to remember again repeatedly the medal-like Italian face, in which every line was an artist's own, in which time told only as tone and consecration; and he was to recall in especial, as the penetrating radiance, as the communication of the illustrious spirit itself, the manner in which, while they stood briefly, in welcome and response, face to face, he was held by the sculptor's eyes. He wasn't soon to forget them, was to think of them, all unconscious, unintending, preoccupied though they were, as the source of the deepest intellectual sounding to which he had ever been exposed. He was in fact quite to cherish his vision of it, to play with it in idle hours; only speaking of it to no one and quite aware he couldn't have spoken

4. One of the very few James characters who appear in more than one novel, Gloriani figures importantly in *Roderick Hudson* (1875). In the extensive revision of that novel, done after *The Ambassadors* was written, Gloriani is described as "an American sculptor of French extraction, or remotely perhaps of Italian" who knew exactly what he was about and was "conscious and compact, unlimitedly intelligent and consummately clever, helpful only as to his own duties, and at once gracefully deferential and profoundly indifferent to those of others." His works "were considered by most people to belong to a very extravagant, and by many to a thoroughly depraved type," and this was largely the result of Gloriani's aesthetics, which maintained "that there is no essential difference between beauty and ugliness; * * * that hideousness grimaces at you suddenly from out of the very bosom of loveliness, and beauty blooms before your eyes in the lap of vileness; * * * that the thing to aim at is the expressive and the way to reach it is by ingenuity" (Chapter VI in the New York Edition of *Roderick Hudson*).

without appearing to talk nonsense. Was what it had told him or
what it had asked him the greater of the mysteries? Was it the most
special flare, unequalled, supreme, of the æsthetic torch, lighting
that wondrous world for ever, or was it above all the long straight
shaft sunk by a personal acuteness that life had seasoned to steel?
Nothing on earth could have been stranger and no one doubtless
more surprised than the artist himself, but it was for all the world
to Strether just then as if in the matter of his accepted duty he had
positively been on trial. The deep human expertness in Gloriani's
charming smile—oh the terrible life behind it!—was flashed upon
him as a test of his stuff.

Chad meanwhile, after having easily named his companion, had
still more easily turned away and was already greeting other persons present. He was as easy, clever Chad, with the great artist as
with his obscure compatriot, and as easy with every one else as with
either: this fell into its place for Strether and made almost a new
light, giving him, as a concatenation, something more he could
enjoy. He liked Gloriani, but should never see him again; of that
he was sufficiently sure. Chad accordingly, who was wonderful with
both of them, was a kind of link for hopeless fancy, an implication
of possibilities—oh if everything had been different! Strether noted
at all events that he was thus on terms with illustrious spirits, and
also that—yes, distinctly—he hadn't in the least swaggered about it.
Our friend hadn't come there only for this figure of Abel Newsome's
son, but that presence threatened to affect the observant mind as
positively central. Gloriani indeed, remembering something and
excusing himself, pursued Chad to speak to him, and Strether was
left musing on many things. One of them was the question of
whether, since he had been tested, he had passed. Did the artist
drop him from having made out that he wouldn't do? He really
felt just to-day that he might do better than usual. Hadn't he done
well enough, so far as that went, in being exactly so dazzled? and
in not having too, as he almost believed, wholly hidden from his
host that he felt the latter's plummet? Suddenly, across the garden,
he saw little Bilham approach, and it was a part of the fit that was
on him that as their eyes met he guessed also *his* knowledge. If he
had said to him on the instant what was uppermost he would have
said: "*Have* I passed?—for of course I know one has to pass here."
Little Bilham would have reassured him, have told him that he
exaggerated, and have adduced happily enough the argument of
little Bilham's own very presence; which, in truth, he could see,
was as easy a one as Gloriani's own or as Chad's. He himself would
perhaps then after a while cease to be frightened, would get the
point of view for some of the faces—types tremendously alien, alien
to Woollett—that he had already begun to take in. Who were they

all, the dispersed groups and couples, the ladies even more unlike those of Woollett than the gentlemen?—this was the enquiry that, when his young friend had greeted him, he did find himself making.

"Oh they're every one—all sorts and sizes; of course I mean within limits, though limits down perhaps rather more than limits up. There are always artists—he's beautiful and inimitable to the *cher confrère;*[5] and then *gros bonnets*[6] of many kinds—ambassadors, cabinet ministers, bankers, generals, what do I know? even Jews. Above all always some awfully nice women—and not too many; sometimes an actress, an artist, a great performer—but only when they're not monsters; and in particular the right *femmes du monde.*[7] You can fancy his history on that side—I believe it's fabulous: they *never* give him up. Yet he keeps them down: no one knows how he manages; it's too beautiful and bland. Never too many—and a mighty good thing too; just a perfect choice. But there are not in any way many bores; it has always been so; he has some secret. It's extraordinary. And you don't find it out. He's the same to every one. He doesn't ask questions."

"Ah doesn't he?" Strether laughed.

Bilham met it with all his candour. "How then should *I* be here?"

"Oh for what you tell me. You're part of the perfect choice."

Well, the young man took in the scene. "It seems rather good to-day."

Strether followed the direction of his eyes. "Are they all, this time, *femmes du monde?*"

Little Bilham showed his competence. "Pretty well."

This was a category our friend had a feeling for; a light, romantic and mysterious, on the feminine element, in which he enjoyed for a little watching it. "Are there any Poles?"

His companion considered. "I think I make out a 'Portuguee.' But I've seen Turks."

Strether wondered, desiring justice. "They seem—all the women —very harmonious."

"Oh in closer quarters they come out!" And then, while Strether was aware of fearing closer quarters, though giving himself again to the harmonies, "Well," little Bilham went on, "it *is* at the worst rather good, you know. If you like it, you feel it, this way, that shows you're not in the least out. But you always know things," he handsomely added, "immediately."

Strether liked it and felt it only too much; so "I say, don't lay traps for me!" he rather helplessly murmured.

"Well," his companion returned, "he's wonderfully kind to *us.*"

"To us Americans you mean?"

5. Dear colleague.
6. Bigwigs.
7. Women of the world.

"Oh no—he doesn't know anything about *that*. That's half the battle here—that you can never hear politics. We don't talk them. I mean to poor young wretches of all sorts. And yet it's always as charming as this; it's as if, by something in the air, our squalor didn't show. It puts us all back—into the last century."

"I'm afraid," Strether said, amused, "that it puts me rather forward: oh ever so far!"

"Into the next? But isn't that only," little Bilham asked, "because you're really of the century before?"

"The century before the last? Thank you!" Strether laughed. "If I ask you about some of the ladies it can't be then that I may hope, as such a specimen of the rococo, to please them."

"On the contrary they adore—we all adore here—the rococo, and where is there a better setting for it than the whole thing, the pavilion and the garden, together? There are lots of people with collections," little Bilham smiled as he glanced round. "You'll be secured!"

It made Strether for a moment give himself again to contemplation. There were faces he scarce knew what to make of. Were they charming or were they only strange? He mightn't talk politics, yet he suspected a Pole or two. The upshot was the question at the back of his head from the moment his friend had joined him. "Have Madame de Vionnet and her daughter arrived?"

"I haven't seen them yet, but Miss Gostrey has come. She's in the pavilion looking at objects. One can see *she's* a collector," little Bilham added without offence.

"Oh yes, she's a collector, and I knew she was to come. Is Madame de Vionnet a collector?" Strether went on.

"Rather, I believe; almost celebrated." The young man met, on it, a little, his friend's eyes. "I happen to know—from Chad, whom I saw last night—that they've come back; but only yesterday. He wasn't sure—up to the last. This, accordingly," little Bilham went on, "will be—if they *are* here—their first appearance after their return."

Strether, very quickly, turned these things over. "Chad told you last night? To me, on our way here, he said nothing about it."

"But did you ask him?"

Strether did him the justice. "I dare say not."

"Well," said little Bilham, "you're not a person to whom it's easy to tell things you don't want to know. Though it *is* easy, I admit—it's quite beautiful," he benevolently added, "when you do want to."

Strether looked at him with an indulgence that matched his intelligence. "Is that the deep reasoning on which—about these ladies—you've been yourself so silent?"

Little Bilham considered the depth of his reasoning. "I haven't been silent. I spoke of them to you the other day, the day we sat together after Chad's tea-party."

Strether came round to it. "They then are the virtuous attachment?"

"I can only tell you that it's what they pass for. But isn't that enough? What more than a vain appearance does the wisest of us know? I commend you," the young man declared with a pleasant emphasis, "the vain appearance."

Strether looked more widely round, and what he saw, from face to face, deepened the effect of his young friend's words. "Is it so good?"

"Magnificent."

Strether had a pause. "The husband's dead?"

"Dear no. Alive."

"Oh!" said Strether. After which, as his companion laughed: "How then can it be so good?"

"You'll see for yourself. One does see."

"Chad's in love with the daughter?"

"That's what I mean."

Strether wondered. "Then where's the difficulty?"

"Why, aren't you and I—with our grander bolder ideas?"

"Oh mine—!" Strether said rather strangely. But then as if to attenuate: "You mean they won't hear of Woollett?"

Little Bilham smiled. "Isn't that just what you must see about?"

It had brought them, as she caught the last words, into relation with Miss Barrace, whom Strether had already observed—as he had never before seen a lady at a party—moving about alone. Coming within sound of them she had already spoken, and she took again, through her long-handled glass, all her amused and amusing possession. "How much, poor Mr. Strether, you seem to have to see about! But you can't say," she gaily declared, "that I don't do what I can to help you. Mr. Waymarsh is placed. I've left him in the house with Miss Gostrey."

"The way," little Bilham exclaimed, "Mr. Strether gets the ladies to work for him! He's just preparing to draw in another; to pounce—don't you see him?—on Madame de Vionnet."

"Madame de Vionnet? Oh, oh, oh!" Miss Barrace cried in a wonderful crescendo. There was more in it, our friend made out, than met the ear. Was it after all a joke that he should be serious about anything? He envied Miss Barrace at any rate her power of not being. She seemed, with little cries and protests and quick recognitions, movements like the darts of some fine high-feathered free-pecking bird, to stand before life as before some full shop-window. You could fairly hear, as she selected and pointed, the tap of her tortoise-shell against the glass. "It's certain that we do need seeing about; only I'm glad it's not I who have to do it. One does, no doubt, begin that way; then suddenly one finds that one has given it up. It's too much, it's too difficult. You're wonderful, you people," she continued to Strether, "for not feeling those things —by which I mean impossibilities. You never feel them. You face them with a fortitude that makes it a lesson to watch you."

"Ah but"—little Bilham put it with discouragement—"what do we achieve after all? We see about you and report—when we even go so far as reporting. But nothing's done."

"Oh you, Mr. Bilham," she replied as with an impatient rap on the glass, "you're not worth sixpence! You come over to convert the savages—for I know you verily did, I remember you—and the savages simply convert *you*."

"Not even!" the young man woefully confessed: "they haven't gone through that form. They've simply—the cannibals!—eaten me; converted me if you like, but converted me into food. I'm but the bleached bones of a Christian."

"Well then there we are! Only"—and Miss Barrace appealed again to Strether—"don't let it discourage you. You'll break down soon enough, but you'll meanwhile have had your moments. *Il faut en avoir.*[8] I always like to see you while you last. And I'll tell you who *will* last."

"Waymarsh?"—he had already taken her up.

She laughed out as at the alarm of it. "He'll resist even Miss Gostrey: so grand is it not to understand. He's wonderful."

"He is indeed," Strether conceded. "He wouldn't tell me of this affair—only said he had an engagement; but with such a gloom, you must let me insist, as if it had been an engagement to be hanged. Then silently and secretly he turns up here with you. Do you call *that* 'lasting'?"

"Oh I hope it's lasting!" Miss Barrace said. "But he only, at the best, bears with me. He doesn't understand—not one little scrap. He's delightful. He's wonderful," she repeated.

"Michelangelesque!"—little Bilham completed her meaning. "He *is* a success. Moses, on the ceiling, brought down to the floor;[9] overwhelming, colossal, but somehow portable."

"Certainly, if you mean by portable," she returned, "looking so well in one's carriage. He's too funny beside me in his corner; he looks like somebody, somebody foreign and famous, *en exil*; so that people wonder—it's very amusing—whom I'm taking about. I show him Paris, show him everything, and he never turns a hair. He's like the Indian chief one reads about, who, when he comes

---

8. It is necessary to have some.
9. The allusions are to Michelangelo Buonarroti (1475–1564), his famous painting on the ceiling of the Sistine Chapel and his equally celebrated statue of Moses, both of which are in Rome.

up to Washington to see the Great Father, stands wrapt in his blanket and gives no sign. *I* might be the Great Father—from the way he takes everything." She was delighted at this hit of her identity with that personage—it fitted so her character; she declared it was the title she meant henceforth to adopt. "And the way he sits, too, in the corner of my room, only looking at my visitors very hard and as if he wanted to start something! They wonder what he does want to start. But he's wonderful," Miss Barrace once more insisted. "He has never started anything yet."

It presented him none the less, in truth, to her actual friends, who looked at each other in intelligence, with frank amusement on Bilham's part and a shade of sadness on Strether's. Strether's sadness sprang—for the image had its grandeur—from his thinking how little he himself was wrapt in his blanket, how little, in marble halls, all too oblivious of the Great Father, he resembled a really majestic aboriginal. But he had also another reflexion. "You've all of you here so much visual sense that you've somehow all 'run' to it. There are moments when it strikes one that you haven't any other."

"Any moral," little Bilham explained, watching serenely, across the garden, the several *femmes du monde.* "But Miss Barrace has a moral distinction," he kindly continued; speaking as if for Strether's benefit not less than for her own.

"*Have* you?" Strether, scarce knowing what he was about, asked of her almost eagerly.

"Oh not a distinction"—she was mightily amused at his tone—"Mr. Bilham's too good. But I think I may say a sufficiency. Yes, a sufficiency. Have you supposed strange things of me?"—and she fixed him again, through all her tortoise-shell, with the droll interest of it. "You *are* all indeed wonderful. I should awfully disappoint you. I do take my stand on my sufficiency. But I know, I confess," she went on, "strange people. I don't know how it happens; I don't do it on purpose; it seems to be my doom—as if I were always one of their habits: it's wonderful! I dare say moreover," she pursued with an interested gravity, "that I do, that we all do here, run too much to mere eye. But how can it be helped? We're all looking at each other—and in the light of Paris one sees what things resemble. That's what the light of Paris seems always to show. It's the fault of the light of Paris—dear old light!"

"Dear old Paris!" little Bilham echoed.

"Everything, every one shows," Miss Barrace went on.

"But for what they really are?" Strether asked.

"Oh I like your Boston 'reallys'! But sometimes—yes."

"Dear old Paris then!" Strether resignedly sighed while for a moment they looked at each other. Then he broke out: "Does

Madame de Vionnet do that? I mean really show for what she is?"
Her answer was prompt. "She's charming. She's perfect."
"Then why did you a minute ago say 'Oh, oh, oh!' at her name?"
She easily remembered. "Why just because—! She's wonderful."
"Ah she too?"—Strether had almost a groan.

But Miss Barrace had meanwhile perceived relief. "Why not put
your question straight to the person who can answer it best?"

"No," said little Bilham; "don't put any question; wait, rather
—it will be much more fun—to judge for yourself. He has come
to take you to her."

II [XI]

On which Strether saw that Chad was again at hand, and he
afterwards scarce knew, absurd as it may seem, what had then
quickly occurred. The moment concerned him, he felt, more
deeply than he could have explained, and he had a subsequent
passage of speculation as to whether, on walking off with Chad,
he hadn't looked either pale or red. The only thing he was clear
about was that, luckily, nothing indiscreet had in fact been said,
and that Chad himself was more than ever, in Miss Barrace's
great sense, wonderful. It was one of the connexions—though
really why it should be, after all, was none so apparent—in which
the whole change in him came out as most striking. Strether recalled as they approached the house that he had impressed him
that first night as knowing how to enter a box. Well, he impressed
him scarce less now as knowing how to make a presentation. It did
something for Strether's own quality—marked it as estimated; so
that our poor friend, conscious and passive, really seemed to feel
himself quite handed over and delivered; absolutely, as he would
have said, made a present of, given away. As they reached the
house a young woman, about to come forth, appeared, unaccom-
panied, on the steps; at the exchange with whom of a word on
Chad's part Strether immediately perceived that, obligingly, kindly,
she was there to meet them. Chad had left her in the house, but she
had afterwards come halfway and then the next moment had joined
them in the garden. Her air of youth, for Strether, was at first almost disconcerting, while his second impression was, not less
sharply, a degree of relief at there not having just been, with the
others, any freedom used about her. It was upon him at a touch
that she was no subject for that, and meanwhile, on Chad's
introducing him, she had spoken to him, very simply and gently,
in an English clearly of the easiest to her, yet unlike any other he
had ever heard. It wasn't as if she tried; nothing, he could see after
they had been a few minutes together, was as if she tried; but her
speech, charming correct and odd, was like a precaution against her
passing for a Pole. There were precautions, he seemed indeed to

see, only when there were really dangers.

Later on he was to feel many more of them, but by that time he was to feel other things besides. She was dressed in black, but in black that struck him as light and transparent; she was exceedingly fair, and, though she was as markedly slim, her face had a round-ness, with eyes far apart and a little strange. Her smile was natural and dim; her hat not extravagant; he had only perhaps a sense of the clink, beneath her fine black sleeves, of more gold bracelets and bangles than he had ever seen a lady wear. Chad was excel-lently free and light about their encounter; it was one of the occa-sions on which Strether most wished he himself might have arrived at such ease and such humour: "Here you are then, face to face at last; you're made for each other—*vous allez voir;*[1] and I bless your union." It was indeed, after he had gone off, as if he had been partly serious too. This latter motion had been determined by an enquiry from him about "Jeanne"; to which her mother had replied that she was probably still in the house with Miss Gostrey, to whom she had lately committed her. "Ah but you know," the young man had rejoined, "he must see her"; with which, while Strether pricked up his ears, he had started as if to bring her, leaving the other objects of his interest together. Strether wondered to find Miss Gostrey already involved, feeling that he missed a link; but feeling also, with small delay, how much he should like to talk with her of Madame de Vionnet on this basis of evidence.

The evidence as yet in truth was meagre; which, for that matter, was perhaps a little why his expectation had had a drop. There was somehow not quite a wealth in her; and a wealth was all that, in his simplicity, he had definitely prefigured. Still, it was too much to be sure already that there was but a poverty. They moved away from the house, and, with eyes on a bench at some distance, he proposed that they should sit down. "I've heard a great deal about you," she said as they went; but he had an answer to it that made her stop short. "Well, about *you*, Madame de Vionnet, I've heard, I'm bound to say, almost nothing"—those struck him as the only words he himself could utter with any lucidity; conscious as he was, and as with more reason, of the determination to be in respect to the rest of his business perfectly plain and go perfectly straight. It hadn't at any rate been in the least his idea to spy on Chad's proper freedom. It was possibly, however, at this very instant and under the impression of Madame de Vionnet's pause, that going straight began to announce itself as a matter for care. She had only after all to smile at him ever so gently in order to make him ask himself if he weren't already going crooked. It might be going crooked to find it of a sudden just only clear that she intended

1. You will see.

very definitely to be what he would have called nice to him. This was what passed between them while, for another instant, they stood still; he couldn't at least remember afterwards what else it might have been. The thing indeed really unmistakeable was its rolling over him as a wave that he had been, in conditions incalculable and unimaginable, a subject of discussion. He had been, on some ground that concerned her, answered for; which gave her an advantage he should never be able to match.

"Hasn't Miss Gostrey," she asked, "said a good word for me?"

What had struck him first was the way he was bracketed with that lady; and he wondered what account Chad would have given of their acquaintance. Something not as yet traceable, at all events, had obviously happened. "I didn't even know of her knowing you."

"Well, now she'll tell you all. I'm so glad you're in relation with her."

This was one of the things—the "all" Miss Gostrey would now tell him—that, with every deference to present preoccupation, was uppermost for Strether after they had taken their seat. One of the others was, at the end of five minutes, that she—oh incontestably, yes—*differed* less; differed, that is, scarcely at all—well, superficially speaking, from Mrs. Newsome or even from Mrs. Pocock. She was ever so much younger than the one and not so young as the other; but what *was* there in her, if anything, that would have made it impossible he should meet her at Woollett? And wherein was her talk during their moments on the bench together not the same as would have been found adequate for a Woollett garden-party?— unless perhaps truly in not being quite so bright. She observed to him that Mr. Newsome had, to her knowledge, taken extraordinary pleasure in his visit; but there was no good lady at Woollett who wouldn't have been at least up to that. Was there in Chad, by chance, after all, deep down, a principle of aboriginal loyalty that had made him, for sentimental ends, attach himself to elements, happily encountered, that would remind him most of the old air and the old soil? Why accordingly be in a flutter—Strether could even put it that way—about this unfamiliar phenomenon of the *femme du monde?* On these terms Mrs. Newsome herself was as much of one. Little Bilham verily had testified that they came out, the ladies of the type, in close quarters; but it was just in these quarters—now comparatively close—that he felt Madame de Vionnet's common humanity. She did come out, and certainly to his relief, but she came out as the usual thing. There might be motives behind, but so could there often be even at Woollett. The only thing was that if she showed him she wished to like him— as the motives behind might conceivably prompt—it would possibly have been more thrilling for him that she should have shown as more vividly alien. Ah she was neither Turk nor Pole!—which would be indeed flat once more for Mrs. Newsome and Mrs. Pocock. A lady and two gentlemen had meanwhile, however, approached their bench, and this accident stayed for the time further developments.

They presently addressed his companion, the brilliant strangers; she rose to speak to them, and Strether noted how the escorted lady, though mature and by no means beautiful, had more of the bold high look, the range of expensive reference, that he had, as might have been said, made his plans for. Madame de Vionnet greeted her as "Duchesse" and was greeted in turn, while talk started in French, as "Ma toute-belle";[2] little facts that had their due, their vivid interest for Strether. Madame de Vionnet didn't, none the less, introduce him—a note he was conscious of as false to the Woollett scale and the Woollett humanity; though it didn't prevent the Duchess, who struck him as confident and free, very much what he had obscurely supposed duchesses, from looking at him as straight and as hard—for it *was* hard—as if she would have liked, all the same, to know him. "Oh yes, my dear, it's all right, it's *me*; and who are *you*, with your interesting wrinkles and your most effective (is it the handsomest, is it the ugliest?) of noses?"—some such loose handful of bright flowers she seemed, fragrantly enough, to fling at him. Strether almost wondered—at such a pace was he going—if some divination of the influence of either party were what determined Madame de Vionnet's abstention. One of the gentlemen, in any case, succeeded in placing himself in close relation with our friend's companion; a gentleman rather stout and importantly short, in a hat with a wonderful wide curl to its brim and a frock coat buttoned with an effect of superlative decision. His French had quickly turned to equal English, and it occurred to Strether that he might well be one of the ambassadors. His design was evidently to assert a claim to Madame de Vionnet's undivided countenance, and he made it good in the course of a minute—led her away with a trick of three words; a trick played with a social art of which Strether, looking after them as the four, whose backs were now all turned, moved off, felt himself no master.

He sank again upon his bench and, while his eyes followed the party, reflected, as he had done before, on Chad's strange communities. He sat there alone for five minutes, with plenty to think of; above all with his sense of having suddenly been dropped by a charming woman overlaid now by other impressions and in fact quite cleared and indifferent. He hadn't yet had so quiet a surrender; he didn't in the least care if nobody spoke to him more. He might have been, by his attitude, in for something of a march

2. My great beauty (*lit.*, my completely beautiful).

so broad that the want of ceremony with which he had just been used could fall into its place as but a minor incident of the procession. Besides, there would be incidents enough, as he felt when this term of contemplation was closed by the reappearance of little Bilham, who stood before him a moment with a suggestive "Well?" in which he saw himself reflected as disorganised, as possibly floored. He replied with a "Well!" intended to show that he wasn't floored in the least. No indeed; he gave it out, as the young man sat down beside him, that if, at the worst, he had been overturned at all, he had been overturned into the upper air, the sublimer element with which he had an affinity and in which he might be trusted a while to float. It wasn't a descent to earth to say after an instant and in sustained response to the reference: "You're quite sure her husband's living?"

"Oh dear, yes."

"Ah then—!"

"Ah then what?"

Strether had after all to think. "Well, I'm sorry for them." But it didn't for the moment matter more than that. He assured his young friend he was quite content. They wouldn't stir; were all right as they were. He didn't want to be introduced; had been introduced already about as far as he could go. He had seen moreover an immensity; liked Gloriani, who, as Miss Barrace kept saying, was wonderful; had made out, he was sure, the half-dozen other men who were distinguished, the artists, the critics and oh the great dramatist—*him* it was easy to spot; but wanted—no, thanks, really—to talk with none of them; having nothing at all to say and finding it would do beautifully as it was; do beautifully because what it was—well, was just simply too late. And when after this little Bilham, submissive and responsive, but with an eye to the consolation nearest, easily threw off some "Better late than never!" all he got in return for it was a sharp "Better early than late!" This note indeed the next thing overflowed for Strether into a quiet stream of demonstration that as soon as he had let himself go he felt as the real relief. It had consciously gathered to a head, but the reservoir had filled sooner than he knew, and his companion's touch was to make the waters spread. There were some things that had to come in time if they were to come at all. If they didn't come in time they were lost for ever. It was the general sense of them that had overwhelmed him with its long slow rush.

"It's not too late for *you*, on any side, and you don't strike me as in danger of missing the train; besides which people can be in general pretty well trusted, of course—with the clock of their freedom ticking as loud as it seems to do here—to keep an eye on the fleeting hour. All the same don't forget that you're young—blessedly young; be glad of it on the contrary and live up to it. Live all you can; it's a mistake not to. It doesn't so much matter what you do in particular, so long as you have your life. If you haven't had that what *have* you had? This place and these impressions—mild as you may find them to wind a man up so; all my impressions of Chad and of people I've seen at *his* place—well, have had their abundant message for me, have just dropped *that* into my mind. I see it now. I haven't done so enough before—and now I'm old; too old at any rate for what I see. Oh I *do* see, at least; and more than you'd believe or I can express. It's too late. And it's as if the train had fairly waited at the station for me without my having had the gumption to know it was there. Now I hear its faint receding whistle miles and miles down the line. What one loses one loses; make no mistake about that. The affair—I mean the affair of life—couldn't, no doubt, have been different for me; for it's at the best a tin mould, either fluted and embossed, with ornamental excrescences, or else smooth and dreadfully plain, into which, a helpless jelly, one's consciousness is poured—so that one 'takes' the form, as the great cook says, and is more or less compactly held by it: one lives in fine as one can. Still, one has the illusion of freedom; therefore don't be, like me, without the memory of that illusion. I was either, at the right time, too stupid or too intelligent to have it; I don't quite know which. Of course at present I'm a case of reaction against the mistake; and the voice of reaction should, no doubt, always be taken with an allowance. But that doesn't affect the point that the right time is now yours. The right time is *any* time that one is still so lucky as to have. You've plenty; that's the great thing; you're, as I say, damn you, so happily and hatefully young. Don't at any rate miss things out of stupidity. Of course I don't take you for a fool, or I shouldn't be addressing you thus awfully. Do what you like so long as you don't make *my* mistake. For it was a mistake. Live!" . . . Slowly and sociably, with full pauses and straight dashes, Strether had so delivered himself; holding little Bilham from step to step deeply and gravely attentive. The end of all was that the young man had turned quite solemn, and that this was a contradiction of the innocent gaiety the speaker had wished to promote. He watched for a moment the consequence of his words, and then, laying a hand on his listener's knee and as if to end with the proper joke: "And now for the eye I shall keep on you!"

"Oh but I don't know that I want to be, at your age, too different from you!"

"Ah prepare while you're about it," said Strether, "to be more amusing."

Little Bilham continued to think, but at last had a smile. "Well, you *are* amusing—to *me*."

"*Impayable*,[3] as you say, no doubt. But what am I to myself?" Strether had risen with this, giving his attention now to an encounter that, in the middle of the garden, was in the act of taking place between their host and the lady at whose side Madame de Vionnet had quitted him. This lady, who appeared within a few minutes to have left her friends, awaited Gloriani's eager approach with words on her lips that Strether couldn't catch, but of which her interesting witty face seemed to give him the echo. He was sure she was prompt and fine, but also that she had met her match, and he liked—in the light of what he was quite sure was the Duchess's latent insolence—the good humour with which the great artist asserted equal resources. Were they, this pair, of the "great world"?—and was he himself, for the moment and thus related to them by his observation, *in* it? Then there was something in the great world covertly tigerish, which came to him across the lawn and in the charming air as a waft from the jungle. Yet it made him admire most of the two, made him envy, the glossy male tiger, magnificently marked. These absurdities of the stirred sense, fruits of suggestion ripening on the instant, were all reflected in his next words to little Bilham. "I know—if we talk of that—whom *I* should enjoy being like!"

Little Bilham followed his eyes; but then as with a shade of knowing surprise: "Gloriani?"

Our friend had in fact already hesitated, though not on the hint of his companion's doubt, in which there were depths of critical reserve. He had just made out, in the now full picture, something and somebody else; another impression had been superimposed. A young girl in a white dress and a softly plumed white hat had suddenly come into view, and what was presently clear was that her course was toward them. What was clearer still was that the handsome young man at her side was Chad Newsome, and what was clearest of all was that she was therefore Mademoiselle de Vionnet, that she was unmistakeably pretty—bright gentle shy happy wonderful— and that Chad now, with a consummate calculation of effect, was about to present her to his old friend's vision. What was clearest of all indeed was something much more than this, something at the single stroke of which—and wasn't it simply juxtaposition?—all vagueness vanished. It was the click of a spring—he saw the truth. He had by this time also met Chad's look; there was more of it in that; and the truth, accordingly, so far as Bilham's enquiry was concerned, had thrust in the answer. "Oh Chad!"—it was that rare youth he should have enjoyed being "like." The virtuous attachment would be all there before him; the virtuous attachment

3. Priceless.

would be in the very act of appeal for his blessing; Jeanne de Vionnet, this charming creature, would be—exquisitely, intensely now
—the object of it. Chad brought her straight up to him, and Chad
was, oh yes, at this moment—for the glory of Woollett or whatever
—better still even than Gloriani. He had plucked this blossom;
he had kept it over-night in water; and at last as he held it up
to wonder he did enjoy his effect. That was why Strether had felt
at first the breath of calculation—and why moreover, as he now
knew, his look at the girl would be, for the young man, a sign of
the latter's success. What young man had ever paraded about that
way, without a reason, a maiden in her flower? And there was
nothing in his reason at present obscure. Her type sufficiently told
of it—they wouldn't, they couldn't, want her to go to Woollett.
Poor Woollett, and what it might miss!—though brave Chad indeed too, and what it might gain! Brave Chad however had just
excellently spoken. "This is a good little friend of mine who
knows all about you and has moreover a message for you. And this,
my dear"—he had turned to the child herself—"is the best man in
the world, who has it in his power to do a great deal for us and
whom I want you to like and revere as nearly as possible as much
as I do."

She stood there quite pink, a little frightened, prettier and prettier and not a bit like her mother. There was in this last particular
no resemblance but that of youth to youth; and here was in fact
suddenly Strether's sharpest impression. It went wondering, dazed,
embarrassed, back to the woman he had just been talking with;
it was a revelation in the light of which he already saw she would
become more interesting. So slim and fresh and fair, she had yet put
forth this perfection; so that for really believing it of her, for seeing
her to any such developed degree as a mother, comparison would be
urgent. Well, what was it now but fairly thrust upon him? "Mamma
wishes me to tell you before we go," the girl said, "that she hopes
very much you'll come to see us very soon. She has something important to say to you."

"She quite reproaches herself," Chad helpfully explained: "you
were interesting her so much when she accidentally suffered you to
be interrupted."

"Ah don't mention it!" Strether murmured, looking kindly from
one to the other and wondering at many things.

"And I'm to ask you for myself," Jeanne continued with her
hands clasped together as if in some small learnt prayer—"I'm to
ask you for myself if you won't positively come."

"Leave it to me, dear—I'll take care of it!" Chad genially declared in answer to this, while Strether himself almost held his
breath. What was in the girl was indeed too soft, too unknown

for direct dealing; so that one could only gaze at it as at a picture, quite staying one's own hand. But with Chad he was now on ground—Chad he could meet; so pleasant a confidence in that and in everything did the young man freely exhale. There was the whole of a story in his tone to his companion, and he spoke indeed as if already of the family. It made Strether guess the more quickly what it might be about which Madame de Vionnet was so urgent. Having seen him then she had found him easy; she wished to have it out with him that some way for the young people must be discovered, some way that would not impose as a condition the transplantation of her daughter. He already saw himself discussing with this lady the attractions of Woollett as a residence for Chad's companion. Was that youth going now to trust her with the affair —so that it would be after all with one of his "lady-friends" that his mother's missionary should be condemned to deal? It was quite as if for an instant the two men looked at each other on this question. But there was no mistaking at last Chad's pride in the display of such a connexion. This was what had made him so carry himself while, three minutes before, he was bringing it into view; what had caused his friend, first catching sight of him, to be so struck with his air. It was, in a word, just when he thus finally felt Chad putting things straight off on him that he envied him, as he had mentioned to little Bilham, most. The whole exhibition however was but a matter of three or four minutes, and the author of it had soon explained that, as Madame de Vionnet was immediately going "on," this could be for Jeanne but a snatch. They would all meet again soon, and Strether was meanwhile to stay and amuse himself—"I'll pick you up again in plenty of time." He took the girl off as he had brought her, and Strether, with the faint sweet foreignness of her "Au revoir, monsieur!" in his ears as a note almost unprecedented, watched them recede side by side and felt how, once more, her companion's relation to her got an accent from it. They disappeared among the others and apparently into the house; whereupon our friend turned round to give out to little Bilham the conviction of which he was full. But there was no little Bilham any more; little Bilham had within the few moments, for reasons of his own, proceeded further: a circumstance by which, in its order, Strether was also sensibly affected.

III [XII]

Chad was not in fact on this occasion to keep his promise of coming back; but Miss Gostrey had soon presented herself with an explanation of his failure. There had been reasons at the last for his going off with *ces dames*; and he had asked her with much instance to come out and take charge of their friend. She did so, Strether felt as she took her place beside him, in a manner that left nothing to desire. He had dropped back on his bench, alone again for a time, and the more conscious for little Bilham's defection of his unexpressed thought; in respect to which however this next converser was a still more capacious vessel. "It's the child!" he had exclaimed to her almost as soon as she appeared; and though her direct response was for some time delayed he could feel in her meanwhile the working of this truth. It might have been simply, as she waited, that they were now in presence altogether of truth spreading like a flood and not for the moment to be offered her in the mere cupful; inasmuch as who should *ces dames* prove to be but persons about whom—once thus face to face with them—she found she might from the first have told him almost everything? This would have freely come had he taken the simple precaution of giving her their name. There could be no better example—and she appeared to note it with high amusement—than the way, making things out already so much for himself, he was at last throwing precautions to the winds. They were neither more nor less, she and the child's mother, than old school-friends—friends who had scarcely met for years but whom this unlooked-for chance had brought together with a rush. It was a relief, Miss Gostrey hinted, to feel herself no longer groping; she was unaccustomed to grope and as a general thing, he might well have seen, made straight enough for her clue. With the one she had now picked up in her hands there need be at least no waste of wonder. "She's coming to see me—that's for *you*," Strether's counsellor continued; "but I don't require it to know where I am."

The waste of wonder might be proscribed; but Strether, characteristically, was even by this time in the immensity of space. "By which you mean that you know where *she* is?"

She just hesitated. "I mean that if she comes to see me I shall —now that I've pulled myself round a bit after the shock—not be at home."

Strether hung poised. "You call it—your recognition—a shock?"

She gave one of her rare flickers of impatience. "It was a surprise, an emotion. Don't be so literal. I wash my hands of her."

Poor Strether's face lengthened. "She's impossible—?"

"She's even more charming than I remembered her."

"Then what's the matter?"

She had to think how to put it. "Well, *I'm* impossible. It's impossible. Everything's impossible."

He looked at her an instant. "I see where you're coming out. Everything's possible." Their eyes had on it in fact an exchange of some duration; after which he pursued: "Isn't it that beautiful child?" Then as she still said nothing: "Why don't you mean to receive her?"

Her answer in an instant rang clear. "Because I wish to keep out of the business."

It provoked in him a weak wail. "You're going to abandon me *now?*"

"No, I'm only going to abandon *her*. She'll want me to help her with you. And I won't."

"You'll only help me with her? Well then—!" Most of the persons previously gathered had, in the interest of tea, passed into the house, and they had the gardens mainly to themselves. The shadows were long, the last call of the birds, who had made a home of their own in the noble interspaced quarter, sounded from the high trees in the other gardens as well, those of the old convent and of the old *hôtels*; it was as if our friends had waited for the full charm to come out. Strether's impressions were still present; it was as if something had happened that "nailed" them, made them more intense; but he was to ask himself soon afterwards, that evening, what really *had* happened—conscious as he could after all remain that for a gentleman taken, and taken the first time, into the "great world," the world of ambassadors and duchesses, the items made a meagre total. It was nothing new to him, however, as we know, that a man might have—at all events such a man as he—an amount of experience out of any proportion to his adventures; so that, though it was doubtless no great adventure to sit on there with Miss Gostrey and hear about Madame de Vionnet, the hour, the picture, the immediate, the recent, the possible—as well as the communication itself, not a note of which failed to reverberate—only gave the moments more of the taste of history.

It was history, to begin with, that Jeanne's mother had been three-and-twenty years before, at Geneva, schoolmate and good girl-friend to Maria Gostrey, who had moreover enjoyed since then, though interruptedly and above all with a long recent drop, other glimpses of her. Twenty-three years put them both on, no doubt; and Madame de Vionnet—though she had married straight after school—couldn't be today an hour less than thirty-eight. This made her ten years older than Chad—though ten years, also, if Strether liked, older than she looked; the least, at any rate, that a prospective mother-in-law could be expected to do with. She would be of all mothers-in-law the most charming; unless indeed, through some perversity as yet insupposeable, she should utterly belie herself in that relation. There was none surely in which, as Maria remembered her, she mustn't be charming; and this frankly in spite of the stigma of failure in the tie where failure always most showed. It was no test there—when indeed *was* it a test there?—for Monsieur de Vionnet had been a brute. She had lived for years apart from him

—which was of course always a horrid position; but Miss Gostrey's impression of the matter had been that she could scarce have made a better thing of it had she done it on purpose to show she was amiable. She was so amiable that nobody had had a word to say; which was luckily not the case for her husband. He was so impossible that she had the advantage of all her merits.

It was still history for Strether that the Comte de Vionnet—it being also history that the lady in question was a Countess—should now, under Miss Gostrey's sharp touch, rise before him as a high distinguished polished impertinent reprobate, the product of a mysterious order; it was history, further, that the charming girl so freely sketched by his companion should have been married out of hand by a mother, another figure of striking outline, full of dark personal motive; it was perhaps history most of all that this company was, as a matter of course, governed by such considerations as put divorce out of the question. "*Ces gens-là*[4] don't divorce, you know, any more than they emigrate or abjure—they think it impious and vulgar"; a fact in the light of which they seemed but the more richly special. It was all special; it was all, for Strether's imagination, more or less rich. The girl at the Genevese school, an isolated interesting attaching creature, then both sensitive and violent, audacious but always forgiven, was the daughter of a French father and an English mother who, early left a widow, had married again—tried afresh with a foreigner; in her career with whom she had apparently given her child no example of comfort. All these people—the people of the English mother's side—had been of condition more or less eminent; yet with oddities and disparities that had often since made Maria, thinking them over, wonder what they really quite rhymed to. It was in any case her belief that the mother, interested and prone to adventure, had been without conscience, had only thought of ridding herself most quickly of a possible, an actual encumbrance. The father, by her impression, a Frenchman with a name one knew, had been a different matter, leaving his child, she clearly recalled, a memory all fondness, as well as an assured little fortune which was unluckily to make her more or less of a prey later on. She had been in particular, at school, dazzlingly, though quite booklessly, clever; as polyglot as a little Jewess (which she wasn't, oh no!) and chattering French, English, German, Italian, anything one would, in a way that made a clean sweep, if not of prizes and parchments, at least of every "part," whether memorised or improvised, in the curtained costumed school repertory, and in especial of all mysteries of race and vagueness of reference, all swagger about "home," among their variegated mates.

4. *Those* people.

It would doubtless be difficult to-day, as between French and English, to name her and place her; she would certainly show, on knowledge, Miss Gostrey felt, as one of those convenient types who don't keep you explaining—minds with doors as numerous as the many-tongued cluster of confessionals at Saint Peter's.[5] You might confess to her with confidence in Roumelian,[6] and even Roumelian sins. Therefore—! But Strether's narrator covered her implication with a laugh; a laugh by which his betrayal of a sense of the lurid in the picture was also perhaps sufficiently protected. He had a moment of wondering, while his friend went on, what sins might be especially Roumelian. She went on at all events to the mention of her having met the young thing—again by some Swiss lake—in her first married state, which had appeared for the few intermediate years not at least violently disturbed. She had been lovely at that moment, delightful to *her*, full of responsive emotion, of amused recognitions and amusing reminders; and then, once more, much later, after a long interval, equally but differently charming—touching and rather mystifying for the five minutes of an encounter at a railway-station *en province*,[7] during which it had come out that her life was all changed. Miss Gostrey had understood enough to see, essentially, what had happened, and yet had beautifully dreamed that she was herself faultless. There were doubtless depths in her, but she was all right; Strether would see if she wasn't. She was another person however—that had been promptly marked—from the small child of nature at the Geneva school; a little person quite made over (as foreign women *were*, compared with American) by marriage. Her situation too had evidently cleared itself up; there would have been—all that was possible—a judicial separation. She had settled in Paris, brought up her daughter, steered her boat. It was no very pleasant boat—especially there—to be in; but Marie de Vionnet would have headed straight. She would have friends, certainly—and very good ones. There she was at all events—and it was very interesting. Her knowing Mr. Chad didn't in the least prove she hadn't friends; what it proved was what good ones *he* had. "I saw that," said Miss Gostrey, "that night at the Français; it came out for me in three minutes. I saw *her* —or somebody like her. And so," she immediately added, "did you."

"Oh no—not anybody like her!" Strether laughed. "But you mean," he as promptly went on, "that she has had such an influence on him?"

Miss Gostrey was on her feet; it was time for them to go. "She has brought him up for her daughter."

5. The cathedral in Vatican City.
6. A form of Greek spoken in those Ottoman territories that are now northern Greece and Bulgaria.
7. In the country.

Their eyes, as so often, in candid conference, through their settled glasses, met over it long; after which Strether's again took in the whole place. They were quite alone there now. "Mustn't she rather—in the time then—have rushed it?"

"Ah she won't of course have lost an hour. But that's just the good mother—the good French one. You must remember that of her—that as a mother she's French, and that for them there's a special providence. It precisely however—that she mayn't have been able to begin as far back as she'd have liked—makes her grateful for aid."

Strether took this in as they slowly moved to the house on their way out. "She counts on me then to put the thing through?"

"Yes—she counts on you. Oh and first of all of course," Miss Gostrey added, "on her—well, convincing you."

"Ah," her friend returned, "she caught Chad young!"

"Yes, but there are women who are for all your 'times of life.' They're the most wonderful sort."

She had laughed the words out, but they brought her companion, the next thing, to a stand. "Is what you mean that she'll try to make a fool of me?"

"Well, I'm wondering what she *will*—with an opportunity—make."

"What do you call," Strether asked, "an opportunity? My going to see her?"

"Ah you must go to see her"—Miss Gostrey was a trifle evasive. "You can't not do that. You'd have gone to see the other woman. I mean if there had been one—a different sort. It's what you came out for."

It might be; but Strether distinguished. "I didn't come out to see *this* sort."

She had a wonderful look at him now. "Are you disappointed she isn't worse?"

He for a moment entertained the question, then found for it the frankest of answers. "Yes. If she were worse she'd be better for our purpose. It would be simpler."

"Perhaps," she admitted. "But won't this be pleasanter?"

"Ah you know," he promptly replied, "I didn't come out—wasn't that just what you originally reproached me with?—for the pleasant."

"Precisely. Therefore I say again what I said at first. You must take things as they come. Besides," Miss Gostrey added, "I'm not afraid for myself."

"For yourself—?"

"Of your seeing her. I trust her. There's nothing she'll say about me. In fact there's nothing she *can.*"

Strether wondered—little as he had thought of this. Then he broke out. "Oh you women!"

There was something in it at which she flushed. "Yes—there we are. We're abysses." At last she smiled. "But I risk her!"

He gave himself a shake. "Well then so do I!" But he added as they passed into the house that he would see Chad the first thing in the morning.

This was the next day the more easily effected that the young man, as it happened, even before he was down, turned up at his hotel. Strether took his coffee, by habit, in the public room; but on his descending for this purpose Chad instantly proposed an adjournment to what he called greater privacy. He had himself as yet had nothing—they would sit down somewhere together; and when after a few steps and a turn into the Boulevard they had, for their greater privacy, sat down among twenty others, our friend saw in his companion's move a fear of the advent of Waymarsh. It was the first time Chad had to that extent given this personage "away"; and Strether found himself wondering of what it was symptomatic. He made out in a moment that the youth was in earnest as he hadn't yet seen him; which in its turn threw a ray perhaps a trifle startling on what they had each up to that time been treating as earnestness. It was sufficiently flattering however that the real thing —if this *was* at last the real thing—should have been determined, as appeared, precisely by an accretion of Strether's importance. For this was what it quickly enough came to—that Chad, rising with the lark, had rushed down to let him know while his morning consciousness was yet young that he had literally made the afternoon before a tremendous impression. Madame de Vionnet wouldn't, couldn't rest till she should have some assurance from him that he *would* consent again to see her. The announcement was made, across their marble-topped table, while the foam of the hot milk was in their cups and its plash still in the air, with the smile of Chad's easiest urbanity; and this expression of his face caused our friend's doubts to gather on the spot into a challenge of the lips. "See here"—that was all; he only for the moment said again "See here." Chad met it with all his air of straight intelligence, while Strether remembered again that fancy of the first impression of him, the happy young Pagan, handsome and hard but oddly indulgent, whose mysterious measure he had under the street-lamp tried mentally to take. The young Pagan, while a long look passed between them, sufficiently understood. Strether scarce needed at last to say the rest—"I want to know where I am." But he said it, adding before any answer something more. "Are you engaged to be married—is that your secret?—to the young lady?"

Chad shook his head with the slow amenity that was one of his ways of conveying that there was time for everything. "I have no secret—though I may have secrets! I haven't at any rate that one. We're not engaged. No."

"Then where's the hitch?"

"Do you mean why I haven't already started with you?" Chad, beginning his coffee and buttering his roll, was quite ready to explain. "Nothing would have induced me—nothing will still induce me—not to try to keep you here as long as you can be made to stay. It's too visibly good for you." Strether had himself plenty to say about this, but it was amusing also to measure the march of Chad's tone. He had never been more a man of the world, and it was always in his company present to our friend that one was seeing how in successive connexions a man of the world acquitted himself. Chad kept it up beautifully. "My idea—*voyons!*[8]—is simply that you should let Madame de Vionnet know you, simply that you should consent to know *her*. I don't in the least mind telling you that, clever and charming as she is, she's ever so much in my confidence. All I ask of you is to let her talk to you. You've asked me about what you call my hitch, and so far as it goes she'll explain it to you. She's herself my hitch, hang it—if you must really have it all out. But in a sense," he hastened in the most wonderful manner to add, "that you'll quite make out for yourself. She's too good a friend, confound her. Too good, I mean, for me to leave without—without—" It was his first hesitation.

"Without what?"

"Well, without my arranging somehow or other the damnable terms of my sacrifice."

"It *will* be a sacrifice then?"

"It will be the greatest loss I ever suffered. I owe her so much."

It was beautiful, the way Chad said these things, and his plea was now confessedly—oh quite flagrantly and publicly—interesting. The moment really took on for Strether an intensity. Chad owed Madame de Vionnet so much? What *did* that do then but clear up the whole mystery? He was indebted for alterations, and she was thereby in a position to have sent in her bill for expenses incurred in reconstruction. What was this at bottom but what had been to be arrived at? Strether sat there arriving at it while he munched toast and stirred his second cup. To do this with the aid of Chad's pleasant earnest face was also to do more besides. No, never before had he been so ready to take him as he was. What was it that had suddenly so cleared up? It was just everybody's character; that is everybody's but—in a measure—his own. Strether felt *his* character receive for the instant a smutch from all the wrong things he had suspected or believed. The person to whom Chad

8. Let us see!

owed it that he could positively turn out such a comfort to other persons—such a person was sufficiently raised above any "breath" by the nature of her work and the young man's steady light. All of which was vivid enough to come and go quickly; though indeed in the midst of it Strether could utter a question. "Have I your word of honour that if I surrender myself to Madame de Vionnet you'll surrender yourself to *me?*"

Chad laid his hand firmly on his friend's. "My dear man, you have it."

There was finally something in his felicity almost embarrassing and oppressive—Strether had begun to fidget under it for the open air and the erect posture. He had signed to the waiter that he wished to pay, and this transaction took some moments, during which he thoroughly felt, while he put down money and pretended —it was quite hollow—to estimate change, that Chad's higher spirit, his youth, his practice, his paganism, his felicity, his assurance, his impudence, whatever it might be, had consciously scored a success. Well, that was all right so far as it went; his sense of the thing in question covered our friend for a minute like a veil through which—as if he had been muffled—he heard his interlocutor ask him if he mightn't take him over about five. "Over" was over the river, and over the river was where Madame de Vionnet lived, and five was that very afternoon. They got at last out of the place— got out before he answered. He lighted, in the street, a cigarette, which again gave him more time. But it was already sharp for him that there was no use in time. "What does she propose to do to me?" he had presently demanded.

Chad had no delays. "Are you afraid of her?"

"Oh immensely. Don't you see it?"

"Well," said Chad, "she won't do anything worse to you than make you like her."

"It's just of that I'm afraid."

"Then it's not fair to me."

Strether cast about. "It's fair to your mother."

"Oh," said Chad, "are you afraid of *her?*"

"Scarcely less. Or perhaps even more. But is this lady against your interests at home?" Strether went on.

"Not directly, no doubt; but she's greatly in favour of them here."

"And what—'here'—does she consider them to be?"

"Well, good relations!"

"With herself?"

"With herself."

"And what is it that makes them so good?"

"What? Well, that's exactly what you'll make out if you'll only go, as I'm supplicating you, to see her."

Strether stared at him with a little of the wanness, no doubt, that the vision of more to "make out" could scarce help producing. "I mean *how* good are they?"

"Oh awfully good."

Again Strether had faltered, but it was brief. It was all very well, but there was nothing now he wouldn't risk. "Excuse me, but I must really—as I began by telling you—know where I am. Is she bad?"

" 'Bad'?"—Chad echoed it, but without a shock. "Is that what's implied—?"

"When relations are good?" Strether felt a little silly, and was even conscious of a foolish laugh, at having it imposed on him to have appeared to speak so. What indeed was he talking about? His stare had relaxed; he looked now all round him. But something in him brought him back, though he still didn't know quite how to turn it. The two or three ways he thought of, and one of them in particular, were, even with scruples dismissed, too ugly. He none the less at last found something. "Is her life without reproach?"

It struck him, directly he had found it, as pompous and priggish; so much so that he was thankful to Chad for taking it only in the right spirit. The young man spoke so immensely to the point that the effect was practically of positive blandness. "Absolutely without reproach. A beautiful life. *Allez donc voir!*"[9]

These last words were, in the liberality of their confidence, so imperative that Strether went through no form of assent; but before they separated it had been confirmed that he should be picked up at a quarter to five.

Book Sixth

I [XIII]

It was quite by half-past five—after the two men had been together in Madame de Vionnet's drawing-room not more than a dozen minutes—that Chad, with a look at his watch and then another at their hostess, said genially, gaily: "I've an engagement, and I know you won't complain if I leave him with you. He'll interest you immensely; and as for her," he declared to Strether, "I assure you, if you're at all nervous, she's perfectly safe."

He had left them to be embarrassed or not by this guarantee, as they could best manage, and embarrassment was a thing that Strether wasn't at first sure Madame de Vionnet escaped. He

9. Go see then!

escaped it himself, to his surprise; but he had grown used by this time to thinking of himself as brazen. She occupied, his hostess, in the Rue de Bellechasse,[1] the first floor of an old house to which our visitors had had access from an old clean court. The court was large and open, full of revelations, for our friend, of the habit of privacy, the peace of intervals, the dignity of distances and approaches; the house, to his restless sense, was in the high homely style of an elder day, and the ancient Paris that he was always looking for—sometimes intensely felt, sometimes more acutely missed—was in the immemorial polish of the wide waxed staircase and in the fine *boiseries*,[2] the medallions, mouldings, mirrors, great clear spaces, of the greyish-white salon into which he had been shown. He seemed at the very outset to see her in the midst of possessions not vulgarly numerous, but hereditary cherished charming. While his eyes turned after a little from those of his hostess and Chad freely talked—not in the least about *him*, but about other people, people he didn't know, and quite as if he did know them—he found himself making out, as a background of the occupant, some glory, some prosperity of the First Empire,[3] some Napoleonic glamour, some dim lustre of the great legend; elements clinging still to all the consular chairs and mythological brasses and sphinxes' heads and faded surfaces of satin striped with alternate silk.

The place itself went further back—that he guessed, and how old Paris continued in a manner to echo there; but the post-revolutionary period, the world he vaguely thought of as the world of Châteaubriand, of Madame de Staël, even of the young Lamartine,[4] had left its stamp of harps and urns and torches, a stamp impressed on sundry small objects, ornaments and relics. He had never before, to his knowledge, had present to him relics, of any special dignity, of a private order—little old miniatures, medallions, pictures, books; books in leather bindings, pinkish and greenish, with gilt garlands on the back, ranged, together with other promiscuous properties, under the glass of brass-mounted cabinets. His attention took them all tenderly into account. They were among the matters that marked Madame de Vionnet's apartment as something quite different from Miss Gostrey's little museum of bargains and from Chad's lovely home; he recognised it as founded much more on old accumulations that had possibly from time to

1. Located in the Faubourg St.-Germain, across the river from the Tuileries. "Bellechasse" literally means beautiful hunt or chase.
2. Wood paneling.
3. The period when Napoléon Bonaparte was Emperor of France (1804–15).
4. François René de Chateaubriand (1768–1848) and Madame de Staël (1776–1817) were the leading French literary figures during the Empire, and their writings did much to spread the influence of Romanticism. Alphonse Marie de Lamartine (1790–1869) was a popular poet during the end of the Empire; he later became a prominent statesman and historian.

time shrunken than on any contemporary method of acquisition or form of curiosity. Chad and Miss Gostrey had rummaged and purchased and picked up and exchanged, sifting, selecting, comparing; whereas the mistress of the scene before him, beautifully passive under the spell of transmission—transmission from her father's line, he quite made up his mind—had only received, accepted and been quiet. When she hadn't been quiet she had been moved at the most to some occult charity for some fallen fortune. There had been objects she or her predecessors might even conceivably have parted with under need, but Strether couldn't suspect them of having sold old pieces to get "better" ones. They would have felt no difference as to better or worse. He could but imagine their having felt—perhaps in emigration, in proscription, for his sketch was slight and confused—the pressure of want or the obligation of sacrifice.

The pressure of want—whatever might be the case with the other force—was, however, presumably not active now, for the tokens of a chastened ease still abounded after all, many marks of a taste whose discriminations might perhaps have been called eccentric. He guessed at intense little preferences and sharp little exclusions, a deep suspicion of the vulgar and a personal view of the right. The general result of this was something for which he had no name on the spot quite ready, but something he would have come nearest to naming in speaking of it as the air of supreme respectability, the consciousness, small, still, reserved, but none the less distinct and diffused, of private honour. The air of supreme respectability—that was a strange blank wall for his adventure to have brought him to break his nose against. It had in fact, as he was now aware, filled all the approaches, hovered in the court as he passed, hung on the staircase as he mounted, sounded in the grave rumble of the old bell, as little electric as possible, of which Chad, at the door, had pulled the ancient but neatly-kept tassel; it formed in short the clearest medium of its particular kind that he had ever breathed. He would have answered for it at the end of a quarter of an hour that some of the glass cases contained swords and epaulettes of ancient colonels and generals; medals and orders once pinned over hearts that had long since ceased to beat; snuffboxes bestowed on ministers and envoys; copies of works presented, with inscriptions, by authors now classic. At bottom of it all for him was the sense of her rare unlikeness to the women he had known. This sense had grown, since the day before, the more he recalled her, and had been above all singularly fed by his talk with Chad in the morning. Everything in fine made her immeasurably new, and nothing so new as the old house and the old objects. There were books, two or three, on a small table near his chair, but they hadn't the lemon-coloured covers with which his eye had begun to dally from the hour of his arrival and to the opportunity of a further acquaintance with which he had for a fortnight now altogether succumbed. On another table, across the room, he made out the great *Revue*;[5] but even that familiar face, conspicuous in Mrs. Newsome's parlours, scarce counted here as a modern note. He was sure on the spot—and he afterwards knew he was right—that this was a touch of Chad's own hand. What would Mrs. Newsome say to the circumstance that Chad's interested "influence" kept her paper-knife in the *Revue?* The interested influence at any rate had, as we say, gone straight to the point—had in fact soon left it quite behind.

She was seated, near the fire, on a small stuffed and fringed chair, one of the few modern articles in the room; and she leaned back in it with her hands clasped in her lap and no movement, in all her person, but the fine prompt play of her deep young face. The fire, under the low white marble, undraped and academic, had burnt down to the silver ashes of light wood; one of the windows, at a distance, stood open to the mildness and stillness, out of which, in the short pauses, came the faint sound, pleasant and homely, almost rustic, of a plash and a clatter of *sabots*[6] from some coach-house on the other side of the court. Madame de Vionnet, while Strether sat there, wasn't to shift her posture by an inch. "I don't think you seriously believe in what you're doing," she said; "but all the same, you know, I'm going to treat you quite as if I did."

"By which you mean," Strether directly replied, "quite as if you didn't! I assure you it won't make the least difference with me how you treat me."

"Well," she said, taking that menace bravely and philosophically enough, "the only thing that really matters is that you shall get on with me."

"Ah but I don't!" he immediately returned.

It gave her another pause; which, however, she happily enough shook off. "Will you consent to go on with me a little—provisionally —as if you did?"

Then it was that he saw how she had decidedly come all the way; and there accompanied it an extraordinary sense of her raising from somewhere below him her beautiful suppliant eyes. He might have been perched at his door-step or at his window and she standing in the road. For a moment he let her stand and couldn't more-over have spoken. It had been sad, of a sudden, with a sadness that was like a cold breath in his face. "What can I do," he finally asked, "but listen to you as I promised Chadwick?"

5. The salmon-colored *Revue des Deux Mondes*, a leading French literary magazine that serialized many of the major nineteenth-century authors.
6. Wooden shoes.

"Ah but what I'm asking you," she quickly said, "isn't what Mr. Newsome had in mind." She spoke at present, he saw, as if to take courageously *all* her risk. "This is my own idea and a different thing."

It gave poor Strether in truth—uneasy as it made him too—something of the thrill of a bold perception justified. "Well," he answered kindly enough, "I was sure a moment since that some idea of your own had come to you."

She seemed still to look up at him, but now more serenely. "I made out you were sure—and that helped it to come. So you see," she continued, "we do get on."

"Oh but it appears to me I don't at all meet your request. How can I when I don't understand it?"

"It isn't at all necessary you should understand; it will do quite well enough if you simply remember it. Only feel I trust you—and for nothing so tremendous after all. Just," she said with a wonderful smile, "for common civility."

Strether had a long pause while they sat again face to face, as they had sat, scarce less conscious, before the poor lady had crossed the stream. She was the poor lady for Strether now because clearly she had some trouble, and her appeal to him could only mean that her trouble was deep. He couldn't help it; it wasn't his fault; he had done nothing; but by a turn of the hand she had somehow made their encounter a relation. And the relation profited by a mass of things that were not strictly in it or of it; by the very air in which they sat, by the high cold delicate room, by the world outside and the little plash in the court, by the First Empire and the relics in the stiff cabinets, by matters as far off as those and by others as near as the unbroken clasp of her hands in her lap and the look her expression had of being most natural when her eyes were most fixed. "You count upon me of course for something really much greater than it sounds."

"Oh it sounds great enough too!" she laughed at this.

He found himself in time on the point of telling her that she was, as Miss Barrace called it, wonderful; but, catching himself up, he said something else instead. "What was it Chad's idea then that you should say to me?"

"Ah his idea was simply what a man's idea always is—to put every effort off on the woman."

"The 'woman'—?" Strether slowly echoed.

"The woman he likes—and just in proportion as he likes her. In proportion too—for shifting the trouble—as she likes *him*."

Strether followed it; then with an abruptness of his own: "How much do you like Chad?"

"Just as much as *that*—to take all, with you, on myself." But she got at once again away from this. "I've been trembling as if we were to stand or fall by what you may think of me; and I'm even now," she went on wonderfully, "drawing a long breath—and, yes, truly taking a great courage—from the hope that I don't in fact strike you as impossible."

"That's at all events, clearly," he observed after an instant, "the way I don't strike *you*."

"Well," she so far assented, "as you haven't yet said you *won't* have the little patience with me I ask for—"

"You draw splendid conclusions? Perfectly. But I don't understand them," Strether pursued. "You seem to me to ask for much more than you need. What, at the worst for you, what at the best for myself, can I after all do? I can use no pressure that I haven't used. You come really late with your request. I've already done all that for myself the case admits of. I've said my say, and here I am."

"Yes, here you are, fortunately!" Madame de Vionnet laughed. "Mrs. Newsome," she added in another tone, "didn't think you can do so little."

He had an hesitation, but he brought the words out. "Well, she thinks so now."

"Do you mean by that—?" But she also hung fire.

"Do I mean what?"

She still rather faltered. "Pardon me if I touch on it, but if I'm saying extraordinary things, why, perhaps, mayn't I? Besides, doesn't it properly concern us to know?"

"To know what?" he insisted as after thus beating about the bush she had again dropped.

She made the effort. "Has she given you up?"

He was amazed afterwards to think how simply and quietly he had met it. "Not yet." It was almost as if he were a trifle disappointed—had expected still more of her freedom. But he went straight on. "Is that what Chad has told you will happen to me?"

She was evidently charmed with the way he took it. "If you mean if we've talked of it—most certainly. And the question's not what has had least to do with my wishing to see you."

"To judge if I'm the sort of man a woman *can*—?"

"Precisely," she exclaimed—"you wonderful gentleman! I do judge—I *have* judged. A woman can't. You're safe—with every right to be. You'd be much happier if you'd only believe it."

Strether was silent a little; then he found himself speaking with a cynicism of confidence of which even at the moment the sources were strange to him. "I try to believe it. But it's a marvel," he exclaimed, "how *you* already get at it!"

Oh she was able to say. "Remember how much I was on the way to it through Mr. Newsome—before I saw you. He thinks everything of your strength."

"Well, I can bear almost anything!" our friend briskly interrupted. Deep and beautiful on this her smile came back, and with the effect of making him hear what he had said just as she had heard it. He easily enough felt that it gave him away, but what in truth had everything done but that? It had been all very well to think at moments that he was holding her nose down and that he had coerced her: what had he by this time done but let her practically see that he accepted their relation? What was their relation moreover—though light and brief enough in form as yet—but whatever she might choose to make it? Nothing could prevent her—certainly he couldn't—from making it pleasant. At the back of his head, behind everything, was the sense that she was—there, before him, close to him, in vivid imperative form—one of the rare women he had so often heard of, read of, thought of, but never met, whose very presence, look, voice, the mere contemporaneous *fact* of whom, from the moment it was at all presented, made a relation of mere recognition. That was not the kind of woman he had ever found Mrs. Newsome, a contemporaneous fact who had been distinctly slow to establish herself; and at present, confronted with Madame de Vionnet, he felt the simplicity of his original impression of Miss Gostrey. She certainly had been a fact of rapid growth; but the world was wide, each day was more and more a new lesson. There were at any rate even among the stranger ones relations and relations. "Of course I suit Chad's grand way," he quickly added. "He hasn't had much difficulty in working me in."

She seemed to deny a little, on the young man's behalf, by the rise of her eyebrows, an intention of any process at all inconsiderate. "You must know how grieved he'd be if you were to lose anything. He believes you can keep his mother patient."

Strether wondered with his eyes on her. "I see. *That's* then what you really want of me. And how am I to do it? Perhaps you'll tell me that."

"Simply tell her the truth."

"And what do you call the truth?"

"Well, *any* truth—about us all—that you see yourself. I leave it to you."

"Thank you very much. I like," Strether laughed with a slight harshness, "the way you leave things!"

But she insisted kindly, gently, as if it wasn't so bad. "Be perfectly honest. Tell her all."

"All?" he oddly echoed.

"Tell her the simple truth," Madame de Vionnet again pleaded.

"But what *is* the simple truth? The simple truth is exactly what I'm trying to discover."

She looked about a while, but presently she came back to him. "Tell her, fully and clearly, about *us*."

Strether meanwhile had been staring. "You and your daughter?"

"Yes—little Jeanne and me. Tell her," she just slightly quavered, "you like us."

"And what good will that do me? Or rather"—he caught himself up—"what good will it do *you?*"

She looked graver. "None, you believe, really?"

Strether debated. "She didn't send me out to 'like' you."

"Oh," she charmingly contended, "she sent you out to face the facts."

He admitted after an instant that there was something in that. "But how can I face them till I know what they are? Do you want him," he then braced himself to ask, "to marry your daughter?"

She gave a headshake as noble as it was prompt. "No—not that."

"And he really doesn't want to himself?"

She repeated the movement, but now with a strange light in her face. "He likes her too much."

Strether wondered. "To be willing to consider, you mean, the question of taking her to America?"

"To be willing to do anything with her but be immensely kind and nice—really tender of her. We watch over her, and you must help us. You must see her again."

Strether felt awkward. "Ah with pleasure—she's so remarkably attractive."

The mother's eagerness with which Madame de Vionnet jumped at this was to come back to him later as beautiful in its grace. "The dear thing *did* please you?" Then as he met it with the largest "Oh!" of enthusiasm: "She's perfect. She's my joy."

"Well, I'm sure that—if one were near her and saw more of her —she'd be mine."

"Then," said Madame de Vionnet, "tell Mrs. Newsome that!"

He wondered the more. "What good will that do you?" As she appeared unable at once to say, however, he brought out something else. "Is your daughter in love with our friend?"

"Ah," she rather startlingly answered, "I wish you'd find out!"

He showed his surprise. "I? A stranger?"

"Oh you won't be a stranger—presently. You shall see her quite, I assure you, as if you weren't."

It remained for him none the less an extraordinary notion. "It seems to me surely that if her mother can't—"

"Ah little girls and their mothers to-day!" she rather inconsequently broke in. But she checked herself with something she seemed to give out as after all more to the point. "Tell her I've been good for him. Don't you think I have?"

It had its effect on him—more than at the moment he quite measured. Yet he was consciously enough touched. "Oh if it's all *you*—!"

"Well, it may not be 'all,'" she interrupted, "but it's to a great extent. Really and truly," she added in a tone that was to take its place with him among things remembered.

"Then it's very wonderful." He smiled at her from a face that he felt as strained, and her own face for a moment kept him so. At last she also got up. "Well, don't you think that for that—"

"I ought to save you?" So it was that the way to meet her—and the way, as well, in a manner, to get off—came over him. He heard himself use the exorbitant word, the very sound of which helped to determine his flight. "I'll save you if I can."

ii [xiv]

In Chad's lovely home, however, one evening ten days later, he felt himself present at the collapse of the question of Jeanne de Vionnet's shy secret. He had been dining there in the company of that young lady and her mother, as well as of other persons, and he had gone into the *petit salon*,[7] at Chad's request, on purpose to talk with her. The young man had put this to him as a favour—"I should like so awfully to know what you think of her. It will really be a chance for you," he had said, "to see the *jeune fille*[8]—I mean the type—as she actually is, and I don't think that, as an observer of manners, it's a thing you ought to miss. It will be an impression that—whatever else you take—you can carry home with you, where you'll find again so much to compare it with."

Strether knew well enough with what Chad wished him to compare it, and though he entirely assented he hadn't yet somehow been so deeply reminded that he was being, as he constantly though mutely expressed it, used. He was as far as ever from making out exactly to what end; but he was none the less constantly accompanied by a sense of the service he rendered. He conceived only that this service was highly agreeable to those who profited by it; and he was indeed still waiting for the moment at which he should catch it in the act of proving disagreeable, proving in some degree intolerable, to himself. He failed quite to see how his situation could clear up at all logically except by some turn of events that would give him the pretext of disgust. He was building from day to day on the possibility of disgust, but each day brought forth meanwhile a new and more engaging bend of the road. That possibility was now ever so much further from sight than on the eve of his arrival, and he perfectly felt that, should it come at all, it would have to be at best inconsequent and violent. He struck himself as a little nearer to it only when he asked himself what service,

---

7. Small drawing room.
8. Young girl.

in such a life of utility, he was after all rendering Mrs. Newsome. When he wished to help himself to believe that he was still all right he reflected—and in fact with wonder—on the unimpaired frequency of their correspondence; in relation to which what was after all more natural than that it should become more frequent just in proportion as their problem became more complicated?

Certain it is at any rate that he now often brought himself balm by the question, with the rich consciousness of yesterday's letter, "Well, what can I do more than that—what can I do more than tell her everything?" To persuade himself that he did tell her, had told her, everything, he used to try to think of particular things he hadn't told her. When at rare moments and in the watches of the night he pounced on one it generally showed itself to be—to a deeper scrutiny—not quite truly of the essence. When anything new struck him as coming up, or anything already noted as re-appearing, he always immediately wrote, as if for fear that if he didn't he would miss something; and also that he might be able to say to himself from time to time "She knows it *now*—even while I worry." It was a great comfort to him in general not to have left past things to be dragged to light and explained; not to have to produce at so late a stage anything not produced, or anything even veiled and attenuated, at the moment. She knew it now: that was what he said to himself to-night in relation to the fresh fact of Chad's acquaintance with the two ladies—not to speak of the fresher one of his own. Mrs. Newsome knew in other words that very night at Woollett that he himself knew Madame de Vionnet and that he had conscientiously been to see her; also that he had found her remarkably attractive and that there would probably be a good deal more to tell. But she further knew, or would know very soon, that, again conscientiously, he hadn't re-peated his visit; and that when Chad had asked him on the Countess's behalf—Strether made her out vividly, with a thought at the back of his head, a Countess—if he wouldn't name a day for dining with her, he had replied lucidly: "Thank you very much —impossible." He had begged the young man would present his excuses and had trusted him to understand that it couldn't really strike one as quite the straight thing. He hadn't reported to Mrs. Newsome that he had promised to "save" Madame de Vionnet; but, so far as he was concerned with that reminiscence, he hadn't at any rate promised to haunt her house. What Chad had under-stood could only, in truth, be inferred from Chad's behaviour, which had been in this connexion as easy as in every other. He was easy, always, when he understood; he was easier still, if pos-sible, when he didn't; he had replied that he would make it all right; and he had proceeded to do this by substituting the present occasion—as he was ready to substitute others—for any, for every occasion as to which his old friend should have a funny scruple.

"Oh but I'm not a little foreign girl; I'm just as English as I can be," Jeanne de Vionnet had said to him as soon as, in the *petit salon*, he sank, shyly enough on his own side, into the place near her vacated by Madame Gloriani at his approach. Madame Gloriani, who was in black velvet, with white lace and powdered hair, and whose somewhat massive majesty melted, at any contact, into the graciousness of some incomprehensible tongue, moved away to make room for the vague gentleman, after benevolent greetings to him which embodied, as he believed, in baffling accents, some recognition of his face from a couple of Sundays before. Then he had remarked—making the most of the advantage of his years—that it frightened him quite enough to find himself dedicated to the entertainment of a little foreign girl. There were girls he wasn't afraid of—he was quite bold with little Americans. Thus it was that she had defended herself to the end—"Oh but I'm almost American too. That's what mamma has wanted me to be —I mean *like* that; for she has wanted me to have lots of freedom. She has known such good results from it."

She was fairly beautiful to him—a faint pastel in an oval frame: he thought of her already as of some lurking image in a long gallery, the portrait of a small old-time princess of whom nothing was known but that she had died young. Little Jeanne wasn't, doubtless, to die young, but one couldn't, all the same, bear on her lightly enough. It was bearing hard, it was bearing as *he*, in any case, wouldn't bear, to concern himself, in relation to her, with the question of a young man. Odious really the question of a young man; one didn't treat such a person as a maid-servant suspected of a "follower." And then young men, young men—well, the thing was their business simply, or was at all events hers. She was fluttered, fairly fevered—to the point of a little glitter that came and went in her eyes and a pair of pink spots that stayed in her cheeks—with the great adventure of dining out and with the greater one still, possibly, of finding a gentleman whom she must think of as very, very old, a gentleman with eye-glasses, wrinkles, a long grizzled moustache. She spoke the prettiest English, our friend thought, that he had ever heard spoken, just as he had believed her a few minutes before to be speaking the prettiest French. He wondered almost wistfully if such a sweep of the lyre didn't react on the spirit itself; and his fancy had in fact, before he knew it, begun so to stray and embroider that he finally found himself, absent and extravagant, sitting with the child in a friendly silence. Only by this time he felt her flutter to have fortunately dropped and that she was more at her ease. She trusted him, liked him, and it was to come back to him afterwards that she had told him things. She had dipped into the waiting medium at last and found neither surge nor chill—nothing but the small splash she could herself make in the pleasant warmth, nothing but the safety of dipping and dipping again. At the end of the ten minutes he was to spend with her his impression—with all it had thrown off and all it had taken in—was complete. She had been free, as she knew freedom, partly to show him that, unlike other little persons she knew, she had imbibed that ideal. She was delightfully quaint about herself, but the vision of what she had imbibed was what most held him. It really consisted, he was soon enough to feel, in just one great little matter, the fact that, whatever her nature, she was thoroughly—he had to cast about for the word, but it came—bred. He couldn't of course on so short an acquaintance speak for her nature, but the idea of breeding was what she had meanwhile dropped into his mind. He had never yet known it so sharply presented. Her mother gave it, no doubt; but her mother, to make that less sensible, gave so much else besides, and on neither of the two previous occasions, extraordinary woman, Strether felt, anything like what she was giving tonight. Little Jeanne was a case, an exquisite case of education; whereas the Countess, whom it so amused him to think of by that denomination, was a case, also exquisite, of—well, he didn't know what.

"He has wonderful taste, *notre jeune homme*":[9] this was what Gloriani said to him on turning away from the inspection of a small picture suspended near the door of the room. The high celebrity in question had just come in, apparently in search of Mademoiselle de Vionnet, but while Strether had got up from beside her their fellow guest, with his eye sharply caught, had paused for a long look. The thing was a landscape, of no size, but of the French school, as our friend was glad to feel he knew, and also of a quality—which he liked to think he should also have guessed; its frame was large out of proportion to the canvas, and he had never seen a person look at anything, he thought, just as Gloriani, with his nose very near and quick movements of the head from side to side and bottom to top, examined this feature of Chad's collection. The artist used that word the next moment, smiling courteously, wiping his nippers and looking round him further—paying the place in short by the very manner of his presence and by something Strether fancied he could make out in this particular glance, such a tribute as, to the latter's sense, settled many things once for all. Strether was conscious at this instant, for that matter, as he hadn't yet been, of how, round about him, quite without him, they *were* consistently settled. Gloriani's smile, deeply

9. Our young man.

Italian, he considered, and finely inscrutable, had had for him, during dinner, at which they were not neighbours, an indefinite greeting; but the quality in it was gone that had appeared on the other occasion to turn him inside out; it was as if even the momentary link supplied by the doubt between them had snapped. He was conscious now of the final reality, which was that there wasn't so much a doubt as a difference altogether; all the more that over the difference the famous sculptor seemed to signal almost condolingly, yet oh how vacantly! as across some great flat sheet of water. He threw out the bridge of a charming hollow civility on which Strether wouldn't have trusted his own full weight a moment. That idea, even though but transient and perhaps belated, had performed the office of putting Strether more at his ease, and the blurred picture had already dropped—dropped with the sound of something else said and with his becoming aware, by another quick turn, that Gloriani was now on the sofa talking with Jeanne, while he himself had in his ears again the familiar friendliness and the elusive meaning of the "Oh, oh, oh!" that had made him, a fortnight before, challenge Miss Barrace in vain. She had always the air, this picturesque and original lady, who struck him, so oddly, as both antique and modern—she had always the air of taking up some joke that one had already had out with her. The point itself, no doubt, was what was antique, and the use she made of it what was modern. He felt just now that her good-natured irony did bear on something, and it troubled him a little that she wouldn't be more explicit, only assuring him, with the pleasure of observation so visible in her, that she wouldn't tell him more for the world. He could take refuge but in asking her what she had done with Waymarsh, though it must be added that he felt himself a little on the way to a clue after she had answered that this personage was, in the other room, engaged in conversation with Madame de Vionnet. He stared a moment at the image of such a conjunction; then, for Miss Barrace's benefit, he wondered. "Is she too then under the charm—?"

"No, not a bit"—Miss Barrace was prompt. "She makes nothing of him. She's bored. She won't help you with him."

"Oh," Strether laughed, "she can't do everything."

"Of course not—wonderful as she is. Besides, he makes nothing of *her*. She won't take him from me—though she wouldn't, no doubt, having other affairs in hand, even if she could. I've never," said Miss Barrace, "seen her fail with any one before. And to-night, when she's so magnificent, it would seem to her strange—if she minded. So at any rate I have him all. *Je suis tranquille!*"[1]

Strether understood, so far as that went; but he was feeling for

1. I am not worried (*lit.*, I am tranquil).

his clue. "She strikes you to-night as particularly magnificent?"

"Surely. Almost as I've never seen her. Doesn't she you? Why it's *for* you."

He persisted in his candour. " 'For' me—?"

"Oh, oh, oh!" cried Miss Barrace, who persisted in the opposite of that quality.

"Well," he acutely admitted, "she *is* different. She's gay."

"She's gay!" Miss Barrace laughed. "And she has beautiful shoulders—though there's nothing different in that."

"No," said Strether, "one was sure of her shoulders. It isn't her shoulders."

His companion, with renewed mirth and the finest sense, between the puffs of her cigarette, of the drollery of things, appeared to find their conversation highly delightful. "Yes, it isn't her shoulders."

"What then is it?" Strether earnestly enquired.

"Why, it's *she*—simply. It's her mood. It's her charm."

"Of course it's her charm, but we're speaking of the difference."

"Well," Miss Barrace explained, "she's just brilliant, as we used to say. That's all. She's various. She's fifty women."

"Ah but only one"—Strether kept it clear—"at a time."

"Perhaps. But in fifty times—!"

"Oh we shan't come to that," our friend declared; and the next moment he had moved in another direction. "Will you answer me a plain question? Will she ever divorce?"

Miss Barrace looked at him through all her tortoise-shell. "Why should she?"

It wasn't what he had asked for, he signified; but he met it well enough. "To marry Chad."

"Why should she marry Chad?"

"Because I'm convinced she's very fond of him. She has done wonders for him."

"Well then, how could she do more? Marrying a man, or a woman either," Miss Barrace sagely went on, "is never the wonder, for any Jack and Jill can bring *that* off. The wonder is their doing such things without marrying."

Strether considered a moment this proposition. "You mean it's so beautiful for our friends simply to go on so?"

But whatever he said made her laugh. "Beautiful."

He nevertheless insisted. "And *that* because it's disinterested?"

She was now, however, suddenly tired of the question. "Yes, then—call it that. Besides, she'll never divorce. Don't, moreover," she added, "believe everything you hear about her husband."

"He's not then," Strether asked, "a wretch?"

"Oh yes. But charming."

"Do you know him?"

"I've met him. He's *bien aimable*."[2]

"To every one but his wife?"

"Oh for all I know, to her too—to any, to every woman. I hope you at any rate," she pursued with a quick change, "appreciate the care I take of Mr. Waymarsh."

"Oh immensely." But Strether was not yet in line. "At all events," he roundly brought out, "the attachment's an innocent one."

"Mine and his? Ah," she laughed, "don't rob it of *all* interest!"

"I mean our friend's here—to the lady we've been speaking of." That was what he had settled to as an indirect but none the less closely involved consequence of his impression of Jeanne. That was where he meant to stay. "It's innocent," he repeated—"I see the whole thing."

Mystified by his abrupt declaration, she had glanced over at Gloriani as at the unnamed subject of his allusion, but the next moment she had understood; though indeed not before Strether had noticed her momentary mistake and wondered what might possibly be behind that too. He already knew that the sculptor admired Madame de Vionnet; but did this admiration also represent an attachment of which the innocence was discussable? He was moving verily in a strange air and on ground not of the firmest. He looked hard for an instant at Miss Barrace, but she had already gone on. "All right with Mr. Newsome? Why of course she is!"—and she got gaily back to the question of her own good friend. "I dare say you're surprised that I'm not worn out with all I see—it being so much!—of Sitting Bull. But I'm not, you know—I don't mind him; I bear up, and we get on beautifully. I'm very strange; I'm like that; and often I can't explain. There are people who are supposed interesting or remarkable or whatever, and who bore me to death; and then there are others as to whom nobody can understand what anybody sees in them—in whom I see no end of things." Then after she had smoked a moment, "He's touching, you know," she said.

" 'Know'?" Strether echoed—"don't I, indeed? We must move you almost to tears."

"Oh but I don't mean *you!*" she laughed.

"You ought to then, for the worst sign of all—as I must have it for you—is that you can't help me. That's when a woman pities."

"Ah but I do help you!" she cheerfully insisted.

Again he looked at her hard, and then after a pause: "No you don't!"

Her tortoise-shell, on its long chain, rattled down. "I help you

2. Very amiable.

with Sitting Bull. That's a good deal."

"Oh that, yes." But Strether hesitated. "Do you mean he talks of me?"

"So that I have to defend you? No, never."

"I see," Strether mused. "It's too deep."

"That's his only fault," she returned—"that everything, with him, is too deep. He has depths of silence—which he breaks only at the longest intervals by a remark. And when the remark comes it's always something he has seen or felt for himself—never a bit banal. *That* would be what one might have feared and what would kill me. But never." She smoked again as she thus, with amused complacency, appreciated her acquisition. "And never about you. We keep clear of you. We're wonderful. But I'll tell you what he does do," she continued: "he tries to make me presents."

"Presents?" poor Strether echoed, conscious with a pang that *he* hadn't yet tried that in any quarter.

"Why you see," she explained, "he's as fine as ever in the victoria; so that when I leave him, as I often do almost for hours—he likes it so—at the doors of shops, the sight of him there helps me, when I come out, to know my carriage away off in the rank. But sometimes, for a change, he goes with me into the shops, and then I've all I can do to prevent his buying me things."

"He wants to 'treat' you?" Strether almost gasped at all he himself hadn't thought of. He had a sense of admiration. "Oh he's much more in the real tradition than I. Yes," he mused; "it's the sacred rage."

"The sacred rage, exactly!"—and Miss Barrace, who hadn't before heard this term applied, recognised its bearing with a clap of her gemmed hands. "Now I do know why he's not banal. But I do prevent him all the same—and if you saw what he sometimes selects—from buying. I save him hundreds and hundreds. I only take flowers."

"Flowers?" Strether echoed again with a rueful reflexion. How many nosegays had her present converser sent?

"Innocent flowers," she pursued, "as much as he likes. And he sends me splendours; he knows all the best places—he has found them for himself; he's wonderful."

"He hasn't told them to *me*," her friend smiled; "he has a life of his own." But Strether had swung back to the consciousness that for himself after all it never would have done. Waymarsh hadn't Mrs. Waymarsh in the least to consider, whereas Lambert Strether had constantly, in the inmost honour of his thoughts, to consider Mrs. Newsome. He liked moreover to feel how much his friend was in the real tradition. Yet he had his conclusion. "*What* a rage it is!" He had worked it out. "It's an opposition."

She followed, but at a distance. "That's what I feel. Yet to what?"

"Well, he thinks, you know, that I've a life of my own. And I haven't!"

"You haven't?" She showed doubt, and her laugh confirmed it. "Oh, oh, oh!"

"No—not for myself. I seem to have a life only for other people."

"Ah for them and *with* them! Just now for instance with—"

"Well, with whom?" he asked before she had had time to say.

His tone had the effect of making her hesitate and even, as he guessed, speak with a difference. "Say with Miss Gostrey. What do you do for *her?*"

It really made him wonder. "Nothing at all!"

III [xv]

Madame de Vionnet, having meanwhile come in, was at present close to them, and Miss Barrace hereupon, instead of risking a rejoinder, became again with a look that measured her from top to toe all mere long-handled appreciative tortoise-shell. She had struck our friend, from the first of her appearing, as dressed for a great occasion, and she met still more than on either of the others the conception reawakened in him at their garden-party, the idea of the *femme du monde* in her habit as she lived. Her bare shoulders and arms were white and beautiful; the materials of her dress, a mixture, as he supposed, of silk and crape, were of a silvery grey so artfully composed as to give an impression of warm splendour; and round her neck she wore a collar of large old emeralds, the green note of which was more dimly repeated, at other points of her apparel, in embroidery, in enamel, in satin, in substances and textures vaguely rich. Her head, extremely fair and exquisitely festal, was like a happy fancy, a notion of the antique, on an old precious medal, some silver coin of the Renaissance; while her slim lightness and brightness, her gaiety, her expression, her decision, contributed to an effect that might have been felt by a poet as half mythological and half conventional. He could have compared her to a goddess still partly engaged in a morning cloud, or to a sea-nymph waist-high in the summer surge. Above all she suggested to him the re-flexion that the *femme du monde*—in these finest developments of the type—was, like Cleopatra in the play, indeed various and multi-fold.[3] She had aspects, characters, days, nights—or had them at least, showed them by a mysterious law of her own, when in addition to everything she happened also to be a woman of genius. She was an obscure person, a muffled person one day, and a showy person, an uncovered person the next. He thought of Madame de

---

3. "Age cannot wither her, nor custom stale/ Her infinite variety." Enobarbus on Cleopatra in Shakespeare's *Antony and Cleopatra* (2. 2. 238–39).

Vionnet to-night as showy and uncovered, though he felt the formula rough, because, thanks to one of the short-cuts of genius, she had taken all his categories by surprise. Twice during dinner he had met Chad's eyes in a longish look; but these communications had in truth only stirred up again old ambiguities—so little was it clear from them whether they were an appeal or an admonition. "You see how I'm fixed," was what they appeared to convey; yet how he was fixed was exactly what Strether didn't see. However, perhaps he should see now.

"Are you capable of the very great kindness of going to relieve Newsome, for a few minutes, of the rather crushing responsibility of Madame Gloriani, while I say a word, if he'll allow me, to Mr. Strether, of whom I've a question to ask? Our host ought to talk a bit to those other ladies, and I'll come back in a minute to your rescue." She made this proposal to Miss Barrace as if her consciousness of a special duty had just flickered up, but that lady's recognition of Strether's little start at it—as at a betrayal on the speaker's part of a domesticated state—was as mute as his own comment; and after an instant, when their fellow guest had good-naturedly left them, he had been given something else to think of. "Why has Maria so suddenly gone? Do you know?" That was the question Madame de Vionnet had brought with her.

"I'm afraid I've no reason to give you but the simple reason I've had from her in a note—the sudden obligation to join in the south a sick friend who has got worse."

"Ah then she has been writing you?"

"Not since she went—I had only a brief explanatory word before she started. I went to see her," Strether explained—"it was the day after I called on you—but she was already on her way, and her concierge told me that in case of my coming I was to be informed she had written to me. I found her note when I got home."

Madame de Vionnet listened with interest and with her eyes on Strether's face; then her delicately decorated head had a small melancholy motion. "She didn't write to *me*. I went to see her," she added, "almost immediately after I had seen you, and as I assured her I would do when I met her at Gloriani's. She hadn't then told me she was to be absent, and I felt at her door as if I understood. She's absent—with all respect to her sick friend, though I know indeed she has plenty—so that I may not see her. She doesn't want to meet me again. Well," she continued with a beautiful conscious mildness, "I liked and admired her beyond every one in the old time, and she knew it—perhaps that's precisely what has made her go—and I dare say I haven't lost her for ever." Strether still said nothing; he had a horror, as he now thought of himself, of being in question between women—was in fact already quite enough on his way to that; and there was moreover, as it came to him, perceptibly, something behind these allusions and professions that, should he take it in, would square but ill with his present resolve to simplify. It was as if, for him, all the same, her softness and sadness were sincere. He felt that not less when she soon went on: "I'm extremely glad of her happiness." But it also left him mute—sharp and fine though the imputation it conveyed. What it conveyed was that *he* was Maria Gostrey's happiness, and for the least little instant he had the impulse to challenge the thought. He could have done so however only by saying "What then do you suppose to be between us?" and he was wonderfully glad a moment later not to have spoken. He would rather seem stupid any day than fatuous, and he drew back as well, with a smothered inward shudder, from the consideration of what women—of highly-developed type in particular—might think of each other. Whatever he had come out for he hadn't come to go into that; so that he absolutely took up nothing his interlocutress had now let drop. Yet, though he had kept away from her for days, had laid wholly on herself the burden of their meeting again, she hadn't a gleam of irritation to show him. "Well, about Jeanne now?" she smiled—it had the gaiety with which she had originally come in. He felt it on the instant to represent her motive and real errand. But he had been schooling her of a truth to say much in proportion to his little. "*Do* you make out that she has a sentiment? I mean for Mr. Newsome."

Almost resentful, Strether could at last be prompt. "How can I make out such things?"

She remained perfectly good-natured. "Ah but they're beautiful little things, and you make out—don't pretend!—everything in the world. Haven't you," she asked, "been talking with her?"

"Yes, but not about Chad. At least not much."

"Oh you don't require 'much'!" she reassuringly declared. But she immediately changed her ground. "I hope you remember your promise of the other day."

"To 'save' you, as you called it?"

"I call it so still. You *will?*" she insisted. "You haven't repented?"

He wondered. "No—but I've been thinking what I meant."

She kept it up. "And not, a little, what *I* did?"

"No—that's not necessary. It will be enough if I know what I meant myself."

"And don't you know," she asked, "by this time?"

Again he had a pause. "I think you ought to leave it to me. But how long," he added, "do you give me?"

"It seems to me much more a question of how long you give *me*. Doesn't our friend here himself, at any rate," she went on, "perpetually make me present to you?"

"Not," Strether replied, "by ever speaking of you to me."

"He never does that?"

"Never."

She considered, and, if the fact was disconcerting to her, effectually concealed it. The next minute indeed she had recovered. "No, he wouldn't. But do you *need* that?"

Her emphasis was wonderful, and though his eyes had been wandering he looked at her longer now. "I see what you mean."

"Of course you see what I mean."

Her triumph was gentle, and she really had tones to make justice weep. "I've before me what he owes you."

"Admit then that that's something," she said, yet still with the same discretion in her pride.

He took in this note but went straight on. "You've made of him what I see, but what I don't see is how in the world you've done it."

"Ah that's another question!" she smiled. "The point is of what use is your declining to know me when to know Mr. Newsome—as you do me the honour to find him—*is* just to know me."

"I see," he mused, still with his eyes on her. "I shouldn't have met you to-night."

She raised and dropped her linked hands. "It doesn't matter. If I trust you why can't you a little trust me too? And why can't you also," she asked in another tone, "trust yourself?" But she gave him no time to reply. "Oh I shall be so easy for you! And I'm glad at any rate you've seen my child."

"I'm glad too," he said; "but she does you no good."

"No good?"—Madame de Vionnet had a clear stare. "Why she's an angel of light."

"That's precisely the reason. Leave her alone. Don't try to find out. I mean," he explained, "about what you spoke to me of—the way she feels."

His companion wondered. "Because one really won't?"

"Well, because I ask you, as a favour to myself, not to. She's the most charming creature I've ever seen. Therefore don't touch her. Don't know—don't want to know. And moreover—yes—you *won't*."

It was an appeal, of a sudden, and she took it in. "As a favour to you?"

"Well—since you ask me."

"Anything, everything you ask," she smiled. "I shan't know then—never. Thank you," she added with peculiar gentleness as she turned away.

The sound of it lingered with him, making him fairly feel as if he had been tripped up and had a fall. In the very act of arranging with her for his independence he had, under pressure from a particular perception, inconsistently, quite stupidly, committed himself, and, with her subtlety sensitive on the spot to an advantage, she had driven in by a single word a little golden nail, the sharp intention of which he signally felt. He hadn't detached, he had more closely connected himself, and his eyes, as he considered with some intensity this circumstance, met another pair which had just come within their range and which struck him as reflecting his sense of what he had done. He recognised them at the same moment as those of little Bilham, who had apparently drawn near on purpose to speak to him, and little Bilham wasn't, in the conditions, the person to whom his heart would be most closed. They were seated together a minute later at the angle of the room obliquely opposite the corner in which Gloriani was still engaged with Jeanne de Vionnet, to whom at first and in silence their attention had been benevolently given. "I can't see for my life," Strether had then observed, "how a young fellow of any spirit—such a one as you for instance—can be admitted to the sight of that young lady without being hard hit. Why don't you go in, little Bilham?" He remembered the tone into which he had been betrayed on the garden-bench at the sculptor's reception, and this might make up for that by being much more the right sort of thing to say to a young man worthy of any advice at all. "There *would* be some reason."

"Some reason for what?"

"Why for hanging on here."

"To offer my hand and fortune to Mademoiselle de Vionnet?"

"Well," Strether asked, "to what lovelier apparition *could* you offer them? She's the sweetest little thing I've ever seen."

"She's certainly immense. I mean she's the real thing. I believe the pale pink petals are folded up there for some wondrous efflorescence in time; to open, that is, to some great golden sun. *I'm* unfortunately but a small farthing candle. What chance in such a field for a poor little painter-man?"

"Oh you're good enough," Strether threw out.

"Certainly I'm good enough. We're good enough, I consider, *nous autres*,[4] for anything. But she's *too* good. There's the difference. They wouldn't look at me."

Strether, lounging on his divan and still charmed by the young girl, whose eyes had consciously strayed to him, he fancied, with a vague smile—Strether, enjoying the whole occasion as with dormant pulses at last awake and in spite of new material thrust upon him, thought over his companion's words. "Whom do you mean by 'they'? She and her mother?"

4. *We.*

"She and her mother. And she has a father too, who, whatever else he may be, certainly can't be indifferent to the possibilities she represents. Besides, there's Chad."

Strether was silent a little. "Ah but he doesn't care for her—not, I mean, it appears, after all, in the sense I'm speaking of. He's *not* in love with her."

"No—but he's her best friend; after her mother. He's very fond of her. He has his ideas about what can be done for her."

"Well, it's very strange!" Strether presently remarked with a sighing sense of fulness.

"Very strange indeed. That's just the beauty of it. Isn't it very much the kind of beauty you had in mind," little Bilham went on, "when you were so wonderful and so inspiring to me the other day? Didn't you adjure me, in accents I shall never forget, to see, while I've a chance, everything I can?—and *really* to see, for it must have been that only you meant. Well, you did me no end of good, and I'm doing my best. I *do* make it out a situation."

"So do I!" Strether went on after a moment. But he had the next minute an inconsequent question. "How comes Chad so mixed up, anyway?"

"Ah, ah, ah!"—and little Bilham fell back on his cushions.

It reminded our friend of Miss Barrace, and he felt again the brush of his sense of moving in a maze of mystic closed allusions. Yet he kept hold of his thread. "Of course I understand really; only the general transformation makes me occasionally gasp. Chad with such a voice in the settlement of the future of a little countess—no," he declared, "it takes more time! You say moreover," he resumed, "that we're inevitably, people like you and me, out of the running. The curious fact remains that Chad himself isn't. The situation doesn't make for it, but in a different one he could have her if he would."

"Yes, but that's only because he's rich and because there's a possibility of his being richer. They won't think of anything but a great name or a great fortune."

"Well," said Strether, "he'll have no great fortune on *these* lines. He must stir his stumps."

"Is that," little Bilham enquired, "what you were saying to Madame de Vionnet?"

"No—I don't say much to her. Of course, however," Strether continued, "he can make sacrifices if he likes."

Little Bilham had a pause. "Oh he's not keen for sacrifices; or thinks, that is, possibly, that he has made enough."

"Well, it *is* virtuous," his companion observed with some decision.

"That's exactly," the young man dropped after a moment, "what

I mean."

It kept Strether himself silent a little. "I've made it out for my-self," he then went on; "I've really, within the last half-hour, got hold of it. I understand it in short at last; which at first—when you originally spoke to me—I didn't. Nor when Chad originally spoke to me either."

"Oh," said little Bilham, "I don't think that at that time you be-lieved me."

"Yes—I did; and I believed Chad too. It would have been odious and unmannerly—as well as quite perverse—if I hadn't. What in-terest have you in deceiving me?"

The young man cast about. "What interest have *I*?"

"Yes. Chad *might* have. But you?"

"Ah, ah, ah!" little Bilham exclaimed.

It might, on repetition, as a mystification, have irritated our friend a little, but he knew, once more, as we have seen, where he was, and his being proof against everything was only another at-testation that he meant to stay there. "I couldn't, without my own impression, realise. She's a tremendously clever brilliant capable woman, and with an extraordinary charm on' top of it all—the charm we surely all of us this evening know what to think of. It isn't every clever brilliant capable woman that has it. In fact it's rare with any woman. So there you are," Strether proceeded as if not for little Bilham's benefit alone. "I understand what a relation with such a woman—what such a high fine friendship—may be. It can't be vulgar or coarse, anyway—and that's the point."

"Yes, that's the point," said little Bilham. "It can't be vulgar or coarse. And, bless us and save us, it *isn't!* It's, upon my word, the very finest thing I ever saw in my life, and the most distinguished."

Strether, from beside him and leaning back with him as he leaned, dropped on him a momentary look which filled a short in-terval and of which he took no notice. He only gazed before him with intent participation. "Of course what it has done for him," Strether at all events presently pursued, "of course what it has done for him—that is as to *how* it has so wonderfully worked—isn't a thing I pretend to understand. I've to take it as I find it. There he is."

"There he is!" little Bilham echoed. "And it's really and truly she. I don't understand either, even with my longer and closer op-portunity. But I'm like you," he added; "I can admire and rejoice even when I'm a little in the dark. You see I've watched it for some three years, and especially for this last. He wasn't so bad before it as I seem to have made out that you think—"

"Oh I don't think anything now!" Strether impatiently broke in: "that is but what I *do* think! I mean that originally, for her to have cared for him—"

"There must have been stuff in him? Oh yes, there was stuff indeed, and much more of it than ever showed, I dare say, at home. Still, you know," the young man in all fairness developed, "there was room for her, and that's where she came in. She saw her chance and took it. That's what strikes me as having been so fine. But of course," he wound up, "he liked her first."

"Naturally," said Strether.

"I mean that they first met somehow and somewhere—I believe in some American house—and she, without in the least then intending it, made her impression. Then with time and opportunity he made his; and after *that* she was as bad as he."

Strether vaguely took it up. "As 'bad'?"

"She began, that is, to care—to care very much. Alone, and in her horrid position, she found it, when once she had started, an interest. It was, it is, an interest; and it did—it continues to do—a lot for herself as well. So she still cares. She cares in fact," said little Bilham thoughtfully, "more."

Strether's theory that it was none of his business was somehow not damaged by the way he took this. "More, you mean, than he?" On which his companion looked round at him, and now for an instant their eyes met. "More than he?" he repeated.

Little Bilham, for as long, hung fire. "Will you never tell any one?"

Strether thought. "Whom should I tell?"

"Why I supposed you reported regularly—"

"To people at home?"—Strether took him up. "Well, I won't tell them this."

The young man at last looked away. "Then she does now care more than he."

"Oh!" Strether oddly exclaimed.

But his companion immediately met it. "Haven't you after all had your impression of it? That's how you've got hold of him."

"Ah but I haven't got hold of him!"

"Oh I say!" But it was all little Bilham said.

"It's at any rate none of my business. I mean," Strether explained, "nothing else than getting hold of him is." It appeared, however, to strike him as his business to add: "The fact remains nevertheless that she has saved him."

Little Bilham just waited. "I thought that was what *you* were to do."

But Strether had his answer ready. "I'm speaking—in connexion with her—of his manners and morals, his character and life. I'm speaking of him as a person to deal with and talk with and live with—speaking of him as a social animal."

"And isn't it as a social animal that you also want him?"

"Certainly; so that it's as if she had saved him *for* us."

"It strikes you accordingly then," the young man threw out, "as for you all to save *her?*"

"Oh for us 'all'—!" Strether could but laugh at that. It brought him back, however, to the point he had really wished to make. "They've accepted their situation—hard as it is. They're not free —at least she's not; but they take what's left to them. It's a friendship, of a beautiful sort; and that's what makes them so strong. They're straight, they feel; and they keep each other up. It's doubtless she, however, who, as you yourself have hinted, feels it most."

Little Bilham appeared to wonder what he had hinted. "Feels most that they're straight?"

"Well, feels that *she* is, and the strength that comes from it. She keeps *him* up—she keeps the whole thing up. When people are able to it's fine. She's wonderful, wonderful, as Miss Barrace says; and he is, in his way, too; however, as a mere man, he may sometimes rebel and not feel that he finds his account in it. She has simply given him an immense moral lift, and what that can explain is prodigious. That's why I speak of it as a situation. It *is* one, if there ever was." And Strether, with his head back and his eyes on the ceiling, seemed to lose himself in the vision of it.

His companion attended deeply. "You state it much better than I could."

"Oh you see it doesn't concern you."

Little Bilham considered. "I thought you said just now that it doesn't concern you either."

"Well, it doesn't a bit as Madame de Vionnet's affair. But as we were again saying just now, what did I come out for but to save him?"

"Yes—to remove him."

"To save him *by* removal; to win him over to *himself* thinking it best he shall take up business—thinking he must immediately do therefore what's necessary to that end."

"Well," said little Bilham after a moment, "you *have* won him over. He does think it best. He has within a day or two again said to me as much."

"And that," Strether asked, "is why you consider that he cares less than she?"

"Cares less for her than she for him? Yes, that's one of the reasons. But other things too have given me the impression. A man, don't you think?" little Bilham presently pursued, "*can't*, in such conditions, care so much as a woman. It takes different conditions to make him, and then perhaps he cares more. Chad," he wound up, "has his possible future before him."

"Are you speaking of his business future?"

"No—on the contrary; of the other, the future of what you so justly call their situation. M. de Vionnet may live for ever."

"So that they can't marry?"

The young man waited a moment. "Not being able to marry is all they've with any confidence to look forward to. A woman—a particular woman—may stand that strain. But can a man?" he propounded.

Strether's answer was as prompt as if he had already, for himself, worked it out. "Not without a very high ideal of conduct. But that's just what we're attributing to Chad. And how, for that matter," he mused, "does his going to America diminish the particular strain? Wouldn't it seem rather to add to it?"

"Out of sight out of mind!" his companion laughed. Then more bravely: "Wouldn't distance lessen the torment?" But before Strether could reply, "The thing is, you see, Chad ought to marry!" he wound up.

Strether, for a little, appeared to think of it. "If you talk of torments you don't diminish mine!" he then broke out. The next moment he was on his feet with a question. "He ought to marry whom?"

Little Bilham rose more slowly. "Well, some one he *can*—some thoroughly nice girl."

Strether's eyes, as they stood together, turned again to Jeanne. "Do you mean *her?*"

His friend made a sudden strange face. "After being in love with her mother? No."

"But isn't it exactly your idea that he *isn't* in love with her mother?"

His friend once more had a pause. "Well, he isn't at any rate in love with Jeanne."

"I dare say not."

"How *can* he be with any other woman?"

"Oh that I admit. But being in love isn't, you know, here"—little Bilham spoke in friendly reminder—"thought necessary, in strictness, for marriage."

"And what torment—to call a torment—can there ever possibly be with a woman like that?" As if from the interest of his own question Strether had gone on without hearing. "Is it for her to have turned a man out so wonderfully, too, only for somebody else?" He appeared to make a point of this, and little Bilham looked at him now. "When it's for each other that people give things up they don't miss them." Then he threw off as with an extravagance of which he was conscious: "Let them face the future together!"

Little Bilham looked at him indeed. "You mean that after all he shouldn't go back?"

"I mean that if he gives her up—!"

"Yes?"

"Well, he ought to be ashamed of himself." But Strether spoke with a sound that might have passed for a laugh.

By Notre Dame

The Ambassadors

Volume II

Book Seventh

1 [XVI]

It wasn't the first time Strether had sat alone in the great dim church—still less was it the first of his giving himself up, so far as conditions permitted, to its beneficent action on his nerves. He had been to Notre Dame[1] with Waymarsh, he had been there with Miss Gostrey, he had been there with Chad Newsome, and had found the place, even in company, such a refuge from the obsession of his problem that, with renewed pressure from that source, he had not unnaturally recurred to a remedy meeting the case, for the moment, so indirectly, no doubt, but so relievingly. He was conscious enough that it was only for the moment, but good moments—if he could call them good—still had their value for a man who by this time struck himself as living almost disgracefully from hand to mouth. Having so well learnt the way, he had lately made the pilgrimage more than once by himself—had quite stolen off, taking an unnoticed chance and making no point of speaking of the adventure when restored to his friends.

His great friend, for that matter, was still absent, as well as remarkably silent; even at the end of three weeks Miss Gostrey hadn't come back. She wrote to him from Mentone,[2] admitting that he must judge her grossly inconsequent—perhaps in fact for the time odiously faithless; but asking for patience, for a deferred sentence, throwing herself in short on his generosity. For her too, she could assure him, life was complicated—more complicated than he could have guessed; she had moreover made certain of him—certain of not wholly missing him on her return—before her disappearance. If furthermore she didn't burden him with letters it was frankly because of her sense of the other great commerce he had to carry on. He himself, at the end of a fortnight, had written twice, to show how his generosity could be trusted; but he reminded himself in each case of Mrs. Newsome's epistolary manner at the

---

1. Located between the banks of the Seine on the Ile de la Cité, the Cathedral of Notre Dame figures indirectly in the frontispiece to the second volume of *The Ambassadors.* The photograph shows a part of the Pont Neuf (New Bridge), which connects the left bank with the Ile de la Cité. (See p. 171. For a discussion of the photograph, see pp. 368–69.)
2. A French seaside resort on the Mediterranean.

times when Mrs. Newsome kept off delicate ground. He sank his problem, he talked of Waymarsh and Miss Barrace, of little Bilham and the set over the river, with whom he had again had tea, and he was easy, for convenience, about Chad and Madame de Vionnet and Jeanne. He admitted that he continued to see them, he was decidedly so confirmed a haunter of Chad's premises and that young man's practical intimacy with them was so undeniably great; but he had his reason for not attempting to render for Miss Gostrey's benefit the impression of these last days. That would be to tell her too much about himself—it being at present just from himself he was trying to escape.

This small struggle sprang not a little, in its way, from the same impulse that had now carried him across to Notre Dame; the impulse to let things be, to give them time to justify themselves or at least to pass. He was aware of having no errand in such a place but the desire not to be, for the hour, in certain other places; a sense of safety, of simplification, which each time he yielded to it he amused himself by thinking of as a private concession to cowardice. The great church had no altar for his worship, no direct voice for his soul; but it was none the less soothing even to sanctity; for he could feel while there what he couldn't elsewhere, that he was a plain tired man taking the holiday he had earned. He was tired, but he wasn't plain—that was the pity and the trouble of it; he was able, however, to drop his problem at the door very much as if it had been the copper piece that he deposited, on the threshold, in the receptacle of the inveterate blind beggar. He trod the long dim nave, sat in the splendid choir, paused before the clustered chapels of the east end, and the mighty monument laid upon him its spell. He might have been a student under the charm of a museum—which was exactly what, in a foreign town, in the afternoon of life, he would have liked to be free to be. This form of sacrifice did at any rate for the occasion as well as another; it made him quite sufficiently understand how, within the precinct, for the real refugee, the things of the world could fall into abeyance. That was the cowardice, probably—to dodge them, to beg the question, not to deal with it in the hard outer light; but his own oblivions were too brief, too vain, to hurt any one but himself, and he had a vague and fanciful kindness for certain persons whom he met, figures of mystery and anxiety, and whom, with observation for his pastime, he ranked as those who were fleeing from justice. Justice was outside, in the hard light, and injustice too; but one was as absent as the other from the air of the long aisles and the brightness of the many altars.

Thus it was at all events that, one morning some dozen days after the dinner in the Boulevard Malesherbes at which Madame de Vionnet had been present with her daughter, he was called upon to play his part in an encounter that deeply stirred his imagination. He had the habit, in these contemplations, of watching a fellow visitant, here and there, from a respectable distance, remarking some note of behaviour, of penitence, of prostration, of the absolved, relieved state; this was the manner in which his vague tenderness took its course, the degree of demonstration to which it naturally had to confine itself. It hadn't indeed so felt its responsibility as when on this occasion he suddenly measured the suggestive effect of a lady whose supreme stillness, in the shade of one of the chapels, he had two or three times noticed as he made, and made once more, his slow circuit. She wasn't prostrate—not in any degree bowed, but she was strangely fixed, and her prolonged immobility showed her, while he passed and paused, as wholly given up to the need, whatever it was, that had brought her there. She only sat and gazed before her, as he himself often sat; but she had placed herself, as he never did, within the focus of the shrine, and she had lost herself, he could easily see, as he would only have liked to do. She was not a wandering alien, keeping back more than she gave, but one of the familiar, the intimate, the fortunate, for whom these dealings had a method and a meaning. She reminded our friend—since it was the way of nine tenths of his current impressions to act as recalls of things imagined—of some fine firm concentrated heroine of an old story, something he had heard, read, something that, had he had a hand for drama, he might himself have written, renewing her courage, renewing her clearness, in splendidly-protected meditation. Her back, as she sat, was turned to him, but his impression absolutely required that she should be young and interesting, and she carried her head moreover, even in the sacred shade, with a discernible faith in herself, a kind of implied conviction of consistency, security, impunity. But what had such a woman come for if she hadn't come to pray? Strether's reading of such matters was, it must be owned, confused; but he wondered if her attitude were some congruous fruit of absolution, of "indulgence." He knew but dimly what indulgence, in such a place, might mean; yet he had, as with a soft sweep, a vision of how it might indeed add to the zest of active rites. All this was a good deal to have been denoted by a mere lurking figure who was nothing to him; but, the last thing before leaving the church, he had the surprise of a still deeper quickening.

He had dropped upon a seat halfway down the nave and, again in the museum mood, was trying with head thrown back and eyes aloft, to reconstitute a past, to reduce it in fact to the convenient terms of Victor Hugo,[3] whom, a few days before, giving the rein for

3. Although Victor Hugo (1802–85), the famous Romantic French poet and novelist, was not one of his favorite authors, James did profess, in his 1866 review of *Les Travailleurs de la*

once in a way to the joy of life, he had purchased in seventy bound volumes, a miracle of cheapness, parted with, he was assured by the shopman, at the price of the red-and-gold alone. He looked, doubtless, while he played his eternal nippers over Gothic glooms, sufficiently rapt in reverence; but what his thought had finally bumped against was the question of where, among packed accumulations, so multiform a wedge would be able to enter. Were seventy volumes in red-and-gold to be perhaps what he should most substantially have to show at Woollett as the fruit of his mission? It was a possibility that held him a minute—held him till he happened to feel that some one, unnoticed, had approached him and paused. Turning, he saw that a lady stood there as for a greeting, and he sprang up as he next took her, securely, for Madame de Vionnet, who appeared to have recognised him as she passed near him on her way to the door. She checked, quickly and gaily, a certain confusion in him, came to meet it, turned it back, by an art of her own; the confusion having threatened him as he knew her for the person he had lately been observing. She was the lurking figure of the dim chapel; she had occupied him more than she guessed; but it came to him in time, luckily, that he needn't tell her and that no harm, after all, had been done. She herself, for that matter, straightway showing she felt their encounter as the happiest of accidents, had for him a "You come here too?" that despoiled surprise of every awkwardness.

"I come often," she said. "I love this place, but I'm terrible, in general, for churches. The old women who live in them all know me; in fact I'm already myself one of the old women. It's like that, at all events, that I foresee I shall end." Looking about for a chair, so that he instantly pulled one nearer, she sat down with him again to the sound of an "Oh, I like so much your also being fond—!"

He confessed the extent of his feeling, though she left the object vague; and he was struck with the tact, the taste of her vagueness, which simply took for granted in him a sense of beautiful things. He was conscious of how much it was affected, this sense, by something subdued and discreet in the way she had arranged herself for her special object and her morning walk—he believed her to have come on foot; the way her slightly thicker veil was drawn—a mere touch, but everything; the composed gravity of her dress, in which, here and there, a dull wine-colour seemed to gleam faintly through black; the charming discretion of her small compact head; the quiet note, as she sat, of her folded, grey-gloved hands. It was, to

mer, an "enormous respect for M. Hugo's heart" (Henry James, "Les Travailleurs de la mer," *Literary Criticism: French Writers. Other European Writers. The Prefaces to the New York Edition,* ed. Leon Edel and Mark Wilson [New York: Library of America, 1984], p. 454). The publication of an edition of Hugo's works in 58 volumes was completed in 1902.

Strether's mind, as if she sat on her own ground, the light honours of which, at an open gate, she thus easily did him, while all the vastness and mystery of the domain stretched off behind. When people were so completely in possession they could be extraordinarily civil; and our friend had indeed at this hour a kind of revelation of her heritage. She was romantic for him far beyond what she could have guessed, and again he found his small comfort in the conviction that, subtle though she was, his impression must remain a secret from her. The thing that, once more, made him uneasy for secrets in general was this particular patience she could have with his own want of colour; albeit that on the other hand his uneasiness pretty well dropped after he had been for ten minutes as colourless as possible and at the same time as responsive.

The moments had already, for that matter, drawn their deepest tinge from the special interest excited in him by his vision of his companion's identity with the person whose attitude before the glimmering altar had so impressed him. This attitude fitted admirably into the stand he had privately taken about her connexion with Chad on the last occasion of his seeing them together. It helped him to stick fast at the point he had then reached; it was there he had resolved that he *would* stick, and at no moment since had it seemed as easy to do so. Unassailably innocent was a relation that could make one of the parties to it so carry herself. If it wasn't innocent why did she haunt the churches?—into which, given the woman he could believe he made out, she would never have come to flaunt an insolence of guilt. She haunted them for continued help, for strength, for peace—sublime support which, if one were able to look at it so, she found from day to day. They talked, in low easy tones and with lifted lingering looks, about the great monument and its history and its beauty—all of which, Madame de Vionnet professed, came to her most in the other, the outer view. "We'll presently, after we go," she said, "walk round it again if you like. I'm not in a particular hurry, and it will be pleasant to look at it well with you." He had spoken of the great romancer and the great romance,[4] and of what, to his imagination, they had done for the whole, mentioning to her moreover the exorbitance of his purchase, the seventy blazing volumes that were so out of proportion.

"Out of proportion to what?"

"Well, to any other plunge." Yet he felt even as he spoke how at that instant he was plunging. He had made up his mind and was impatient to get into the air; for his purpose was a purpose to be uttered outside, and he had a fear that it might with delay still slip

---

4. Hugo's *Notre-Dame de Paris* (1831)—better known to moviegoers as *The Hunchback of Notre Dame*.

away from him. She however took her time; she drew out their quiet gossip as if she had wished to profit by their meeting, and this confirmed precisely an interpretation of her manner, of her mystery. While she rose, as he would have called it, to the question of Victor Hugo, her voice itself, the light low quaver of her deference to the solemnity about them, seemed to make her words mean something that they didn't mean openly. Help, strength, peace, a sublime support—she hadn't found so much of these things as that the amount wouldn't be sensibly greater for any scrap his appearance of faith in her might enable her to feel in her hand. Every little, in a long strain, helped, and if he happened to affect her as a firm object she could hold on by, he wouldn't jerk himself out of her reach. People in difficulties held on by what was nearest, and he was perhaps after all not further off than sources of comfort more abstract. It was as to this he had made up his mind; he had made it up, that is, to give her a sign. The sign would be that—though it was her own affair—he understood; the sign would be that—though it was her own affair—she was free to clutch. Since she took him for a firm object—much as he might to his own sense appear at times to rock—he would do his best to *be* one.

The end of it was that half an hour later they were seated together for an early luncheon at a wonderful, a delightful house of entertainment on the left bank—a place of pilgrimage for the knowing, they were both aware, the knowing who came, for its great renown, the homage of restless days, from the other end of the town. Strether had already been there three times—first with Miss Gostrey, then with Chad, then with Chad again and with Waymarsh and little Bilham, all of whom he had himself sagaciously entertained; and his pleasure was deep now on learning that Madame de Vionnet hadn't yet been initiated. When he had said, as they strolled round the church, by the river, acting at last on what, within, he had made up his mind to, "Will you, if you have time, come to déjeuner with me somewhere? For instance, if you know it, over there on the other side, which is so easy a walk"— and then had named the place; when he had done this she stopped short as for quick intensity, and yet deep difficulty, of response. She took in the proposal as if it were almost too charming to be true; and there had perhaps never yet been for her companion so unexpected a moment of pride—so fine, so odd a case, at any rate, as his finding himself thus able to offer to a person in such universal possession a new, a rare amusement. She had heard of the happy spot, but she asked him in reply to a further question how in the world he could suppose her to have been there. He supposed himself to have supposed that Chad might have taken her, and she guessed this the next moment, to his no small discomfort.

"Ah, let me explain," she smiled, "that I don't go about with him in public; I never have such chances—not having them otherwise—and it's just the sort of thing that, as a quiet creature living in my hole, I adore." It was more than kind of him to have thought of it—though, frankly, if he asked whether she had time she hadn't a single minute. That however made no difference—she'd throw everything over. Every duty at home, domestic, maternal, social, awaited her; but it was a case for a high line. Her affairs would go to smash, but hadn't one a right to one's snatch of scandal when one was prepared to pay? It was on this pleasant basis of costly disorder, consequently, that they eventually seated themselves, on either side of a small table, at a window adjusted to the busy quay and the shining barge-burdened Seine; where, for an hour, in the matter of letting himself go, of diving deep, Strether was to feel he had touched bottom. He was to feel many things on this occasion, and one of the first of them was that he had travelled far since that evening in London, before the theatre, when his dinner with Maria Gostrey, between the pink-shaded candles, had struck him as requiring so many explanations. He had at that time gathered them in, the explanations—he had stored them up; but it was at present as if he had either soared above or sunk below them—he couldn't tell which; he could somehow think of none that didn't seem to leave the appearance of collapse and cynicism easier for him than lucidity. How could he wish it to be lucid for others, for any one, that he, for the hour, saw reasons enough in the mere way the bright clean ordered water-side life came in at the open window?—the mere way Madame de Vionnet, opposite him over their intensely white table-linen, their *omelette aux tomates*,[5] their bottle of straw-coloured Chablis,[6] thanked him for everything almost with the smile of a child, while her grey eyes moved in and out of their talk, back to the quarter of the warm spring air, in which early summer had already begun to throb, and then back again to his face and their human questions.

Their human questions became many before they had done—many more, as one after the other came up, than our friend's free fancy had at all foreseen. The sense he had had before, the sense he had had repeatedly, the sense that the situation was running away with him, had never been so sharp as now; and all the more that he could perfectly put his finger on the moment it had taken the bit in its teeth. That accident had definitely occurred, the other evening, after Chad's dinner; it had occurred, as he fully knew, at the moment when he interposed between this lady and her child, when he suffered himself so to discuss with her a matter closely concerning them that her own subtlety, marked by its

5. Tomato omelet.
6. A white Burgundy wine.

significant "Thank you!" instantly sealed the occasion in her favour. Again he had held off for ten days, but the situation had continued out of hand in spite of that; the fact that it was running so fast being indeed just *why* he had held off. What had come over him as he recognised her in the nave of the church was that holding off could be but a losing game from the instant she was worked for not only by her subtlety, but by the hand of fate itself. If all the accidents were to fight on her side—and by the actual showing they loomed large—he could only give himself up. This was what he had done in privately deciding then and there to propose she should breakfast with him. What did the success of his proposal in fact resemble but the smash in which a regular runaway properly ends? The smash was their walk, their déjeuner, their omelette, the Chablis, the place, the view, their present talk and his present pleasure in it—to say nothing, wonder of wonders, of her own. To this tune and nothing less, accordingly, was his surrender made good. It sufficiently lighted up at least the folly of holding off. Ancient proverbs sounded, for his memory, in the tone of their words and the clink of their glasses, in the hum of the town and the plash of the river. It *was* clearly better to suffer as a sheep than as a lamb. One might as well perish by the sword as by famine.

"Maria's still away?"—that was the first thing she had asked him; and when he had found the frankness to be cheerful about it in spite of the meaning he knew her to attach to Miss Gostrey's absence, she had gone on to enquire if he didn't tremendously miss her. There were reasons that made him by no means sure, yet he nevertheless answered "Tremendously"; which she took in as if it were all she had wished to prove. Then, "A man in trouble *must* be possessed somehow of a woman," she said; "if she doesn't come in one way she comes in another."

"Why do you call me a man in trouble?"

"Ah because that's the way you strike me." She spoke ever so gently and as if with all fear of wounding him while she sat partaking of his bounty. "*Aren't* you in trouble?"

He felt himself colour at the question, and then hated that—hated to pass for anything so idiotic as woundable. Woundable by Chad's lady, in respect to whom he had come out with such a fund of indifference—was he already at that point? Perversely, none the less, his pause gave a strange air of truth to her supposition; and what was he in fact but disconcerted at having struck her just in the way he had most dreamed of not doing? "I'm not in trouble yet," he at last smiled. "I'm not in trouble now."

"Well, I'm always so. But that you sufficiently know." She was a woman who, between courses, could be graceful with her elbows on the table. It was a posture unknown to Mrs. Newsome, but it was easy for a *femme du monde.* "Yes—I am 'now'!"

"There was a question you put to me," he presently returned, "the night of Chad's dinner. I didn't answer it then, and it has been very handsome of you not to have sought an occasion for pressing me about it since."

She was instantly all there. "Of course I know what you allude to. I asked you what you had meant by saying, the day you came to see me, just before you left me, that you'd save me. And you then said —at our friend's—that you'd have really to wait to see, for yourself, what you did mean."

"Yes, I asked for time," said Strether. "And it sounds now, as you put it, like a very ridiculous speech."

"Oh!" she murmured—she was full of attenuation. But she had another thought. "If it does sound ridiculous why do you deny that you're in trouble?"

"Ah if I were," he replied, "it wouldn't be the trouble of fearing ridicule. I don't fear it."

"What then do you?"

"Nothing—now." And he leaned back in his chair.

"I like your 'now'!" she laughed across at him.

"Well, it's precisely that it fully comes to me at present that I've kept you long enough. I know by this time, at any rate, what I meant by my speech; and I really knew it the night of Chad's dinner."

"Then why didn't you tell me?"

"Because it was difficult at the moment. I had already at that moment done something for you, in the sense of what I had said the day I went to see you; but I wasn't then sure of the importance I might represent this as having."

She was all eagerness. "And you're sure now?"

"Yes; I see that, practically, I've done for you—had done for you when you put me your question—all that it's as yet possible to me to do. I feel now," he went on, "that it may go further than I thought. What I did after my visit to you," he explained, "was to write straight off to Mrs. Newsome about you, and I'm at last, from one day to the other, expecting her answer. It's this answer that will represent, as I believe, the consequences."

Patient and beautiful was her interest. "I see—the consequences of your speaking for me." And she waited as if not to hustle him.

He acknowledged it by immediately going on. "The question, you understand, was *how* I should save you. Well, I'm trying it by thus letting her know that I consider you worth saving."

"I see—I see." Her eagerness broke through.

"How can I thank you enough?" He couldn't tell her that, however, and she quickly pursued. "You do really, for yourself, consider it?"

His only answer at first was to help her to the dish that had been freshly put before them. "I've written to her again since then —I've left her in no doubt of what I think. I've told her all about you."

"Thanks—not so much. 'All about' me," she went on—"yes."

"All it seems to me you've done for him."

"Ah and you might have added all it seems to *me!*" She laughed again, while she took up her knife and fork, as in the cheer of these assurances. "But you're not sure how she'll take it."

"No, I'll not pretend I'm sure."

"Voilà." And she waited a moment. "I wish you'd tell me about her."

"Oh," said Strether with a slightly strained smile, "all that need concern you about her is that she's really a grand person."

Madame de Vionnet seemed to demur. "Is that all that need concern me about her?"

But Strether neglected the question. "Hasn't Chad talked to you?"

"Of his mother? Yes, a great deal—immensely. But not from your point of view."

"He can't," our friend returned, "have said any ill of her."

"Not the least bit. He has given me, like you, the assurance that she's really grand. But her being really grand is somehow just what hasn't seemed to simplify our case. Nothing," she continued, "is further from me than to wish to say a word against her; but of course I feel how little she can like being told of her owing me anything. No woman ever enjoys such an obligation to another woman."

This was a proposition Strether couldn't contradict. "And yet what other way could I have expressed to her what I felt? It's what there was most to say about you."

"Do you mean then that she *will* be good to me?"

"It's what I'm waiting to see. But I've little doubt she would," he added, "if she could comfortably see you."

It seemed to strike her as a happy, a beneficent thought. "Oh then couldn't that be managed? Wouldn't she come out? Wouldn't she if you so put it to her? *Did* you by any possibility?" she faintly quavered.

"Oh no"—he was prompt. "Not that. It would be, much more, to give an account of you that—since there's no question of *your* paying the visit—I should go home first."

It instantly made her graver. "And are you thinking of that?"

"Oh all the while, naturally."

"Stay with us—stay with us!" she exclaimed on this. "That's your only way to make sure."

"To make sure of what?"

"Why that he doesn't break up. You didn't come out to do that to him."

"Doesn't it depend," Strether returned after a moment, "on what you mean by breaking up?"

"Oh you know well enough what I mean!"

His silence seemed again for a little to denote an understanding. "You take for granted remarkable things."

"Yes, I do—to the extent that I don't take for granted vulgar ones. You're perfectly capable of seeing that what you came out for wasn't really at all to do what you'd now have to do."

"Ah it's perfectly simple," Strether good-humouredly pleaded. "I've had but one thing to do—to put our case before him. To put it as it could only be put here on the spot—by personal pressure. My dear lady," he lucidly pursued, "my work, you see, is really done, and my reasons for staying on even another day are none of the best. Chad's in possession of our case and professes to do it full justice. What remains is with himself. I've had my rest, my amusement and refreshment; I've had, as we say at Woollett, a lovely time. Nothing in it has been more lovely than this happy meeting with you—in these fantastic conditions to which you've so delightfully consented. I've a sense of success. It's what I wanted. My getting all this good is what Chad has waited for, and I gather that if I'm ready to go he's the same."

She shook her head with a finer deeper wisdom. "You're not ready. If you're ready why did you write to Mrs. Newsome in the sense you've mentioned to me?"

Strether considered. "I shan't go before I hear from her. You're too much afraid of her," he added.

It produced between them a long look from which neither shrank. "I don't think you believe that—believe I've not really reason to fear her."

"She's capable of great generosity," Strether presently stated.

"Well then let her trust me a little. That's all I ask. Let her recognise in spite of everything what I've done."

"Ah remember," our friend replied, "that she can't effectually recognise it without seeing it for herself. Let Chad go over and show her what you've done, and let him plead with her there for it and, as it were, for *you*."

She measured the depth of this suggestion. "Do you give me your word of honour that if she once has him there she won't do her best to marry him?"

It made her companion, this enquiry, look again a while out at the view; after which he spoke without sharpness. "When she sees for herself what he is—"

But she had already broken in. "It's when she sees for herself what he is that she'll want to marry him most."

Strether's attitude, that of due deference to what she said, permitted him to attend for a minute to his luncheon. "I doubt if that will come off. It won't be easy to make it."

"It will be easy if he remains there—and he'll remain for the money. The money appears to be, as a probability, so hideously much."

"Well," Strether presently concluded, "nothing *could* really hurt you but his marrying."

She gave a strange light laugh. "Putting aside what may really hurt *him.*"

But her friend looked at her as if he had thought of that too. "The question will come up, of course, of the future that you yourself offer him."

She was leaning back now, but she fully faced him. "Well, let it come up!"

"The point is that it's for Chad to make of it what he can. His being proof against marriage will show what he does make."

"If he *is* proof, yes"—she accepted the proposition. "But for myself," she added, "the question is what *you* make."

"Ah I make nothing. It's not my affair."

"I beg your pardon. It's just there that, since you've taken it up and are committed to it, it most intensely becomes yours. You're not saving me, I take it, for your interest in myself, but for your interest in our friend. The one's at any rate wholly dependent on the other. You can't in honour not see me through," she wound up, "because you can't in honour not see *him.*"

Strange and beautiful to him was her quiet soft acuteness. The thing that most moved him was really that she was so deeply serious. She had none of the portentous forms of it, but he had never come in contact, it struck him, with a force brought to so fine a head. Mrs. Newsome, goodness knew, was serious; but it was nothing to this. He took it all in, he saw it all together. "No," he mused, "I can't in honour not see him."

Her face affected him as with an exquisite light. "You *will* then?"

"I will."

At this she pushed back her chair and was the next moment on her feet. "Thank you!" she said with her hand held out to him across the table and with no less a meaning in the words than her lips had so particularly given them after Chad's dinner. The golden nail she had then driven in pierced a good inch deeper. Yet he reflected that he himself had only meanwhile done what he had made up his mind to on the same occasion. So far as the essence of the matter went he had simply stood fast on the spot on which he had then planted his feet.

II [XVII]

He received three days after this a communication from America, in the form of a scrap of blue paper folded and gummed, not reaching him through his bankers, but delivered at his hotel by a small boy in uniform, who, under instructions from the concierge, approached him as he slowly paced the little court. It was the evening hour, but daylight was long now and Paris more than ever penetrating. The scent of flowers was in the streets, he had the whiff of violets perpetually in his nose; and he had attached himself to sounds and suggestions, vibrations of the air, human and dramatic, he imagined, as they were not in other places, that came out for him more and more as the mild afternoons deepened —a far-off hum, a sharp near click on the asphalt, a voice calling, replying, somewhere and as full of tone as an actor's in a play. He was to dine at home, as usual, with Waymarsh—they had settled to that for thrift and simplicity; and he now hung about before his friend came down.

He read his telegram in the court, standing still a long time where he had opened it and giving five minutes afterwards to the renewed study of it. At last, quickly, he crumpled it up as if to get it out of the way; in spite of which, however, he kept it there —still kept it when, at the end of another turn, he had dropped into a chair placed near a small table. Here, with his scrap of paper compressed in his fist and further concealed by his folding his arms tight, he sat for some time in thought, gazed before him so straight that Waymarsh appeared and approached him without catching his eye. The latter in fact, struck with his appearance, looked at him hard for a single instant and then, as if determined to that course by some special vividness in it, dropped back into the *salon de lecture*[7] without addressing him. But the pilgrim from Milrose permitted himself still to observe the scene from behind the clear glass plate of that retreat. Strether ended, as he sat, by a fresh scrutiny of his compressed missive, which he smoothed out carefully again as he placed it on his table. There it remained for some minutes, until, at last looking up, he saw Waymarsh watching him from within. It was on this that their eyes met—met for a moment during which neither moved. But Strether then got up, folding his telegram more carefully and putting it into his waistcoat pocket.

A few minutes later the friends were seated together at dinner; but Strether had meanwhile said nothing about it, and they

7. Reading room.

eventually parted, after coffee in the court, with nothing said on either side. Our friend had moreover the consciousness that even less than usual was on this occasion said between them, so that it was almost as if each had been waiting for something from the other. Waymarsh had always more or less the air of sitting at the door of his tent, and silence, after so many weeks, had come to play its part in their concert. This note indeed, to Strether's sense, had lately taken a fuller tone, and it was his fancy to-night that they had never quite so drawn it out. Yet it befell, none the less, that he closed the door to confidence when his companion finally asked him if there were anything particular the matter with him. "Nothing," he replied, "more than usual."

On the morrow, however, at an early hour, he found occasion to give an answer more in consonance with the facts. What was the matter had continued to be so all the previous evening, the first hours of which, after dinner, in his room, he had devoted to the copious composition of a letter. He had quitted Waymarsh for this purpose, leaving him to his own resources with less ceremony than their wont, but finally coming down again with his letter un-concluded and going forth into the streets without enquiry for his comrade. He had taken a long vague walk, and one o'clock had struck before his return and his re-ascent to his room by the aid of the glimmering candle-end left for him on the shelf outside the porter's lodge. He had possessed himself, on closing his door, of the numerous loose sheets of his unfinished composition, and then, without reading them over, had torn them into small pieces. He had thereupon slept—as if it had been in some measure thanks to that sacrifice—the sleep of the just, and had prolonged his rest considerably beyond his custom. Thus it was that when, between nine and ten, the tap of the knob of a walking-stick sounded on his door, he had not yet made himself altogether presentable. Chad Newsome's bright deep voice determined quickly enough none the less the admission of the visitor. The little blue paper of the evening before, plainly an object the more precious for its escape from premature destruction, now lay on the sill of the open window, smoothed out afresh and kept from blowing away by the superincumbent weight of his watch. Chad, looking about with careless and competent criticism, as he looked wherever he went, immediately espied it and permitted himself to fix it for a moment rather hard. After which he turned his eyes to his host. "It has come then at last?"

Strether paused in the act of pinning his necktie. "Then you know—? You've had one too?"

"No, I've had nothing, and I only know what I see. I see that thing and I guess. Well," he added, "it comes as pat as in a play, for I've precisely turned up this morning—as I would have done yesterday, but it was impossible—to take you."

"To take me?" Strether had turned again to his glass.

"Back, at last, as I promised. I'm ready—I've really been ready this month. I've only been waiting for you—as was perfectly right. But you're better now; you're safe—I see that for myself; you've got all your good. You're looking, this morning, as fit as a flea."

Strether, at his glass, finished dressing; consulting that witness moreover on this last opinion. Was he looking preternaturally fit? There was something in it perhaps for Chad's wonderful eye, but he had felt himself for hours rather in pieces. Such a judgement, however, was after all but a contribution to his resolve; it testified unwittingly to his wisdom. He was still firmer, apparently—since it shone in him as a light—than he had flattered himself. His firmness indeed was slightly compromised, as he faced about to his friend, by the way this very personage looked—though the case would of course have been worse hadn't the secret of personal magnificence been at every hour Chad's unfailing possession. There he was in all the pleasant morning freshness of it—strong and sleek and gay, easy and fragrant and fathomless, with happy health in his colour, and pleasant silver in his thick young hair, and the right word for everything on the lips that his clear brownness caused to show as red. He had never struck Strether as personally such a success; it was as if now, for his definite surrender, he had gathered himself vividly together. This, sharply and rather strangely, was the form in which he was to be presented to Woollett. Our friend took him in again—he was always taking him in and yet finding that parts of him still remained out; though even thus his image showed through a mist of other things. "I've had a cable," Strether said, "from your mother."

"I dare say, my dear man. I hope she's well."

Strether hesitated. "No—she's not well, I'm sorry to have to tell you."

"Ah," said Chad, "I must have had the instinct of it. All the more reason then that we should start straight off."

Strether had now got together hat, gloves and stick, but Chad had dropped on the sofa as if to show where he wished to make his point. He kept observing his companion's things; he might have been judging how quickly they could be packed. He might even have wished to hint that he'd send his own servant to assist. "What do you mean," Strether enquired, "by 'straight off'?"

"Oh by one of next week's boats. Everything at this season goes out so light that berths will be easy anywhere."

Strether had in his hand his telegram, which he had kept there after attaching his watch, and he now offered it to Chad, who, however, with an odd movement, declined to take it. "Thanks, I'd rather not. Your correspondence with Mother's your own affair. I'm only *with* you both on it, whatever it is." Strether, at this, while their eyes met, slowly folded the missive and put it in his pocket; after which, before he had spoken again, Chad broke fresh ground. "Has Miss Gostrey come back?"

But when Strether presently spoke it wasn't in answer. "It's not, I gather, that your mother's physically ill; her health, on the whole, this spring, seems to have been better than usual. But she's worried, she's anxious, and it appears to have risen within the last few days to a climax. We've tired out, between us, her patience."

"Oh it isn't *you!*" Chad generously protested.

"I beg your pardon—it *is* me." Strether was mild and melancholy, but firm. He saw it far away and over his companion's head. "It's very particularly me."

"Well then all the more reason. *Marchons, marchons!*"[8] said the young man gaily. His host, however, at this, but continued to stand agaze; and he had the next thing repeated his question of a moment before. "Has Miss Gostrey come back?"

"Yes, two days ago."

"Then you've seen her?"

"No—I'm to see her to-day." But Strether wouldn't linger now on Miss Gostrey. "Your mother sends me an ultimatum. If I can't bring you I'm to leave you; I'm to come at any rate myself."

"Ah but you *can* bring me now," Chad, from his sofa, reassuringly replied.

Strether had a pause. "I don't think I understand you. Why was it that, more than a month ago, you put it to me so urgently to let Madame de Vionnet speak for you?"

" 'Why'?" Chad considered, but he had it at his fingers' ends. "Why but because I knew how well she'd do it? It was the way to keep you quiet and, to that extent, do you good. Besides," he happily and comfortably explained, "I wanted you really to know her and to get the impression of her—and you see the good that *has* done you."

"Well," said Strether, "the way she has spoken for you, all the same—so far as I've given her a chance—has only made me feel how much she wishes to keep you. If you make nothing of that I don't see why you wanted me to listen to her."

"Why my dear man," Chad exclaimed, "I make everything of it! How can you doubt—?"

"I doubt only because you come to me this morning with your

---

8. "Let us march, let us march!"—from the refrain of *Le Marseillaise*, the French national anthem.

signal to start."

Chad stared, then gave a laugh. "And isn't my signal to start just what you've been waiting for?"

Strether debated; he took another turn. "This last month I've been awaiting, I think, more than anything else, the message I have here."

"You mean you've been afraid of it?"

"Well, I was doing my business in my own way. And I suppose your present announcement," Strether went on, "isn't merely the result of your sense of what I've expected. Otherwise you wouldn't have put me in relation—" But he paused, pulling up.

At this Chad rose. "Ah *her* wanting me not to go has nothing to do with it! It's only because she's afraid—afraid of the way that, over there, I may get caught. But her fear's groundless."

He had met again his companion's sufficiently searching look. "Are you tired of her?"

Chad gave him in reply to this, with a movement of the head, the strangest slow smile he had ever had from him. "Never."

It had immediately, on Strether's imagination, so deep and soft an effect that our friend could only for the moment keep it before him. "Never?"

"Never," Chad obligingly and serenely repeated.

It made his companion take several more steps. "Then *you're* not afraid."

"Afraid to go?"

Strether pulled up again. "Afraid to stay."

The young man looked brightly amazed. "You want me now to 'stay'?"

"If I don't immediately sail the Pococks will immediately come out. That's what I mean," said Strether, "by your mother's ultimatum."

Chad showed a still livelier, but not an alarmed interest. "She has turned on Sarah and Jim?"

Strether joined him for an instant in the vision. "Oh and you may be sure Mamie. *That's* whom she's turning on."

This also Chad saw—he laughed out. "Mamie—to corrupt me?"

"Ah," said Strether, "she's very charming."

"So you've already more than once told me. I should like to see her."

Something happy and easy, something above all unconscious, in the way he said this, brought home again to his companion the facility of his attitude and the enviability of his state. "See her then by all means. And consider too," Strether went on, "that you really give your sister a lift in letting her come to you. You give her a couple of months of Paris, which she hasn't seen, if I'm not mistaken, since just after she was married, and which I'm sure she wants but the pretext to visit."

Chad listened, but with all his own knowledge of the world. "She has had it, the pretext, these several years, yet she has never taken it."

"Do you mean *you?*" Strether after an instant enquired.

"Certainly—the lone exile. And whom do you mean?" said Chad.

"Oh I mean *me*. I'm her pretext. That is—for it comes to the same thing—I'm your mother's."

"Then why," Chad asked, "doesn't Mother come herself?"

His friend gave him a long look. "Should you like her to?" And as he for the moment said nothing: "It's perfectly open to you to cable for her."

Chad continued to think. "Will she come if I do?"

"Quite possibly. But try, and you'll see."

"Why don't *you* try?" Chad after a moment asked.

"Because I don't want to."

Chad thought. "Don't desire her presence here?"

Strether faced the question, and his answer was the more emphatic. "Don't put it off, my dear boy, on *me!*"

"Well—I see what you mean. I'm sure you'd behave beautifully, but you *don't* want to see her. So I won't play you that trick."

"Ah," Strether declared, "I shouldn't call it a trick. You've a perfect right, and it would be perfectly straight of you." Then he added in a different tone: "You'd have moreover, in the person of Madame de Vionnet, a very interesting relation prepared for her."

Their eyes, on this proposition, continued to meet, but Chad's, pleasant and bold, never flinched for a moment. He got up at last, and he said something with which Strether was struck. "She wouldn't understand her, but that makes no difference. Madame de Vionnet would like to see her. She'd like to be charming to her. She believes she could work it."

Strether thought a moment, affected by this, but finally turning away. "She couldn't!"

"You're quite sure?" Chad asked.

"Well, risk it if you like!"

Strether, who uttered this with serenity, had urged a plea for their now getting into the air; but the young man still waited. "Have you sent your answer?"

"No, I've done nothing yet."

"Were you waiting to see me?"

"No, not that."

"Only waiting"—and Chad, with this, had a smile for him—"to

see Miss Gostrey?"

"No—not even Miss Gostrey. I wasn't waiting to see any one. I had only waited, till now, to make up my mind—in complete solitude; and, since I of course absolutely owe you the information, was on the point of going out with it quite made up. Have therefore a little more patience with me. Remember," Strether went on, "that that's what you originally asked *me* to have. I've had it, you see, and you see what has come of it. Stay on with me."

Chad looked grave. "How much longer?"

"Well, till I make you a sign. I can't myself, you know, at the best, or at the worst, stay for ever. Let the Pococks come," Strether repeated.

"Because it gains you time?"

"Yes—it gains me time."

Chad, as if it still puzzled him, waited a minute. "You don't want to get back to Mother?"

"Not just yet. I'm not ready."

"You feel," Chad asked in a tone of his own, "the charm of life over here?"

"Immensely." Strether faced it. "You've helped me so to feel it that that surely needn't surprise you."

"No, it doesn't surprise me, and I'm delighted. But what, my dear man," Chad went on with conscious queerness, "does it all lead to for you?"

The change of position and of relation, for each, was so oddly betrayed in the question that Chad laughed out as soon as he had uttered it—which made Strether also laugh. "Well, to my having a certitude that has been tested—that has passed through the fire. But oh," he couldn't help breaking out, "if within my first month here you had been willing to move with me—!"

"Well?" said Chad, while he broke down as for weight of thought.

"Well, we should have been over there by now."

"Ah but you wouldn't have had your fun!"

"I should have had a month of it; and I'm having now, if you want to know," Strether continued, "enough to last me for the rest of my days."

Chad looked amused and interested, yet still somewhat in the dark; partly perhaps because Strether's estimate of fun had required of him from the first a good deal of elucidation. "It wouldn't do if I left you—?"

"Left me?"—Strether remained blank.

"Only for a month or two—time to go and come. Madame de Vionnet," Chad smiled, "would look after you in the interval."

"To go back by yourself, I remaining here?" Again for an instant their eyes had the question out; after which Strether said: "Grotesque!"

"But I want to see Mother," Chad presently returned. "Remember how long it is since I've seen Mother."

"Long indeed; and that's exactly why I was originally so keen for moving you. Hadn't you shown us enough how beautifully you could do without it?"

"Oh but," said Chad wonderfully, "I'm better now."

There was an easy triumph in it that made his friend laugh out again. "Oh if you were worse I *should* know what to do with you. In that case I believe I'd have you gagged and strapped down, carried on board resisting, kicking. How *much*," Strether asked, "do you want to see Mother?"

"How much?"—Chad seemed to find it in fact difficult to say.

"How much."

"Why as much as you've made me. I'd give anything to see her. And you've left me," Chad went on, "in little enough doubt as to how much *she* wants it."

Strether thought a minute. "Well then if those things are really your motive catch the French steamer and sail to-morrow. Of course, when it comes to that, you're absolutely free to do as you choose. From the moment you can't hold yourself I can only accept your flight."

"I'll fly in a minute then," said Chad, "if you'll stay here."

"I'll stay here till the next steamer—then I'll follow you."

"And do you call that," Chad asked, "accepting my flight?"

"Certainly—it's the only thing to call it. The only way to keep me here, accordingly," Strether explained, "is by staying yourself."

Chad took it in. "All the more that I've really dished you, eh?"

"Dished me?" Strether echoed as inexpressively as possible.

"Why if she sends out the Pococks it will be that she doesn't trust you, and if she doesn't trust you, that bears upon—well, you know what."

Strether decided after a moment that he did know what, and in consonance with this he spoke. "You see then all the more what you owe me."

"Well, if I do see, how can I pay?"

"By not deserting me. By standing by me."

"Oh I say—!" But Chad, as they went downstairs, clapped a firm hand, in the manner of a pledge, upon his shoulder. They descended slowly together and had, in the court of the hotel, some further talk, of which the upshot was that they presently separated. Chad Newsome departed, and Strether, left alone, looked about, superficially, for Waymarsh. But Waymarsh hadn't yet, it appeared, come down, and our friend finally went forth without sight of him.

III [XVIII]

At four o'clock that afternoon he had still not seen him, but he was then, as to make up for this, engaged in talk about him with Miss Gostrey. Strether had kept away from home all day, given himself up to the town and to his thoughts, wandered and mused, been at once restless and absorbed—and all with the present climax of a rich little welcome in the Quartier Marbœuf. "Waymarsh has been, 'unbeknown' to me, I'm convinced"—for Miss Gostrey had enquired—"in communication with Woollett: the consequence of which was, last night, the loudest possible call for me."

"Do you mean a letter to bring you home?"

"No—a cable, which I have at this moment in my pocket: a 'Come back by the first ship.' "

Strether's hostess, it might have been made out, just escaped changing colour. Reflexion arrived but in time and established a provisional serenity. It was perhaps exactly this that enabled her to say with duplicity: "And you're going—?"

"You almost deserve it when you abandon me so."

She shook her head as if this were not worth taking up. "My absence has helped you—as I've only to look at you to see. It was my calculation, and I'm justified. You're not where you were. And the thing," she smiled, "was for me not to be there either. You can go of yourself."

"Oh but I feel to-day," he comfortably declared, "that I shall want you yet."

She took him all in again. "Well, I promise you not again to leave you, but it will only be to follow you. You've got your momentum and can toddle alone."

He intelligently accepted it. "Yes—I suppose I can toddle. It's the sight of that in fact that has upset Waymarsh. He can bear it —the way I strike him as going—no longer. That's only the climax of his original feeling. He wants me to quit; and he must have written to Woollett that I'm in peril of perdition."

"Ah good!" she murmured. "But is it only your supposition?"

"I make it out—it explains."

"Then he denies?—or you haven't asked him?"

"I've not had time," Strether said; "I made it out but last night, putting various things together, and I've not been since then face to face with him."

She wondered. "Because you're too disgusted? You can't trust yourself?"

He settled his glasses on his nose. "Do I look in a great rage?"

"You look divine!"

"There's nothing," he went on, "to be angry about. He has done me on the contrary a service."

She made it out. "By bringing things to a head?"

"How well you understand!" he almost groaned. "Waymarsh won't in the least, at any rate, when I have it out with him, deny or extenuate. He has acted from the deepest conviction, with the best conscience and after wakeful nights. He'll recognise that he's fully responsible, and will consider that he has been highly successful; so that any discussion we may have will bring us quite together again—bridge the dark stream that has kept us so thoroughly apart. We shall have at last, in the consequences of his act, something we can definitely talk about."

She was silent a little. "How wonderfully you take it! But you're always wonderful."

He had a pause that matched her own; then he had, with an adequate spirit, a complete admission. "It's quite true. I'm extremely wonderful just now. I dare say in fact I'm quite fantastic, and I shouldn't be at all surprised if I were mad."

"Then tell me!" she earnestly pressed. As he, however, for the time answered nothing, only returning the look with which she watched him, she presented herself where it was easier to meet her. "What will Mr. Waymarsh exactly have done?"

"Simply have written a letter. One will have been quite enough. He has told them I want looking after."

"And *do* you?"—she was all interest.

"Immensely. And I shall get it."

"By which you mean you don't budge?"

"I don't budge."

"You've cabled?"

"No—I've made Chad do it."

"That you decline to come?"

"That *he* declines. We had it out this morning and I brought him round. He had come in, before I was down, to tell me he was ready—ready, I mean, to return. And he went off, after ten minutes with me, to say he wouldn't."

Miss Gostrey followed with intensity. "Then you've *stopped* him?"

Strether settled himself afresh in his chair. "I've stopped him. That is for the time. That"—he gave it to her more vividly—"is where I am."

"I see, I see. But where's Mr. Newsome? He was ready," she asked, "to go?"

"All ready."

"And sincerely—believing *you'd* be?"

"Perfectly, I think; so that he was amazed to find the hand I had laid on him to pull him over suddenly converted into an engine for keeping him still."

It was an account of the matter Miss Gostrey could weigh. "Does he think the conversion sudden?"

"Well," said Strether, "I'm not altogether sure what he thinks. I'm not sure of anything that concerns him, except that the more I've seen of him the less I've found him what I originally expected. He's obscure, and that's why I'm waiting."

She wondered. "But for what in particular?"

"For the answer to his cable."

"And what was his cable?"

"I don't know," Strether replied; "it was to be, when he left me, according to his own taste. I simply said to him: 'I want to stay, and the only way for me to do so is for *you* to.' That I wanted to stay seemed to interest him, and he acted on that."

Miss Gostrey turned it over. "He wants then himself to stay."

"He half wants it. That is he half wants to go. My original appeal has to that extent worked in him. Nevertheless," Strether pursued, "he won't go. Not, at least, so long as I'm here."

"But you can't," his companion suggested, "stay here always. I wish you could."

"By no means. Still, I want to see him a little further. He's not in the least the case I supposed; he's quite another case. And it's as such that he interests me." It was almost as if for his own intelligence that, deliberate and lucid, our friend thus expressed the matter. "I don't want to give him up."

Miss Gostrey but desired to help his lucidity. She had however to be light and tactful. "Up, you mean—a—to his mother?"

"Well, I'm not thinking of his mother now. I'm thinking of the plan of which I was the mouthpiece, which, as soon as we met, I put before him as persuasively as I knew how, and which was drawn up, as it were, in complete ignorance of all that, in this last long period, has been happening to him. It took no account whatever of the impression I was here on the spot immediately to begin to receive from him—impressions of which I feel sure I'm far from having had the last."

Miss Gostrey had a smile of the most genial criticism. "So your idea is—more or less—to stay out of curiosity?"

"Call it what you like! I don't care what it's called—"

"So long as you do stay? Certainly not then. I call it, all the same, immense fun," Maria Gostrey declared; "and to see you work it out will be one of the sensations of my life. It *is* clear you can toddle alone!"

He received this tribute without elation. "I shan't be alone when the Pococks have come."

Her eyebrows went up. "The Pococks are coming?"

"That, I mean, is what will happen—and happen as quickly as possible—in consequence of Chad's cable. They'll simply embark. Sarah will come to speak for her mother—with an effect different from *my* muddle."

Miss Gostrey more gravely wondered. "*She* then will take him back?"

"Very possibly—and we shall see. She must at any rate have the chance, and she may be trusted to do all she can."

"And do you *want* that?"

"Of course," said Strether, "I want it. I want to play fair."

But she had lost for a moment the thread. "If it devolves on the Pococks why do you stay?"

"Just to see that I *do* play fair—and a little also, no doubt, that they do." Strether was luminous as he had never been. "I came out to find myself in presence of new facts—facts that have kept striking me as less and less met by our old reasons. The matter's perfectly simple. New reasons—reasons as new as the facts themselves—are wanted; and of this our friends at Woollett—Chad's and mine—were at the earliest moment definitely notified. If any are producible Mrs. Pocock will produce them; she'll bring over the whole collection. They'll be," he added with a pensive smile, "a part of the 'fun' you speak of."

She was quite in the current now and floating by his side. "It's Mamie—so far as I've had it from you—who'll be their great card." And then as his contemplative silence wasn't a denial she significantly added: "I think I'm sorry for her."

"I think I am!"—and Strether sprang up, moving about a little as her eyes followed him. "But it can't be helped."

"You mean her coming out can't be?"

He explained after another turn what he meant. "The only way for her not to come is for me to go home—as I believe that on the spot I could prevent it. But the difficulty as to that is that if I do go home—"

"I see, I see"—she had easily understood. "Mr. Newsome will do the same, and that's not"—she laughed out now—"to be thought of."

Strether had no laugh; he had only a quiet comparatively placid look that might have shown him as proof against ridicule. "Strange, isn't it?"

They had, in the matter that so much interested them, come so far as this without sounding another name—to which however their present momentary silence was full of a conscious reference. Strether's question was a sufficient implication of the weight it had gained with him during the absence of his hostess; and just for that reason a single gesture from her could pass for him as a vivid answer. Yet he was answered still better when she said in a moment: "Will Mr. Newsome introduce his sister—?"

"To Madame de Vionnet?" Strether spoke the name at last. "I shall be greatly surprised if he doesn't."

She seemed to gaze at the possibility. "You mean you've thought of it and you're prepared."

"I've thought of it and I'm prepared."

It was to her visitor now that she applied her consideration. "Bon! You *are* magnificent!"

"Well," he answered after a pause and a little wearily, but still standing there before her—"well, that's what, just once in all my dull days, I think I shall like to have been!"

Two days later he had news from Chad of a communication from Woollett in response to their determinant telegram, this missive being addressed to Chad himself and announcing the immediate departure for France of Sarah and Jim and Mamie. Strether had meanwhile on his own side cabled; he had but delayed that act till after his visit to Miss Gostrey, an interview by which, as so often before, he felt his sense of things cleared up and settled. His message to Mrs. Newsome, in answer to her own, had consisted of the words: "Judge best to take another month, but with full appreciation of all re-enforcements." He had added that he was writing, but he was of course always writing; it was a practice that continued, oddly enough, to relieve him, to make him come nearer than anything else to the consciousness of doing something: so that he often wondered if he hadn't really, under his recent stress, acquired some hollow trick, one of the specious arts of make-believe. Wouldn't the pages he still so freely dispatched by the American post have been worthy of a showy journalist, some master of the great new science of beating the sense out of words? Wasn't he writing against time, and mainly to show he was kind? —since it had become quite his habit not to like to read himself over. On those lines he could still be liberal, yet it was at best a sort of whistling in the dark. It was unmistakeable moreover that the sense of being in the dark now pressed on him more sharply— creating thereby the need for a louder and livelier whistle. He whistled long and hard after sending his message; he whistled again and again in celebration of Chad's news; there was an interval of a fortnight in which this exercise helped him. He had no great notion of what, on the spot, Sarah Pocock would have to say, though he had indeed confused premonitions; but it shouldn't be in her power to say—it shouldn't be in any one's anywhere to say— that he was neglecting her mother. He might have written before more freely, but he had never written more copiously; and he frankly gave for a reason at Woollett that he wished to fill the void created there by Sarah's departure.

The increase of his darkness, however, and the quickening, as I have called it, of his tune, resided in the fact that he was hearing almost nothing. He had for some time been aware that he was hearing less than before, and he was now clearly following a process by which Mrs. Newsome's letters could but logically stop. He hadn't had a line for many days, and he needed no proof—though he was, in time, to have plenty—that she wouldn't have put pen to paper after receiving the hint that had determined her telegram. She wouldn't write till Sarah should have seen him and reported on him. It was strange, though it might well be less so than his own behaviour appeared at Woollett. It was at any rate significant, and what *was* remarkable was the way his friend's nature and manner put on for him, through this very drop of demonstration, a greater intensity. It struck him really that he had never so lived with her as during this period of her silence; the silence was a sacred hush, a finer clearer medium, in which her idiosyncrasies showed. He walked about with her, sat with her, drove with her and dined face-to-face with her—a rare treat "in his life," as he could perhaps have scarce escaped phrasing it; and if he had never seen her so soundless he had never, on the other hand, felt her so highly, so almost austerely, herself: pure and by the vulgar estimate "cold," but deep devoted delicate sensitive noble. Her vividness in these respects became for him, in the special conditions, almost an obsession; and though the obsession sharpened his pulses, adding really to the excitement of life, there were hours at which, to be less on the stretch, he directly sought forgetfulness. He knew it for the queerest of adventures—a circumstance capable of playing such a part only for Lambert Strether—that in Paris itself, of all places, he should find this ghost of the lady of Woollett more importunate than any other presence.

When he went back to Maria Gostrey it was for the change to something else. And yet after all the change scarcely operated, for he talked to her of Mrs. Newsome in these days as he had never talked before. He had hitherto observed in that particular a discretion and a law; considerations that at present broke down quite as if relations had altered. They hadn't *really* altered, he said to himself, so much as that came to; for if what had occurred was of course that Mrs. Newsome had ceased to trust him, there was nothing on the other hand to prove that he shouldn't win back her confidence. It was quite his present theory that he would leave no stone unturned to do so; and in fact if he now told Maria things about her that he had never told before this was largely because it kept before him the idea of the honour of such a woman's esteem. His relation with Maria as well was, strangely enough, no longer quite the same; this truth—though not too disconcertingly—had come up between them on the renewal of their meetings. It was all contained in what she had then almost immediately said to him; it was represented by the remark she had needed but ten minutes to make and that he hadn't been disposed to gainsay. He could toddle alone, and the difference that showed was extraordinary. The turn taken by their talk had promptly confirmed this difference; his larger confidence on the score of Mrs. Newsome did the rest; and the time seemed already far off when he had held out his small thirsty cup to the spout of her pail. Her pail was scarce touched now, and other fountains had flowed for him; she fell into her place as but one of his tributaries; and there was a strange sweetness— a melancholy mildness that touched him—in her acceptance of the altered order.

It marked for himself the flight of time, or at any rate what he was pleased to think of with irony and pity as the rush of experi- ence; it having been but the day before yesterday that he sat at her feet and held on by her garment and was fed by her hand. It was the proportions that were changed, and the proportions were at all times, he philosophised, the very conditions of perception, the terms of thought. It was as if, with her effective little entresol and her wide acquaintance, her activities, varieties, promiscuities, the duties and devotions that took up nine tenths of her time and of which he got, guardedly, but the side-wind—it was as if she had shrunk to a secondary element and had consented to the shrinkage with the perfection of tact. This perfection had never failed her; it had originally been greater than his prime measure for it; it had kept him quite apart, kept him out of the shop, as she called her huge general acquaintance, made their commerce as quiet, as much a thing of the home alone—the opposite of the shop—as if she had never another customer. She had been wonderful to him at first, with the memory of her little entresol, the image to which, on most mornings at that time, his eyes directly opened; but now she mainly figured for him as but part of the bristling total—though of course always as a person to whom he should never cease to be indebted. It would never be given to him certainly to inspire a greater kindness. She had decked him out for others, and he saw at this point at least nothing she would ever ask for. She only wondered and ques- tioned and listened, rendering him the homage of a wistful specula- tion. She expressed it repeatedly; he was already far beyond her, and she must prepare herself to lose him. There was but one little chance for her.

Often as she had said it he met it—for it was a touch he liked—

each time the same way. "My coming to grief?"

"Yes—then I might patch you up."

"Oh for my real smash, if it takes place, there will be no patching."

"But you surely don't mean it will kill you."

"No—worse. It will make me old."

"Ah nothing can do that! The wonderful and special thing about you is that you *are*, at this time of day, youth." Then she always made, further, one of those remarks that she had completely ceased to adorn with hesitations or apologies, and that had, by the same token, in spite of their extreme straightness, ceased to produce in Strether the least embarrassment. She made him believe them, and they became thereby as impersonal as truth itself. "It's just your particular charm."

His answer too was always the same. "Of course I'm youth—youth for the trip to Europe. I began to be young, or at least to get the benefit of it, the moment I met you at Chester, and that's what has been taking place ever since. I never had the benefit at the proper time—which comes to saying that I never had the thing itself. I'm having the benefit at this moment; I had it the other day when I said to Chad 'Wait'; I shall have it still again when Sarah Pocock arrives. It's a benefit that would make a poor show for many people; and I don't know who else but you and I, frankly, could begin to see in it what I feel. I don't get drunk; I don't pursue the ladies; I don't spend money; I don't even write sonnets. But nevertheless I'm making up late for what I didn't have early. I cultivate my little benefit in my own little way. It amuses me more than anything that has happened to me in all my life. They may say what they like—it's my surrender, it's my tribute, to youth. One puts that in where one can—it has to come in somewhere, if only out of the lives, the conditions, the feelings of other persons. Chad gives me the sense of it, for all his grey hairs, which merely make it solid in him and safe and serene; and *she* does the same, for all her being older than he, for all her marriageable daughter, her separated husband, her agitated history. Though they're young enough, my pair, I don't say they're, in the freshest way, their *own* absolutely prime adolescence; for that has nothing to do with it. The point is that they're mine. Yes, they're my youth; since somehow at the right time nothing else ever was. What I meant just now therefore is that it would all go—go before doing its work—if they were to fail me."

On which, just here, Miss Gostrey inveterately questioned. "What do you, in particular, call its work?"

"Well, to see me through."

"But through what?"—she liked to get it all out of him.

"Why through this experience." That was all that would come.

It regularly gave her none the less the last word. "Don't you remember how in those first days of our meeting it was *I* who was to see you through?"

"Remember? Tenderly, deeply"—he always rose to it. "You're just doing your part in letting me maunder to you thus."

"Ah don't speak as if my part were small; since whatever else fails you—"

"*You* won't, ever, ever, ever?"—he thus took her up. "Oh I beg your pardon; you necessarily, you inevitably *will*. Your conditions—that's what I mean—won't allow me anything to do for you."

"Let alone—I see what you mean—that I'm drearily dreadfully old. I *am*, but there's a service—possible for you to render—that I know, all the same, I shall think of."

"And what will it be?"

This, in fine, however, she would never tell him. "You shall hear only if your smash takes place. As that's really out of the question, I won't expose myself"—a point at which, for reasons of his own, Strether ceased to press.

He came round, for publicity—it was the easiest thing—to the idea that his smash *was* out of the question, and this rendered idle the discussion of what might follow it. He attached an added importance, as the days elapsed, to the arrival of the Pococks; he had even a shameful sense of waiting for it insincerely and incorrectly. He accused himself of making believe to his own mind that Sarah's presence, her impression, her judgement would simplify and harmonise; he accused himself of being so afraid of what they *might* do that he sought refuge, to beg the whole question, in a vain fury. He had abundantly seen at home what they were in the habit of doing, and he had not at present the smallest ground. His clearest vision was when he made out that what he most desired was an account more full and free of Mrs. Newsome's state of mind than any he felt he could now expect from herself; that calculation at least went hand in hand with the sharp consciousness of wishing to prove to himself that he was not afraid to look his behaviour in the face. If he was by an inexorable logic to pay for it he was literally impatient to know the cost, and he held himself ready to pay in instalments. The first instalment would be precisely this entertainment of Sarah; as a consequence of which, moreover, he should know vastly better how he stood.

Book Eighth

1 [XIX]

Strether rambled alone during these few days, the effect of the incident of the previous week having been to simplify in a marked fashion his mixed relations with Waymarsh. Nothing had passed between them in reference to Mrs. Newsome's summons but that our friend had mentioned to his own the departure of the deputation actually at sea—giving him thus an opportunity to confess to the occult intervention he imputed to him. Waymarsh however in the event confessed to nothing; and though this falsified in some degree Strether's forecast the latter amusedly saw in it the same depth of good conscience out of which the dear man's impertinence had originally sprung. He was patient with the dear man now and delighted to observe how unmistakeably he had put on flesh; he felt his own holiday so successfully large and free that he was full of allowances and charities in respect to those cabined and confined[1] his instinct toward a spirit so strapped down as Waymarsh's was to walk round it on tiptoe for fear of waking it up to a sense of losses by this time irretrievable. It was all very funny, he knew, and but the difference, as he often said to himself, of tweedledum and tweedledee—an emancipation so purely comparative that it was like the advance of the door-mat on the scraper; yet the present crisis was happily to profit by it and the pilgrim from Milrose to know himself more than ever in the right.

Strether felt that when he heard of the approach of the Pococks the impulse of pity quite sprang up in him beside the impulse of triumph. That was exactly why Waymarsh had looked at him with eyes in which the heat of justice was measured and shaded. He had looked very hard, as if affectionately sorry for the friend—the friend of fifty-five—whose frivolity had had thus to be recorded; becoming, however, but obscurely sententious and leaving his companion to formulate a charge. It was in this general attitude that he had of late altogether taken refuge; with the drop of discussion they were solemnly sadly superficial; Strether recognised in him the mere portentous rumination to which Miss Barrace had so good-humouredly described herself as assigning a corner of her salon. It was quite as if he knew his surreptitious step had been divined, and it was also as if he missed the chance to explain the purity of his motive; but this privation of relief should be precisely his small penance: it was not amiss for Strether that he should find himself to that degree uneasy. If he had been challenged or accused, rebuked for meddling or otherwise pulled up, he would probably have

1. "But now I am cabined, cribbed, confined, bound in / To saucy doubts and fears." *Macbeth* 3. 4. 23–24.

shown, on his own system, all the height of his consistency, all the depth of his good faith. Explicit resentment of his course would have made him take the floor, and the thump of his fist on the table would have affirmed him as consciously incorruptible. Had what now really prevailed with Strether been but a dread of that thump—a dread of wincing a little painfully at what it might invidiously demonstrate? However this might be, at any rate, one of the marks of the crisis was a visible, a studied lapse, in Waymarsh, of betrayed concern. As if to make up to his comrade for the stroke by which he had played providence he now conspicuously ignored his movements, withdrew himself from the pretension to share them, stiffened up his sensibility to neglect, and, clasping his large empty hands and swinging his large restless foot, clearly looked to another quarter for justice.

This made for independence on Strether's part, and he had in truth at no moment of his stay been so free to go and come. The early summer brushed the picture over and blurred everything but the near; it made a vast warm fragrant medium in which the elements floated together on the best of terms, in which rewards were immediate and reckonings postponed. Chad was out of town again, for the first time since his visitor's first view of him; he had explained this necessity—without detail, yet also without embarrassment; the circumstance was one of those which, in the young man's life, testified to the variety of his ties. Strether wasn't otherwise concerned with it than for its so testifying—a pleasant multitudinous image in which he took comfort. He took comfort, by the same stroke, in the swing of Chad's pendulum back from that other swing, the sharp jerk towards Woollett, so stayed by his own hand. He had the entertainment of thinking that if he had for that moment stopped the clock it was to promote the next minute this still livelier motion. He himself did what he hadn't done before; he took two or three times whole days off—irrespective of others, of two or three taken with Miss Gostrey, two or three taken with little Bilham: he went to Chartres[2] and cultivated, before the front of the cathedral, a general easy beatitude; he went to Fontainebleau[3] and imagined himself on the way to Italy; he went to Rouen[4] with a little handbag and inordinately spent the night.

One afternoon he did something quite different; finding himself in the neighbourhood of a fine old house across the river, he passed under the great arch of its doorway and asked at the porter's lodge

2. At Chartres (app. 45 miles southwest of Paris) is perhaps the greatest of all Gothic cathedrals, especially renowned for its stained glass.
3. Fontainebleau (app. 35 miles southeast of Paris) is famous for its Renaissance palace.
4. Rouen (app. 85 miles northwest of Paris) is celebrated for its Gothic cathedral and its smaller Gothic Church of St. Ouen.

for Madame de Vionnet. He had already hovered more than once about that possibility, been aware of it, in the course of ostensible strolls, as lurking but round the corner. Only it had perversely happened, after his morning at Notre Dame, that his consistency, as he considered and intended it, had come back to him; whereby he had reflected that the encounter in question had been none of his making; clinging again intensely to the strength of his position, which was precisely that there was nothing in it for himself. From the moment he actively pursued the charming associate of his adventure, from that moment his position weakened, for he was then acting in an interested way. It was only within a few days that he had fixed himself a limit: he promised himself his consistency should end with Sarah's arrival. It was arguing correctly to feel the title to a free hand conferred on him by this event. If he wasn't to be let alone he should be merely a dupe to act with delicacy. If he wasn't to be trusted he could at least take his ease. If he was to be placed under control he gained leave to try what his position *might* agreeably give him. An ideal rigour would perhaps postpone the trial till after the Pococks had shown their spirit; and it was to an ideal rigour that he had quite promised himself to conform.

Suddenly, however, on this particular day, he felt a particular fear under which everything collapsed. He knew abruptly that he was afraid of himself—and yet not in relation to the effect on his sensibilities of another hour of Madame de Vionnet. What he dreaded was the effect of a single hour of Sarah Pocock, as to whom he was visited, in troubled nights, with fantastic waking dreams. She loomed at him larger than life; she increased in volume as she drew nearer; she so met his eyes that, his imagination taking, after the first step, all, and more than all, the strides, he already felt her come down on him, already burned, under her reprobation, with the blush of guilt, already consented, by way of penance, to the instant forfeiture of everything. He saw himself, under her direction, recommitted to Woollett as juvenile offenders are committed to reformatories. It wasn't of course that Woollett was really a place of discipline; but he knew in advance that Sarah's salon at the hotel would be. His danger, at any rate, in such moods of alarm, was some concession, on this ground, that would involve a sharp rupture with the actual; therefore if he waited to take leave of that actual he might wholly miss his chance. It was represented with supreme vividness by Madame de Vionnet, and that is why, in a word, he waited no longer. He had seen in a flash that he must anticipate Mrs. Pocock. He was accordingly much disappointed on now learning from the portress that the lady of his quest was not in Paris. She had gone for some days to the country. There was nothing in this accident but what was natural; yet it produced for poor

Strether a drop of all confidence. It was suddenly as if he should never see her again, and as if moreover he had brought it on himself by not having been quite kind to her.

It was the advantage of his having let his fancy lose itself for a little in the gloom that, as by reaction, the prospect began really to brighten from the moment the deputation from Woollett alighted on the platform of the station. They had come straight from Havre,[5] having sailed from New York to that port, and having also, thanks to a happy voyage, made land with a promptitude that left Chad Newsome, who had meant to meet them at the dock, belated. He had received their telegram, with the announcement of their immediate further advance, just as he was taking the train for Havre, so that nothing had remained for him but to await them in Paris. He hastily picked up Strether, at the hotel, for this purpose, and he even, with easy pleasantry, suggested the attendance of Waymarsh as well—Waymarsh, at the moment his cab rattled up, being engaged, under Strether's contemplative range, in a grave perambulation of the familiar court. Waymarsh had learned from his companion, who had already had a note, delivered by hand, from Chad, that the Pococks were due, and had ambiguously, though, as always, impressively, glowered at him over the circumstance; carrying himself in a manner in which Strether was now expert enough to recognise his uncertainty, in the premises, as to the best tone. The only tone he aimed at with confidence was a full tone—which was necessarily difficult in the absence of a full knowledge. The Pococks were a quantity as yet unmeasured, and, as he had practically brought them over, so this witness had to that extent exposed himself. He wanted to feel right about it, but could only, at the best, for the time, feel vague. "I shall look to you, you know, immensely," our friend had said, "to help me with them," and he had been quite conscious of the effect of the remark, and of others of the same sort, on his comrade's sombre sensibility. He had insisted on the fact that Waymarsh would quite like Mrs. Pocock—one could be certain he would: he would be with her about everything, and she would also be with *him*, and Miss Barrace's nose, in short, would find itself out of joint.

Strether had woven this web of cheerfulness while they waited in the court for Chad; he had sat smoking cigarettes to keep himself quiet while, caged and leonine, his fellow traveller paced and turned before him. Chad Newsome was doubtless to be struck, when he arrived, with the sharpness of their opposition at this particular hour; he was to remember, as a part of it, how Waymarsh came with him and with Strether to the street and stood

5. The principal French seaport on the Atlantic Ocean.

there with a face half-wistful and half-rueful. They talked of him, the two others, as they drove, and Strether put Chad in possession of much of his own strained sense of things. He had already, a few days before, named to him the wire he was convinced their friend had pulled—a confidence that had made on the young man's part quite hugely for curiosity and diversion. The action of the matter, moreover, Strether could see, was to penetrate; he saw, that is, how Chad judged a system of influence in which Waymarsh had served as a determinant—an impression just now quickened again; with the whole bearing of such a fact on the youth's view of his relatives. As it came up between them that they might now take their friend for a feature of the control of these latter now sought to be exerted from Woollett, Strether felt indeed how it would be stamped all over him, half an hour later, for Sarah Pocock's eyes, that he was as much on Chad's "side" as Waymarsh had probably described him. He was letting himself, at present, go; there was no denying it; it might be desperation, it might be confidence; he should offer himself to the arriving travellers bristling with all the lucidity he had cultivated.

He repeated to Chad what he had been saying in the court to Waymarsh; how there was no doubt whatever that his sister would find the latter a kindred spirit, no doubt of the alliance, based on an exchange of views, that the pair would successfully strike up. They would become as thick as thieves—which moreover was but a development of what Strether remembered to have said in one of his first discussions with his mate, struck as he had then already been with the elements of affinity between that personage and Mrs. Newsome herself. "I told him, one day, when he had questioned me on your mother, that she was a person who, when he should know her, would rouse in him, I was sure, a special enthusiasm; and that hangs together with the conviction we now feel—this certitude that Mrs. Pocock will take him into her boat. For it's your mother's own boat that she's pulling."

"Ah," said Chad, "Mother's worth fifty of Sally!"

"A thousand; but when you presently meet her, all the same, you'll be meeting your mother's representative—just as I shall. I feel like the outgoing ambassador," said Strether, "doing honour to his appointed successor." A moment after speaking as he had just done he felt he had inadvertently rather cheapened Mrs. Newsome to her son; an impression audibly reflected, as at first seen, in Chad's prompt protest. He had recently rather failed of apprehension of the young man's attitude and temper—remaining principally conscious of how little worry, at the worst, he wasted; and he studied him at this critical hour with renewed interest. Chad had done exactly what he had promised him a fortnight previous

—had accepted without another question his plea for delay. He was waiting cheerfully and handsomely, but also inscrutably and with a slight increase perhaps of the hardness originally involved in his acquired high polish. He was neither excited nor depressed; was easy and acute and deliberate—unhurried unflurried unworried, only at most a little less amused than usual. Strether felt him more than ever a justification of the extraordinary process of which his own absurd spirit had been the arena; he knew as their cab rolled along, knew as he hadn't even yet known, that nothing else than what Chad had done and had been would have led to his present showing. They had made him, these things, what he was, and the business hadn't been easy; it had taken time and trouble, it had cost, above all, a price. The result at any rate was now to be offered to Sally; which Strether, so far as that was concerned, was glad to be there to witness. Would she in the least make it out or take it in, the result, or would she in the least care for it if she did? He scratched his chin as he asked himself by what name, when challenged—as he was sure he should be—he could call it for her. Oh those were determinations she must herself arrive at; since she wanted so much to see, let her see then and welcome. She had come out in the pride of her competence, yet it hummed in Strether's inner sense that she practically wouldn't see.

That this was moreover what Chad shrewdly suspected was clear from a word that next dropped from him. "They're children; they play at life!"—and the exclamation was significant and reassuring. It implied that he hadn't then, for his companion's sensibility, appeared to give Mrs. Newsome away; and it facilitated our friend's presently asking him if it were his idea that Mrs. Pocock and Madame de Vionnet should become acquainted. Strether was still more sharply struck, hereupon, with Chad's lucidity. "Why, isn't that exactly—to get a sight of the company I keep—what she has come out for?"

"Yes—I'm afraid it is," Strether unguardedly replied.

Chad's quick rejoinder lighted his precipitation. "Why do you say you're afraid?"

"Well, because I feel a certain responsibility. It's my testimony, I imagine, that will have been at the bottom of Mrs. Pocock's curiosity. My letters, as I've supposed you to understand from the beginning, have spoken freely. I've certainly said my little say about Madame de Vionnet."

All that, for Chad, was beautifully obvious. "Yes, but you've only spoken handsomely."

"Never more handsomely of any woman. But it's just that tone—!"

"That tone," said Chad, "that has fetched her? I dare say;

but I've no quarrel with you about it. And no more has Madame de Vionnet. Don't you know by this time how she likes you?"

"Oh!"—and Strether had, with his groan, a real pang of melancholy. "For all I've done for her!"

"Ah you've done a great deal."

Chad's urbanity fairly shamed him, and he was at this moment absolutely impatient to see the face Sarah Pocock would present to a sort of thing, as he synthetically phrased it to himself, with no adequate forecast of which, despite his admonitions, she would certainly arrive. "I've done *this!*"

"Well, this is all right. She likes," Chad comfortably remarked, "to be liked."

It gave his companion a moment's thought. "And she's sure Mrs. Pocock *will*—?"

"No, I say that for you. She likes your liking her; it's so much, as it were," Chad laughed, "to the good. However, she doesn't despair of Sarah either, and is prepared, on her own side, to go all lengths."

"In the way of appreciation?"

"Yes, and of everything else. In the way of general amiability, hospitality and welcome. She's under arms," Chad laughed again; "she's prepared."

Strether took it in; then as if an echo of Miss Barrace were in the air: "She's wonderful."

"You don't begin to know *how* wonderful!"

There was a depth in it, to Strether's ear, of confirmed luxury—almost a kind of unconscious insolence of proprietorship; but the effect of the glimpse was not at this moment to foster speculation: there was something so conclusive in so much graceful and generous assurance. It was in fact a fresh evocation; and the evocation had before many minutes another consequence. "Well, I shall see her oftener now. I shall see her as much as I like—by your leave; which is what I hitherto haven't done."

"It has been," said Chad, but without reproach, "only your own fault. I tried to bring you together, and *she*, my dear fellow—I never saw her more charming to any man. But you've got your extraordinary ideas."

"Well, I *did* have," Strether murmured; while he felt both how they had possessed him and how they had now lost their authority. He couldn't have traced the sequence to the end, but it was all because of Mrs. Pocock. Mrs. Pocock might be because of Mrs. Newsome, but that was still to be proved. What came over him was the sense of having stupidly failed to profit where profit would have been precious. It had been open to him to see so much more of her, and he had but let the good days pass. Fierce in him almost

was the resolve to lose no more of them, and he whimsically reflected, while at Chad's side he drew nearer to his destination,
that it was after all Sarah who would have quickened his chance.
What her visit of inquisition might achieve in other directions was
as yet all obscure—only not obscure that it would do supremely
much to bring two earnest persons together. He had but to listen
to Chad at this moment to feel it; for Chad was in the act of remarking to him that they of course both counted on him—he
himself and the other earnest person—for cheer and support. It
was brave to Strether to hear him talk as if the line of wisdom they
had struck out was to make things ravishing to the Pococks. No,
if Madame de Vionnet compassed *that*, compassed the ravishment
of the Pococks, Madame de Vionnet would be prodigious. It would
be a beautiful plan if it succeeded, and it all came to the question of
Sarah's being really bribeable. The precedent of his own case helped
Strether perhaps but little to consider she might prove so; it being
distinct that her character would rather make for every possible
difference. This idea of his own bribeability set him apart for
himself; with the further mark in fact that his case was absolutely
proved. He liked always, where Lambert Strether was concerned,
to know the worst, and what he now seemed to know was not only
that he was bribeable, but that he had been effectually bribed.
The only difficulty was that he couldn't quite have said with what.
It was as if he had sold himself, but hadn't somehow got the cash.
That, however, was what, characteristically, *would* happen to him.
It would naturally be his kind of traffic. While he thought of these
things he reminded Chad of the truth they mustn't lose sight of—
the truth that, with all deference to her susceptibility to new interests, Sarah would have come out with a high firm definite purpose.
"She hasn't come out, you know, to be bamboozled. We may all be
ravishing—nothing perhaps can be more easy for us; but she hasn't
come out to be ravished. She has come out just simply to take you
home."

"Oh well, with *her* I'll go," said Chad good-humouredly. "I suppose you'll allow *that*." And then as for a minute Strether said
nothing: "Or is your idea that when I've seen her I shan't want to
go?" As this question, however, again left his friend silent he presently went on: "My own idea at any rate is that they shall have
while they're here the best sort of time."

It was at this that Strether spoke. "Ah there you are! I think
if you really wanted to go—!"

"Well?" said Chad to bring it out.

"Well, you wouldn't trouble about our good time. You wouldn't
care what sort of a time we have."

Chad could always take in the easiest way in the world any

ingenious suggestion. "I see. But can I help it? I'm too decent."

"Yes, you're too decent!" Strether heavily sighed. And he felt for the moment as if it were the preposterous end of his mission.

It ministered for the time to this temporary effect that Chad made no rejoinder. But he spoke again as they came in sight of the station. "Do you mean to introduce her to Miss Gostrey?"

As to this Strether was ready. "No."

"But haven't you told me they know about her?"

"I think I've told you your mother knows."

"And won't she have told Sally?"

"That's one of the things I want to see."

"And if you find she *has*—?"

"Will I then, you mean, bring them together?"

"Yes," said Chad with his pleasant promptness: "to show her there's nothing in it."

Strether hesitated. "I don't know that I care very much what she may think there's in it."

"Not if it represents what Mother thinks?"

"Ah what *does* your mother think?" There was in this some sound of bewilderment.

But they were just driving up, and help, of a sort, might after all be quite at hand. "Isn't that, my dear man, what we're both just going to make out?"

ii [xx]

Strether quitted the station half an hour later in different company. Chad had taken charge, for the journey to the hotel, of Sarah, Mamie, the maid and the luggage, all spaciously installed and conveyed; and it was only after the four had rolled away that his companion got into a cab with Jim. A strange new feeling had come over Strether, in consequence of which his spirits had risen; it was as if what had occurred on the alighting of his critics had been something other than his fear, though his fear had yet not been of an instant scene of violence. His impression had been nothing but what was inevitable—he said that to himself; yet relief and reassurance had softly dropped upon him. Nothing could be so odd as to be indebted for these things to the look of faces and the sound of voices that had been with him to satiety, as he might have said, for years; but he now knew, all the same, how uneasy he had felt; that was brought home to him by his present sense of a respite. It had come moreover in the flash of an eye; it had come in the smile with which Sarah, whom, at the window of her compartment, they had effusively greeted from the platform, rustled down to them a moment later, fresh and handsome from her cool June progress through the charming land. It was only a sign, but enough: she was going to be gracious and unallusive, she was going to play

the larger game—which was still more apparent, after she had
emerged from Chad's arms, in her direct greeting to the valued
friend of her family.

Strether *was* then as much as ever the valued friend of her
family; it was something he could at all events go on with; and the
manner of his response to it expressed even for himself how little
he had enjoyed the prospect of ceasing to figure in that likeness.
He had always seen Sarah gracious—had in fact rarely seen her
shy or dry; her marked thin-lipped smile, intense without brightness
and as prompt to act as the scrape of a safety-match; the protrusion
of her rather remarkably long chin, which in her case represented
invitation and urbanity, and not, as in most others, pugnacity and
defiance; the penetration of her voice to a distance, the general encouragement and approval of her manner, were all elements with
which intercourse had made him familiar, but which he noted to-
day almost as if she had been a new acquaintance. This first
glimpse of her had given a brief but vivid accent to her resemblance
to her mother; he could have taken her for Mrs. Newsome while
she met his eyes as the train rolled into the station. It was an impression that quickly dropped; Mrs. Newsome was much handsomer, and while Sarah inclined to the massive her mother had, at
an age, still the girdle of a maid; also the latter's chin was rather
short, than long, and her smile, by good fortune, much more, oh
ever so much more, mercifully vague. Strether had seen Mrs. Newsome reserved; he had literally heard her silent, though he had
never known her unpleasant. It was the case with Mrs. Pocock that
he had known *her* unpleasant, even though he had never known her
not affable. She had forms of affability that were in a high degree
assertive; nothing for instance had ever been more striking than that
she was affable to Jim.

What had told in any case at the window of the train was her
high clear forehead, that forehead which her friends, for some
reason, always thought of as a "brow"; the long reach of her eyes
—it came out at this juncture in such a manner as to remind him,
oddly enough, also of that of Waymarsh's; and the unusual gloss
of her dark hair, dressed and hatted, after her mother's refined
example, with such an avoidance of extremes that it was always
spoken of at Woollett as "their own." Though this analogy dropped
as soon as she was on the platform it had lasted long enough to
make him feel all the advantage, as it were, of his relief. The
woman at home, the woman to whom he was attached, was before him just long enough to give him again the measure of the
wretchedness, in fact really of the shame, of their having to recognise the formation, between them, of a "split." He had taken this
measure in solitude and meditation; but the catastrophe, as Sarah

steamed up, looked for its seconds unprecedentedly dreadful—
or proved, more exactly, altogether unthinkable; so that his finding
something free and familiar to respond to brought with it an instant
renewal of his loyalty. He had suddenly sounded the whole depth,
had gasped at what he might have lost.

Well, he could now, for the quarter of an hour of their detention,
hover about the travellers as soothingly as if their direct message to
him was that he had lost nothing. He wasn't going to have Sarah
write to her mother that night that he was in any way altered or
strange. There had been times enough for a month when it had
seemed to him that he was strange, that he was altered, in every
way; but that was a matter for himself; he knew at least whose
business it was *not*; it was not at all events such a circumstance
as Sarah's own unaided lights would help her to. Even if she had
come out to flash those lights more than yet appeared she wouldn't
make much headway against mere pleasantness. He counted on
being able to be merely pleasant to the end, and if only from in-
capacity moreover to formulate anything different. He couldn't
even formulate to himself his being changed and queer; it had taken
place, the process, somewhere deep down; Maria Gostrey had
caught glimpses of it; but how was he to fish it up, even if he
desired, for Mrs. Pocock? This was then the spirit in which he
hovered, and with the easier throb in it much indebted furthermore
to the impression of high and established adequacy as a pretty girl
promptly produced in him by Mamie. He had wondered vaguely—
turning over many things in the fidget of his thoughts—if Mamie
were as pretty as Woollett published her; as to which issue seeing
her now again was to be so swept away by Woollett's opinion that
this consequence really let loose for the imagination an avalanche
of others. There were positively five minutes in which the last word
seemed of necessity to abide with a Woollett represented by a
Mamie. This was the sort of truth the place itself would feel; it
would send her forth in confidence; it would point to her with
triumph; it would take its stand on her with assurance; it would
be conscious of no requirements she didn't meet, of no question
she couldn't answer.

Well, it was right, Strether slipped smoothly enough into the
cheerfulness of saying: granted that a community *might* be best
represented by a young lady of twenty-two, Mamie perfectly played
the part, played it as if she were used to it, and looked and spoke
and dressed the character. He wondered if she mightn't, in the
high light of Paris, a cool full studio-light, becoming yet treacher-
ous, show as too conscious of these matters; but the next moment he
felt satisfied that her consciousness was after all empty for its size,
rather too simple than too mixed, and that the kind way with her

would be not to take many things out of it, but to put as many as possible in. She was robust and conveniently tall; just a trifle too bloodlessly fair perhaps, but with a pleasant public familiar radiance that affirmed her vitality. She might have been "receiving" for Woollett, wherever she found herself, and there was something in her manner, her tone, her motion, her pretty blue eyes, her pretty perfect teeth and her very small, too small, nose, that immediately placed her, to the fancy, between the windows of a hot bright room in which voices were high—up at that end to which people were brought to be "presented." They were there to congratulate, these images, and Strether's renewed vision, on this hint, completed the idea. What Mamie was like was the happy bride, the bride after the church and just before going away. She wasn't the mere maiden, and yet was only as much married as that quantity came to. She was in the brilliant acclaimed festal stage. Well, might it last her long!

Strether rejoiced in these things for Chad, who was all genial attention to the needs of his friends, besides having arranged that his servant should re-enforce him; the ladies were certainly pleasant to see, and Mamie would be at any time and anywhere pleasant to exhibit. She would look extraordinarily like his young wife—the wife of a honeymoon, should he go about with her; but that was his own affair—or perhaps it was hers; it was at any rate something she couldn't help. Strether remembered how he had seen him come up with Jeanne de Vionnet in Gloriani's garden, and the fancy he had had about that—the fancy obscured now, thickly overlaid with others; the recollection was during these minutes his only note of trouble. He had often, in spite of himself, wondered if Chad but too probably were not with Jeanne the object of a still and shaded flame. It was on the cards that the child *might* be tremulously in love, and this conviction now flickered up not a bit the less for his disliking to think of it, for its being, in a complicated situation, a complication the more, and for something indescribable in Mamie, something at all events straightway lent her by his own mind, something that gave her value, gave her intensity and purpose, as the symbol of an opposition. Little Jeanne wasn't really at all in question—how *could* she be?—yet from the moment Miss Pocock had shaken her skirts on the platform, touched up the immense bows of her hat and settled properly over her shoulder the strap of her morocco-and-gilt travelling-satchel, from that moment little Jeanne was opposed.

It was in the cab with Jim that impressions really crowded on Strether, giving him the strangest sense of length of absence from people among whom he had lived for years. Having them thus come out to him was as if he had returned to find them; and the

droll promptitude of Jim's mental reaction threw his own initiation
far back into the past. Whoever might or mightn't be suited by
what was going on among them, Jim, for one, would certainly be:
his instant recognition—frank and whimsical—of what the affair
was for *him* gave Strether a glow of pleasure. "I say, you know, this
is about my shape, and if it hadn't been for *you*—!" so he broke
out as the charming streets met his healthy appetite; and he wound
up, after an expressive nudge, with a clap of his companion's knee
and an "Oh you, you—you *are* doing it!" that was charged with
rich meaning. Strether felt in it the intention of homage, but,
with a curiosity otherwise occupied, postponed taking it up. What
he was asking himself for the time was how Sarah Pocock, in the
opportunity already given her, had judged her brother—from whom
he himself, as they finally, at the station, separated for their different conveyances, had had a look into which he could read more
than one message. However Sarah was judging her brother, Chad's
conclusion about his sister, and about her husband and her husband's sister, was at the least on the way not to fail of confidence.
Strether felt the confidence, and that, as the look between them
was an exchange, what he himself gave back was relatively vague.
This comparison of notes however could wait; everything struck
him as depending on the effect produced by Chad. Neither Sarah
nor Mamie had in any way, at the station—where they had had
after all ample time—broken out about it; which, to make up for
this, was what our friend had expected of Jim as soon as they
should find themselves together.

It was queer to him that he had that noiseless brush with Chad;
an ironic intelligence with this youth on the subject of his relatives,
an intelligence carried on under their nose and, as might be said,
at their expense—such a matter marked again for him strongly
the number of stages he had come; albeit that if the number seemed
great the time taken for the final one was but the turn of a hand.
He had before this had many moments of wondering if he himself
weren't perhaps changed even as Chad was changed. Only what
in Chad was conspicuous improvement—well, he had no name
ready for the working, in his own organism, of his own more timid
dose. He should have to see first what this action would amount to.
And for his occult passage with the young man, after all, the directness of it had no greater oddity than the fact that the young man's
way with the three travellers should have been so happy a mani-
festation. Strether liked him for it, on the spot, as he hadn't yet
liked him; it affected him while it lasted as he might have been
affected by some light pleasant perfect work of art: to that degree
that he wondered if they were really worthy of it, took it in and did
it justice; to that degree that it would have been scarce a miracle

if, there in the luggage-room, while they waited for their things, Sarah had pulled his sleeve and drawn him aside. "You're right; we haven't quite known what you mean, Mother and I, but now we see. Chad's magnificent; what can one want more? If *this* is the kind of thing—!" On which they might, as it were, have embraced and begun to work together.

Ah how much, as it was, for all her bridling brightness—which was merely general and noticed nothing—*would* they work together? Strether knew he was unreasonable; he set it down to his being nervous: people couldn't notice everything and speak of everything in a quarter of an hour. Possibly, no doubt, also, he made too much of Chad's display. Yet, none the less, when, at the end of five minutes, in the cab, Jim Pocock had said nothing either—hadn't said, that is, what Strether wanted, though he had said much else—it all suddenly bounced back to their being either stupid or wilful. It was more probably on the whole the former; so that that would be the drawback of the bridling brightness. Yes, they would bridle and be bright; they would make the best of what was before them, but their observation would fail; it would be beyond them; they simply wouldn't understand. Of what use would it be then that they had come?—if they weren't to be intelligent up to *that* point: unless indeed he himself were utterly deluded and extravagant? Was he, on this question of Chad's improvement, fantastic and away from the truth? Did he live in a false world, a world that had grown simply to suit him, and was his present slight irritation—in the face now of Jim's silence in particular—but the alarm of the vain thing menaced by the touch of the real? Was this contribution of the real possibly the mission of the Pococks?—had they come to make the work of observation, as *he* had practised observation, crack and crumble, and to reduce Chad to the plain terms in which honest minds could deal with him? Had they come in short to be sane where Strether was destined to feel that he himself had only been silly?

He glanced at such a contingency, but it failed to hold him long when once he had reflected that he would have been silly, in this case, with Maria Gostrey and little Bilham, with Madame de Vionnet and little Jeanne, with Lambert Strether, in fine, and above all with Chad Newsome himself. Wouldn't it be found to have made more for reality to be silly with these persons than sane with Sarah and Jim? Jim in fact, he presently made up his mind, was individually out of it; Jim didn't care; Jim hadn't come out either for Chad or for him; Jim in short left the moral side to Sally and indeed simply availed himself now, for the sense of recreation, of the fact that he left almost everything to Sally. He was nothing compared to Sally, and not so much by reason of Sally's temper and will as by that of her more developed type and greater acquaintance with the world. He quite frankly and serenely confessed, as he sat there with Strether, that he felt his type hang far in the rear of his wife's and still further, if possible, in the rear of his sister's. Their types, he well knew, were recognised and acclaimed; whereas the most a leading Woollett business-man could hope to achieve socially, and for that matter industrially, was a certain freedom to play into this general glamour.

The impression he made on our friend was another of the things that marked our friend's road. It was a strange impression, especially as so soon produced; Strether had received it, he judged, all in the twenty minutes; it struck him at least as but in a minor degree the work of the long Woollett years. Pocock was normally and consentingly though not quite wittingly out of the question. It was despite his being normal; it was despite his being cheerful; it was despite his being a leading Woollett business-man; and the determination of his fate left him thus perfectly usual—as everything else about it was clearly, to his sense, not less so. He seemed to say that there was a whole side of life on which the perfectly usual *was* for leading Woollett business-men to be out of the question. He made no more of it than that, and Strether, so far as Jim was concerned, desired to make no more. Only Strether's imagination, as always, worked, and he asked himself if this side of life were not somehow connected, for those who figured on it, with the fact of marriage. Would *his* relation to it, had he married ten years before, have become now the same as Pocock's? Might it even become the same should he marry in a few months? Should he ever know himself as much out of the question for Mrs. Newsome as Jim knew himself—in a dim way—for Mrs. Jim?

To turn his eyes in that direction was to be personally reassured; he was different from Pocock; he had affirmed himself differently and was held after all in higher esteem. What none the less came home to him, however, at this hour, was that the society over there, that of which Sarah and Mamie—and, in a more eminent way, Mrs. Newsome herself—were specimens, was essentially a society of women, and that poor Jim wasn't in it. He himself, Lambert Strether, *was* as yet in some degree—which was an odd situation for a man; but it kept coming back to him in a whimsical way that he should perhaps find his marriage had cost him his place. This occasion indeed, whatever that fancy represented, was not a time of sensible exclusion for Jim, who was in a state of manifest response to the charm of his adventure. Small and fat and constantly facetious, straw-coloured and destitute of marks, he would have been practically indistinguishable hadn't his constant preference for light-grey clothes, for white hats, for very big cigars and very little stories, done what it could for his identity. There were signs in him, though none of them plaintive, of always paying for others; and the principal one perhaps was just this failure of type. It was with this that he paid, rather than with fatigue or waste; and also doubtless a little with the effort of humour—never irrelevant to the conditions, to the relations, with which he was acquainted.

He gurgled his joy as they rolled through the happy streets; he declared that his trip was a regular windfall, and that he wasn't there, he was eager to remark, to hang back from anything: he didn't know quite what Sally had come for, but *he* had come for a good time. Strether indulged him even while wondering if what Sally wanted her brother to go back for was to become like her husband. He trusted that a good time was to be, out and out, the programme for all of them; and he assented liberally to Jim's proposal that, disencumbered and irresponsible—his things were in the omnibus with those of the others—they should take a further turn round before going to the hotel. It wasn't for *him* to tackle Chad—it was Sally's job; and as it would be like her, he felt, to open fire on the spot, it wouldn't be amiss of them to hold off and give her time. Strether, on his side, only asked to give her time; so he jogged with his companion along boulevards and avenues, trying to extract from meagre material some forecast of his catastrophe. He was quick enough to see that Jim Pocock declined judgement, had hovered quite round the outer edge of discussion and anxiety, leaving all analysis of their question to the ladies alone and now only feeling his way toward some small droll cynicism. It broke out afresh, the cynicism—it had already shown a flicker—in a but slightly deferred: "Well, hanged if I would if *I* were he!"

"You mean you wouldn't in Chad's place—?"

"Give up this to go back and boss the advertising!" Poor Jim, with his arms folded and his little legs out in the open fiacre, drank in the sparkling Paris noon and carried his eyes from one side of their vista to the other. "Why I want to come right out and live here myself. And I want to live while I *am* here too. I feel with *you* —oh you've been grand, old man, and I've twigged—that it ain't right to worry Chad. *I* don't mean to persecute him; I couldn't in conscience. It's thanks to you at any rate that I'm here, and I'm sure I'm much obliged. You're a lovely pair."

There were things in this speech that Strether let pass for the time. "Don't you then think it important the advertising should be thoroughly taken in hand? Chad *will* be, so far as capacity is concerned," he went on, "the man to do it."

"Where did he get his capacity," Jim asked, "over here?"

"He didn't get it over here, and the wonderful thing is that over here he hasn't inevitably lost it. He has a natural turn for business, an extraordinary head. He comes by that," Strether explained, "honestly enough. He's in that respect his father's son, and also—for she's wonderful in her way too—his mother's. He has other tastes and other tendencies; but Mrs. Newsome and your wife are quite right about his having that. He's very remarkable."

"Well, I guess he is!" Jim Pocock comfortably sighed. "But if you've believed so in his making us hum, why have you so prolonged the discussion? Don't you know we've been quite anxious about you?"

These questions were not informed with earnestness, but Strether saw he must none the less make a choice and take a line. "Because, you see, I've greatly liked it. I've liked my Paris. I dare say I've liked it too much."

"Oh you old wretch!" Jim gaily exclaimed.

"But nothing's concluded," Strether went on. "The case is more complex than it looks from Woollett."

"Oh well, it looks bad enough from Woollett!" Jim declared.

"Even after all I've written?"

Jim bethought himself. "Isn't it what you've written that has made Mrs. Newsome pack us off? That at least and Chad's not turning up?"

Strether made a reflexion of his own. "I see. That she should do something was, no doubt, inevitable, and your wife has therefore of course come out to act."

"Oh yes," Jim concurred—"to act. But Sally comes out to act, you know," he lucidly added, "every time she leaves the house. She never comes out but she *does* act. She's acting moreover now for her mother, and that fixes the scale." Then he wound up, opening all his senses to it, with a renewed embrace of pleasant Paris. "We haven't all the same at Woollett got anything like this."

Strether continued to consider. "I'm bound to say for you all that you strike me as having arrived in a very mild and reasonable frame of mind. You don't show your claws. I felt just now in Mrs. Pocock no symptom of that. She isn't fierce," he went on. "I'm such a nervous idiot that I thought she might be."

"Oh don't you know her well enough," Pocock asked, "to have noticed that she never gives herself away, any more than her mother ever does? They ain't fierce, either of 'em; they let you come quite close. They wear their fur the smooth side out—the warm side in. Do you know what they are?" Jim pursued as he looked about him, giving the question, as Strether felt, but half his care—"do you know what they are? They're about as intense as they can live."

"Yes"—and Strether's concurrence had a positive precipitation;

"they're about as intense as they can live."

"They don't lash about and shake the cage," said Jim, who seemed pleased with his analogy; "and it's at feeding-time that they're quietest. But they always get there."

"They do indeed—they always get there!" Strether replied with a laugh that justified his confession of nervousness. He disliked to be talking sincerely of Mrs. Newsome with Pocock; he could have talked insincerely. But there was something he wanted to know, a need created in him by her recent intermission, by his having given from the first so much, as now more than ever appeared to him, and got so little. It was as if a queer truth in his companion's metaphor had rolled over him with a rush. She *had* been quiet at feeding-time; she had fed, and Sarah had fed with her, out of the big bowl of all his recent free communication, his vividness and pleasantness, his ingenuity and even his eloquence, while the current of her response had steadily run thin. Jim meanwhile however, it was true, slipped characteristically into shallowness from the moment he ceased to speak out of the experience of a husband.

"But of course Chad has now the advantage of being there before her. If he doesn't work that for all it's worth—!" He sighed with contingent pity at his brother-in-law's possible want of resource. "He has worked it on *you*, pretty well, eh?" and he asked the next moment if there were anything new at the Varieties,[6] which he pronounced in the American manner. They talked about the Varieties—Strether confessing to a knowledge which produced again on Pocock's part a play of innuendo as vague as a nursery-rhyme, yet as aggressive as an elbow in his side; and they finished their drive under the protection of easy themes. Strether waited to the end, but still in vain, for any show that Jim had seen Chad as different; and he could scarce have explained the discouragement he drew from the absence of this testimony. It was what he had taken his own stand on, so far as he had taken a stand; and if they were all only going to see nothing he had only wasted his time. He gave his friend till the very last moment, till they had come into sight of the hotel; and when poor Pocock only continued cheerful and envious and funny he fairly grew to dislike him, to feel him extravagantly common. If they were *all* going to see nothing!— Strether knew, as this came back to him, that he was also letting Pocock represent for him what Mrs. Newsome wouldn't see. He went on disliking, in the light of Jim's commonness, to talk to him about that lady; yet just before the cab pulled up he knew the extent of his desire for the real word from Woollett.

"Has Mrs. Newsome at all given way—?"

6. At the Variétés were staged—according to a guidebook of the time—"vaudevilles, farces, operettas, and similar lively pieces of essentially Parisian character." Karl Baedeker, *Paris* (Leipsic: Karl Baedeker, Publishers, 1900), 34.

" 'Given way'?"—Jim echoed it with the practical derision of his sense of a long past.

"Under the strain, I mean, of hope deferred, of disappointment repeated and thereby intensified."

"Oh is she prostrate, you mean?"—he had his categories in hand. "Why yes, she's prostrate—just as Sally is. But they're never so lively, you know, as when they're prostrate."

"Ah Sarah's prostrate?" Strether vaguely murmured.

"It's when they're prostrate that they most sit up."

"And Mrs. Newsome's sitting up?"

"All night, my boy—for *you!*" And Jim fetched him, with a vulgar little guffaw, a thrust that gave relief to the picture. But he had got what he wanted. He felt on the spot that this *was* the real word from Woollett. "So don't you go home!" Jim added while he alighted and while his friend, letting him profusely pay the cabman, sat on in a momentary muse. Strether wondered if that were the real word too.

III [XXI]

As the door of Mrs. Pocock's salon was pushed open for him, the next day, well before noon, he was reached by a voice with a charming sound that made him just falter before crossing the threshold. Madame de Vionnet was already on the field, and this gave the drama a quicker pace than he felt it as yet—though his suspense had increased—in the power of any act of his own to do. He had spent the previous evening with all his old friends together; yet he would still have described himself as quite in the dark in respect to a forecast of their influence on his situation. It was strange now, none the less, that in the light of this unexpected note of her presence he felt Madame de Vionnet a part of that situation as she hadn't even yet been. She was alone, he found himself assuming, with Sarah, and there was a bearing in that— somehow beyond his control—on his personal fate. Yet she was only saying something quite easy and independent—the thing she had come, as a good friend of Chad's, on purpose to say. "There isn't anything at all—? I should be so delighted."

It was clear enough, when they were there before him, how she had been received. He saw this, as Sarah got up to greet him, from something fairly hectic in Sarah's face. He saw furthermore that they weren't, as had first come to him, alone together; he was at no loss as to the identity of the broad high back presented to him in the embrasure of the window furthest from the door. Waymarsh, whom he had to-day not yet seen, whom he only knew to have left the hotel before him, and who had taken part, the night previous, on Mrs. Pocock's kind invitation, conveyed by Chad, in the entertainment, informal but cordial, promptly offered by that lady

—Waymarsh had anticipated him even as Madame de Vionnet had done, and, with his hands in his pockets and his attitude unaffected by Strether's entrance, was looking out, in marked detachment, at the Rue de Rivoli. The latter felt it in the air—it was immense how Waymarsh could mark things—that he had remained deeply dissociated from the overture to their hostess that we have recorded on Madame de Vionnet's side. He had, conspicuously, tact, besides a stiff general view; and this was why he had left Mrs. Pocock to struggle alone. He would outstay the visitor; he would unmistakeably wait; to what had he been doomed for months past but waiting? Therefore she was to feel that she had him in reserve. What support she drew from this was still to be seen, for, although Sarah was vividly bright, she had given herself up for the moment to an ambiguous flushed formalism. She had had to reckon more quickly than she expected; but it concerned her first of all to signify that she was not to be taken unawares. Strether arrived precisely in time for her showing it. "Oh you're too good; but I don't think I feel quite helpless. I have my brother—and these American friends. And then you know I've been to Paris. I *know* Paris," said Sally Pocock in a tone that breathed a certain chill on Strether's heart.

"Ah but a woman, in this tiresome place where everything's always changing, a woman of good will," Madame de Vionnet threw off, "can always help a woman. I'm sure you 'know'—but we know perhaps different things." She too, visibly, wished to make no mistake; but it was a fear of a different order and more kept out of sight. She smiled in welcome at Strether; she greeted him more familiarly than Mrs. Pocock; she put out her hand to him without moving from her place; and it came to him in the course of a minute and in the oddest way that—yes, positively—she was giving him over to ruin. She was all kindness and ease, but she couldn't help so giving him; she was exquisite, and her being just as she was poured for Sarah a sudden rush of meaning into his own equivocations. How could she know how she was hurting him? She wanted to show as simple and humble—in the degree compatible with operative charm; but it was just this that seemed to put him on her side. She struck him as dressed, as arranged, as prepared infinitely to conciliate—with the very poetry of good taste in her view of the conditions of her early call. She was ready to advise about dressmakers and shops; she held herself wholly at the disposition of Chad's family. Strether noticed her card on the table— her coronet and her "Comtesse"—and the imagination was sharp in him of certain private adjustments in Sarah's mind. She had never, he was sure, sat with a "Comtesse" before, and such was the specimen of that class he had been keeping to play on her. She had

crossed the sea very particularly for a look at her; but he read in
Madame de Vionnet's own eyes that this curiosity hadn't been so
successfully met as that she herself wouldn't now have more than
ever need of him. She looked much as she had looked to him that
morning at Notre Dame; he noted in fact the suggestive sameness
of her discreet and delicate dress. It seemed to speak—perhaps a
little prematurely or too finely—of the sense in which she would
help Mrs. Pocock with the shops. The way that lady took her in,
moreover, added depth to his impression of what Miss Gostrey, by
their common wisdom, had escaped. He winced as he saw himself
but for that timely prudence ushering in Maria as a guide and an
example. There was however a touch of relief for him in his glimpse,
so far as he had got it, of Sarah's line. She "knew Paris." Madame
de Vionnet had, for that matter, lightly taken this up. "Ah then
you've a turn for that, an affinity that belongs to your family. Your
brother, though his long experience makes a difference, I admit,
has become one of us in a marvellous way." And she appealed to
Strether in the manner of a woman who could always glide off with
smoothness into another subject. Wasn't *he* struck with the way
Mr. Newsome had made the place his own, and hadn't he been in
a position to profit by his friend's wondrous expertness?

Strether felt the bravery, at the least, of her presenting herself
so promptly to sound that note, and yet asked himself what other
note, after all, she *could* strike from the moment she presented
herself at all. She could meet Mrs. Pocock only on the ground of
the obvious, and what feature of Chad's situation was more eminent
than the fact that he had created for himself a new set of circumstances? Unless she hid herself altogether she could show but as
one of these, an illustration of his domiciled and indeed of his
confirmed condition. And the consciousness of all this in her charming eyes was so clear and fine that as she thus publicly drew him
into her boat she produced in him such a silent agitation as he was
not to fail afterwards to denounce as pusillanimous. "Ah don't be
so charming to me!—for it makes us intimate, and after all what *is*
between us when I've been so tremendously on my guard and have
seen you but half a dozen times?" He recognised once more the
perverse law that so inveterately governed his poor personal aspects:
it would be exactly *like* the way things always turned out for him
that he should affect Mrs. Pocock and Waymarsh as launched in a
relation in which he had really never been launched at all. They
were at this very moment—they could only be—attributing to him
the full licence of it, and all by the operation of her own tone with
him; whereas his sole licence had been to cling with intensity to
the brink, not to dip so much as a toe into the flood. But the flicker
of his fear on this occasion was not, as may be added, to repeat itself;

it sprang up, for its moment, only to die down and then go out for ever. To meet his fellow visitor's invocation and, with Sarah's brilliant eyes on him, answer, *was* quite sufficiently to step into her boat. During the rest of the time her visit lasted he felt himself proceed to each of the proper offices, successively, for helping to keep the adventurous skiff afloat. It rocked beneath him, but he settled himself in his place. He took up an oar and, since he was to have the credit of pulling, pulled.

"That will make it all the pleasanter if it so happens that we *do* meet," Madame de Vionnet had further observed in reference to Mrs. Pocock's mention of her initiated state; and she had immediately added that, after all, her hostess couldn't be in need with the good offices of Mr. Strether so close at hand. "It's he, I gather, who has learnt to know his Paris, and to love it, better than any one ever before in so short a time; so that between him and your brother, when it comes to the point, how can you possibly want for good guidance? The great thing, Mr. Strether will show you," she smiled, "is just to let one's self go."

"Oh I've not let myself go very far," Strether answered, feeling quite as if he had been called upon to hint to Mrs. Pocock how Parisians could talk. "I'm only afraid of showing I haven't let myself go far enough. I've taken a good deal of time, but I must quite have had the air of not budging from one spot." He looked at Sarah in a manner that he thought she might take as engaging, and he made, under Madame de Vionnet's protection, as it were, his first personal point. "What has really happened has been that, all the while, I've done what I came out for."

Yet it only at first gave Madame de Vionnet a chance immediately to take him up. "You've renewed acquaintance with your friend—you've learnt to know him again." She spoke with such cheerful helpfulness that they might, in a common cause, have been calling together and pledged to mutual aid.

Waymarsh, at this, as if he had been in question, straightway turned from the window. "Oh yes, Countess—he has renewed acquaintance with *me*, and he *has*, I guess, learnt something about me, though I don't know how much he has liked it. It's for Strether himself to say whether he has felt it justifies his course."

"Oh but *you*," said the Countess gaily, "are not in the least what he came out for—is he really, Strether? and I hadn't you at all in my mind. I was thinking of Mr. Newsome, of whom we think so much and with whom, precisely, Mrs. Pocock has given herself the opportunity to take up threads. What a pleasure for you both!" Madame de Vionnet, with her eyes on Sarah, bravely continued.

Mrs. Pocock met her handsomely, but Strether quickly saw she

meant to accept no version of her movements or plans from any
other lips. She required no patronage and no support, which were
but other names for a false position; she would show in her own way
what she chose to show, and this she expressed with a dry glitter
that recalled to him a fine Woollett winter morning. "I've never
wanted for opportunities to see my brother. We've many things to
think of at home, and great responsibilities and occupations, and
our home's not an impossible place. We've plenty of reasons,"
Sarah continued a little piercingly, "for everything we do"—and
in short she wouldn't give herself the least little scrap away. But
she added as one who was always bland and who could afford a
concession: "I've come because—well, because we do come."

"Ah then fortunately!"—Madame de Vionnet breathed it to the
air. Five minutes later they were on their feet for her to take leave,
standing together in an affability that had succeeded in surviving a
further exchange of remarks; only with the emphasised appearance
on Waymarsh's part of a tendency to revert, in a ruminating manner and as with an instinctive or a precautionary lightening of his
tread, to an open window and his point of vantage. The glazed and
gilded room, all red damask, ormolu, mirrors, clocks, looked south,
and the shutters were bowed upon the summer morning; but the
Tuileries garden and what was beyond it, over which the whole place
hung, were things visible through gaps; so that the far-spreading
presence of Paris came up in coolness, dimness and invitation, in
the twinkle of gilt-tipped palings, the crunch of gravel, the click of
hoofs, the crack of whips, things that suggested some parade of the
circus. "I think it probable," said Mrs. Pocock, "that I shall have
the opportunity of going to my brother's. I've no doubt it's very
pleasant indeed." She spoke as to Strether, but her face was turned
with an intensity of brightness to Madame de Vionnet, and there
was a moment during which, while she thus fronted her, our
friend expected to hear her add: "I'm much obliged to you, I'm
sure, for inviting me there." He guessed that for five seconds these
words were on the point of coming; he heard them as clearly as if
they had been spoken; but he presently knew they had just failed
—knew it by a glance, quick and fine, from Madame de Vionnet,
which told him that she too had felt them in the air, but that the
point had luckily not been made in any manner requiring notice.
This left her free to reply only to what had been said.

"That the Boulevard Malesherbes may be common ground for
us offers me the best prospect I see for the pleasure of meeting
you again."

"Oh I shall come to see you, since you've been so good": and
Mrs. Pocock looked her invader well in the eyes. The flush in
Sarah's cheeks had by this time settled to a small definite crimson

spot that was not without its own bravery; she held her head a good deal up, and it came to Strether that of the two, at this moment, she was the one who most carried out the idea of a Countess. He quite took in, however, that she would really return her visitor's civility: she wouldn't report again at Woollett without at least so much producible history as that in her pocket.

"I want extremely to be able to show you my little daughter." Madame de Vionnet went on; "and I should have brought her with me if I hadn't wished first to ask your leave. I was in hopes I should perhaps find Miss Pocock, of whose being with you I've heard from Mr. Newsome and whose acquaintance I should so much like my child to make. If I have the pleasure of seeing her and you do permit it I shall venture to ask her to be kind to Jeanne. Mr. Strether will tell you"—she beautifully kept it up—"that my poor girl is gentle and good and rather lonely. They've made friends, he and she, ever so happily, and he doesn't, I believe, think ill of her. As for Jeanne herself he has had the same success with her that I know he has had here wherever he has turned." She seemed to ask him for permission to say these things, or seemed rather to take it, softly and happily, with the ease of intimacy, for granted, and he had quite the consciousness now that not to meet her at any point more than halfway would be odiously, basely to abandon her. Yes, he was *with* her, and, opposed even in this covert, this semi-safe fashion to those who were not, he felt, strangely and confusedly, but excitedly, inspiringly, how much and how far. It was as if he had positively waited in suspense for something from her that would let him in deeper, so that he might show her how he could take it. And what did in fact come as she drew out a little her farewell served sufficiently the purpose. "As his success is a matter that I'm sure he'll never mention for himself, I feel, you see, the less scruple; which it's very good of me to say, you know, by the way," she added as she addressed herself to him; "considering how little direct advantage I've gained from your triumphs with *me*. When does one ever see you? I wait at home and I languish. You'll have rendered me the service, Mrs. Pocock, at least," she wound up, "of giving me one of my much-too-rare glimpses of this gentleman."

"I certainly should be sorry to deprive you of anything that seems so much, as you describe it, your natural due. Mr. Strether and I are very old friends," Sarah allowed, "but the privilege of his society isn't a thing I shall quarrel about with any one."

"And yet, dear Sarah," he freely broke in, "I feel, when I hear you say that, that you don't quite do justice to the important truth of the extent to which—as you're also mine—I'm *your* natural

due. I should like much better," he laughed, "to see you fight for
me."

She met him, Mrs. Pocock, on this, with an arrest of speech—
with a certain breathlessness, as he immediately fancied, on the
score of a freedom for which she wasn't quite prepared. It had
flared up—for all the harm he had intended by it—because, con-
foundedly, he didn't want any more to be afraid about her than he
wanted to be afraid about Madame de Vionnet. He had never, naturally, called her anything but Sarah at home, and though he had
perhaps never quite so markedly invoked her as his "dear," that
was somehow partly because no occasion had hitherto laid so effective a trap for it. But something admonished him now that it
was too late—unless indeed it were possibly too early; and that he
at any rate shouldn't have pleased Mrs. Pocock the more by it.
"Well, Mr. Strether—!" she murmured with vagueness, yet with
sharpness, while her crimson spot burned a trifle brighter and he was
aware that this must be for the present the limit of her response.
Madame de Vionnet had already, however, come to his aid, and
Waymarsh, as if for further participation, moved again back to
them. It was true that the aid rendered by Madame de Vionnet was
questionable; it was a sign that, for all one might confess to with
her, and for all she might complain of not enjoying, she could still
insidiously show how much of the material of conversation had
accumulated between them.

"The real truth is, you know, that you sacrifice one without
mercy to dear old Maria. She leaves no room in your life for anybody else. Do you know," she enquired of Mrs. Pocock, "about
dear old Maria? The worst is that Miss Gostrey is really a wonderful woman."

"Oh yes indeed," Strether answered for her, "Mrs. Pocock knows
about Miss Gostrey. Your mother, Sarah, must have told you about
her; your mother knows everything," he sturdily pursued. "And I
cordially admit," he added with his conscious gaiety of courage,
"that she's as wonderful a woman as you like."

"Ah it isn't *I* who 'like,' dear Mr. Strether, anything to do with
the matter!" Sarah Pocock promptly protested; "and I'm by no
means sure I have—from my mother or from any one else—a notion of whom you're talking about."

"Well, he won't let you see her, you know," Madame de Vionnet
sympathetically threw in. "He never lets *me*—old friends as we
are: I mean as I am with Maria. He reserves her for his best hours;
keeps her consummately to himself; only gives us others the crumbs
of the feast."

"Well, Countess, *I've* had some of the crumbs," Waymarsh observed with weight and covering her with his large look; which led her to break in before he could go on.

"*Comment donc,* he shares her with *you?*" she exclaimed in droll stupefaction. "Take care you don't have, before you go much further, rather more of all *ces dames* than you may know what to do with!"

But he only continued in his massive way. "I can post you about the lady, Mrs. Pocock, so far as you may care to hear. I've seen her quite a number of times, and I was practically present when they made acquaintance. I've kept my eye on her right along, but I don't know as there's any real harm in her."

" 'Harm'?" Madame de Vionnet quickly echoed. "Why she's the dearest and cleverest of all the clever and dear."

"Well, you run her pretty close, Countess," Waymarsh returned with spirit; "though there's no doubt she's pretty well up in things. She knows her way round Europe. Above all there's no doubt she does love Strether."

"Ah but we all do that—we all love Strether: it isn't a merit!" their fellow visitor laughed, keeping to her idea with a good conscience at which our friend was aware that he marvelled, though he trusted also for it, as he met her exquisitely expressive eyes, to some later light.

The prime effect of her tone, however—and it was a truth which his own eyes gave back to her in sad ironic play—could only be to make him feel that, to say such things to a man in public, a woman must practically think of him as ninety years old. He had turned awkwardly, responsively red, he knew, at her mention of Maria Gostrey; Sarah Pocock's presence—the particular quality of it— had made this inevitable; and then he had grown still redder in proportion as he hated to have shown anything at all. He felt indeed that he was showing much, as, uncomfortably and almost in pain, he offered up his redness to Waymarsh, who, strangely enough, seemed now to be looking at him with a certain explanatory yearning. Something deep—something built on their old old relation—passed, in this complexity, between them; he got the side-wind of a loyalty that stood behind all actual queer questions. Waymarsh's dry bare humour—as it gave itself to be taken— gloomed out to demand justice. "Well, if you talk of Miss Barrace I've *my* chance too," it appeared stiffly to nod, and it granted that it was giving him away, but struggled to add that it did so only to save him. The sombre glow stared it at him till it fairly sounded out —"to save you, poor old man, to save you; to save you in spite of yourself." Yet it was somehow just this communication that showed him to himself as more than ever lost. Still another result of it was to put before him as never yet that between his comrade and the

interest represented by Sarah there was already a basis. Beyond all
question now, yes: Waymarsh had been in occult relation with
Mrs. Newsome—out, out it all came in the very effort of his face.
"Yes, you're feeling my hand"—he as good as proclaimed it; "but
only because this at least I *shall* have got out of the damned Old
World: that I shall have picked up the pieces into which it has
caused you to crumble." It was as if in short, after an instant,
Strether had not only had it from him, but had recognised that so
far as this went the instant had cleared the air. Our friend understood and approved; he had the sense that they wouldn't otherwise
speak of it. This would be all, and it would mark in himself a kind
of intelligent generosity. It was with grim Sarah then—Sarah grim
for all her grace—that Waymarsh had begun at ten o'clock in the
morning to save him. Well—if he *could*, poor dear man, with his
big bleak kindness! The upshot of which crowded perception was
that Strether, on his own side, still showed no more than he
absolutely had to. He showed the least possible by saying to Mrs.
Pocock after an interval much briefer than our glance at the picture
reflected in him: "Oh it's as true as they please!—There's no Miss
Gostrey for any one but me—not the least little peep. I keep her to
myself."

"Well, it's very good of you to notify me," Sarah replied without looking at him and thrown for a moment by this discrimination,
as the direction of her eyes showed, upon a dimly desperate little
community with Madame de Vionnet. "But I hope I shan't miss
her too much."

Madame de Vionnet instantly rallied. "And you know—though
it might occur to one—it isn't in the least that he's ashamed of
her. She's really—in a way—extremely good-looking."

"Ah but extremely!" Strether laughed while he wondered at the
odd part he found thus imposed on him.

It continued to be so by every touch from Madame de Vionnet.
"Well, as I say, you know, I wish you would keep *me* a little more
to yourself. Couldn't you name some day for me, some hour—and
better soon than late? I'll be at home whenever it best suits you.
There—I can't say fairer."

Strether thought a moment while Waymarsh and Mrs. Pocock
affected him as standing attentive. "I did lately call on you. Last
week—while Chad was out of town."

"Yes—and I was away, as it happened, too. You choose your
moments well. But don't wait for my next absence, for I shan't
make another," Madame de Vionnet declared, "while Mrs. Pocock's
here."

"That vow needn't keep you long, fortunately," Sarah observed
with reasserted suavity. "I shall be at present but a short time in

Paris. I have my plans for other countries. I meet a number of charming friends"—and her voice seemed to caress that description of these persons.

"Ah then," her visitor cheerfully replied, "all the more reason! To-morrow, for instance, or next day?" she continued to Strether. "Tuesday would do for me beautifully."

"Tuesday then with pleasure."

"And at half-past five?—or at six?"

It was ridiculous, but Mrs. Pocock and Waymarsh struck him as fairly waiting for his answer. It was indeed as if they were arranged, gathered for a performance, the performance of "Europe" by his confederate and himself. Well, the performance could only go on. "Say five forty-five."

"Five forty-five—good." And now at last Madame de Vionnet must leave them, though it carried, for herself, the performance a little further. "I *did* hope so much also to see Miss Pocock. Mayn't I still?"

Sarah hesitated, but she rose equal. "She'll return your visit with me. She's at present out with Mr. Pocock and my brother."

"I see—of course Mr. Newsome has everything to show them. He has told me so much about her. My great desire's to give my daughter the opportunity of making her acquaintance. I'm always on the lookout for such chances for her. If I didn't bring her to-day it was only to make sure first that you'd let me." After which the charming woman risked a more intense appeal. "It wouldn't suit *you* also to mention some near time, so that we shall be sure not to lose you?" Strether on his side waited, for Sarah likewise had, after all, to perform; and it occupied him to have been thus reminded that she had stayed at home—and on her first morning of Paris—while Chad led the others forth. Oh she was up to her eyes; if she had stayed at home she had stayed by an understanding, arrived at the evening before, that Waymarsh would come and find her alone. This was beginning well—for a first day in Paris; and the thing might be amusing yet. But Madame de Vionnet's earnestness was meanwhile beautiful. "You may think me indiscreet, but I've *such* a desire my Jeanne shall know an American girl of the really delightful kind. You see I throw myself for it on your charity."

The manner of this speech gave Strether such a sense of depths below it and behind it as he hadn't yet had—ministered in a way that almost frightened him to his dim divinations of reasons; but if Sarah still, in spite of it, faltered, this was why he had time for a sign of sympathy with her petitioner. "Let me say then, dear lady, to back your plea, that Miss Mamie is of the most delightful kind of all—is charming among the charming."

Even Waymarsh, though with more to produce on the subject,

could get into motion in time. "Yes, Countess, the American girl's a thing that your country must at least allow ours the privilege to say we *can* show you. But her full beauty is only for those who know how to make use of her."

"Ah then," smiled Madame de Vionnet, "that's exactly what I want to do. I'm sure she has much to teach us."

It was wonderful, but what was scarce less so was that Strether found himself, by the quick effect of it, moved another way. "Oh that may be! But don't speak of your own exquisite daughter, you know, as if she weren't pure perfection. *I* at least won't take that from you. Mademoiselle de Vionnet," he explained, in considerable form, to Mrs. Pocock, "*is* pure perfection. Mademoiselle de Vionnet *is* exquisite."

It had been perhaps a little portentous, but "Ah?" Sarah simply glittered.

Waymarsh himself, for that matter, apparently recognised, in respect to the facts, the need of a larger justice, and he had with it an inclination to Sarah. "Miss Jane's strikingly handsome—in the regular French style."

It somehow made both Strether and Madame de Vionnet laugh out, though at the very moment he caught in Sarah's eyes, as glancing at the speaker, a vague but unmistakeable "You too?" It made Waymarsh in fact look consciously over her head. Madame de Vionnet meanwhile, however, made her point in her own way. "I wish indeed I could offer you my poor child as a dazzling attraction: it would make one's position simple enough! She's as good as she can be, but of course she's different, and the question is now—in the light of the way things seem to go—if she isn't after all *too* different: too different I mean from the splendid type every one is so agreed that your wonderful country produces. On the other hand of course Mr. Newsome, who knows it so well, has, as a good friend, dear kind man that he is, done everything he can—to keep us from fatal benightedness—for my small shy creature. Well," she wound up after Mrs. Pocock had signified, in a murmur still a little stiff, that she would speak to her own young charge on the question—"well, we shall sit, my child and I, and wait and wait and wait for you." But her last fine turn was for Strether. "Do speak of us in such a way—!"

"As that something can't but come of it? Oh something *shall* come of it! I take a great interest!" he further declared; and in proof of it, the next moment, he had gone with her down to her carriage.

Book Ninth

I [XXII]

"The difficulty is," Strether said to Madame de Vionnet a couple of days later, "that I can't surprise them into the smallest sign of his not being the same old Chad they've been for the last three years glowering at across the sea. They simply won't give any, and as a policy, you know—what you call a *parti pris*,[1] a deep game—that's positively remarkable."

It was so remarkable that our friend had pulled up before his hostess with the vision of it; he had risen from his chair at the end of ten minutes and begun, as a help not to worry, to move about before her quite as he moved before Maria. He had kept his appointment with her to the minute and had been intensely impatient, though divided in truth between the sense of having everything to tell her and the sense of having nothing at all. The short interval had, in the face of their complication, multiplied his impressions—it being meanwhile to be noted, moreover, that he already frankly, already almost publicly, viewed the complication as common to them. If Madame de Vionnet, under Sarah's eyes, had pulled him into her boat, there was by this time no doubt whatever that he had remained in it and that what he had really most been conscious of for many hours together was the movement of the vessel itself. They were in it together this moment as they hadn't yet been, and he hadn't at present uttered the least of the words of alarm or remonstrance that had died on his lips at the hotel. He had other things to say to her than that she had put him in a position; so quickly had his position grown to affect him as quite excitingly, altogether richly, inevitable. That the outlook, however—given the point of exposure—hadn't cleared up half so much as he had reckoned was the first warning she received from him on his arrival. She had replied with indulgence that he was in too great a hurry, and had remarked soothingly that if she knew how to be patient surely *he* might be. He felt her presence, on the spot, he felt her tone and everything about her, as an aid to that effort; and it was perhaps one of the proofs of her success with him that he seemed so much to take his ease while they talked. By the time he had explained to her why his impressions, though multiplied, still baffled him, it was as if he had been familiarly talking for hours. They baffled him because Sarah—well, Sarah was deep, deeper than she had ever yet had a chance to show herself. He didn't say that this was partly the effect of her opening so straight down, as it

---

1. An obstinate purpose or prejudice.

were, into her mother, and that, given Mrs. Newsome's profundity, the shaft thus sunk might well have a reach; but he wasn't without a resigned apprehension that, at such a rate of confidence between the two women, he was likely soon to be moved to show how already, at moments, it had been for him as if he were dealing directly with Mrs. Newsome. Sarah, to a certainty, would have begun herself to feel it in him—and this naturally put it in her power to torment him the more. From the moment she knew he *could* be tormented—!

"But *why* can you be?"—his companion was surprised at his use of the word.

"Because I'm made so—I think of everything."

"Ah one must never do that," she smiled. "One must think of as few things as possible."

"Then," he answered, "one must pick them out right. But all I mean is—for I express myself with violence—that she's in a position to watch me. There's an element of suspense for me, and she can see me wriggle. But my wriggling doesn't matter," he pursued. "I can bear it. Besides, I shall wriggle out."

The picture at any rate stirred in her an appreciation that he felt to be sincere. "I don't see how a man can be kinder to a woman than you are to me."

Well, kind was what he wanted to be; yet even while her charming eyes rested on him with the truth of this he none the less had his humour of honesty. "When I say suspense I mean, you know," he laughed, "suspense about my own case too!"

"Oh yes—about your own case too!" It diminished his magnanimity, but she only looked at him the more tenderly.

"Not, however," he went on, "that I want to talk to you about that. It's my own little affair, and I mentioned it simply as part of Mrs. Pocock's advantage." No, no; though there was a queer present temptation in it, and his suspense was so real that to fidget was a relief, he wouldn't talk to her about Mrs. Newsome, wouldn't work off on her the anxiety produced in him by Sarah's calculated omissions of reference. The effect she produced of representing her mother had been produced—and that was just the immense, the uncanny part of it—without her having so much as mentioned that lady. She had brought no message, had alluded to no question, had only answered his enquiries with hopeless limited propriety. She had invented a way of meeting them—as if he had been a polite perfunctory poor relation, of distant degree—that made them almost ridiculous in him. He couldn't moreover on his own side ask much without appearing to publish how he had lately lacked news; a circumstance of which it was Sarah's profound policy not to betray a suspicion. These things, all the same, he wouldn't breathe to

Madame de Vionnet—much as they might make him walk up and
down. And what he didn't say—as well as what *she* didn't, for she
had also her high decencies—enhanced the effect of his being there
with her at the end of ten minutes more intimately on the basis
of saving her than he had yet had occasion to be. It ended in fact
by being quite beautiful between them, the number of things they
had a manifest consciousness of not saying. He would have liked to
turn her, critically, to the subject of Mrs. Pocock, but he so stuck
to the line he felt to be the point of honour and of delicacy that
he scarce even asked her what her personal impression had been.
He knew it, for that matter, without putting her to trouble: that
she wondered how, with such elements, Sarah could still have no
charm, was one of the principal things she held her tongue about.
Strether would have been interested in her estimate of the elements
—indubitably there, some of them, and to be appraised according to
taste—but he denied himself even the luxury of this diversion. The
way Madame de Vionnet affected him to-day was in itself a kind of
demonstration of the happy employment of gifts. How could a
woman think Sarah had charm who struck one as having arrived at
it herself by such different roads? On the other hand of course
Sarah wasn't obliged to have it. He felt as if somehow Madame de
Vionnet *was*. The great question meanwhile was what Chad thought
of his sister; which was naturally ushered in by that of Sarah's apprehension of Chad. *That* they could talk of, and with a freedom
purchased by their discretion in other senses. The difficulty however was that they were reduced as yet to conjecture. He had given
them in the day or two as little of a lead as Sarah, and Madame de
Vionnet mentioned that she hadn't seen him since his sister's
arrival.

"And does that strike you as such an age?"

She met it in all honesty. "Oh I won't pretend I don't miss him.
Sometimes I see him every day. Our friendship's like that. Make
what you will of it!" she whimsically smiled; a little flicker of the
kind, occasional in her, that had more than once moved him to
wonder what he might best make of *her*. "But he's perfectly right,"
she hastened to add, "and I wouldn't have him fail in any way at
present for the world. I'd sooner not see him for three months. I
begged him to be beautiful to them, and he fully feels it for himself."

Strether turned away under his quick perception; she was so odd
a mixture of lucidity and mystery. She fell in at moments with the
theory about her he most cherished, and she seemed at others to
blow it into air. She spoke now as if her art were all an innocence,
and then again as if her innocence were all an art. "Oh he's giving
himself up, and he'll do so to the end. How can he but want, now

that it's within reach, his full impression?—which is much more important, you know, than either yours or mine. But he's just soaking," Strether said as he came back; "he's going in conscientiously for a saturation. I'm bound to say he *is* very good."

"Ah," she quietly replied, "to whom do you say it?" And then more quietly still: "He's capable of anything."

Strether more than reaffirmed—"Oh he's excellent. I more and more like," he insisted, "to see him with them;" though the oddity of this tone between them grew sharper for him even while they spoke. It placed the young man so before them as the result of her interest and the product of her genius, acknowledged so her part in the phenomenon and made the phenomenon so rare, that more than ever yet he might have been on the very point of asking her for some more detailed account of the whole business than he had yet received from her. The occasion almost forced upon him some question as to how she had managed and as to the appearance such miracles presented from her own singularly close place of survey. The moment in fact however passed, giving way to more present history, and he continued simply to mark his appreciation of the happy truth. "It's a tremendous comfort to feel how one can trust him." And then again while for a little she said nothing—as if after all to *her* trust there might be a special limit: "I mean for making a good show to them."

"Yes," she thoughtfully returned—"but if they shut their eyes to it!"

Strether for an instant had his own thought. "Well perhaps that won't matter!"

"You mean because he probably—do what they will—won't like them?"

"Oh 'do what they will'—! They won't do much; especially if Sarah hasn't more—well, more than one has yet made out—to give."

Madame de Vionnet weighed it. "Ah she has all her grace!" It was a statement over which, for a little, they could look at each other sufficiently straight, and though it produced no protest from Strether the effect was somehow as if he had treated it as a joke. "She may be persuasive and caressing with him; she may be eloquent beyond words. She may get hold of him," she wound up—"well, as neither you nor I have."

"Yes, she *may*"—and now Strether smiled. "But he has spent all his time each day with Jim. He's still showing Jim round."

She visibly wondered. "Then how about Jim?"

Strether took a turn before he answered. "Hasn't he given you Jim? Hasn't he before this 'done' him for you?" He was a little at a loss. "Doesn't he tell you things?"

She hesitated. "No"—and their eyes once more gave and took.
"Not as you do. You somehow make me see them—or at least feel
them. And I haven't asked too much," she added; "I've of late
wanted so not to worry him."

"Ah for that, so have I," he said with encouraging assent; so
that—as if she had answered everything—they were briefly sociable
on it. It threw him back on his other thought, with which he took
another turn; stopping again, however, presently with something
of a glow. "You see Jim's really immense. I think it will be Jim
who'll do it."

She wondered. "Get hold of him?"

"No—just the other thing. Counteract Sarah's spell." And he
showed now, our friend, how far he had worked it out. "Jim's intensely cynical."

"Oh dear Jim!" Madame de Vionnet vaguely smiled.

"Yes, literally—dear Jim! He's awful. What _he_ wants, heaven
forgive him, is to help us."

"You mean"—she was eager—"help _me?_"

"Well, Chad and me in the first place. But he throws you in
too, though without as yet seeing you much. Only, so far as he
does see you—if you don't mind—he sees you as awful."

" 'Awful'?"—she wanted it all.

"A regular bad one—though of course of a tremendously superior kind. Dreadful, delightful, irresistible."

"Ah dear Jim! I should like to know him. I _must._"

"Yes, naturally. But will it do? You may, you know," Strether
suggested, "disappoint him."

She was droll and humble about it. "I can but try. But my
wickedness then," she went on, "is my recommendation for him?"

"Your wickedness and the charms with which, in such a degree
as yours, he associates it. He understands, you see, that Chad and
I have above all wanted to have a good time, and his view is simple
and sharp. Nothing will persuade him—in the light, that is, of my
behaviour—that I really didn't, quite as much as Chad, come over
to have one before it was too late. He wouldn't have expected it of
me; but men of my age, at Woollett—and especially the least likely
ones—have been noted as liable to strange outbreaks, belated uncanny clutches at the unusual, the ideal. It's an effect that a lifetime of Woollett has quite been observed as having; and I thus give
it to you, in Jim's view, for what it's worth. Now his wife and his
mother-in-law," Strether continued to explain, "have, as in honour
bound, no patience with such phenomena, late or early—which
puts Jim, as against his relatives, on the other side. Besides," he
added, "I don't think he really wants Chad back. If Chad doesn't
come—"

"He'll have"—Madame de Vionnet quite apprehended—"more of the free hand?"

"Well, Chad's the bigger man."

"So he'll work now, *en dessous*,[2] to keep him quiet?"

"No—he won't 'work' at all, and he won't do anything *en dessous*. He's very decent and won't be a traitor in the camp. But he'll be amused with his own little view of our duplicity, he'll sniff up what he supposes to be Paris from morning till night, and he'll be, as to the rest, for Chad—well, just what he is."

She thought it over. "A warning?"

He met it almost with glee. "You *are* as wonderful as everybody says!" And then to explain all he meant: "I drove him about for his first hour, and do you know what—all beautifully unconscious—he most put before me? Why that something like *that* is at bottom, as an improvement to his present state, as in fact the real redemption of it, what they think it may not be too late to make of our friend." With which, as, taking it in, she seemed, in her recurrent alarm, bravely to gaze at the possibility, he completed his statement. "But it *is* too late. Thanks to you!"

It drew from her again one of her indefinite reflexions. "Oh 'me' —after all!"

He stood before her so exhilarated by his demonstration that he could fairly be jocular. "Everything's comparative. You're better than *that*."

"You"—she could but answer him—"are better than anything." But she had another thought. "*Will* Mrs. Pocock come to me?"

"Oh yes—she'll do that. As soon, that is, as my friend Waymarsh—*her* friend now—leaves her leisure."

She showed an interest. "Is he so much her friend as that?"

"Why, didn't you see it all at the hotel?"

"Oh"—she was amused—" 'all' is a good deal to say. I don't know—I forget. I lost myself in *her*."

"You were splendid," Strether returned—"but 'all' isn't a good deal to say: it's only a little. Yet it's charming so far as it goes. She wants a man to herself."

"And hasn't she got *you*?"

"Do you think she looked at me—or even at you—as if she had?" Strether easily dismissed that irony. "Every one, you see, must strike her as having somebody. You've got Chad—and Chad has got you."

"I see"—she made of it what she could. "And you've got Maria."

Well, he on his side accepted that. "I've got Maria. And Maria has got me. So it goes."

"But Mr. Jim—whom has he got?"

"Oh he has got—or it's as *if* he had—the whole place."

"But for Mr. Waymarsh"—she recalled—"isn't Miss Barrace before any one else?"

He shook his head. "Miss Barrace is a *raffinée*,[3] and her amusement won't lose by Mrs. Pocock. It will gain rather—especially if Sarah triumphs and she comes in for a view of it."

"How well you know us!" Madame de Vionnet, at this, frankly sighed.

"No—it seems to me it's we that I know. I know Sarah—it's perhaps on that ground only that my feet are firm. Waymarsh will take her round while Chad takes Jim—and I shall be, I assure you, delighted for both of them. Sarah will have had what she requires —she will have paid her tribute to the ideal; and he will have done about the same. In Paris it's in the air—so what can one do less? If there's a point that, beyond any other, Sarah wants to make, it's that she didn't come out to be narrow. We shall feel at least that."

"Oh," she sighed, "the quantity we seem likely to 'feel'! But what becomes, in these conditions, of the girl?"

"Of Mamie—if we're all provided? Ah for that," said Strether, "you can trust Chad."

"To be, you mean, all right to her?"

"To pay her every attention as soon as he has polished off Jim. He wants what Jim can give him—and what Jim really won't— though he has had it all, and more than all, from me. He wants in short his own personal impression, and he'll get it—strong. But as soon as he has got it Mamie won't suffer."

"Oh Mamie mustn't *suffer!*" Madame de Vionnet soothingly emphasised.

But Strether could reassure her. "Don't fear. As soon as he has done with Jim, Jim will fall to me. And then you'll see."

It was as if in a moment she saw already; yet she still waited. Then "Is she really quite charming?" she asked.

He had got up with his last words and gathered in his hat and gloves. "I don't know; I'm watching. I'm studying the case, as it were—and I dare say I shall be able to tell you."

She wondered. "Is it a case?"

"Yes—I think so. At any rate I shall see."

"But haven't you known her before?"

"Yes," he smiled—"but somehow at home she wasn't a case. She has become one since." It was as if he made it out for himself. "She has become one here."

"So very very soon?"

He measured it, laughing. "Not sooner than I did."

"And you became one—?"

3. Person of refinement.

"Very very soon. The day I arrived."

Her intelligent eyes showed her thought of it. "Ah but the day you arrived you met Maria. Whom has Miss Pocock met?"

He paused again, but he brought it out. "Hasn't she met Chad?"

"Certainly—but not for the first time. He's an old friend." At which Strether had a slow amused significant headshake that made her go on: "You mean that for *her* at least he's a new person—that she sees him as different?"

"She sees him as different."

"And how does she see him?"

Strether gave it up. "How can one tell how a deep little girl sees a deep young man?"

"Is every one so deep? Is she too?"

"So it strikes me—deeper than I thought. But wait a little—between us we'll make it out. You'll judge for that matter yourself."

Madame de Vionnet looked for the moment fairly bent on the chance. "Then she *will* come with her?—I mean Mamie with Mrs. Pocock?"

"Certainly. Her curiosity, if nothing else, will in any case work that. But leave it all to Chad."

"Ah," wailed Madame de Vionnet, turning away a little wearily, "the things I leave to Chad!"

The tone of it made him look at her with a kindness that showed his vision of her suspense. But he fell back on his confidence. "Oh well—trust him. Trust him all the way." He had indeed no sooner so spoken than the queer displacement of his point of view appeared again to come up for him in the very sound, which drew from him a short laugh, immediately checked. He became still more advisory. "When they do come give them plenty of Miss Jeanne. Let Mamie see her well."

She looked for a moment as if she placed them face to face. "For Mamie to hate her?"

He had another of his corrective headshakes. "Mamie won't. Trust *them*."

She looked at him hard, and then as if it were what she must always come back to: "It's *you* I trust. But I was sincere," she said, "at the hotel. I did, I do, want my child—"

"Well?"—Strether waited with deference while she appeared to hesitate as to how to put it.

"Well, to do what she can for me."

Strether for a little met her eyes on it; after which something that might have been unexpected to her came from him. "Poor little duck!"

Not more expected for himself indeed might well have been her echo of it. "Poor little duck! But she immensely wants herself," she said, "to see our friend's cousin."

"Is that what she thinks her?"

"It's what we call the young lady."

He thought again; then with a laugh: "Well, your daughter will help you."

And now at last he took leave of her, as he had been intending for five minutes. But she went part of the way with him, accompanying him out of the room and into the next and the next. Her noble old apartment offered a succession of three, the first two of which indeed, on entering, smaller than the last, but each with its faded and formal air, enlarged the office of the antechamber and enriched the sense of approach. Strether fancied them, liked them, and, passing through them with her more slowly now, met a sharp renewal of his original impression. He stopped, he looked back; the whole thing made a vista, which he found high melancholy and sweet—full, once more, of dim historic shades, of the faint far-away cannon-roar of the great Empire. It was doubtless half the projection of his mind, but his mind was a thing that, among old waxed parquets, pale shades of pink and green, pseudo-classic candelabra, he had always needfully to reckon with. They could easily make him irrelevant. The oddity, the originality, the poetry—he didn't know what to call it—of Chad's connexion reaffirmed for him its romantic side. "They ought to see this, you know. They *must*."

"The Pococks?"—she looked about in deprecation; she seemed to see gaps he didn't.

"Mamie and Sarah—Mamie in particular."

"My shabby old place? But *their* things—!"

"Oh their things! You were talking of what will do something for you—"

"So that it strikes you," she broke in, "that my poor place may? Oh," she ruefully mused, "that *would* be desperate!"

"Do you know what I wish?" he went on. "I wish Mrs. Newsome herself could have a look."

She stared, missing a little his logic. "It would make a difference?"

Her tone was so earnest that as he continued to look about he laughed. "It might!"

"But you've told her, you tell me—"

"All about you? Yes, a wonderful story. But there's all the indescribable—what one gets only on the spot."

"Thank you!" she charmingly and sadly smiled.

"It's all about me here," he freely continued. "Mrs. Newsome feels things."

But she seemed doomed always to come back to doubt. "No one feels so much as *you*. No—not any one."

"So much the worse then for every one. It's very easy."

They were by this time in the antechamber, still alone together, as she hadn't rung for a servant. The antechamber was high and square, grave and suggestive too, a little cold and slippery even in summer, and with a few old prints that were precious, Strether divined, on the walls. He stood in the middle, slightly lingering, vaguely directing his glasses, while, leaning against the door-post of the room, she gently pressed her cheek to the side of the recess. "*You* would have been a friend."

"I?"—it startled him a little.

"For the reason you say. You're not stupid." And then abruptly, as if bringing it out were somehow founded on that fact: "We're marrying Jeanne."

It affected him on the spot as a move in a game, and he was even then not without the sense that that wasn't the way Jeanne should be married. But he quickly showed his interest, though— as quickly afterwards struck him—with an absurd confusion of mind. " 'You'? You and—a—not Chad?" Of course it was the child's father who made the 'we,' but to the child's father it would have cost him an effort to allude. Yet didn't it seem the next minute that Monsieur de Vionnet was after all not in question?—since she had gone on to say that it was indeed to Chad she referred and that he had been in the whole matter kindness itself.

"If I must tell you all, it is he himself who has put us in the way. I mean in the way of an opportunity that, so far as I can yet see, is all I could possibly have dreamed of. For all the trouble Monsieur de Vionnet will ever take!" It was the first time she had spoken to him of her husband, and he couldn't have expressed how much more intimate with her it suddenly made him feel. It wasn't much, in truth—there were other things in what she was saying that were far more; but it was as if, while they stood there together so easily in these cold chambers of the past, the single touch had shown the reach of her confidence. "But our friend," she asked, "hasn't then told you?"

"He has told me nothing."

"Well, it has come with rather a rush—all in a very few days; and hasn't moreover yet taken a form that permits an announcement. It's only for you—absolutely you alone—that I speak; I so want you to know." The sense he had so often had, since the first hour of his disembarkment, of being further and further "in," treated him again at this moment to another twinge; but in this wonderful way of her putting him in there continued to be something exquisitely remorseless. "Monsieur de Vionnet will accept what he *must* accept. He has proposed half a dozen things—each one more impossible than the other; and he wouldn't have found this if he lives to a hundred. Chad found it," she continued with her lighted, faintly flushed, her conscious confidential face, "in the quietest way in the world. Or rather it found *him*—for everything finds him; I mean finds him right. You'll think we do such things strangely—but at my age," she smiled, "one has to accept one's conditions. Our young man's people had seen her; one of his sisters, a charming woman—we know all about them—had observed her somewhere with me. She had spoken to her brother—turned him on; and we were again observed, poor Jeanne and I, without our in the least knowing it. It was at the beginning of the winter; it went on for some time; it outlasted our absence; it began again on our return; and it luckily seems all right. The young man had met Chad, and he got a friend to approach him—as having a decent interest in us. Mr. Newsome looked well before he leaped; he kept beautifully quiet and satisfied himself fully; then only he spoke. It's what has for some time past occupied us. It seems as if it were what would do; really, really all one could wish. There are only two or three points to be settled—they depend on her father. But this time I think we're safe."

Strether, consciously gaping a little, had fairly hung upon her lips. "I hope so with all my heart." And then he permitted himself: "Does nothing depend on *her*?"

"Ah naturally; everything did. But she's pleased *comme tout*.[4] She has been perfectly free; and he—our young friend—is really a combination. I quite adore him."

Strether just made sure. "You mean your future son-in-law?"

"Future if we all bring it off."

"Ah well," said Strether decorously, "I heartily hope you may." There seemed little else for him to say, though her communication had the oddest effect on him. Vaguely and confusedly he was troubled by it; feeling as if he had even himself been concerned in something deep and dim. He had allowed for depths, but these were greater: and it was as if, oppressively—indeed absurdly—he was responsible for what they had now thrown up to the surface. It was— through something ancient and cold in it—what he would have called the real thing. In short his hostess's news, though he couldn't have explained why, was a sensible shock, and his oppression a weight he felt he must somehow or other immediately get rid of. There were too many connexions missing to make it tolerable he should do anything else. He was prepared to suffer—before his own inner tribunal—for Chad; he was prepared to suffer even for Madame de Vionnet. But he wasn't prepared to suffer for the little girl. So now having said the proper thing, he wanted to get away. She held him an instant, however, with another appeal.

4. Completely.

"Do I seem to you very awful?"

"Awful? Why so?" But he called it to himself, even as he spoke, his biggest insincerity yet.

"Our arrangements are so different from yours."

"Mine?" Oh he could dismiss that too! "I haven't any arrangements."

"Then you must accept mine; all the more that they're excellent. They're founded on a *vieille sagesse*.[5] There will be much more, if all goes well, for you to hear and to know, and everything, believe me, for you to like. Don't be afraid; you'll be satisfied." Thus she could talk to him of what, of her innermost life—for that was what it came to—he must "accept"; thus she could extraordinarily speak as if in such an affair his being satisfied had an importance. It was all a wonder and made the whole case larger. He had struck himself at the hotel, before Sarah and Waymarsh, as being in her boat; but where on earth was he now? This question was in the air till her own lips quenched it with another. "And do you suppose *he*— who loves her so—would do anything reckless or cruel?"

He wondered what he supposed. "Do you mean your young man—?"

"I mean yours. I mean Mr. Newsome." It flashed for Strether the next moment a finer light, and the light deepened as she went on. "He takes, thank God, the truest tenderest interest in her."

It deepened indeed. "Oh I'm sure of that!"

"You were talking," she said, "about one's trusting him. You see then how I do."

He waited a moment—it all came. "I see—I see." He felt he really did see.

"He wouldn't hurt her for the world, nor—assuming she marries at all—risk anything that might make against her happiness. And —willingly, at least—he would never hurt *me*."

Her face, with what he had by this time grasped, told him more than her words; whether something had come into it, or whether he only read clearer, her whole story—what at least he then took for such—reached out to him from it. With the initiative she now attributed to Chad it all made a sense, and this sense— a light, a lead, was what had abruptly risen before him. He wanted, once more, to get off with these things; which was at last made easy, a servant having, for his assistance, on hearing voices in the hall, just come forward. All that Strether had made out was, while the man opened the door and impersonally waited, summed up in his last word. "I don't think, you know, Chad will tell me anything."

"No—perhaps not yet."

5. Ancient wisdom.

"And I won't as yet speak to him."

"Ah that's as you'll think best. You must judge."

She had finally given him her hand, which he held a moment. "How *much* I have to judge!"

"Everything," said Madame de Vionnet: a remark that was indeed—with the refined disguised suppressed passion of her face—what he most carried away.

II [XXIII]

So far as a direct approach was concerned Sarah had neglected him, for the week now about to end, with a civil consistency of chill that, giving him a higher idea of her social resource, threw him back on the general reflexion that a woman could always be amazing. It indeed helped a little to console him that he felt sure she had for the same period also left Chad's curiosity hanging; though on the other hand, for his personal relief, Chad could at least go through the various motions—and he made them extraordinarily numerous—of seeing she had a good time. There wasn't a motion on which, in her presence, poor Strether could so much as venture, and all he could do when he was out of it was to walk over for a talk with Maria. He walked over of course much less than usual, but he found a special compensation in a certain half-hour during which, toward the close of a crowded empty expensive day, his several companions seemed to him so disposed of as to give his forms and usages a rest. He had been with them in the morning and had nevertheless called on the Pococks in the afternoon; but their whole group, he then found, had dispersed after a fashion of which it would amuse Miss Gostrey to hear. He was sorry again, gratefully sorry she was so out of it—she who had really put him in; but she had fortunately always her appetite for news. The pure flame of the disinterested burned in her cave of treasures as a lamp in a Byzantine vault. It was just now, as happened, that for so fine a sense as hers a near view would have begun to pay. Within three days, precisely, the situation on which he was to report had shown signs of an equilibrium; the effect of his look in at the hotel was to confirm this appearance. If the equilibrium might only prevail! Sarah was out with Waymarsh, Mamie was out with Chad, and Jim was out alone. Later on indeed he himself was booked to Jim, was to take him that evening to the Varieties—which Strether was careful to pronounce as Jim pronounced them.

Miss Gostrey drank it in. "What then to-night do the others do?"

"Well, it has been arranged. Waymarsh takes Sarah to dine at Bignon's."[6]

She wondered. "And what do they do after? They can't come

<hr/>

6. Louis Bignon, a great nineteenth-century French restaurateur, managed the Café Riche (see p. 57).

straight home."

"No, they can't come straight home—at least Sarah can't. It's their secret, but I think I've guessed it." Then as she waited: "The circus."

It made her stare a moment longer, then laugh almost to extravagance. "There's no one like you!"

"Like *me?*"—he only wanted to understand.

"Like all of you together—like all of us: Woollett, Milrose and their products. We're abysmal—but may we never be less so! Mr. Newsome," she continued, "meanwhile takes Miss Pocock—?"

"Precisely—to the Français: to see what *you* took Waymarsh and me to, a family-bill."

"Ah then may Mr. Chad enjoy it as *I* did!" But she saw so much in things. "Do they spend their evenings, your young people, like that, alone together?"

"Well, they're young people—but they're old friends."

"I see, I see. And do *they* dine—for a difference—at Brébant's?"[7]

"Oh where they dine is their secret too. But I've my idea that it will be, very quietly, at Chad's own place."

"She'll come to him there alone?"

They looked at each other a moment. "He has known her from a child. Besides," said Strether with emphasis, "Mamie's remarkable. She's splendid."

She wondered. "Do you mean she expects to bring it off?"

"Getting hold of him? No—I think not."

"She doesn't want him enough?—or doesn't believe in her power?" On which as he said nothing she continued: "She finds she doesn't care for him?"

"No—I think she finds she does. But that's what I mean by so describing her. It's *if* she does that she's splendid. But we'll see," he wound up, "where she comes out."

"You seem to show me sufficiently," Miss Gostrey laughed, "where she goes in! But is her childhood's friend," she asked, "permitting himself recklessly to flirt with her?"

"No—not that. Chad's also splendid. They're *all* splendid!" he declared with a sudden strange sound of wistfulness and envy. "They're at least *happy.*"

"Happy?"—it appeared, with their various difficulties, to surprise her.

"Well—I seem to myself among them the only one who isn't."

She demurred. "With your constant tribute to the ideal?"

He had a laugh at his tribute to the ideal, but he explained after a moment his impression. "I mean they're living. They're rushing about. I've already had my rushing. I'm waiting."

7. A well-known tavern on the right bank.

"But aren't you," she asked by way of cheer, "waiting with *me?*"

He looked at her in all kindness. "Yes—if it weren't for that!"

"And you help me to wait," she said. "However," she went on, "I've really something for you that will help you to wait and which you shall have in a minute. Only there's something more I want from you first. I revel in Sarah."

"So do I. If it weren't," he again amusedly sighed, "for *that—!*"

"Well, you owe more to women than any man I ever saw. We do seem to keep you going. Yet Sarah, as I see her, must be great."

"She *is*"—Strether fully assented: "great! Whatever happens, she won't, with these unforgettable days, have lived in vain."

Miss Gostrey had a pause. "You mean she has fallen in love?"

"I mean she wonders if she hasn't—and it serves all her purpose."

"It has indeed," Maria laughed, "served women's purposes before!"

"Yes—for giving in. But I doubt if the idea—as an idea—has ever up to now answered so well for holding out. That's *her* tribute to the ideal—we each have our own. It's her romance—and it seems to me better on the whole than mine. To have it in Paris too," he explained—"on this classic ground, in this charged infectious air, with so sudden an intensity: well, it's more than she expected. She has had in short to recognise the breaking out for her of a real affinity—and with everything to enhance the drama."

Miss Gostrey followed. "Jim for instance?"

"Jim. Jim hugely enhances. Jim was made to enhance. And then Mr. Waymarsh. It's the crowning touch—it supplies the colour. He's positively separated."

"And she herself unfortunately isn't—that supplies the colour too." Miss Gostrey was all there. But somehow—! "Is *he* in love?"

Strether looked at her a long time; then looked all about the room; then came a little nearer. "Will you never tell any one in the world as long as ever you live?"

"Never." It was charming.

"He thinks Sarah really is. But he has no fear," Strether hastened to add.

"Of her being affected by it?"

"Of *his* being. He likes it, but he knows she can hold out. He's helping her, he's floating her over, by kindness."

Maria rather funnily considered it. "Floating her over in champagne? The kindness of dining her, nose to nose, at the hour when all Paris is crowding to profane delights, and in the—well, in the great temple, as one hears of it, of pleasure?"

"That's just *it*, for both of them," Strether insisted—"and all of a supreme innocence. The Parisian place, the feverish hour, the putting before her of a hundred francs' worth of food and drink, which they'll scarcely touch—all that's the dear man's own romance; the expensive kind, expensive in francs and centimes, in which he abounds. And the circus afterwards—which is cheaper, but which he'll find some means of making as dear as possible—that's also *his* tribute to the ideal. It does for him. He'll see her through. They won't talk of anything worse than you and me."

"Well, we're bad enough perhaps, thank heaven," she laughed. "to upset them! Mr. Waymarsh at any rate is a hideous old coquette." And the next moment she had dropped everything for a different pursuit. "What you don't appear to know is that Jeanne de Vionnet has become engaged. She's to marry—it has been definitely arranged—young Monsieur de Montbron."

He fairly blushed. "Then—if you know it—it's 'out'?"

"Don't I often know things that are *not* out? However," she said, "this will be out to-morrow. But I see I've counted too much on your possible ignorance. You've been before me, and I don't make you jump as I hoped."

He gave a gasp at her insight. "You never fail! I've *had* my jump. I had it when I first heard."

"Then if you knew why didn't you tell me as soon as you came in?"

"Because I had it from her as a thing not yet to be spoken of."

Miss Gostrey wondered. "From Madame de Vionnet herself?"

"As a probability—not quite a certainty: a good cause in which Chad has been working. So I've waited."

"You need wait no longer," she returned. "It reached me yesterday—roundabout and accidental, but by a person who had had it from one of the young man's own people—as a thing quite settled. I was only keeping it for you."

"You thought Chad wouldn't have told me?"

She hesitated. "Well, if he hasn't—"

"He hasn't. And yet the thing appears to have been practically his doing. So there we are."

"There we are!" Maria candidly echoed.

"That's why I jumped. I jumped," he continued to explain, "because it means, this disposition of the daughter, that there's now nothing else: nothing else but him and the mother."

"Still—it simplifies."

"It simplifies"—he fully concurred. "But that's precisely where we are. It marks a stage in his relation. The act is his answer to Mrs. Newsome's demonstration."

"It tells," Maria asked, "the worst?"

"The worst."

"But is the worst what he wants Sarah to know?"

"He doesn't care for Sarah."

At which Miss Gostrey's eyebrows went up. "You mean she has already dished herself?"

Strether took a turn about; he had thought it out again and again before this, to the end; but the vista seemed each time longer. "He wants his good friend to know the best. I mean the measure of his attachment. She asked for a sign, and he thought of that one. There it is."

"A concession to her jealousy?"

Strether pulled up. "Yes—call it that. Make it lurid—for that makes my problem richer."

"Certainly, let us have it lurid—for I quite agree with you that we want none of our problems poor. But let us also have it clear. Can he, in the midst of such a preoccupation, or on the heels of it, have seriously cared for Jeanne?—cared, I mean, as a young man at liberty would have cared?"

Well, Strether had mastered it. "I think he can have thought it would be charming if he *could* care. It would be nicer."

"Nicer than being tied up to Marie?"

"Yes—than the discomfort of an attachment to a person he can never hope, short of a catastrophe, to marry. And he was quite right," said Strether. "It would certainly have been nicer. Even when a thing's already nice there mostly *is* some other thing that would have been nicer—or as to which we wonder if it wouldn't. But his question was all the same a dream. He *couldn't* care in that way. He *is* tied up to Marie. The relation is too special and has gone too far. It's the very basis, and his recent lively contribution toward establishing Jeanne in life has been his definite and final acknowledgement to Madame de Vionnet that he has ceased squirming. I doubt meanwhile," he went on, "if Sarah has at all directly attacked him."

His companion brooded. "But won't he wish for his own satisfaction to make his ground good to her?"

"No—he'll leave it to me, he'll leave everything to me. I 'sort of' feel"—he worked it out—"that the whole thing will come upon me. Yes, I shall have every inch and every ounce of it. I shall be *used* for it—!" And Strether lost himself in the prospect. Then he fancifully expressed the issue. "To the last drop of my blood."

Maria, however, roundly protested. "Ah you'll please keep a drop for *me*. I shall have a use for it!"—which she didn't however follow up. She had come back the next moment to another matter. "Mrs. Pocock, with her brother, is trusting only to her general charm?"

"So it would seem."

"And the charm's not working?"

Well, Strether put it otherwise, "She's sounding the note of home—which is the very best thing she can do."

"The best for Madame de Vionnet?"

"The best for home itself. The natural one; the right one."

"Right," Maria asked, "when it fails?"

Strether had a pause. "The difficulty's Jim. Jim's the note of home."

She debated. "Ah surely not the note of Mrs. Newsome."

But he had it all. "The note of the home for which Mrs. Newsome wants him—the home of the business. Jim stands, with his little legs apart, at the door of *that* tent; and Jim *is*, frankly speaking, extremely awful."

Maria stared. "And you in, you poor thing, for your evening with him?"

"Oh he's all right for *me*!" Strether laughed. "Any one's good enough for *me*. But Sarah shouldn't, all the same, have brought him. She doesn't appreciate him."

His friend was amused with this statement of it. "Doesn't know, you mean, how bad he is?"

Strether shook his head with decision. "Not really."

She wondered. "Then doesn't Mrs. Newsome?"

It made him frankly do the same. "Well, no—since you ask me."

Maria rubbed it in. "Not really either?"

"Not at all. She rates him rather high." With which indeed, immediately, he took himself up. "Well, he *is* good too, in his way. It depends on what you want him for."

Miss Gostrey, however, wouldn't let it depend on anything—wouldn't have it, and wouldn't want him, at any price. "It suits my book," she said, "that he should be impossible; and it suits it still better," she more imaginatively added, "that Mrs. Newsome doesn't know he is."

Strether, in consequence, had to take it from her, but he fell back on something else. "I'll tell you who does really know."

"Mr. Waymarsh? Never!"

"Never indeed. I'm not *always* thinking of Mr. Waymarsh; in fact I find now I never am." Then he mentioned the person as if there were a good deal in it. "Mamie."

"His own sister?" Oddly enough it but let her down. "What good will that do?"

"None perhaps. But there—as usual—we are!"

III [XXIV]

There they were yet again, accordingly, for two days more; when Strether, on being, at Mrs. Pocock's hotel, ushered into that lady's salon, found himself at first assuming a mistake on the part of the servant who had introduced him and retired. The occupants hadn't

come in, for the room looked empty as only a room can look in
Paris, of a fine afternoon, when the faint murmur of the huge
collective life, carried on out of doors, strays among scattered objects even as a summer air idles in a lonely garden. Our friend
looked about and hesitated; observed, on the evidence of a table
charged with purchases and other matters, that Sarah had become
possessed—by no aid from *him*—of the last number of the salmon-
coloured Revue; noted further that Mamie appeared to have received a present of Fromentin's "Maîtres d'Autrefois"[8] from Chad,
who had written her name on the cover; and pulled up at the sight
of a heavy letter addressed in a hand he knew. This letter, for-
warded by a banker and arriving in Mrs. Pocock's absence, had
been placed in evidence, and it drew from the fact of its being un-
opened a sudden queer power to intensify the reach of its author.
It brought home to him the scale on which Mrs. Newsome—for
she had been copious indeed this time—was writing to her daughter
while she kept *him* in durance; and it had altogether such an effect
upon him as made him for a few minutes stand still and breathe
low. In his own room, at his own hotel, he had dozens of well-filled
envelopes superscribed in that character; and there was actually
something in the renewal of his interrupted vision of the character
that played straight into the so frequent question of whether he
weren't already disinherited beyond appeal. It was such an assurance as the sharp downstrokes of her pen hadn't yet had occasion
to give him; but they somehow at the present crisis stood for a
probable absoluteness in any decree of the writer. He looked at
Sarah's name and address, in short, as if he had been looking hard
into her mother's face, and then turned from it as if the face had
declined to relax. But since it was in a manner as if Mrs. Newsome
were thereby all the more, instead of the less, in the room, and
were conscious, sharply and sorely conscious, of himself, so he
felt both held and hushed, summoned to stay at least and take his
punishment. By staying, accordingly, he took it—creeping softly
and vaguely about and waiting for Sarah to come in. She *would*
come in if he stayed long enough, and he had now more than
ever the sense of her success in leaving him a prey to anxiety. It
wasn't to be denied that she had had a happy instinct, from the
point of view of Woollett, in placing him thus at the mercy of her
own initiative. It was very well to try to say he didn't care—that
she might break ground when she would, might never break it at
all if she wouldn't, and that he had no confession whatever to wait
upon her with: he breathed from day to day an air that damnably

---

8. Eugène Fromentin, French painter, writer, and art critic, published his studies of painters in
1876, and James, reviewing it the same year, found the book brilliantly written, exquisitely
charming—and over subtle. See Henry James, *"Les Maîtres d'autrefois," The Painter's Eye*,
ed. John L. Sweeney (London: Rupert Hart-Davis, 1956), 116–21.

required clearing, and there were moments when he quite ached to precipitate that process. He couldn't doubt that, should she only oblige him by surprising him just as he then was, a clarifying scene of some sort would result from the concussion.

He humbly circulated in this spirit till he suddenly had a fresh arrest. Both the windows of the room stood open to the balcony, but it was only now that, in the glass of the leaf of one of them, folded back, he caught a reflexion quickly recognised as the colour of a lady's dress. Somebody had been then all the while on the balcony, and the person, whoever it might be, was so placed between the windows as to be hidden from him; while on the other hand the many sounds of the street had covered his own entrance and movements. If the person were Sarah he might on the spot therefore be served to his taste. He might lead her by a move or two up to the remedy for his vain tension; as to which, should he get nothing else from it, he would at least have the relief of pulling down the roof on their heads. There was fortunately no one at hand to observe—in respect to his valour—that even on this completed reasoning he still hung fire. He had been waiting for Mrs. Pocock and the sound of the oracle; but he had to gird himself afresh—which he did in the embrasure of the window, neither advancing nor retreating—before provoking the revelation. It was apparently for Sarah to come more into view; he was in that case there at her service. She did however, as meanwhile happened, come more into view; only she luckily came at the last minute as a contradiction of Sarah. The occupant of the balcony was after all quite another person, a person presented, on a second look, by a charming back and a slight shift of her position, as beautiful brilliant unconscious Mamie—Mamie alone at home, Mamie passing her time in her own innocent way, Mamie in short rather shabbily used, but Mamie absorbed interested and interesting. With her arms on the balustrade and her attention dropped to the street she allowed Strether to watch her, to consider several things, without her turning round.

But the oddity was that when he *had* so watched and considered he simply stepped back into the room without following up his advantage. He revolved there again for several minutes, quite as with something new to think of and as if the bearings of the possibility of Sarah had been superseded. For frankly, yes, it *had* bearings thus to find the girl in solitary possession. There was something in it that touched him to a point not to have been reckoned beforehand, something that softly but quite pressingly spoke to him, and that spoke the more each time he paused again at the edge of the balcony and saw her still unaware. Her companions were plainly scattered; Sarah would be off somewhere with Waymarsh and Chad off somewhere with Jim. Strether didn't at

all mentally impute to Chad that he was with his "good friend";
he gave him the benefit of supposing him involved in appearances
that, had he had to describe them—for instance to Maria—he
would have conveniently qualified as more subtle. It came to him
indeed the next thing that there was perhaps almost an excess of
refinement in having left Mamie in such weather up there alone;
however she might in fact have extemporised, under the charm of
the Rue de Rivoli, a little makeshift Paris of wonder and fancy.
Our friend in any case now recognised—and it was as if at the
recognition Mrs. Newsome's fixed intensity had suddenly, with
a deep audible gasp, grown thin and vague—that day after day he
had been conscious in respect to his young lady of something odd
and ambiguous, yet something into which he could at last read a
meaning. It had been at the most, this mystery, an obsession—
oh an obsession agreeable; and it had just now fallen into its place
as at the touch of a spring. It had represented the possibility between them of some communication baffled by accident and delay
—the possibility even of some relation as yet unacknowledged.
    There was always their old relation, the fruit of the Woollett
years; but that—and it was what was strangest—had nothing
whatever in common with what was now in the air. As a child, as a
"bud," and then again as a flower of expansion, Mamie had
bloomed for him, freely, in the almost incessantly open doorways
of home; where he remembered her as first very forward, as then
very backward—for he had carried on at one period, in Mrs. Newsome's parlours (oh Mrs. Newsome's phases and his own!) a
course of English Literature re-enforced by exams and teas—and
once more, finally, as very much in advance. But he had kept no
great sense of points of contact; it not being in the nature of things
at Woollett that the freshest of the buds should find herself in the
same basket with the most withered of the winter apples. The child
had given sharpness, above all, to his sense of the flight of time;
it was but the day before yesterday that he had tripped up on her
hoop, yet his experience of remarkable women—destined, it would
seem, remarkably to grow—felt itself ready this afternoon, quite
braced itself, to include her. She had in fine more to say to him
than he had ever dreamed the pretty girl of the moment *could*
have; and the proof of the circumstance was that, visibly, unmistakeably, she had been able to say it to no one else. It was something she
could mention neither to her brother, to her sister-in-law nor to
Chad; though he could just imagine that had she still been at home
she might have brought it out, as a supreme tribute to age, authority and attitude, for Mrs. Newsome. It was moreover something in
which they all took an interest; the strength of their interest was in
truth just the reason of her prudence. All this then, for five minutes,

was vivid to Strether, and it put before him that, poor child, she
had now but her prudence to amuse her. That, for a pretty girl in
Paris, struck him, with a rush, as a sorry state; so that under the
impression he went out to her with a step as hypocritically alert, he
was well aware, as if he had just come into the room. She turned
with a start at his voice; preoccupied with him though she might
be, she was just a scrap disappointed. "Oh I thought you were
Mr. Bilham!"

The remark had been at first surprising and our friend's private
thought, under the influence of it, temporarily blighted; yet we are
able to add that he presently recovered his inward tone and that
many a fresh flower of fancy was to bloom in the same air. Little
Bilham—since little Bilham was, somewhat incongruously, expected—appeared behindhand; a circumstance by which Strether
was to profit. They came back into the room together after a little,
the couple on the balcony, and amid its crimson-and-gold elegance,
with the others still absent, Strether passed forty minutes that he
appraised even at the time as far, in the whole queer connexion,
from his idlest. Yes indeed, since he had the other day so agreed
with Maria about the inspiration of the lurid, here was something
for his problem that surely didn't make it shrink and that was
floated in upon him as part of a sudden flood. He was doubtless not
to know till afterwards, on turning them over in thought, of how
many elements his impression was composed; but he none the less
felt, as he sat with the charming girl, the signal growth of a confidence. For she *was* charming, when all was said—and none the less
so for the visible habit and practice of freedom and fluency. She
was charming, he was aware, in spite of the fact that if he hadn't
found her so he would have found her something he should have
been in peril of expressing as "funny." Yes, she was funny, wonderful Mamie, and without dreaming it; she was bland, she was bridal
—with never, that he could make out as yet, a bridegroom to support it; she was handsome and portly and easy and chatty, soft and
sweet and almost disconcertingly reassuring. She was dressed, if
we might so far discriminate, less as a young lady than as an old
one—had an old one been supposable to Strether as so committed
to vanity; the complexities of her hair missed moreover also the
looseness of youth; and she had a mature manner of bending a
little, as to encourage and reward, while she held neatly together
in front of her a pair of strikingly polished hands: the combination
of all of which kept up about her the glamour of her "receiving,"
placed her again perpetually between the windows and within
sound of the ice-cream plates, suggested the enumeration of all the
names, all the Mr. Brookses and Mr. Snookses, gregarious specimens of a single type, she was happy to "meet."

But if all this was where she was funny, and if what was funnier than the rest was the contrast between her beautiful benevolent patronage—such a hint of the polysyllabic as might make her something of a bore toward middle age—and her rather flat little voice, the voice, naturally, unaffectedly yet, of a girl of fifteen; so Strether, none the less, at the end of ten minutes, felt in her a quiet dignity that pulled things bravely together. If quiet dignity, almost more than matronly, with voluminous, too voluminous clothes, was the effect she proposed to produce, that was an ideal one could like in her when once one had got into relation. The great thing now for her visitor was that this was exactly what he had done; it made so extraordinary a mixture of the brief and crowded hour. It was the mark of a relation that he had begun so quickly to find himself sure she was, of all people, as might have been said, on the side and of the party of Mrs. Newsome's original ambassador. She was in *his* interest and not in Sarah's; and some sign of that was precisely what he had been feeling in her, these last days, as imminent. Finally placed, in Paris, in immediate presence of the situation and of the hero of it—by whom Strether was incapable of meaning any one but Chad—she had accomplished, and really in a manner all unexpected to herself, a change of base; deep still things had come to pass within her, and by the time she had grown sure of them Strether had become aware of the little drama. When she knew where she was, in short, he had made it out; and he made it out at present still better; though with never a direct word passing between them all the while on the subject of his own predicament. There had been at first, as he sat there with her, a moment during which he wondered if she meant to break ground in respect to his prime undertaking. That door stood so strangely ajar that he was half-prepared to be conscious, at any juncture, of her having, of any one's having, quite bounced in. But, friendly, familiar, light of touch and happy of tact, she exquisitely stayed out; so that it was for all the world as if to show she could deal with him without being reduced to—well, scarcely anything.

It fully came up for them then, by means of their talking of everything *but* Chad, that Mamie, unlike Sarah, unlike Jim, knew perfectly what had become of him. It fully came up that she had taken to the last fraction of an inch the measure of the change in him, and that she wanted Strether to know what a secret she proposed to make of it. They talked most conveniently—as if they had had no chance yet—about Woollett; and that had virtually the effect of their keeping the secret more close. The hour took on for Strether, little by little, a queer sad sweetness of quality; he had such a revulsion in Mamie's favour and on behalf of her social value as might have come from remorse at some early injustice. She made him, as under the breath of some vague western whiff, homesick and freshly restless; he could really for the time have fancied himself stranded with her on a far shore, during an ominous calm, in a quaint community of shipwreck. Their little interview was like a picnic on a coral strand; they passed each other, with melancholy smiles and looks sufficiently allusive, such cupfuls of water as they had saved. Especially sharp in Strether meanwhile was the conviction that his companion really knew, as we have hinted, where she had come out. It was at a very particular place— only *that* she would never tell him; it would be above all what he should have to puzzle for himself. This was what he hoped for, because his interest in the girl wouldn't be complete without it. No more would the appreciation to which she was entitled—so assured was he that the more he saw of her process the more he should see of her pride. She saw, herself, everything; but she knew what she didn't want, and that it was that had helped her. What didn't she want?—there was a pleasure lost for her old friend in not yet knowing, as there would doubtless be a thrill in getting a glimpse. Gently and sociably she kept that dark to him, and it was as if she soothed and beguiled him in other ways to make up for it. She came out with her impression of Madame de Vionnet—of whom she had "heard so much"; she came out with her impression of Jeanne, whom she had been "dying to see": she brought it out with a blandness by which her auditor was really stirred that she had been with Sarah early that very afternoon, and after dreadful delays caused by all sorts of things, mainly, eternally, by the purchase of clothes—clothes that unfortunately wouldn't be themselves eternal—to call in the Rue de Bellechasse.

At the sound of these names Strether almost blushed to feel that he couldn't have sounded them first—and yet couldn't either have justified his squeamishness. Mamie made them easy as he couldn't have begun to do, and yet it could only have cost her more than he should ever have had to spend. It was as friends of Chad's, friends special, distinguished, desirable, enviable, that she spoke of them, and she beautifully carried it off that much as she had heard of them—though she didn't say how or where, which was a touch of her own—she had found them beyond her supposition. She abounded in praise of them, and after the manner of Woollett—which made the manner of Woollett a loveable thing again to Strether. He had never so felt the true inwardness of it as when his blooming companion pronounced the elder of the ladies of the Rue de Bellechasse too fascinating for words and declared of the younger that she was perfectly ideal, a real little monster of charm. "Nothing," she said of Jeanne, "ought ever

to happen to her—she's so awfully right as she is. Another touch
will spoil her—so she oughtn't to *be* touched."

"Ah but things, here in Paris," Strether observed, "do happen
to little girls." And then for the joke's and the occasion's sake:
"Haven't you found that yourself?"

"That things happen—? Oh I'm not a little girl. I'm a big battered blowsy one. *I* don't care," Mamie laughed, "*what* happens."

Strether had a pause while he wondered if it mightn't happen
that he should give her the pleasure of learning that he found her
nicer than he had really dreamed—a pause that ended when he had
said to himself that, so far as it at all mattered for her, she had in
fact perhaps already made this out. He risked accordingly a different question—though conscious, as soon as he had spoken, that he
seemed to place it in relation to her last speech. "But that Mademoiselle de Vionnet is to be married—I suppose you've heard of
that."

For all, he then found, he need fear! "Dear, yes; the gentleman
was there: Monsieur de Montbron, whom Madame de Vionnet
presented to us."

"And was he nice?"

Mamie bloomed and bridled with her best reception manner.
"Any man's nice when he's in love."

It made Strether laugh. "But is Monsieur de Montbron in love
—already—with *you*?"

"Oh that's not necessary—it's so much better he should be so
with *her*: which, thank goodness, I lost no time in discovering
for myself. He's perfectly gone—and I couldn't have borne it for
her if he hadn't been. She's just too sweet."

Strether hesitated. "And through being in love too?"

On which with a smile that struck him as wonderful Mamie
had a wonderful answer. "She doesn't know if she is or not."

It made him again laugh out. "Oh but *you* do!"

She was willing to take it that way. "Oh yes, I know everything." And as she sat there rubbing her polished hands and making the best of it—only holding her elbows perhaps a little too
much out—the momentary effect for Strether was that every one
else, in all their affair, seemed stupid.

"Know that poor little Jeanne doesn't know what's the matter
with her?"

It was as near as they came to saying that she was probably in
love with Chad; but it was quite near enough for what Strether
wanted; which was to be confirmed in his certitude that, whether
in love or not, she appealed to something large and easy in the girl
before him. Mamie would be fat, too fat, at thirty; but she would
always be the person who, at the present sharp hour, had been

disinterestedly tender. "If I see a little more of her, as I hope I shall, I think she'll like me enough—for she seemed to like me to-day—to want me to tell her."

"And *shall* you?"

"Perfectly. I shall tell her the matter with her is that she wants only too much to do right. To do right for her, naturally," said Mamie, "is to please."

"Her mother, do you mean?"

"Her mother first."

Strether waited. "And then?"

"Well, 'then'—Mr. Newsome."

There was something really grand for him in the serenity of this reference. "And last only Monsieur de Montbron?"

"Last only"—she good-humouredly kept it up.

Strether considered. "So that every one after all then will be suited?"

She had one of her few hesitations, but it was a question only of a moment; and it was her nearest approach to being explicit with him about what was between them. "I think I can speak for myself. *I* shall be."

It said indeed so much, told such a story of her being ready to help him, so committed to him that truth, in short, for such use as he might make of it toward those ends of his own with which, patiently and trustfully, she had nothing to do—it so fully achieved all this that he appeared to himself simply to meet it in its own spirit by the last frankness of admiration. Admiration was of itself almost accusatory, but nothing less would serve to show her how nearly he understood. He put out his hand for good-bye with a "Splendid, splendid, splendid!" And he left her, in her splendour, still waiting for little Bilham.

Book Tenth

I [xxv]

Strether occupied beside little Bilham, three evenings after his interview with Mamie Pocock, the same deep divan they had enjoyed together on the first occasion of our friend's meeting Madame de Vionnet and her daughter in the apartment of the Boulevard Malesherbes, where his position affirmed itself again as ministering to an easy exchange of impressions. The present evening had a different stamp; if the company was much more numerous, so, inevitably, were the ideas set in motion. It was on the other hand, however, now strongly marked that the talkers moved, in respect to such matters, round an inner, a protected circle. They knew at any rate what really concerned them to-night, and Strether had begun by keeping his companion close to it. Only a few of Chad's guests had dined—that is fifteen or twenty, a few compared with the large concourse offered to sight by eleven o'clock; but number and mass, quantity and quality, light, fragrance, sound, the overflow of hospitality meeting the high tide of response, had all from the first pressed upon Strether's consciousness, and he felt himself somehow part and parcel of the most festive scene, as the term was, in which he had ever in his life been engaged. He had perhaps seen, on Fourths of July and on dear old domestic Commencements, more people assembled, but he had never seen so many in proportion to the space, or had at all events never known so great a promiscuity to show so markedly as picked. Numerous as was the company, it had still been made so by selection, and what was above all rare for Strether was that, by no fault of his own, he was in the secret of the principle that had worked. He hadn't enquired, he had averted his head, but Chad had put him a pair of questions that themselves smoothed the ground. He hadn't answered the questions, he had replied that they were the young man's own affair; and he had then seen perfectly that the latter's direction was already settled.

Chad had applied for counsel only by way of intimating that he knew what to do; and he had clearly never known it better than in now presenting to his sister the whole circle of his society. This was all in the sense and the spirit of the note struck by him on that lady's arrival; he had taken at the station itself a line that led him without a break, and that enabled him to lead the Pococks —though dazed a little, no doubt, breathless, no doubt, and bewildered—to the uttermost end of the passage accepted by them perforce as pleasant. He had made it for them violently pleasant and mercilessly full; the upshot of which was, to Strether's vision, that they had come all the way without discovering it to be really no passage at all. It was a brave blind alley, where to pass was impossible and where, unless they stuck fast, they would have— which was always awkward—publicly to back out. They were touching bottom assuredly tonight; the whole scene represented the terminus of the *cul-de-sac*.[1] So could things go when there was a hand to keep them consistent—a hand that pulled the wire with a skill at which the elder man more and more marvelled. The elder man felt responsible, but he also felt successful, since what had taken place was simply the issue of his own contention, six weeks before, that they properly should wait to see what their friends would have really to say. He had determined Chad to wait, he had determined him to see; he was therefore not to quarrel with

1. Blind alley.

the time given up to the business. As much as ever, accordingly, now that a fortnight had elapsed, the situation created for Sarah, and against which she had raised no protest, was that of her having accommodated herself to her adventure as to a pleasure-party surrendered perhaps even somewhat in excess to bustle and to "pace." If her brother had been at any point the least bit open to criticism it might have been on the ground of his spicing the draught too highly and pouring the cup too full. Frankly treating the whole occasion of the presence of his relatives as an opportunity for amusement, he left it, no doubt, but scant margin as an opportunity for anything else. He suggested, invented, abounded—yet all the while with the loosest easiest rein. Strether, during his own weeks, had gained a sense of knowing Paris; but he saw it afresh, and with fresh emotion, in the form of the knowledge offered to his colleague.

A thousand unuttered thoughts hummed for him in the air of these observations; not the least frequent of which was that Sarah might well of a truth not quite know whither she was drifting. She was in no position not to appear to expect that Chad should treat her handsomely; yet she struck our friend as privately stiffening a little each time she missed the chance of marking the great *nuance*. The great *nuance* was in brief that of course her brother must treat her handsomely—she should like to see him not; but that treating her handsomely, none the less, wasn't all in all—treating her handsomely buttered no parsnips; and that in fine there were moments when she felt the fixed eyes of their admirable absent mother fairly screw into the flat of her back. Strether, watching, after his habit, and overscoring with thought, positively had moments of his own in which he found himself sorry for her—occasions on which she affected him as a person seated in a runaway vehicle and turning over the question of a possible jump. *Would* she jump, could she, would *that* be a safe place?—this question, at such instants, sat for him in her lapse into pallor, her tight lips, her conscious eyes. It came back to the main point at issue: would she be, after all, to be squared? He believed on the whole she would jump; yet his alternations on this subject were the more especial stuff of his suspense. One thing remained well before him—a conviction that was in fact to gain sharpness from the impressions of this evening: that if she *should* gather in her skirts, close her eyes and quit the carriage while in motion, he would promptly enough become aware. She would alight from her headlong course more or less directly upon him; it would be appointed to him, unquestionably, to receive her entire weight. Signs and portents of the experience thus in reserve for him had, as it happened, multiplied even through the dazzle of Chad's party. It was partly under the nervous consciousness of such a prospect that, leaving almost every one in the two other rooms, leaving those of the guests already known to him as well as a mass of brilliant strangers of both sexes and of several varieties of speech, he had desired five quiet minutes with little Bilham, whom he always found soothing and even a little inspiring, and to whom he had actually moreover something distinct and important to say.

He had felt of old—for it already seemed long ago—rather humiliated at discovering he could learn in talk with a personage so much his junior the lesson of a certain moral ease; but he had now got used to that—whether or no the mixture of the fact with other humiliations had made it indistinct, whether or no directly from little Bilham's example, the example of his being contentedly just the obscure and acute little Bilham he was. It worked so for him, Strether seemed to see; and our friend had at private hours a wan smile over the fact that he himself, after so many more years, was still in search of something that would work. However, as we have said, it worked just now for them equally to have found a corner a little apart. What particularly kept it apart was the circumstance that the music in the salon was admirable, with two or three such singers as it was a privilege to hear in private. Their presence gave a distinction to Chad's entertainment, and the interest of calculating their effect on Sarah was actually so sharp as to be almost painful. Unmistakeably, in her single person, the motive of the composition and dressed in a splendour of crimson which affected Strether as the sound of a fall through a skylight, she would now be in the forefront of the listening circle and committed by it up to her eyes. Those eyes during the wonderful dinner itself he hadn't once met; having confessedly—perhaps a little pusillanimously—arranged with Chad that he should be on the same side of the table. But there was no use in having arrived now with little Bilham at an unprecedented point of intimacy unless he could pitch everything into the pot. "You who sat where you could see her, what does she make of it all? By which I mean on what terms does she take it?"

"Oh she takes it, I judge, as proving that the claim of his family is more than ever justified."

"She isn't then pleased with what he has to show?"

"On the contrary; she's pleased with it as with his capacity to do this kind of thing—more than she has been pleased with anything for a long time. But she wants him to show it *there*. He has no right to waste it on the likes of us."

Strether wondered. "She wants him to move the whole thing over?"

"The whole thing—with an important exception. Everything

he has 'picked up'—and the way he knows how. She sees no difficulty in that. She'd run the show herself, and she'll make the handsome concession that Woollett would be on the whole in some ways the better for it. Not that it wouldn't be also in some ways the better for Woollett. The people there are just as good."

"Just as good as you and these others? Ah that may be. But such an occasion as this, whether or no," Strether said, "isn't the people. It's what has made the people possible."

"Well then," his friend replied, "there you are; I give you my impression for what it's worth. Mrs. Pocock has *seen*, and that's to-night how she sits there. If you were to have a glimpse of her face you'd understand me. She has made up her mind—to the sound of expensive music."

Strether took it freely in. "Ah then I shall have news of her."

"I don't want to frighten you, but I think that likely. However," little Bilham continued, "if I'm of the least use to you to hold on by—!"

"You're not of the least!"—and Strether laid an appreciative hand on him to say it. "No one's of the least." With which, to mark how gaily he could take it, he patted his companion's knee. "I must meet my fate alone, and I *shall*—oh you'll see! And yet," he pursued the next moment, "you *can* help me too. You once said to me"—he followed this further—"that you held Chad should marry. I didn't see then so well as I know now that you meant he should marry Miss Pocock. Do you still consider that he should? Because if you do"—he kept it up—"I want you immediately to change your mind. You can help me that way."

"Help you by thinking he should *not* marry?"

"Not marry at all events Mamie."

"And who then?"

"Ah," Strether returned, "that I'm not obliged to say. But Madame de Vionnet—I suggest—when he can."

"Oh!" said little Bilham with some sharpness.

"Oh precisely! But he needn't marry at all—I'm at any rate not obliged to provide for it. Whereas in your case I rather feel that I *am*."

Little Bilham was amused. "Obliged to provide for my marrying?"

"Yes—after all I've done to you!"

The young man weighed it. "Have you done as much as that?"

"Well," said Strether, thus challenged, "of course I must remember what you've also done to *me*. We may perhaps call it square. But all the same," he went on, "I wish awfully you'd marry Mamie Pocock yourself."

Little Bilham laughed out. "Why it was only the other night, in this very place, that you were proposing to me a different union altogether."

"Mademoiselle de Vionnet?" Well, Strether easily confessed it. "That, I admit, was a vain image. *This* is practical politics. I want to do something good for both of you—I wish you each so well; and you can see in a moment the trouble it will save me to polish you off by the same stroke. She likes you, you know. You console her. And she's splendid."

Little Bilham stared as a delicate appetite stares at an over-heaped plate. "What do I console her for?"

It just made his friend impatient. "Oh come, you know!"

"And what proves for you that she likes me?"

"Why the fact that I found her three days ago stopping at home alone all the golden afternoon on the mere chance that you'd come to her, and hanging over her balcony on that of seeing your cab drive up. I don't know what you want more."

Little Bilham after a moment found it. "Only just to know what proves to you that I like *her*."

"Oh if what I've just mentioned isn't enough to make you do it, you're a stony-hearted little fiend. Besides"—Strether encouraged his fancy's flight—"you showed your inclination in the way you kept her waiting, kept her on purpose to see if she cared enough for you."

His companion paid his ingenuity the deference of a pause. "I didn't keep her waiting. I came at the hour. I wouldn't have kept her waiting for the world," the young man honourably declared.

"Better still—then there you are!" And Strether, charmed, held him the faster. "Even if you didn't do her justice, moreover," he continued, "I should insist on your immediately coming round to it. I want awfully to have worked it. I want"—and our friend spoke now with a yearning that was really earnest—"at least to have done *that*."

"To have married me off—without a penny?"

"Well, I shan't live long; and I give you my word, now and here, that I'll leave you every penny of my own. I haven't many, un-fortunately, but you shall have them all. And Miss Pocock, I think, has a few. I want," Strether went on, "to have been at least to that extent constructive—even expiatory. I've been sacrificing so to strange gods that I feel I want to put on record, somehow, my fidelity—fundamentally unchanged after all—to our own. I feel as if my hands were embrued with the blood of monstrous alien altars—of another faith altogether. There it is—it's done." And then he further explained. "It took hold of me because the idea of getting her quite out of the way for Chad helps to clear my ground."

The young man, at this, bounced about, and it brought them

face to face in admitted amusement. "You want me to marry as a convenience to Chad?"

"No," Strether debated—"*he* doesn't care whether you marry or not. It's as a convenience simply to my own plan *for* him."

"'Simply'!"—and little Bilham's concurrence was in itself a lively comment. "Thank you. But I thought," he continued, "you had exactly *no* plan 'for' him."

"Well then call it my plan for myself—which may be well, as you say, to have none. His situation, don't you see? is reduced now to the bare facts one has to recognise. Mamie doesn't want him, and he doesn't want Mamie: so much as that these days have made clear. It's a thread we can wind up and tuck in."

But little Bilham still questioned. "*You* can—since you seem so much to want to. But why should I?"

Poor Strether thought it over, but was obliged of course to admit that his demonstration did superficially fail. "Seriously, there *is* no reason. It's my affair—I must do it alone. I've only my fantastic need of making my dose stiff."

Little Bilham wondered. "What do you call your dose?"

"Why what I have to swallow. I want my conditions unmitigated."

He had spoken in the tone of talk for talk's sake, and yet with an obscure truth lurking in the loose folds; a circumstance presently not without its effect on his young friend. Little Bilham's eyes rested on him a moment with some intensity; then suddenly, as if everything had cleared up, he gave a happy laugh. It seemed to say that if pretending, or even trying, or still even hoping, to be able to care for Mamie would be of use, he was all there for the job. "I'll do anything in the world for you!"

"Well," Strether smiled, "anything in the world is all I want. I don't know anything that pleased me in her more," he went on, "than the way that, on my finding her up there all alone, coming on her unawares and feeling greatly for her being so out of it, she knocked down my tall house of cards with her instant and cheerful allusion to the next young man. It was somehow so the note I needed—her staying at home to receive him."

"It was Chad of course," said little Bilham, "who asked the next young man—I like your name for me!—to call."

"So I supposed—all of which, thank God, is in our innocent and natural manners. But do you know," Strether asked, "if Chad knows—?" And then as this interlocutor seemed at a loss: "Why where she has come out."

Little Bilham, at this, met his face with a conscious look; it was as if, more than anything yet, the allusion had penetrated. "Do you know yourself?"

Strether lightly shook his head. "There I stop. Oh, odd as it may appear to you, there *are* things I don't know. I only got the sense from her of something very sharp, and yet very down, that she was keeping all to herself. That is I had begun with the belief that she *had* kept it to herself; but face to face with her there I soon made out that there was a person with whom she would have shared it. I had thought she possibly might with *me*—but I saw then that I was only half in her confidence. When, turning to me to greet me—for she was on the balcony and I had come in without her knowing it—she showed me she had been expecting *you* and was proportionately disappointed, I got hold of the tail of my conviction. Half an hour later I was in possession of all the rest of it. You know what has happened." He looked at his young friend hard—then he felt sure. "For all you say, you're up to your eyes. So there you are."

Little Bilham after an instant pulled half round. "I assure you she hasn't told me anything."

"Of course she hasn't. For what do you suggest that I suppose her to take you? But you've been with her every day, you've seen her freely, you've liked her greatly—I stick to that—and you've made your profit of it. You know what she has been through as well as you know that she has dined here to-night—which must have put her, by the way, through a good deal more."

The young man faced this blast; after which he pulled round the rest of the way. "I haven't in the least said she hasn't been nice to me. But she's proud."

"And quite properly. But not too proud for that."

"It's just her pride that has made her. Chad," little Bilham loyally went on, "has really been as kind to her as possible. It's awkward for a man when a girl's in love with him."

"Ah but she isn't—now."

Little Bilham sat staring before him; then he sprang up as if his friend's penetration, recurrent and insistent, made him really after all too nervous. "No—she isn't now. It isn't in the least," he went on, "Chad's fault. He's really all right. I mean he would have been willing. But she came over with ideas. Those she had got at home. They had been her motive and support in joining her brother and his wife. She was to *save* our friend."

"Ah like me, poor thing?" Strether also got to his feet.

"Exactly—she had a bad moment. It was very soon distinct to her, to pull her up, to let her down, that, alas, he was, he *is*, saved. There's nothing left for her to do."

"Not even to love him?"

"She would have loved him better as she originally believed him."

Strether wondered. "Of course one asks one's self what notion a little girl forms, where a young man's in question, of such a history and such a state."

"Well, this little girl saw them, no doubt, as obscure, but she saw them practically as wrong. The wrong for her *was* the obscure. Chad turns out at any rate right and good and disconcerting, while what she was all prepared for, primed and girded and wound up for, was to deal with him as the general opposite."

"Yet wasn't her whole point"—Strether weighed it—"that he was to be, that he *could* be, made better, redeemed?"

Little Bilham fixed it all a moment, and then with a small head-shake that diffused a tenderness: "She's too late. Too late for the miracle."

"Yes"—his companion saw enough. "Still, if the worst fault of his condition is that it may be all there for her to profit by—?"

"Oh she doesn't want to 'profit,' in that flat way. She doesn't want to profit by another woman's work—she wants the miracle to have been her own miracle. *That's* what she's too late for."

Strether quite felt how it all fitted, yet there seemed one loose piece. "I'm bound to say, you know, that she strikes one, on these lines, as fastidious—what you call here *difficile*."[2]

Little Bilham tossed up his chin. "Of course she's *difficile*—on any lines! What else in the world *are* our Mamies—the real, the right ones?"

"I see, I see," our friend repeated, charmed by the responsive wisdom he had ended by so richly extracting. "Mamie is one of the real and the right."

"The very thing itself."

"And what it comes to then," Strether went on, "is that poor awful Chad is simply too good for her."

"Ah too good was what he was after all to be; but it was she herself, and she herself only, who was to have made him so."

It hung beautifully together, but with still a loose end. "Wouldn't he do for her even if he should after all break—"

"With his actual influence?" Oh little Bilham had for this enquiry the sharpest of all his controls. "How can he 'do'—on any terms whatever—when he's flagrantly spoiled?"

Strether could only meet the question with his passive, his receptive pleasure. "Well, thank goodness, *you're* not! *You* remain for her to save, and I come back, on so beautiful and full a demonstration, to my contention of just now—that of your showing distinct signs of her having already begun."

The most he could further say to himself—as his young friend turned away—was that the charge encountered for the moment no renewed denial. Little Bilham, taking his course back to the music,

2. Difficult to please.

only shook his good-natured ears an instant, in the manner of a terrier who has got wet; while Strether relapsed into the sense—which had for him in these days most of comfort—that he was free to believe in anything that from hour to hour kept him going. He had positively motions and flutters of this conscious hour-to-hour kind, temporary surrenders to irony, to fancy, frequent instinctive snatches at the growing rose of observation, constantly stronger for him, as he felt, in scent and colour, and in which he could bury his nose even to wantonness. This last resource was offered him, for that matter, in the very form of his next clear perception—the vision of a prompt meeting, in the doorway of the room, between little Bilham and brilliant Miss Barrace, who was entering as Bilham withdrew. She had apparently put him a question, to which he had replied by turning to indicate his late interlocutor; toward whom, after an interrogation further aided by a resort to that optical machinery which seemed, like her other ornaments, curious and archaic, the genial lady, suggesting more than ever for her fellow guest the old French print, the historic portrait, directed herself with an intention that Strether instantly met. He knew in advance the first note she would sound, and took in as she approached all her need of sounding it. Nothing yet had been so "wonderful" between them as the present occasion; and it was her special sense of this quality in occasions that she was there, as she was in most places, to feed. That sense had already been so well fed by the situation about them that she had quitted the other room, forsaken the music, dropped out of the play, abandoned, in a word, the stage itself, that she might stand a minute behind the scenes with Strether and so perhaps figure as one of the famous augurs replying, behind the oracle, to the wink of the other. Seated near him presently where little Bilham had sat, she replied in truth to many things; beginning as soon as he had said to her—what he hoped he said without fatuity—"All you ladies are extraordinarily kind to me."

She played her long handle, which shifted her observation; she saw in an instant all the absences that left them free. "How can we be anything else? But isn't that exactly your plight? 'We ladies'—oh we're nice, and you must be having enough of us! As one of us, you know, I don't pretend I'm crazy about us. But Miss Gostrey at least to-night has left you alone, hasn't she?" With which she again looked about as if Maria might still lurk.

"Oh yes," said Strether; "she's only sitting up for me at home." And then as this elicited from his companion her gay "Oh, oh, oh!" he explained that he meant sitting up in suspense and prayer. "We thought it on the whole better she shouldn't be present; and either way of course it's a terrible worry for her." He abounded in the sense of his appeal to the ladies, and they might take their choice of his doing so from humility or from pride. "Yet she inclines to believe I shall come out."

"Oh I incline to believe too you'll come out!"—Miss Barrace, with her laugh, was not to be behind. "Only the question's about *where*, isn't it? However," she happily continued, "if it's anywhere at all it must be very far on, mustn't it? To do us justice, I think, you know," she laughed, "we do, among us all, want you rather far on. Yes, yes," she repeated in her quick droll way; "we want you very, *very* far on!" After which she wished to know why he had thought it better Maria shouldn't be present.

"Oh," he replied, "it was really her own idea. I should have wished it. But she dreads responsibility."

"And isn't that a new thing for her?"

"To dread it? No doubt—no doubt. But her nerve has given way."

Miss Barrace looked at him a moment. "She has too much at stake." Then less gravely: "Mine, luckily for me, holds out."

"Luckily for me too"—Strether came back to that. "My own isn't so firm, *my* appetite for responsibility isn't so sharp, as that I haven't felt the very principle of this occasion to be 'the more the merrier.' If we *are* so merry it's because Chad has understood so well."

"He has understood amazingly," said Miss Barrace.

"It's wonderful!"—Strether anticipated for her.

"It's wonderful!" she, to meet it, intensified; so that, face to face over it, they largely and recklessly laughed. But she presently added: "Oh I see the principle. If one didn't one would be lost. But when once one has got hold of it—"

"It's as simple as twice two! From the moment he had to do something—"

"A crowd"—she took him straight up—"was the only thing? Rather, rather: a rumpus of sound," she laughed, "or nothing. Mrs. Pocock's built in, or built out—whichever you call it; she's packed so tight she can't move. She's in splendid isolation"—Miss Barrace embroidered the theme.

Strether followed, but scrupulous of justice. "Yet with every one in the place successively introduced to her."

"Wonderfully—but just so that it does build her out. She's bricked up, she's buried alive!"

Strether seemed for a moment to look at it; but it brought him to a sigh. "Oh but she's not dead! It will take more than this to kill her."

His companion had a pause that might have been for pity. "No, I can't pretend I think she's finished—or that it's for more

than to-night." She remained pensive as if with the same compunction. "It's only up to her chin." Then again for the fun of it:
"She can breathe."

"She can breathe!"—he echoed it in the same spirit. "And
do you know," he went on, "what's really all this time happening
to me?—through the beauty of music, the gaiety of voices, the
uproar in short of our revel and the felicity of your wit? The
sound of Mrs. Pocock's respiration drowns for me, I assure you,
every other. It's literally all I hear."

She focussed him with her clink of chains. "Well—!" she
breathed ever so kindly.

"Well, what?"

"She *is* free from her chin up," she mused; "and that *will* be
enough for her."

"It will be enough for me!" Strether ruefully laughed. "Waymarsh has really," he then asked, "brought her to see you?"

"Yes—but that's the worst of it. I could do you no good. And
yet I tried hard."

Strether wondered. "And how did you try?"

"Why I didn't speak of you."

"I see. That was better."

"Then what would have been worse? For speaking or silent,"
she lightly wailed, "I somehow 'compromise.' And it has never
been any one but you."

"That shows"—he was magnanimous—"that it's something
not in you, but in one's self. It's *my* fault."

She was silent a little. "No, it's Mr. Waymarsh's. It's the fault
of his having brought her."

"Ah then," said Strether good-naturedly, "why *did* he bring
her?"

"He couldn't afford not to."

"Oh you were a trophy—one of the spoils of conquest? But why
in that case, since you do 'compromise'—"

"Don't I compromise *him* as well? I do compromise him as well,"
Miss Barrace smiled. "I compromise him as hard as I can. But
for Mr. Waymarsh it isn't fatal. It's—so far as his wonderful relation with Mrs. Pocock is concerned—favourable." And then, as he
still seemed slightly at sea: "The man who had succeeded with *me*,
don't you see? For her to get him from me was such an added
incentive."

Strether saw, but as if his path was still strewn with surprises.
"It's 'from' you then that she has got him?"

She was amused at his momentary muddle. "You can fancy my
fight! She believes in her triumph. I think it has been part of her
joy."

"Oh her joy!" Strether sceptically murmured.

"Well, she thinks she has had her own way. And what's to-night for her but a kind of apotheosis? Her frock's really good."

"Good enough to go to heaven in? For after a real apotheosis," Strether went on, "there's nothing *but* heaven. For Sarah there's only to-morrow."

"And you mean that she won't find to-morrow heavenly?"

"Well, I mean that I somehow feel to-night—on her behalf—too good to be true. She has had her cake; that is she's in the act now of having it, of swallowing the largest and sweetest piece. There won't be another left for her. Certainly *I* haven't one. It can only, at the best, be Chad." He continued to make it out as for their common entertainment. "He may have one, as it were, up his sleeve; yet it's borne in upon me that if he had—"

"He wouldn't"—she quite understood—"have taken all *this* trouble? I dare say not, and, if I may be quite free and dreadful, I very much hope he won't take any more. Of course I won't pretend now," she added, "not to know what it's a question of."

"Oh every one must know now," poor Strether thoughtfully admitted; "and it's strange enough and funny enough that one should feel everybody here at this very moment to be knowing and watching and waiting."

"Yes—isn't it indeed funny?" Miss Barrace quite rose to it. "That's the way we *are* in Paris." She was always pleased with a new contribution to that queerness. "It's wonderful! But, you know," she declared, "it all depends on you. I don't want to turn the knife in your vitals, but that's naturally what you just now meant by our all being on top of you. We know you as the hero of the drama, and we're gathered to see what you'll do."

Strether looked at her a moment with a light perhaps slightly obscured. "I think that must be why the hero has taken refuge in this corner. He's scared at his heroism—he shrinks from his part."

"Ah but we nevertheless believe he'll play it. That's why," Miss Barrace kindly went on, "we take such an interest in you. We feel you'll come up to the scratch." And then as he seemed perhaps not quite to take fire: "Don't let him do it."

"Don't let Chad go?"

"Yes, keep hold of him. With all this"—and she indicated the general tribute—"he has done enough. We love him here—he's charming."

"It's beautiful," said Strether, "the way you all can simplify when you will."

But she gave it to him back. "It's nothing to the way *you* will when you must."

He winced at it as at the very voice of prophecy, and it kept him a moment quiet. He detained her, however, on her appearing about to leave him alone in the rather cold clearance their talk had made. "There positively isn't a sign of a hero to-night; the hero's dodging and shirking, the hero's ashamed. Therefore, you know, I think, what you must all *really* be occupied with is the heroine."

Miss Barrace took a minute. "The heroine?"

"The heroine. I've treated her," said Strether, "not a bit like a hero. Oh," he sighed, "I don't do it well!"

She eased him off. "You do it as you can." And then after another hesitation: "I think she's satisfied."

But he remained compunctious. "I haven't been near her. I haven't looked at her."

"Ah then you've lost a good deal!"

He showed he knew it. "She's more wonderful than ever?"

"Than ever. With Mr. Pocock."

Strether wondered. "Madame de Vionnet—with Jim?"

"Madame de Vionnet—with 'Jim.' " Miss Barrace was historic.

"And what's she doing with him?"

"Ah you must ask *him!*"

Strether's face lighted again at the prospect. "It *will* be amusing to do so." Yet he continued to wonder. "But she must have some idea."

"Of course she has—she has twenty ideas. She has in the first place," said Miss Barrace, swinging a little her tortoise-shell, "that of doing her part. Her part is to help *you.*"

It came out as nothing had come yet; links were missing and connexions unnamed, but it was suddenly as if they were at the heart of their subject. "Yes; how much more she does it," Strether gravely reflected, "than I help *her!*" It all came over him as with the near presence of the beauty, the grace, the intense, dissimulated spirit with which he had, as he said, been putting off contact. "*She* has courage."

"Ah she has courage!" Miss Barrace quite agreed; and it was as if for a moment they saw the quantity in each other's face.

But indeed the whole thing was present. "How much she must care!"

"Ah there it is. She does care. But it isn't, is it," Miss Barrace considerately added, "as if you had ever had any doubt of that?"

Strether seemed suddenly to like to feel that he really never had. "Why of course it's the whole point."

"Voilà!" Miss Barrace smiled.

"It's why one came out," Strether went on. "And it's why one has stayed so long. And it's also"—he abounded—"why one's going home. It's why, it's why—"

"It's why everything!" she concurred. "It's why she might be to-night—for all she looks and shows, and for all your friend 'Jim' does—about twenty years old. That's another of her ideas; to be for him, and to be quite easily and charmingly, as young as a little girl."

Strether assisted at his distance. " 'For him'? For Chad—?"

"For Chad, in a manner, naturally, always. But in particular to-night for Mr. Pocock." And then as her friend still stared: "Yes, it *is* of a bravery! But that's what she has: her high sense of duty." It was more than sufficiently before them. "When Mr. Newsome has his hands so embarrassed with his sister—"

"It's quite the least"—Strether filled it out—"that she should take his sister's husband? Certainly—quite the least. So she has taken him."

"She has taken him." It was all Miss Barrace had meant.

Still it remained enough. "It must be funny."

"Oh it *is* funny." That of course essentially went with it.

But it brought them back. "How indeed then she must care!" In answer to which Strether's entertainer dropped a comprehensive "Ah!" expressive perhaps of some impatience for the time he took to get used to it. She herself had got used to it long before.

II [XXVI]

When one morning within the week he perceived the whole thing to be really at last upon him Strether's immediate feeling was all relief. He had known this morning that something was about to happen—known it, in a moment, by Waymarsh's manner when Waymarsh appeared before him during his brief consumption of coffee and a roll in the small slippery *salle-à-manger* so associated with rich rumination. Strether had taken there of late various lonely and absent-minded meals; he communed there, even at the end of June, with a suspected chill, the air of old shivers mixed with old savours, the air in which so many of his impressions had perversely matured; the place meanwhile renewing its message to him by the very circumstance of his single state. He now sat there, for the most part, to sigh softly, while he vaguely tilted his carafe, over the vision of how much better Waymarsh was occupied. That was really his success by the common measure—to have led this companion so on and on. He remembered how at first there had been scarce a squatting-place he could beguile him into passing; the actual outcome of which at last was that there was scarce one that could arrest him in his rush. His rush—as Strether vividly and amusedly figured it—continued to be all with Sarah, and contained perhaps moreover the word of the whole enigma, whipping up in its fine full-flavoured froth the very principle, for good or for ill, of his own, of Strether's destiny. It might after all, to the end, only be that they had united to save him, and indeed, so far as

Waymarsh was concerned, that *had* to be the spring of action. Strether was glad at all events, in connexion with the case, that the saving he required was not more scant; so constituted a luxury was it in certain lights just to lurk there out of the full glare. He had moments of quite seriously wondering whether Waymarsh wouldn't in fact, thanks to old friendship and a conceivable indulgence, make about as good terms for him as he might make for himself. They wouldn't be the same terms of course; but they might have the advantage that he himself probably should be able to make none at all.

He was never in the morning very late, but Waymarsh had already been out, and, after a peep into the dim refectory, he presented himself with much less than usual of his large looseness. He had made sure, through the expanse of glass exposed to the court, that they would be alone; and there was now in fact that about him that pretty well took up the room. He was dressed in the garments of summer; and save that his white waistcoat was redundant and bulging these things favoured, they determined, his expression. He wore a straw hat such as his friend hadn't yet seen in Paris, and he showed a buttonhole freshly adorned with a magnificent rose. Strether read on the instant his story—how, astir for the previous hour, the sprinkled newness of the day, so pleasant at that season in Paris, he was fairly panting with the pulse of adventure and had been with Mrs. Pocock, unmistakeably, to the Marché aux Fleurs.[3] Strether really knew in this vision of him a joy that was akin to envy; so reversed as he stood there did their old positions seem; so comparatively doleful now showed, by the sharp turn of the wheel, the posture of the pilgrim from Woollett. He wondered, this pilgrim, if he had originally looked to Waymarsh so brave and well, so remarkably launched, as it was at present the latter's privilege to appear. He recalled that his friend had remarked to him even at Chester that his aspect belied his plea of prostration; but there certainly couldn't have been, for an issue, an aspect less concerned than Waymarsh's with the menace of decay. Strether had at any rate never resembled a Southern planter of the great days—which was the image picturesquely suggested by the happy relation between the fuliginous face and the wide panama of his visitor. This type, it further amused him to guess, had been, on Waymarsh's part, the object of Sarah's care; he was convinced that her taste had not been a stranger to the conception and purchase of the hat, any more than her fine fingers had been guiltless of the bestowal of the rose. It came to him in the current of thought, as things so oddly did come, that *he* had never risen with the lark to attend a brilliant woman to the Marché aux Fleurs;

3. Flower market.

this could be fastened on him in connexion neither with Miss Gostrey nor with Madame de Vionnet; the practice of getting up early for adventures could indeed in no manner be fastened on him. It came to him in fact that just here was his usual case: he was for ever missing things through his general genius for missing them, while others were for ever picking them up through a contrary bent. And it was others who looked abstemious and he who looked greedy; it was he somehow who finally paid, and it was others who mainly partook. Yes, he should go to the scaffold yet for he wouldn't know quite whom. He almost, for that matter, felt on the scaffold now and really quite enjoying it. It worked out as *because* he was anxious there—it worked out as for this reason that Waymarsh was so blooming. It was *his* trip for health, for a change, that proved the success—which was just what Strether, planning and exerting himself, had desired it should be. That truth already sat full-blown on his companion's lips; benevolence breathed from them as with the warmth of active exercise, and also a little as with the bustle of haste.

"Mrs. Pocock, whom I left a quarter of an hour ago at her hotel, has asked me to mention to you that she would like to find you at home here in about another hour. She wants to see you; she has something to say—or considers, I believe, that you may have: so that I asked her myself why she shouldn't come right round. She hasn't *been* round yet—to see our place; and I took upon myself to say that I was sure you'd be glad to have her. The thing's therefore, you see, to keep right here till she comes."

The announcement was sociably, even though, after Waymarsh's wont, somewhat solemnly made; but Strether quickly felt other things in it than these light features. It was the first approach, from that quarter, to admitted consciousness; it quickened his pulse; it simply meant at last that he should have but himself to thank if he didn't know where he was. He had finished his breakfast; he pushed it away and was on his feet. There were plenty of elements of surprise, but only one of doubt. "The thing's for *you* to keep here too?" Waymarsh had been slightly ambiguous.

He wasn't ambiguous, however, after this enquiry; and Strether's understanding had probably never before opened so wide and effective a mouth as it was to open during the next five minutes. It was no part of his friend's wish, as appeared, to help to receive Mrs. Pocock; he quite understood the spirit in which she was to present herself, but his connexion with her visit was limited to his having —well, as he might say—perhaps a little promoted it. He had thought, and had let her know it, that Strether possibly would think she might have been round before. At any rate, as turned out, she had been wanting herself, quite a while, to come. "I told her," said Waymarsh, "that it would have been a bright idea if she had only carried it out before."

Strether pronounced it so bright as to be almost dazzling. "But why *hasn't* she carried it out before? She has seen me every day—she had only to name her hour. I've been waiting and waiting."

"Well, I told her you had. And she has been waiting too." It was, in the oddest way in the world, on the showing of this tone, a genial new pressing coaxing Waymarsh; a Waymarsh conscious with a different consciousness from any he had yet betrayed, and actually rendered by it almost insinuating. He lacked only time for full persuasion, and Strether was to see in a moment why. Meantime, however, our friend perceived, he was announcing a step of some magnanimity on Mrs. Pocock's part, so that he could deprecate a sharp question. It was his own high purpose in fact to have smoothed sharp questions to rest. He looked his old comrade very straight in the eyes, and he had never conveyed to him in so mute a manner so much kind confidence and so much good advice. Everything that was between them was again in his face, but matured and shelved and finally disposed of. "At any rate," he added, "she's coming now."

Considering how many pieces had to fit themselves, it all fell, in Strether's brain, into a close rapid order. He saw on the spot what had happened, and what probably would yet; and it was all funny enough. It was perhaps just this freedom of appreciation that wound him up to his flare of high spirits. "What is she coming *for?* —to kill me?"

"She's coming to be very *very* kind to you, and you must let me say that I greatly hope you'll not be less so to herself."

This was spoken by Waymarsh with much gravity of admonition, and as Strether stood there he knew he had but to make a movement to take the attitude of a man gracefully receiving a present. The present was that of the opportunity dear old Waymarsh had flattered himself he had divined in him the slight soreness of not having yet thoroughly enjoyed; so he had brought it to him thus, as on a little silver breakfast-tray, familiarly though delicately—without oppressive pomp; and he was to bend and smile and acknowledge, was to take and use and be grateful. He was not—that was the beauty of it—to be asked to deflect too much from his dignity. No wonder the old boy bloomed in this bland air of his own distillation. Strether felt for a moment as if Sarah were actually walking up and down outside. Wasn't she hanging about the porte-cochère while her friend thus summarily opened a way? Strether would meet her but to take it, and everything would be for the best in the best of possible worlds. He had never so much known what any one meant as, in the light of this demonstration, he knew what

Mrs. Newsome did. It had reached Waymarsh from Sarah, but it had reached Sarah from her mother, and there was no break in the chain by which it reached *him*. "Has anything particular happened," he asked after a minute—"so suddenly to determine her? Has she heard anything unexpected from home?"

Waymarsh, on this, it seemed to him, looked at him harder than ever. " 'Unexpected'?" He had a brief hesitation; then, however, he was firm. "We're leaving Paris."

"Leaving? That *is* sudden."

Waymarsh showed a different opinion. "Less so than it may seem. The purpose of Mrs. Pocock's visit is to explain to you in fact that it's *not*."

Strether didn't at all know if he had really an advantage—anything that would practically count as one; but he enjoyed for the moment—as for the first time in his life—the sense of so carrying it off. He wondered—it was amusing—if he felt as the impudent feel. "I shall take great pleasure, I assure you, in any explanation. I shall be delighted to receive Sarah."

The sombre glow just darkened in his comrade's eyes; but he was struck with the way it died out again. It was too mixed with another consciousness—it was too smothered, as might be said, in flowers. He really for the time regretted it—poor dear old sombre glow! Something straight and simple, something heavy and empty, had been eclipsed in its company; something by which he had best known his friend. Waymarsh wouldn't *be* his friend, somehow, without the occasional ornament of the sacred rage, and the right to the sacred rage—inestimably precious for Strether's charity—he also seemed in a manner, and at Mrs. Pocock's elbow, to have forfeited. Strether remembered the occasion early in their stay when on that very spot he had come out with his earnest, his ominous "Quit it!"—and, so remembering, felt it hang by a hair that he didn't himself now utter the same note. Waymarsh was having a good time—this was the truth that was embarrassing for him, and he was having it then and there, he was having it in Europe, he was having it under the very protection of circumstances of which he didn't in the least approve; all of which placed him in a false position, with no issue possible—none at least by the grand manner. It was practically in the manner of any one—it was all but in poor Strether's own—that instead of taking anything up he merely made the most of having to be himself explanatory. "I'm not leaving for the United States direct. Mr. and Mrs. Pocock and Miss Mamie are thinking of a little trip before their own return, and we've been talking for some days past of our joining forces. We've settled it that we do join and that we sail together the end of next month. But we start to-morrow for Switzerland. Mrs. Pocock wants some scenery. She hasn't had much yet."

He was brave in his way too, keeping nothing back, confessing all there was, and only leaving Strether to make certain connexions. "Is what Mrs. Newsome had cabled her daughter an injunction to break off short?"

The grand manner indeed at this just raised its head a little. "I know nothing about Mrs. Newsome's cables."

Their eyes met on it with some intensity—during the few seconds of which something happened quite out of proportion to the time. It happened that Strether, looking thus at his friend, didn't take his answer for truth—and that something more again occurred in consequence of *that*. Yes—Waymarsh just *did* know about Mrs. Newsome's cables: to what other end than that had they dined together at Bignon's? Strether almost felt for the instant that it was to Mrs. Newsome herself the dinner had been given; and, for that matter, quite felt how she must have known about it and, as he might think, protected and consecrated it. He had a quick blurred view of daily cables, questions, answers, signals: clear enough was his vision of the expense that, when so wound up, the lady at home was prepared to incur. Vivid not less was his memory of what, during his long observation of her, some of her attainments of that high pitch had cost her. Distinctly she was at the highest now, and Waymarsh, who imagined himself an independent performer, was really, forcing his fine old natural voice, an overstrained accompanist. The whole reference of his errand seemed to mark her for Strether as by this time consentingly familiar to him, and nothing yet had so despoiled her of a special shade of consideration. "You don't know," he asked, "whether Sarah has been directed from home to try me on the matter of my also going to Switzerland?"

"I know," said Waymarsh as manfully as possible, "nothing whatever about her private affairs; though I believe her to be acting in conformity with things that have my highest respect." It was as manful as possible, but it was still the false note—as it had to be to convey so sorry a statement. He knew everything, Strether more and more felt, that he thus disclaimed, and his little punishment was just in this doom to a second fib. What falser position—given the man—could the most vindictive mind impose? He ended by squeezing through a passage in which three months before he would certainly have stuck fast. "Mrs Pocock will probably be ready herself to answer any enquiry you may put to her. But," he continued, "*but*—!" He faltered on it.

"But what? Don't put her too many?"

Waymarsh looked large, but the harm was done; he couldn't, do what he would, help looking rosy. "Don't do anything you'll be sorry for."

It was an attenuation, Strether guessed, of something else that had been on his lips; it was a sudden drop to directness, and was thereby the voice of sincerity. He had fallen to the supplicating note, and that immediately, for our friend, made a difference and reinstated him. They were in communication as they had been, that first morning, in Sarah's salon and in her presence and Madame de Vionnet's; and the same recognition of a great good will was again, after all, possible. Only the amount of response Waymarsh had then taken for granted was doubled, decupled now. This came out when he presently said: "Of course I needn't assure you I hope you'll come with us." Then it was that his implications and expectations loomed up for Strether as almost pathetically gross.

The latter patted his shoulder while he thanked him, giving the go-by to the question of joining the Pococks; he expressed the joy he felt at seeing him go forth again so brave and free, and he in fact almost took leave of him on the spot. "I shall see you again of course before you go; but I'm meanwhile much obliged to you for arranging so conveniently for what you've told me. I shall walk up and down in the court there—dear little old court which we've each bepaced so, this last couple of months, to the tune of our flights and our drops, our hesitations and our plunges: I shall hang about there, all impatience and excitement, please let Sarah know, till she graciously presents herself. Leave me with her without fear," he laughed; "I assure you I shan't hurt her. I don't think either she'll hurt *me*: I'm in a situation in which damage was some time ago discounted. Besides, *that* isn't what worries you—but don't, don't explain! We're all right as we are: which was the degree of success our adventure was pledged to for each of us. We weren't, it seemed, all right as we were before; and we've got over the ground, all things considered, quickly. I hope you'll have a lovely time in the Alps."

Waymarsh fairly looked up at him as from the foot of them. "I don't know as I *ought* really to go."

It was the conscience of Milrose in the very voice of Milrose, but, oh it was feeble and flat! Strether suddenly felt quite ashamed for him; he breathed a greater boldness. "*Let* yourself, on the contrary, go—in all agreeable directions. These are precious hours—at our age they mayn't recur. Don't have it to say to yourself at Milrose, next winter, that you hadn't courage for them." And then as his comrade queerly stared: "Live up to Mrs. Pocock."

"Live up to her?"

"You're a great help to her."

Waymarsh looked at it as at one of the uncomfortable things that were certainly true and that it was yet ironical to say. "It's more then than you are."

"That's exactly your own chance and advantage. Besides," said Strether, "I do in my way contribute. I know what I'm about."

Waymarsh had kept on his great panama, and, as he now stood nearer the door, his last look beneath the shade of it had turned again to darkness and warning. "So do I! See here, Strether."

"I know what you're going to say. 'Quit this'?"

"Quit this!" But it lacked its old intensity; nothing of it remained; it went out of the room with him.

III [XXVII]

Almost the first thing, strangely enough, that, about an hour later, Strether found himself doing in Sarah's presence was to remark articulately on this failure, in their friend, of what had been superficially his great distinction. It was as if—he alluded of course to the grand manner—the dear man had sacrificed it to some other advantage; which would be of course only for himself to measure. It might be simply that he was physically so much more sound than on his first coming out; this was all prosaic, comparatively cheerful and vulgar. And fortunately, if one came to that, his improvement in health was really itself grander than any manner it could be conceived as having cost him. "You yourself alone, dear Sarah"—Strether took the plunge—"have done him, it strikes me, in these three weeks, as much good as all the rest of his time together."

It was a plunge because somehow the range of reference was, in the conditions, "funny," and made funnier still by Sarah's attitude, by the turn the occasion had, with her appearance, so sensibly taken. Her appearance was really indeed funnier than anything else—the spirit in which he felt her to be there as soon as she *was* there, the shade of obscurity that cleared up for him as soon as he was seated with her in the small *salon de lecture* that had, for the most part, in all the weeks, witnessed the wane of his early vivacity of discussion with Waymarsh. It was an immense thing, quite a tremendous thing, for her to have come: this truth opened out to him in spite of his having already arrived for himself at a fairly vivid view of it. He had done exactly what he had given Waymarsh his word for—had walked and re-walked the court while he awaited her advent; acquiring in this exercise an amount of light that affected him at the time as flooding the scene. She had decided upon the step in order to give him the benefit of a doubt, in order to be able to say to her mother that she had, even to abjectness, smoothed the way for him. The doubt had been as to whether he mightn't take her as not having smoothed it—and the admonition had possibly come from Waymarsh's more detached spirit. Waymarsh had at any rate, certainly, thrown his weight into the scale—he had pointed to the importance of depriving their friend of a grievance. She had done justice to the plea, and it was to set herself right with a high ideal that she actually sat there in her state. Her calculation was sharp in the immobility with which she held her tall parasol-stick upright and at arm's length, quite as if she had struck the place to plant her flag; in the separate precautions she took not to show as nervous; in the aggressive repose in which she did quite nothing but wait for him. Doubt ceased to be possible from the moment he had taken in that she had arrived with no proposal whatever; that her concern was simply to show what she had come to receive. She had come to receive his submission, and Waymarsh was to have made it plain to him that she would expect nothing less. He saw fifty things, her host, at this convenient stage; but one of those he most saw was that their anxious friend hadn't quite had the hand required of him. Waymarsh *had*, however, uttered the request that she might find him mild, and while hanging about the court before her arrival he had turned over with zeal the different ways in which he could be so. The difficulty was that if he was mild he wasn't, for her purpose, conscious. If she wished him conscious—as everything about her cried aloud that she did—she must accordingly be at costs to make him so. Conscious he *was*, for himself—but only of too many things; so she must choose the one she required.

Practically, however, it at last got itself named, and when once that had happened they were quite at the centre of their situation. One thing had really done as well as another; when Strether had spoken of Waymarsh's leaving him, and that had necessarily brought on a reference to Mrs. Pocock's similar intention, the jump was but short to supreme lucidity. Light became indeed after that so intense that Strether would doubtless have but half made out, in the prodigious glare, by which of the two the issue had been in fact precipitated. It was, in their contracted quarters, as much there between them as if it had been something suddenly spilled with a crash and a splash on the floor. The form of his submission was to be an engagement to acquit himself within the twenty-four hours. "He'll go in a moment if you give him the word—he assures me on his honour he'll do that": this came in its order, out of its order, in respect to Chad, after the crash had occurred. It came repeatedly during the time taken by Strether to feel that he was even more fixed in his rigour than he had supposed—the time he was not above adding to a little by telling her that such a way of putting it on her brother's part left him sufficiently surprised. She wasn't at all funny at last—she was really fine; and he felt easily where she was strong—strong for herself. It hadn't yet so come home to him that she was nobly and appointedly officious. She was acting in interests grander and clearer than that of her poor little personal,

poor little Parisian equilibrium, and all his consciousness of her
mother's moral pressure profited by this proof of its sustaining
force. She would be held up; she would be strengthened; he needn't
in the least be anxious for her. What would once more have been
distinct to him had he tried to make it so was that, as Mrs. Newsome was essentially all moral pressure, the presence of this element
was almost identical with her own presence. It wasn't perhaps that
he felt he was dealing with her straight, but it was certainly as if she
had been dealing straight with *him*. She was reaching him somehow by the lengthened arm of the spirit, and he was having to that
extent to take her into account; but he wasn't reaching her in turn,
not making her take *him*; he was only reaching Sarah, who appeared
to take so little of him. "Something has clearly passed between
you and Chad," he presently said, "that I think I ought to know
something more about. Does he put it all," he smiled, "on me?"

"Did you come out," she asked, "to put it all on *him*?"

But he replied to this no further than, after an instant, by saying: "Oh it's all right. Chad I mean's all right in having said to
you—well anything he may have said. I'll *take* it all—what he does
put on me. Only I must see him before I see you again."

She hesitated, but she brought it out. "Is it absolutely necessary you should see me again?"

"Certainly, if I'm to give you any definite word about anything."

"Is it your idea then," she returned, "that I shall keep on meeting you only to be exposed to fresh humiliation?"

He fixed her a longer time. "Are your instructions from Mrs.
Newsome that you shall, even at the worst, absolutely and irretrievably break with me?"

"My instructions from Mrs. Newsome are, if you please, my affair. You know perfectly what your own were, and you can judge
for yourself of what it can do for you to have made what you have
of them. You can perfectly see, at any rate, I'll go so far as to say,
that if I wish not to expose myself I must wish still less to expose
her." She had already said more than she had quite expected; but,
though she had also pulled up, the colour in her face showed him
he should from one moment to the other have it all. He now indeed felt the high importance of his having it. "What is your
conduct," she broke out as if to explain—"what is your conduct
but an outrage to women like *us*? I mean your acting as if there can
be a doubt—as between us and such another—of his duty?"

He thought a moment. It was rather much to deal with at once;
not only the question itself, but the sore abysses it revealed. "Of
course they're totally different kinds of duty."

"And do you pretend that he has any at all—to such another?"

"Do you mean to Madame de Vionnet?" He uttered the name

not to affront her, but yet again to gain time—time that he needed
for taking in something still other and larger than her demand of
a moment before. It wasn't at once that he could see all that was
in her actual challenge; but when he did he found himself just
checking a low vague sound, a sound which was perhaps the nearest
approach his vocal chords had ever known to a growl. Everything
Mrs. Pocock had failed to give a sign of recognising in Chad as a
particular part of a transformation—everything that had lent intention to this particular failure—affected him as gathered into a
large loose bundle and thrown, in her words, into his face. The
missile made him to that extent catch his breath; which however he
presently recovered. "Why when a woman's at once so charming
and so beneficent—"

"You can sacrifice mothers and sisters to her without a blush,
and can make them cross the ocean on purpose to feel the more,
and take from you the straighter, *how* you do it?"

Yes, she had taken him up as short and as sharply as that; but
he tried not to flounder in her grasp. "I don't think there's anything I've done in any such calculated way as you describe. Everything has come as a sort of indistinguishable part of everything
else. Your coming out belonged closely to my having come before
you, and my having come was a result of our general state of mind.
Our general state of mind had proceeded, on its side, from our
queer ignorance, our queer misconceptions and confusions—from
which, since then, an inexorable tide of light seems to have floated
us into our perhaps still queerer knowledge. Don't you *like* your
brother as he is," he went on, "and haven't you given your mother
an intelligible account of all that that comes to?"

It put to her also, doubtless, his own tone, too many things; this
at least would have been the case hadn't his final challenge directly helped her. Everything, at the stage they had reached, directly helped her, because everything betrayed in him such a basis
of intention. He saw—the odd way things came out!—that he would
have been held less monstrous had he only been a little wilder.
What exposed him was just his poor old trick of quiet inwardness,
what exposed him was his *thinking* such offence. He hadn't in the
least however the desire to irritate that Sarah imputed to him, and
he could only at last temporise, for the moment, with her indignant view. She was altogether more inflamed than he had expected, and he would probably understand this better when he
should learn what had occurred for her with Chad. Till then her
view of his particular blackness, her clear surprise at his not clutching the pole she held out, must pass as extravagant. "I leave you to
flatter yourself," she returned, "that what you speak of is what
you've beautifully done. When a thing has been already described

in such a lovely way—!" But she caught herself up, and her comment on his description rang out sufficiently loud. "Do you consider her even an apology for a decent woman?"

Ah there it was at last! She put the matter more crudely than, for his own mixed purposes, he had yet had to do; but essentially it was all one matter. It was so much—so much; and she treated it, poor lady, as so little. He grew conscious, as he was now apt to do, of a strange smile, and the next moment he found himself talking like Miss Barrace. "She has struck me from the first as wonderful. I've been thinking too moreover that, after all, she would probably have represented even for yourself something rather new and rather good."

He was to have given Mrs. Pocock with this, however, but her best opportunity for a sound of derision. "Rather new? I hope so with all my heart!"

"I mean," he explained, "that she might have affected you by her exquisite amiability—a real revelation, it has seemed to myself; her high rarity, her distinction of every sort."

He had been, with these words, consciously a little "precious"; but he had had to be—he couldn't give her the truth of the case without them; and it seemed to him moreover now that he didn't care. He had at all events not served his cause, for she sprang at its exposed side. "A 'revelation'—to me: I've come to such a woman for a revelation? You talk to me about 'distinction'—you, you who've had your privilege?—when the most distinguished woman we shall either of us have seen in this world sits there insulted, in her loneliness, by your incredible comparison!"

Strether forbore, with an effort, from straying; but he looked all about him. "Does your mother herself make the point that she sits insulted?"

Sarah's answer came so straight, so "pat," as might have been said, that he felt on the instant its origin. "She has confided to my judgement and my tenderness the expression of her personal sense of everything, and the assertion of her personal dignity."

They were the very words of the lady of Woollett—he would have known them in a thousand; her parting charge to her child. Mrs. Pocock accordingly spoke to this extent by book, and the fact immensely moved him. "If she does really feel as you say it's of course very very dreadful. I've given sufficient proof, one would have thought," he added, "of my deep admiration for Mrs. Newsome."

"And pray what proof would one have thought you'd *call* sufficient? That of thinking this person here so far superior to her?"

He wondered again; he waited. "Ah dear Sarah, you must *leave* me this person here!"

In his desire to avoid all vulgar retorts, to show how, even perversely, he clung to his rag of reason, he had softly almost wailed this plea. Yet he knew it to be perhaps the most positive declaration he had ever made in his life, and his visitor's reception of it virtually gave it that importance. "That's exactly what I'm delighted to do. God knows *we* don't want her! You take good care not to meet," she observed in a still higher key, "my question about their life. If you do consider it a thing one can even *speak* of, I congratulate you on your taste!"

The life she alluded to was of course Chad's and Madame de Vionnet's, which she thus bracketed together in a way that made him wince a little; there being nothing for him but to take home her full intention. It was none the less his inconsequence that while he had himself been enjoying for weeks the view of the brilliant woman's specific action, he just suffered from any characterisation of it by other lips. "I think tremendously well of her, at the same time that I seem to feel her 'life' to be really none of my business. It's my business, that is, only so far as Chad's own life is affected by it; and what has happened, don't you see? is that Chad's has been affected so beautifully. The proof of the pudding's in the eating" —he tried, with no great success, to help it out with a touch of pleasantry, while she let him go on as if to sink and sink. He went on however well enough, as well as he could do without fresh counsel; he indeed shouldn't stand quite firm, he felt, till he should have re-established his communications with Chad. Still, he could always speak for the woman he had so definitely promised to "save." This wasn't quite for her the air of salvation; but as that chill fairly deepened what did it become but a reminder that one might at the worst perish *with* her? And it was simple enough—it was rudimentary: not, not to give her away. "I find in her more merits than you would probably have patience with my counting over. And do you know," he enquired, "the effect you produce on me by alluding to her in such terms? It's as if you had some motive in not recognising all she has done for your brother, and so shut your eyes to each side of the matter, in order, whichever side comes up, to get rid of the other. I don't, you must allow me to say, see how you can with any pretence to candour get rid of the side nearest you."

"Near me—*that* sort of thing?" And Sarah gave a jerk back of her head that well might have nullified any active proximity.

It kept her friend himself at his distance, and he respected for a moment the interval. Then with a last persuasive effort he bridged it. "You don't, on your honour, appreciate Chad's fortunate development?"

"Fortunate?" she echoed again. And indeed she was prepared. "I call it hideous."

Her departure had been for some minutes marked as imminent, and she was already at the door that stood open to the court, from the threshold of which she delivered herself of this judgement. It rang out so loud as to produce for the time the hush of everything else. Strether quite, as an effect of it, breathed less bravely; he could acknowledge it, but simply enough. "Oh if you think *that*—!"

"Then all's at an end? So much the better. I do think that!" She passed out as she spoke and took her way straight across the court, beyond which, separated from them by the deep arch of the porte-cochère the low victoria that had conveyed her from her own hotel was drawn up. She made for it with decision, and the manner of her break, the sharp shaft of her rejoinder, had an intensity by which Strether was at first kept in arrest. She had let fly at him as from a stretched cord, and it took him a minute to recover from the sense of being pierced. It was not the penetration of surprise; it was that, much more, of certainty; his case being put for him as he had as yet only put it to himself. She was away at any rate; she had distanced him—with rather a grand spring, an effect of pride and ease, after all; she had got into her carriage before he could overtake her, and the vehicle was already in motion. He stopped halfway; he stood there in the court only seeing her go and noting that she gave him no other look. The way he had put it to himself was that all quite *might* be at an end. Each of her movements, in this resolute rupture, reaffirmed, re-enforced that idea. Sarah passed out of sight in the sunny street while, planted there in the centre of the comparatively grey court, he continued merely to look before him. It probably *was* all at an end.

Book Eleventh

I [xxviii]

He went late that evening to the Boulevard Malesherbes, having his impression that it would be vain to go early, and having also, more than once in the course of the day, made enquiries of the concierge. Chad hadn't come in and had left no intimation; he had affairs, apparently, at this juncture—as it occurred to Strether he so well might have—that kept him long abroad. Our friend asked once for him at the hotel in the Rue de Rivoli, but the only contribution offered there was the fact that every one was out. It was with the idea that he would have to come home to sleep that Strether went up to his rooms, from which however he was still absent, though, from the balcony, a few moments later, his visitor heard eleven o'clock strike. Chad's servant had by this time answered for his reappearance; he *had*, the visitor learned, come quickly in to dress for dinner and vanish again. Strether spent an hour in waiting for him—an hour full of strange suggestions, persuasions, recognitions; one of those that he was to recall, at the end of his adventure, as the particular handful that most had counted. The mellowest lamplight and the easiest chair had been placed at his disposal by Baptiste, subtlest of servants; the novel half-uncut, the novel lemon-coloured and tender, with the ivory knife athwart it like the dagger in a contadina's [1] hair, had been pushed within the soft circle—a circle which, for some reason, affected Strether as softer still after the same Baptiste had remarked that in the absence of a further need of anything by Monsieur he would betake himself to bed. The night was hot and heavy and the single lamp sufficient; the great flare of the lighted city, rising high, spending itself afar, played up from the Boulevard and, through the vague vista of the successive rooms, brought objects into view and added to their dignity. Strether found himself in possession as he never yet had been; he had been there alone, had turned over books and prints, had invoked, in Chad's absence, the spirit of the place, but never at the witching hour and never with a relish quite so like a pang.

He spent a long time on the balcony; he hung over it as he had seen little Bilham hang the day of his first approach, as he had seen Mamie hang over her own the day little Bilham himself might have seen her from below; he passed back into the rooms, the three that occupied the front and that communicated by wide doors; and, while he circulated and rested, tried to recover the impression that they had made on him three months before, to catch again the voice in which they had seemed then to speak to him. That voice, he had to note, failed audibly to sound; which he took as the proof of all the change in himself. He had heard, of old, only what he *could* then hear; what he could do now was to think of three months ago as a point in the far past. All voices had grown thicker and meant more things; they crowded on him as he moved about—it was the way they sounded together that wouldn't let him be still. He felt, strangely, as sad as if he had come for some wrong, and yet as excited as if he had come for some freedom. But the freedom was what was most in the place and the hour; it was the freedom that most brought him round again to the youth of his own that he had long ago missed. He could have explained little enough to-day either why he had missed it or why, after years and years, he should care that he had; the main truth of the actual appeal of everything was none the less that everything represented the substance of his loss put it within reach, within touch, made it, to a degree it had never

---

1. Italian peasant woman.

been, an affair of the senses. That was what it became for him at
this singular time, the youth he had long ago missed—a queer concrete presence, full of mystery, yet full of reality, which he could
handle, taste, smell, the deep breathing of which he could positively
hear. It was in the outside air as well as within; it was in the long
watch, from the balcony, in the summer night, of the wide late life
of Paris, the unceasing soft quick rumble, below, of the little lighted
carriages that, in the press, always suggested the gamblers he had
seen of old at Monte Carlo pushing up to the tables. This image
was before him when he at last became aware that Chad was behind.

"She tells me you put it all on *me*"—he had arrived after this
promptly enough at that information; which expressed the case
however quite as the young man appeared willing for the moment
to leave it. Other things, with this advantage of their virtually having the night before them, came up for them, and had, as well, the
odd effect of making the occasion, instead of hurried and feverish,
one of the largest, loosest and easiest to which Strether's whole
adventure was to have treated him. He had been pursuing Chad
from an early hour and had overtaken him only now; but now the
delay was repaired by their being so exceptionally confronted. They
had foregathered enough of course in all the various times; they had
again and again, since that first night at the theatre, been face to
face over their question; but they had never been so alone together
as they were actually alone—their talk hadn't yet been so supremely
for themselves. And if many things moreover passed before them,
none passed more distinctly for Strether than that striking truth
about Chad of which he had been so often moved to take note: the
truth that everything came happily back with him to his knowing
how to live. It had been seated in his pleased smile—a smile that
pleased exactly in the right degree—as his visitor turned round, on
the balcony, to greet his advent; his visitor in fact felt on the spot
that there was nothing their meeting would so much do as bear
witness to that facility. He surrendered himself accordingly to so
approved a gift; for what was the meaning of the facility but that
others *did* surrender themselves? He didn't want, luckily, to prevent Chad from living; but he was quite aware that even if he had
he would himself have thoroughly gone to pieces. It was in truth
essentially by bringing down his personal life to a function all
subsidiary to the young man's own that he held together. And the
great point, above all, the sign of how completely Chad possessed
the knowledge in question, was that one thus became, not only
with a proper cheerfulness, but with wild native impulses, the
feeder of his stream. Their talk had accordingly not lasted three
minutes without Strether's feeling basis enough for the excitement

in which he had waited. This overflow fairly deepened, wastefully
abounded, as he observed the smallness of anything corresponding
to it on the part of his friend. That was exactly this friend's happy
case; he "put out" his excitement, or whatever other emotion the
matter involved, as he put out his washing; than which no arrangement could make more for domestic order. It was quite for Strether
himself in short to feel a personal analogy with the laundress bringing home the triumphs of the mangle.

When he had reported on Sarah's visit, which he did very fully,
Chad answered his question with perfect candour. "I positively referred her to you—told her she must absolutely see you. This was
last night, and it all took place in ten minutes. It was our first free
talk—really the first time she had tackled me. She knew I also
knew what her line had been with yourself; knew moreover how
little you had been doing to make anything difficult for her. So I
spoke for you frankly—assured her you were all at her service. I
assured her I was too," the young man continued; "and I pointed
out how she could perfectly, at any time, have got at me. Her difficulty has been simply her not finding the moment she fancied."

"Her difficulty," Strether returned, "has been simply that she
finds she's afraid of you. She's not afraid of *me*, Sarah, one little
scrap; and it was just because she has seen how I can fidget when I
give my mind to it that she has felt her best chance, rightly enough,
to be in making me as uneasy as possible. I think she's at bottom
as pleased to *have* you put it on me as you yourself can possibly be
to put it."

"But what in the world, my dear man," Chad enquired in objection to this luminosity, "have I done to make Sally afraid?"

"You've been 'wonderful, wonderful,' as we say—we poor people who watch the play from the pit; and that's what has, admirably, made her. Made her all the more effectually that she
could see you didn't set about it on purpose—I mean set about
affecting her as with fear."

Chad cast a pleasant backward glance over his possibilities of
motive. "I've only wanted to be kind and friendly, to be decent
and attentive—and I still only want to be."

Strether smiled at his comfortable clearness. "Well, there can
certainly be no way for it better than by my taking the onus. It
reduces your personal friction and your personal offence to almost
nothing."

Ah but Chad, with his completer conception of the friendly,
wouldn't quite have this! They had remained on the balcony,
where, after their day of great and premature heat, the midnight air
was delicious; and they leaned back in turn against the balustrade,
all in harmony with the chairs and the flower-pots, the cigarettes

and the starlight. "The onus isn't *really* yours—after our agreeing so to wait together and judge together. That was all my answer to Sally," Chad pursued—"that we have been, that we are, just judging together."

"I'm not afraid of the burden," Strether explained; "I haven't come in the least that you should take it off me. I've come very much, it seems to me, to double up my fore legs in the manner of the camel when he gets down on his knees to make his back convenient. But I've supposed you all this while to have been doing a lot of special and private judging—about which I haven't troubled you; and I've only wished to have your conclusion first from you. I don't ask more than that; I'm quite ready to take it as it has come."

Chad turned up his face to the sky with a slow puff of his smoke. "Well, I've seen."

Strether waited a little. "I've left you wholly alone; haven't, I think I may say, since the first hour or two—when I merely preached patience—so much as breathed on you."

"Oh you've been awfully good!"

"We've both been good then—we've played the game. We've given them the most liberal conditions."

"Ah," said Chad, "splendid conditions! It was open to them, open to them"—he seemed to make it out, as he smoked, with his eyes still on the stars. He might in quiet sport have been reading their horoscope. Strether wondered meanwhile what had been open to them, and he finally let him have it. "It was open to them simply to let me alone; to have made up their minds, on really seeing me for themselves, that I could go on well enough as I was."

Strether assented to this proposition with full lucidity, his companion's plural pronoun, which stood all for Mrs. Newsome and her daughter, having no ambiguity for him. There was nothing, apparently, to stand for Mamie and Jim; and this added to our friend's sense of Chad's knowing what he thought. "But they've made up their minds to the opposite—that you *can't* go on as you are."

"No," Chad continued in the same way; "they won't have it for a minute."

Strether on his side also reflectively smoked. It was as if their high place really represented some moral elevation from which they could look down on their recent past. "There never was the smallest chance, do you know, that they *would* have it for a moment."

"Of course not—no real chance. But if they were willing to think there was—!"

"They weren't willing." Strether had worked it all out. "It wasn't for you they came out, but for me. It wasn't to see for themselves what you're doing, but what I'm doing. The first branch of their curiosity was inevitably destined, under my culpable delay, to give way to the second; and it's on the second that, if I may use the expression and you don't mind my marking the invidious fact, they've been of late exclusively perched. When Sarah sailed it was me, in other words, they were after."

Chad took it in both with intelligence and with indulgence. "It *is* rather a business then—what I've let you in for!"

Strether had again a brief pause; which ended in a reply that seemed to dispose once for all of this element of compunction. Chad was to treat it, at any rate, so far as they were again together, as having done so. "I was 'in' when you found me."

"Ah but it was you," the young man laughed, "who found *me*."

"I only found you out. It was you who found me in. It was all in the day's work for them, at all events, that they should come. And they've greatly enjoyed it," Strether declared.

"Well, I've tried to make them," said Chad.

His companion did himself presently the same justice. "So have I. I tried even this very morning—while Mrs. Pocock was with me. She enjoys for instance, almost as much as anything else, not being, as I've said, afraid of me; and I think I gave her help in that."

Chad took a deeper interest. "Was she very very nasty?"

Strether debated. "Well, she was the most important thing—she was definite. She was—at last—crystalline. And I felt no remorse. I saw that they must have come."

"Oh I wanted to see them for myself; so that if it were only for *that*—!" Chad's own remorse was as small.

This appeared almost all Strether wanted. "Isn't your having seen them for yourself then *the* thing, beyond all others, that has come of their visit?"

Chad looked as if he thought it nice of his old friend to put it so. "Don't you count it as anything that you're dished—if you *are* dished? Are you, my dear man, dished?"

It sounded as if he were asking if he had caught cold or hurt his foot, and Strether for a minute but smoked and smoked. "I want to see her again. I must see her."

"Of course you must." Then Chad hesitated. "Do you mean—a —Mother herself?"

"Oh your mother—that will depend."

It was as if Mrs. Newsome had somehow been placed by the words very far off. Chad however endeavoured in spite of this to reach the place. "What do you mean it will depend on?"

Strether, for all answer, gave him a longish look. "I was speaking of Sarah. I must positively—though she quite cast me off—see *her* again. I can't part with her that way."

"Then she was awfully unpleasant?"

Again Strether exhaled. "She was what she had to be. I mean that from the moment they're not delighted they can only be—well what I admit she was. We gave them," he went on, "their chance to be delighted, and they've walked up to it, and looked all round it, and not taken it."

"You can bring a horse to water—!" Chad suggested.

"Precisely. And the tune to which this morning Sarah wasn't delighted—the tune to which, to adopt your metaphor, she refused to drink—leaves us on that side nothing more to hope."

Chad had a pause, and then as if consolingly: "It was never of course really the least on the cards that they would be 'delighted.'"

"Well, I don't know, after all," Strether mused. "I've had to come as far round. However"—he shook it off—"it's doubtless *my* performance that's absurd."

"There are certainly moments," said Chad, "when you seem to me too good to be true. Yet if you are true," he added, "that seems to be all that need concern me."

"I'm true, but I'm incredible. I'm fantastic and ridiculous—I don't explain myself even *to* myself. How can they then," Strether asked, "understand me? So I don't quarrel with them."

"I see. They quarrel," said Chad rather comfortably, "with *us*." Strether noted once more the comfort, but his young friend had already gone on. "I should feel greatly ashamed, all the same, if I didn't put it before you again that you ought to think, after all, tremendously well. I mean before giving up beyond recall—" With which insistence, as from a certain delicacy, dropped.

Ah but Strether wanted it. "Say it all, say it all."

"Well, at your age, and with what—when all's said and done—Mother might do for you and be for you."

Chad had said it all, from his natural scruple, only to that extent; so that Strether after an instant himself took a hand. "My absence of an assured future. The little I have to show toward the power to take care of myself. The way, the wonderful way, she would certainly take care of me. Her fortune, her kindness, and the constant miracle of her having been disposed to go even so far. Of course, of course"—he summed it up. "There are those sharp facts."

Chad had meanwhile thought of another still. "And don't you really care—?"

His friend slowly turned round to him. "Will you go?"

"I'll go if you'll say you now consider I should. You know," he went on, "I was ready six weeks ago."

"Ah," said Strether, "that was when you didn't know I wasn't! You're ready at present because you do know it."

"That may be," Chad returned; "but all the same I'm sincere. You talk about taking the whole thing on your shoulders, but in what light do you regard me that you think me capable of letting you pay?" Strether patted his arm, as they stood together against the parapet, reassuringly—seeming to wish to contend that he *had* the wherewithal; but it was again round this question of purchase and price that the young man's sense of fairness continued to hover. "What it literally comes to for you, if you'll pardon my putting it so, is that you give up money. Possibly a good deal of money."

"Oh," Strether laughed, "if it were only just enough you'd still be justified in putting it so! But I've on my side to remind you too that *you* give up money; and more than 'possibly'—quite certainly, as I should suppose—a good deal."

"True enough; but I've got a certain quantity," Chad returned after a moment. "Whereas you, my dear man, you—"

"I can't be at all said"—Strether took him up—"to have a 'quantity' certain or uncertain? Very true. Still, I shan't starve."

"Oh you mustn't *starve!*" Chad pacifically emphasised; and so, in the pleasant conditions, they continued to talk; though there was, for that matter, a pause in which the younger companion might have been taken as weighing again the delicacy of his then and there promising the elder some provision against the possibility just mentioned. This, however, he presumably thought best not to do, for at the end of another minute they had moved in quite a different direction. Strether had broken in by returning to the subject of Chad's passage with Sarah and enquiring if they had arrived, in the event, at anything in the nature of a "scene." To this Chad replied that they had on the contrary kept tremendously polite; adding moreover that Sally was after all not the woman to have made the mistake of not being. "Her hands are a good deal tied, you see. I got so, from the first," he sagaciously observed, "the start of her."

"You mean she has taken so much from you?"

"Well, I couldn't of course in common decency give less: only she hadn't expected, I think, that I'd give her nearly so much. And she began to take it before she knew it."

"And she began to like it," said Strether, "as soon as she began to take it!"

"Yes, she has liked it—also more than she expected." After which Chad observed: "But she doesn't like *me*. In fact she hates me."

Strether's interest grew. "Then why does she want you at home?"

"Because when you hate you want to triumph, and if she should get me neatly stuck there she *would* triumph."

Strether followed afresh, but looking as he went. "Certainly—in a manner. But it would scarce be a triumph worth having if, once entangled, feeling her dislike and possibly conscious in time of a certain quantity of your own, you should on the spot make yourself unpleasant to her."

"Ah," said Chad, "she can bear *me*—could bear me at least at home. It's my being there that would be her triumph. She hates me in Paris."

"She hates in other words—"

"Yes, *that's* it!"—Chad had quickly understood this understanding; which formed on the part of each as near an approach as they had yet made to naming Madame de Vionnet. The limitations of their distinctness didn't, however, prevent its fairly lingering in the air that it was this lady Mrs. Pocock hated. It added one more touch moreover to their established recognition of the rare intimacy of Chad's association with her. He had never yet more twitched away the last light veil from this phenomenon than in presenting himself as confounded and submerged in the feeling she had created at Woollett. "And I'll tell you who hates me too," he immediately went on.

Strether knew as immediately whom he meant, but with as prompt a protest. "Ah no! Mamie doesn't hate—well," he caught himself in time—"anybody at all. Mamie's beautiful."

Chad shook his head. "That's just why I mind it. She certainly doesn't like me."

"How much do you mind it? What would you do for her?"

"Well, I'd like her if she'd like me. Really, really," Chad declared.

It gave his companion a moment's pause. "You asked me just now if I don't, as you said, 'care' about a certain person. You rather tempt me therefore to put the question in my turn. Don't *you* care about a certain other person?"

Chad looked at him hard in the lamplight of the window. "The difference is that I don't want to."

Strether wondered. " 'Don't want' to?"

"I try not to—that is I *have* tried. I've done my best. You can't be surprised," the young man easily went on, "when you yourself set me on it. I was indeed," he added, "already on it a little; but you set me harder. It was six weeks ago that I thought I had come out."

Strether took it well in. "But you haven't come out!"

"I don't know—it's what I *want* to know," said Chad. "And if I could have sufficiently wanted—by myself—to go back, I think I might have found out."

"Possibly"—Strether considered. "But all you were able to achieve was to want to want to! And even then," he pursued, "only till our friends there came. Do you want to want to still?" As with a sound half-dolorous, half-droll and all vague and equivocal, Chad buried his face for a little in his hands, rubbing it in a whimsical way that amounted to an evasion, he brought it out more sharply: "*Do* you?"

Chad kept for a time his attitude, but at last he looked up, and then abruptly, "Jim *is* a damned dose!" he declared.

"Oh I don't ask you to abuse or describe or in any way pronounce on your relatives; I simply put it to you once more whether you're *now* ready. You say you've 'seen.' Is what you've seen that you can't resist?"

Chad gave him a strange smile—the nearest approach he had ever shown to a troubled one. "Can't you make me *not* resist?"

"What it comes to," Strether went on very gravely now and as if he hadn't heard him, "what it comes to is that more has been done for you, I think, than I've ever seen done—attempted perhaps, but never so successfully done—by one human being for another."

"Oh an immense deal certainly"—Chad did it full justice. "And you yourself are adding to it."

It was without heeding this either that his visitor continued. "And our friends there won't have it."

"No, they simply won't."

"They demand you on the basis, as it were, of repudiation and ingratitude; and what has been the matter with me," Strether went on, "is that I haven't seen my way to working with you for repudiation."

Chad appreciated this. "Then as you haven't seen yours you naturally haven't seen mine. There it is." After which he proceeded, with a certain abruptness, to a sharp interrogation. "*Now* do you say she doesn't hate me?"

Strether hesitated. " 'She'—?"

"Yes—Mother. We called it Sarah, but it comes to the same thing."

"Ah," Strether objected, "not to the same thing as her hating *you*."

On which—though as if for an instant it had hung fire—Chad remarkably replied: "Well, if they hate my good friend, *that* comes to the same thing." It had a note of inevitable truth that made Strether take it as enough, feel he wanted nothing more. The young man spoke in it for his "good friend" more than he had ever yet directly spoken, confessed to such deep identities between them as he might play with the idea of working free from, but which at a given moment could still draw him down like a whirlpool. And meanwhile he had gone on. "Their hating you too moreover—that also comes to a good deal."

"Ah," said Strether, "your mother doesn't."

Chad, however, loyally stuck to it—loyally, that is, to Strether.

"She will if you don't look out."

"Well, I do look out. I am, after all, looking out. That's just why," our friend explained, "I want to see her again."

It drew from Chad again the same question. "To see Mother?"

"To see—for the present—Sarah."

"Ah then there you are! And what I don't for the life of me make out," Chad pursued with resigned perplexity, "is what you *gain* by it."

Oh it would have taken his companion too long to say! "That's because you have, I verily believe, no imagination. You've other qualities. But no imagination, don't you see? at all."

"I dare say. I do see." It was an idea in which Chad showed interest. "But haven't you yourself rather too much?"

"Oh *rather*—!" So that after an instant, under this reproach and as if it were at last a fact really to escape from, Strether made his move for departure.

II [XXIX]

One of the features of the restless afternoon passed by him after Mrs. Pocock's visit was an hour spent, shortly before dinner, with Maria Gostrey, whom of late, in spite of so sustained a call on his attention from other quarters, he had by no means neglected. And that he was still not neglecting her will appear from the fact that he was with her again at the same hour on the very morrow—with no less fine a consciousness moreover of being able to hold her ear. It continued inveterately to occur, for that matter, that whenever he had taken one of his greater turns he came back to where she so faithfully awaited him. None of these excursions had on the whole been livelier than the pair of incidents—the fruit of the short interval since his previous visit—on which he had now to report to her. He had seen Chad Newsome late the night before, and he had had that morning, as a sequel to this conversation, a second interview with Sarah. "But they're all off," he said, "at last."

It puzzled her a moment. "All?—Mr. Newsome with them?"

"Ah not yet! Sarah and Jim and Mamie. But Waymarsh with them—for Sarah. It's too beautiful," Strether continued; "I find I don't get over that—it's always a fresh joy. But it's a fresh joy too," he added, "that—well, what do you think? Little Bilham also goes. But he of course goes for Mamie."

Miss Gostrey wondered. " 'For' her? Do you mean they're already engaged?"

"Well," said Strether, "say then for *me*. He'll do anything for me; just as I will, for that matter—anything I can—for him. Or for Mamie either. *She'll* do anything for me."

Miss Gostrey gave a comprehensive sigh. "The way you reduce people to subjection!"

"It's certainly, on one side, wonderful. But it's quite equalled, on another, by the way I don't. I haven't reduced Sarah, since yesterday; though I've succeeded in seeing her again, as I'll presently tell you. The others however are really all right. Mamie, by that blessed law of ours, absolutely must have a young man."

"But what must poor Mr. Bilham have? Do you mean they'll *marry* for you?"

"I mean that, by the same blessed law, it won't matter a grain if they don't—I shan't have in the least to worry."

She saw as usual what he meant. "And Mr. Jim?—who goes for him?"

"Oh," Strether had to admit, "I couldn't manage *that*. He's thrown, as usual, on the world; the world which, after all, by his account—for he has prodigious adventures—seems very good to him. He fortunately—'over here,' as he says—finds the world everywhere; and his most prodigious adventure of all," he went on, "has been of course of the last few days."

Miss Gostrey, already knowing, instantly made the connexion. "He has seen Marie de Vionnet again?"

"He went, all by himself, the day after Chad's party—didn't I tell you?—to tea with her. By her invitation—all alone."

"Quite like yourself!" Maria smiled.

"Oh but he's more wonderful about her than I am!" And then as his friend showed how she could believe it, filling it out, fitting it on to old memories of the wonderful woman: "What I should have liked to manage would have been *her* going."

"To Switzerland with the party?"

"For Jim—and for symmetry. If it had been workable moreover for a fortnight she'd have gone. She's ready"—he followed up his renewed vision of her—"for anything."

Miss Gostrey went with him a minute. "She's too perfect!"

"She *will*, I think," he pursued, "go to-night to the station."

"To see him off?"

"With Chad—marvellously—as part of their general attention. And she does it"—it kept before him—"with a light, light grace, a free, free gaiety, that may well softly bewilder Mr. Pocock."

It kept her so before him that his companion had after an instant a friendly comment. "As in short it has softly bewildered a saner man. Are you really in love with her?" Maria threw off.

"It's of no importance I should know," he replied. "It matters so little—has nothing to do, practically, with either of us."

"All the same"—Maria continued to smile—"they go, the five, as I understand you, and you and Madame de Vionnet stay."

"Oh and Chad." To which Strether added: "And you."

"Ah 'me'!"—she gave a small impatient wail again, in which

something of the unreconciled seemed suddenly to break out. "I don't stay, it somehow seems to me, much to my advantage. In the presence of all you cause to pass before me I've a tremendous sense of privation."

Strether hesitated. "But your privation, your keeping out of everything, has been—hasn't it?—by your own choice."

"Oh yes; it has been necessary—that is it has been better for you. What I mean is only that I seem to have ceased to serve you."

"How can you tell that?" he asked. "You don't know how you serve me. When you cease—"

"Well?" she said as he dropped.

"Well, I'll *let* you know. Be quiet till then."

She thought a moment. "Then you positively like me to stay?"

"Don't I treat you as if I did?"

"You're certainly very kind to me. But that," said Maria, "is for myself. It's getting late, as you see, and Paris turning rather hot and dusty. People are scattering, and some of them, in other places, want me. But if you want me here—!"

She had spoken as resigned to his word, but he had of a sudden a still sharper sense than he would have expected of desiring not to lose her. "I want you here."

She took it as if the words were all she had wished; as if they brought her, gave her something that was the compensation of her case. "Thank you," she simply answered. And then as he looked at her a little harder, "Thank you very much," she repeated.

It had broken as with a slight arrest into the current of their talk, and it held him a moment longer. "Why, two months, or whatever the time was, ago, did you so suddenly dash off? The reason you afterwards gave me for having kept away three weeks wasn't the real one."

She recalled. "I never supposed you believed it was. Yet," she continued, "if you didn't guess it that was just what helped you."

He looked away from her on this; he indulged, so far as space permitted, in one of his slow absences. "I've often thought of it, but never to feel that I could guess it. And you see the consideration with which I've treated you in never asking till now."

"Now then why *do* you ask?"

"To show you how I miss you when you're not here, and what it does for me."

"It doesn't seem to have done," she laughed, "all it might! However," she added, "if you've really never guessed the truth I'll tell it you."

"I've never guessed it," Strether declared.

"Never?"

"Never."

"Well then I dashed off, as you say, so as not to have the confusion of being there if Marie de Vionnet should tell you anything to my detriment."

He looked as if he considerably doubted. "You even then would have had to face it on your return."

"Oh if I had found reason to believe it something very bad I'd have left you altogether."

"So then," he continued, "it was only on guessing she had been on the whole merciful that you ventured back?"

Maria kept it together. "I owe her thanks. Whatever her temptation she didn't separate us. That's one of my reasons," she went on, "for admiring her so."

"Let it pass then," said Strether, "for one of mine as well. But what would have been her temptation?"

"What are ever the temptations of women?"

He thought—but hadn't, naturally, to think too long. "Men?"

"She would have had you, with it, more for herself. But she saw she could have you without it."

"Oh 'have' me!" Strether a trifle ambiguously sighed. "*You*," he handsomely declared, "would have had me at any rate *with* it."

"Oh 'have' you!"—she echoed it as he had done. "I do have you, however," she less ironically said, "from the moment you express a wish."

He stopped before her, full of the disposition. "I'll express fifty."

Which indeed begot in her, with a certain inconsequence, a return of her small wail. "Ah there you are!"

There, if it were so, he continued for the rest of the time to be, and it was as if to show her how she could still serve him that, coming back to the departure of the Pococks, he gave her the view, vivid with a hundred more touches than we can reproduce, of what had happened for him that morning. He had had ten minutes with Sarah at her hotel, ten minutes reconquered, by irresistible pressure, from the time over which he had already described her to Miss Gostrey as having, at the end of their interview on his own premises, passed the great sponge of the future. He had caught her by not announcing himself, had found her in her sitting-room with a dressmaker and a *lingère*[2] whose accounts she appeared to have been more or less ingenuously settling and who soon withdrew. Then he had explained to her how he had succeeded, late the night before, in keeping his promise of seeing Chad. "I told her I'd take it all."

"You'd 'take' it?"

"Why if he doesn't go."

2. Seamstress.

Maria waited. "And who takes it if he does?" she enquired with a certain grimness of gaiety.

"Well," said Strether, "I think I take, in any event, everything."

"By which I suppose you mean," his companion brought out after a moment, "that you definitely understand you now lose everything."

He stood before her again. "It does come perhaps to the same thing. But Chad, now that he has seen, doesn't really want it."

She could believe that, but she made, as always, for clearness. "Still, what, after all, *has* he seen?"

"What they want of him. And it's enough."

"It contrasts so unfavourably with what Madame de Vionnet wants?"

"It contrasts—just so; all round, and tremendously."

"Therefore, perhaps, most of all with what *you* want?"

"Oh," said Strether, "what I want is a thing I've ceased to measure or even to understand."

But his friend none the less went on. "Do you want Mrs. Newsome—after such a way of treating you?"

It was a straighter mode of dealing with this lady than they had as yet—such was their high form—permitted themselves; but it seemed not wholly for this that he delayed a moment. "I dare say it has been, after all, the only way she could have imagined."

"And does that make you want her any more?"

"I've tremendously disappointed her," Strether thought it worth while to mention.

"Of course you have. That's rudimentary; that was plain to us long ago. But isn't it almost as plain," Maria went on, "that you've even yet your straight remedy? Really drag him away, as I believe you still can, and you'd cease to have to count with her disappointment."

"Ah then," he laughed, "I should have to count with yours!"

But this barely struck her now. "What, in that case, should you call counting? You haven't come out where you are, I think, to please *me*."

"Oh," he insisted, "that too, you know, has been part of it. I can't separate—it's all one; and that's perhaps why, as I say, I don't understand." But he was ready to declare again that this didn't in the least matter; all the more that, as he affirmed, he *hadn't* really as yet "come out." "She gives me after all, on its coming to the pinch, a last mercy, another chance. They don't sail, you see, for five or six weeks more, and they haven't—she admits that —expected Chad would take part in their tour. It's still open to him to join them, at the last, at Liverpool."

Miss Gostrey considered. "How in the world is it 'open' unless you open it? How can he join them at Liverpool if he but sinks deeper into his situation here?"

"He has given her—as I explained to you that she let me know yesterday—his word of honour to do as I say."

Maria stared. "But if you say nothing!"

Well, he as usual walked about on it. "I did say something this morning. I gave her my answer—the word I had promised her after hearing from himself what *he* had promised. What she demanded of me yesterday, you'll remember, was the engagement then and there to make him take up this vow."

"Well then," Miss Gostrey enquired, "was the purpose of your visit to her only to decline?"

"No; it was to ask, odd as that may seem to you, for another delay."

"Ah that's weak!"

"Precisely!" She had spoken with impatience, but, so far as that at least, he knew where he was. "If I *am* weak I want to find it out. If I don't find it out I shall have the comfort, the little glory, of thinking I'm strong."

"It's all the comfort, I judge," she returned, "that you *will* have!"

"At any rate," he said, "it will have been a month more. Paris may grow, from day to day, hot and dusty, as you say; but there are other things that are hotter and dustier. I'm not afraid to stay on; the summer here must be amusing in a wild—if it isn't a tame— way of its own; the place at no time more picturesque. I think I shall like it. And then," he benevolently smiled for her, "there will be always you."

"Oh," she objected, "it won't be as a part of the picturesqueness that I shall stay, for I shall be the plainest thing about you. You may, you see, at any rate," she pursued, "have nobody else. Madame de Vionnet may very well be going off, mayn't she?—and Mr. Newsome by the same stroke: unless indeed you've had an assurance from them to the contrary. So that if your idea's to stay for them"—it was her duty to suggest it—"you may be left in the lurch. Of course if they do stay"—she kept it up—"they would be part of the picturesqueness. Or else indeed you might join them somewhere."

Strether seemed to face it as if it were a happy thought; but the next moment he spoke more critically. "Do you mean that they'll probably go off together?"

She just considered. "I think it will be treating you quite without ceremony if they do; though after all," she added, "it would be difficult to see now quite what degree of ceremony properly meets your case."

"Of course," Strether conceded, "my attitude toward them is extraordinary."

"Just so; so that one may ask one's self what style of proceeding on their own part can altogether match it. The attitude of their own that won't pale in its light they've doubtless still to work out. The really handsome thing perhaps," she presently threw off, "*would* be for them to withdraw into more secluded conditions, offering at the same time to share them with you." He looked at her, on this, as if some generous irritation—all in his interest—had suddenly again flickered in her; and what she next said indeed half-explained it. "Don't really be afraid to tell me if what now holds you *is* the pleasant prospect of the empty town, with plenty of seats in the shade, cool drinks, deserted museums, drives to the Bois³ in the evening, and our wonderful woman all to yourself." And she kept it up still more. "The handsomest thing of *all*, when one makes it out, would, I dare say, be that Mr. Chad should for a while go off by himself. It's a pity, from that point of view," she wound up, "that he doesn't pay his mother a visit. It would at least occupy your interval." The thought in fact held her a moment. "Why doesn't he pay his mother a visit? Even a week, at this good moment, would do."

"My dear lady," Strether replied—and he had it even to himself surprisingly ready—"my dear lady, his mother has paid *him* a visit. Mrs. Newsome has been with him, this month, with an intensity that I'm sure he has thoroughly felt; he has lavishly entertained her, and she has let him have her thanks. Do you suggest he shall go back for more of them?"

Well, she succeeded after a little in shaking it off. "I see. It's what you don't suggest—what you haven't suggested. And you know."

"So would you, my dear," he kindly said, "if you had so much as seen her."

"As seen Mrs. Newsome?"

"No, Sarah—which, both for Chad and for myself, has served all the purpose."

"And served it in a manner," she responsively mused, "so extraordinary!"

"Well, you see," he partly explained, "what it comes to is that she's all cold thought—which Sarah could serve to us cold without its really losing anything. So it is that we know what she thinks of us."

Maria had followed, but she had an arrest. "What I've never made out, if you come to that, is what you think—I mean you personally—of *her*. Don't you so much, when all's said, as care a

─────

3. The Bois de Boulogne, a large wooded park on the outskirts of Paris.

little?"

"That," he answered with no loss of promptness, "is what even Chad himself asked me last night. He asked me if I don't mind the loss—well, the loss of an opulent future. Which moreover," he hastened to add, "was a perfectly natural question."

"I call your attention, all the same," said Miss Gostrey, "to the fact that I don't ask it. What I venture to ask is whether it's to Mrs. Newsome herself that you're indifferent."

"I haven't been so"—he spoke with all assurance. "I've been the very opposite. I've been, from the first moment, preoccupied with the impression everything might be making on her—quite oppressed, haunted, tormented by it. I've been interested *only* in her seeing what I've seen. And I've been as disappointed in her refusal to see it as she has been in what has appeared to her the perversity of my insistence."

"Do you mean that she has shocked you as you've shocked her?"

Strether weighed it. "I'm probably not so shockable. But on the other hand I've gone much further to meet her. She, on her side, hasn't budged an inch."

"So that you're now at last"—Maria pointed the moral—"in the sad stage of recriminations."

"No—it's only to you I speak. I've been like a lamb to Sarah. I've only put my back to the wall. It's to *that* one naturally staggers when one has been violently pushed there."

She watched him a moment. "Thrown over?"

"Well, as I feel I've landed somewhere I think I must have been thrown."

She turned it over, but as hoping to clarify much rather than to harmonise. "The thing is that I suppose you've been disappointing—"

"Quite from the very first of my arrival? I dare say. I admit I was surprising even to myself."

"And then of course," Maria went on, "I had much to do with it."

"With my being surprising—?"

"That will do," she laughed, "if you're too delicate to call it *my* being! Naturally," she added, "you came over more or less for surprises."

"Naturally!"—he valued the reminder.

"But they were to have been all for you"—she continued to piece it out—"and none of them for *her*."

Once more he stopped before her as if she had touched the point. "That's just her difficulty—that she doesn't admit surprises. It's a fact that, I think, describes and represents her; and it falls in with what I tell you—that she's all, as I've called it, fine cold thought.

She had, to her own mind, worked the whole thing out in advance, and worked it out for me as well as for herself. Whenever she has done that, you see, there's no room left; no margin, as it were, for any alteration. She's filled as full, packed as tight, as she'll hold, and if you wish to get anything more or different either out or in—"

"You've got to make over altogether the woman herself?"

"What it comes to," said Strether, "is that you've got morally and intellectually to get rid of her."

"Which would appear," Maria returned, "to be practically what you've done."

But her friend threw back his head. "I haven't touched her. She won't *be* touched. I see it now as I've never done; and she hangs together with a perfection of her own," he went on, "that does suggest a kind of wrong in *any* change of her composition. It was at any rate," he wound up, "the woman herself, as you call her, the whole moral and intellectual being or block, that Sarah brought me over to take or to leave."

It turned Miss Gostrey to deeper thought. "Fancy having to take at the point of the bayonet a whole moral and intellectual being or block!"

"It was in fact," said Strether, "what, at home, I *had* done. But somehow over there I didn't quite know it."

"One never does, I suppose," Miss Gostrey concurred, "realise in advance, in such a case, the size, as you may say, of the block. Little by little it looms up. It has been looming for you more and more till at last you see it all."

"I see it all," he absently echoed, while his eyes might have been fixing some particularly large iceberg in a cool blue northern sea. "It's magnificent!" he then rather oddly exclaimed.

But his friend, who was used to this kind of inconsequence in him, kept the thread. "There's nothing so magnificent—for making others feel you—as to have no imagination."

It brought him straight round. "Ah there you are! It's what I said last night to Chad. That he himself, I mean, has none."

"Then it would appear," Maria suggested, "that he has, after all, something in common with his mother."

"He has in common that he makes one, as you say, 'feel' him. And yet," he added, as if the question were interesting, "one feels others too, even when they have plenty."

Miss Gostrey continued suggestive. "Madame de Vionnet?"

"*She* has plenty."

"Certainly—she had quantities of old. But there are different ways of making one's self felt."

"Yes, it comes, no doubt, to that. You now—"

He was benevolently going on, but she wouldn't have it. "Oh I *don't* make myself felt; so my quantity needn't be settled. Yours, you know," she said, "is monstrous. No one has ever had so much."

It struck him for a moment. "That's what Chad also thinks."

"There *you* are then—though it isn't for him to complain of it!"

"Oh he doesn't complain of it," said Strether.

"That's all that would be wanting! But apropos of what," Maria went on, "did the question come up?"

"Well, of his asking me what it is I gain."

She had a pause. "Then as I've asked you too it settles *my* case. Oh you *have*," she repeated, "treasures of imagination."

But he had been for an instant thinking away from this, and he came up in another place. "And yet Mrs. Newsome—it's a thing to remember—*has* imagined, did, that is, imagine, and apparently still does, horrors about what I should have found. I was booked, by her vision—extraordinarily intense, after all—to find them; and that I didn't, that I couldn't, that, as she evidently felt, I wouldn't—this evidently didn't at all, as they say, 'suit' her book. It was more than she could bear. That was her disappointment."

"You mean you were to have found Chad himself horrible?"

"I was to have found the woman."

"Horrible?"

"Found her as she imagined her." And Strether paused as if for his own expression of it he could add no touch to that picture.

His companion had meanwhile thought. "She imagined stupidly —so it comes to the same thing."

"Stupidly? Oh!" said Strether.

But she insisted. "She imagined meanly."

He had it, however, better. "It couldn't but be ignorantly."

"Well, intensity with ignorance—what do you want worse?"

This question might have held him, but he let it pass. "Sarah isn't ignorant—now; she keeps up the theory of the horrible."

"Ah but she's intense—and that by itself will do sometimes as well. If it doesn't do, in this case, at any rate, to deny that Marie's charming, it will do at least to deny that she's good."

"What I claim is that she's good for Chad."

"You don't claim"—she seemed to like it clear—"that she's good for *you*."

But he continued without heeding. "That's what I wanted them to come out for—to see for themselves if she's bad for him."

"And now that they've done so they won't admit that she's good even for anything?"

"They do think," Strether presently admitted, "that she's on the whole about as bad for me. But they're consistent of course, inasmuch as they've their clear view of what's good for both of us."

"For you, to begin with"—Maria, all responsive, confined the question for the moment—"to eliminate from your existence and if possible even from your memory the dreadful creature that I must gruesomely shadow forth for them, even more than to eliminate the distincter evil—thereby a little less portentous—of the person whose confederate you've suffered yourself to become. However, that's comparatively simple. You can easily, at the worst, after all, give me up."

"I can easily at the worst, after all, give you up." The irony was so obvious that it needed no care. "I can easily at the worst, after all, even forget you."

"Call that then workable. But Mr. Newsome has much more to forget. How can *he* do it?"

"Ah there again we are! That's just what I was to have made him do; just where I was to have worked with him and helped."

She took it in silence and without attenuation—as if perhaps from very familiarity with the facts; and her thought made a connexion without showing the links. "Do you remember how we used to talk at Chester and in London about my seeing you through?" She spoke as of far-off things and as if they had spent weeks at the places she named.

"It's just what you *are* doing."

"Ah but the worst—since you've left such a margin—may be still to come. You may yet break down."

"Yes, I may yet break down. But will you take me—?"

He had hesitated, and she waited. "Take you?"

"For as long as I can bear it."

She also debated. "Mr. Newsome and Madame de Vionnet may, as we were saying, leave town. How long do you think you can bear it without them?"

Strether's reply to this was at first another question. "Do you mean in order to get away from me?"

Her answer had an abruptness. "Don't find me rude if I say I should think they'd want to!"

He looked at her hard again—seemed even for an instant to have an intensity of thought under which his colour changed. But he smiled. "You mean after what they've done to me?"

"After what *she* has."

At this, however, with a laugh, he was all right again. "Ah but she hasn't done it yet!"

III [XXX]

He had taken the train a few days after this from a station—as well as *to* a station—selected almost at random; such days, what-

ever should happen, were numbered, and he had gone forth under
the impulse—artless enough, no doubt—to give the whole of one
of them to that French ruralism, with its cool special green, into
which he had hitherto looked only through the little oblong window
of the picture-frame. It had been as yet for the most part but a
land of fancy for him—the background of fiction, the medium of
art, the nursery of letters; practically as distant as Greece, but practically also well-nigh as consecrated. Romance could weave itself,
for Strether's sense, out of elements mild enough; and even after
what he had, as he felt, lately "been through," he could thrill a
little at the chance of seeing something somewhere that would remind him of a certain small Lambinet[4] that had charmed him,
long years before, at a Boston dealer's and that he had quite absurdly never forgotten. It had been offered, he remembered, at a
price he had been instructed to believe the lowest ever named for
a Lambinet, a price he had never felt so poor as on having to
recognise, all the same, as beyond a dream of possibility. He had
dreamed—had turned and twisted possibilities for an hour: it had
been the only adventure of his life in connexion with the purchase
of a work of art. The adventure, it will be perceived, was modest;
but the memory, beyond all reason and by some accident of association, was sweet. The little Lambinet abode with him as the
picture he *would* have bought—the particular production that had
made him for the moment overstep the modesty of nature. He
was quite aware that if he were to see it again he should perhaps
have a drop or a shock, and he never found himself wishing that
the wheel of time would turn it up again, just as he had seen it
in the maroon-coloured, sky-lighted inner shrine of Tremont
Street.[5] It would be a different thing, however, to see the remembered mixture resolved back into its elements—to assist at the
restoration to nature of the whole far-away hour: the dusty day in
Boston, the background of the Fitchburg Depot, of the maroon-
coloured sanctum, the special-green vision, the ridiculous price,
the poplars, the willows, the rushes, the river, the sunny silvery
sky, the shady woody horizon.

He observed in respect to his train almost no condition save
that it should stop a few times after getting out of the *banlieue;*[6]

---

4. Emile Lambinet (1815–77), a French Romantic landscape painter, was remembered by James
in *A Small Boy and Others: Autobiography*, ed. F. W. Dupee (New York: Criterion, 1956),
193, as one of the "so finely interesting landscapists" of his youth who "summed up for the
American collector and in the New York and Boston markets the idea of the modern in the
masterly." For an example of Lambinet's art, see the front cover.
5. A principal street in Boston and the location of at least one commercial gallery. (See *The
Painter's Eye*, p. 43n.) The Fitchburg train station was located nearby.
6. Suburb.

he threw himself on the general amiability of the day for the hint
of where to alight. His theory of his excursion was that he could
alight anywhere—not nearer Paris than an hour's run—on catching a suggestion of the particular note required. It made its sign,
the suggestion—weather, air, light, colour and his mood all favour-
ing—at the end of some eighty minutes; the train pulled up just
at the right spot, and he found himself getting out as securely as
if to keep an appointment. It will be felt of him that he could
amuse himself, at his age, with very small things if it be again
noted that his appointment was only with a superseded Boston
fashion. He hadn't gone far without the quick confidence that it
would be quite sufficiently kept. The oblong gilt frame disposed
its enclosing lines; the poplars and willows, the reeds and river—
a river of which he didn't know, and didn't want to know, the name
—fell into a composition, full of felicity, within them; the sky was
silver and turquoise and varnish; the village on the left was white
and the church on the right was grey; it was all there, in short—
it was what he wanted: it was Tremont Street, it was France, it was
Lambinet. Moreover he was freely walking about in it. He did
this last, for an hour, to his heart's content, making for the shady
woody horizon and boring so deep into his impression and his idleness that he might fairly have got through them again and reached
the maroon-coloured wall. It was a wonder, no doubt, that the
taste of idleness for him shouldn't need more time to sweeten;
but it had in fact taken the few previous days; it had been sweeten-
ing in truth ever since the retreat of the Pococks. He walked and
walked as if to show himself how little he had now to do; he had
nothing to do but turn off to some hillside where he might stretch
himself and hear the poplars rustle, and whence—in the course
of an afternoon so spent, an afternoon richly suffused too with
the sense of a book in his pocket—he should sufficiently command the scene to be able to pick out just the right little rustic
inn for an experiment in respect to dinner. There was a train back
to Paris at 9.20, and he saw himself partaking, at the close of the
day, with the enhancements of a coarse white cloth and a sanded
floor, of something fried and felicitous, washed down with authentic
wine; after which he might, as he liked, either stroll back to his
station in the gloaming or propose for the local *carriole*[7] and
converse with his driver, a driver who naturally wouldn't fail of a
stiff clean blouse, of a knitted nightcap and of the genius of response—who, in fine, would sit on the shafts, tell him what the
French people were thinking, and remind him, as indeed the whole
episode would incidentally do, of Maupassant.[8] Strether heard his

7. A small cart or carriage.
8. In an 1888 essay on Guy de Maupassant (1850–93), the great French short story writer and
   novelist, James gave high but qualified praise to his sensuous point of view and sensual subjects;

lips, for the first time in French air, as this vision assumed consistency, emit sounds of expressive intention without fear of his company. He had been afraid of Chad and of Maria and of Madame de Vionnet; he had been most of all afraid of Waymarsh, in whose presence, so far as they had mixed together in the light of the town, he had never without somehow paying for it aired either his vocabulary or his accent. He usually paid for it by meeting immediately afterwards Waymarsh's eye.

Such were the liberties with which his fancy played after he had turned off to the hillside that did really and truly, as well as most amiably, await him beneath the poplars, the hillside that made him feel, for a murmurous couple of hours, how happy had been his thought. He had the sense of success, of a finer harmony in things; nothing but what had turned out as yet according to his plan. It most of all came home to him, as he lay on his back on the grass, that Sarah had really gone, that his tension was really relaxed; the peace diffused in these ideas might be delusive, but it hung about him none the less for the time. It fairly, for half an hour, sent him to sleep; he pulled his straw hat over his eyes—he had bought it the day before with a reminiscence of Waymarsh's—and lost himself anew in Lambinet. It was as if he had found out he was tired—tired not from his walk, but from that inward exercise which had known, on the whole, for three months, so little intermission. That was it—when once they were off he had dropped; this moreover was what he had dropped to, and now he was touching bottom. He was kept luxuriously quiet, soothed and amused by the consciousness of what he had found at the end of his descent. It was very much what he had told Maria Gostrey he should like to stay on for, the hugely-distributed Paris of summer, alternately dazzling and dusky, with a weight lifted for him off its columns and cornices and with shade and air in the flutter of awnings as wide as avenues. It was present to him without attenuation that, reaching out, the day after making the remark, for some proof of his freedom, he had gone that very afternoon to see Madame de Vionnet. He had gone again the next day but one, and the effect of the two visits, the after-sense of the couple of hours spent with her, was almost that of fulness and frequency. The brave intention of frequency, so great with him from the moment of his finding himself unjustly suspected at Woollett, had remained rather theoretic, and one of the things he could muse about under his poplars was the source of the special shyness that had still made him careful. He had surely got rid of it now, this special shyness; what had

prominent among the latter were the Normandy peasants. See Henry James, "Guy de Maupassant," *Literary Criticism: French Writers, Other European Writers. The Prefaces to the New York Edition*, ed. Leon Edel and Mark Wilson (New York: Library of America, 1984), 521-49.

become of it if it hadn't precisely, within the week, rubbed off?

It struck him now in fact as sufficiently plain that if he had still been careful he had been so for a reason. He had really feared, in his behaviour, a lapse from good faith; if there was a danger of one's liking such a woman too much one's best safety was in waiting at least till one had the right to do so. In the light of the last few days the danger was fairly vivid; so that it was proportionately fortunate that the right was likewise established. It seemed to our friend that he had on each occasion profited to the utmost by the latter: how could he have done so more, he at all events asked himself, than in having immediately let her know that, if it was all the same to her, he preferred not to talk about anything tiresome? He had never in his life so sacrificed an armful of high interests as in that remark; he had never so prepared the way for the comparatively frivolous as in addressing it to Madame de Vionnet's intelligence. It hadn't been till later that he quite recalled how in conjuring away everything but the pleasant he had conjured away almost all they had hitherto talked about; it was not till later even that he remembered how, with their new tone, they hadn't so much as mentioned the name of Chad himself. One of the things that most lingered with him on his hillside was this delightful facility, with such a woman, of arriving at a new tone; he thought, as he lay on his back, of all the tones she might make possible if one were to try her, and at any rate of the probability that one could trust her to fit them to occasions. He had wanted her to feel that, as he was disinterested now, so she herself should be, and she had showed she felt it, and he had showed he was grateful, and it had been for all the world as if he were calling for the first time. They had had other, but irrelevant, meetings; it was quite as if, had they sooner known how much they *really* had in common, there were quantities of comparatively dull matters they might have skipped. Well, they were skipping them now, even to graceful gratitude, even to handsome "Don't mention it!"—and it was amazing what could still come up without reference to what had been going on between them. It might have been, on analysis, nothing more than Shakespeare and the musical glasses;[9] but it had served all the purpose of his appearing to have said to her: "Don't like me, if it's a question of liking me, for anything obvious and clumsy that I've, as they call it, 'done' for you: like me—well, like me, hang it, for anything else you choose. So, by the same propriety, don't be for me simply the person I've come to know through my awkward connexion with Chad—was ever anything,

9. The Vicar in *The Vicar of Wakefield* (see above, p. 37) describes the conversation of his supposedly fashionable visitors as "talk of nothing but high life, and high lived company; with other fashionable topics, such as pictures, taste, Shakespeare, and the musical glasses." "Musical glasses" probably refers to Benjamin Franklin's 1761 invention of a musical instrument (also called a glass harmonica) that produces sound through friction on glass.

by the way, *more* awkward? Be for me, please, with all your admirable tact and trust, just whatever I may show you it's a present pleasure to me to think you." It had been a large indication to meet; but if she hadn't met it what *had* she done, and how had their time together slipped along so smoothly, mild but not slow, and melting, liquefying, into his happy illusion of idleness? He could recognise on the other hand that he had probably not been without reason, in his prior, his restricted state, for keeping an eye on his liability to lapse from good faith.

He really continued in the picture—that being for himself his situation—all the rest of this rambling day; so that the charm was still, was indeed more than ever upon him when, toward six o'clock, he found himself amicably engaged with a stout white-capped deep-voiced woman at the door of the *auberge*[1] of the biggest village, a village that affected him as a thing of whiteness, blueness and crookedness, set in coppery green, and that had the river flowing behind or before it—one couldn't say which; at the bottom, in particular, of the inn-garden. He had had other adventures before this; had kept along the height, after shaking off slumber; had admired, had almost coveted, another small old church, all steep roof and dim slate-colour without and all whitewash and paper flowers within; had lost his way and had found it again; had conversed with rustics who struck him perhaps a little more as men of the world than he had expected; had acquired at a bound a fearless facility in French; had had, as the afternoon waned, a watery *bock*, all pale and Parisian, in the café of the furthest village, which was not the biggest; and had meanwhile not once overstepped the oblong gilt frame. The frame had drawn itself out for him, as much as you please; but that was just his luck. He had finally come down again to the valley, to keep within touch of stations and trains, turning his face to the quarter from which he had started; and thus it was that he had at last pulled up before the hostess of the Cheval Blanc,[2] who met him, with a rough readiness that·was like the clatter of *sabots* over stones, on their common ground of a *côtelette de veau à l'oseille*[3] and a subsequent lift. He had walked many miles and didn't know he was tired; but he still knew he was amused, and even that, though he had been alone all day, he had never yet so struck himself as engaged with others and in midstream of his drama. It might have passed for finished, his drama, with its catastrophe all but reached: it had, however, none the less been vivid again for him as he thus gave it its fuller chance. He had only had to be at last well out of it to feel it, oddly enough, still going on.

1. Inn.
2. White Horse.
3. Veal cutlet with purée of sorrel.

For this had been all day at bottom the spell of the picture—
that it was essentially more than anything else a scene and a stage,
that the very air of the play was in the rustle of the willows and the
tone of the sky. The play and the characters had, without his
knowing it till now, peopled all his space for him, and it seemed
somehow quite happy that they should offer themselves, in the
conditions so supplied, with a kind of inevitability. It was as if the
conditions made them not only inevitable, but so much more nearly
natural and right as that they were at least easier, pleasanter, to
put up with. The conditions had nowhere so asserted their difference
from those of Woollett as they appeared to him to assert it in the
little court of the Cheval Blanc while he arranged with his hostess
for a comfortable climax. They were few and simple, scant and
humble, but they were *the thing*, as he would have called it, even
to a greater degree than Madame de Vionnet's old high salon
where the ghost of the Empire walked. "The" thing was the thing
that implied the greatest number of other things of the sort he had
had to tackle; and it was queer of course, but so it was—the implication here was complete. Not a single one of his observations
but somehow fell into a place in it; not a breath of the cooler
evening that wasn't somehow a syllable of the text. The text was
simply, when condensed, that in *these* places such things were,
and that if it was in them one elected to move about one had to
make one's account with what one lighted on. Meanwhile at all
events it was enough that they did affect one—so far as the village
aspect was concerned—as whiteness, crookedness and blueness set
in coppery green; there being positively, for that matter, an outer
wall of the White Horse that was painted the most improbable
shade. That was part of the amusement—as if to show that the
fun was harmless; just as it was enough, further, that the picture
and the play seemed supremely to melt together in the good
woman's broad sketch of what she could do for her visitor's appetite.
He felt in short a confidence, and it was general, and it was all he
wanted to feel. It suffered no shock even on her mentioning that
she had in fact just laid the cloth for two persons who, unlike
Monsieur, had arrived by the river—in a boat of their own; who
had asked her, half an hour before, what she could do for them,
and had then paddled away to look at something a little further up
—from which promenade they would presently return. Monsieur
might meanwhile, if he liked, pass into the garden, such as it was,
where she would serve him, should he wish it—for there were tables
and benches in plenty—a "bitter" before his repast. Here she
would also report to him on the possibility of a conveyance to his
station, and here at any rate he would have the *agrément*[4] of the

4. Pleasure.

river.

It may be mentioned without delay that Monsieur had the *agrément* of everything, and in particular, for the next twenty minutes, of a small and primitive pavilion that, at the garden's edge, almost overhung the water, testifying, in its somewhat battered state, to much fond frequentation. It consisted of little more than a platform, slightly raised, with a couple of benches and a table, a protecting rail and a projecting roof; but it raked the full grey-blue stream, which, taking a turn a short distance above, passed out of sight to reappear much higher up; and it was clearly in esteemed requisition for Sundays and other feasts. Strether sat there and, though hungry, felt at peace; the confidence that had so gathered for him deepened with the lap of the water, the ripple of the surface, the rustle of the reeds on the opposite bank, the faint diffused coolness and the slight rock of a couple of small boats attached to a rough landing-place hard by. The valley on the further side was all copper-green level and glazed pearly sky, a sky hatched across with screens of trimmed trees, which looked flat, like espaliers; and though the rest of the village straggled away in the near quarter the view had an emptiness that made one of the boats suggestive. Such a river set one afloat almost before one could take up the oars— the idle play of which would be moreover the aid to the full impression. This perception went so far as to bring him to his feet; but that movement, in turn, made him feel afresh that he was tired, and while he leaned against a post and continued to look out he saw something that gave him a sharper arrest.

IV [XXXI]

What he saw was exactly the right thing—a boat advancing round the bend and containing a man who held the paddles and a lady, at the stern, with a pink parasol. It was suddenly as if these figures, or something like them, had been wanted in the picture, had been wanted more or less all day, and had now drifted into sight, with the slow current, on purpose to fill up the measure. They came slowly, floating down, evidently directed to the landing-place near their spectator and presenting themselves to him not less clearly as the two persons for whom his hostess was already preparing a meal. For two very happy persons he found himself straightway taking them—a young man in shirt-sleeves, a young woman easy and fair, who had pulled pleasantly up from some other place and, being acquainted with the neighbourhood, had known what this particular retreat could offer them. The air quite thickened, at their approach, with further intimations; the intimation that they were expert, familiar, frequent—that this wouldn't at all events be the first time. They knew how to do it, he vaguely felt— and it made them but the more idyllic, though at the very moment

of the impression, as happened, their boat seemed to have begun to
drift wide, the oarsman letting it go. It had by this time none the
less come much nearer—near enough for Strether to dream the
lady in the stern had for some reason taken account of his being
there to watch them. She had remarked on it sharply, yet her companion hadn't turned round; it was in fact almost as if our
friend had felt her bid him keep still. She had taken in something
as a result of which their course had wavered, and it continued to
waver while they just stood off. This little effect was sudden and
rapid, so rapid that Strether's sense of it was separate only for an
instant from a sharp start of his own. He too had within the minute
taken in something, taken in that he knew the lady whose parasol,
shifting as if to hide her face, made so fine a pink point in the
shining scene. It was too prodigious, a chance in a million, but,
if he knew the lady, the gentleman, who still presented his back
and kept off, the gentleman, the coatless hero of the idyll, who
had responded to her start, was, to match the marvel, none other
than Chad.

Chad and Madame de Vionnet were then like himself taking
a day in the country—though it was as queer as fiction, as farce,
that their country could happen to be exactly his; and she had been
the first at recognition, the first to feel, across the water, the shock
—for it appeared to come to that—of their wonderful accident.
Strether became aware, with this, of what was taking place—that
her recognition had been even stranger for the pair in the boat, that
her immediate impulse had been to control it, and that she was
quickly and intensely debating with Chad the risk of betrayal.
He saw they would show nothing if they could feel sure he hadn't
made them out; so that he had before him for a few seconds his own
hesitation. It was a sharp fantastic crisis that had popped up as if
in a dream, and it had had only to last the few seconds to make
him feel it as quite horrible. They were thus, on either side, *trying*
the other side, and all for some reason that broke the stillness
like some unprovoked harsh note. It seemed to him again, within
the limit, that he had but one thing to do—to settle their common question by some sign of surprise and joy. He hereupon gave
large play to these things, agitating his hat and his stick and loudly
calling out—a demonstration that brought him relief as soon as he
had seen it answered. The boat, in mid-stream, still went a little
wild—which seemed natural, however, while Chad turned round,
half springing up; and his good friend, after blankness and wonder,
began gaily to wave her parasol. Chad dropped afresh to his paddles
and the boat headed round, amazement and pleasantry filling the
air meanwhile, and relief, as Strether continued to fancy, superseding mere violence. Our friend went down to the water under

this odd impression as of violence averted—the violence of their having "cut" him, out there in the eye of nature, on the assumption that he wouldn't know it. He awaited them with a face from which he was conscious of not being able quite to banish this idea that they would have gone on, not seeing and not knowing, missing their dinner and disappointing their hostess, had he himself taken a line to match. That at least was what darkened his vision for the moment. Afterwards, after they had bumped at the landing-place and he had assisted their getting ashore, everything found itself sponged over by the mere miracle of the encounter.

They could so much better at last, on either side, treat it as a wild extravagance of hazard, that the situation was made elastic by the amount of explanation called into play. Why indeed—apart from oddity—the situation should have been really stiff was a question naturally not practical at the moment, and in fact, so far as we are concerned, a question tackled, later on and in private, only by Strether himself. He was to reflect later on and in private that it was mainly *he* who had explained—as he had had moreover comparatively little difficulty in doing. He was to have at all events meanwhile the worrying thought of their perhaps secretly suspecting him of having plotted this coincidence, taking such pains as might be to give it the semblance of an accident. That possibility —as their imputation—didn't of course bear looking into for an instant; yet the whole incident was so manifestly, arrange it as they would, an awkward one, that he could scarce keep disclaimers in respect to his own presence from rising to his lips. Disclaimers of intention would have been as tactless as his presence was practically gross; and the narrowest escape they either of them had was his lucky escape, in the event, from making any. Nothing of the sort, so far as surface and sound were involved, was even in question; surface and sound all made for their common ridiculous good fortune, for the general *invraisemblance*[5] of the occasion, for the charming chance that they had, the others, in passing, ordered some food to be ready, the charming chance that he had himself not eaten, the charming chance, even more, that their little plans, their hours, their train, in short, from *là-bas*,[6] would all match for their return together to Paris. The chance that was most charming of all, the chance that drew from Madame de Vionnet her clearest, gayest "*Comme cela se trouve!*"[7] was the announcement made to Strether after they were seated at table, the word given him by their hostess in respect to his carriage for the station, on which he might now count. It settled the matter for his friends as well; the con-

5. Unlikelihood.
6. Over there.
7. How it works out!

veyance—it *was* all too lucky!—would serve for them; and nothing
was more delightful than his being in a position to make the train
so definite. It might have been, for themselves—to hear Madame
de Vionnet—almost unnaturally vague, a detail left to be fixed;
though Strether indeed was afterwards to remember that Chad
had promptly enough intervened to forestall this appearance, laughing at his companion's flightiness and making the point that he had,
after all, in spite of the bedazzlement of a day out with her, known
what he was about.

Strether was to remember afterwards further that this had had
for him the effect of forming Chad's almost sole intervention; and
indeed he was to remember further still, in subsequent meditation,
many things that, as it were, fitted together. Another of them was
for instance that the wonderful woman's overflow of surprise and
amusement was wholly into French, which she struck him as speaking with an unprecedented command of idiomatic turns, but in
which she got, as he might have said, somewhat away from him,
taking all at once little brilliant jumps that he could but lamely
match. The question of his own French had never come up for
them; it was the one thing she wouldn't have permitted—it belonged, for a person who had been through much, to mere bore-
dom; but the present result was odd, fairly veiling her identity,
shifting her back into a mere voluble class or race to the intense
audibility of which he was by this time inured. When she spoke
the charming slightly strange English he best knew her by he
seemed to feel her as a creature, among all the millions, with a
language quite to herself, the real monopoly of a special shade of
speech, beautifully easy for her, yet of a colour and a cadence that
were both inimitable and matters of accident. She came back to
these things after they had shaken down in the inn-parlour and
knew, as it were, what was to become of them; it was inevitable
that loud ejaculation over the prodigy of their convergence should
at last wear itself out. Then it was that his impression took fuller
form—the impression, destined only to deepen, to complete
itself, that they had something to put a face upon, to carry off
and make the best of, and that it was she who, admirably on the
whole, was doing this. It was familiar to him of course that they had
something to put a face upon; their friendship, their connexion,
took any amount of explaining—that would have been made familiar
by his twenty minutes with Mrs. Pocock if it hadn't already been so.
Yet his theory, as we know, had bountifully been that the facts
were specifically none of his business, and were, over and above,
so far as one had to do with them, intrinsically beautiful; and this
might have prepared him for anything, as well as rendered him
proof against mystification. When he reached home that night,

however, he knew he had been, at bottom, neither prepared nor proof; and since we have spoken of what he was, after his return, to recall and interpret, it may as well immediately be said that his real experience of these few hours put on, in that belated vision—for he scarce went to bed till morning—the aspect that is most to our purpose.

He then knew more or less how he had been affected—he but half knew at the time. There had been plenty to affect him even after, as has been said, they had shaken down; for his consciousness, though muffled, had its sharpest moments during this passage, a marked drop into innocent friendly Bohemia. They then had put their elbows on the table, deploring the premature end of their two or three dishes; which they had tried to make up with another bottle while Chad joked a little spasmodically, perhaps even a little irrelevantly, with the hostess. What it all came to had been that fiction and fable *were*, inevitably, in the air, and not as a simple term of comparison, but as a result of things said; also that they were blinking it, all round, and that they yet needn't, so much as that, have blinked it—though indeed if they hadn't Strether didn't quite see what else they could have done. Strether didn't quite see *that* even at an hour or two past midnight, even when he had, at his hotel, for a long time, without a light and without undressing, sat back on his bedroom sofa and stared straight before him. He was, at that point of vantage, in full possession, to make of it all what he could. He kept making of it that there had been simply a *lie* in the charming affair—a lie on which one could now, detached and deliberate, perfectly put one's finger. It was with the lie that they had eaten and drunk and talked and laughed, that they had waited for their *carriole* rather impatiently, and had then got into the vehicle and, sensibly subsiding, driven their three or four miles through the darkening summer night. The eating and drinking, which had been a resource, had had the effect of having served its turn; the talk and laughter had done as much; and it was during their somewhat tedious progress to the station, during the waits there, the further delays, their submission to fatigue, their silences in the dim compartment of the much-stopping train, that he prepared himself for reflexions to come. It had been a performance, Madame de Vionnet's manner, and though it had to that degree faltered toward the end, as through her ceasing to believe in it, as if she had asked herself, or Chad had found a moment surreptitiously to ask her, what after all was the use, a performance it had none the less quite handsomely remained, with the final fact about it that it was on the whole easier to keep up than to abandon.

From the point of view of presence of mind it had been very

wonderful indeed, wonderful for readiness, for beautiful assurance, for the way her decision was taken on the spot, without time to confer with Chad, without time for anything. Their only conference could have been the brief instants in the boat before they confessed to recognising the spectator on the bank, for they hadn't been alone together a moment since and must have communicated all in silence. It was a part of the deep impression for Strether, and not the least of the deep interest, that they *could* so communicate —that Chad in particular could let her know he left it to her. He habitually left things to others, as Strether was so well aware, and it in fact came over our friend in these meditations that there had been as yet no such vivid illustration of his famous knowing how to live. It was as if he had humoured her to the extent of letting her lie without correction—almost as if, really, he would be coming round in the morning to set the matter, as between Strether and himself, right. Of course he couldn't quite come; it was a case in which a man was obliged to accept the woman's version, even when fantastic; if she had, with more flurry than she cared to show, elected, as the phrase was, to represent that they had left Paris that morning, and with no design but of getting back within the day—if she had so sized-up, in the Woollett phrase, their necessity, she knew best her own measure. There were things, all the same, it was impossible to blink and which made this measure an odd one —the too evident fact for instance that she hadn't started out for the day dressed and hatted and shod, and even, for that matter, pink parasol'd, as she had been in the boat. From what did the drop in her assurance proceed as the tension increased—from what did this slightly baffled ingenuity spring but from her consciousness of not presenting, as night closed in, with not so much as a shawl to wrap her round, an appearance that matched her story? She admitted that she was cold, but only to blame her imprudence, which Chad suffered her to give such account of as she might. Her shawl and Chad's overcoat and her other garments, and his, those they had each worn the day before, were at the place, best known to themselves—a quiet retreat enough, no doubt—at which they had been spending the twenty-four hours, to which they had fully meant to return that evening, from which they had so remarkably swum into Strether's ken, and the tacit repudiation of which had been thus the essence of her comedy. Strether saw how she had perceived in a flash that they couldn't quite look to going back there under his nose; though, honestly, as he gouged deeper into the matter, he was somewhat surprised, as Chad likewise had perhaps been, at the uprising of this scruple. He seemed even to divine that she had entertained it rather for Chad than for herself, and that, as the young man had lacked the chance to enlighten her, she had had to go on with it, he meanwhile mistaking her motive.

He was rather glad, none the less, that they had in point of fact not parted at the Cheval Blanc, that he hadn't been reduced to giving them his blessing for an idyllic retreat down the river. He had had in the actual case to make-believe more than he liked, but this was nothing, it struck him, to what the other event would have required. Could he, literally, quite have faced the other event? Would he have been capable of making the best of it with them? This was what he was trying to do now; but with the advantage of his being able to give more time to it a good deal counteracted by his sense of what, over and above the central fact itself, he had to swallow. It was the quantity of make-believe involved and so vividly exemplified that most disagreed with his spiritual stomach. He moved, however, from the consideration of that quantity—to say nothing of the consciousness of that organ—back to the other feature of the show, the deep, deep truth of the intimacy revealed. That was what, in his vain vigil, he oftenest reverted to: intimacy, at such a point, was *like* that—and what in the world else would one have wished it to be like? It was all very well for him to feel the pity of its being so much like lying; he almost blushed, in the dark, for the way he had dressed the possibility in vagueness, as a little girl might have dressed her doll. He had made them—and by no fault of their own—momentarily pull it for him, the possibility, out of this vagueness; and must he not therefore take it now as they had had simply, with whatever thin attenuations, to give it to him? The very question, it may be added, made him feel lonely and cold. There was the element of the awkward all round, but Chad and Madame de Vionnet had at least the comfort that they could talk it over together. With whom could *he* talk of such things? —unless indeed always, at almost any stage, with Maria? He foresaw that Miss Gostrey would come again into requisition on the morrow; though it wasn't to be denied that he was already a little afraid of her "What on earth—that's what I want to know now—had you then supposed?" He recognised at last that he had really been trying all along to suppose nothing. Verily, verily, his labour had been lost. He found himself supposing innumerable and wonderful things.

Book Twelfth

I [XXXII]

Strether couldn't have said he had during the previous hours definitely expected it; yet when, later on, that morning—though

no later indeed than for his coming forth at ten o'clock—he saw
the concierge produce, on his approach, a *petit bleu*[1] delivered since
his letters had been sent up, he recognised the appearance as the
first symptom of a sequel. He then knew he had been thinking of
some early sign from Chad as more likely, after all, than not;
and this would be precisely the early sign. He took it so for granted
that he opened the *petit bleu* just where he had stopped, in the
pleasant cool draught of the porte-cochère—only curious to see
where the young man would, at such a juncture, break out. His
curiosity, however, was more than gratified; the small missive,
whose gummed edge he had detached without attention to the address, not being from the young man at all, but from the person
whom the case gave him on the spot as still more worth while.
Worth while or not, he went round to the nearest telegraph-office,
the big one on the Boulevard, with a directness that almost confessed to a fear of the danger of delay. He might have been thinking
that if he didn't go before he could think he wouldn't perhaps go
at all. He at any rate kept, in the lower side-pocket of his morning
coat, a very deliberate hand on his blue missive, crumpling it up
rather tenderly than harshly. He wrote a reply, on the Boulevard,
also in the form of a *petit bleu*—which was quickly done, under
pressure of the place, inasmuch as, like Madame de Vionnet's own
communication, it consisted of the fewest words. She had asked
him if he could do her the very great kindness of coming to see her
that evening at half-past nine, and he answered, as if nothing were
easier, that he would present himself at the hour she named. She
had added a line of postscript, to the effect that she would come to
him elsewhere and at his own hour if he preferred; but he took no
notice of this, feeling that if he saw her at all half the value of it
would be in seeing her where he had already seen her best. He
mightn't see her at all; that was one of the reflexions he made
after writing and before he dropped his closed card into the box;
he mightn't see any one at all any more at all; he might make an
end as well now as ever, leaving things as they were, since he was
doubtless not to leave them better, and taking his way home so
far as should appear that a home remained to him. This alternative
was for a few minutes so sharp that if he at last did deposit his
missive it was perhaps because the pressure of the place had an
effect.

There was none other, however, than the common and constant pressure, familiar to our friend under the rubric of *Postes et
Télégraphes*[2]—the something in the air of these establishments;

---

1. A special-delivery letter transmitted within Paris through pneumatic tubes (*lit.*, little blue).
2. The Postal and Telegraph Offices are combined in France.

the vibration of the vast strange life of the town, the influence of the types, the performers concocting their messages; the little prompt Paris women, arranging, pretexting goodness knew what, driving the dreadful needle-pointed public pen at the dreadful sand-strewn public table: implements that symbolised for Strether's too interpretative innocence something more acute in manners, more sinister in morals, more fierce in the national life. After he had put in his paper he had ranged himself, he was really amused to think, on the side of the fierce, the sinister, the acute. He was carrying on a correspondence, across the great city, quite in the key of the *Postes et Télégraphes* in general; and it was fairly as if the acceptance of that fact had come from something in his state that sorted with the occupation of his neighbours. He was mixed up with the typical tale of Paris, and so were they, poor things— how could they all together help being? They were no worse than he, in short, and he no worse than they—if, queerly enough, no better; and at all events he had settled his hash, so that he went out to begin, from that moment, his day of waiting. The great settlement was, as he felt, in his preference for seeing his correspondent in her own best conditions. *That* was part of the typical tale, the part most significant in respect to himself. He liked the place she lived in, the picture that each time squared itself, large and high and clear, around her: every occasion of seeing it was a pleasure of a different shade. Yet what precisely was he doing with shades of pleasure now, and why hadn't he properly and logically compelled her to commit herself to whatever of disadvantage and penalty the situation might throw up? He might have proposed, as for Sarah Pocock, the cold hospitality of his own *salon de lecture*, in which the chill of Sarah's visit seemed still to abide and shades of pleasure were dim; he might have suggested a stone bench in the dusty Tuileries or a penny chair at the back part of the Champs Elysées.[3] These things would have been a trifle stern, and sternness alone now wouldn't be sinister. An instinct in him cast about for some form of discipline in which they might meet— some awkwardness they would suffer from, some danger, or at least some grave inconvenience, they would incur. This would give a sense—which the spirit required, rather ached and sighed in the absence of—that somebody was paying something somewhere and somehow, that they were at least not all floating together on the silver stream of impunity. Just instead of that to go and see her late in the evening, as if, for all the world—well, as if he were as much in the swim as anybody else: this had as little as possible in common with the penal form.

Even when he had felt that objection melt away, however, the

---

3. A park at the end of the Avenue Champs-Élysées, near the Tuileries.

practical difference was small; the long stretch of his interval took the colour it would, and if he lived on thus with the sinister from hour to hour it proved an easier thing than one might have supposed in advance. He reverted in thought to his old tradition, the one he had been brought up on and which even so many years of life had but little worn away; the notion that the state of the wrongdoer, or at least this person's happiness, presented some special difficulty. What struck him now rather was the ease of it—for nothing in truth appeared easier. It was an ease he himself fairly tasted of for the rest of the day; giving himself quite up; not so much as trying to dress it out, in any particular whatever, as a difficulty; not after all going to see Maria—which would have been in a manner a result of such dressing; only idling, lounging, smoking, sitting in the shade, drinking lemonade and consuming ices. The day had turned to heat and eventual thunder, and he now and again went back to his hotel to find that Chad hadn't been there. He hadn't yet struck himself, since leaving Woollett, so much as a loafer, though there had been times when he believed himself touching bottom. This was a deeper depth than any, and with no foresight, scarcely with a care, as to what he should bring up. He almost wondered if he didn't *look* demoralised and disreputable; he had the fanciful vision, as he sat and smoked, of some accidental, some motived, return of the Pococks, who would be passing along the Boulevard and would catch this view of him. They would have distinctly, on his appearance, every ground for scandal. But fate failed to administer even that sternness; the Pococks never passed and Chad made no sign. Strether meanwhile continued to hold off from Miss Gostrey, keeping her till to-morrow; so that by evening his irresponsibility, his impunity, his luxury, had become—there was no other word for them—immense.

Between nine and ten, at last, in the high clear picture—he was moving in these days, as in a gallery, from clever canvas to clever canvas—he drew a long breath: it was so presented to him from the first that the spell of his luxury wouldn't be broken. He wouldn't have, that is, to become responsible—this was admirably in the air: she had sent for him precisely to let him feel it, so that he might go on with the comfort (comfort already established, hadn't it been?) of regarding his ordeal, the ordeal of the weeks of Sarah's stay and of their climax, as safely traversed and left behind him. Didn't she just wish to assure him that *she* now took it all and so kept it; that he was absolutely not to worry any more, was only to rest on his laurels and continue generously to help her? The light in her beautiful formal room was dim, though it would do, as everything would always do; the hot night had kept out lamps, but there was a pair of clusters of candles that glim-

mered over the chimney-piece like the tall tapers of an altar. The
windows were all open, their redundant hangings swaying a little,
and he heard once more, from the empty court, the small plash of
the fountain. From beyond this, and as from a great distance—
beyond the court, beyond the *corps de logis*[4] forming the front—
came, as if excited and exciting, the vague voice of Paris. Strether
had all along been subject to sudden gusts of fancy in connexion
with such matters as these—odd starts of the historic sense, suppositions and divinations with no warrant but their intensity. Thus
and so, on the eve of the great recorded dates, the days and nights
of revolution, the sounds had come in, the omens, the beginnings
broken out. They were the smell of revolution, the smell of the
public temper—or perhaps simply the smell of blood.

It was at present queer beyond words, "subtle," he would have
risked saying, that such suggestions should keep crossing the scene;
but it was doubtless the effect of the thunder in the air, which had
hung about all day without release. His hostess was dressed as for
thunderous times, and it fell in with the kind of imagination we
have just attributed to him that she should be in simplest coolest
white, of a character so old-fashioned, if he were not mistaken, that
Madame Roland[5] must on the scaffold have worn something like it.
This effect was enhanced by a small black fichu or scarf, of crape
or gauze, disposed quaintly round her bosom and now completing as
by a mystic touch the pathetic, the noble analogy. Poor Strether
in fact scarce knew what analogy was evoked for him as the charming woman, receiving him and making him, as she could do such
things, at once familiarly and gravely welcome, moved over her
great room with her image almost repeated in its polished floor,
which had been fully bared for summer. The associations of the
place, all felt again; the gleam here and there, in the subdued
light, of glass and gilt and parquet, with the quietness of her own
note as the centre—these things were at first as delicate as if they
had been ghostly, and he was sure in a moment that, whatever he
should find he had come for, it wouldn't be for an impression that
had previously failed him. That conviction held him from the outset, and, seeming singularly to simplify, certified to him that the
objects about would help him, would really help them both. No,
he might never see them again—this was only too probably the
last time; and he should certainly see nothing in the least degree
like them. He should soon be going to where such things were not,
and it would be a small mercy for memory, for fancy, to have, in
that stress, a loaf on the shelf. He knew in advance he should look

4. Main part of the building.
5. A famous intellectual and moderate French revolutionary executed in 1793 during the Reign
of Terror. She dressed in simple white for her execution, and her last words were "O Liberty!
What crimes are committed in your name."

back on the perception actually sharpest with him as on the view
of something old, old, old, the oldest thing he had ever personally
touched; and he also knew, even while he took his companion in
as the feature among features, that memory and fancy couldn't help
being enlisted for her. She might intend what she would, but this
was beyond anything she could intend, with things from far back
—tyrannies of history, facts of type, values, as the painters said,
of expression—all working for her and giving her the supreme
chance, the chance of the happy, the really luxurious few, the
chance, on a great occasion, to be natural and simple. She had never,
with him, been more so; or if it was the perfection of art it would
never—and that came to the same thing—be proved against her.

What was truly wonderful was her way of differing so from
time to time without detriment to her simplicity. Caprices, he was
sure she felt, were before anything else bad manners, and that
judgement in her was by itself a thing making more for safety of
intercourse than anything that in his various own past inter-
courses he had had to reckon on. If therefore her presence was now
quite other than the one she had shown him the night before,
there was nothing of violence in the change—it was all harmony
and reason. It gave him a mild deep person, whereas he had had
on the occasion to which their interview was a direct reference a
person committed to movement and surface and abounding in them;
but she was in either character more remarkable for nothing than
for her bridging of intervals, and this now fell in with what he
understood he was to leave to her. The only thing was that, if he
was to leave it *all* to her, why exactly had she sent for him? He had
had, vaguely, in advance, his explanation, his view of the probability of her wishing to set something right, to deal in some way with
the fraud so lately practised on his presumed credulity. Would she
attempt to carry it further or would she blot it out? Would she
throw over it some more or less happy colour; or would she do
nothing about it at all? He perceived soon enough at least that,
however reasonable she might be, she wasn't vulgarly confused, and
it herewith pressed upon him that their eminent "lie," Chad's and
hers, was simply after all such an inevitable tribute to good taste as
he couldn't have wished them not to render. Away from them, during his vigil, he had seemed to wince at the amount of comedy involved; whereas in his present posture he could only ask himself
how he should enjoy any attempt from her to take the comedy
back. He shouldn't enjoy it at all; but, once more and yet once
more, he could trust her. That is he could trust her to make deception right. As she presented things the ugliness—goodness knew
why—went out of them; none the less too that she could present
them, with an art of her own, by not so much as touching them.

She let the matter, at all events, lie where it was—where the previous twenty-four hours had placed it; appearing merely to circle about it respectfully, tenderly, almost piously, while she took up another question.

She knew she hadn't really thrown dust in his eyes; this, the previous night, before they separated, had practically passed between them; and, as she had sent for him to see what the difference thus made for him might amount to, so he was conscious at the end of five minutes that he had been tried and tested. She had settled with Chad after he left them that she would, for her satisfaction, assure herself of this quantity, and Chad had, as usual, let her have her way. Chad was always letting people have their way when he felt that it would somehow turn his wheel for him; it somehow always did turn his wheel. Strether felt, oddly enough, before these facts, freshly and consentingly passive; they again so rubbed it into him that the couple thus fixing his attention were intimate, that his intervention had absolutely aided and intensified their intimacy, and that in fine he must accept the consequence of that. He had absolutely become, himself, with his perceptions and his mistakes, his concessions and his reserves, the droll mixture, as it must seem to them, of his braveries and his fears, the general spectacle of his art and his innocence, almost an added link and certainly a common priceless ground for them to meet upon. It was as if he had been hearing their very tone when she brought out a reference that was comparatively straight. "The last twice that you've been here, you know, I never asked you," she said with an abrupt transition—they had been pretending before this to talk simply of the charm of yesterday and of the interest of the country they had seen. The effort was confessedly vain; not for such talk had she invited him; and her impatient reminder was of their having done for it all the needful on his coming to her after Sarah's flight. What she hadn't asked him then was to state to her where and how he stood for her; she had been resting on Chad's report of their midnight hour together in the Boulevard Malesherbes. The thing therefore she at present desired was ushered in by this recall of the two occasions on which, disinterested and merciful, she hadn't worried him. To-night truly she *would* worry him, and this was her appeal to him to let her risk it. He wasn't to mind if she bored him a little: she had behaved, after all—hadn't she?—so awfully, awfully well.

II [XXXIII]

"Oh, you're all right, you're all right," he almost impatiently declared; his impatience being moreover not for her pressure, but for her scruple. More and more distinct to him was the tune to which she would have had the matter out with Chad; more and more vivid for him the idea that she had been nervous as to what he might be able to "stand." Yes, it had been a question if he had "stood" what the scene on the river had given him, and, though the young man had doubtless opined in favour of his recuperation, her own last word must have been that she should feel easier in seeing for herself. That was it, unmistakeably; she *was* seeing for herself. What he could stand was thus, in these moments, in the balance for Strether, who reflected, as he became fully aware of it, that he must properly brace himself. He wanted fully to appear to stand all he might; and there was a certain command of the situation for him in this very wish not to look too much at sea. She was ready with everything, but so, sufficiently, was he; that is he was at one point the more prepared of the two, inasmuch as, for all her cleverness, she couldn't produce on the spot—and it was surprising—an account of the motive of her note. He had the advantage that his pronouncing her "all right" gave him for an enquiry. "May I ask, delighted as I've been to come, if you've wished to say something special?" He spoke as if she might have seen he had been waiting for it—not indeed with discomfort, but with natural interest. Then he saw that she was a little taken aback, was even surprised herself at the detail she had neglected—the only one ever yet; having somehow assumed he would know, would recognise, would leave some things not to be said. She looked at him, however, an instant as if to convey that if he wanted them *all*—!

"Selfish and vulgar—that's what I must seem to you. You've done everything for me, and here I am as if I were asking for more. But it isn't," she went on, "because I'm afraid—though I *am* of course afraid, as a woman in my position always is. I mean it isn't because one lives in terror—it isn't because of that one is selfish, for I'm ready to give you my word to-night that I don't care; don't care what still may happen and what I may lose. I don't ask you to raise your little finger for me again, nor do I wish so much as to mention to you what we've talked of before, either my danger or my safety, or his mother, or his sister, or the girl he may marry, or the fortune he may make or miss, or the right or the wrong, of any kind, he may do. If after the help one has had from you one can't either take care of one's self or simply hold one's tongue, one must renounce all claim to be an object of interest. It's in the name of what I *do* care about that I've tried still to keep hold of you. How can I be indifferent," she asked, "to how I appear to you?" And as he found himself unable immediately to say: "Why, if you're going, *need* you, after all? Is it impossible you should stay on—so that one mayn't lose you?"

"Impossible I should live with you here instead of going home?"

"Not 'with' us, if you object to that, but near enough to us, somewhere, for us to see you—well," she beautifully brought out, "when we feel we *must*. How shall we not sometimes feel it? I've wanted to see you often when I couldn't," she pursued, "all these last weeks. How shan't I then miss you now, with the sense of your being gone forever?" Then as if the straightness of this appeal, taking him unprepared, had visibly left him wondering: "Where *is* your 'home' moreover now—what has become of it? I've made a change in your life, I know I have; I've upset everything in your mind as well; in your sense of—what shall I call it?—all the decencies and possibilities. It gives me a kind of detestation—" She pulled up short.

Oh but he wanted to hear. "Detestation of what?"

"Of everything—of life."

"Ah that's too much," he laughed—"or too little!"

"Too little, precisely"—she was eager. "What I hate is myself —when I think that one has to take so much, to be happy, out of the lives of others, and that one isn't happy even then. One does it to cheat one's self and to stop one's mouth—but that's only at the best for a little. The wretched self is always there, always making one somehow a fresh anxiety. What it comes to is that it's not, that it's never, a happiness, any happiness at all, to *take*. The only safe thing is to give. It's what plays you least false." Interesting, touching, strikingly sincere as she let these things come from her, she yet puzzled and troubled him—so fine was the quaver of her quietness. He felt what he had felt before with her, that there was always more behind what she showed, and more and more again behind that. "You know so, at least," she added, "where you are!"

"*You* ought to know it indeed then; for isn't what you've been giving exactly what has brought us together this way? You've been making, as I've so fully let you know I've felt," Strether said, "the most precious present I've ever seen made, and if you can't sit down peacefully on that performance you *are*, no doubt, born to torment yourself. But you ought," he wound up, "to be easy."

"And not trouble you any more, no doubt—not thrust on you even the wonder and the beauty of what I've done; only let you regard our business as over, and well over, and see you depart in a peace that matches my own? No doubt, no doubt, no doubt," she nervously repeated—"all the more that I don't really pretend I believe you couldn't, for yourself, *not* have done what you have. I don't pretend you feel yourself victimised, for this evidently is the way you live, and it's what—we're agreed—is the best way. Yes, as you say," she continued after a moment, "I ought to be easy and rest on my work. Well then here am I doing so. I *am* easy. You'll have it for your last impression. When is it you say you go?" she asked with a quick change.

He took some time to reply—his last impression was more and more so mixed a one. It produced in him a vague disappointment, a drop that was deeper even than the fall of his elation the previous night. The good of what he had done, if he had done so much, wasn't there to enliven him quite to the point that would have been ideal for a grand gay finale. Women were thus endlessly absorbent, and to deal with them was to walk on water. What was at bottom the matter with her, embroider as she might and disclaim as she might—what was at bottom the matter with her was simply Chad himself. It was of Chad she was after all renewedly afraid; the strange strength of her passion was the very strength of her fear; she clung to *him*, Lambert Strether, as to a source of safety she had tested, and, generous graceful truthful as she might try to be, exquisite as she was, she dreaded the term of his being within reach. With this sharpest perception yet, it was like a chill in the air to him, it was almost appalling, that a creature so fine could be, by mysterious forces, a creature so exploited. For at the end of all things they *were* mysterious: she had but made Chad what he was—so why could she think she had made him infinite? She had made him better, she had made him best, she had made him anything one would; but it came to our friend with supreme queerness that he was none the less only Chad. Strether had the sense that *he*, a little, had made him too; his high appreciation had, as it were, consecrated her work. The work, however admirable, was nevertheless of the strict human order, and in short it was marvellous that the companion of mere earthly joys, of comforts, aberrations (however one classed them) within the common experience, should be so transcendently prized. It might have made Strether hot or shy, as such secrets of others brought home sometimes do make us; but he was held there by something so hard that it was fairly grim. This was not the discomposure of last night; that had quite passed—such discomposures were a detail; the real coercion was to see a man ineffably adored. There it was again—it took women, it took women; if to deal with them was to walk on water what wonder that the water rose? And it had never surely risen higher than round this woman. He presently found himself taking a long look from her, and the next thing he knew he had uttered all his thought. "You're afraid for your life!"

It drew out her long look, and he soon enough saw why. A spasm came into her face, the tears she had already been unable to hide overflowed at first in silence, and then, as the sound suddenly comes from a child, quickened to gasps, to sobs. She sat and covered her face with her hands, giving up all attempt at a manner. "It's how you see me, it's how you see me"—she caught her breath with it—"and it's as I *am*, and as I must take myself, and of

course it's no matter." Her emotion was at first so incoherent that
he could only stand there at a loss, stand with his sense of having
upset her, though of having done it by the truth. He had to listen
to her in a silence that he made no immediate effort to attenuate,
feeling her doubly woeful amid all her dim diffused elegance; consenting to it as he had consented to the rest, and even conscious of
some vague inward irony in the presence of such a fine free range
of bliss and bale. He couldn't say it was *not* no matter; for he was
serving her to the end, he now knew, anyway—quite as if what he
thought of her had nothing to do with it. It was actually moreover as if he didn't think of her at all, as if he could think of nothing
but the passion, mature, abysmal, pitiful, she represented, and the
possibilities she betrayed. She was older for him to-night, visibly
less exempt from the touch of time; but she was as much as ever
the finest and subtlest creature, the happiest apparition, it had been
given him, in all his years, to meet; and yet he could see her there
as vulgarly troubled, in very truth, as a maidservant crying for her
young man. The only thing was that she judged herself as the maid-
servant wouldn't; the weakness of which wisdom too, the dishonour
of which judgement, seemed but to sink her lower. Her collapse,
however, no doubt, was briefer and she had in a manner recovered
herself before he intervened. "Of course I'm afraid for my life. But
that's nothing. It isn't that."

He was silent a little longer, as if thinking what it might be.
"There's something I have in mind that I can still do."

But she threw off at last, with a sharp sad headshake, drying her
eyes, what he could still do. "I don't care for that. Of course, as
I've said, you're acting, in your wonderful way, for yourself; and
what's for yourself is no more my business—though I may reach
out unholy hands so clumsily to touch it—than if it were something
in Timbuctoo. It's only that you don't snub me, as you've had
fifty chances to do—it's only your beautiful patience that makes
one forget one's manners. In spite of your patience, all the same,"
she went on, "you'd do anything rather than be with us here, even
if that were possible. You'd do everything for us but be mixed up
with us—which is a statement you can easily answer to the advantage of your own manners. You can say 'What's the use of
talking of things that at the best are impossible?' What *is* of course
the use? It's only my little madness. You'd talk if you were tormented. And I don't mean now about *him*. Oh for him—!" Positively, strangely, bitterly, as it seemed to Strether, she gave "him,"
for the moment, away. "You don't care what I think of you; but I
happen to care what you think of me. And what you *might*," she
added. "What you perhaps even did."

He gained time. "What I did—?"

"Did think before. Before this. *Didn't* you think—?"

But he had already stopped her. "I didn't think anything. I never think a step further than I'm obliged to."

"That's perfectly false, I believe," she returned—"except that you may, no doubt, often pull up when things become *too* ugly; or even, I'll say, to save you a protest, too beautiful. At any rate, even so far as it's true, we've thrust on you appearances that you've had to take in and that have therefore made your obligation. Ugly or beautiful—it doesn't matter what we call them—you were getting on without them, and that's where we're detestable. We bore you —that's where we are. And we may well—for what we've cost you. All you can do *now* is not to think at all. And I who should have liked to seem to you—well, sublime!"

He could only after a moment re-echo Miss Barrace. "You're wonderful!"

"I'm old and abject and hideous"—she went on as without hearing him. "Abject above all. Or old above all. It's when one's old that it's worst. I don't care what becomes of it—let what *will*; there it is. It's a doom—I know it; you can't see it more than I do myself. Things have to happen as they will." With which she came back again to what, face to face with him, had so quite broken down. "Of course you wouldn't, even if possible, and no matter what may happen to you, be near us. But think of me, think of me—!" She exhaled it into air.

He took refuge in repeating something he had already said and that she had made nothing of. "There's something I believe I can still do." And he put his hand out for good-bye.

She again made nothing of it; she went on with her insistence. "That won't help you. There's nothing to help you."

"Well, it may help *you*," he said.

She shook her head. "There's not a grain of certainty in my future—for the only certainty is that I shall be the loser in the end."

She hadn't taken his hand, but she moved with him to the door. "That's cheerful," he laughed, "for your benefactor!"

"What's cheerful for *me*," she replied, "is that we might, you and I, have been friends. That's it—that's it. You see how, as I say, I want everything. I've wanted you too."

"Ah but you've *had* me!" he declared, at the door, with an emphasis that made an end.

III [XXXIV]

His purpose had been to see Chad the next day, and he had prefigured seeing him by an early call; having in general never stood on ceremony in respect to visits at the Boulevard Malesherbes. It had been more often natural for him to go there than for Chad to come to the small hotel, the attractions of which were scant; yet it nevertheless, just now, at the eleventh hour, did suggest itself to Strether to begin by giving the young man a chance. It struck him that, in the inevitable course, Chad would be "round," as Waymarsh used to say—Waymarsh who already, somehow, seemed long ago. He hadn't come the day before, because it had been arranged between them that Madame de Vionnet should see their friend first; but now that this passage had taken place he would present himself, and their friend wouldn't have long to wait. Strether assumed, he became aware, on this reasoning, that the interesting parties to the arrangement would have met betimes, and that the more interesting of the two—as she was after all—would have communicated to the other the issue of her appeal. Chad would know without delay that his mother's messenger had been with her, and, though it was perhaps not quite easy to see how she could qualify what had occurred, he would at least have been sufficiently advised to feel he could go on. The day, however, brought, early or late, no word from him, and Strether felt, as a result of this, that a change had practically come over their intercourse. It was perhaps a premature judgement; or it only meant perhaps—how could he tell?—that the wonderful pair he protected had taken up again together the excursion he had accidentally checked. They might have gone back to the country, and gone back but with a long breath drawn; that indeed would best mark Chad's sense that reprobation hadn't rewarded Madame de Vionnet's request for an interview. At the end of the twenty-four hours, at the end of the forty-eight, there was still no overture; so that Strether filled up the time, as he had so often filled it before, by going to see Miss Gostrey.

He proposed amusements to her; he felt expert now in proposing amusements; and he had thus, for several days, an odd sense of leading her about Paris, of driving her in the Bois, of showing her the penny steamboats—those from which the breeze of the Seine was to be best enjoyed—that might have belonged to a kindly uncle doing the honours of the capital to an intelligent niece from the country. He found means even to take her to shops she didn't know, or that she pretended she didn't; while she, on her side, was, like the country maiden, all passive modest and grateful—going in fact so far as to emulate rusticity in occasional fatigues and bewilderments. Strether described these vague proceedings to himself, described them even to her, as a happy interlude; the sign of which was that the companions said for the time no further word about the matter they had talked of to satiety. He proclaimed satiety at the outset, and she quickly took the hint; as docile both in this and in everything else as the intelligent obedient niece. He told her as yet

nothing of his late adventure—for as an adventure it now ranked
with him; he pushed the whole business temporarily aside and
found his interest in the fact of her beautiful assent. She left questions unasked—she who for so long had been all questions; she
gave herself up to him with an understanding of which mere mute
gentleness might have seemed the sufficient expression. She knew
his sense of his situation had taken still another step—of that he
was quite aware; but she conveyed that, whatever had thus happened for him, it was thrown into the shade by what was happening for herself. This—though it mightn't to a detached spirit have
seemed much—was the major interest, and she met it with a new
directness of response, measuring it from hour to hour with her
grave hush of acceptance. Touched as he had so often been by her
before, he was, for his part too, touched afresh; all the more that
though he could be duly aware of the principle of his own mood he
couldn't be equally so of the principle of hers. He knew, that is, in
a manner—knew roughly and resignedly—what he himself was
hatching; whereas he had to take the chance of what he called to
himself Maria's calculations. It was all he needed that she liked
him enough for what they were doing, and even should they do a
good deal more would still like him enough for that; the essential
freshness of a relation so simple was a cool bath to the soreness
produced by other relations. These others appeared to him now
horribly complex; they bristled with fine points, points all unimaginable beforehand, points that pricked and drew blood; a fact that
gave to an hour with his present friend on a *bateau-mouche*,[6] or in
the afternoon shade of the Champs Elysées, something of the innocent pleasure of handling rounded ivory. His relation with Chad
personally—from the moment he had got his point of view—had
been of the simplest; yet this also struck him as bristling, after a
third and a fourth blank day had passed. It was as if at last however his care for such indications had dropped; there came a fifth
blank day and he ceased to enquire or to heed.

They now took on to his fancy, Miss Gostrey and he, the image
of the Babes in the Wood;[7] they could trust the merciful elements
to let them continue at peace. He had been great already, as he
knew, at postponements; but he had only to get afresh into the
rhythm of one to feel its fine attraction. It amused him to say to
himself that he might for all the world have been going to die—
die resignedly; the scene was filled for him with so deep a death-bed
hush, so melancholy a charm. That meant the postponement of
everything else—which made so for the quiet lapse of life; and the

6. A Seine passenger-steamer.
7. An anonymous (sixteenth-century?) ballad—actually entitled *Children in the Wood*—in which
   two orphaned and abandoned children perish in the woods and are covered with leaves by the
   robins.

postponement in especial of the reckoning to come—unless indeed the reckoning to come were to be one and the same thing with extinction. It faced him, the reckoning, over the shoulder of much interposing experience—which also faced him; and one would float to it doubtless duly through these caverns of Kubla Khan.[8] It was really behind everything; it hadn't merged in what he had done; his final appreciation of what he had done—his appreciation on the spot—would provide it with its main sharpness. The spot so focussed was of course Woollett, and he was to see, at the best, what Woollett would be with everything there changed for him. Wouldn't *that* revelation practically amount to the wind-up of his career? Well, the summer's end would show; his suspense had meanwhile exactly the sweetness of vain delay; and he had with it, we should mention, other pastimes than Maria's company—plenty of separate musings in which his luxury failed him but at one point. He was well in port, the outer sea behind him, and it was only a matter of getting ashore. There was a question that came and went for him, however, as he rested against the side of his ship, and it was a little to get rid of the obsession that he prolonged his hours with Miss Gostrey. It was a question about himself, but it could only be settled by seeing Chad again; it was indeed his principal reason for wanting to see Chad. After that it wouldn't signify—it was a ghost that certain words would easily lay to rest. Only the young man must be there to take the words. Once they were taken he wouldn't have a question left; none, that is, in connexion with this particular affair. It wouldn't then matter even to himself that he might now have been guilty of speaking *because* of what he had forfeited. That was the refinement of his supreme scruple—he wished so to leave what he had forfeited out of account. He wished not to do anything because he had missed something else, because he was sore or sorry or impoverished, because he was maltreated or desperate; he wished to do everything because he was lucid and quiet, just the same for himself on all essential points as he had ever been. Thus it was that while he virtually hung about for Chad he kept mutely putting it: "You've been chucked, old boy; but what has that to do with it?" It would have sickened him to feel vindictive.

These tints of feeling indeed were doubtless but the iridescence of his idleness, and they were presently lost in a new light from Maria. She had a fresh fact for him before the week was out, and she practically met him with it on his appearing one night. He hadn't on this day seen her, but had planned presenting himself in due course to ask her to dine with him somewhere out of doors, on

---

8. "In Xanadu did Kubla Khan / A stately pleasure-dome decree: / Where Alph, the sacred river, ran / Through caverns measureless to man / Down to a sunless sea." Samuel Taylor Coleridge, *Kubla Khan* ll. 1–5.

one of the terraces, in one of the gardens, of which the Paris of
summer was profuse. It had then come on to rain, so that, disconcerted, he changed his mind; dining alone at home, a little
stuffily and stupidly, and waiting on her afterwards to make up his
loss. He was sure within a minute that something had happened; it
was so in the air of the rich little room that he had scarcely to
name his thought. Softly lighted, the whole colour of the place, with
its vague values, was in cool fusion—an effect that made the visitor
stand for a little agaze. It was as if in doing so now he had felt a
recent presence—his recognition of the passage of which his hostess
in turn divined. She had scarcely to say it—"Yes, she has been here,
and this time I received her." It wasn't till a minute later that she
added: "There being, as I understand you, no reason *now*—!"

"None for your refusing?"

"No—if you've done what you've had to do."

"I've certainly so far done it," Strether said, "as that you needn't
fear the effect, or the appearance of coming between us. There's
nothing between us now but what we ourselves have put there,
and not an inch of room for anything else whatever. Therefore
you're only beautifully *with* us as always—though doubtless now,
if she has talked to you, rather more with us than less. Of course if
she came," he added, "it was to talk to you."

"It was to talk to me," Maria returned; on which he was further
sure that she was practically in possession of what he himself hadn't
yet told her. He was even sure she was in possession of things he
himself couldn't have told; for the consciousness of them was now
all in her face and accompanied there with a shade of sadness that
marked in her the close of all uncertainties. It came out for him
more than ever yet that she had had from the first a knowledge she
believed him not to have had, a knowledge the sharp acquisition of
which might be destined to make a difference for him. The difference for him might not inconceivably be an arrest of his independence and a change in his attitude—in other words a revulsion
in favour of the principles of Woollett. She had really prefigured
the possibility of a shock that would send him swinging back to
Mrs. Newsome. He hadn't, it was true, week after week, shown
signs of receiving it, but the possibility had been none the less in
the air. What Maria accordingly had had now to take in was that
the shock had descended and that he hadn't, all the same, swung
back. He had grown clear, in a flash, on a point long since settled
for herself; but no reapproximation to Mrs. Newsome had occurred
in consequence. Madame de Vionnet had by her visit held up the
torch to these truths, and what now lingered in poor Maria's face
was the somewhat smoky light of the scene between them. If the
light however wasn't, as we have hinted, the glow of joy, the rea-

sons for this also were perhaps discernible to Strether even through the blur cast over them by his natural modesty. She had held herself for months with a firm hand; she hadn't interfered on any chance—and chances were specious enough—that she might interfere to her profit. She had turned her back on the dream that Mrs. Newsome's rupture, their friend's forfeiture—the engagement, the relation itself, broken beyond all mending—might furnish forth her advantage; and, to stay her hand from promoting these things, she had, on private, difficult, but rigid, lines, played strictly fair. She couldn't therefore but feel that, though, as the end of all, the facts in question had been stoutly confirmed, her ground for personal, for what might have been called interested, elation remained rather vague. Strether might easily have made out that she had been asking herself, in the hours she had just sat through, if there were still for her, or were only not, a fair shade of uncertainty. Let us hasten to add, however, that what he at first made out on this occasion he also at first kept to himself. He only asked what in particular Madame de Vionnet had come for; and as to this his companion was ready.

"She wants tidings of Mr. Newsome, whom she appears not to have seen for some days."

"Then she hasn't been away with him again?"

"She seemed to think," Maria answered, "that he might have gone away with *you*."

"And did you tell her I know nothing of him?"

She had her indulgent headshake. "I've known nothing of what you know. I could only tell her I'd ask you."

"Then I've not seen him for a week—and of course I've wondered." His wonderment showed at this moment as sharper, but he presently went on. "Still, I dare say I can put my hand on him. Did she strike you," he asked, "as anxious?"

"She's always anxious."

"After all I've done for her?" And he had one of the last flickers of his occasional mild mirth. "To think that was just what I came out to prevent!"

She took it up but to reply. "You don't regard him then as safe?"

"I was just going to ask you how in that respect you regard Madame de Vionnet."

She looked at him a little. "What woman was *ever* safe? She told me," she added—and it was as if at the touch of the connexion—"of your extraordinary meeting in the country. After that *à quoi se fier?*"[9]

"It was, as an accident, in all the possible or impossible chapter," Strether conceded, "amazing enough. But still, but still—!"

9. What can be relied upon?

"But still she didn't mind?"

"She doesn't mind anything."

"Well, then, as you don't either, we may all sink to rest!"

He appeared to agree with her, but he had his reservation. "I do mind Chad's disappearance."

"Oh you'll get him back. But now you know," she said, "why I went to Mentone." He had sufficiently let her see that he had by this time gathered things together, but there was nature in her wish to make them clearer still. "I didn't want you to put it to me."

"To put it to you—?"

"The question of what you were at last—a week ago—to see for yourself. I didn't want to have to lie for her. I felt that to be too much for me. A man of course is always expected to do it—to do it, I mean, for a woman; but not a woman for another woman; unless perhaps on the tit-for-tat principle, as an indirect way of protecting herself. I don't need protection, so that I was free to 'funk' you—simply to dodge your test. The responsibility was too much for me. I gained time, and when I came back the need of a test had blown over."

Strether thought of it serenely. "Yes; when you came back little Bilham had shown me what's expected of a gentleman. Little Bilham had lied like one."

"And like what you believed him?"

"Well," said Strether, "it was but a technical lie—he classed the attachment as virtuous. That was a view for which there was much to be said—and the virtue came out for me hugely. There was of course a great deal of it. I got it full in the face, and I haven't, you see, done with it yet."

"What I see, what I saw," Maria returned, "is that you dressed up even the virtue. You were wonderful—you were beautiful, as I've had the honour of telling you before; but, if you wish really to know," she sadly confessed, "I never quite knew *where* you were. There were moments," she explained, "when you struck me as grandly cynical; there were others when you struck me as grandly vague."

Her friend considered. "I had phases. I had flights."

"Yes, but things must have a basis."

"A basis seemed to me just what her beauty supplied."

"Her beauty of person?"

"Well, her beauty of everything. The impression she makes. She has such variety and yet such harmony."

She considered him with one of her deep returns of indulgence —returns out of all proportion to the irritations they flooded over. "You're complete."

"You're always too personal," he good-humouredly said; "but

that's precisely how I wondered and wandered."

"If you mean," she went on, "that she was from the first for you the most charming woman in the world, nothing's more simple. Only that was an odd foundation."

"For what I reared on it?"

"For what you didn't!"

"Well, it was all not a fixed quantity. And it had for me—it has still—such elements of strangeness. Her greater age than his, her different world, traditions, association; her other opportunities, liabilities, standards."

His friend listened with respect to his enumeration of these disparities; then she disposed of them at a stroke. "Those things are nothing when a woman's hit. It's very awful. She was hit."

Strether, on his side, did justice to that plea. "Oh of course I saw she was hit. That she was hit was what we were busy with; that she was hit was our great affair. But somehow I couldn't think of her as down in the dust. And as put there by *our* little Chad!"

"Yet wasn't 'your' little Chad just your miracle?"

Strether admitted it. "Of course I moved among miracles. It was all phantasmagoric. But the great fact was that so much of it was none of my business—as I saw my business. It isn't even now."

His companion turned away on this, and it might well have been yet again with the sharpness of a fear of how little his philosophy could bring her personally. "I wish *she* could hear you!"

"Mrs. Newsome?"

"No—not Mrs. Newsome; since I understand you that it doesn't matter now what Mrs. Newsome hears. Hasn't she heard everything?"

"Practically—yes." He had thought a moment, but he went on. "You wish Madame de Vionnet could hear me?"

"Madame de Vionnet." She had come back to him. "She thinks just the contrary of what you say. That you distinctly judge her."

He turned over the scene as the two women thus placed together for him seemed to give it. "She might have known—!"

"Might have known you don't?" Miss Gostrey asked as he let it drop. "She was sure of it at first," she pursued as he said nothing; "she took it for granted, at least, as any woman in her position would. But after that she changed her mind; she believed you believed—"

"Well?"—he was curious.

"Why in her sublimity. And that belief had remained with her, I make out, till the accident of the other day opened your eyes. For that it did," said Maria, "open them—"

"She can't help"—he had taken it up—"being aware? No," he mused; "I suppose she thinks of that even yet."

"Then they *were* closed? There you are! However, if you see her
as the most charming woman in the world it comes to the same
thing. And if you'd like me to tell her that you do still so see
her—!" Miss Gostrey, in short, offered herself for service to the end.

It was an offer he could temporarily entertain; but he decided.
"She knows perfectly how I see her."

"Not favourably enough, she mentioned to me, to wish ever to
see her again. She told me you had taken a final leave of her. She
says you've done with her."

"So I have."

Maria had a pause; then she spoke as if for conscience. "She
wouldn't have done with *you*. She feels she has lost you—yet that
she might have been better for you."

"Oh she has been quite good enough!" Strether laughed.

"She thinks you and she might at any rate have been friends."

"We might certainly. That's just"—he continued to laugh—
"why I'm going."

It was as if Maria could feel with this then at last that she had
done her best for each. But she had still an idea. "Shall I tell her
that?"

"No. Tell her nothing."

"Very well then." To which in the next breath Miss Gostrey
added: "Poor dear thing!"

Her friend wondered; then with raised eyebrows: "Me?"

"Oh no. Marie de Vionnet."

He accepted the correction, but he wondered still. "Are you so
sorry for her as that?"

It made her think a moment—made her even speak with a smile.
But she didn't really retract. "I'm sorry for us all!"

IV [XXXV]

He was to delay no longer to re-establish communication with
Chad, and we have just seen that he had spoken to Miss Gostrey of
this intention on hearing from her of the young man's absence. It
was not moreover only the assurance so given that prompted him;
it was the need of causing his conduct to square with another profession still—the motive he had described to her as his sharpest
for now getting away. If he was to get away because of some of the
relations involved in staying, the cold attitude toward them might
look pedantic in the light of lingering on. He must do both things;
he must see Chad, but he must go. The more he thought of the
former of these duties the more he felt himself make a subject of
insistence of the latter. They were alike intensely present to him as
he sat in front of a quiet little café into which he had dropped on
quitting Maria's entresol. The rain that had spoiled his evening
with her was over; for it was still to him as if his evening *had* been

spoiled—though it mightn't have been wholly the rain. It was late when he left the café, yet not too late; he couldn't in any case go straight to bed, and he would walk round by the Boulevard Malesherbes—rather far round—on his way home. Present enough always was the small circumstance that had originally pressed for him the spring of so big a difference—the accident of little Bilham's appearance on the balcony of the mystic troisième at the moment of his first visit, and the effect of it on his sense of what was then before him. He recalled his watch, his wait, and the recognition that had proceeded from the young stranger, that had played frankly into the air and had presently brought him up—things smoothing the way for his first straight step. He had since had occasion, a few times, to pass the house without going in; but he had never passed it without again feeling how it had then spoken to him. He stopped short to-night on coming to sight of it: it was as if his last day were oddly copying his first. The windows of Chad's apartment were open to the balcony—a pair of them lighted; and a figure that had come out and taken up little Bilham's attitude, a figure whose cigarette-spark he could see leaned on the rail and looked down at him. It denoted however no reappearance of his younger friend; it quickly defined itself in the tempered darkness as Chad's more solid shape; so that Chad's was the attention that, after he had stepped forward into the street and signalled, he easily engaged; Chad's was the voice that, sounding into the night with promptness and seemingly with joy, greeted him and called him up.

That the young man had been visible there just in this position expressed somehow for Strether that, as Maria Gostrey had reported, he had been absent and silent; and our friend drew breath on each landing—the lift, at that hour, having ceased to work—before the implications of the fact. He had been for a week intensely away, away to a distance and alone; but he was more back than ever, and the attitude in which Strether had surprised him was something more than a return—it was clearly a conscious surrender. He had arrived but an hour before, from London, from Lucerne, from Homburg, from no matter where—though the visitor's fancy, on the staircase, liked to fill it out; and after a bath, a talk with Baptiste and a supper of light cold clever French things, which one could see the remains of there in the circle of the lamp, pretty and ultra-Parisian, he had come into the air again for a smoke, was occupied at the moment of Strether's approach in what might have been called taking up his life afresh. His life, his life!—Strether paused anew, on the last flight, at this final rather breathless sense of what Chad's life was doing with Chad's mother's emissary. It was dragging him, at strange hours, up the staircases of the rich;

it was keeping him out of bed at the end of long hot days; it was transforming beyond recognition the simple, subtle, conveniently uniform thing that had anciently passed with him for a life of his own. Why should it concern him that Chad was to be fortified in the pleasant practice of smoking on balconies, of supping on salads, of feeling his special conditions agreeably reaffirm themselves, of finding reassurance in comparisons and contrasts? There was no answer to such a question but that he was still practically committed—he had perhaps never yet so much known it. It made him feel old, and he would buy his railway-ticket—feeling, no doubt, older—the next day; but he had meanwhile come up four flights, counting the entresol, at midnight and without a lift, for Chad's life. The young man, hearing him by this time, and with Baptiste sent to rest, was already at the door; so that Strether had before him in full visibility the cause in which he was labouring and even, with the troisième fairly gained, panting a little.

Chad offered him, as always, a welcome in which the cordial and the formal—so far as the formal was the respectful—handsomely met; and after he had expressed a hope that he would let him put him up for the night Strether was in full possession of the key, as it might have been called, to what had lately happened. If he had just thought of himself as old Chad was at sight of him thinking of him as older: he wanted to put him up for the night just because he was ancient and weary. It could never be said the tenant of these quarters wasn't nice to him; a tenant who, if he might indeed now keep him, was probably prepared to work it all still more thoroughly. Our friend had in fact the impression that with the minimum of encouragement Chad would propose to keep him indefinitely; an impression in the lap of which one of his own possibilities seemed to sit. Madame de Vionnet had wished him to stay—so why didn't that happily fit? He could enshrine himself for the rest of his days in his young host's *chambre d'ami*[1] and draw out these days at his young host's expense: there could scarce be greater logical expression of the countenance he had been moved to give. There was literally a minute—it was strange enough—during which he grasped the idea that as he *was* acting, as he could only act, he was inconsistent. The sign that the inward forces he had obeyed really hung together would be that—in default always of another career—he should promote the good cause by mounting guard on it. These things, during his first minutes, came and went; but they were after all practically disposed of as soon as he had mentioned his errand. He had come to say good-bye—yet that was only a part; so that from the moment Chad accepted his farewell the question of a more ideal affirmation gave way to something else. He proceeded

1. Spare room (*lit.*, friend's room).

with the rest of his business. "You'll be a brute, you know—you'll be guilty of the last infamy—if you ever forsake her."

That, uttered there at the solemn hour, uttered in the place that was full of her influence, was the rest of his business; and when once he had heard himself say it he felt that his message had never before been spoken. It placed his present call immediately on solid ground, and the effect of it was to enable him quite to play with what we have called the key. Chad showed no shade of embarrassment, but had none the less been troubled for him after their meeting in the country; had had fears and doubts on the subject of his comfort. He was disturbed, as it were, only *for* him, and had positively gone away to ease him off, to let him down—if it wasn't indeed rather to screw him up—the more gently. Seeing him now fairly jaded he had come, with characteristic good humour, all the way to meet him, and what Strether thereupon supremely made out was that he would abound for him to the end in conscientious assurances. This was what was between them while the visitor remained; so far from having to go over old ground he found his entertainer keen to agree to everything. It couldn't be put too strongly for him that he'd be a brute. "Oh rather!—if I should do anything of *that* sort. I hope you believe I really feel it."

"I want it," said Strether, "to be my last word of all to you. I can't say more, you know; and I don't see how I can do more, in every way, than I've done."

Chad took this, almost artlessly, as a direct allusion. "You've seen her?"

"Oh yes—to say good-bye. And if I had doubted the truth of what I tell you—"

"She'd have cleared up your doubt?" Chad understood—"rather" —again! It even kept him briefly silent. But he made that up. "She must have been wonderful."

"She *was*," Strether candidly admitted—all of which practically told as a reference to the conditions created by the accident of the previous week.

They appeared for a little to be looking back at it; and that came out still more in what Chad next said. "I don't know what you've really thought, all along; I never did know—for anything, with you, seemed to be possible. But of course—of course—" Without confusion, quite with nothing but indulgence, he broke down, he pulled up. "After all, you understand. I spoke to you originally only as I *had* to speak. There's only one way—isn't there?—about such things. However," he smiled with a final philosophy, "I see it's all right."

Strether met his eyes with a sense of multiplying thoughts. What was it that made him at present, late at night and after journeys, so renewedly, so substantially young? Strether saw in a moment what it was—it was that he was younger again than Madame de Vionnet. He himself said immediately none of the things that he was thinking; he said something quite different. "You *have* really been to a distance?"

"I've been to England." Chad spoke cheerfully and promptly, but gave no further account of it than to say: "One must sometimes get off."

Strether wanted no more facts—he only wanted to justify, as it were, his question. "Of course you do as you're free to do. But I hope, this time, that you didn't go for *me*."

"For very shame at bothering you really too much? My dear man," Chad laughed, "what *wouldn't* I do for you?"

Strether's easy answer for this was that it was a disposition he had exactly come to profit by. "Even at the risk of being in your way I've waited on, you know, for a definite reason."

Chad took it in. "Oh yes—for us to make if possible a still better impression." And he stood there happily exhaling his full general consciousness. "I'm delighted to gather that you feel we've made it."

There was a pleasant irony in the words, which his guest, preoccupied and keeping to the point, didn't take up. "If I had my sense of wanting the rest of the time—the time of their being still on this side," he continued to explain—"I know now why I wanted it."

He was as grave, as distinct, as a demonstrator before a blackboard, and Chad continued to face him like an intelligent pupil. "You wanted to have been put through the whole thing."

Strether again, for a moment, said nothing; he turned his eyes away, and they lost themselves, through the open window, in the dusky outer air. "I shall learn from the Bank here where they're now having their letters, and my last word, which I shall write in the morning and which they're expecting as my ultimatum, will so immediately reach them." The light of his plural pronoun was sufficiently reflected in his companion's face as he again met it; and he completed his demonstration. He pursued indeed as if for himself. "Of course I've first to justify what I shall do."

"You're justifying it beautifully!" Chad declared.

"It's not a question of advising you not to go," Strether said, "but of absolutely preventing you, if possible, from so much as thinking of it. Let me accordingly appeal to you by all you hold sacred."

Chad showed a surprise. "What makes you think me capable—?"

"You'd not only be, as I say, a brute; you'd be," his companion went on in the same way, "a criminal of the deepest dye."

Chad gave a sharper look, as if to gauge a possible suspicion. "I don't know what should make you think I'm tired of her."

Strether didn't quite know either, and such impressions, for the imaginative mind, were always too fine, too floating, to produce on the spot their warrant. There was none the less for him, in the very manner of his host's allusion to satiety as a thinkable motive, a slight breath of the ominous. "I feel how much more she can do for you. She hasn't done it all yet. Stay with her at least till she has."

"And leave her *then?*"

Chad had kept smiling, but its effect in Strether was a shade of dryness. "Don't leave her *before.* When you've got all that can be got—I don't say," he added a trifle grimly. "That will be the proper time. But as, for you, from such a woman, there will always be something to be got, my remark's not a wrong to her." Chad let him go on, showing every decent deference, showing perhaps also a candid curiosity for this sharper accent. "I remember you, you know, as you were."

"An awful ass, wasn't I?"

The response was as prompt as if he had pressed a spring; it had a ready abundance at which he even winced; so that he took a moment to meet it. "You certainly then wouldn't have seemed worth all you've let me in for. You've defined yourself better. Your value has quintupled."

"Well then, wouldn't that be enough—?"

Chad had risked it jocosely, but Strether remained blank. "Enough?"

"If one *should* wish to live on one's accumulations?" After which, however, as his friend appeared cold to the joke, the young man as easily dropped it. "Of course I really never forget, night or day, what I owe her. I owe her everything. I give you my word of honour," he frankly rang out, "that I'm not a bit tired of her." Strether at this only gave him a stare: the way youth could express itself was again and again a wonder. He meant no harm, though he might after all be capable of much; yet he spoke of being "tired" of her almost as he might have spoken of being tired of roast mutton for dinner. "She has never for a moment yet bored me—never been wanting, as the cleverest women sometimes are, in tact. She has never talked about her tact—as even they too sometimes talk; but she has always had it. She has never had it more"—he handsomely made the point—"than just lately." And he scrupulously went further. "She has never been anything I could call a burden."

Strether for a moment said nothing; then he spoke gravely, with his shade of dryness deepened. "Oh if you didn't do her justice—!"

"I *should* be a beast, eh?"

Strether devoted no time to saying what he would be; *that,* visibly, would take them far. If there was nothing for it but to repeat, however, repetition was no mistake. "You owe her everything —very much more than she can ever owe you. You've in other words duties to her, of the most positive sort; and I don't see what other duties—as the others are presented to you—can be held to go before them."

Chad looked at him with a smile. "And you know of course about the others, eh?—since it's you yourself who have done the presenting."

"Much of it—yes—and to the best of my ability. But not all— from the moment your sister took my place."

"She didn't," Chad returned. "Sally took a place, certainly; but it was never, I saw from the first moment, to be yours. No one— with us—will ever take yours. It wouldn't be possible."

"Ah of course," sighed Strether, "I knew it. I believe you're right. No one in the world, I imagine, was ever so portentously solemn. There I am," he added with another sigh, as if weary enough, on occasion, of this truth. "I was made so."

Chad appeared for a little to consider the way he was made; he might for this purpose have measured him up and down. His conclusion favoured the fact. "You have never needed any one to make you better. There has never been any one good enough. They couldn't," the young man declared.

His friend hesitated. "I beg your pardon. They *have*."

Chad showed, not without amusement, his doubt. "Who then?"

Strether—though a little dimly—smiled at him. "Women—too."

" 'Two'?"—Chad stared and laughed. "Oh I don't believe, for such work, in any more than one! So you're proving too much. And what *is* beastly, at all events," he added, "is losing you."

Strether had set himself in motion for departure, but at this he paused. "Are you afraid?"

"Afraid—?"

"Of doing wrong. I mean away from my eye." Before Chad could speak, however, he had taken himself up. "I *am*, certainly," he laughed, "prodigious."

"Yes, you spoil us for all the stupid—!" This might have been, on Chad's part, in its extreme emphasis, almost too freely extravagant; but it was full, plainly enough, of the intention of comfort, it carried with it a protest against doubt and a promise, positively, of performance. Picking up a hat in the vestibule he came out with his friend, came downstairs, took his arm, affectionately, as to help and guide him, treating him if not exactly as aged and infirm, yet as a noble eccentric who appealed to tenderness, and keeping on with him, while they walked, to the next corner and the next. "You needn't tell me, you needn't tell me!"—this again as they proceeded, he wished to make Strether feel. What he needn't tell him was now at last, in the geniality of separation, anything at all it concerned him to know. He knew, up to the hilt—that really came over Chad; he understood, felt, recorded his vow; and they lingered on it as they had lingered in their walk to Strether's hotel the night of their first meeting. The latter took, at this hour, all he could get; he had given all he had had to give; he was as depleted as if he had spent his last sou. But there was just one thing for which, before they broke off, Chad seemed disposed slightly to bargain. His companion needn't, as he said, tell him, but he might himself mention that he had been getting some news of the art of advertisement. He came out quite suddenly with this announcement, while Strether wondered if his revived interest were what had taken him, with strange inconsequence, over to London. He appeared at all events to have been looking into the question and had encountered a revelation. Advertising scientifically worked presented itself thus as the great new force. "It really does the thing, you know."

They were face to face under the street-lamp as they had been the first night, and Strether, no doubt, looked blank. "Affects, you mean, the sale of the object advertised?"

"Yes—but affects it extraordinarily; really beyond what one had supposed. I mean of course when it's done as one makes out that, in our roaring age, it *can* be done. I've been finding out a little; though it doubtless doesn't amount to much more than what you originally, so awfully vividly—and all, very nearly, that first night— put before me. It's an art like another, and infinite like all the arts." He went on as if for the joke of it—almost as if his friend's face amused him. "In the hands, naturally, of a master. The right man must take hold. With the right man to work it *c'est un monde.*"[2]

Strether had watched him quite as if, there on the pavement, without a pretext, he had begun to dance a fancy step. "Is what you're thinking of that you yourself, in the case you have in mind, would be the right man?"

Chad had thrown back his light coat and thrust each of his thumbs into an armhole of his waistcoat; in which position his fingers played up and down. "Why, what is he but what you yourself, as I say, took me for when you first came out?"

Strether felt a little faint, but he coerced his attention. "Oh yes, and there's no doubt that, with your natural parts, you'd have much in common with him. Advertising is clearly at this time of day the secret of trade. It's quite possible it will be open to you—giving the whole of your mind to it—to make the whole place hum with you. Your mother's appeal is to the whole of your mind, and that's exactly the strength of her case."

2. It's a (whole) world.

Chad's fingers continued to twiddle, but he had something of a drop. "Ah we've been through my mother's case!"

"So I thought. Why then do you speak of the matter?"

"Only because it was part of our original discussion. To wind up where we began, my interest's purely platonic. There at any rate the fact is—the fact of the possible. I mean the money in it."

"Oh damn the money in it!" said Strether. And then as the young man's fixed smile seemed to shine out more strange: "Shall you give your friend up for the money in it?"

Chad preserved his handsome grimace as well as the rest of his attitude. "You're not altogether—in your so great 'solemnity'—kind. Haven't I been drinking you in—showing you all I feel you're worth to me? What have I done, what am I doing, but cleave to her to the death? The only thing is," he good-humouredly explained, "that one can't but have it before one, in the cleaving—the point where the death comes in. Don't be afraid for *that*. It's pleasant to a fellow's feelings," he developed, "to 'size-up' the bribe he applies his foot to."

"Oh then if all you want's a kickable surface the bribe's enormous."

"Good. Then there it goes!" Chad administered his kick with fantastic force and sent an imaginary object flying. It was accordingly as if they were once more rid of the question and could come back to what really concerned him. "Of course I shall see you to-morrow."

But Strether scarce heeded the plan proposed for this; he had still the impression—not the slighter for the simulated kick—of an irrelevant hornpipe or jig. "You're restless."

"Ah," returned Chad as they parted, "you're exciting."

v [xxxvi]

He had, however, within two days, another separation to face. He had sent Maria Gostrey a word early, by hand, to ask if he might come to breakfast; in consequence of which, at noon, she awaited him in the cool shade of her little Dutch-looking dining-room. This retreat was at the back of the house, with a view of a scrap of old garden that had been saved from modern ravage; and though he had on more than one other occasion had his legs under its small and peculiarly polished table of hospitality, the place had never before struck him as so sacred to pleasant knowledge, to intimate charm, to antique order, to a neatness that was almost august. To sit there was, as he had told his hostess before, to see life reflected for the time in ideally kept pewter; which was somehow becoming, improving to life, so that one's eyes were held and comforted. Strether's were comforted at all events now—and the more that it was the last time—with the charming effect, on the board bare of a cloth and proud of its perfect surface, of the small old crockery and old silver, matched by the more substantial pieces happily disposed about the room. The specimens of vivid Delf, in particular, had the dignity of family portraits; and it was in the midst of them that our friend resignedly expressed himself. He spoke even with a certain philosophic humour. "There's nothing more to wait for; I seem to have done a good day's work. I've let them have it all round. I've seen Chad, who has been to London and come back. He tells me I'm 'exciting,' and I seem indeed pretty well to have upset every one. I've at any rate excited *him*. He's distinctly restless."

"You've excited *me*," Miss Gostrey smiled. "*I'm* distinctly restless."

"Oh you were that when I found you. It seems to me I've rather got you out of it. What's this," he asked as he looked about him, "but a haunt of ancient peace?"

"I wish with all my heart," she presently replied, "I could make you treat it as a haven of rest." On which they fronted each other, across the table, as if things unuttered were in the air.

Strether seemed, in his way, when he next spoke, to take some of them up. "It wouldn't give me—that would be the trouble—what it will, no doubt, still give you. I'm not," he explained, leaning back in his chair, but with his eyes on a small ripe round melon —"in real harmony with what surrounds me. You *are*. I take it too hard. You *don't*. It makes—that's what it comes to in the end—a fool of me." Then at a tangent, "What has he been doing in London?" he demanded.

"Ah one may go to London," Maria laughed. "You know *I* did."

Yes—he took the reminder. "And you brought *me* back." He brooded there opposite to her, but without gloom. "Whom has Chad brought? He's full of ideas. And I wrote to Sarah," he added, "the first thing this morning. So I'm square. I'm ready for them."

She neglected certain parts of this speech in the interest of others. "Marie said to me the other day that she felt him to have the makings of an immense man of business."

"There it is. He's the son of his father!"

"But *such* a father!"

"Ah just the right one from that point of view! But it isn't his father in him," Strether added, "that troubles me."

"What is it then?" He came back to his breakfast; he partook presently of the charming melon, which she liberally cut for him; and it was only after this that he met her question. Then moreover it was but to remark that he'd answer her presently. She waited, she watched, she served him and amused him, and it was perhaps with this last idea that she soon reminded him of his having never even yet named to her the article produced at Woollett. "Do you remember our talking of it in London—that night at the play?" Before he could say yes, however, she had put it to him for other matters. Did he remember, did he remember—this and that of their first days? He remembered everything, bringing up with humour even things of which she professed no recollection, things she vehemently denied; and falling back above all on the great interest of their early time, the curiosity felt by both of them as to where he would "come out." They had so assumed it was to be in some wonderful place—they had thought of it as so very *much* out. Well, that was doubtless what it had been—since he had come out just there. He was out, in truth, as far as it was possible to be, and must now rather bethink himself of getting in again. He found on the spot the image of his recent history; he was like one of the figures of the old clock at Berne.[3] *They* came out, on one side, at their hour, jigged along their little course in the public eye, and went in on the other side. He too had jigged his little course—him too a modest retreat awaited. He offered now, should she really like to know, to name the great product of Woollett. It would be a great commentary on everything. At this she stopped him off; she not only had no wish to know, but she wouldn't know for the world. She had done with the products of Woollett—for all the good she had got from them. She desired no further news of them, and she mentioned that Madame de Vionnet herself had, to her knowledge, lived exempt from the information he was ready to supply. She had never consented to receive it, though she would have taken it, under stress, from Mrs. Pocock. But it was a matter about which Mrs. Pocock appeared to have had little to say—never sounding the word—and it didn't signify now. There was nothing clearly for Maria Gostrey that signified now—save one sharp point, that is, to which she came in time. "I don't know whether it's before you as a possibility that, left to himself, Mr. Chad may after all go back. I judge that it *is* more or less so before you, from what you just now said of him."

Her guest had his eyes on her, kindly but attentively, as if foreseeing what was to follow this. "I don't think it will be for the money." And then as she seemed uncertain: "I mean I don't believe it will be for that he'll give her up."

"Then he *will* give her up?"

Strether waited a moment, rather slow and deliberate now, drawing out a little this last soft stage, pleading with her in various suggestive and unspoken ways for patience and understanding. "What were you just about to ask me?"

3. Probably the clock on the Zeitglockenthurm in the center of Berne, Switzerland. The clock announces the hour by means of a group of mechanical bears that appear from the clock and parade around a seated figure.

"Is there anything he can do that would make you patch it up?"

"With Mrs. Newsome?"

Her assent, as if she had had a delicacy about sounding the name, was only in her face; but she added with it: "Or is there anything he can do that would make *her* try it?"

"To patch it up with me?" His answer came at last in a conclusive headshake. "There's nothing any one can do. It's over. Over for both of us."

Maria wondered, seemed a little to doubt. "Are you so sure for her?"

"Oh yes—sure now. Too much has happened. I'm different for her."

She took it in then, drawing a deeper breath. "I see. So that as she's different for *you*—"

"Ah but," he interrupted, "she's not." And as Miss Gostrey wondered again: "She's the same. She's more than ever the same. But I do what I didn't before—I *see* her."

He spoke gravely and as if responsibly—since he had to pronounce; and the effect of it was slightly solemn, so that she simply exclaimed "Oh!" Satisfied and grateful, however, she showed in her own next words an acceptance of his statement. "What then do you go home to?"

He had pushed his plate a little away, occupied with another side of the matter; taking refuge verily in that side and feeling so moved that he soon found himself on his feet. He was affected in advance by what he believed might come from her, and he would have liked to forestall it and deal with it tenderly; yet in the presence of it he wished still more to be—though as smoothly as possible—deterrent and conclusive. He put her question by for the moment; he told her more about Chad. "It would have been impossible to meet me more than he did last night on the question of the infamy of not sticking to her."

"Is that what you called it for him—'infamy'?"

"Oh rather! I described to him in detail the base creature he'd be, and he quite agrees with me about it."

"So that it's really as if you had nailed him?"

"Quite really as if—! I told him I should curse him."

"Oh," she smiled, "you *have* done it." And then having thought again: "You *can't* after that propose—!" Yet she scanned his face.

"Propose again to Mrs. Newsome?"

She hesitated afresh, but she brought it out. "I've never believed, you know, that you did propose. I always believed it was really she —and, so far as that goes, I can understand it. What I mean is," she explained, "that with such a spirit—the spirit of curses!—your breach is past mending. She has only to know what you've done to him never again to raise a finger."

"I've done," said Strether, "what I could—one can't do more. He protests his devotion and his horror. But I'm not sure I've saved him. He protests too much. He asks how one can dream of his being tired. But he has all life before him."

Maria saw what he meant. "He's formed to please."

"And it's our friend who has formed him." Strether felt in it the strange irony.

"So it's scarcely his fault!"

"It's at any rate his danger. I mean," said Strether, "it's hers. But she knows it."

"Yes, she knows it. And is your idea," Miss Gostrey asked, "that there was some other woman in London?"

"Yes. No. That is I *have* no ideas. I'm afraid of them. I've done with them." And he put out his hand to her. "Good-bye."

It brought her back to her unanswered question. "To what do you go home?"

"I don't know. There will always be something."

"To a great difference," she said as she kept his hand.

"A great difference—no doubt. Yet I shall see what I can make of it."

"Shall you make anything so good—?" But, as if remembering what Mrs. Newsome had done, it was as far as she went.

He had sufficiently understood. "So good as this place at this moment? So good as what *you* make of everything you touch?" He took a moment to say, for, really and truly, what stood about him there in her offer—which was as the offer of exquisite service, of lightened care, for the rest of his days—might well have tempted. It built him softly round, it roofed him warmly over, it rested, all so firm, on selection. And what ruled selection was beauty and knowledge. It was awkward, it was almost stupid, not to seem to prize such things; yet, none the less, so far as they made his opportunity they made it only for a moment. She'd moreover understand—she always understood.

That indeed might be, but meanwhile she was going on. "There's nothing, you know, I wouldn't do for you."

"Oh yes—I know."

"There's nothing," she repeated, "in all the world."

"I know. I know. But all the same I must go." He had got it at last. "To be right."

"To be right?"

She had echoed it in vague deprecation, but he felt it already clear for her. "That, you see, is my only logic. Not, out of the whole affair, to have got anything for myself."

She thought. "But with your wonderful impressions you'll have got a great deal."

"A great deal"—he agreed. "But nothing like *you*. It's you who would make me wrong!"

Honest and fine, she couldn't greatly pretend she didn't see it. Still she could pretend just a little. "But why should you be so dreadfully right?"

"That's the way that—if I must go—you yourself would be the first to want me. And I can't do anything else."

So then she had to take it, though still with her defeated protest. "It isn't so much your *being* 'right'—it's your horrible sharp eye for what makes you so."

"Oh but you're just as bad yourself. You can't resist me when I point that out."

She sighed it at last all comically, all tragically, away. "I can't indeed resist you."

"Then there we are!" said Strether.

Textual Notes

Henry James revised *The Ambassadors* three times in six years, and two of these revisions were, to some extent, made independently of each other. The original periodical version of the novel, published in twelve installments of *The North American Review* from January through December 1903, was revised and supplemented with additional chapters for the first American edition, which was published in November 1903. Before this volume appeared, however, James again revised and supplemented the periodical text for the first English edition, which was published in September 1903, two months before the publication of the first American edition. Around 1908 James made a third and final revision of *The Ambassadors* for *The Novels and Tales of Henry James*, the collected New York Edition of his works, and the text in which he made these last revisions was that of the first American edition. The changes that had been made separately in the second revision (the first English edition) were either forgotten or ignored in the final revision of the novel.

The story of how these different texts came into being and a general description of the differences between them is given in the discussion of the editions and revisions of *The Ambassadors*, pp. 354–70. The following textual notes record the most substantial or interesting of these differences[1] by keying the principal variants in the periodical text and in the two first editions to the New York Edition, from which the text for this Norton Critical Edition of *The Ambassadors* is taken. The textual notes also record emendations—such as the change of the famous inverted chapter—in the New York Edition, holograph changes made by James in his own copy of the first English edition, and brief editorial comments on corrupt or omitted passages.

In the following notes the words in boldface type give the reading of the Norton–New York Edition text for which variants from earlier editions are given. Ellipses are used in readings of any length taken from the present text. The numbers preceding an entry give the page and line numbers of the Norton text from which the reading is taken. Variant readings are given in regular type below a boldface entry, and each

---

1. These have been selected from changes in wording; differences in punctuation, syntax, paragraphing, and spelling have not been given except when accompanyig a change in wording.

348

separate reading is preceded by an italicized capital letter identifying the text. These letters and the texts for which they stand are as follows:

P   the periodical text published in twelve installments in *The North American Review*, vols. CLXXVI–CLXXVII, from January through December 1903.

A   the first American edition, published in New York by Harper and Brothers in November 1903.

E   the first English edition, published in London by Methuen and Company, September 1903.

N   *The Novels and Tales of Henry James*, New York Edition, vols. XXI–XXII, published in New York by Charles Scribner's Sons and issued in London by Macmillan and Company in 1909.

The texts following an entry are given in the chronological order of their revision. Minor differences—such as American and English spelling—between variants that appear in otherwise identical form in several texts have not been recorded. Texts not referred to in a given entry—and not noted earlier as lacking the passage in question—agree with the New York Edition reading. And unless otherwise noted, the installments of the serial and the "parts" of the first edition correspond to the "books" of the New York Edition. Editorial comment on variants is given in italic type, and emendations in the New York Edition have been marked with an asterisk. Occasionally words common to variant readings have been added at the beginning or end of an entry to help identify the variant.

*16 *"The Luxembourg Gardens" frontispiece originally appeared in the second volume of the novel.*

17.22 **it**
E he

18.35 **but on happy terms with each other**
P A E but expressive and agreeable

19.22 **She appeared to have no reserves**
P A E She was frank

19.39 **under this unsought protection**
P A E with his new friend

19.41–43 **to meet * * * assurances**
P A E to meet her there again as soon as he should have made himself tidy

20.26 **expensive**
E expansive

20.33 **sense of himself as**
P A E feeling

21.8 **thoroughly. * * * thoroughly**
P A E subtly. * * * subtly

21.12 **intenser**
P A E more subtle

30.17 **during years**
P A E for some five years

30.17 **brief**
E breach

38.27 **just**
E unjust

40.28 **hideous**
E ignoble

46.27 **American**
P A E bad

46.29–33 **but she. * * * delicate**
These lines appear only in N. *P A E have simply*
But she's delicate

46.41 **she forged ahead**
P A she reappeared further on E she took the subject up further on

*46.42 **money?"**
N *originally reads* money?'

*49.31 **Comment donc?**
N *does not originally italicize this phrase here, although it is italicized elsewhere in the novel.*

50.30 **now**
E not

*55.3 **good-humouredly**
N *originally reads* good-humoredly *here but* good-humouredly *elsewhere.*

55.12 **the real**
P E the truth

56.14 **groaned**
P A E murmured

60.4–5 **plentitude**
P A E enormity

*61.22 **short road**

N *originally reads* short load, *which does not make much sense;* P A E *all read* short road
61.31 itself
E himself
63.38 in confession
P A E with the fancy
64.14–67.19
This whole section is omitted in P.
64.14 This suggested the question of whether
E *adds the following:* With his letters in his lap then, in his Luxembourg nook—letters held with nervous, unconscious intensity—he thought of things in a stange, vast order, swinging at moments off into space, into past and future, and then dropping fast, with some loss of breath, but with a soft, reassuring thud, down to yesterday and to-day. Thus it was that he came back to his puzzle of the evening, the question of whether
64.34 possible processes
A processes E things
65.32 five
E five or six
65.33 six
E several
67.6 irresistibly sharp: he
E overwhelmingly intense; the wretched youth
67.9 somewhere of a
E somewhere in Théophile Gautier of a
67.12 three
E three—through numbers indeed as to which it might be a question whether those of mere modest clock-faces wouldn't be exceeded.
67.16–17 migration, the expensive
E migration, the journey retraced, that is, in the sense of demoralisation, the expensive
67.18–19 French for some special variety of the worst.
E French for something that might in a manner be a part of that ambiguous ideal, but was certainly not the part permitting publicity, either of appreciation or of discussion, in respect to varieties of quality. All Mrs. Newsome had now for a long time known of her son was that he had renewed his career in the expensive district—it was so, she felt, that she sufficiently designated it—and that he had not so established himself without intimate countenance. He had travelled, in the dreadful direction, almost like a Pasha—save that his palanquins had been by no means curtained and their occupants far from veiled; he had, in short, had company—scandalous, notorious company—across the bridges, company making with him, in the cynical journey, from stage to stage and from period to period, bolder pushes and taking larger freedoms: traces, echoes, almost legends, all these things, left in the wake of the pair.
68.7 three or four
E four or five
*****70.28 porte-cochère**
N *originally italicizes these words here but not where they are often used elsewhere in the novel.*
*****71.21 salle-à-manger**
N *does not originally italicize these words here,*

although they are italicized elsewhere in the novel.
73.28–29
There is an x *marked by these lines in the margin of James's own copy of* E.
87.14–15, 87.22–23
The figures 200 *and* 300 *respectively were written opposite these lines in the margins of James's copy of* E.
98.28 feet.
E *adds* He knew he showed he was glad to bring his effort to an end.
104.30 sacrifice
P A E present
*****105.16 look**
N *originally reads* book, *which does not make good sense in the context;* P A E *all read* look
105.18–19 her discrimination
P E *her* fearless sense
106.2 uncanny
P E abnormal
106.9 never barren, nor even dull
P A E never dull
106.40 wretch
P E brute *This change is also made three times in the next paragraph.*
107.37–38 things. You
E things. It may really become extraordinary. You
109.34 brute
P E wretch
110.11 sadly
P A awkwardly E deplorably
110.40 "Where do you see him come out?"
E "When shall I really catch him?"
112.31 had been
In his copy of E *James crossed this out and wrote* were *in the margin.*
114.33 his
E her
115.40 "I wish they'd send
E "If only, for the excellent use I could make of her, they would send
*****117.32 success. Well,"**
N *originally reads* success, Well,"
118.23 in profusely dispensing
P E in the offered bribe A in the offer
118.25 flowers
P E sensations
118.27 ascetic
P E inbred
119.34 of
P A E to
121.34 he felt the latter's plummet
P A E he knew of the latter's inquiry
130.27–28 importantly short
P A E not very tall
134.13 they wouldn't, they couldn't, want
P A E they wouldn't want
134.33–34 important
P A E particular
135.7–8 so urgent
P A E "particular"
136.28 in the immensity of space
P E quite in the air
*****136.37 charming**

N *originally reads* charmng
*138.37 **polyglot**
N *originally reads* polgylot
140.16 **for all your 'times of life'**
P E for all ages
143.18–19 **his sense of the thing in question covered**
P E they covered
143.42–43
Omitted in P and E.
144.17 **ways**
P E days
148.15 **it**
P A him *In James's copy of E* him *is crossed out and* it *written in the margin.*
155.24 **notre jeune homme**
P E our young friend
157.38 **our**
E your
158.10 **interest**
P A E romance
161.19 **their fellow guest**
P the spinster E their friend
162.21–22 **to represent her motive and real errand**
P A E to have been, for her, her real errand
163.42 **then**
E them
164.34 **painter-man**
P A E artist-man
*165.37 **to**
N *originally reads* fo
*166.12 **I?"**
N *originally reads* I?'
169.45 **Little Bilham looked at him indeed.**
P and E lack this sentence.
*171 **The "By Notre Dame" frontispiece originally appeared in the first volume of the novel.**
172.13–14 **a remedy * * * relievingly**
P A E a remedy that seemed so, for the moment, to meet the case
172.20 **making no point**
E feeling no need
176.3 **domain**
P A E property
180.7 **you allude**
E you always allude
183.34–35 **with a force brought to so fine a head**
P A with a spirit brought to so fine a point E with a spirit whose lightest throbs were so full
190.4 **elucidation**
P E interpretation
192 **Book Seventh: III**
E *begins Part Eighth here.*
192.4 **that afternoon he had still not seen him**
E the same afternoon Strether had still not seen his old friend
193.1 **divine**
E exquisite
194.4 **weigh**
E be absorbed by
196.10 **It was to her visitor now that she applied her consideration.**

Omitted from P.
196.14 **been?"**
P *ends the seventh installment and Chapter XVIII at this point and begins the eighth installment and Chapter XIX with the next paragraph.*
196.15 **later**
P after the talk with Miss Gostrey that we have last commemorated
197.28 **life**
E time
*198.34 **entresol**
N *originally italicizes this word here but not elsewhere in the novel.*
199.14 **charm**
E attraction
201 **Book Eighth [XIX]**
This chapter is completely omitted from P.
201.1 **rambled alone**
E rambled largely alone
201.35 **his surreptitious step**
A E the step
201.37 **relief**
A E opportunity
202.8–9 **crisis * * * concern**
A E situation was a visible lapse, in Waymarsh, of expectation.
202.14 **justice**
A E relief
203.9 **actively**
E eagerly
204.24 **he aimed at with confidence**
A E he really liked
204.27 **this witness**
A Waymarsh E he
205.3 **strained**
E heavy
207.7–8 **present to a sort of thing, as he synthetically phrased it to himself,**
A E present to a force
208.30 **bamboozled**
E beguiled
209.1–2 **decent * * * decent**
E nice. * * * nice
209.24 **Strether quitted the station**
P He had driven to the station on the momentous day with Chad, but he quitted it
209.30 **his critics**
P A E the travellers
210.22 **girdle of a maid**
E waist of a girl
210.24 **mercifully vague**
E restfully dim
210.26–27 **unpleasant. * * * unpleasant**
P A E disagreeable. * * * disagreeable
212.2 **robust**
E erect
213.18–19 **the way not to fail of confidence. * * * confidence**
P A E the way to be sharp. * * * sharpness
214.25 **a world that had grown**
E a rank world that he had grown
215.35 **Newsome**
E Newcome
216.32 **boss**
E run

222.13 **good offices**
E aid and comfort
225.42 **consummately**
E thoroughly
227.5 **the damned**
E your stale
227.15 **bleak**
P A E narrow
*228.37 **charity."**
N originally reads charity.'
229.10–11 *I* **at least won't take that from**
   you.
This sentence appears only in N.
230.27 **point of exposure**
P A E standpoint
231.3–4 **between the two women**
This phrase appears only in N.
231.4 **show**
P E betray
231.28 **the more tenderly**
E with the greater indulgence
231.43 **lacked news**
E lacked the direct and intimate news
to which he would have been so conspicuously
entitled
234.21–22 **awful.** ° ° ° **'Awful'**
E very advanced. ° ° ° 'Advanced'
234.28 **droll**
P A funny
234.42 **phenomena**
P doings *E* performances
235.8 **he supposes**
E he ecstatically supposes
239.11 **not stupid**
E not, like almost everyone, stupid
240.33 **she's pleased** *comme tout*
P A E she's as pleased as Punch
242.23 **forms and usages**
P A E manners
243.9 **but may we never be less so!**
P but long may we wave! *A* but may we never
fill up! *E* but long may we play our parts!
243.25 **"Getting hold of him?**
E "Winning him over and making him her
own?
244.37 **affected**
E demoralised
244.40 **Maria rather funnily considered it**
E Maria considered it in the light of comedy
247.12 **awful**
E fearsome
248.31 **sorely**
E solely
249.25–26 **as a contradiction of Sarah**
E not in the form he had conceived
251.44 **all the Mr. Brookses and Mr.**
   Snookses
E all the Mr. Coxes and Mr. Coleses
253.22–25 **She came out with** ° ° ° **she**
   came out with ° ° ° **she**
   brought it out
E she aired for him ° ° ° she threw off ° ° °
she produced it
253.45 **monster**
E miracle
254.34–37 **And** ° ° ° **stupid**

Omitted from P.
255.31 **beside little Bilham**
E next this appreciated youth
257.12 **easiest**
E lightest
257.14–15 **the knowledge offered to his**
   colleague
E the knowledge, the *panem et circenses* again,
offered to his fellow-emissary
264.35 **absences that**
E absences, all the diverted attentions, that
269.44 **destiny**
P A E outlook
271.29–30 **approach, from that quarter, to**
   admitted consciousness
P A E approach to a meaning
272.8 **genial**
P E bright
272.36–37 **he.** ° ° ° **He**
E one. ° ° ° One
274.19 **so wound up**
P A E so exalted
274.22–25 **Distinctly** ° ° ° **accompanist.**
P A E Distinctly, she was exalted now, and
Waymarsh, who imagined himself standing
there on his own feet, was truly but suspended
in an air of her making.
274.33 **the false note**
P A the small manner *E* the same manner
279.24–26 **queerer** ° ° ° **queer** ° ° °
   queerer
P E funny ° ° ° funny ° ° ° funnier
281.40 **have nullified any active proximity**
P have paralyzed any active approach *E* have
placed a penalty on any active approach
*282 **Book Eleventh: I [XXVIII]**
This chapter was completely omitted from P and
then inserted and numbered in A and N after
Chapter XXIX or Book Eleventh: II. Chapter
XXIX was then numbered XXVIII in A, and
II in N was numbered I. The chapter followed
XXVII in E, but was put into Part Tenth.
288.37–38 **"And don't you really care**
E "And then isn't there your liking her so
290.14–15 **feeling she had created**
A E sentiment she had engendered
*292 **II [XXIX]**
N and A inserted XXVIII here. P and E begin
Part Eleventh here, and P numbers this chapter
XXVIII, having omitted the previous chapter.
292.18 **visit**
E descent
293.23 **wonderful**
E comfortable
293.38–39 **bewildered a saner man**
P A E bewildered *you*
295.5 **considerably doubted**
P A E still doubted
299.7–8 **it's to Mrs. Newsome**
E it's to the forfeiture of possession of Mrs.
Newsome
299.13 **I've been as disappointed in her**
E I've been as disconcerted, as disappointed,
as disillusioned by her
299.17 **probably**
P A E doubtless

299.24 **violently**
E indignantly
299.26 **I've landed**
E I've violently landed
301.13 **treasures of imagination**
E treasures
301.25 **she imagined**
E she insistently imagined
302.5 **the dreadful creature that** *I*
E the dreadful insidious parasite that *I*
302.10–11 **give me up.** * * * **give you up**
E give up the creature that I am. * * * give
up the creature that you are
302.13 **you**
E the creature
302 **[XX]**
P XXIX
303.17–18 **beyond.** * * * **twisted**
*The words in these lines were dropped from A
at this point and inserted below.*
303.17 **a dream of possibility**
A any dream of his
303.22–23 **as the picture he would have
bought**
E as the material acquisition that, in all his
time, he had most sharply failed of
303.26 **himself**
*The dropped words of A mentioned above were
reinserted at this point.*
304.10–11 **superseded Boston fashion**
E faded Boston enthusiasm
306.36 **nothing more than Shakespeare and
the musical glasses; but it**
E nothing more than such questions as the
difference between Victor Hugo and the English poets; Victor Hugo, for whom one could
have but a plural comparison, and the English
poets, whom his friend quite surprisingly,
rather quaintly and archaically, knew. Yet it
*307.34 *sabots*
N *does not originally italicize this word here
although it is italicized elsewhere in the novel.*
*309.3 **twenty**
N *originally reads* twenty twenty
309 **[XXXI]**
P XXX
311.12 **wild extravagance of hazard**
E wild fable than as anything else
311.29–30 **from making any. Nothing of
the sort**
E from so blundering. Nothing either like a
challenge or like an apology
312.32 **loud**
P E mere
314.20 **no design but of getting**
E omits but
315.21 **a little**
E a prattling little
315.36–37 **supposing   innumerable   and
wonderful things**
P A E supposing everything
315 **[XXXII]**
P XXXI
317.43 **penal**
P A E disciplinary
320.14 **Caprices**

E Inequalities
321.20 **droll**
P A funny E ridiculous
321.36 **two occasions**
E late occasions
321 **[XXXIII]**
P XXXII
322.9 **must properly brace himself**
P E must pull himself up
323.20 **one**
E us
326.7–8 **you've had to take in**
P A E you've had to see
326 **[XXXIV]**
P XXXIII
327.1 **small**
E same
327.25–26 **that   reprobation   * * *   interview.**
P E that violence had not awaited the presentation of Mme. de Vionnet's plea.
327.27 **overture**
P E demonstration
328.4 **all questions**
E all question
329.38 **These tints of feeling**
P E These shades
329.43–330.2 **on one * * * profuse.**
P and E lack these lines.
330.40 **He had grown clear, in a flash, on**
E He had shut to, with a click, on
331.9 **difficult but rigid lines**
P E passionate lines
331.29 **as sharper**
P E as confirmed
332.34 **grandly * * * grandly**
P superbly * * * sublimely
332.39 **Her beauty of person?**
P Her beauty—?
332.40 **Well, her beauty of everything.**
P Well, I can't call it anything else.
332.44 **complete**
P E magnificent
332.45 **You're always too personal**
E You're too much struck with everything
332.45–333.1 **but that's precisely how I
wondered and wandered**
P E but that then is where I was
333.13 **hit**
P taken *This change is repeated four times
below.*
333.13 **It's very awful.**
P and E lack this sentence.
333.32 **That you distinctly judge her**
P That you judge her E That you judge her
differently now
333.38 **would. But**
E would. Nothing else could occur to her. But
333.45 **I suppose she thinks of that even yet**
E I can see that she must have liked better the
other idea
334.1 **Then they** *were* **closed?**
E Then you *had* the other idea.
334.5 **temporarily entertain**
P weigh E estimate
334 **Book Twelfth: IV [XXXV]**

This chapter was completely omitted from P.

334.31 Chad, and we have just seen that he
E Chad, and he
335.8 his sense of what was then before him
E his curiosity
335.24 voice that, sounding into the night, with
E voice that, with
335.25 joy, greeted him and called him up
E joy, called him straight up
335.43 with Chad's mother's emissary
E with him
336.19–20 that he would let him put him up
E that Strether would let himself be put up
336.31 enshrine
E instal
336.32 host's *chambre d'ami*
E friend's spare room
336.37 the inward forces
E the inspiration
337.12–13 to let ° ° ° gently.
Omitted from E.
337.19 entertainer keen to
E host quite ready to
337.20–21 if I should do anything of *that* sort.
Omitted from E.
339.2 the imaginative mind
E the sensitive spirit
339.21 You've defined yourself better.
Omitted from E.
340.20–37 "You. ° ° ° extravagant;
These lines are completely omitted from E.

340.37–39 but   it   ° ° °   performance. Picking
E The intention of kindness was, at any rate all there; Chad continued to show it as a protest and a promise, and, picking
341.24–26 though ° ° ° me
Omitted from E.
342.11 in your so great 'solemnity'
Omitted from E.
342.12–13 haven't ° ° ° me?
Omitted from E.
342.14 to the death?
Omitted from E.
342.15–16 that one. ° ° ° for *that*
Omitted from E.
342 [XXXVI]
P XXXIV
342.30 separation to face
E report to make
343.18 you treat it as a haven of rest
P E you find it so
343.34 Marie
P She E A certain person
344.37–38 I mean I don't believe it will be for that he'll
P A E I mean that he'll
345.33 "Is that
E Well, he could hold poor Maria with this too. "Is that
347.7 "That's the
E He considered, but he kept it straight. "That's the

S. P. ROSENBAUM

Editions and Revisions

The story of the writing of *The Ambassadors*, as revealed in James's notebooks and letters, is given in "The Author on the Novel" section of this Norton Critical Edition. The story of the novel's publication is to be found in other letters of James's as well as in the preceding textual notes, which record the most important differences between the four versions of *The Ambassadors* that were published in James's lifetime. The following account of these editions and their revisions is relevant to the study of the novel because the conditions surrounding the publication of each version clearly affected the text and because James's three sets of revisions constitute, when interpreted, a form of commentary by the author on his work.

Even if nothing unusual had happened to *The Ambassadors*, the history of its publication would have been complex because of the customary arrangements James sought to make for his fiction. As a professional author whose livelihood depended in part on income from his writings, James naturally sought the best financial arrangements he could obtain. Ideally for a novel, these would have been concurrent serial publication in English and American magazines and then, as the serials drew to a close, simultaneous publication of the book in England and the United States. Through these arrangements—which in the case of joint periodical publication were rarely attained—James would have received payment for serial rights in both countries and then royalties from the English and American first editions. And even if the royalties were small, as they were likely to be with James's diminishing popularity in the latter part of his career, these arrangements would at least have protected his literary property from pirating publishers who had previously defrauded him and other nineteenth-century authors in the absence of international copyright agreement.

The story of the publication of *The Ambassadors* begins, then, with the nearly abortive arrangements for the publication of the novel in installments.

Serial Publication

On May 9, 1901, approximately a year after James had begun *The Ambassadors*, he wrote to James B. Pinker, his literary agent in London, that he was sending him nine of the twelve installments of the novel.[1] Several weeks later James signed an agreement with Harper and Brothers in New York, which was also the publisher of *Harper's New Monthly Magazine* and *The North American Review*. James had sent his lengthy "Project of Novel" (see pp. 377–404) to Harper the previous autumn, and the agreement he now signed with the publisher included the serialization of *The Ambassadors*. In July James sent off the twelfth installment of the novel to Pinker, noting that he was keeping back three and a half chapters: "I have withheld them only for the shortness of the Parts, and they will be indispensable in the book."[2] James kept back these chapters because the parts of *The Ambassadors* were running longer than the ten thousand words he had agreed to for each installment. In September of 1901 James sent Pinker another copy of his typescript of *The Ambassadors*, perhaps for Pinker to circulate among potential English publishers, and at the same time he "put it on witnessed record that I formally ask for duplicate *Proofs* of the serial, and that I as formally give warning that the volume is to contain a small quantity of additional material."[3]

Harper, however, was to supply James with no proofs at all in the near future because it delayed serializing the novel. The editor of *Harper's New Monthly Magazine*, H. M. Alden, had rejected the serial,

1. James's letters to Pinker are now in the library at Yale University.
2. *Letters*, ed. Leon Edel (Cambridge, Mass.: Harvard University Press, 1984), 4: 194.
3. Quoted in Leon Edel, Dan H. Laurence, and James Rambeau, *A Bibliography of Henry James*, 3rd ed. (Oxford: Oxford University Press, 1982), 124–25.

though James does not seem to have known this.[4] Why the firm signed
a contract for serialization when the editor of one of its magazines had
turned down the novel is unclear; perhaps the confusion that followed
Harper's bankruptcy in 1899 remained in the reorganized company.
Whatever the causes, Pinker suggested to James in June 1902, after he
had completed his next novel, *The Wings of the Dove*, that they try to
find another publisher for *The Ambassadors*, and James agreed. This
move seems to have had some financial results, for Harper then sent
£500, the second half of the payment for the serial rights to *The Ambassadors*. At the same time the publisher indicated that serialization of
the novel was now uncertain! It must have been exasperating for James
to find that after carefully constructing the novel around the interrupted
installments of a serial, it now seemed that *The Ambassadors* would not
appear in serial form.[5] Some hope temporarily reappeared in July when
Pinker sold the English serial rights and book publication to Methuen,
Harper having given up the English rights. But *The Ambassadors* never
appeared in an English magazine.

   The Wings of the Dove was published in August 1902, and still Harper
held back the novel James had written before it. Then suddenly in
January 1903, James heard that Harper had begun to serialize *The
Ambassadors*—but not, as he had expected, in *Harper's Monthly*. The
novel was appearing instead in *The North American Review*, one of the
most prestigious journals in the United States, and, more surprisingly,
one that did not publish prose fiction. The review also did not publish
pictures, yet the fourth installment of *The Ambassadors* began with the
signed photograph of the formidable, buttoned-up author that is reproduced on p. ix of this Norton Critical Edition. Apart from the abruptness
with which Harper had acted, James was delighted with the arrangements, which he discovered had been made for his novel by the same
person who had inadvertently provided the initial inspiration for *The
Ambassadors*. To his friend the novelist William Dean Howells, now
an adviser to Harper and a regular contributor to the firm's magazines,
James expressed his gratitude not only for the arrangements but also for
the essay "Mr. Henry James's Later Work," which immediately preceded
the first installment of *The Ambassadors* in *The North American Review*:

> I *like*, extremely, the place the N.A.R. makes for my novel; it meets
> quite my ideal in respect to that isolation and relief one has always
> fondly conceived as the proper *due* of one's productions, and yet
> never, amid the promiscuous petticoats and other low company of
> the usual magazine table-of-contents, seen them in the remotest
> degree attended with. One had dreamed, in private fatuity, that

4. See Alden's memorandum to Harper on p. 415.
5. James had planned to write *The Wings of the Dove* the same way, but when its preliminary
   statement failed to interest any magazine editors, he wrote the novel "on a more free and
   independent scale" (see p. 407).

one would really be the better for "standing out" a little; but one had, to one's own sense, never really "stood" at all, but simply lain very flat, for the petticoats and all the foolish feet aforesaid to trample over with the best conscience in the world. Charming to me also is the idea of your own beneficent paper in the same quarter—the complete detachment of which, however, from the current fiction itself I equally apprehend and applaud.[6]

James's serialized fiction frequently had to compete for attention with sentimental romances, often by women, whose literary petticoats James complained about. Howells had also remarked at the opening of his essay, which does not mention *The Ambassadors* but discusses James's three most recent novels, that "the enmity to Mr. James's fiction among his readers is mostly feminine because the men who do not like him are not his readers." Part of Howells's essay consists of a dialogue with a woman reader who complains that James is "of a tremendosity, but he worries me to death; he kills me; he really gives me a headache. He fascinates me, but I have no patience with him." In the course of his appreciation, Howells suggests ways of patiently approaching James's recent fiction.

In some respects *The North American Review* in 1903 resembled Strether's Woollett review, which "comprised, by the law of [its] purpose, no tribute to letters; it was of a mere rich kernel of economics, politics, ethics" (see p. 63). The twelve issues in which *The Ambassadors* appeared are rich in discussions of current issues and recent history, but there were also some tributes to letters. Mark Twain wrote on Christian Science, Hamlin Garland on "Sanity in Fiction," Edith Wharton on reading in general, and Howells himself again on Chicago fiction and then Hawthorne. There were also essays on Emerson, Tennyson, and Mrs. Humphry Ward, as well as a poem by Thomas Hardy, letters by John Ruskin, and a one-act play by William Butler Yeats. This was decidedly not low magazine company. *The North American Review* was, if anything, closer to the great salmon-colored *Revue des Deux Mondes* than Strether's green Woollett review.

Also unlike the usual magazine practice of the time, *The North American Review* appears to have treated James's text with some respect, though it did cut words and sometimes sentences at the end of several installments to fit them into the pages of the magazine.[7] The serial has surprisingly few typographical errors, and the punctuation and spelling were not significantly altered to conform with a magazine style. Aside from the omitted chapters, the twelve parts into which James divided his novel correspond—with one exception—to the twelve installments

6. *The Letters of Henry James*, ed. Percy Lubbock (New York: Charles Scribner's Sons, 1920), 1: 414.
7. Brian Birch, "Henry James: Some Bibliographical and Textual Matters," *The Library* 20 (1965): 116.

of *The North American Review*. The exception was the splitting of Chapter XVIII (which consists of two discussions with Maria Gostrey about the significance of the Pococks' impending arrival) into two chapters that were then placed in different installments. Even here there is no reason to suppose the changes were not made by James himself to keep the installments approximately the same length. Yet the serial version of *The Ambassadors* is the least satisfactory of the four texts of the novel published in James's lifetime, not just because it is three stages removed from the author's final revisions of the novel, but because it lacks the three and a half "indispensable" chapters.

The omission of these chapters may be an oblique authorial comment on what in *The Ambassadors* James considered to be, if not less important, at least separate and detachable. The omitted parts, which actually consist of less than three and a quarter chapters, all share one dimension of the story. Chapter V, half of the omitted Chapter XIX, and all of the omitted Chapters XXVIII and XXXV concern Strether's relations with Chad Newsome. In removing these chapters James first left out Strether's initial speculations (which retrospectively included Chad's history in Paris) on how he was to handle Chad, next Strether and Chad's conversation on the way to meet the Pococks at the railroad station, then the interview with Chad after Strether had been confronted by Sarah Pocock, and finally the meeting of Strether and Chad after Strether's last visit to Madame de Vionnet. Also cut was Strether's solitary wait for the Pococks to arrive—a wait in which James prepares for Strether's final discovery by having him find Chad and then Madame de Vionnet out of town at the same time.

The main consequence of these cuts is that Chad becomes a much vaguer character. At the end of his preface to the final edition of *The Ambassadors*, James regretted the "disguised and repaired losses" of the author's relation to Chad. For the readers of *The North American Review*, this relation was reduced even more. Strether's bitter realization that Chad had not really changed as much as Strether supposed is blander in the periodical version. The implicit father-son relationship is also more limited, and a significant part of the motive for Strether's action in the novel disappears along with the descriptions of Chad's extraordinary charm. The charge of moral perversity that might have come from Woollett-oriented readers of *The North American Review* is a little easier to support without these chapters. Also, the later criticism that the significance of Paris—which Chad in some measure represents—is essentially empty in *The Ambassadors* could be more easily argued in the serial version of the novel (see pp. 439–42). With the cutting of Strether's relationship with Chad, Strether's other relationships receive proportionately more emphasis. That James chose to remove scenes with Chad rather than those with Maria Gostrey or Madame de Vionnet seems to suggest the greater importance of their relationships with him, at least in *The North American Review*.

James's cutting of *The Ambassadors* for its serialization had another effect, however, and one that James did not foresee. It resulted in "a curious error which probably has no parallel in the annals of American literature."[8]

First American Edition

When Harper abruptly announced to James early in 1903 that *The Ambassadors* was being serialized in *The North American Review*, the publisher asked him for the opening pages of the first American edition, which it was also to publish. James felt there was no rush for these; more important, as he wrote to Pinker, was that Harper should send him duplicate proofs so that he could correct the serial and also prepare proofs for the book at the same time. In returning the proofs for the February installment of the serial, James repeated this request to Harper, but to no avail. By July he was complaining to his agent that Harper had delayed sending him proofs for the last three or four parts of both the serial and first edition—a delay that was creating new problems because James intended to send the sheets from the corrected proofs of the first American edition to his English publisher so that it could set its edition from them. By August he had finished proofing the rest of the novel for Harper, which included two of the chapters omitted from the serial that were to be restored in the volume. Harper did not publish the novel in book form until November 6, 1903, when the serial had one more installment to run, and James seems not to have noticed that two of the chapters in the first American edition were not in chronological sequence.

In 1950 Robert E. Young, an undergraduate student of Yvor Winters at Stanford University, finally noticed that Chapters XXVIII and XXIX of the Harper edition were in reverse order: Strether's evening conversation with Chad at the Boulevard Malesherbes (following Sarah Pocock's criticism of Chad and Strether) was placed after the chapter in which Strether talks with Maria Gostrey the next afternoon. By noticing that in Strether's talk with Gostrey there were allusions to the scene with Chad which had not yet been described in the novel, Young was able to deduce the inverted order of the chapters.[9] What Young did not

---

8. Robert E. Young, "An Error in *The Ambassadors*," *American Literature* 22 (1950): 245.
9. In their inverted chronological order the words "that evening" at the beginning of Chapter XXVIII (p. 282) appear to refer to the evening following Strether's talk with Gostrey, when they actually refer to the previous evening after Strether's meeting with Sarah Pocock at his hotel. There are also allusions in Strether's conversation with Gostrey to his and Chad's talk about imagination, which had not yet happened (pp. 292 and 300). Furthermore, Strether describes to Gostrey his second interview with Sarah at her hotel and says the Pococks have now left Paris. In the conversation with Chad, Strether has not yet seen Sarah again, and the

realize is that these chapters were in chronological order in the first English edition of *The Ambassadors*.

Having made his brilliant discovery, Young went on to draw a moral: "Indeed, there must be something radically wrong with a writing style that has managed to obscure an error of this magnitude for so many years from the probing eyes of innumerable readers, publishers, editors, critics, and even the author himself."[1] How the chronological sequence of Chapters XXVIII and XXIX was reversed may never be known. It seems unlikely that James himself would have placed the chapter out of order—assuming he finally received the duplicate proofs for which he repeatedly asked. It may have been left to an editor at Harper to insert the chapters James had kept back from the serial for the book. The editor perhaps noticed that Chapter XXVIII consists of an evening conversation, whereas Chapter XXIX opens by referring to an afternoon conversation; what he may not have noticed is that there were actually two afternoon talks mentioned, and the second took place the next day. The opening references to afternoon and evening conversations in the chronologically inverted chapters seem also to explain why so many subsequent readers failed to notice that the time of these two chapters is out of joint.

However the mistake came about, it is rather unreasonable to blame it simply on James's style. Presumably the chronological sequence would have been more obvious if James had made the transitions between chapters more explicit. The reason he did not is clear, and it lies not in James's style but in the necessity to cut the novel for its serialized version. The very fact of serialization meant that the various installments of the novel had to be separable, if not independent from one another. James must have realized as he was writing Chapters XXVIII and XXIX that he was exceeding the length estimated for each serial part. Had he made Strether's afternoon conversation with Maria Gostrey depend more directly on his conversation with Chad the night before, it would not have been possible to make the simple deletion of Chapter XXVIII from the serial. Thus if there is something "radically wrong" with *The Ambassadors*, it stems more from the conditions of publication imposed on it by Harper and *The North American Review* than from the author's style. Any fair account of the textual history of *The Ambassadors* needs to take into account the origins of the novel as a serial.

Recently it has been playfully maintained that James intended to have

---

Pococks have not yet left. Some of these and other inconsistencies were independently noticed by Susan M. Humphreys ("Henry James's Revisions for *The Ambassadors*," *Notes and Queries* 199 [1954]: 397–99), but she concluded that they were the results of faulty revision rather than inverted chapters.

1. "An Error in *The Ambassadors*," p. 253. See the ensuing controversy over Young's discovery in Leon Edel, "A Further Note on 'An Error in *The Ambassadors*,'" *American Literature* 23 (1951): 128–30; Young, "A Final Note on *The Ambassadors*," *American Literature* 23 (1952): 487–90; and Yvor Winters, "Problems for the Modern Critic of Literature," *Hudson Review* 9 (1956): 348–50.

Chapters XXVIII and XXIX in reverse chronological order, as their continued inversion in the carefully revised New York Edition confirms, and it was a mistake of the first English edition to have them in their temporal sequence. To argue away the possibility that James committed or failed to notice an error in the ordering of his chapters in two editions of *The Ambassadors*, Jerome McGann finds the interview with Maria Gostrey serving as "a kind of textual flash forward" with ironical anticipations. The irony arises when Strether "fails utterly to register" Maria Gostrey's love for him although he has been so perceptive about Madame de Vionnet and Chad's love in the earlier discussion with Chad that is presented in the chapter following his visit with Gostrey.[2]

Whether Strether is actually that unaware of Maria Gostrey's feelings is another question, but even if he is, it seems a slender critical basis for insisting on the inversion of temporal sequence in the novel's chapters. And why does the supposed irony of what Strether sees and fails to see have to be anticipatory? McGann also believes that the normal chronological order of Chapters XXVIII and XXIX was the "fearful though much patched over fault or weakness" that James referred to in a letter to Mrs. Humphry Ward about the first English edition of *The Ambassadors* (see p. 408). The difficulty with this claim is James's description of the fault as "much patched over," which hardly seems to describe just the interchanging of two chapters. A more plausible indication of the fault or weakness referred to is suggested later by James at the end of his preface to *The Ambassadors*, where he describes the direct presentation of Chad Newsome in the novel as "diminished and compromised—despoiled, that is, of its *proportional* advantage; so that, in a word, the whole economy of his author's relation to him has at important points to be redetermined" (see p. 14).

In preparing the serial text of *The Ambassadors* for its book publication, James did more than insert deleted chapters, restore smaller editorial cuts, and correct typographical errors. James habitually revised his works as they passed from manuscript or typescript (if he dictated them as he did *The Ambassadors*) to print, from serial to first editions, and then to subsequent editions. Often the changes were minor, but they involved more than simply altering the punctuation. Generally, the changes for the Harper edition of *The Ambassadors* consisted of removing repeated words, making the diction of a speaker more characteristic, and sharpening an occasional descriptive word. Examples of the last two kinds of changes can be found in the textual notes. Longer, but not necessarily more important, changes were made when James added sentences to intensify the questioning in a dialogue or to note a speaker's reaction. Despite these changes, the first American edition is closer to *The North*

2. Jerome McGann, "Revision, Rewriting, Rereading: or, 'An Error [Not] in *The Ambassadors*,' " *American Literature* 64 (1992): 105–6.

American Review text than the other two editions of *The Ambassadors* that James published, yet it has defects. In addition to the reversed chapters, for example, the opening of Chapter XXX became garbled when a line of type dropped out and was reinserted eight lines below. The chapter sequence and typographical errors of the Harper text survived through numerous reissues and reprints even after the edition's inverted chronology was discovered.

First English Edition

Harper's delay in sending the proof sheets for the first American edition began to worry James early in the summer of 1903 because he intended to forward duplicates of the corrected proof sheets through his agent to Methuen, which was to bring out the first English edition of *The Ambassadors*. By July Methuen had received no copy for a book it was to publish in the autumn. To help the firm out, James wrote to Pinker that he could send Methuen the first six or seven installments in *The North American Review*, though in doing this he would again have to revise the serial version, as he had for Harper. James thus provided a text for the first English edition that was revised independently of the text for the first American edition. In August, just after he had sent Harper revised and corrected proofs for the last third of the novel, James heard from Pinker that Methuen was now ready for more copy. Once again Harper's "mortal slowness" in sending proofs had created difficulties for James that he declared could have been avoided if Harper had initially sent him the duplicate proofs of the serial he had repeatedly asked for.

James resolved these new difficulties by having Pinker cable Harper for an identical set of the proofs for the last third of *The Ambassadors*, though they would be uncorrected, while James himself revised the eighth installment of the serial for Methuen. James then asked Pinker to send him a copy of this installment in *The North American Review* so that he could make "a small interpolation," which was probably Chapter XIX. James also offered to send through Pinker to Methuen "a duplicate Type-Copy of my MS., which I fortunately have clung to, and have not sent him hitherto because the printed text of the Serial contains inevitable little amendments and alterations. (Besides this I am afraid I lack duplicate of some passages omitted in the serial form and subsequently supplied to Harpers for insertion in the Book.)"[3] Later the same day, August 13, James wrote Pinker again, saying he could send Methuen a large section of his duplicate typescript, though this would involve him in "a quantity of double amending and correcting."

The result of these seemingly trivial details about the publication of the first English edition of *The Ambassadors* can be seen in the ways in which the text of that edition differs from the Harper text. Methuen

3. James, *Letters*, ed. Edel, 4:282–83.

published *The Ambassadors* in England on September 24, 1903, six weeks before the American edition appeared.[4] Because of the difficulties created by Harper's not sending James the duplicate proofs and then delaying the proofs it did send him, the first English edition differs from the American edition, and not just in the repeated corrections and emendations he was forced to make. The first important difference to be noted between the two first editions of *The Ambassadors* is that Chapters XXVIII and XXIX are in chronological sequence in the Methuen edition. Yet when James inserted the deleted chapters of the serial into the English edition, he put two of the chapters into parts different from those of the American edition. Part Seventh of Methuen consists of two chapters and Part Eighth of four, instead of the three chapters each that these parts have in Harper's edition. And the famous transposed conversation with Chad that is Chapter XXVIII was put at the end of Part Tenth (making four chapters there) instead of at the beginning of Part Eleventh (which now had three). In addition to making Methuen's Part Seventh considerably shorter than Part Eighth, these changes reduced somewhat the suspense created between the parts of the novel in the American edition. In the publication history of *The Ambassadors*, then, problems were created for the Harper as well as the Methuen editions in the order of chapters and the length of parts by the necessity of inserting chapters or parts of chapters that had been omitted from the serialized novel.

Beyond these structural differences, there are also a number of additional passages to be found in the Methuen but not the Harper edition. Because the typescript that James had to send to Methuen has not survived, it is not possible to tell with certainty whether these passages were additions to the first English edition or deletions from the first American that James then ignored or forgot about. The longest of the passages found in Methuen's text but not Harper's concerns the history of Chad in Paris that was omitted from Chapter V in *The North American Review*. In putting Chad's history back into the English edition, James added or restored to the beginning of it an account of Strether's awareness of the whirling of events into time, and then put in or left at the end three long sentences describing the view from Woollett of Chad's progress as a kind of Parisian Pasha (see textual notes 64:14 and 67:18–19). Other Methuen phrases in this section also emphasize Woollett's vision of Chad's degeneration.

These and numerous other brief passages and phrases appearing only in the English edition led Leon Edel to describe Methuen's edition as "more prolix" than the others.[5] But the first English edition

4. Methuen, which did not need to hold the novel back because of a serial, apparently also wanted as long an interval of time as possible between *The Ambassadors* and *The Golden Bowl*, which it was scheduled to publish in 1904.
5. Leon Edel, "The Text of *The Ambassadors*," *Harvard Library Bulletin* 14 (1960): 459.

also lacks passages found in other editions, and its overall length does not significantly differ from the American edition. The passages missing from the Methuen edition occur in the last third of the novel, which James had to supply from his typescript and from *The North American Review*—particularly in Chapter XXXV, which is Strether's last scene with Chad. With one exception, the passages omitted from the English edition (or restored in the American edition) are not as interesting as the additions to the Methuen edition. The exception somethingis ten lines of dialogue in which Strether suggests to Chad that something has been done for Strether himself by "Women—too." Chad's response of " 'Two'?" touches more directly than anywhere else in *The Ambassadors* on the way Madame de Vionnet and Maria Gostrey have affected Strether (see textual notes 340:20–37).

Apart from passages found only in or absent from the English edition, there are numerous places where James appears to have made revisions for that edition alone. They involve such things as the altering of a mixed metaphor, the removing of repeated words, or the changing of an adjective to make a description more telling. Sarah Pocock's "visit" to Strether, for example, is changed to a "descent," and the possibility of Waymarsh's being "affected" by his attachment to Sarah is changed to "demoralized." Some of the changes seem to have been made for an English audience, as in the revision of "bamboozled" to "beguiled," "boss" to "run," and perhaps "all the Mr. Brookses and Mr. Snookses" to "all the Mr. Coxes and Mr. Coleses."

Methuen's edition of *The Ambassadors* has occasionally been considered to be the best text of the novel published in James's lifetime. James resided in England, he saw the edition through the press himself instead of having to rely on transatlantic instructions to editors, and Chapters XXVÏII and XXIX are in chronological sequence. Yet there are more serious typographical errors in the first English edition than in the other three texts of the novel.[6] James's own copy of Methuen's edition survives, and in it he made two corrections as well as writing in the margin of one page a series of numbers that appear to be a word count.[7] When James revised *The Ambassadors* for his collected edition several years later, he incorporated only one of the corrections he had made. More important, the text he selected for his final revisions was not Methuen's but Harper's. The English edition with its additions and deletions was

---

6. Among the more obvious mistakes are "itself" for "himself," "your" for "our," "no design of getting" instead of "no design but of getting," "breach" for "brief," "expansive" for "expensive," "solely" for "sorely," "not" for "now," and "same" for "small." The Methuen text also repeats two errors ("days" instead of "ways" and "an" instead of "as") that were made in *The North American Review* but corrected in the Harper edition.
7. See textual notes 112:31 and 150:15. There is also a mysterious "X" at 73:28–29. James's copy is preserved in the Houghton Library of Harvard University.

abandoned, possibly because James had had to put the last third of it together from different sources.[8]

New York Edition

When the first editions of *The Ambassadors* were published, James was sixty years old. In 1904 he finished *The Golden Bowl*, his last major novel, and then revisited the United States for the first time in twenty years. While there he interested Charles Scribner's Sons in publishing a collected edition of his works that James himself named the "New York Edition" in homage to his native city. The edition, as James later described it to a friend, was to be

> a (severely-sifted) Collective and Definitive Edition. * * * A "handsome"—I hope really handsome and not too cheap—in fact sufficiently dear—array * * * owing much to close amendment (and even "rewriting") of the four earliest novels and to illuminatory classification, collocation, juxtaposition and separation through the whole series. The work on the earlier novels has involved much labour; * * * but the real tussle is in writing the Prefaces (to each vol. or book,) which are to be long—very long!—and loquacious —and competent perhaps to *pousser à la vente* [increase sales]. The Edition is to be of 23 vols. and there are to be some 15 Prefaces (as some of the books are in two,) and twenty-three lovely frontispieces.[9]

James began revising for the edition when he returned to England in 1905, and the volumes started to appear, two at a time, in 1907. Volumes XXI and XXII containing *The Ambassadors* were published in 1909.

James's method of revising for Scribner's New York Edition was to mark up an earlier edition of the novel by canceling passages in the text and then floating "balloon" insertions in the margins. As the revising proceeded, James began to lament in his letters the amount of labor involved, but by the time he reached the late novels he found, as he says in his last preface, the need for revision "reduced to nothing * * * in the presence of the altogether better literary manners of 'The Ambassadors' and 'The Golden Bowl.' "[1] Compared with the revisions of his earlier works, James's final revision of *The Ambassadors* might seem to be insignificant, but as the textual notes show, James still

8. On the relative merits of the American and English editions of *The Ambassadors*, see Birch's article referred to above. For my reply and his response, see "The Editions of *The Ambassadors*," *The Library* 31(1966): 248–52. Some of the changes I have made in revising this discussion of editions and revisions take account of Birch's criticism.

9. *Letters of Henry James*, ed. Lubbock, 2:70. (A marked-up page of James's revision of *The American* is reproduced on the facing page.) The edition actually came to twenty-four volumes with eighteen prefaces. An English issue of the edition was published by Macmillan.

1. Henry James, *Literary Criticism: French Writers, Other European Writers. The Prefaces to the New York Edition*, ed. Leon Edel and Mark Wilson (New York: Library of America, 1984), 1337. (Cited hereafter as *Prefaces*.)

found opportunities to improve the novel's manners. And these notes do not include certain kinds of changes made throughout the New York Edition, like the use of contractions and the omission of numerous relative pronouns and especially commas. James himself described another type of change as the addition of an "immense array of terms, perceptional and expressional, that * * * simply looked over the heads of the standing terms."[2] Included among "perceptional" terms are words describing the reactions of James's perceivers, such as "hesitated," which was changed seven times in *The Ambassadors*. Among the revised "expressional" terms were the various names given to the speakers in a dialogue, such as "interlocutress," which James removed four times.

The differences between the last revised text of *The Ambassadors* and its three earlier versions are not limited to these relatively minor types of alteration. By using the first American edition as the basis for his revisions, James incorporated most of the changes made when he revised the serial for Harper, while ignoring the changes made separately for the first English edition.[3] Yet in revising the American edition for the New York Edition, James appears not to have noticed that two of its chapters were in reverse chronological order. Considering the care he took in revising for his collected edition (he corrected the garbled opening of Chapter XXX, for example), it remains surprising that he did not notice this. It may have been a case of not seeing the chapters for the commas. James did take enough care to renumber all the chapters, changing them from a single sequence running throughout the novel to a series of sequences within each of the novel's twelve parts, or "books" as he called them in the Scribner edition. The effect of this renumbering de-emphasizes the succession of chapters and re-emphasizes the twelve books, thus bringing the novel's structure closer to James's original metaphor of twelve rounded medallions on a wall (see p. 404). (The chapter numbers of the first editions have been included in brackets after the New York Edition numbering in this Norton Critical Edition.) But in revising *The Ambassadors* for Scribner's, James did not do the entire novel before he sent it off. He did groups of books at a time, sending, for example, Books IX and X to Scribner's in January 1909; the publisher received the remainder of the novel, including the books with the inverted chapters, the next month.[4]

The changes that James did make in Harper's text as he revised it for the New York Edition appear for the most part to be improvements.

2. *Prefaces*, pp. 1332–33.
3. Not all the New York Edition revisions were based on American texts. In revising *The Spoils of Poynton*, for example, James picked the later revised first English edition rather than the earlier revised American one, thus establishing more of a continuity of revised texts than with *The Ambassadors*. See my "*The Spoils of Poynton*: Revisions and Editions," *Studies in Bibliography* 19 (1966): 161–74.
4. James's correspondence with Scribner's is summarized in Philip Horne's *Henry James and Revision: The New York Edition* (Oxford: Oxford University Press, 1990), 327–57.

James continued to make his descriptions somewhat more precise, as illustrated by the revision of Waymarsh's uncharacteristic murmur to a groan, of the "enormity" of Strether's consciousness to its "plentitude," of vaguer "inequalities" of behavior to "caprices," and the change of an ambassador's stature from "not very tall" to "importantly short." Sometimes the retouching of descriptions involved changes in imagery, such as in the introduction of a metaphor at the start of the novel to describe the features of Maria Gostrey's face as being "on happy terms with each other." Another example is the revision of an image describing Waymarsh's relation to Mrs. Newsome from something suggesting a puppet to the image of an overstrained vocal accompanist. Usually these changes involved separate nuances of meaning, but occasionally a slight shift in characterization emerges from their cumulative effect. Mrs. Newsome, for instance, is more faintly ridiculous and pathetic in the New York Edition as James changed the description of her as "exalted" to "wound up" and added five lines of dialogue about her between Strether and Gostrey in London; the gist of this most substantial revision in the New York Edition is that Mrs. Newsome would probably consent to be an invalid in order to be an American (see textual note 46:29–33).

Not all the changes in the final revision of *The Ambassadors* are clearly meaningful. James's hunt for the right phrase to use in Maria Gostrey's exclamation over Americans reads like a parody of his stylistic mannerisms, as he changed the serial version of "long may we wave" to "but may we never fill up" in the American edition, to "but long may we play our parts" in the English edition, and finally to "but may we never be less so" in the New York Edition. At least one alteration in James's last revision is not obviously an improvement, and that is in the concluding sentences of Book Eleventh, where James changed Strether's concise "supposing everything" to his "supposing innumerable and wonderful things." Scribner's edition is also not without misprints, though they are not as numerous as in Methuen's.

Despite these blemishes and the inverted chapters, the New York Edition of *The Ambassadors* is still the best of the novel's four texts. It embodies James's final revisions, and there is no sound reason for not choosing it, especially when it is possible, as in this edition, to include the more significant variants from earlier versions in the textual notes. Critics have sometimes objected to the New York Edition revisions, their reasons being similar to those of Little Bilham's in *The Ambassadors* when he compares Chad's development to "the new edition of an old book that one has been fond of—revised and brought up to date, but not quite the thing one knew and loved" (p. 111). Yet clearly this kind of objection does not apply to the six-year-old *The Ambassadors* as it does, say, to the extensively revised *The American* or even *The Portrait of a Lady*, which were written decades before. Nevertheless, it is worth noting here again for readers who prefer writers' first visions to their

revisions why James felt he had to revise his works for the New York
Edition. The question of revision for him was a moral one:

> As the whole of life consists of things done, which do other things
> in their turn, just so our behaviour and its fruits are essentially
> one and continuous and persistent and unquenchable, so the act
> has its way of abiding and showing and testifying, and so, among
> our innumerable acts, are no arbitrary, no senseless separations.
> * * * Not to *be* disconnected, for the tradition of behaviour, he
> [the artist] has but to feel that he is not; by his lightest touch
> the whole chain of relation and responsibility is reconsti-
> tuted. * * * On all the ground to which the pretension of per-
> formance by a series of exquisite laws may apply there reigns one
> sovereign truth—which decrees that, as art is nothing if not ex-
> emplary, care nothing if not active, finish nothing if not consistent,
> the proved error is the base apologetic deed, the helpless regret is
> the barren commentary, and "connexions" are employable for finer
> purposes than mere gaping contrition.[5]

James's eloquent justification has been the inspiration as well for this
revised Norton Critical Edition of his novel.

Two other important features of the New York Edition—the frontispieces, which have already been mentioned, and the prefaces—remain
to be described in this survey of editions and revisions of *The Ambassadors*. James's prefaces have been justly celebrated as a major contribution to the theory of fiction, but the frontispieces have generally been
ignored. The significance of the beautiful photographs that appear in
the front of each volume of the New York Edition lies in James's su-
pervision of their selection, and thus they serve as another oblique
comment by the author on his work. When Scribner's originally suggested drawings as the frontispieces, James was reluctant. Throughout
his career he had had misgivings about the illustration of fiction because,
as he said while discussing the photographs in his final preface to the
Scribner's edition, "anything that relieves responsible prose of the duty
of being, while placed before us, good enough, interesting enough and,
if the question be of picture, pictorial enough, above all *in itself*, does
it the worst of services, and may well inspire in the lover of literature
certain lively questions as to the future of that institution." But after
meeting and seeing the work of the young American photographer Alvin
Langdon Coburn, James agreed to work with him in finding suitable
subjects for photographic frontispieces.[6] The results of this collaboration
were also described by James in his preface to *The Golden Bowl*:

---

5. *Prefaces*, pp. 1340–41.
6. James's collaboration is discussed in Ralph F. Bogardus, *Pictures and Texts: Henry James, A.
   L. Coburn, and New Ways of Seeing in Literary Culture* (Ann Arbor, Mich.: UMI Research
   Press, 1984). Bogardus includes a portfolio of all the frontispieces for the New York Edition.

Nothing in fact could more have amused the author than the opportunity of a hunt for a series of reproducible subjects—such moreover as might best consort with photography—the reference of which to Novel or Tale should exactly be *not* competitive and obvious, should on the contrary plead its case with some shyness, that of images always confessing themselves mere optical symbols or echoes, expressions of no particular thing in the text, but only of the type or idea of this or that thing. They were to remain at the most small pictures of our "set" stage with the actors left out.[7]

For *The Ambassadors* James first suggested to Coburn in a memorandum on Paris subjects that some view of Notre Dame would serve, or perhaps a picture of the bookstalls under the arcade of the Odéon theater, where Strether lingers. The result was a picture of the Pont Neuf, connecting the left bank with the Ile de la Cité, which James entitled "By Notre Dame." Then James wanted a picture from the Luxembourg Gardens, as he explained in some detail to Coburn in his memorandum (where he identified himself with Strether—see p. 410). The second photograph was entitled simply "The Luxembourg Gardens." The photographs are reproduced here on pp. 16 and 371—but *not* in the order in which they appear in the New York Edition. As printed in Volumes XXI and XXII of the New York Edition, the frontispieces appear to be reversed. The Luxembourg Gardens photograph should reasonably be the frontispiece to Volume I, where the crucial scene in those gardens takes place in Book Second, Chapter II (pp. 59ff. of this edition). And the photograph of the Pont Neuf entitled "By Notre Dame" should clearly accompany the opening of Volume II, where Strether encounters Madame de Vionnet in Notre Dame and then has lunch with her in a restaurant nearby. But in the New York Edition we have the Pont Neuf as the illustration for Volume I and the Luxembourg Gardens for Volume II.

None of the frontispieces for the other two-volume novels in the New York Edition are out of narrative sequence the way they are in *The Ambassadors*.[8] This additional anomaly in the ordering of the frontispieces for *The Ambassadors* in the New York Edition clearly throws more doubt on the care with which—apart from his painstaking revisions—James supervised this edition of *The Ambassadors*, or perhaps on the control he was able to exercise over the way that edition of his novel was assembled.

The most direct and sustained commentary that James made on *The Ambassadors* is his preface to the novel. The prefaces, James explained

7. *Prefaces*, pp. 1326–27.
8. See Bogardus's discussion of *The Portrait of a Lady* and *The Princess Casamassima* in *Pictures and Texts*, pp. 187–90, and James's own description of the two frontispieces for *The Golden Bowl* in *Prefaces*, pp. 1327–29.

to Howells in 1908, were intended to be "in general, a sort of plea for Criticism, for Discrimination, for Appreciation on other than infantile lines—as against the so almost universal Anglo-Saxon absence of these things. * * * They ought, collected together, * * *to form a sort of comprehensive manual or *vademecum* for aspirants in our arduous profession."[9] In the preface to *The Ambassadors* James developed two fundamental principles of the novel. The first concerns his celebrated point of view technique. Strether was at once "hero and historian," yet he does not and cannot tell his own story because James refused to sacrifice subtleties and discriminations to "the terrible *fluidity* of self-revelation" in the first person point of view. Strether's view, as presented by the novelist, gave the larger form of *The Ambassadors*, the smaller being the "compositional law" of serial installments. Strether's point of view required, however, the use of Maria Gostrey as "the most unmitigated and abandoned of *ficelles*," but she aided substantially in the development of the second major principle of the novel, which was the alternation of pictorial description and scenic drama. The changes of picture and scene in *The Ambassadors* showed once again to James that "the Novel remains still, under the right persuasion, the most independent, most elastic, most prodigious of literary forms" (see p. 15).

The plea for criticism, discrimination, and appreciation that the preface to *The Ambassadors* makes is not confined to generalized formal considerations. As he tells "the story of one's story itself" in the earlier part of his preface, James emphasizes the main concerns of his novel. Howells's inspiring remark, the question of whether there would be time to live, the demonstration of what Strether sees, the breakdown of his moral scheme before the facts of the case—all these and other developments are touched upon by James in his account of the novel he considered his best. About other important matters in *The Ambassadors*, however, James is vague or silent. What the prefaces do not say, and the involuted prose used not to say it, can exhaust the patience of readers expecting a statement of the author's creative intentions. But if James's prefaces are taken *as* prefaces to novels or stories that are about to be read or (since all the works in the edition had been published before) reread, then the prefaces are what James described them to be: not an exhaustive commentary to end criticism but rather an introduction suggesting where criticism might illuminatingly begin. And the place for it to begin with *The Ambassadors* is the text for which the preface was written.

---

9. *Letters of Henry James*, ed. Lubbock, 2:99. For an outline of ideas about the nature and techniques of fiction that James found as he reviewed his own novels and tales, see R. P. Blackmur's introduction to the collected prefaces in Henry James, *The Art of the Novel* (New York: Charles Scribner's Sons, 1953), vii–xxxix.

THE AUTHOR ON THE NOVEL

NOTEBOOK ENTRIES†

When he recorded the inspiration for *The Ambassadors* in 1895 James had been keeping his notebooks for over fifteen years. Among the various purposes he used them for, two are most important. First, James habitually noted down what he called the "germs" of his fiction—the brief anecdotes, ideas, situations which he might later take up and develop into a story or a novel. Secondly, he practiced in his notebooks what he called "the art of *reflection*"—the actual working out of the possibilities latent in the germs. The first and main entry on *The Ambassadors* shows how both these functions could often be combined, for here James noted down the actual inspiration of Howells's words as reported to him and then went on to explore the possible situation that would give rise to them in a work of fiction. In doing this James returned to a cluster of ideas that had been in his mind since his painful failure as a dramatist in January, 1895. At the beginning of a note made in February, 1895, James asked himself "What is there in the idea of *Too late*—of some friendship or passion or bond—some affection long desired and waited for, that is formed too late?—I mean too late in life altogether" (*Notebooks*, pp. 182–83). James then went on to speculate briefly on the conditions of previous marriage or impending death that would prevent this relationship. On October 28, 1895, James noted another idea that was to be included in a possible group of stories that, in the entry on *The Ambassadors*, James classified as "*Les Vieux*—The Old." Here the peaceful and secure end of a man's life is suddenly destroyed by the return of a wife, the source of past unrest, who drives him out and takes over his haven of retirement. Three days later James noted down the idea for *The Ambassadors*. At the time of the entry he was still staying at a resort hotel in Torquay, Cornwall, where he had gone earlier in the summer to work quietly on *The Spoils of Poynton*, his first novel in five years.

By the time *The Ambassadors* was written James had developed the habit of dictating his novels to a typist as he composed them. Consequently there are no notebook entries on *The Ambassadors*—as there are for such earlier works as *The Spoils of Poynton* and *What Maisie Knew*—in which the ideas for the novel are actually worked out. Apart from the initial note on the inspiration for the novel, the only other entry that refers directly to *The Ambassadors* was written about three months after the novel was finished. Scattered throughout James's notebooks, however, are various names that appear in *The Ambassadors*. One of the minor uses James made of his notebooks was to list names, usually taken from the London *Times*, that might be of future use in his fiction. The following names that appear in *The Ambassadors* are taken from these undated lists; the date preceding each given below is that of the entry immediately preceding the list from which the name is taken:

> August 6, 1884: "Chad"; March 4, 1895: "Mme de Vionnet"; May 11, 1895: "Gostrey"; May 16, 1899: "Newsome," "Milrose," "Waymark" (the last is the name James used for Waymarsh in his preliminary statement for *The Ambassadors*); August 9, 1900: "Strether"; September 11, 1900: "Bilham," "Barrace."

† Excerpted from *The Notebooks of Henry James*, ed. F. O. Matthiessen and Kenneth B. Murdock, copyright (©) 1947 by Oxford University Press, Inc.; renewed 1974 by Kenneth B. Murdock and Mrs. Peters Putnam. Reprinted by permission of Oxford University Press. Pages 225–28, 313, 372, 374–75, 379–80, 381–84, 386, 391–401, 402–3, 405–7, 408, 409–12. Minor errors in the manuscripts and published text of the notebooks have been silently corrected.

Torquay, October 31st, 1895.

I was struck last evening with something that Jonathan Sturges,[1] who has been staying here 10 days, mentioned to me: it was only 10 words, but I seemed, as usual, to catch a glimpse of a *sujet de nouvelle*[2] in it. We were talking of W.D.H.[3] and of his having seen him during a short and interrupted stay H. had made 18 months ago in Paris—called away—back to America, when he had just come—at the end of 10 days by the news of the death—or illness—of his father. He had scarcely been in Paris, ever, in former days, and he had come there to see his domiciled and initiated son, who was at the Beaux Arts. Virtually in the evening, as it were, of life, it was all new to him: all, all, all. Sturges said he seemed sad—rather brooding; and I asked him what gave him (Sturges) that impression. 'Oh—somewhere—I forget, when I was with him—he laid his hand on my shoulder and said *à propos* of some remark of mine: "Oh, you are young, you are young—be glad of it: be glad of it and *live*. Live all you can: it's a mistake not to. It doesn't so much matter what you do—but live. This place makes it all come over me. I see it now. I haven't done so—and now I'm old. It's too late. It has gone past me—I've lost it. You have time. You are young. Live!" '[4] I amplify and improve a little—but that was the tone. It touches me—I can see him—I can hear him. Immediately, of course—as everything, thank God, does—it suggests a little situation. I seem to see something, of a tiny kind, springing out of it, that would take its place in the little group I should like to do of *Les Vieux*—The Old. (What should I call it in English—*Old Fellows*? No, that's trivial and common.) At any rate, it gives me the little idea of the figure of an elderly man who hasn't 'lived,' hasn't at all, in the sense of sensations, passions, impulses, pleasures—and to whom, in the presence of some great human spectacle, some great organization for the Immediate, the Agreeable, for curiosity, and experiment and perception, for Enjoyment, in a word,

1. Jonathan Sturges (1864–1911), a crippled, expatriated American man of letters, was an intimate friend of James's who admired his wit and intelligence. Leon Edel has suggested he was an inspiration for the character of little Bilham. See Leon Edel, "Jonathan Sturges," *Princeton University Library Chronicle* XV (Autumn 1953): 1–9.
2. Subject for a *nouvelle*. For James the *nouvelle* occupied the territory between a short story (five to twenty thousand words) and a short novel (sixty to one hundred thousand words).
3. William Dean Howells (1837–1920) was, in addition to being a major American novelist, a prominent editor and literary critic. As James's friend and colleague he was associated with both the inspiration for and publication of *The Ambassadors*. See James's letters to Howells on pp. 404–6.
4. These words should be compared not only with James's use of them in his preface to *The Ambassadors* and in the novel itself, but also with the following excerpt from a letter Howells wrote from the States to his son, who was studying architecture at the École des Beaux-Arts. (The garden referred to was that of the American painter James McNeill Whistler, and it was there that Howells made his remarks to Sturges.) "Perhaps it was as well I was called home. The poison of Europe was getting into my soul. You must look out for that. They live much more fully than we do. Life here is still for the future,—it is a land of Emersons—and I like a little present moment in mine. When I think of the Whistler garden!—" From *Life in Letters of William Dean Howells*, ed. Mildred Howells (New York: Doubleday Doran, 1928), 2:52.

becomes, *sur la fin*, [5] or toward it, sorrowfully aware. He has never really enjoyed—he has lived only for Duty and conscience—his conception of them; for pure appearances and daily tasks—lived for effort, for surrender, abstention, sacrifice. I seem to see his history, his temperament, his circumstances, his figure, his life. I don't see him as having battled with his passions—I don't see him as harassed by his temperament or as having, in the past, suspected, very much, what he was losing, what he was not doing. The alternative wasn't present to him. He may be an American—he might be an Englishman. I don't altogether like the *banal* side of the revelation of Paris—it's so obvious, so usual to make Paris the vision that opens his eyes, makes him feel his mistake. It might be London—it might be Italy—it might be the general impression of a summer in Europe—abroad. Also, it *may* be Paris. He has been a great worker, a local worker. But of what kind? I can't make him a novelist —too like W. D. H., and too generally *invraisemblable*. [6] But I want him 'intellectual,' I want him *fine*, clever, literary almost: it deepens the irony, the tragedy. A clergyman is too obvious and *usé*[7] and otherwise impossible. A journalist, a lawyer—these men WOULD in a manner have 'lived,' through their contact with life, with the complications and turpitudes and general vitality of mankind. A doctor—an artist too. A mere man of business—he's possible; but not of the intellectual grain that I mean. The Editor of a Magazine—that would come nearest: not at all of a newspaper. A Professor in a college would imply some knowledge of the lives of the young—though there might be a tragic effect in his seeing at the last that he hasn't even suspected what those lives might contain. (They had passed by him—he had passed them by.) He has married very young, and austerely. Happily enough, but charmlessly, and oh, so conscientiously: a wife replete with the New England conscience. But all this must be—oh, so light, so delicately summarized, so merely touched. What I seem to see is the possibility of some little illustrative action. The idea of the tale being the revolution that takes place in the poor man, the impression made on him by the particular experience, the incident in which this revolution and this impression embody themselves, is the point *à trouver*. [8] They are determined by certain circumstances, and they produce a situation, his issue from which is the little drama. I am supposing him, I think, to have 'illustrated,' as I say, in the past, by his issue from some *other* situation, the opposite conditions, those that have determined him in the sense of the sort of life and feeling I have sketched and the memory, the consciousness of which roll over him now with force. He has sacrificed some one, some friend, some son, some younger brother, to his failure to feel, to un-

5. At the end.
6. Unlikely.
7. Worn.
8. To be found.

derstand, all that his new experience causes to come home to him in a wave of reaction, of compunction. He has not allowed for these things, the new things, new sources of emotion, new influences and appeals— didn't realize them at all. It was in communication with *them* that the spirit, the sense, the nature, the temperament of this victim (as now seems to him) of his old ignorance, struggled and suffered. He was wild—he was free—he was passionate; but there would have been a way of taking him. Our friend never saw it—never, never: he perceives that—ever so sadly, so bitterly, now. The young man is dead: it's all over. Was he a son, was he a ward, a younger brother—or an elder one? Points to settle: though I'm not quite sure I like the *son*. Well, my vague little fancy is that he 'comes out,' as it were (to London, to Paris—I'm afraid it *must* be Paris; if he's an American), to take some step, decide some question with regard to some one, in the sense of his old feelings and habits, and that the new influences, to state it roughly, make him act just in the opposite spirit—make him accept on the spot, with a *volte-face*,[9] a wholly different inspiration. It is a case of some other person or persons, it is some other young life in regard to which it's a question of his interfering, rescuing, bringing home. Say he 'goes out' (partly) to look after, to bring home, some young man whom his family are anxious about, who won't *come* home, etc.—and under the operation of the change *se range du côté du jeune homme*,[1] says to him: 'No; STAY:—*don't* come home.' Say our friend is a widower, and that the *jeune homme* is the son of a widow to whom he is engaged to be married. *She* is of the strenuous pattern—she is the reflection of his old self. She has money—she admires and approves him: 5 years have elapsed since his 1st wife's death, 10 since his own son's. He is 55. He married at 20! Displeasing the strenuous widow is a sacrifice—an injury to him. To marry her means rest and security *pour ses vieux jours*.[2] The 'revolution' endangers immensely his situation with her. But of course my denouement is that it takes place—that he makes the sacrifice, does the thing I have, vaguely, represented him, *supra*,[3] as doing, and loses the woman he was to marry and all the advantages attaching to her. It is too late, too late *now*, for HIM to live—but what stirs in him with a dumb passion of desire, of I don't know what, is the sense that he may have a little supersensual hour in the vicarious freedom of another. His little drama is the administration of the touch that contributes to—that prolongs—that freedom.

9. About-face.
1. Sides with the young man.
2. For his old age.
3. Earlier.

October 19th, 1901, Lamb House.

Something in reference to man who, like W.D.H. (say), has never known *at all* any woman BUT his wife—and at 'time of life' somehow sees it, is face to face with it: little situation *on* it. *Ça rentre,*[4] however, rather, into the idea (is a small side of it) of *The Ambassadors*. But *never*, NEVER—in any degree to call a relation at all: *and on American lines.* x x x x x[5]

"PROJECT OF NOVEL BY HENRY JAMES"†

The most remarkable document relating to *The Ambassadors* is the 20,000-word statement composed for magazine editors *before* he had written the novel. Together with the original "germ" of the story and the later preface this preliminary statement forms a sequence of the novelist's plans and commentary that is unique in James's writings and almost unparalleled in the history of fiction. James referred to this statement as a scenario in a letter to Howells (p. 405), but in describing the "wondrous and copious preliminary statements" to H. G. Wells (pp. 406–7) James distinguished between two kinds of documents: the public "manifesto" addressed to "the dim editorial mind" and the very private "interminable garrulous letter addressed to my own fond fancy." The "*private* outpouring" on which the preliminary statement of *The Ambassadors* was based has not survived, although there are similar documents to be found in the working out of *The Spoils of Poynton* and *What Maisie Knew* in James's notebooks and in his notes for the unfinished *The Sense of the Past* and *The Ivory Tower*. These statements show even more clearly than the "project" of *The Ambassadors* how, after his failure as a playwright, James came to plan his fiction through what he called the "divine principle of the Scenario." (See James's *Notebooks*, p. 188, for his formulation of the principle.) The scenario principle led James to think and write out the plans for his novels through a series of dramatic scenes which were prepared for by an alternating series of narrative summaries or pictures. The resulting structure of picture and scene was justly celebrated by James himself in the preface to *The Ambassadors*. James also mentioned in his preface the "small compositional law" of serial installments which governed both the planning of his "project" and the writing of the novel.

Compared to the finished novel James's preliminary statement reveals

4. That returns.
5. James frequently used x's at the end of a notebook entry.
† This preliminary statement was first published in its entirety in *The Notebooks of Henry James*, ed. F. O. Matthiessen and Kenneth B. Murdock (New York: Oxford University Press, 1947), 372–415. The original typescript that James dictated bears the title given above. Several errors of typing or dictation have been either silently corrected or, where James's intention is unclear, simply noted.

numerous and important differences not only in the arrangement of pictures and scenes but also in the conceptions of major characters in *The Ambassadors*. At times the statement reads like a supplement to the novel with its account of events that never take place; almost as interesting is the absence of certain characters and crucial complications in the plot. Beyond these changes there is the fundamental difference in the telling itself. The "project" for *The Ambassadors* demonstrates by contrast just what is involved in James's reflection of a character's point of view because here the story is related not through a mirroring of Strether's consciousness but rather through the intruding, confiding, omniscient author himself.

Certain passages have been omitted from the "project" as it appears below. The first of these omissions is the introduction, in which James recounts the "germ" of *The Ambassadors* that he recorded in his notebooks and retold in his preface. For the response of the editor of *Harper's Magazine* to this preliminary statement, see p. 415.

I

* * * My subject may be most simply described, then, as the picture of a certain momentous and interesting period, of some six months or so, in the history of a man no longer in the prime of life, yet still able to live with sufficient intensity to be a source of what may be called excitement to himself, not less than to the reader of his record. Lambert Strether (to give him, for our purpose here, a name, even if it be not final) has behind him so much past that I perforce accept him, and undertake to create on his behalf all the romantic sympathy necessary, just as his fifty-fifth year has struck. He is an American, of the present hour and of sufficiently typical New England origin, who has, at the point of his career that he has reached, the consciousness of a good deal of prolonged effort and tension, the memory of a good many earnest and anxious experiments—professional, practical, intellectual, moral, personal—to look back upon, without, for himself, any very proportionate sense of acknowledged or achieved success. However, he is, in the rather provincial, the somewhat contracted world in which he lives, a highly esteemed figure and influence. Educated, with excellent gifts, intelligent, having passed, for the most part, as exceptionally 'clever,' he has had a life by no means wasted, but not happily concentrated; and rather makes on himself the impression of having come in for many of the drawbacks, even perhaps for the little of the discredit, of an incoherent existence, without, unfortunately, any of the accompanying entertainment or 'fun.' He feels tired, in other words, without having a great deal to show for it; disenchanted without having known any great enchantments, enchanters, or, above all, enchantresses; and even before the action in which he is engaged launches him, is vaguely haunted by the feeling of what he has missed, though this is a quantity, and a quality, that he would be rather at a loss to name. His traditions, associations, sympathies, have all been the liberal and instructed sort, on a due basis of culture and curiosity; he has not been too much mixed up with vulgar things; he has always been occupied, and preoccupied, in one way and another, but has always, in all relations and connections, been ridden by his 'New England conscience.' He has known no extremes of fortune; has never been very poor, yet still less had any but the most limited enjoyment of money; has had always rather urgently to 'do something,' yet has never been without the thing—in a decently remunerative way—to do.

So much for him in a very general way, for everything that further concerns us about his conditions and antecedents is given, immediately, by the unfolding of the action itself—the action of which my story essentially consists and which of itself involves and achieves all presentation and explanation. This action takes him up at the moment of his arrival, one evening of early spring, in England—arrival in connection with a matter, and as the first note of a situation, with everything that has prepared and led up to which we become *dramatically*, so to speak, acquainted. My first Part or two are expository, presentative (on these lines of present picture and movement); and are primarily concerned with his encounter and relation with two persons his portrayed intercourse with whom throws up to the surface what it concerns us to learn. * * *[1]

* * * Waymark will not be wholly ignorant of who Mrs. Newsome is. Who she is comes up, at any rate, lucidly, for ourselves; and with it, in brief, the full evocation of Strether's background and setting. These things put before us, by their implications, an American city of the second order—not such a place either as New York, as Boston or as Chicago, but a New England 'important local centre' like Providence, R.I., like Worcester, Mass., or like Hartford, Conn.; an old and enlightened Eastern community, in short, which is yet not the seat of one of the bigger colleges (which for special reasons I don't want). The place of course to be designated with sufficient intensity. Mrs. Newsome is the widow, there domiciled and dominant, of one of the local rich men, a man known to Strether in his time—and not all too agreeably or handsomely; the late Mr. Newsome, hard, sharp and the reverse of overscrupulous, not having left a name (for those who *know*—and Strether is abundantly one of them) of a savour ideally sweet. Mrs. Newsome herself, however, is a very different affair and a really remarkable woman: high, strenuous, nervous, 'intense' (oh, a type!)—full

1. In the omitted sections James describes the characters and functions of Waymark (Waymarsh)—a "contrast and foil" to Strether—and Miss Gostrey, "Another agent, operative on this expository ground." And Strether's tour of Chester is taken with Waymark rather than Miss Gostrey.

of ideals and activities, many of them really, in respect to her husband's career, of a decidedly fine expiatory or compensatory nature. She is many other things besides; invalidical, exalted, depressed, at once shrill and muffled, at once extremely abounding and extremely narrow, and of an especial austerity (in spite of herself almost, as it were, and of some of her imaginations), an especial refined hardness and dryness of grain and strain. She is old enough to have had by her early marriage, a marriage when she was barely twenty, two children, a son now of about twenty-eight, the one who remains in Europe, and predominantly in Paris, where she can't, for reasons, get at him; and a daughter of thirty, Mrs. Pocock, who lives in the same place as her mother and near her, in close communion with her, being married, to a man somewhat older than herself, actually a partner in the considerable family business, a business, the manufacture of some small, convenient, homely, in fact distinctly vulgar article of domestic use (to be duly specified), to which the late Newsome gave in his time such an impulse that his family derive a large income from it and will continue to do so if their interests are sharply guarded and the working of the thing thoroughly kept up. * * *[2]

* * * [Mrs. Newsome] is a particularly intense and energetic invalid, moreover, but still an invalid, never sure of herself in advance, and with recollections of Europe gathered from an early infelicitous round or two with her late husband, memories not of an order to leave traditions of ease. In short, for two or three years past she has, from year to year and from month to month, failed to achieve the move; in connection with which there has been another deterrent still. This deterrent has been the part more and more played in her life by Lambert Strether (full name Lewis Lambert Strether), and to which we catch on wholly through the lights given us by Strether himself. What we have is his depicted, betrayed, communicated consciousness and picture of it. We see Mrs. Newsome, in fine, altogether in this reflected manner, as she figures in our hero's relation to her and in his virtual projection, for us, *of* her. I may as well say at once, that, lively element as she is in the action, we deal with her presence and personality only as an affirmed influence, only in their deputed, represented form; and nothing, of course, can be more artistically interesting than such a little problem as to make her always out of it, yet always *of* it, always absent, yet always felt. But the realities, the circumstances—as they are evoked by Strether first for Waymark—are not the less distinctly before us. Waymark doesn't learn all—it's Miss Gostrey who presently makes all *out*; but Waymark elicits a good deal. Mrs. Newsome has begun by being immensely indebted to Strether, but Strether has also ended by contracting a sense of no small obligation to herself. He has helped her originally with her char-

2. James goes on to sketch Chad's financial independence and Mrs. Newsome's view of his selfish and immoral stay in Paris, which she attributes in her ignorance of life to the lure of "a dreadful woman."

ities, her reforms, her good works—twenty manifestations of that restless conscience which I have called in a measure unwittingly expiatory; he has been advisory, sympathetic, suggestive, been an influence, for her, making in fact altogether for sanity and success. He has controlled and moderated her, been, in short, in these connections, exactly the clever, competent man needed by a peculiarly high-strung woman. Cleverness, competence, soundness, the thing to do and the thing not to, the way and the way not—these have been, by a happy constitution in our interesting friend, matters easy and natural to him; so that he has played, without great inconvenience to himself, and with an interest too in her subjects and ideals, straight into the current of his earnest neighbour's activity.

What we further learn about him helps to explain it. He himself has, in the New England way, married young, married, at an age not much greater than Mrs. Newsome's (who at present, I've omitted to note, is in her fifty-first year), emphatically for love, married happily for all save the fact of the death of his wife, in a second confinement, at the end of some five years. Left with a little boy of less than that age, Strether has then known such a period of helpless and discomfortable paternity as has deepened the bitterness of his bereavement; a period at once unrelieved and unspoiled by a second marriage, but brought to a term by the death—through an accident (while swimming)—of his boy at the age of about sixteen, an age sufficient to have unfortunately marked the fact that they (the boy and he) had not wholly hit it off together. There have been special facts about the boy, his nature, temperament, tendencies, that Strether has subsequently accused himself, with bitter compunction, of not having understood and allowed for, not handled with sufficient tenderness and tact. Deep and silent penance has he privately performed ever since; and the loss of his son, and the particular conditions and particular consequent feelings, are things that have constituted one of the sharpest elements of his life. It's all a history as to which Mrs. Newsome has repeatedly accused him of being morbid—as if, it is true, in a measure to make up as she can for all the occasions on which he has called *her* the same. He has thought her a little so—or in fact a good deal so—about her son, though holding a good deal himself the impression that Chad, whom he has known a bit as a boy, and in earlier youth, is not a little, really, alas, of an egotist and even a brute. He has *his* theory about Chad, which differs from the mother's, and is, as he considers, the theory of a man of the world as distinguished from such a person as Mrs. Newsome of Hartford, Conn. His own boy, at all events, *wasn't* a brute; he has ached, at times, with the sense that he himself was, in the doomed relation, the brute—unconscious of tender and sensitive things in the lad, stupidly, harshly blundering about them.

And there have been other things in his career—but things of labour

and effort mainly, things in which he has tried to steep his disappointments, disillusionments, depressions. It had been his idea of himself,
above all, that he has been fundamentally indifferent and detached,
fatally unable really to care for anything. What more proof of it has he
needed, to his own mind, than that he has tried half-a-dozen things
and successively, rather, as he calls it to himself, sneakingly given them
up? He tutored at college, after graduating, for a while, and gave that
up. He studied law, and was admitted, and provincially, drearily practised for a time, but made little of that, had hankerings for 'study,' for
serious literature, for serious journalism, and threw himself, with characteristic intensity, into experiments in that direction. They failed, in a
manner, yet left him still with his yearnings, so that even after accepting
and exercising, with a good deal of continuity, a salaried, an authoritative
post in connection with the control of a large 'Home,' or some such
other beneficent or economic institution founded, patronised, promoted
by Mrs. Newsome these aspirations have again, a few years previous to
our opening, in the form of an expensive Review, devoted to serious
questions and inquiries, economic, social, sanitary, humanitary,
Strether carries with some financial ruefulness and Mrs. Newsome sub-
sidises with much public pride [*sic*]. She gave him his chance, at a given
moment, and he accepted it from her. Between them they keep the
thing going. It has been an alliance, a united superior effort. What they
both feel about it is that the thing is of course too good, too enlightened
to succeed, but not, uncontestably, to *do* good. It's a great beneficent
endeavour, equally honourable to both. It has, moreover, a few hundred
subscribers, and all the colleges, all the cultivated groups scattered about
the country, take it in and esteem it. It goes to Europe—where they
believe it to have attracted attention in high quarters. Strether's name,
as the editor, is on the cover, where it has been one of the few frank
pleasures of his somewhat straightened life to have liked to see it. He is
known by that pale, costly cover—it has become his principal identity.
A man of moods and of a very variable imagination, he has sometimes
thought this identity small, poor, miserable; while at others thinking it
as good as most of the others around him. It's on the cover, at any rate,
that Mrs. Newsome has liked to see him—this has been a greater joy
to her than she has ever even betrayed; and the common interest, the
most especial of many, has done much to bind them together. The
feelings connected for her with this intimacy form precisely the subject
of my reference just above to her practically deterred condition in respect
to breaking in and going off. She has been under a spell from poor fine
melancholy, missing, striving Strether. To be plain (though we are not
plain at first), she's in love with him. She's fifty, and he's fifty-five; but
he's the secret romance—secret, that is, up to a given point; then sufficiently public—that she has never otherwise had. To say that she plays
a similar part very exactly for himself would be to say too much; but he

likes, admires and esteems her; she is much the most remarkable woman, in her way the most distinguished, the highest, keenest spirit, within his social range; and in their sufficiently 'awake' community she passes for very remarkable indeed. She is *the* personage, almost the great lady, certainly the 'prominent woman' of that community. Indeed her name is in the local papers much more than he, secretly, can like. However, *she* likes it, and the upshot of everything (for I am expatiating here, for you, far too much) is that, certain things having, at home, happened in certain ways, certain symptoms in regard to Chad, in Paris, having multiplied—in regard to Chad and in regard to other matters besides— the situation has taken the form of Strether's having offered Mrs. Newsome the service, as a loyal and grateful friend, of coming out to Paris to see what, in the premises, he can do. There has been a plan of *her* coming, but many personal and other things, complications, of sorts, indisposition, nervousness, moral and other apprehensions, have interposed and again checked her; a particular consideration which presently comes out for us has in fact above all interfered. There had been a question, if she *had* come, of Strether's coming with her; then there had been a question of her coming, as it were, with *him*. But the particular consideration I speak of has interposed especially as to *that*; and in the event Strether, tired, overstrained, chronically deficient in holidays and in 'a little change,' has taken his course by himself. It fits in, in short, with a kind of crisis in his personal history, which it may, in a manner, contribute to ease off, to produce an interruption, a suspension, a possible practical evaporation of. He comes on a kind of moral and sentimental mission, but committed to nothing more than to get hold of Chad tactfully, kindly, to try to fish him out of his deep waters. He is to act only within his full discretion, and he is to report on the situation and enlighten Mrs. Newsome's darkness. In particular, at any rate, they have both fully felt, and in almost equal good faith, that it will have been, on the possible bad issue, but a small honour to them if the boy be lost without some earnest, some practical, personal effort to save him. The case has been virtually as simple for them as that. Perdition on one side, salvation on the other. * * *[3]

[Strether] is really touched at the way Miss Gostrey has entered into his life—at the feelings he has about certain things in it. He does deny—deny the offer as directly made by Mrs. Newsome, but his new friend makes what she likes of that. She has the whole thing—she reconstructs and fairly illumines it. She puts it all there to him—almost as if speaking of others. She even urges with exaggeration, almost with extravagance, his not disappointing a person who has made such an effort for him. Of course she's in love with him, Mrs. Newsome; but

---

3. In the paragraph omitted here James notes the developing relationship between Strether and Miss Gostrey, which culminates in Strether's admission that Mrs. Newsome has, in effect, proposed to him.

for many women that wouldn't have availed—the proceeding would have been too unusual. She herself, she, Miss Gostrey, would really like to know the person capable of it: she must be quite too wonderful. She will be, at all events, clearly, this heroic lady, his providence. Rich, clever, powerful, she will look after him in all sorts of charming ways, and guarantee and protect his future. Therefore he mustn't let her back out. He must *do* the thing he came out for. He must carry the young man home in triumph and be led to the altar as his reward. She gives the whole thing a humourous turn but we get from it all we need. Strether disclaims, deprecates, but really shows himself as so bewildered—that is, so affected both with dazzlement and doubt—over this particular element of his situation, that his condition constitutes of itself a kind of testimony. Yet, superficially, he refuses to recognize in Miss Gostrey's picture anything but a free joke; and to make his disclaimer appear the more sincere, he abounds in her sense and jokes *with* her. 'She won't then, you feel, if I *don't*?'

'Won't, you mean, stick to her offer if you don't capture the child? Surely not, no song no supper. So you *must* capture him. Oh, I see what you're thinking—that Paris is an awful place, and that it may be awfully difficult. But it will be all the more fun.'

'Fun?' poor Strether rather ruefully echoes.

'It's just the sort of job,' she replies, 'that's really, I assure you, in my line and that I should be quite ready to hand in an estimate for. Upon my word, I'd take the order.'

'I wish to goodness then you would!' her companion laughs. 'It would save me a lot of trouble!'

'Well, I'll save you,' she responds, 'all the trouble I can.' And the little scene, with its climax, marks the culmination, as I have indicated, of my Preliminary.

II[4]

* * * There is in other words a particular occasion on which everything—by which I mean a lot of accumulated perception and emotion—seems to culminate for Strether. I 'do' the occasion and the picture, evoke the place and influences, multiply so far as may be, the different sources of impression for our poor fermenting friend—the persons, figures, strangenesses, newnesses there present; give, above all, the wonderful intensity, oddity, amenity of the general intellectual, colloquial air. It's a real date for Strether. Chad's two friends, Mme de

---

4. At the beginning of Part II James describes Strether's sense of ease and refreshment in Paris. He inquires immediately after Chad and meets Glenn Burbage (little Bilham) and other friends. (James notes that their general fondness for Strether is "a bad note for his intensity of identity.") When Chad finally appears Strether is astonished to find him so changed, so "saved" as Maria Gostrey claims by the woman in question. James then leads up to the garden scene of his original "germ."

Vionnet and her daughter, are, happily, at last there; and there it is, very much in the same beautiful old garden that my original anecdote gives me, that our hero's introduction to them takes place. But this is an occasion on which, through relations already existing for her, Miss Gostrey is also on the ground; whereupon, lo and behold, once in presence, it turns out that Mme de Vionnet is a person she has already known, an acquaintance of a previous time—a time both previous to Mme de Vionnet's marriage and subsequent to it—whom she has lost sight of. The identity of this lady—through Strether's not having got her name right in speaking of her, or having forgotten it or not pro-nounced it—has not, antecedently to this encounter, come up between them sharply enough for Miss Gostrey to have been guided: so that when she does meet, in Strether's company, Chad's vaunted ladies, she finds it a surprise to be able to fit them in to facts actually known to her. These facts she produces afterwards for Strether, and they are indeed all to Mme de Vionnet's credit—in spite of the circumstance that she is living apart from her husband. By the time, at any rate, they are known in this measure to Strether, the impression, as it were, has been made upon him by the charming woman herself: inasmuch as it now becomes of the essence of the business, becomes vividly and importantly so, that Mme de Vionnet *is* charming, and that he fully recognizes her as such. She is young (that is, she is thirty-eight), bright, graceful, kind, sym-pathetic, interesting—and doesn't alarm him by being dazzlingly clever (which is the cleverest thing *in* her!). Without having anything that he immediately feels to be positive beauty, she has a face, and a general air and aspect, that singularly speak to him. He likes no less, also, the way she receives him, lends herself to the reference made to him by Chad for her, and to the reference made to *her* by Chad for Strether himself. She lends herself to everything, in short, with the friendliest ease, and strikes our hero from the first—which is the most particular note of all—as a kind of person he has absolutely never seen, nor ever, with any distinctness, dreamed of.

And yet it's not in the least that he has fallen in love with her, or is at all likely to do so. Her charm is independent of that for him, and gratifies some more distinctively disinterested aesthetic, intellectual, so-cial, even, so to speak, historic sense in him, which has never yet been *à pareille fête,*[5] never found itself so called to the front. She shows him her daughter, a girl of seventeen, who strikes him as almost as much of a revelation; a little tender flower of shy and exquisite good-breeding; different again, in her way and degree, from pretty little girls of seventeen as hitherto known to him. Above all she speaks to him of Chad after a fashion that intensifies his consciousness, his suspicion, as it were, of differences. Chad's being in confirmed relation with her at all, her being

5. At such a feast.

interested in Chad and at all socially bound up with him: these things have for Strether—and with all due deference, with all allowance made, for the young man's improved and transformed state—an element of mystification, of slight perplexity, even from the first hour: such an odd sort of personal, or social promotion or transposition do they seem to represent for the boy as known to him in other lights. However, this whole occasion puts so many new meanings into things, does its little part toward shifting so many landmarks and confounding so many small assumptions, that perhaps one case of ambiguity doesn't count much more than another. His judgments, conclusions, discriminations are more or less in solution—in the pot, on the fire, stewing and simmering again, waiting to come up in what will be doubtless new combinations. This whole occasion, I repeat, is a picture and an admonition for him; and among the things it does, it throws him again with the young artist-man, Chad's friend, whom he likes, who is acuter, more 'intellectual' and aesthetic, than Chad, and with whom he has some amusing and suggestive moments. With his enlarged and intensified vision of a life containing—though indeed, by what he makes out, also more or less lacking—ingredients and influences closed to him and, at his actual age, forfeited and foregone, the 'too late' comes immensely home to him, yet only to stir in him the impulse to do the whole thing at least an imaginative justice. He can't, at such a time of day, begin to live—for he feels, besides, with all the rush of the reaction against his past, that he *hasn't* lived: yet there stirs in him a dumb passion of desire, of rebellion, of God knows what, in respect to his still snatching a little super-sensual hour, a kind of vicarious joy, in that *freedom of another* which he has found himself, by an extraordinary turn of the wheel, committed to weigh in the balance: a connection not, however, on the spot, so much taking in Chad's case as that of young Burbage before-mentioned, whose own sense of his opportunities strikes him as perhaps not quite adequate. It's to young Burbage, at any rate, that he indulges in some such little outburst as the one retailed in my preliminary pages—the conditions and effect of which my story more or less repro-duces. I leave nothing untouched in fine, that may make of this Sunday afternoon in the old Paris garden, in a circle profuse in intimations, the kind of moral 'dishing' for Strether that I have already glanced at.

When they separate he feels that a relation, a link, of a sort, that will have both more to give him and to ask of him, has formed itself for him with Mme de Vionnet. She asks him to come and see her; she wants to see him again; she is gracious, encouraging, benevolent: and yet all for what? Mysteries, mysteries: he stands in a world of mystery. He doesn't at all know her really—he feels that; but queerer yet is it that he feels he doesn't at all really, at this time of day, know even himself. Has she addressed herself to some conception of him purely delusive and erroneous?—or to some element in him of which he has himself been unconscious, but which she has, with prodigious penetration, made out, in half an hour, as a possibility? Well, he will see.

He walks away, through the grave and impressive old streets of the Faubourg Saint-Germain, with Miss Gostrey, and as soon as they have got, after a spell of silence at first, to a certain distance, he puts her, stopping short, the abrupt question, full of tacit references: 'Isn't it for her daughter . . . ?'

'That she's nursing your young friend?' They have stopped on a quiet corner of the Rue de l'Université; the day and the hour are tranquil there, and the straight, narrow vista of the austere, aristocratic street stretches before them. For a moment they look at each other, and Strether's companion just visibly hesitates. 'Yes,' she then brings out with decision; and after their eyes have again met they resume their walk; in the course of which—for he sees her home—she is very interesting about Mme de Vionnet, whom she also particularly rejoices to have encountered again. Their acquaintance goes back to old days of school at Geneva, where this charming woman was a *pensionnaire*[6] slightly older, but not much, than herself; a rather isolated young thing, the daughter of a French father and an English mother who, left a widow, had married again—married some second foreigner. The girl was then clever, already charming, polyglot, speaking French and English, and even German, equally well, doing everything, in fact, well that she touched. Afterwards, however, it appeared that she had not had a happy hand at marrying. Miss Gostrey, after a considerable interval, had again met her; by which time her mother, otherwise engaged and entangled, impatient, preoccupied, precipitate, had made for her a summary match, assisted by her possession of a certain sufficient *dot*,[7] with a Frenchman of supposedly the best condition, who yet, in spite of it, had not at all turned out well. Miss Gostrey has lights on the Comte de Vionnet, with whom his young wife was still living at the moment of this second period of observation. But things had even then been ominous, and the tolerably prompt separation, of which she had also heard, was not a thing to surprise her. She believes the husband still to be living and the pair to be on irreconcileable terms; but she also knows how little there can be a question for them of divorce, each of them belonging to the kind of *monde* that, in France, doesn't practice it. Of the kind of *monde* they do belong to she gives Strether all due, all manageable or communicable, notion, putting the presumptions before him vividly and interestingly enough. She particularises, makes him understand it—all of which, however, are processes rather concerning the author than the reader. Strether's acquaintance with Mme de Vionnet, and the conditions of the lady's identity and existence, are, in fine, ushered in—as to which it is sufficient that Miss Gostrey is helpful.

6. Boarder.
7. Dowry.

Strether, at all events, on the occasion I speak of, sees her home, but doesn't go in, having at the moment another engagement. So, before her door, reverting, taking things up again, they have another word. 'Yes, you *do* see,' he asks, 'don't you? that charming little girl as having done it?'

But she is not, for the instant, all there. 'Done what?'

'Why, saved Chad.'

'Oh yes—as we said. One sees it. The charming little girl has done it. It's *she* who has saved Chad.' And on this they separate.[8]

* * * But meanwhile Strether has had to report to his mother— finding it more and more difficult to do so with lucidity; and meanwhile, further, he has been to see Mme de Vionnet. From this latter moment his own attitude, mission, simplicity and cogency of position on the whole question in which his presence in Paris has originated—from this latter moment these things undergo inevitable modification. A whole process begins to take form in him which is of the core of the subject, and the steps and shade in the representation of which I cannot pretend here to adumbrate. Chad's case becomes for him a concrete case in a kind of big general question that his actual experience keeps more and more putting to him; so that he finds himself each day more in the presence of a responsibility much less simple than the one he had braced himself to incur. And Mme de Vionnet becomes the most determinant cause of this revolution, this interesting process—becomes so simply by being, and by showing herself, exactly what she is. Though there are always, and more than enough, round about Strether, mysteries, am-biguities and things equivocal, yet one or two convictions and impres-sions thicken for him, stiffen, harden—and one of these is the estimate of the value of such a relation, for any young man, as such a woman as Mme de Vionnet represents. The value of this relation grows clear and high, to his eyes; and almost grotesque becomes the kind of revision he has to make of the bundle of notions with which he started from home. They all cluster about a woman, and there *is* a woman, most unmistakeably and strikingly. But it's a different thing from what he has mapped out to come to plead, to come to pull, against *her.* The person of most personal charm, indisputably, that poor Strether has ever met, arrays herself on one side, and the group of interests and associations on behalf of which he has proposed to carry Chad off arrays itself on the other. The bustling business at home, the mercantile mandate, the counter, the ledger, the bank, the 'advertising interest,' embody mainly the special phase of civilization to which he must recall his charge— and a totally other cluster of forces weave the adverse tangle. Singularly, admirably Mme de Vionnet comes after a little to stand, with Strether, for most of the things that make the *charm* of civilization as he now

8. James goes on to explain Strether's new theory that Chad is in love with Mlle de Vionnet.

revises and imaginatively reconstructs, morally reconsiders, so to speak, civilization.

This is a summary sketch of what takes place in my hero's spirit in consequence of this new contact—and I needn't insist on the necessity weighing on the author to paint the contact in a manner to justify it. The whole thing must more or less stand or fall by the way in which both Strether and Mme de Vionnet are done. The latter, of course, is a magnificent little subject, and the artist must be left alone with her. There is much in her—alas, for the artist's ease, *too* much. But the thing none the less works out. One of its workings is that, even to Strether's consciousness, she *knows* what she wishes and tries for. She isn't spoiled for him by his analysis of the situation. What is spoiled for him, on the other hand, is his freedom of communication with Mrs. Newsome, which he has sought to make possible by making it really candid, by throwing his whole vision of the matter upon her intelligence and her sympathy. He tells her what he sees. He tells her what he does. He tells her what he thinks. He tells her what he feels. The more, at this point, everything grows, the more he tries, by letter, to keep her in touch with it. Of course he reflects that, after all, what he is doing isn't the very definite thing he came out to do—which was to bring Chad home. Instead of there being representable for her in his life a detachment, a removal, from the female element, there can only strike her as being a greater and stranger abundance of it, and in forms difficult to give her, really, a just notion of. As things go, none the less, Strether has by this time been in a manner frank with Chad as well—only, by the time that hour is able to strike, the young man is shrewd enough himself to make out that, for consistency on his friend's part, the assault is made, the charge sounded, too late. Chad has had a kind of happy instinct in making things play on to the juncture at which poor Strether has become sceptical—at which, accordingly, consequently, he can only do his business at a sore disadvantage. The young man declines to meet any of the propositions with which his visitor is charged—and yet has the covert triumph of seeing that visitor not throw up the game. Strether doesn't break off and go home—Strether stays on and fairly consecrates the situation by his anxious presence. This is what Chad sees, and what Mme de Vionnet sees, and what Strether himself sees, and sees that they see, and sees above all that the lady at home sees. He isn't straight, as it may be called, and he knows it; isn't at all straight after he finds himself not only consenting, but liking, to discuss the question with Mme de Vionnet herself—or even with Miss Gostrey. It isn't a question he came out to discuss at all. He came out to do what he could, but everything is altered for him by the fact that nothing, damn it, is as simple as his scheme. Chad was to have been simple, for instance; but even Chad isn't. Least of all is he now himself. What would have been straight would have been so almost equally, as it were, in either case.

If it would have been simple to be able to 'write back': 'It's all right; he consents to come; I come with him, I bring him, only just taking a little turn off with him—perhaps to Norway and Sweden; in which case we sail about the middle of next month': so likewise it would have been comparatively plain-going to have to say: 'He absolutely won't come at all—and you'll have to come out yourself; so that, so far as I'm concerned, it's a failure, and I shall just look about me a bit on my own hook and take ship to rejoin you three or four weeks hence'—so likewise, I repeat, *that* would have been, though disappointing, yet manageable, natural and final. But somehow, on what *does* take place everything is different. Nothing is manageable, nothing final—nothing, above all, for poor Strether, natural. I repeat that he has almost a sense of the uncanny. I repeat, as a good little note of his fallacious forecast, that he has really thought, as a 'resource,' as a clever stroke, of the way it might have eased difficulties off just to *coax* Chad aside for some small sanitary and, as it were, disinfecting jaunt through some one of those regions vaguely figuring to Strether as the more marked homes and haunts of earnestness. If there are smiles for this *naïveté* later, the first smiles are yet all his very own. There is a passage of irony for him, in the connection, with Miss Gostrey. Well, he finds himself sinking, as I say, up to his middle in the Difference—difference from what he expected, difference in Chad, difference in everything; and the Difference, I also again say, is what I give.

'No: Chad won't come'—he has, accordingly, presently to communicate that. But what he has *not* to communicate with it is that he will therefore reappear without him. He won't reappear without him—that is practically what he has very soon to let Mrs. Newsome see; and as he can't reappear *with* him the complication is one that takes, so far as she is concerned, a good deal of explaining. Candid and explicit as he meanwhile tries to be, there are things he *can't* explain. It has been part of his characteristic understanding with the lady at home, and part of her own with him, that if Chad is really, as may be so well on the cards, painfully unamenable, he himself is not—out of any excessive conscience in respect to service or duty owing, to remain too long mixed up, too long in a state of contact that was originally at best rather to be deprecated. That last is a distinct note, one of a great many even, in the relation of Strether and Mrs. Newsome—the feeling she has so much had *for* him, the anxious, scrupulous feeling; which is not wholly unlike, moreover, the state of mind he has really, beforehand, rather been in about himself. They have between them—they had it, at least, to begin with almost equally—a sense that he can't morally, or even personally, cheapen himself too much in the business, can't too long hang about it, rub against it, give himself away for it. *She,* in fact, is very high and fine in all this view of it; is very high and fine indeed altogether—to the point even of being ready rather to let Chad go than to regard with any complacency the prostitution, so to speak, of poor Strether. Reflections and reverberations of all this play over the scene. Chad has meanwhile continued to deny, however, to our friend that he has his eye on Mlle de Vionnet, that her mother has, to any such end, hers on him, and that the question of his marrying the girl has come up between them. They are simply all three the best of friends, and they have made for him a kind of charming second home. Isn't that enough? He puts the case to Strether with every appearance of frankness—pleads quite explicitly for the kind of privilege it is to be *as* he is with *ces dames*, who weren't at all likely to have taken up with one of his type, and who have been, simply, incredibly nice and charming to him. He speaks of the matter as really quite a recognized anomaly—but that doesn't diminish the value he sets on it. His effect on Strether is, curiously, that of moving him without really quite convincing him; the latter assents, in a word, without quite believing. He throws himself moreover again, as it were, on Miss Gostrey; and she again tells him to let her shrewdness answer for it that the question of the marriage is really—though disavowed for whatever reasons of prudence and diplomacy, whatever precautions required by the possible interference of the obnoxious Monsieur de Vionnet—the tie. Strether takes this from her, fitting it fairly into impressions of his own; though there is one thing that does stick in his crop: the question, namely, of why Chad won't at least go home for long enough to see his mother herself and have things out with her at Worcester. Chad promises of course to do this—admits the propriety of it; yet evidently has no intention of doing it at all soon. His perpetual postponement has therefore a motive—is the result of some obscure coercion; and Strether of course connects Mme de Vionnet with it. Yet at the same time he doesn't see her own reasons, or why she should have so peculiarly much to fear. In fine he goes on from day to day and from week to week; only, when he has done so a certain time, he finds himself landed in the *volte-face*[9] in which the process I have described as taking place in him is practically to culminate. Various special things, a business-chance of importance in particular, depend for Chad upon an immediate change of life, a general radical rupture; and yet one fine day, in the presence of news from home that has brought everything immensely to a head, Strether's emphatic word to him is suddenly: 'No then—don't. I seem to see my "mission" differently. Stay as you are.'

'And will you then,' says the young man, wonderfully pleased and impressed, 'see me through?'

Strether has to think another moment; then he takes his jump. 'I'll see you through.'

But immediately afterwards, to make up for this grave inconsequence, he cables to his friend at home that his recommendation to her is, if

9. About-face.

she at all conveniently can, to come straight out. He more than half then, for a day or two, expects her; but two or three things may happen, and he holds himself in suspense—as also in readiness. She will either cable that she starts, or she will cable to him, more or less emphatically, and rather more than less, to come straight back to *her*. He has thought it over, and if she does so, believes that he will do it: though now really seeing how little he wants to. However, at the expectant word from her he *will*—yes, positively, he will. He gets no answer for three or four days, during which he is awfully restless, and yet with it all has a queer sense of freedom hitherto unknown to him. He *will* go—yes, again, if she calls; but even if he does go things will be somehow, and rather strangely, different: and his sense of freedom is partly just in *that*. Then at the end of the waiting a reply comes. But it proves to be neither a summons to Strether nor an announcement of Mrs. Newsome's embarkation. It is different—something he hadn't thought of. It announces the immediate departure of the Pococks—which is a surprise. But Strether sees a good deal in it—sees more the more he thinks.

III

Mrs. Pocock, as has been mentioned, is the daughter of Mrs. Newsome, Chad's elder sister, married to a partner in the family business, whose own young sister, a girl of about the same age as Mlle de Vionnet, accompanies them. They promptly arrive—a young couple of extremely marked attributes—as little Mamie Pocock is, in her way, the same: a lively (in their way) young American pair, who have been to Europe once before—immediately after their marriage; and consider (so far at least as Mrs. Pocock is concerned) that they know it very well. I can't 'do' this trio for you here—and they will take all proper doing in the book, where they will be adequately attended to; I limit myself to designating their office, which is in a manner that of rather tacitly, coldly and austerely superseding and suspending Strether in *his* function; that at all events of representing Mrs. Newsome on the spot and putting in their plea on behalf of the business, on behalf of the family, on behalf of propriety, on behalf of his country, on behalf of all the claims that Strether appears to have handled so ineffectually. As Mrs. Newsome remains personally out of the action, so now she is represented in it by these fresh emissaries. But Mrs. Pocock herself is the one who principally, or exclusively, counts in this respect; Mrs. Pocock is a sharp type and (D.V.)[1] a vivid picture; Mrs. Pocock makes for interest and entertainment. She brings, as it were, her mother's ultimatum—which is that if Chad doesn't come home immediately he needn't, so far as his material advantage is concerned, ever come home at all; Mrs. Newsome being in possession of options and having command of alternatives upon

1. *Deo Volente*—God willing.

which she is actually free to close. Strether is confronted thus with the whole crisis and, most sharply of all, with what it means for himself. This latter element is more or less implied—or even, doubtless, I shall make it explicit; the remarkable young woman, who has nothing in common with her brother, being fully *au courant* of the state of affairs between her mother and their friend, and empowered to speak and act, conscientiously, lucidly, indignantly, if necessary, *for* that lady. Mrs. Pocock arrives, in other words, with a great deal of accumulated resentment, disapproval, virtue, surprise. Her husband, in truth, is on quite another foot; her husband is an example, in characteristically vulgar form, and with all due humourous effect, of the same 'fatal' effect of European opportunities on characters giving way too freely, which Strether more subtly embodies. Pocock, a traitor in the camp, a humourous, surreptitious backer of his brother-in-law and their friend does, in short, all he can to amuse us. He has his personal function, in a word—for which he must be trusted. All the complexities of the drama deepen here; things grow closer and more tense. Poor Waymark, thrown off from Strether, whose strange laxities and perversities he deplores, whose general sensibility and surrender, as he can't help thinking them, he regards as the reverse of edifying, rebounds to Mrs. Pocock, who strikes up with him an alliance that they both regard as rather a fine, free intimacy—almost a 'European' affair. They stand together, they confer together, they exult and lament together, go about together generally, hold the same opinions and invoke the same conclusions, cheer and comfort and sustain each other. The whole comedy, or tragedy, the drama, whatever we call it, of Strether's and Chad's encounter of the new complications and relations springing from the Pococks' presence, from the necessity, for instance, bravely to confront them with Mme de Vionnet and her daughter, and to confront Mme de Vionnet and her daughter with *them*—this is a thing, I need scarcely say, I am not trying thus, *currente calamo*[2] to formulate. Mme de Vionnet, in it all, is magnificent; Mme de Vionnet is wonderful; but these things are no more than what she is throughout. I repeat that, little as I project her here—for the smallest development of that attempt would take me too far—I must be trusted with her. Mrs. Newsome and Mrs. Pocock have hatched it between them that *one* aid to the recovery of Chad may be possibly just this putting in his path of the little Pocock girl. Strange and ignorant complacencies, fathomless fallacies, have attended this idea. She is thus produced in Paris for the young man's benefit, and is thus seen to figure face to face with and in opposition to the little Vionnet girl—who is as wonderful, in her way, about this introduced representative of a different type of manners, as her mother. Contrasts and oppositions naturally here play straight up. The Vionnets and the Po-

---

2. Writing offhand (*lit.*, with a running pen).

cocks, Chad and his sister, Pocock and his brother-in-law, Chad and
Pocock's sister, Strether and Pocock, Pocock and Strether, Strether and
everyone and everything, but Strether and Mrs. Pocock in especial, with
everything brought to a head by *her*—there is no lack of stuff; above all
as, on the very eve of the last-named lady's arrival, a sharp thing has
happened for Strether. * * *[3]

She has gone, but meanwhile the fact of Chad's definite *non-*
engagement, and with it the breakdown of the most presentable of the
grounds for promoting, for condoning, his recalcitrance has had to be
produced, has had inevitably to come straight up, for Mrs. Pocock. It
facilitates, of course, her position, puts an arm in her hand. What motive
that can conceivably remain *is* then presentable? She is moreover more
fully armed now—or by so much the less obstructed—in respect to her
putting forward her little sister-in-law. But we see what comes of that.
She sees, and has to make her mother see—constantly, as she is, communicating and cabling (nothing having ever been known like the cabling that goes on—alarming even to Chad, immensely amusing to
Pocock, fraught with strange possibilities for Strether and prodigious to
Mme de Vionnet). Precipitated thus is the kind of *crux* in his position
that Mrs. Pocock's manner of acting for her mother has already prepared.
More than she has yet done, as it were, she has it out with Strether why
they have come. She puts it in its light, and she gives him the warning
that she herself believes to be admirably disinterested and magnanimous,
purely conscientious and solicitous. I should premise that her brother
has put it to her, on her having to recognize the humiliating futility of
her attempt to catch him with any such bait as Miss Pocock, that, in
respect to his consenting to do what appears to them all so imperative
at home, he will stand or fall then by what Strether now says, will let
the latter absolutely answer for him, determine his line, determine,
quite, as it practically is, his fate. This is a special and superior stroke
of Chad's—this inspiration of throwing himself, at the psychological
moment, thus completely on our friend. But the inspiration has come,
he has taken the measure of the dependence that, for backing him up,
he can really place on Strether; and now, acting *on* that dependence,
he passes to his sister his word of honour. The scene between them
moreover has had other elements—elements rather confounding to some
of Mrs. Pocock's complacencies: he really lets fly at her, that is, for the
folly of her supposing him amenable to her ridiculous view of the little
Pocock. He is fairly angry with her—in respect to what she has thus
taken *him* for; and, though he has, to do him justice, tried not to be
rude, he has raised for her a sufficiently startling and bewildering curtain,
revealed to her, in a manner that she feels to be quite lurid and that

3. James explains here Strether's learning of Mlle de Vionnet's approaching marriage. When he
   reproaches Maria Gostrey about this, she admits misleading him for his own good—but won't
   say why.

makes her shudder off across the sea, the intimate difference now existing in their standards of value. She is *proud* of the little Pocock. *Why* the inspiration just mentioned—the inspiration of standing or falling by Strether's final word—has thus operated in Chad, we also interestingly know. The reason is partly the result of definite passages between them—at one of which I have already glanced; passages from which Chad had eagerly snatched Strether's general sense that, really, the young man has succeeded in growing, by whatever obscure, whatever nefarious process, comparatively too civilized for *him*, Strether, to find it in his responsible conscience to urge as a substitute for that process a mere relapse to the precious place—beautiful business-place, with a big chance for any, for every, new assertion of the paternal smartness, though it may be—which has, at much inconvenience to the family interest, been kept, or rather been all but lost, for him at home. That vision of Strether's attitude is part of the ground, I say, on which Chad's stand to Mrs. Pocock is made; but he has also been confirmed and illuminated by the so considerable acuter judgment and observation of Mme de Vionnet, who has not lost, not wasted her time with Strether, and has answered to Chad for the degree to which they can count on him. She has worked, in fine, and the necessary effect has been produced. What takes place accordingly is, as I have indicated, Mrs. Pocock's supreme appeal to their good friend, in which she gives her point, all her deputed meaning, its full value.

We know what this full value is, what Strether 'stands to lose' by any perversity or, as Mrs. Newsome's daughter really takes upon herself to brand it, disloyalty. * * *[4] These things, as I say, he can only turn well over—which we assist (as we assist at everything) at the process of his doing. The upshot is, none the less, only the intenser impossibility, to his spirit, of the step just defined. He *can't* go home with Mrs. Pocock, he *won't* go home with Mrs. Pocock; above all it's impossible to him to throw Chad over. He has given him his word that he will see him through—though, at the same time, Chad has given Mrs. Pocock *his* word that he will surrender, once his summons is distinctly pronounced, to Strether's decision. Strether has, in this tighter squeeze of his crisis, to take again a little time, to put every question to himself once again, and clear up, so far as he can, his ambiguities. There are one or two that won't clear up: the fact that the supposition of Chad's designs on Mlle de Vionnet has been dispelled leaves, for instance, a vague residuum of the discomfortable, the equivocal, that he doesn't quite know what to do with. What does anything, what does everything, in the intimacy of a youth after all comparatively crude and a woman after all much older and admirably fine and subtle, mean if it doesn't mean—

---

4. James describes here Mrs. Pocock's rather vulgar account of what Strether will lose. She insists Chad is playing a game, and she urges Strether to abandon Chad and return alone if he can't bring Chad with him.

well, what it might at the worst? There is one thing indeed that it *may* signify, and to this explanation Strether sufficiently clings. It *is*, in the light of it, the mother, not the daughter, that Chad has all the while been in love with, and it's in respect to the mother that he is hanging on and on. He has the inextinguishable hope of some turn of the situation that may render their marriage possible. She may consent to a divorce, or M. de Vionnet may, by a kind and just Providence, suddenly and happily be snuffed out. Such are conceivably, to Chad's mind, by Strether's interpretation, the possibilities; and others, that match them, may prevail in that of Mme de Vionnet herself: though *her* 'hanging on' is, at the best, a phenomenon requiring at once more analysis and more elucidation. What requires very little of either, however, and what thereby has most to contribute to our friend's growing stiffness of back, is that—confound the whole thing—he has by this time *seen* too much, felt too much, to retrace his steps to his old standpoint. The distance that separates him from it is, measured by mere dates, of the slightest, but it is virtually ground that he has got for ever behind him. He is conscious of his evolution; he likes it—wouldn't for the world not have had it; albeit that he fully sees how fatal, in a manner, it has been for him. But if he's dished, he *is*, and all that is left for him is to say what he can as mere interesting, inconvenient experience. He is out of pocket by it, clearly, materially; but he has a handful of gold-pieces for imagination and memory. Mrs. Pocock has signified to him that she awaits his supreme reply, awaits his final beneficent interposition with Chad; and, for congruity, he conforms by appearing to take three days for the benefit of the doubt. His intention is to cultivate, during this period, such detachment as he may; to get off somewhere by himself; to see, for a little, nothing of Chad, of Mme de Vionnet, or of Mrs. Newsome's representative—and then come back with his reply. He's rather bored with them all, *en fin de compte*,[5] as the people about him say; he is even a little overdone with other people's adventures, and wouldn't mind a trifling one on his own account, which should yield him a little less worry. Miss Gostrey, after the absence on the eve of which he took leave of her, has, to his knowledge, returned; but he doesn't want particularly to see even *her*. Still less does he wish to see Waymark, who, for that matter, has ended, as a result of the spectacle of his behaviour, by cultivating an estrangement from him that makes Strether half melancholy (so almost insanely odd, or madly morbid, it is) and half merry.

What does in fact befall during this little interval is that he tumbles for two or three days, in spite of himself, into the arms of poor solitarily-prowling Pocock, whom the preoccupations of the latter's wife, her earnest exchange of impressions and convictions with Waymark in es-

5. Taking everything into account.

pecial, have left at the mercy of a good deal of more or less consoled[?][6] leisure. Strether is kind to him, easy with him, amused at him, and, above all, abundantly conscious of *his* reactions and 'game.' Pocock doesn't at all really want Chad brought back—doesn't believe in him as an active element in the business, and doesn't require him as an additional participant in what has been roughly denominated the general and particular 'pickings.' But this is one side, and Pocock has his mixture. He is amused at his mother-in-law's baffled state—a state rare for her and which he has never known the joy, so much as he would have liked it, of directly promoting. All his instinct is to promote it now by acting on his rather coarse divination of the nature of Strether's independence, and above all on his still livelier perception of the character of Chad's own. For Strether, at all events, he performs the present function, while they go about together and Strether shows him bits of Paris, things in it that he mightn't otherwise see—though not always the very things he wants; performs the function of representing as vulgarly as possible the whole particular mass of interests at home on behalf of which the long arm has reached itself out for Chad. * * *[7] What this reflection, roughly stated, amounts to then is: 'No, I'll be hanged if I purchase the certainty of being coddled for the rest of my days by going straight against the way in which all these impressions and suggestions of the last three months have made me feel, and like to feel, and want to feel. Whatever is the matter with Chad, it strikes me as having done more for him as a man and a gentleman than would have been done, or than will yet be done, by his having remained in, or being again introduced and compressed into, the box that we have flattered ourselves can be once more made to contain him. It has really made him quite over. As between Mme de Vionnet and the advertising-department, then, I decide for Mme de Vionnet, and if my expression, my action *is* to tip down the scale, why, let it tip, and I'll take the consequences. They will really, whatever they may be, immensely interest, and in their way, doubtless, even amuse me. They will represent something—meagre and belated and indirect and absurd as it may be—that I shall have done for my poor old infatuated and imaginative self. I didn't know I had it in me, and it's worth all the journey and all the worry to have found out. It will have cost me—I feel sure, it's in my bones, I forecast the whole thing—everything that my engagement to that wonderful woman at home, so full of high qualities too, represents and promises; but I'm not going to let such a circumstance prevent me. I'll keep my promise to Chad; I'll say to him: "Do as the interest of your situation *here* most

6. James's typescript has "concoled" here.
7. James describes here how Pocock and Pocock's talk of Chad's father's unsavory practices affect Strether, who realizes that the wavering Chad is being summoned home to this heritage. Strether also recognizes that marriage to Mrs. Newsome means that he too will have to accept some of this heritage.

prescribes—and say frankly and freely that it's the sense in which I've positively advised you." I stand by that—and *vogue la galère!*[8] * * *
* * * Strether has it then, as I say, all ready, and in this condition he has taken the train to one of the suburbs of Paris quite at random, scarce knowing, and not much caring, where he is. The effect of his complete decision is a queer sense of freedom and almost of amusement. It's a lovely day of early summer; the aspect of things is such as to charm and beguile him—the air full of pictures and felicities and hints for future memory. Suddenly, with these predispositions, in a suburban village by the river, a place where people come out from Paris to boat, to dine, to dance, to make love, to do anything they like, he comes upon Mme de Vionnet and Chad together—Mme de Vionnet and Chad presented somehow in a light that, in spite of all preparation and previous perplexity, of all embarrassing questions and satisfactory and unsatisfactory answers, considerably startles and pulls him up. The case shows them, somehow, as they have not yet been shown; it represents them as positively and indubitably intimate with the last intimacy; it is, in a word, full, for Strether, of informing and convincing things. He meets it then and there as he can—which is the way they also, conscious, inconvenienced, but carrying the whole thing bravely off, deal, on their side, with the encounter. Each side acquits itself with such discretion and ease as it can command; and the passage between them is in fine full of interest. Of course I am not attempting in any degree whatever to represent or render it here, or to do more than thus glance at it and pass. They separate, on pretexts, and Strether goes back to Paris alone. But he goes back with a deeper and stranger sense, a sense that his responsibility is verily deep and sharp. It staggers him a little, and he has to brace himself afresh; he doesn't back down from his decision, but he rather wishes the incident hadn't occurred. At the same time he feels rather ashamed—ashamed, I mean, of his regret; for the essence of his attitude to himself on the whole business has been that what he *is* moved to he wants not to shirk. Here is a beautiful chance then not to shirk. He looks what he has seen in the face; he passes a discomfortable night on it; that is one way not to shirk. There are other ways too, and he vigorously cultivates them, for the next twenty-four hours, all. He shakes himself, snubs and scolds himself, brings himself sternly and rigidly into line. Why should he pusillanimously wish he mightn't so sharply have *known*, since all the value of his total episode, and all the enjoyment of it, has precisely been that 'knowing' was the effect of it? He is, all the same, rather inconsequently disposed not to go to Mrs. Pocock that very day with his answer; and while, exactly, he is hesitating as to the positively final immediacy and urgency of this step, another incident,

8. Let's risk it! (*lit.*, row the galley). James notes here that Strether finally leaves Pocock. Meanwhile Mme de Vionnet now knows that Strether has the deciding vote as to whether Chad stays or goes.

not, superficially, at least, more simplifying than the previous, somewhat surprisingly overtakes him. He receives a visit from Mme de Vionnet, and Mme de Vionnet's visit is a wonderful affair, but which, again, I can, beyond naming it, really give you here no more than I have given you anything else. It gives her away to him—which is the last thing he had expected anything to do; and gives her away as the consequence of her fears. It's her fears, her weakness now, her surprising spilling of her cards, that definitely tell him, face to face, what he had previously neither really made out for himself, nor really dismissed: the strange fact—of an order both so obscure and so recorded—of the passion of this accomplished woman of almost forty for their so imperfectly accomplished young friend of a dozen years less. Strether is in the presence of more things than he has yet had to count with, things by no means, doubtless, explicitly in his book; but with which, pitying the remarkable woman all the more that her present proceeding reduces her, for the hour, in some respects, to a tolerably common category, he does his best to get, as it were, into relation. He sees and understands, and such is the force in him of his alien and awkward tradition, that he has, almost like a gasping spectator at a thrilling play, to *see* himself see and understand. Mme de Vionnet is, precisely like some woman less clever and less rare, in a 'funk' about the possible loss of Chad. He has become a cherished necessity to her. Her passion simplifies and abases her; ranges her in a category; presents her as a case; does, in short, more things than I can now enumerate. Infinite tact and delicacy of *presentation* of course lavished on all this. But the upshot of it, after all, is but to confirm Strether's vision of the influence and the benefit the situation has represented for Chad. If he has found him transformed, that effect ceases to be wonderful in the presence, so vividly, of the forces making for it. Mme de Vionnet's visit is at any rate a frightened appeal. She comes to entreat him to *keep* Chad for her. They have both got scared the day before, but she in particular, and the more, all night, her fears and her imagination have dwelt on it, as to the way their friend may be practically affected by the impression they were conscious of making on him. She beseeches him not to be practically affected. She tells him, shows him, proves to him, how good she is for Chad. He is rueful as to assenting to that, but he is helpless as to denying it, and, not to multiply my words here, he at all events dismisses her with the reassurance that his view is his view, that he doesn't mean to take back any word he has given, that his mind was in fact, the day before, all made up to confirm it; and that, in fine, no 'impression' of anything or anybody now will have made any difference. Besides, for that matter, what has she supposed he had supposed? He has, really and truly, in his 'secret heart,' not known what he has supposed—and hence his sharp emotion, the upset to his nerves, on the previous day. But he doesn't tell Mme de Vionnet that.

She leaves him, and he does nothing that day—Chad, meanwhile, 'lying low' very markedly; but on the morrow he goes and reports himself to Mrs. Pocock. If his responsibility has been complicated and thickened it proves, none the less, not, after all, too much for him. He tells her —and the announcement is practically made to Mrs. Newsome—that he has thought over everything he has owed it to her to think over since their last interview, but that his attitude remains just what he was then obliged to let her fear it to be. He 'sides,' so to speak, with Chad; he holds that Chad, by meeting his mother's views, will give up more than he gains, and he has frankly expressed himself to him in that sense. He recognizes the effect his words, of which he has counted the cost, will probably have; but he has not been able to act in any other way. I pass briefly, for you, over this juncture, and over the effect of it on the Pocock party, who, with Waymark, shocked and scandalised—approximately or vulgarly speaking—in their train, are quickly determined by it to departure and disappearance. They withdraw from the scene, they return straightway home, with all the proper circumstances and concomitants. Strether has immediately afterwards gone to Chad and told him what he has done; his sentiment about him being that he can't quite, all the same, wash his hands of him. On the other hand, what can he do more for him than he has already done? He lingers in Paris a little—he has wanted to see the situation 'through.' But with the direction events have taken from him, it sufficiently comes over him that they *are* through. His imagination of them drops, and if he rather glosses over for the pair the quantity they have cost him, the last tribute strikes him, at last, as the very most he can manage. He does gloss it over—with Chad at least; he carries out, to his utmost, the spirit of his promise to 'make it all right.' That is a pious misrepresentation, in the interest of Chad's sta- bility, absolutely precious, now, to Strether's imagination: but it is a part of the amusement and the harmless *panache*[9] of his proceeding. He measures exactly, himself, the situation. He knows he won't make it all right. He knows he can't make it all right. He knows that, for Mrs. Newsome, it's all hideously wrong and must remain so. But he only (that is as with Chad) knows this; and he misrepresents, as I say, the question with what he believes to be a certain success—making the matter, at all events, and without much difficulty, none of Chad's busi- ness. It's the last thing moreover, naturally, that he conceives Chad as being touched by, or conceives, with any intensity, Mme de Vionnet.

After these things have happened, however, and especially after the departure of the Pococks, he has a kind of moral and intellectual drop or arrest—of the whole range of feeling that has kept him up hitherto —which makes him feel that his work is done, that his so strange, half-

9. Flourish.

bitter, half-sweet experience is at an end, that what has happened, through him, has really happened *for* him, for his own spirit, for his own queer sense of things, more than for anyone or anything else, and that now he has no reason for stopping any longer. Now he *will* go back, and he gathers himself up, and he's ready. He has waited till the moment he wished—he couldn't have gone before; the whole affair had become as a thing of his own that he had to watch and accompany, as it were, out of a deep inward necessity, sympathy, curiosity, perversity, if need were, to its conclusion; but he recognizes the conclusion, so far as *he* is concerned with it, when he sees it—recognizes that his hour has sounded. The sound is like the bell of the steamer calling him, from its place at the dock, aboard again, and by the same act ringing down the curtain on the play. He goes back to all the big Difference, over there, that he foresees—the big Difference of his having spoiled himself for any future favour from Mrs. Newsome, and spoiled the poor fatuous Review, as an implication and a consequence, for any future subsidy. These things, and many more things, are before him—evoked, projected, made vivid, made certain. But before he goes, on the eve of his departure, two other things happen which mark, to the extent of their interest and importance, that the curtain has *not* yet quite dropped, the play is not *yet* quite over. The first of these is an interview that he has with Mme de Vionnet, who either comes to see him again or addresses him an earnest request, which he complies with, to come to *her* (I've not yet determined which) after that last scene with Chad to which I have just referred. Of what has passed between them on this occasion she has, of course, immediately received from Chad all tidings, and, affected by it in more than one interesting manner, and moved, in particular, to the deepest gratitude, she has placed herself, in what she feels to be for the last time, in relation with him. On what Chad has told her, repeated to her, of his making everything 'all right,' as regards himself, his personal situation and responsibility, at home, she has her own impressions, suspicions, divinations, and, though she can do nothing *for* poor Strether, as it were, though she sees in him and in his behaviour more things than she can even be explicit about with him, she obeys an irresistible instinct in desiring once more to see him and, however poorly, to thank him. He has not, frankly, from a feeling quite absolute, though difficult to justify or—in this place, for instance—explain, wanted any further vision of Chad or contact with him, and he seeks none, and practically makes any, for the young man himself, impossible, after the just-above-mentioned passage. He has done with *him*, or at any rate feels that Chad has done, and that Chad (immensely, though perhaps after all a trifle ruefully, just a shade regretfully and anxiously, obliged) is ready, on his side, to let him pass away. But as to Mme de Vionnet, it's another affair, and to just a last sight of everything in her that he has found wonderful and abysmal, strange and charming, beautiful and rather dreadful, he thus finally adjusts and treats himself. The meeting, the scene, then, takes place, and is the happy and harmonious *pendant* (from the point of view, I mean, of interest and effect) of the previous one, the one referred to a moment ago, the scene of 'appeal' after Strether's encounter with the pair in the country and her consequent apprehension and commotion. But don't imagine I pretend to give it to you here. I merely mark it with this little cross as probably the most beautiful and interesting morsel in the book, and I would say most handsomely 'done'—say so did I admit that there can be any *difference* of morsels in any self-respecting work-of-art, where the morsel *not* handsomely done simply incurs one's own pity long before the critic—if there *were* a critic!—has cut the eye-teeth of any knowledge of *how* competently to kick it. You must leave me accordingly with this passage and with my treatment of it. It is really the climax— for all it can be made to give and to do, for the force with which it may illustrate and illuminate the subject—toward which the action marches straight from the first. So there it is.

The second of the two situations of which the one just noted is the first deals scarcely less handsomely with Strether's relation with poor Maria Gostrey, and with hers with him—taking it up again effectively, I should say, if it were correct to speak of it as having really at all dropped. But it hasn't really at all dropped; it has only seemed, here, to fall into the background through my not wanting to risk too much to confuse and complicate my statement by insistence, at every point, on its quite continuous function. I have not named Miss Gostrey in sketching the stages of the business after the arrival of the Pococks, but it is, from step to step, with the aid of her confirmed relation to Strether that I show what I need to show. It's a relation the fortunate friction of which projects light, the light of interpretation and illustration, upon all that passes before them, upon all causes and effects. After his question is settled, after the Pococks have gone and Waymark, as a sequel to a final brush with Strether and a presumably-not-at-all final sign from Mrs. Pocock, has gone with them; after Strether has seen Chad for the wind-up I have noted and then, as it were, washed his hands of him; after he has seen Mme de Vionnet on corresponding lines, there are two things he is left face to face with. One of these is what I have already so much more than sufficiently evoked, his end, the end of his play, of his stay, and his domestic penalty and consequences—all another busi- ness, all for him, on the spot, only taken for granted and accepted; the other is the presence, the personality, the general form and pressure of Maria Gostrey. *She* is his residuum—that of the three or four months' experience and drama after everything else has come and gone. He is there with her in Paris now alone, as it were; and I see a particular moment of the place and season: the midsummer emptiness reached, the flight of everyone, the rather stale hot, empty city—but with the sense of freedom and of a now strangely full initiation interfusing it all, which the pair seem, as it were, to have quite to themselves. Miss Gostrey, poor dear, but vivid and all herself to the last, is informed with the principle of standing by her friend, so to speak, to the end, and the meaning and moral of what she has done for him, the play of the circumstance that, all the while, she has just purely and simply fallen in love with him—these things gild with their declining rays this last of his complications. Here again I have something that I can't fully trot out for you; here again I can only put in the picture with a single touch of the brush. It will be brushed in another fashion in its order and proper light. Fate gives poor Strether, before she has done with him, just this other chance; and we see him see it and look it in the face and hold out his hand to it with half a kindness and half a renouncement; we see him all touched and intelligent about it, but we don't do anything so vulgar as make him 'take up,' save for a friendship that he quite sincerely hopes may last, with poor convenient, amusing, unforgettable, impossible Gostrey. Very pretty, very charming and pleasant and droll and sad all this concluding but I don't want to represent every woman in the book, beginning with Mrs. Newsome, as having, of herself, 'made up' to my hero; for vivid and concrete and interesting as I desire to make him, the mark of the real never ceases to show in him, and with the real only the real—of verisimilitude, of consistency—consorts. But it's none the less a fact that Mrs. Newsome, Miss Gostrey, and poor magnificent Mme de Vionnet herself (though this last is a secret of secrets) have been, in the degree involved, agreeably and favourably affected by him. Mrs. Newsome has—as we fairly figure to ourselves—'proposed.' Mme de Vionnet has been, only, exquisite over what *might* have been! Miss Gostrey, at all events, doesn't repeat Mrs. Newsome by proposing, but Strether has as clear a vision of his opportunity as if she did—and he has even his moment of hesitation. This moment of hesitation is what we get—what I give. He shows her that he has it—that is, that he sees he can marry her on the morrow if he will—at all events on the morrow of his return to America, or (since she in that case will follow) on the morrow of *that*; is, as I say, everything that is pleasant and appreciative about it—everything but what he would be if he assented or accepted. He *can't* accept or assent. He won't. He doesn't. It's too late. It mightn't have been, sooner—but it is, yes, distinctly, now. He has come so far through his total little experience that he has come out on the other side—on the other side, even, of a union with Miss Gostrey. He must go back as he came—or rather, really, so quite other that, in comparison, marrying Miss Gostrey would be almost of the old order. Yes, he goes back other—and to other things. We see him on the eve of departure, with whatever awaits him *là-bas,* and their lingering, ripe separation is the last note.

P.S. —I should mention that I see the foregoing in a tolerable certitude of Ten Parts, each of 10,000 words, making thus a total of 100,000. But I should very much like my option of stretching to 120,000[1] if necessary—that is, adding an Eleventh and Twelfth Parts. Each Part I rather definitely see in Two Chapters, and each very full, as it were, and charged—like a rounded medallion, in a series of a dozen, hung, with its effect of high relief, on a wall. Such are my general lines. Of course there's a lot to say about the matter that I haven't said—but I have doubtless said a great deal more than it may seem to you at first easy to find your way about in. The way is really, however, very straight. Only the difficulty with one's having made so very full a Statement as the present is that one seems to have gone far toward saying *all*: which I needn't add that I haven't in the least pretended to do. Reading these pages over, for instance, I find I haven't at all placed in a light what I make of the nature of Strether's feeling—his affianced, indebted, and other, consciousness—about Mrs. Newsome. But I need scarcely add, after this, that everything will in fact be in its place and of its kind. September 1st 1900. *Henry James*

COMMENTS FROM JAMES'S LETTERS†

To William Dean Howells[1]

[*"The greatest obsession * * * of all"*]

Lamb House, Rye,
August 9, 1900

* * * I've two or three things begun ever so beautifully in such a key (and only awaiting the rush of the avid bidder!)—each affecting me with its particular obsession, and one, the most started, affecting me with the greatest obsession, for the time (till I can do it, work it off, get it out of the way and fall with still-accumulated intensity upon the *others,*) of all. * * * The scheme to which I am *now* alluding is lovely—

1. James took the option, but the periodical version ran to some 150,000 words. The complete novel was approximately 165,000 words long.

† Unless otherwise indicated, James's letters are quoted from *The Letters of Henry James,* ed. Percy Lubbock, (New York: Charles Scribner's Sons, 1920), 1:357–58, 376–77, 404–5; 2:10, 245, 332–33.

1. In response to Howells's request for "a little 'tale of terror,' " presumably on the order of *The Turn of the Screw* only international in scope, James had begun his uncompleted *The Sense of the Past,* which grew beyond Howells's 50,000 word limit. James asked Howells earlier in this letter if he wanted a short international novel of manners and then added that this idea was "compromised" by the other things he was writing.

human, dramatic, international, exquisitely "pure," exquisitely everything; only absolutely condemned, from the germ up, to be workable
in not less than 100,000 words. If 100,000 were what you had asked
me for, I would fall back upon it ("terror" failing) like a flash; and even
send you, without delay, a detailed Scenario of it that I drew up a year
ago; beginning then—a year ago—to *do* the thing—immediately afterwards; and then again pausing for reasons extraneous and economic. * * * It really constitutes, at any rate, the work I intimately
want actually to be getting on with; and—if you are not overdone with
the profusion of my confidence—I dare say I best put my case by
declaring that, if you don't in another month or two hear from me either
as a Terrorist or as a Cheerful Internationalist, it will be that intrinsic
difficulties will in each case have mastered me; the difficulty in the one
having been to keep my Terror down by *any* ingenuity to the 50,000;
and the difficulty in the *other* form of Cheer than the above-mentioned
obsessive hundred-thousander. I only wish you wanted *him*. But I have
now in all probability a decent outlet for him. * * *

To William Dean Howells

["*You are responsible for the whole business*"]

Lamb House, Rye.
August 10th, 1901

* * * I lately finished a tolerably long novel, and I've written a third
of another—with still another begun and two or three more subjects
awaiting me thereafter like carriages drawn up at the door and horses
champing their bits. And àpropos of the first named of these, which is
in the hands of the Harpers, I have it on my conscience to let you know
that the idea of the fiction in question had its earliest origin in a circumstance mentioned to me—years ago—in respect to no less a person
than yourself. At Torquay, once, our young friend Jon. Sturges came
down to spend some days near me, and, lately from Paris, repeated to
me five words you had said to him one day on his meeting you during
a call at Whistler's. I thought the words charming—you have probably
quite forgotten them; and the whole incident suggestive—so far as it was
an incident; and, more than this, they presently caused me to see in
them the faint vague germ, the mere point of the *start*, of a subject. I
noted them,[2] to that end, as I note everything; and years afterwards (that
is three or four) the subject sprang at me, one day, out of my notebook.
I don't know if it be good; at any rate it has been treated, now, for
whatever it is; and my point is that it had long before—it had in the
very act of striking me as a germ—got away from *you* or from anything

2. See pp. 374–76.

like you! had become impersonal and independent. Nevertheless your initials figure in my little note; and if you hadn't said the five words to Jonathan he wouldn't have had them (most sympathetically and interestingly) to relate, and I shouldn't have had them to work in my imagination. The moral is that you are responsible for the whole business. But I've had it, since the book was finished, much at heart to tell you so. May you carry the burden bravely! * * *

To H. G. Wells

["*Those wondrous and copious preliminary* statements"]

Lamb House, Rye, Sussex.
November 15th, 1902.

MY DEAR WELLS,

It is too horribly long that I have neglected an interesting (for I can't say an interested) inquiry of yours—in your last note; and neglected precisely *because* the acknowledgment involved had to be an explanation. I have somehow, for the last month, not felt capable of explanations, it being my infirmity that when "finishing a book" (and that seems my chronic condition) my poor enfeebled cerebration becomes incapable of the least extra effort, however slight and simple. My correspondence then shrinks and shrinks—only the least explicit of my letters get themselves approximately written. And somehow it has seemed highly explicit to tell you that (in reply to your suggestive last) those wondrous and copious preliminary *statements* (of my fictions that are to be,) don't really exist in any form in which they can be imparted. I think I know to whom you allude as having seen their semblance—and indeed their very substance; but in two exceptional (as it were) cases. In these cases what was seen was the statement drawn up on the basis of the serialization of the work—drawn up in one case with extreme detail and at extreme length (in 20,000 words!) Pinker saw that: it referred to a long novel, afterwards (this more than a year,) written and finished, but not yet, to my great inconvenience, published; but it went more than two years ago, to America, to the Harpers, and there it remained and has probably been destroyed. Were it here I would with pleasure transmit it to you; for, though I say it who should not, it *was*, the statement, full and vivid, I think, as a statement could be, of a subject as worked out. Then CONRAD[3] saw a shorter one of the *Wings of the D[ove]*—also well enough in its way, but only half as long and proportionately less developed. *That* had been prepared so that the book might be serialized in another American periodical, but this wholly failed (what secrets and shames I

---

3. The novelist Joseph Conrad, also a friend of James's.

reveal to you!) and the thing (the book) was then written, the subject treated, on a more free and independent scale. But *that* synopsis too has been destroyed; it was returned from the U.S., but I had then no occasion to preserve it. And evidently no fiction of mine can or *will* now be serialized; certainly I shall not again draw up detailed and explicit plans for unconvinced and ungracious editors; so that I fear I shall have nothing of that sort to show. A plan for *myself*, as copious and developed as possible, I always do draw up—that is the two documents I speak of were based upon, and extracted from, such a preliminary *private* out-pouring. But this latter voluminous effusion is, ever, so extremely familiar, confidential and intimate—in the form of an interminable garrulous letter addressed to my own fond fancy—that, though I always, for easy reference, have it carefully typed, it isn't a thing I would willingly expose to any eye but my own. And even *then*, sometimes, I shrink! So there it is. I am greatly touched by your respectful curiosity, but I haven't, you see, anything coherent to produce. Let me promise however that if I ever do, within any calculable time, address a manifesto to the dim editorial mind, you shall certainly have the benefit of a copy. Candour compels me to add that that consummation has now become unlikely. It is too wantonly expensive a treat to them. In the first place they will none of me, and in the second the relief, and greater intellectual dignity, so to speak, of working on one's own scale, one's own line of continuity and in one's own absolutely independent *tone*, is too precious to me to be again forfeited. Pardon my too many words. I only add that I hope the domestic heaven bends blue above you. Yours, my dear Wells, always,

HENRY JAMES

To Jocelyn Persse†

[*"A vague resemblance * * * to yours always"*]

Rye, Sussex. Monday p.m.

My dear Jocelyn,

This is but a poor word, omitted three days ago, very stupidly, to say that I have written to have a copy of *The Ambassadors* sent you—every copy I have succeeded in being possessed of here having successively melted away. Don't write to 'thank' me for it—but if you are able successfully to struggle with it try to like the poor old hero, in whom you will perhaps find a vague resemblance (though not facial!) to yours always   HENRY JAMES

† From Henry James, *Letters*, ed. Leon Edel (Cambridge, Mass.: Harvard University Press, 1984), 4:286.

To Mrs. Humphry Ward†

["A *fearful* * * * *fault or weakness*"]

Dec 16th 1903

Dear Mrs. Ward—

Please believe in the very great pleasure given me by your kind & generous letter. It belongs to the area of acts that touch deeply, & of which the remembrance abides. I felt a good deal of despair after "The Ambassadors" were launched, & said to myself "what can be expected for a novel with a hero of 55, & properly no heroine at all?" But I have slowly felt a little better, & the book is, intrinsically, I daresay, the best I have written in spite of a fearful though much patched over[4] fault or weakness in it (which, however, I seem to see no one has noticed & which nothing will induce me *now* ever to reveal not at least till some one does spot it). It is in general meritorious for its conformation & composition—*that* I make bold to say. But it was written 4 years ago, & I feel myself rather away & "off" from it. What gives me particular pleasure is your feeling that one is in a fresh & a larger period which I really hope and believe (D. V., absit omen unberufen.[5] etc. etc.!) may prove to be the case. Yet I find it all a too damnably difficult art & have so to pretend that it isn't. However, we pretend life isn't either & toward that such good friends as you exceedingly help. I rejoice to think of finding you before very long in town & I am, dear Mrs. Ward, yours very constantly,

Henry James

To the Duchess of Sutherland‡

["*Don't break the thread*"]

Rye, *Dec. 23rd*, 1903

* * * Take, meanwhile pray, the *Ambassadors* very easily and gently: read five pages a day—be even as deliberate as that—but *don't break the thread.* The thread is really stretched quite scientifically tight. Keep along with it step by step—and then the full charm will come out. I *want* the charm, you see, to come out for you—so convinced am I that it's there! Besides, I find that the very most difficult thing in the art of the novelist is to give the impression and illusion of the real *lapse of time, the quantity* of time, represented by our poor few phrases and

---

† From *American Literature* 64 (March 1992): 108.
4. The phrase "though much patched over" was inserted later by James.
5. God willing, may no ominous meaning attach to these words, without summoning bad luck.
† From James, *Letters*, ed. Edel, 4:302–3.

pages, and all the drawing-out the reader can contribute helps a little perhaps the production of that spell. * * *

To William Dean Howells

["The 'International' "]

January 8, 1904

* * * This is all, or almost all, to-day—all except to reassure you of the pleasure you give me by your remarks about *The Ambassadors* and cognate topics. The "International" is very presumably indeed, and in fact quite inevitably, what I am *chronically* booked for. * * *

To Alvin Langdon Coburn†

["Paris Subjects"]

[2 October 1906]

Memoranda to A. L. Coburn
For the Paris Subjects
This is to make definite to you that the principal streets to look in for the portal of the old "aristocratic" *hôtel* are the R. de l'Université, the R. de Lille, and the R. Bellechasse, the R. du Faubourg St. Germain, and even the short Rue Monsieur and (possibly) Rue Madame. There are even possibly three or four such *portes-cochère* on the quays of the Left Bank: the Quai Malaquais, for instance, the Quai Voltaire, the Quai d'Orsay, and etc., which are over there very much together. But look, for a grand specimen of the *type*, as I told you, at the British Embassy, in the R. du Faubourg St. Honoré. You will know it by its being on your left, in that street, not long after you have passed the Rue Royale, and by its having the big escutcheon of lion and unicorn above it. Ask for *l'ambassade d'Angleterre*: anyone thereabouts, most of all your cabman, will show you. And there are two or three others, very nearly as majestic, in the same street: only these are too modern, and also too majestic. But I repeat for you that, once you get the Type into your head, you will easily recognise specimens by walking about in the *old* residential and "noble" parts of the city: by which I mean particularly Faubourg St. Germain. (Not but what there are there plenty of featureless houses too.) Tell a cabman that you want to drive through every street in it, and then, having got that notion, go back and walk and stare at your ease. Add to the streets I named above, the R. *St. Dominique* and

† From James, *Letters*, ed. Edel, 4:416–18. Henry James met the distinguished American photographer Alvin Langdon Coburn early in his career. For their collaboration on the frontispieces of the New York Edition, see pp. 368–69.

the R. *de Varenne*, which both cross the R. de Bellechasse, as does also the possible R. *de Grenelle*. So there you are for *that*.

Place de la Concorde, etc.

Look out *there* for some combination of objects that won't be hackneyed and commonplace and panoramic; some fountain or statue or balustrade or vista or suggestion (of some damnable sort or other) that will serve in connection with *The Ambassadors*, perhaps; just as some view, rightly arrived at, of *Notre Dame* would also serve—if sufficiently bedimmed and refined and glorified; especially as to its Side on the River and Back ditto. Above all don't forget I yearn for some outside aspect of the Théâtre-Français, for possible use in *The Tragic Muse*; but something of course of the same transfigured nature; some ingeniously-hit-upon angle of presentment of its rather majestic big square mass and classic colonnade. If by the same token, you could do something of the *Odéon Theatre* and *its* classic colonnade (the bookstalls are haunted by students of the Latin Quarter), there is a passage in *The Ambassadors*, where the hero lingers under the arcade, which might enable me to work it in.

Note that the Odéon is close to the *Luxembourg Gardens*, and there is another passage in the same book about his sitting *there* against the pedestal of some pleasant old garden-statue, to read over certain letters with which the story is concerned. Go into the sad Luxembourg Garden, straight across from the arcade of the Odéon, to look for my right garden-statue (composing with other interesting objects)—against which my chair was tilted back. Do bring me something right, in short, from the Luxembourg. These are the principal things I think of; though if you could rake in one or two big generalising glimpses or fragments (even of the Arc de Triomphe say) there are one or two other places—as second volume of *Princess Casamassima*, where suchlike might come in. My blessing on your inspiration and your weather!

Henry James

To Hugh Walpole

["*How can you say I* * * * '*state*'?"]

Lamb House, Rye.
Aug. 14th, 1912

* * * It's charming to me to hear that *The Ambassadors* have again engaged and still beguile you; it *is* probably a very *packed* production, with a good deal of one thing within another; I remember sitting on it, when I wrote it, with that intending weight and presence with which you probably often sit in these days on your trunk to make the lid close

and *all* your trousers and boots go in. I remember putting in a good deal about Chad and Strether, or Strether and Chad, rather; and am not sure that I quite understand what in that connection you miss—I mean in the way of what *could* be there. The whole thing is of course, to intensity, a picture of relations—and among them is, though not on the first line, the relation of Strether to Chad. The relation of Chad to Strether is a limited and according to my method only implied and indicated thing, sufficiently there; but Strether's to Chad consists above all in a charmed and yearning and wondering sense, a dimly envious sense, of all Chad's young living and easily-taken *other* relations; other not only than the one to him, but than the one to Mme de Vionnet and whoever else; this very sense, and the sense of Chad, generally, is a part, a large part, of poor dear Strether's discipline, development, adventure and general history. All of it that is of my subject seems to me given—given by dramatic projection, as all the rest is given: how can you say I do anything so foul and abject as to "state"? You deserve that I should condemn you to read the book over once again! * * *

To Mrs. G. W. Prothero

[*"More 'advanced'* "]

Rye. Sept. 14th, 1913

This, please, for the delightful young man from Texas[6] who shews such excellent dispositions. I only want to meet him half way, and I hope very much he won't think I don't when I tell him that the following indications as to five of my productions (splendid number—I glory in the tribute of his appetite!) are all on the basis of the Scribner's (or Macmillan's) collective and revised and prefaced edition of my things, and that if he is not minded somehow to obtain access to *that* form of them, ignoring any others, he forfeits half, or much more than half, my confidence. So I thus amicably beseech him——! I suggest to give him as alternatives these two slightly different lists:

1. Roderick Hudson.
2. The Portrait of a Lady.
3. The Princess Casamassima.
4. The Wings of the Dove.
5. The Golden Bowl.

———————

1. The American.
2. The Tragic Muse.
3. The Wings of the Dove.

6. Mrs. Prothero, a friend of James's, had been asked by Stark Young, later a well-known drama critic, for assistance in choosing what to read of James's works.

4. The Ambassadors.
5. The Golden Bowl.

The second list is, as it were, the more "advanced." And when it comes to the shorter Tales the question is more difficult (for characteristic selection) and demands separate treatment. Come to me about that, dear young man from Texas, later on—you shall have your little tarts when you have eaten your beef and potatoes. Meanwhile receive this from your admirable friend Mrs. Prothero.

HENRY JAMES

CRITICISM

H. M. ALDEN (1900)

[Memorandum on "Project of Novel by Henry James"]†

The scenario is interesting, but it does not promise a popular novel. The tissues of it are too subtly fine for general appreciation. It is subjective, fold within fold of a complex mental web, in which the reader is lost if his much-wearied attention falters. A good proportion of the characters are American, but the scene is chiefly in Paris. The story (in its mere plot) centres about an American youth in Paris who has been captivated by a charming French woman (separated from her husband) and the critical situations are developed in connection with the efforts of his friends and relatives to rescue him. The moral in the end is that he is better off in this captivity than in the conditions to which his friends would restore him. I do not advise acceptance. We ought to do better.

PERCY LUBBOCK (1921)

[Point of View in *The Ambassadors*]‡

And now for the method by which the picture of a mind is fully dramatized, the method which is to be seen consistently applied in The Ambassadors and the other later novels of Henry James. How is the author to withdraw, to stand aside, and to let Strether's thought tell its own story? The thing must be seen from our own point of view and no other. Author and hero, Thackeray and Esmond, Meredith and Harry Richmond, have given their various accounts of emotional and intellectual adventure; but they might do more, they might bring the facts of the adventure upon the scene and leave them to make their impression. The story passes in an invisible world, the events take place in the man's mind; and we might have to conclude that they lie beyond our reach, and that we cannot attain to them save by the help of the man himself, or of the author who knows all about him. We might have to make the best of an account at second hand, and it would not occur to

† From *The Notebooks of Henry James*, ed. F. O. Matthiessen and Kenneth B. Murdock, copyright (©) 1947 by Oxford University Press, Inc.; renewed 1974 by Kenneth B. Murdock and Mrs. Peters Putnam. Reprinted by permission of Oxford University Press, p. 372. H. M. Alden, the editor of *Harper's New Monthly Magazine*, sent his report on James's preliminary project (see pp. 355–56) to the magazine's publisher.

‡ From *The Craft of Fiction* (London: Jonathan Cape, 1954), 156–71. Reprinted by permission of the Estate of Percy Lubbock and the publisher.

us, I dare say, that anything more could be forthcoming; we seem to touch the limit of the possibilities of drama in fiction. But it is not the final limit—there is fiction here to prove it; and it is this further stroke of the art that I would now examine.

The world of silent thought is thrown open, and instead of telling the reader what happened there, the novelist uses the look and behaviour of thought as the vehicle by which the story is rendered. Just as the writer of a play embodies his subject in visible action and audible speech, so the novelist, dealing with a situation like Strether's, represents it by means of the movement that flickers over the surface of his mind. The impulses and reactions of his mood are the players upon the new scene. In drama of the theatre a character must bear his part unaided; if he is required to be a desperate man, harbouring thoughts of crime, he cannot look to the author to appear at the side of the stage and inform the audience of the fact; he must express it for himself through his words and deeds, his looks and tones. The playwright so arranges the matter that these will be enough, the spectator will make the right inference. But suppose that instead of a man upon the stage, concealing and betraying his thought, we watch the thought itself, the hidden thing, as it twists to and fro in his brain—watch it without any other aid to understanding but such as its own manner of bearing may supply. The novelist, more free than the playwright, could of course *tell* us, if he chose, what lurks behind this agitated spirit; he could step forward and explain the restless appearance of the man's thought. But if he prefers the dramatic way, admittedly the more effective, there is nothing to prevent him from taking it. The man's thought, in its turn, can be made to reveal its own inwardness.

Let us see how this plan is pursued in The Ambassadors. That book is entirely concerned with Strether's experience of his peculiar mission to Europe, and never passes outside the circle of his thought. Strether is despatched, it will be remembered, by a resolute New England widow, whose son is living lightly in Paris instead of attending to business at home. To win the hand of the widow, Strether must succeed in snatching the young man from the siren who is believed to have beguiled him. The mission is undertaken in all good faith, Strether descends upon Paris with a mind properly disposed and resolved. He comes as an ambassador representing principle and duty, to treat with the young man, appeal to him convincingly and bear him off. The task before him may be difficult, but his purpose is simple. Strether has reckoned, however, without his imagination; he had scarcely been aware of possessing one before, but everything grows complicated as it is touched and awakened on the new scene. By degrees and degrees he changes his opinion of the life of freedom; it is most unlike his prevision of it, and at last his purpose is actually inverted. He no longer sees a misguided young man to be saved from disaster, he sees an exquisite, bountiful world laid at a young man's feet; and now the only question is whether the young man is capable of meeting and grasping his opportunity. He is incapable, as it turns out; when the story ends he is on the verge of rejecting his freedom and going back to the world of commonplace; Strether's mission has ended successfully. But in Strether's mind the revolution is complete; there is nothing left for him, no reward and no future. The world of commonplace is no longer *his* world, and he is too late to seize the other; he is old, he has missed the opportunity of youth.

This is a story which must obviously be told from Strether's point of view, in the first place. The change in his purpose is due to a change in his vision, and the long slow process could not be followed unless his vision were shared by the reader. Strether's predicament, that is to say, could not be placed upon the stage; his outward behaviour, his conduct, his talk, do not express a tithe of it. Only the brain behind his eyes can be aware of the colour of his experience, as it passes through its innumerable gradations; and all understanding of his case depends upon seeing these. The way of the author, therefore, who takes this subject in hand, is clear enough at the outset. It is a purely pictorial subject, covering Strether's field of vision and bounded by its limits; it consists entirely of an impression received by a certain man. There can accordingly be no thought of rendering him as a figure seen from without; nothing that any one else could discern, looking at him and listening to his conversation, would give the full sense of the eventful life he is leading within. The dramatic method, as we ordinarily understand it, is ruled out at once. Neither as an action set before the reader without interpretation from within, nor yet as an action pictured for the reader by some other onlooker in the book, can this story possibly be told.

Strether's real situation, in fact, is not his open and visible situation, between the lady in New England and the young man in Paris; his grand adventure is not expressed in its incidents. These, as they are devised by the author, are secondary, they are the extension of the moral event that takes place in the breast of the ambassador, his change of mind. That is the very middle of the subject; it is a matter that lies solely between Strether himself and his vision of the free world. It is a delightful effect of irony, indeed, that he should have accomplished his errand after all, in spite of himself; but the point of the book is not there, the ironic climax only serves to bring out the point more sharply. The reversal of his own idea is underlined and enhanced by the reversal of the young man's idea in the opposite sense; but essentially the subject of the book would be unchanged if the story ended differently, if the young man held to his freedom and refused to go home. Strether would still have passed through the same cycle of unexpected experience; his errand might have failed, but still it would not have been any the more impossible for him to claim his reward, for his part, than it is impossible as things are, with the quest achieved and the young man ready to hasten back to duty of his own accord. And so the subject can only be reached through Strether's consciousness, it is plain; that way alone will command the impression that the scene makes on him. Nothing in the scene has any importance, any value in itself; what Strether sees in it—that is the whole of its meaning.

But though in The Ambassadors the point of view is primarily Strether's, and though it *appears* to be his throughout the book, there is in fact an insidious shifting of it, so artfully contrived that the reader may arrive at the end without suspecting the trick. The reader, all unawares, is placed in a better position for an understanding of Strether's history, better than the position of Strether himself. Using his eyes, we see what *he* sees, we are possessed of the material on which his patient thought sets to work; and that is so far well enough, and plainly necessary. All the other people in the book face towards him, and it is that aspect of them, and that only, which is shown to the reader; still more important, the beautiful picture of Paris and spring-time, the stir and shimmer of life in the Rue de Rivoli and the gardens of the Tuileries, is Strether's picture, *his* vision, rendered as the time and the place strike upon his senses. All this on which his thought ruminates, the stuff that occupies it, is represented from his point of view. To see it, even for a moment, from some different angle—if, for example, the author interposed with a vision of his own—would patently disturb the right impression. The author does no such thing, it need hardly be said.

When it comes to Strether's treatment of this material, however, when it is time to learn what he makes of it, turning his experience over and over in his mind, then his own point of view no longer serves. How is anybody, even Strether, to *see* the working of his own mind? A mere account of its working, after the fact, has already been barred; we have found that this of necessity is lacking in force, it is statement where we look for demonstration. And so we must see for ourselves, the author must so arrange matters that Strether's thought will all be made intelligible by a direct view of its surface. The immediate flaw or ripple of the moment, and the next and the next, will then take up the tale, like the speakers in a dialogue which gradually unfolds the subject of the play. Below the surface, behind the outer aspect of his mind, we do not penetrate; this is drama, and in drama the spectator must judge by appearances. When Strether's mind is dramatized, nothing is shown but the passing images that anybody might detect, looking down upon a mind grown visible. There is no drawing upon extraneous sources of information; Henry James knows all there is to know of Strether, but he most carefully refrains from using his knowledge. He wishes us to accept nothing from him, on authority—only to watch and learn.

For suppose him to begin sharing the knowledge that he alone possesses, as the author and inventor of Strether; suppose that instead of representing only the momentary appearance of Strether's thought he begins to expound its substance: he must at once give us the whole of it, must let us into every secret without delay, or his exposition is plainly misleading. It is assumed that he tells all, if he once begins. And so, too, if the book were cast autobiographically and Strether spoke in person; he could not hold back, he could not heighten the story of his thought with that touch of suspense, waiting to be resolved, which stamps the impression so firmly into the memory of the onlooker. In a tale of murder and mystery there is one man who cannot possibly be the narrator, and that is the murderer himself; for if he admits us into his mind at all he must do so without reserve, thereby betraying the secret that we ought to be guessing at for ourselves. But by this method of The Ambassadors the mind of which the reader is made free, Strether's mind, is not given away; there is no need for it to yield up all its secrets at once. The story in it is played out by due degrees, and there may be just as much deliberation, refrainment, suspension, as in a story told scenically upon the stage. All the effect of true drama is thus at the disposal of the author, even when he seems to be describing and picturing the consciousness of one of his characters. He arrives at the point where apparently nothing but a summary and a report should be possible, and even there he is precluded from none of the privileges of a dramatist.

It is necessary to show that in his attitude towards his European errand Strether is slowly turning upon himself and looking in another direction. To announce the fact, with a tabulation of his reasons, would be the historic, retrospective, undramatic way of dealing with the matter. To bring his mind into view at the different moments, one after another, when it is brushed by new experience—to make a little scene of it, without breaking into hidden depths where the change of purpose is proceeding—to multiply these glimpses until the silent change is apparent, though no word has actually been said of it: this is Henry James's way, and though the *method* could scarcely be more devious and roundabout, always refusing the short cut, yet by these very qualities and precautions it finally produces the most direct impression, for the reader has *seen*. That is why the method is adopted. The author has so fashioned his book that his own part in the narration is now unobtrusive to the last degree; he, the author, could not imaginably figure there more discreetly. His part in the effect is no more than that of the playwright, who vanishes and leaves his people to act the story; only instead of men and women talking together, in Strether's case there are innumerable images of thought crowding across the stage, expressing the story in their behaviour.

But there is more in the book, as I suggested just now, than Strether's vision and the play of his mind. In the *scenic* episodes, the colloquies that Strether holds, for example, with his sympathetic friend Maria Gostrey, another turn appears in the author's procedure. Throughout these clear-cut dialogues Strether's point of view still reigns; the only eyes in the matter are still his, there is no sight of the man himself as his companion sees him. Miss Gostrey is clearly visible, and Madame de Vionnet and little Bilham, or whoever it may be; the face of Strether himself is never turned to the reader. On the evening of the first encounter between the elderly ambassador and the young man, they sat together in a café of the boulevards and walked away at midnight through quiet streets; and all through their interview the fact of the young man's appearance is strongly dominant, for it is this that first reveals to Strether how the young man has been transformed by his commerce with the free world; and so his figure is sharply before the reader as they talk. How Strether seemed to Chad—this, too, is represented, but only by implication, through Chad's speech and manner. It is essential, of course, that it should be so, the one-sided vision is strictly enjoined by the method of the whole book. But though the seeing eye is still with Strether, there is a noticeable change in the author's way with him.

In these scenic dialogues, on the whole, we seem to have edged away from Strether's consciousness. He sees, and we with him; but when he *talks* it is almost as though we were outside him and away from him altogether. Not always, indeed; for in many of the scenes he is busily brooding and thinking throughout, and we share his mind while he joins in the talk. But still, on the whole, the author is inclined to leave Strether alone when the scene is set. He talks the matter out with Maria, he sits and talks with Madame de Vionnet, he strolls along the boulevards with Chad, he lounges on a chair in the Champs Elysées with some one else—we know the kind of scene that is set for Strether, know how very few accessories he requires, and know that the scene marks a certain definite climax, wherever it occurs, for all its everyday look. The occasion is important, there is no doubt about that; its importance is in the air. And Strether takes his part in it as though he had almost become what he cannot be, an objective figure for the reader. Evidently he cannot be that, since the centre of vision is still within him; but by an easy sleight of hand the author gives him almost the value of an independent person, a man to whose words we may listen expectantly, a man whose mind is screened from us. Again and again the stroke is accomplished, and indeed there is nothing mysterious about it. Simply it consists in treating the scene as dramatically as possible—keeping it framed in Strether's vision, certainly, but keeping his consciousness out of sight, his thought unexplored. He talks to Maria; and to us, to the reader, his voice seems as much as hers to belong to somebody whom we are *watching*—which is impossible, because our point of view is his.

A small matter, perhaps, but it is interesting as a sign, still another, of the perpetual tendency of the novel to capture the advantages which it appears to forego. The Ambassadors is without doubt a book that deals with an entirely non-dramatic subject; it is the picture of an *état d'âme*.

But just as the chapters that are concerned with Strether's soul are in the key of drama, after the fashion I have described, so too the episode, the occasion, the scene that crowns the impression, is always more dramatic in its method than it apparently has the means to be. Here, for instance, is the central scene of the whole story, the scene in the old Parisian garden, where Strether, finally filled to the brim with the sensation of all the life for which his own opportunity has passed, overflows with his passionate exhortation to little Bilham—warning him, adjuring him not to make *his* mistake, not to let life slide away ungrasped. It is the hour in which Strether touches his crisis, and the first necessity of the chapter is to show the sudden lift and heave of his mood within; the voices and admonitions of the hour, that is to say, must be heard and felt as he hears and feels them himself. The scene, then, will be given as Strether's impression, clearly, and so it is; the old garden and the evening light and the shifting company of people appear as their reflection in his thought. But the scene is *also* a piece of drama, it strikes out of the book with the strong relief of dramatic action; which is evidently an advantage gained, seeing the importance of the hour in the story, but which is an advantage that it could not enjoy, one might have said.

The quality of the scene becomes clear if we imagine the story to be told by Strether himself, narrating in the first person. Of the damage that this would entail for the picture of his brooding mind I have spoken already; but suppose the book to have taken the form of autobiography, and suppose that Strether has brought the story up to this point, where he sits beside little Bilham in Gloriani's garden. He describes the deep and agitating effect of the scene upon him, calling to him of the world he has missed; he tells what he thought and felt; and then, he says, I broke out with the following tirade to little Bilham—and we have the energetic outburst which Henry James has put into his mouth. But is it not clear how the incident would be weakened, so rendered? That speech, word for word as we have it, would lose its unexpected and dramatic quality, because Strether, arriving at it by narration, could not suddenly spring away from himself and give the impression of the worn, intelligent, clear-sighted man sitting there in the evening sun, strangely moved to unwonted eloquence. His narration must have discounted the effect of his outburst, leading us up to the very edge of it, describing how it arose, explaining where it came from. He would be *subjective*, and committed to remain so all the time.

Henry James, by his method, can secure this effect of drama, even though his Strether is apparently in the position of a narrator throughout. Strether's are the eyes, I said, and they are more so than ever during this hour in the garden; he is the sentient creature in the scene. But the author, who all through the story has been treating Strether's consciousness as a play, as an action proceeding, can at any moment use his talk almost as though the source from which it springs were unknown to us from within. I remember that he himself, in his critical preface to the book, calls attention to the way in which a conversation between Strether and Maria Gostrey, near the beginning, puts the reader in possession of all the past facts of the situation which it is necessary for him to know; a *scene* thus takes the place of that "harking back to make up," as he calls it, which is apt to appear as a lump of narrative shortly after the opening of a story. If Strether were really the narrator, whether in the first person or the third, he could not use his own talk in this manner; he would have to tell us himself about his past. But he has never *told* us his thought, we have looked at it and drawn our inferences; and so there is still some air of dramatic detachment about him, and his talk may seem on occasion to be that of a man whom we know from outside. The advantage is peculiarly felt on that crucial occasion at Gloriani's, where Strether's sudden flare of vehemence, so natural and yet so unlike him, breaks out with force unimpaired. It strikes freshly on the ear, the speech of a man whose inmost perturbations we have indeed inferred from many glimpses of his mind, but still without ever learning the full tale of them from himself.

The Ambassadors, then, is a story which is seen from one man's point of view, and yet a story in which that point of view is itself a matter for the reader to confront and to watch constructively. Everything in the novel is now dramatically rendered, whether it is a page of dialogue or a page of description, because even in the page of description nobody is addressing us, nobody is reporting his impression to the reader. The impression is enacting itself in the endless series of images that play over the outspread expanse of the man's mind and memory. When the story passes from these to the scenes of dialogue—from the silent drama of Strether's meditation to the spoken drama of the men and women— there is thus no break in the method. The same law rules everywhere —that Strether's changing sense of his situation shall appeal directly to the onlooker, and not by way of any summarizing picture-maker. And yet *as a whole* the book is all pictorial, an indirect impression received through Strether's intervening consciousness, beyond which the story never strays. I conclude that on this paradox the art of dramatizing the picture of somebody's experience—the art I have been considering in these last chapters—touches its limit. There is indeed no further for it to go.

E. M. FORSTER (1927)

[Pattern in *The Ambassadors*]†

Let us examine at some length another book of the rigid type, a book with a unity, and in this sense an easy book, although it is by Henry James. We shall see in it pattern triumphant, and we shall also be able to see the sacrifices an author must make if he wants his pattern and nothing else to triumph.

The Ambassadors, like *Thaïs*,[1] is the shape of an hour-glass. Strether and Chad, like Paphnuce and Thaïs, change places, and it is the realization of this that makes the book so satisfying at the close. The plot is elaborate and subtle, and proceeds by action or conversation or meditation through every paragraph. Everything is planned, everything fits; none of the minor characters are just decorative like the talkative Alexandrians at Nicias' banquet; they elaborate on the main theme, they work. The final effect is prearranged, dawns gradually on the reader, and is completely successful when it comes. Details of intrigue, of the various missions from America, may be forgotten, but the symmetry they have created is enduring.

Let us trace the growth of this symmetry.[2]

Strether, a sensitive middle-aged American, is commissioned by his old friend, Mrs. Newsome, whom he hopes to marry, to go to Paris and rescue her son Chad, who has gone to the bad in that appropriate city. The Newsomes are sound commercial people, who have made money over manufacturing a small article of domestic utility. Henry James never tells us what the small article is, and in a moment we shall understand why. Wells spits it out in *Tono Bungay*, Meredith reels it out in *Evan Harrington*, Trollope prescribes it freely for Miss Dunstable, but for James to indicate how his characters made their pile—it would not do. The article is somewhat ignoble and ludicrous—that is enough. If you choose to be coarse and daring and visualize it for yourself as, say, a button-hook, you can, but you do so at your own risk: the author remains uninvolved.

Well, whatever it is, Chad Newsome ought to come back and help make it, and Strether undertakes to fetch him. He has to be rescued from a life which is both immoral and unremunerative.

Strether is a typical James character—he recurs in nearly all the books

† From *Aspects of the Novel* (1927; London: Edward Arnold, 1974), 104–12. Reprinted by permission of King's College, Cambridge, and The Society of Authors as the literary representatives of the E. M. Forster Estate.
1. By Anatole France, discussed earlier in *Aspects of the Novel* [*Editor*].
2. There is a masterly analysis of *The Ambassadors* from another standpoint in *The Craft of Fiction* [pp. 415–22].

and is an essential part of their construction. He is the observer who tries to influence the action, and who through his failure to do so gains extra opportunities for observation. And the other characters are such as an observer like Strether is capable of observing—through lenses procured from a rather too first-class oculist. Everything is adjusted to his vision, yet he is not a quietist—no, that is the strength of the device; he takes us along with him, we move as well as look on.

When he lands in England (and a landing is an exalted and enduring experience for James, it is as vital as Newgate for Defoe; poetry and life crowd round a landing): when Strether lands, though it is only old England, he begins to have doubts of his mission, which increase when he gets to Paris. For Chad Newsome, far from going to the bad, has improved; he is distinguished, he is so sure of himself that he can be kind and cordial to the man who has orders to fetch him away; his friends are exquisite, and as for "women in the case" whom his mother antic- ipated, there is no sign of them whatever. It is Paris that has enlarged and redeemed him—and how well Strether himself understands this!

> His greatest uneasiness seemed to peep at him out of the possible impression that almost any acceptance of Paris might give one's authority away. It hung before him this morning, the vast bright Babylon, like some huge iridescent object, a jewel brilliant and hard, in which parts were not to be discriminated nor differences comfortably marked. It twinkled and trembled and melted together; and what seemed all surface one moment seemed all depth the next. It was a place of which, unmistakably, Chad was fond; where- fore, if he, Strether, should like it too much, what on earth, with such a bond, would become of either of them?

Thus, exquisitely and firmly, James sets his atmosphere—Paris irra- diates the book from end to end, it is an actor though always unembodied, it is a scale by which human sensibility can be measured, and when we have finished the novel and allow its incidents to blur that we may see the pattern plainer, it is Paris that gleams at the centre of the hour-glass shape—Paris—nothing so crude as good or evil. Strether sees this soon, and sees that Chad realizes it better than he himself can; and when he has reached this stage of initiation the novel takes a turn: there is, after all, a woman in the case; behind Paris, interpreting it for Chad, is the adorable and exalted figure of Mme. de Vionnet. It is now impossible for Strether to proceed. All that is noble and refined in life concentrates in Mme. de Vionnet and is reinforced by her pathos. She asks him not to take Chad away. He promises—without reluctance, for his own heart has already shown him as much—and he remains in Paris not to fight it but to fight for it.

For the second batch of ambassadors now arrives from the New World. Mrs. Newsome, incensed and puzzled by the unseemly delay, has despatched Chad's sister, his brother-in-law, and Mamie, the girl whom he is supposed to marry. The novel now becomes, within its ordained limits, most amusing. There is a superb set-to between Chad's sister and Mme. de Vionnet, while as for Mamie—here is disastrous Mamie, seen as we see all things, through Strether's eyes.

> As a child, as a "bud," and then again as a flower of expansion, Mamie had bloomed for him, freely, in the almost incessantly open doorways of home; where he remembered her at first very forward, as then very backward—for he had carried on at one period, in Mrs. Newsome's parlours, a course of English literature reinforced by exams and teas—and once more, finally, as very much in advance. But he had kept no great sense of points of contact; it not being in the nature of things at Woollett that the freshest of the buds should find herself in the same basket with the most withered of the winter apples. . . . He none the less felt now, as he sat with the charming girl, the signal growth of a confidence. For she *was* charming, when all was said, and none the less so for the visible habit and practice of freedom and fluency. She was charming, he was aware, in spite of the fact that if he hadn't found her so he would have found her something he should have been in peril of expressing as "funny." Yes, she was funny, wonderful Mamie, and without dreaming it; she was bland, she was bridal—with never, that he could make out as yet, a bridegroom to support it; she was handsome and portly, and easy and chatty, soft and sweet and almost disconcertingly reassuring. She was dressed, if we might so far discriminate, less as a young lady than as an old one—had an old one been supposable to Strether as so committed to vanity; the complexities of her hair missed moreover also the looseness of youth; and she had a mature manner of bending a little, as to encourage and reward, while she held neatly in front of her a pair of strikingly polished hands: the combination of all of which kept up about her the glamour of her "receiving," placed her again perpetually between the windows and within sound of the ice cream plates, suggested the enumeration of all the names, gregarious specimens of a single type, she was happy to "meet."

Mamie! She is another Henry James type; nearly every novel contains a Mamie—Mrs. Gereth in *The Spoils of Poynton* for instance, or Henrietta Stackpole in *The Portrait of a Lady*. He is so good at indicating instantaneously and constantly that a character is second rate, deficient in sensitiveness, abounding in the wrong sort of worldliness; he gives such a character so much vitality that its absurdity is delightful.

So Strether changes sides and loses all hopes of marrying Mrs. Newsome. Paris is winning—and then he catches sight of something new. Is not Chad, as regards any fineness in him, played out? Is not Chad's Paris after all just a place for a spree? This fear is confirmed. He goes for a solitary country walk, and at the end of the day he comes across Chad and Mme. de Vionnet. They are in a boat, they pretend not to see him, because their relation is at bottom an ordinary liaison, and they are ashamed. They were hoping for a secret week-end at an inn while their passion survived; for it will not survive, Chad will tire of the exquisite Frenchwoman, she is part of his fling; he will go back to his mother and make the little domestic article and marry Mamie. They know all this, and it is revealed to Strether though they try to hide it; they lie, they are vulgar—even Mme. de Vionnet, even her pathos, once so exquisite, is stained with commonness.

It was like a chill in the air to him, it was almost appalling, that a creature so fine could be, by mysterious forces, a creature so exploited. For, at the end of all things, they *were* mysterious; she had but made Chad what he was—so why could she think she had made him infinite? She had made him better, she had made him best, she had made him anything one would; but it came to our friend with supreme queerness that he was none the less only Chad. The work, however admirable, was nevertheless of the strict human order, and in short it was marvellous that the companion of mere earthly joys, of comforts, aberrations—however one classed them —within the common experience, should be so transcendently prized.

She was older for him tonight, visibly less exempt from the touch of time; but she was as much as ever the finest and subtlest creature, the happiest apparition, it had been given him, in all his years, to meet; and yet he could see her there as vulgarly troubled, in very truth, as a maidservant crying for a young man. The only thing was that she judged herself as the maidservant wouldn't; the weakness of which wisdom too, the dishonour of which judgment, seemed but to sink her lower.

So Strether loses them too. As he says: "I have lost everything—it is my only logic." It is not that they have gone back. It is that he has gone on. The Paris they revealed to him—he could reveal it to them now, if they had eyes to see, for it is something finer than they could ever notice for themselves, and his imagination has more spiritual value than their youth. The pattern of the hour-glass is complete; he and Chad have changed places, with more subtle steps than Thaïs and Paphnuce, and the light in the clouds proceeds not from the well-lit Alexandria, but from the jewel which "twinkled and trembled and melted together, and what seemed all surface one moment seemed all depth the next."

The beauty that suffuses *The Ambassadors* is the reward due to a fine artist for hard work. James knew exactly what he wanted, he pursued the narrow path of æsthetic duty, and success to the full extent of his possibilities has crowned him. The pattern has woven itself with modulation and reservations Anatole France will never attain. Woven itself wonderfully. But at what sacrifice!

So enormous is the sacrifice that many readers cannot get interested in James, although they can follow what he says (his difficulty has been much exaggerated), and can appreciate his effects. They cannot grant his premise, which is that most of human life has to disappear before he can do us a novel.

He has, in the first place, a very short list of characters. I have already mentioned two—the observer who tries to influence the action, and the second-rate outsider (to whom, for example, all the brilliant opening of *What Maisie Knew* is entrusted). Then there is the sympathetic foil—very lively and frequently female—in *The Ambassadors*. Maria Gostrey plays this part; there is the wonderful rare heroine, whom Mme. de Vionnet approached and who is consummated by Milly in *The Wings of the Dove*; there is sometimes a villain, sometimes a young artist with generous impulses; and that is about all. For so fine a novelist it is a poor show.

In the second place, the characters, beside being few in number, are constructed on very stingy lines. They are incapable of fun, of rapid motion, of carnality, and of nine-tenths of heroism. Their clothes will not take off, the diseases that ravage them are anonymous, like the sources of their income, their servants are noiseless or resemble themselves, no social explanation of the world we know is possible for them, for there are no stupid people in their world, no barriers of language, and no poor. Even their sensations are limited. They can land in Europe and look at works of art and at each other, but that is all. Maimed creatures can alone breathe in Henry James's pages—maimed yet specialized. They remind one of the exquisite deformities who haunted Egyptian art in the reign of Akhenaton—huge heads and tiny legs, but nevertheless charming. In the following reign they disappear.

Now this drastic curtailment, both of the numbers of human beings and of their attributes, is in the interests of the pattern. The longer James worked, the more convinced he grew that a novel should be a whole—not necessarily geometric like *The Ambassadors*, but it should accrete round a single topic, situation, gesture, which should occupy the characters and provide a plot, and should also fasten up the novel on the outside—catch its scattered statements in a net, make them cohere like a planet, and swing through the skies of memory. A pattern must emerge, and anything that emerged from the pattern must be pruned off as wanton distraction. Who so wanton as human beings? Put Tom Jones or Emma or even Mr. Casaubon into a Henry James book, and the book will burn to ashes, whereas we could put them into one another's books and only cause local inflammation. Only a Henry James character will suit, and though they are not dead—certain selected recesses of experience he explores very well—they are gutted of the common stuff that fills characters in other books, and ourselves. And this castrating is not in the interests of the Kingdom of Heaven, there is no philosophy in the novels, no religion (except an occasional touch of superstition), no prophecy, no benefit for the superhuman at all. It is for the sake of a particular æsthetic effect which is certainly gained, but at this heavy price.

H. G. Wells has been amusing on this point, and perhaps profound. In *Boon*—one of his liveliest works—he had Henry James much upon his mind, and wrote a superb parody of him.

> James begin by taking it for granted that a novel is a work of art that must be judged by its oneness. Some one gave him that idea in the beginning of things and he has never found it out. He doesn't find things out. He doesn't even seem to want to find things out. He accepts very readily and then—elaborates. . . . The only living human motives left in his novels are a certain avidity and an entirely superficial curiosity. . . . His people nose out suspicions, hint by hint, link by link. Have you ever known living human beings do that? The thing his novel is *about* is always there. It is like a church lit but with no congregation to distract you, with every light and line focussed on the high altar. And on the altar, very reverently placed, intensely there, is a dead kitten, an egg shell, a piece of string. . . . Like his *Altar of the Dead* with nothing to the dead at all. . . . For if there was, they couldn't all be candles, and the effect would vanish.

Wells sent *Boon* as a present to James, apparently thinking the master would be as much pleased by such heartiness and honesty as was he himself. The master was far from pleased, and a most interesting correspondence ensued.[3] Each of the eminent men becomes more and more himself as it proceeds. James is polite, reminiscent, bewildered, and exceedingly formidable: he admits that the parody has not "filled him with a fond elation," and regrets in conclusion that he can sign himself "only yours faithfully, Henry James." Wells is bewildered too, but in a different way; he cannot understand why the man should be upset. And, beyond the personal comedy, there is the great literary importance of the issue. It is this question of the rigid pattern: hourglass or grand chain or converging lines of the cathedral or diverging lines of the Catherine wheel, or bed of Procrustes—whatever image you like as long as it implies unity. Can it be combined with the immense richness of material which life provides? Wells and James would agree it cannot, Wells would go on to say that life should be given the preference, and must not be whittled or distended for a pattern's sake. My own prejudices are with Wells. The James novels are a unique possession and the reader who cannot accept his premises misses some valuable and exquisite sensations. But I do not want more of his novels, especially

3. See the *Letters of H. James*, vol. II.

when they are written by some one else, just as I do not want the art of Akhenaton to extend into the reign of Tutankhamen.

F. O. MATTHIESSEN (1944)

The Ambassadors†

* * * What caused James' preference for the book was not its theme, but its roundness of structure. On the same grounds of ' "architectural" competence' his second favorite was *The Portrait of a Lady*. In *The Ambassadors* we have a fine instance of the experienced artist taking an external convention, and, instead of letting it act as a handicap, turning it to his own signal advantage. James had always been uneasy—as well he might have been!—with his age's demand for serialized fiction. But here for once he felt a great stimulus to his ingenuity, and he laid out his novel organically in twelve books, each of which could serve for a month's installment. His subject was well fitted to such treatment, since it consisted in Strether's gradual initiation into a world of new values, and a series of small climaxes could therefore best articulate this hero's successive discoveries. * * *

* * * What most concerned James in this structure was also his principal contribution to the art of the novel, his development in Strether of a center of consciousness. What Strether *sees* is the entire content, and James thus perfected a device both for framing and for interpreting experience. All art must give the effect of putting a frame around its subject, in the sense that it must select a significant design, and, by concentrating upon it, thus empower us to share in the essence without being distracted by irrelevant details. James' device serves greatly to reinforce such concentration, since if every detail must be observed and analysed by Strether, we obtain a heightened singleness of vision. We obtain both 'the large unity' and 'the grace of intensity' which James held to be the final criteria for a novel. His contribution here has been fully assessed by critics, and has been assimilated in varying degrees by many subsequent novelists. Indeed, some have gone so far as to declare *The Ambassadors* the most skillfully planned novel ever written. The chief reminder we need now is that there is a vast difference between James' method and that of the novels of 'the stream of consciousness.' That phrase was used by William James in his *Principles of Psychology*, but in his brother's novels there is none of the welling up of the darkly subconscious life that has characterized the novel since Freud. James'

† Excerpted from *Henry James: The Major Phase* by F. O. Matthiessen, copyright (©) 1944 by Oxford University Press, Inc.; renewed 1971 by Mrs. Peters Putnam. Reprinted by permission of Oxford University Press, Inc. Pages 19–41. The chapter has been abridged.

novels are strictly novels of intelligence rather than of full consciousness; and in commenting on the focus of attention that he had achieved through Strether, he warned against 'the terrible *fluidity* of self-revelation.' * * *

The challenge to *live*, in its short initial form [in James's notebooks], had dwelt solely on the elderly man's warning—James stipulated his age as fifty-five—against the repetition of his mistake. James' immense elaboration of this challenge tells how much it meant to him. As Strether delivers it in Gloriani's garden, it becomes in fact the quintessential expression of a dominant theme that runs throughout James' work. * * *

Strether introduces into his version of this declaration for life a highly complex image, which serves to reveal his Puritan heritage. It is the image of life as a tin mould, be it plain or fluted and embossed, into which the 'helpless jelly' of one's consciousness is poured by 'the great cook.' In this way Strether symbolizes the illusion of free will: the form of the individual consciousness has been predetermined and limited, not, to be sure, by the Puritans' God, but by every force in the individual's background and environment. Yet Strether insists that we make the most of life by enjoying our illusion, that we should act as though we were free. * * *

James himself did not have the heritage of American Puritanism. He spoke of his not being a New Englander 'as a danger after all escaped.' He remarked also, 'Boston is absolutely nothing to me—I don't even dislike it.' But to understand all the overtones with which he charged the imperative *live*, we must remember that his grandfather was an Irish Presbyterian. Against that background James' father was in revolt. Yet even as he responded to Emerson's rejection of the old restrictions, he found that philosopher dangerously limited by his refusal to reckon with Calvinism 'as a fact at all' in his sublime superiority to evil. Most of Henry James Senior's own declarations, as he ripened into his version of Swedenborgianism, were on the side of optimism and expansion. In that he proved himself a child of his age, but the strong residue of his concern with the nature of evil was to be transmitted to his sons, though ultimately more to the brooding novelist than to the hopeful philosopher.

Yet Strether's declaration, except for its qualifying of free will, continues, essentially, the transcendental mood of liberation. What had proved so heartening to Emerson's contemporaries was his insistence that life for Americans no longer needed to be starved. The most intense expression of that conviction, perhaps the most intense single passage in American writing, is Thoreau's development of a theme extraordinarily like Strether's. When Thoreau declared why he went to the woods, he too revealed the depth of the New England dread that a man might die without ever having lived. But Thoreau's will was in dynamic response to the challenge, and he expressed his desire 'to suck out all the marrow of life' in a series of physical images, the energy of which was quite beyond Strether—or James.

The relative attenuation of Strether's desire, its passive rather than active scope, is one of the most striking consequences of James' own peculiar conditioning. No experimental child of the nineteenth century, not even John Stuart Mill, was brought up more deliberately on a theory. That theory, as James described it in *Notes of a Son and Brother*, sprang from his father's profound aversion to the narrow competitive drives of American life. What he wanted for his sons was the greatest possible range of spiritual experience—'spiritual,' as Henry noted, was his father's 'most living' word—before they should be limited by the dictates of a career. In fact, as Henry was humorously aware, his father carried his dread of their being circumscribed to such lengths as to deplore their decision upon any career at all, and continued in the hope that they were instead 'just to *be* something, something unconnected with specific doing, something free and uncommitted . . .'

Such a theory could have resulted in utter dispersion in a group with less passion for ideas than the James family possessed. But as it affected both the older boys, it induced a slow but richer ripening. It may well have caused some of William's early nervous tensions, as he struggled to find himself by turning from painting to experimental science to medicine, and only finally to psychology and philosophy. But it meant that when he finally wrote his first book, at the age of forty-seven, in the same year as Henry's *Tragic Muse*, he produced a masterpiece, *The Principles of Psychology*. Henry's tensions were less apparent but extremely acute, and the more glimpses we catch of them, the more we perceive why a declaration like Strether's spoke so much for himself as well. On the verge of manhood, the injury to his back that kept him from participating in the Civil War made him feel that his was the peculiar case of having to live inwardly at a time of 'immense and prolonged outwardness.' For many years thereafter his health continued to be so precarious that he was afraid he might never be able to bring his expression of life to the fullness for which he longed, an anxiety which found its way into such a story of an artist's frustration as *The Madonna of the Future*. As he came through to middle age, he began to find stability, and though in his 'summing up' he could recall that his twenties had been 'a time of suffering so keen that that fact might seem to pin its dark colours to the whole period,' nevertheless the dominant strain in his memories was quite other. He could feel at last the satisfaction of having 'wanted to do very much what I have done, and success, if I may say so, now stretches back a tender hand to its younger brother, desire.'

But he was still to have many hours of his old anxiety, of feeling merely on the verge of completion. And though, unlike Strether, he had not been shut out from the opportunity for impressions of life, still he was to come back again and again to a central dilemma. He made his most complete declaration of it shortly after he had started to work for the stage. His advice to himself should be put beside Strether's advice to Bilham: 'The upshot of all such reflections is that I have only to let myself *go*. So I have said to myself all my life—so I said to myself in the far-off days of my fermenting and passionate youth. Yet I have never fully done it. The taste of it—of the need of it—rolls over me at times with commanding force: it seems the formula of my salvation, of what remains to me of a future. I am in full possession of accumulated resources—I have only to use them, to insist, to persist, to do something more,—to do much more,—than I *have* done. The way to do it—to affirm one's self *sur la fin*—is to strike as many notes, deep, full, and rapid, as one can. All life is—at my age, with all one's artistic soul the record of it—in one's pocket, as it were. Go on, my boy, and strike hard; have a rich and long St. Martin's Summer. Try everything, do everything, render everything—be an artist, be distinguished to the last.'

Another decade was to elapse before he was able to let himself go to his full extent, and to say finally the most that he had to say. His Saint Martin's summer really began with *The Ambassadors*. It is notable that the two New England minds of his own generation with whom he had most enjoyed friendship during his Boston years were to come to equally late flowering. Henry Adams was not to write his *Mont-Saint-Michel and Chartres* until he was past sixty-five and his *Education* until he was almost seventy. Wendell Holmes was to arrive at his full stature only after he reached the Supreme Court, at sixty-one, in the same year as *The Ambassadors* appeared. These other late harvests, along with those of the James brothers, are evidence against the current belief that American talents always burn themselves out after an early promise. They may indicate too that the older New England strain could come to valuable expression, in the period of New England's cultural decline, only if it had the stamina to survive its arid surroundings and so mature at last the rich juices for which Adams in particular felt himself parched.

What Strether awakened to in Paris was not unlike the aesthetic experience that Adams came finally to know only as he discovered the beauty of the cathedrals. Strether keeps emphasizing the importance of seeing, and we know that James himself lived in large measure by his eyes. He developed very early the feeling that intense life concentrated itself into scenes of which he was the absorbed spectator. This was to mean that of the two types into which Yeats divides artists, those who, like Blake, celebrate their own immediate share in the energy that 'is eternal delight,' and those who, like Keats, give us a poignant sense of being separated from what they present, James belonged to the latter. He described his own early romantic longing for 'otherness' in terms very close to those Yeats was to use for Keats:

'I see a schoolboy when I think of him,
With face and nose pressed to a sweet shop window . . .

James said that in his childhood 'to *be* other, other almost anyhow, seemed as good as the probable taste of the bright compound wistfully watched in the confectioner's window, unattainable, impossible . . .' His account too of the kind of delight he took in his first 'pedestrian gaping' along Broadway delineates even more sharply the type to which he belonged. For at this very same time, in the early eighteen-fifties, an incipient American poet had also been drinking in the sights of this same street. But Whitman was to make his poetry out of passionate identification with everything he saw, not out of detachment. James, on the other hand, came to believe that 'the only form of riot or revel' his temperament would ever know would be that 'of the visiting mind,' and that he could attain the longed for 'otherness' of the world outside himself only by imaginative projection which, by framing his vision, could give it permanence.

What Strether sees is what James saw, the Europe of the tourist. But James conceived of seeing in a multiple sense, as an act of the inward even more than of the outward eye. An interesting chapter of cultural history could be written about the nineteenth century's stress on sight. When Emerson declared that 'the age is ocular,' and delighted in the fact that the poet is the seer, he was overwhelmingly concerned with the spiritual and not the material vision. But concern with the external world came to mark every phase of the century's increasing closeness of observation, whether in such scientific achievements as the lenses for the telescope and the microscope, or in the painters' new experiments with light, or in the determination of the photographers and the realistic novelists to record every specific surface detail. Matthew Arnold was to note that 'curiosity' had a good sense in French, but unfortunately only a bad one in English. James, an early convert to Arnold's culture, set himself to prove the value of the farthest reaches of curiosity. The distance that he had travelled from Emerson may be measured by the fact that though both knew their chief subject matter to be consciousness, the mind's awareness of its processes, for Emerson that awareness reaffirmed primarily the moral laws. James was also a moralist, but aesthetic experience was primarily for him, since αἰσθητικός meant perceptive. He had turned that double-edged word 'seer' back to this world. As he said in the preface to *The Ambassadors*, 'art deals with what we see, it must first contribute full-handed that ingredient; it plucks its material, otherwise expressed, in the garden of life—which material elsewhere grown is stale and uneatable.' But what distinguished him from French naturalists and English aesthetes alike was that he never forgot the further kind of seeing, the transcendent passage to the world behind appearance and beyond the senses.

Emerson had exulted that the eye was 'the best of painters,' but his poetry and prose were both woefully lacking in plastic quality. James deliberately cultivated the skills of the painter. The first form he had experimented with as a small boy was what he called in his reminiscences 'dramatic, accompanied by pictorial composition,' short scenes each followed by its illustration. * * * Henry at seventeen had shown his own shy curiosity in sketching. And although he soon realized that he had no talent, and turned to fiction, 'it was to feel, with reassurance, that the picture was still in essence one's aim.' He was to continue to train his eye by means of his long series of 'portraits of places,' wherein he followed the lead of Gautier and other Frenchmen who were bringing literature closer to the art of the Impressionists. He was finally to arrive at the explicit statement that he wanted such a story as *The Coxon Fund* to be 'an Impression—as one of Sargent's pictures is an impression.'

The perfected instance of his belief that the novelist should 'catch the colour of life' is the way he initiates both Strether and the reader into Paris. His accuracy of presentation is such that he can really suggest the quality of Chad's existence through the very look of his house, 'its cold fair grey, warmed and polished a little by life.' James makes such a magnificently functional use of his architectural details that his hero is persuaded—and thousands of his countrymen have had the same yearning belief—that the life which goes on behind those windows and that balcony must also be characterized by tact and taste, by 'the fine relation of part to part and space to space.' And when Strether throws to the winds all scruples as to what Mrs. Newsome would think, and invites Madame de Vionnet to lunch, James presents us with a fully achieved canvas: 'How could he wish it to be lucid for others, for any one, that he, for the hour, saw reasons enough in the mere way the bright clean ordered water-side life came in at the open window?—the mere way Madame de Vionnet, opposite him over their intensely white table-linen, their *omelette aux tomates*, their bottle of straw-colored Chablis, thanked him for everything almost with the smile of a child, while her grey eyes moved in and out of their talk, back to the quarter of the warm spring air, in which early summer had already begun to throb, and then back again to his face and their human questions.'

Here he has come to the essence, not of Sargent's effects but of Renoir's, in the wonderful sense of open air; in the sensuous relish of all the surfaces, with exactly the right central spot of color in that *omelette aux tomates*; in the exquisite play of light around his figures. And when James added a further accent, it made for the very kind of charm by which the Impressionists declared their art a release from stuffy manners as well as from stale techniques: Madame de Vionnet 'was a woman who, between courses, could be graceful with her elbows on the table. It was a posture unknown to Mrs. Newsome . . .'

James' cities, unlike Balzac's or Joyce's, focus on the inviting vistas

presented to the well-to-do visitor. The very air of Strether's Paris has
the taste 'of something mixed with art, something that presented nature
as a white-capped master-chef.' But James was not ignorant of what he
called 'the huge collective life' going on beyond his charmed circle; and
at the end, when Strether is meditating on Madame de Vionnet's suffering, he thinks too of the vast suffering Paris has witnessed, and senses
in the streets their long ineradicable 'smell of revolution, the smell of
the public temper—or perhaps simply the smell of blood.' Yet such
omens are black shadows looming only at the very edge of James' pictures. What he chose to frame, specially selected though it is, takes on
an intensity to the degree that he could realize the multiple kinds of
seeing in which he had striven to perfect himself, and could demonstrate
that he had mastered 'the art of reflection' in both senses of that
phrase—both as a projector of the luminous surfaces of life, and as an
interpreter of their significance. Perhaps the most brilliant instance of
this double skill in all James' work is the recognition scene on the river,
a scene which reveals also his extraordinary awareness of how art frames
experience. He took great delight in adapting plastic devices for a highly
developed, wholly unexpected illustration of this aesthetic process.

When Strether decides on a day in the country, what leads him there
is his far-off memory 'of a certain small Lambinet that had charmed
him, long years before, at a Boston dealer's.' It is interesting to recall
that this nearly forgotten painter of scenes along the Seine was of the
era of Rousseau and Daubigny, all of whom James noted as having been
first shown to him in the early days by Hunt.

On one plane, Strether's being drawn by art to nature to verify an
old impression, shows the curious reversal of order in the modern sensibility. On another plane, as he dwells on how much that canvas, not
expensive but far beyond his purse, had meant to him in the Tremont
Street gallery, we have a sharp contrast between Strether's New England
actuality and his long smothered French ideal. But James doesn't leave
it at that. Strether's entire day progresses as though he had 'not once
overstepped the oblong gilt frame.' The whole scene was there, the
clustered houses and the poplars and the willows: 'it was Tremont Street,
it was France, it was Lambinet.' In the late afternoon, as he sits at a
village café overlooking a reach of the river, his landscape takes on a
further interest. It becomes a Landscape with Figures, as a boat appears
around the bend, a man rowing, a lady with a pink parasol. There, in
an instant, was 'the lie in the charming affair.' The skill with which
James has held our eyes within his frame has so heightened the significance of every slight detail that such a recognition scene leaps out with
the force of the strongest drama.

What Strether has seen comes to him as a great shock, but it does
not cause him to waver in his judgment of how much Chad has improved. What he is anxious about now is whether Chad is really worthy

of what Madame de Vionnet has given him, and there are plenty of undeveloped hints at the close that he is not, that he is already restive, that he will not be happy permanently without the business world, and that he may even soon be turning to a younger woman. What then finally is the positive content of Strether's challenge to Bilham? As far as that young painter is concerned, the possibilities seem very slight. His eye has taken in so much of the beautiful surface of Paris that his productive power has faltered before it; and though he is happy with his vision, his is certainly a mild version of the doctrine of being rather than of doing.

What then of Strether himself, what has he gained from his initiation? Waymarsh warned him at the outset that he was 'a very attractive man,' and Maria Gostrey says that he owes more to women than any man she ever saw. Yet when he encounters Gloriani, Strether is acutely conscious of his own 'rather grey interior.' He expresses his sense of the Italian sculptor's vitality through an image of the sexual jungle: he both admires and envies 'the glossy male tiger, magnificently marked.' How far James himself had advanced in his penetration into character may be instanced by his different handling of this same Gloriani in *Roderick Hudson* nearly thirty years before. There the worldly sculptor had been somewhat cheap in his sophistication as he played the rôle of a Mephistopheles to Roderick's Faust. But now James suggests an unfathomable depth of 'human expertness' in his eyes, an enormous fund of 'terrible' energy behind his smile.

It is revelatory of the careful pattern that James worked out in *The Ambassadors* to note the sequence of events in this crucial scene in Gloriani's garden. As he first takes in the beauty of his surroundings in the heart of the Faubourg Saint-Germain, Strether reflects to Bilham: 'You've all of you here so much visual sense that you've somehow all "run" to it. There are moments when it strikes one that you haven't any other.' Almost at once thereafter Strether is presented to Madame de Vionnet, and when she moves on after a few moments' conversation, he faces Bilham with his declaration for life. This, in turn, he follows with his expressed envy of Gloriani. None of these connections are made explicit, a sign that James' way of creating Madame de Vionnet's charm is to render it more pervasive in its operation than anything he says about it. Before the close of this scene he remarks that Strether is the kind of man who receives 'an amount of experience out of any proportion to his adventures.' That, we recall, is what James also rejoiced over in his preface, that in Strether he had had his full chance 'to "do" a man of imagination.'

But what does Strether finally make of his experience? The issue at the close shows how rigorously James believed that an author should hold to his structure. He had posited his hero's sense that it was too late for him to live; and had reinforced this with Strether's New England scrupulosity that in siding with Chad his conscience could be clear, since there was to be 'nothing in it for himself.' And no matter how bewilderingly iridescent he finds the jewel-image of Paris, since 'what seemed all surface one moment seemed all depth the next,' Strether never loses his moral sense. James seems to have taken his own special pleasure in avoiding the banal by not making Paris the usual scene of seduction but instead the center of an ethical drama. Another aspect of the structure—and its most artificial—is the rôle of *ficelle* conceived for Maria Gostrey. She exists only as a confidante for Strether, only as a means of letting him comment on his experience. Consequently, as James himself noted, she had a 'false connexion' with the plot which he had to bend his ingenuity to make appear as a real one. But his device of having her fall in love with Strether and hope wistfully to marry him does not achieve such reality.

It serves rather to exaggerate the negative content of Strether's renunciation. He has come at last, as he says, to *see* Mrs. Newsome, and we know by now how much is involved in that word. But he leaves Paris and Maria to go back to no prospect of life at all. We are confronted here with what will strike us much more forcibly in *The Golden Bowl*, the contrast in James between imputed and actual values. The burden of *The Ambassadors* is that Strether has awakened to a wholly new sense of life. Yet he does nothing at all to fulfill that sense. Therefore, fond as James is of him, we cannot help feeling his relative emptiness. At times, even, as when James describes how 'he went to Rouen with a little handbag and inordinately spent the night,' it is forced upon us that, despite James' humorous awareness of the inadequacy of his hero's adventures, neither Strether nor his creator escape a certain soft fussiness.

What gives this novel the stamina to survive the dated flavor of Strether's liberation is the quality that James admired most in Turgenieff, the ability to endow some of his characters with such vitality that they seem to take the plot into their own hands, or rather, to continue to live beyond its exigencies. The center of that vitality here is the character not reckoned with in James' initial outline. For what pervades the final passages is Strether's unacknowledged love for Madame de Vionnet. James has succeeded in making her so attractive that, quite apart from the rigid requirement of his structure, there can really be no question of Strether's caring deeply for any other woman. The means that James used to evoke her whole way of life is a supreme instance of how he went about to give concrete embodiment to his values. Just as he devoted the greatest care to the surroundings for Strether's declaration and explicitly drew on his own memories of the garden behind the house where Madame Récamier had died, so he created Madame de Vionnet entirely in terms of and inseparable from old Paris. Every distinction in her manner is related to Strether's impression of her house, where each chair and cabinet suggests 'some glory, some prosperity of the First Empire, some Napoleonic glamour, some dim lustre of the great legend.' In his 'summing up' James had attempted to convey why the great English houses had grown to mean so much to him. It was primarily their 'accumulations of expression': 'the soil over which so much has passed, and out of which so much has come,' they 'rose before me like a series of visions . . . I thought of stories, of dramas, of all the life of the past—of things one can hardly speak of; speak of, I mean at the time. It is art that speaks of those things; and the idea makes me adore her more and more.'

That gives us insight into why James, to a greater degree than any other American artist, was a spokesman for the imagination as a conserving force. He believed that art is the great conserver, since it alone can give permanence to the more perishable order of society. Yet, despite the usual view of him, James dwelt very little in the past. His impressions and his reading were preponderantly, almost oppressively, contemporary. His one living tap-root to the past was through his appreciation of such an exquisite product of tradition as Madame de Vionnet. Yet, as he created her, she was the very essence of the aesthetic sensibility of his own day. Strether can hardly find enough comparisons for her splendor. Her head is like that on 'an old precious medal of the Renaissance.' She is 'a goddess still partly engaged in a morning cloud,' or 'a sea-nymph waist-high in the summer surge.' She is so 'various and multifold' that he hardly needs to mention Cleopatra. And though Mona Lisa is not mentioned, James is evoking something very like Pater's spell. Although James' moral residues are considerably different from Pater's, both Strether and James could have subscribed to much of Pater's famous exhortation for fullness of life, particularly to the sentence which urges that one's passion should yield 'this fruit of a quickened, multiplied consciousness.'

But Madame de Vionnet is more human than Pater's evocation. On the last night that Strether sees her, she seems older, 'visibly less exempt from the touch of time.' And though she is still 'the finest and subtlest creature' he has ever met, she is, even as Shakespeare's Cleopatra, troubled like 'a maid servant crying for her young man.' In an image which enables him to fuse the qualities with which he especially wants to endow her, James makes Strether think that her dress of 'simplest coolest white' is so old fashioned 'that Madame Roland must on the scaffold have worn something like it.' Madame de Vionnet's end is also to be tragic. She has learned from life that no real happiness comes from taking: 'the only safe thing is to give.' Such a nature is far too good for Chad, and she realizes now that 'the only certainty' for the future is that she will be 'the loser in the end.' Her positive suffering and loss are far more affecting than Strether's tenuous renunciation.

THE MEANING OF PARIS IN *THE AMBASSADORS*: A DISAGREEMENT

F. R. LEAVIS† (1948)

* * * *The Ambassadors,* * * * which [James] seems to have thought his greatest success, produces an effect of disproportionate "doing"—of a technique the subtleties and elaborations of which are not sufficiently controlled by a feeling for value and significance in living. What, we ask, is this, symbolized by Paris, that Strether feels himself to have missed in his own life? Has James himself sufficiently inquired? Is it anything adequately realized? If we are to take the elaboration of the theme in the spirit in which we are meant to take it, haven't we to take the symbol too much at the glamorous face-value it has for Strether? Isn't, that is, the energy of the "doing" (and the energy demanded for the reading) disproportionate to the issues—to any issues that are concretely held and presented?

JOSEPH WARREN BEACH‡ (1954)

* * * One is quite at a loss to understand how this enlightened critic [F. R. Leavis] should so resolutely decline to read what is written in capitals on every page of this book. Does James need to tell us in so many words that Paris is, for Strether, as it has been for many generations of Americans, and Englishmen too—the *Ville Lumière,* the place where ideas are everywhere in circulation, and subject to free and animated discussion—and that in this respect it is the absolute antithesis to Woollett, Mass., where Strether had been spending his starved life? Does he need to tell us—but this he does plainly—that it is physically and socially a seat of great amenity, where one can exercise and communicate with "an ideal civilized sensibility; a humanity capable of the finest shades of inflection and implication," where "a nuance may engage a whole complex moral economy and the perceptive response be the index of a major valuation or choice"? Is it not clear that what Paris gives to Strether, under the helpful direction of Maria Gostrey, is a "glimpse of a possible 'civilization' in which the manners belonging to a ripe social intercourse shall be the index of a moral refinement"—well, if not "of the best American kind" as conceived in Woollett, at least of the kind that was implicit in every turn of James's father's ethical philosophy? For the elder James was determined to cultivate the spirit and substance

---

† From *The Great Tradition* (London: Chattox Windus, 1948), 161.
‡ From "Introduction: 1954," *The Method of Henry James* (Philadelphia: Albert Saifer, 1954), xlviii–li. Reprinted with the kind permission of Northrop and Warren Beach.

of the moral life, and was highly scornful of the "flagrant moralism" which he found so often taking the place of true ethical judgment. And so Strether.

He went to Paris to fetch back Chad Newsome, so that the young man might go into the business and further augment the family fortune; and he was expected to pry him loose from some low sexual involvement. It took some time to determine just what this involvement was, but it soon became evident that it was not so low but what it had made a thoroughly "civilized" man of Chad. To Strether it was clear that Chad owed something to a relationship so serious and of such long standing, which involved so genuine and deep a love on the part of the woman, and in the end he is greatly disappointed with Chad for his willingness to ditch his love so irresponsibly, so that he can return to Woollett and go into the advertising end of the business.

In the course of the series of occasions necessary to bring about these successive changes of view in regard to Chad, Strether has had an opportunity to revise his opinion of Mrs. Newsome and to take a good dose of the Woollett tone in the persons of the Pococks, sent over to keep him in line. None of this is too subtle for any interested reader to take in, but it does take a good deal of "doing." For it involves nothing less than the formal opposition of a commercial, utilitarian and narrowly puritan way of living and thinking to that "possible 'civilization' in which the manners, etc., shall be the index, etc." That is, for Strether it involves his instinct to judge moral situations from the inside by their quality and substance rather than by the labels attached to them by conventional opinion from the outside.

Perhaps the unsureness of James's moral touch is betrayed, for Mr. Leavis, by the fact that, when Strether is thoroughly persuaded of the rightness of Chad's attachment to Mme. de Vionnet, and of the obligation to loyalty which it entails for Chad, he is scarcely perturbed by his accidental discovery that their relation is a "guilty" one. But that can hardly be what troubles a critic like Mr. Leavis, who prefers genuine though "guilty" love relations to sentimental platonic ones. * * *

Or perhaps the unsureness of touch is shown in the several changes of attitude undergone by Strether between the first page and the last. It is here that we may have come to the heart of the matter. For the great peculiarity of James's later narratives is that we do not arrive at his final valuations without going through a long course of "visions and revisions." And while it may seem to some of us that this is the very way that, in actual life, we do win through to our valuations, and that indeed such is the true essence of a live and working ethical experience, it may appear to others to be the sign of a radical unsureness of touch in author and character, and a fertile source of obscurity and obfuscation for the reader.

JOAN BENNETT† (1956)

* * * It is characteristic of Leavis that he goes straight to the heart of the matter. Certainly these questions are the ones we should ask ourselves. The only adequate answers are contained in the novel itself —the work of art in which James unearths his buried bone. But some reader may be deterred from looking there by Leavis' implication that he will find nothing worth while. In case that should happen I will attempt to counterattack.

During the seven years that intervened between his hearing the anecdote and his writing *The Ambassadors* James was asking himself what it was "symbolized by Paris" that Strether felt himself to have missed. The answer is in the whole series of impressions we are made to share with him through the novel. Little more can be said, in other terms than James's own, except that he had missed those spontaneous joys that come from the contemplation of beauty, the culture of the mind and uncalculating love for a fellow-creature. It does not seem to James—and it does not seem to a reader who responds to his novel— that Paris has, by the end, a "glamorous face value" for Strether. It had something like that at the beginning of the book. But the Paris he renounces for himself contains cruelty, greed, and suffering as well as generosity, courage, and joy. The issues "concretely held and presented" are not, to my mind, disproportionate to the labor of writing or of reading because they are ever-relevant issues between true and false human values. Finally I should like to add that the "energy demanded for reading" is rewarded at every turn, not only because we share with James the discovery of important truths; but because we are continuously spellbound by his story and amused by his irony, his wit, and his charm in presenting what he sees.

LEON EDEL‡ (1960)

* * * But is it merely the "glamorous face value" of Paris? Mr. Leavis is under the impression that the traditional symbol of the French capital as a glittering Babylon is the whole of Strether's vision. This is decidedly not the case. It is *seeing* that is the subject of the novel, perception at the pitch of awareness; and this could have been treated in any scene, as James remarked in his notebooks when he debated the merits of Paris as against England or Italy. As Joan Bennett has pointed out, we are made to share a "whole series of impressions" with Strether throughout the novel—his feelings in the green countryside, his sympathy with Madame de Vionnet, his grasp of the ideal and the ugly, his balancing

† From *Chicago Review* (Winter 1956) 9:26. Reprinted by permission of *Chicago Review*.
‡ From "Introduction," *The Ambassadors* (Boston: Houghton Mifflin, 1972), xv–xvi. *The Ambassadors by Henry James*, Riverside Edition. Copyright (©) 1972 by Houghton Mifflin Company. Used by permission.

of the parochial and the cosmopolitan, his appraisal of an entire code of values as between Woollett and Paris, and his refusal to dance to the trite little tune of Sarah Pocock. All this is a great deal more than the "face value" of the French capital. "Awareness" is made by James the very essence of life itself.

Miss Bennett leaves partly unanswered the other aspect of Mr. Leavis's statement: "the energy demanded for the reading." If we are to start measuring such energies, we would find ourselves indeed in an uncritical muscle-flexing world. * * * Personal "energy" cannot, it seems to me, be invoked in this way; it is, critically speaking, irrelevant. There are readers for whom certain books will always remain closed; and others for whom the same books cannot be opened too often. James wrote *The Ambassadors* for the attentive reader, and a reader capable of *seeing* with him —and accepting his painter-sense, his brush-work, his devotion to picture and to scene and above all his need to render this in a highly colored and elaborate style, so as to capture the nuances of his perceptions. The reader who is able to give him "attention of perusal," will discover soon enough the particular rewards of this book. When he meets James on the ground proper to the novelist, and walks with him over it, he will recognize, after fifty years, that *The Ambassadors* possesses a singular perfection—the novel converted from mere storytelling to work of art.

IAN WATT (1960)

The First Paragraph of *The Ambassadors*: An Explication†

* * * [The first paragraph of *The Ambassadors* (p. 17)] seems a fairly ordinary sort of prose, but for its faint air of elaborate portent; and on second reading its general quality reminds one of what Strether is later to observe—approvingly—in Maria Gostrey: an effect of 'expensive, subdued suitability'. There's certainly nothing particularly striking in the diction or syntax; none of the immediate drama or rich description that we often get at the beginning of novels; and certainly none of the sensuous concreteness that, until recently, was regarded as a chief criterion of good prose in our long post-imagistic phase: if anything, the passage is conspicuously un-sensuous and un-concrete, a little dull perhaps, and certainly not easy reading.

The difficulty isn't one of particularly long or complicated sentences:

† From *Essays in Criticism* X (July 1960): 250–74. The opening discussion of the theory of explication has been omitted here; discussions of Dickens and Conrad have also been abridged later on. Reprinted by permission of the author and *Essays in Criticism*.

actually they're of fairly usual length: I make it an average of 41 words; a little, but not very much, longer than James' average of 35 (in Book 2, ch. 2 of *The Ambassadors*, according to R. W. Short's count, in his very useful article 'The Sentence Structure of Henry James', *American Literature*, XVIII [March 1946], 71–88).[1] The main cause of difficulty seems rather to come from what may be called the delayed specification of referents: 'Strether' and 'the hotel' and 'his friend' are mentioned before we are told who or where they are. But this difficulty is so intimately connected with James's general narrative technique that it may be better to begin with purely verbal idiosyncrasies, which are more easily isolated. The most distinctive ones in the passage seem to be these: a preference for non-transitive verbs; many abstract nouns; much use of 'that'; a certain amount of elegant variation to avoid piling up personal pronouns and adjectives such as 'he', 'his' and 'him'; and the presence of a great many negatives and near-negatives.

By the preference for non-transitive verbs I mean three related habits: a great reliance on copulatives—'Strether's first question *was* about his friend'; '*was* apparently not to arrive': a frequent use of the passive voice—'*was* not wholly *disconcerted*'; 'a telegram . . . *was produced*'; 'his business *would be* a trifle *bungled*': and the employment of many intransitive verbs—'the understanding . . . remained . . . sound'; 'the . . . principle . . . operated to'. My count of all the verbs in the indicative would give a total of 14 passive, copulative or intransitive uses as opposed to only 6 transitive ones: and there are in addition frequent infinitive, participial, or gerundial uses of transitive verbs, in all of which the active nature of the subject-verb-and-object sequence is considerably abated— 'on his learning'; 'bespeaking a room'; 'not absolutely to desire'; 'led him thus to postpone'.

This relative infrequency of transitive verbal usages in the passage is associated with the even more pronounced tendency towards using abstract nouns as subjects of main or subordinate clauses: 'question'; 'understanding'; 'the same secret principle'; 'the principle'; 'his business'. If one takes only the main clauses, there are four such abstract nouns as subjects, while only three main clauses have concrete and particular subjects ('he', or 'they').[2]

I detail these features only to establish that in this passage, at least, there is a clear quantitative basis for the common enough view that James's late prose style is characteristically abstract; more explicitly, that the main grammatical subjects are very often nouns for mental ideas, 'question', 'principle', etc.; and that the verbs—because they are mainly

1. I am also indebted to the same author's 'Henry James's World of Images', *PMLA* LXVIII (Dec., 1953), 943–960.
2. Sentences one and four are compound or multiple, but in my count I haven't included the second clause in the latter—'there was little fear': though if we can talk of the clause having a subject it's an abstract one—'fear'.

used either non-transitively, or in infinitive, participial and gerundial forms,—tend to express states of being rather than particular finite actions affecting objects.

The main use of abstractions is to deal at the same time with many objects or events rather than single and particular ones: and we use verbs that denote states of being rather than actions for exactly the same reason—their much more general applicability. But in this passage, of course, James isn't in the ordinary sense making abstract or general statements; it's narrative, not expository prose; what need exploring, therefore, are the particular literary imperatives which impose on his style so many of the verbal and syntactical qualities of abstract and general discourse; of expository rather than narrative prose.

Consider the first sentence. The obvious narrative way of making things particular and concrete would presumably be 'When Strether reached the hotel, he first asked "Has Mr. Waymarsh arrived yet?" ' Why does James say it the way he does? One effect is surely that, instead of a sheer stated event, we get a very special view of it; the mere fact that actuality has been digested into reported speech—the question 'was about his friend'—involves a narrator to do the job, to interpret the action, and also a presumed audience that he does it for: and by implication, the heat of the action itself must have cooled off somewhat for the translation and analysis of the events into this form of statement to have had time to occur. Lastly, making the subject of the sentence 'question' rather than 'he' has the effect of subordinating the particular actor, and therefore the particular act, to a much more general perspective: mental rather than physical, and subjective rather than objective; 'question' is a word which involves analysis of a physical event into terms of meaning and intention: it involves, in fact, both Strether's mind and the narrator's. The narrator's, because he interprets Strether's act: if James had sought the most concrete method of taking us into Strether's mind—' "Has Mr. Waymarsh come yet?" I at once asked'—he would have obviated the need for the implied external categoriser of Strether's action. But James disliked the 'mere platitude of statement' involved in first-person narrative; partly, presumably, because it would merge Strether's consciousness into the narrative, and not isolate it for the reader's inspection. For such isolation, a more expository method is needed: no confusion of subject and object, as in first-person narration, but a narrator forcing the reader to pay attention to James's primary objective—Strether's mental and subjective state.

The 'multidimensional' quality of the narrative, with its continual implication of a community of three minds—Strether's, James's, and the reader's—isn't signalled very obviously until the fourth sentence—'The principle I have just mentioned as operating . . .'; but it's already been established tacitly in every detail of diction and structure, and it remains pervasive. One reason for the special demand James's fictional prose makes on our attention is surely that there are always at least three levels of development—all of them subjective: the characters' awareness of events; the narrator's seeing of them; and our own trailing perception of the relation between these two.

The primary location of the narrative in a mental rather than a physical continuum gives the narrative a great freedom from the restrictions of particular time and place. Materially, we are, of course, in Chester, at the hotel—characteristically 'the hotel' because a fully particularised specification—'The Pied Bull Inn' say—would be an irrelevant brute fact which would distract attention from the mental train of thought we are invited to partake in. But actually we don't have any pressing sense of time and place: we feel ourselves to be spectators, rather specifically, of Strether's thought processes, which easily and imperceptibly range forwards and backwards both in time and space. Sentence three, for example, begins in the past, at the Liverpool dock; sentence four looks forward to the reunion later that day, and to its many sequels: such transitions of time and place are much easier to effect when the main subjects of the sentences are abstract: a 'principle' exists independently of its context.

The multiplicity of relations—between narrator and object, and between the ideas in Strether's mind—held in even suspension throughout the narrative, is presumably the main explanation for the number of 'thats' in the passage, as well as of the several examples of elegant variation. There are 9 'thats'—only two of them demonstrative and the rest relative pronouns (or conjunctions or particles if you prefer those terms); actually there were no less than three more of them in the first edition, which James removed from the somewhat more colloquial and informal New York edition; while there are several other 'thats' implied—in 'the principle [that] I have just mentioned', for instance.

The number of 'thats' follows from two habits already noted in the passage. 'That' characteristically introduces relative clauses dealing not with persons but with objects, including abstractions; and it is also used to introduce reported speech—'on his learning that Waymarsh'—not 'Mr. Waymarsh isn't here'. Both functions are combined in the third sentence where we get a triple definition of a timeless idea based on the report of three chronologically separate events: 'the same secret principle, however, that had prompted Strether not absolutely to desire Waymarsh's presence at the dock, that had led him thus to postpone for a few hours his enjoyment of it, now operated to make him feel that he could still wait without disappointment'.

Reported rather than direct speech also increases the pressure towards elegant variation: the use, for example, in sentence 1 of 'his friend', where in direct speech it would be 'Mr. Waymarsh' (and the reply— '*He* hasn't come yet'). In the second sentence—'a telegram . . . was produced for the inquirer'—'inquirer' is needed because 'him' has already been used for Waymarsh just above; of course, 'the inquirer' is logical enough after the subject of the first sentence has been an abstract noun—'question'; and the epithet also gives James an opportunity for underlining the ironic distance and detachment with which we are invited to view his dedicated 'inquirer', Strether. Later, when Strether is 'the most newly disembarked of the two men', we see how both elegant variation and the grammatical subordination of physical events are related to the general Jamesian tendency to present characters and actions on a plane of abstract categorisation; the mere statement, 'Mr. Waymarsh had already been in England for [so many] months', would itself go far to destroy the primarily mental continuum in which the paragraph as a whole exists.

The last general stylistic feature of the passage to be listed above was the use of negative forms. There are 6 'noes' or 'nots' in the first 4 sentences; four implied negatives—'postpone'; 'without disappointment'; 'at the worst'; 'there was little fear': and two qualifications that modify positiveness of affirmation—'not wholly', and 'to that extent'. This abundance of negatives has no doubt several functions: it enacts Strether's tendency to hesitation and qualification; it puts the reader into the right judicial frame of mind; and it has the further effect of subordinating concrete events to their mental reflection; 'Waymarsh was not to arrive', for example, is not a concrete statement of a physical event: it is subjective—because it implies an expectation in Strether's mind (which was not fulfilled); and it has an abstract quality—because while Waymarsh's arriving would be particular and physical, his *not* arriving is an idea, a non-action. More generally, James's great use of negatives or near-negatives may also, perhaps, be regarded as part of his subjective and abstractive tendency: there are no negatives in nature but only in the human consciousness.

II

The most obvious grammatical features of what Richard Chase has called Henry James's 'infinitely syntactical language' (*The American Novel and its Tradition*, New York, 1957), can, then, be shown to reflect the essential imperatives of his narrative point of view; and they could therefore lead into a discussion of the philosophical qualities of his mind, as they are discussed, for example, by Dorothea Krook in her notable article 'The Method of the Later Works of Henry James' (*London Magazine*, I [1954], 55–70); our passage surely exemplifies James's power 'to generalise to the furthest limit the particulars of experience', and with it the characteristic way in which both his 'perceptions of the world itself and his perceptions of the logic of his perceptions of the world . . . happen simultaneously, are the parts of a single comprehensive experience'. Another aspect of the connection between James's metaphysic and his method as a novelist has inspired a stimulating stylistic study— Carlo Izzo's 'Henry James, Scrittore Sintattico' (*Studi Americani*, II [1956], 127–142). The connection between thought and style finds its historical perspective in John Henry Raleigh's illuminating study 'Henry James: The Poetics of Empiricism' (*PMLA*, LXVI [1951], 107–123), which establishes connections between Lockean epistemology and James's extreme, almost anarchic, individualism; while this epistemological preoccupation, which is central to Quentin Anderson's view of how James worked out his father's cosmology in fictional terms (*The American Henry James*, New Brunswick, 1957), also leads towards another large general question, the concern with 'point of view', which became a crucial problem in the history and criticism of fiction under the influence of the sceptical relativism of the late nineteenth-century.

In James's case, the problem is fairly complicated. He may be classed as an 'Impressionist', concerned, that is, to show not so much the events themselves, but the impressions which they make on the characters. But James's continual need to generalise and place and order, combined with his absolute demand for a point of view that would be plastic enough to allow him freedom for the formal 'architectonics' of the novelist's craft, eventually involved him in a very idiosyncratic kind of multiple Impressionism: idiosyncratic because the dual presence of Strether's consciousness and of that of the narrator, who translates what he sees there into more general terms, makes the narrative point of view both intensely individual and yet ultimately social.

Another possible direction of investigation would be to show that the abstractness and indirection of James's style are essentially the result of this characteristic multiplicity of his vision. There is, for example, the story reported by Edith Wharton that after his first stroke James told Lady Prothero that 'in the very act of falling . . . he heard in the room a voice which was distinctly, it seemed, not his own, saying: "So here it is at last, the distinguished thing".' James, apparently, could not but see even his own most fateful personal experience, except as evoked by some other observer's voice in terms of the long historical and literary tradition of death. Carlo Izzo regards this tendency as typical of the Alexandrian style, where there is a marked disparity between the rich inheritance of the means of literary expression, and the meaner creative world which it is used to express; but the defence of the Jamesian habit of mind must surely be that what the human vision shares with that of animals is presumably the perception of concrete images, not the power to conceive universals: such was Aristotle's notion of man's distinguishing capacity. The universals in the present context are presumably the awareness that behind every petty individual circumstance there ramifies an endless network of general moral, social and historical relations. Henry

James's style can therefore be seen as a supremely civilised effort to relate every event and every moment of life to the full complexity of its circumambient conditions.

Obviously James's multiple awareness can go too far; and in the later novels it often poses the special problem that we do not quite know whether the awareness implied in a given passage is the narrator's or that of his character. Most simply, a pronoun referring to the subject of a preceding clause is always liable to give trouble if one hasn't been very much aware of what the grammatical subject of that preceding clause was; in the last sentence of the paragraph, for example, 'the apprehension, already, on Strether's part, that . . . it would, at best, . . . prove the "note" of Europe,' 'it' refers to Waymarsh's countenance: but this isn't at first obvious; which is no doubt why, in his revision of the periodical version for the English edition James replaced 'it' by 'he'—simpler, grammatically, but losing some of the ironic visual precision of the original. More seriously, because the narrator's consciousness and Strether's are both present, we often don't know whose mental operations and evaluative judgments are involved in particular cases. We pass, for instance, from the objective analysis of sentence 3 where the analytic terminology of 'the same secret principle' must be the responsibility of the narrator, to what must be a verbatim quotation of Strether's mind in sentence 4: 'with all respect to dear old Waymarsh' is obviously Strether's licensed familiarity.

But although the various difficulties of tense, voice, and reference require a vigilance of attention in the reader which some have found too much to give, they are not in themselves very considerable: and what perhaps is much more in need of attention is how the difficulties arising from the multiplicity of points of view don't by any means prevent James from ordering all the elements of his narrative style into an amazingly precise means of expression: and it is this positive, and in the present case, as it seems to me, triumphant, mastery of the difficulties which I want next to consider.

Our passage is not, I think, James either at his most memorable or at his most idiosyncratic: *The Ambassadors* is written with considerable sobriety and has, for example, little of the vivid and direct style of the early part of *The Wings of the Dove*, or of the happy symbolic complexities of *The Golden Bowl*. Still, the passage is fairly typical of the later James; and I think it can be proved that all or at least nearly all the idiosyncrasies of diction or syntax in the present passage are fully justified by the particular emphases they create.

The most flagrant eccentricity of diction is presumably that where James writes 'the most newly disembarked of the two men' (lines 15–16). 'Most' may very well be a mere slip; and it must certainly seem indefensible to any one who takes it as an absolute rule that the comparative must always be used when only two items are involved.[3] But a defence is at least possible. 'Most newly disembarked' means something rather different from 'more newly disembarked'. James, it may be surmised, did not want to compare the recency of the two men's arrival, but to inform us that Strether's arrival was 'very' or as we might say, 'most' recent; the use of the superlative also had the advantage of suggesting the long and fateful tradition of transatlantic disembarcations in general.

The reasons for the other main syntactical idiosyncrasies in the passage are much clearer. In the first part of the opening sentence, for example, the separation of subject—'question'—from verb—'was'—by the longish temporal clause 'when he reached the hotel', is no doubt a dislocation of normal sentence structure; but, of course, 'Strether' must be the first word of the novel: while, even more important, the delayed placing of the temporal clause forces a pause after 'question' and thus gives it a very significant resonance. Similarly with the last sentence; it has several peculiarities, of which the placing of 'throughout' seems the most obvious. The sentence has three parts: the first and last are comparatively straightforward, but the middle is a massed block of portentous qualifications: 'Mixed with everything was the apprehension—already, on Strether's part, that he would, at best, throughout,—prove the note of Europe in quite a sufficient degree.' The echoing doom started by the connotation of 'apprehension'—reverberates through 'already' ('much more to come later'), 'on Strether's part' ('even he knows') and 'at best' ('the worst has been envisaged, too'); but it is the final collapse of the terse rhythm of the parenthesis that isolates the rather awkwardly placed 'throughout', and thus enables James to sound the fine full fatal note; there is no limit to the poignant eloquence of 'throughout'. It was this effect, of course, which dictated the preceding inversion which places 'apprehension' not at the start of the sentence, but in the middle where, largely freed from its syntactical nexus, it may be directly exposed to its salvos of qualification.

The mockingly fateful emphasis on 'throughout' tells us, if nothing had before, that James's tone is in the last analysis ironic, comic, or better, as I shall try to suggest, humorous. The general reasons for this have already been suggested. To use Maynard Mack's distinction (in his Preface to *Joseph Andrews*, Rinehart Editions, New York, 1948), 'the comic artist subordinates the presentation of life as experience, where the relationship between ourselves and the characters experiencing it is a primary one, to the presentation of life as a spectacle, where the primary relation is between himself and us as onlookers'. In the James passage, the primacy of the relation between the narrator and the reader has already been noted, as has its connection with the abstraction of the diction, which brings home the distance between the narrator and

3. Though consider *Rasselas*, ch. xxviii: 'Both conditions may be bad, but they cannot both be worst'.

Strether. Of course, the application of abstract diction to particular persons always tends towards irony,[4] because it imposes a dual way of looking at them: few of us can survive being presented as general representatives of humanity.

The paragraph, of course, is based on one of the classic contradictions in psychological comedy—Strether's reluctance to admit to himself that he has very mixed feelings about his friend: and James develops this with the narrative equivalent of *commedia dell'arte* technique: virtuoso feats of ironic balance, comic exaggeration, and deceptive hesitation conduct us on a complicated progress towards the foreordained illumination.

In structure, to begin with, the six sentences form three groups of two: each pair of them gives one aspect of Strether's delay; and they are arranged in an ascending order of complication so that the fifth sentence—72 words—is almost twice as long as any other, and is succeeded by the final sentence, the punch line, which is noticeably the shortest—26 words. The development of the ideas is as controlled as the sentence structure. Strether is obviously a man with an enormous sense of responsibility about personal relationships; so his first question is about his friend. That loyal *empressement*, however, is immediately checked by the balanced twin negatives that follow: 'on his learning that Waymarsh *was not* to arrive till evening, he *was not* wholly disconcerted': one of the diagnostic elements of irony, surely, is hyperbole qualified with mock-scrupulousness, such as we get in 'not wholly disconcerted'. Why there are limits to Lambert Strether's consternation is to transpire in the next sentence; Waymarsh's telegram bespeaking a room 'only if not noisy' is a laconic suggestion of that inarticulate worthy's habitually gloomy expectations—from his past experiences of the indignities of European hotel noise we adumbrate the notion that the cost of their friendly *rencontre* may be his sleeping in the street. In the second part of the sentence we have another similar, though more muted, hint: 'the understanding that they should meet in Chester rather than at Liverpool remained to that extent sound'; 'to that extent', no doubt, but to *any other?*—echo seems to answer 'No'.

In the second group of sentences we are getting into Strether's mind, and we have been prepared to relish the irony of its ambivalences. The negatived hyperbole of 'not absolutely to desire' turns out to mean 'postpone'; and, of course, a voluntarily postponed 'enjoyment' itself denotes a very modified rapture, although Strether's own consciousness of the problem is apparently no further advanced than that 'he could still wait without disappointment'. Comically loyal to what he would like to feel, therefore, we have him putting in the consoling reflection that 'they would dine together at the worst'; and the ambiguity of 'at the worst' is

---

4. As I have argued in 'The Ironic Tradition in Augustan Prose from Swift to Johnson', *Restoration and Augustan Prose* (Los Angeles, 1957).

followed by the equally dubious thought: 'there was little fear that in the sequel they shouldn't see enough of each other'. That they should, in fact, see too much of each other; but social decorum and Strether's own loyalties demand that the outrage of the open statement be veiled in the obscurity of formal negation.

By the time we arrive at the climactic pair of sentences, we have been told enough for more ambitious effects to be possible. The twice-mentioned 'secret principle', it appears, is actually wholly 'instinctive' (line 16); but in other ways Strether is almost ludicrously self-conscious. The qualified hyperbole of 'his business would be a trifle bungled', underlined as it is by the alliteration, prepares us for a half-realised image which amusingly defines Strether's sense of his role: he sees himself, it appears, as the stage-manager of an enterprise in which his solemn obligations as an implicated friend are counterbalanced by his equally ceremonious sense that due decorums must also be attended to when he comes face to face with another friend of long ago—no less a person than Europe. It is, of course, silly of him, as James makes him acknowledge in the characteristic italicising of 'the "note" of Europe';[5] but still, he does have a comically ponderous sense of protocol which leads him to feel that 'his business would be a trifle bungled' should he simply arrange for this countenance to present itself to the nearing steamer as the first 'note' of Europe. The steamer, one imagines, would not have turned hard astern at the proximity of Waymarsh's sacred rage; but Strether's fitness for ambassadorial functions is defined by his thinking in terms of 'arranging' for a certain countenance at the docks to give just the right symbolic greeting.

Strether's notion of what Europe demands also shows us the force of his aesthetic sense. But in the last sentence the metaphor, though it remains equally self-conscious, changes its mode of operation from the dramatic, aesthetic, and diplomatic, to something more scientific: for, although ten years ago I should not have failed to point out, and my readers would not, I suppose, have failed to applaud, the ambiguity of 'prove', it now seems to me that we must chose between its two possible meanings. James may be using 'prove' to mean that Waymarsh's face will 'turn out to be' the 'note of Europe' for Strether. But 'prove' in this sense is intransitive, and 'to be' would have to be supplied; it therefore seems more likely that James is using 'prove' in the older sense of 'to test': Waymarsh is indeed suited to the role of being the sourly acid test of the siren songs of Europe 'in quite a sufficient degree', as Strether puts it with solemn but arch understatement.

The basic development structure of the passage, then, is one of progressive and yet artfully delayed clarification; and this pattern is also typical of James's general novelistic method. The reasons for this are

5. See George Knox, 'James's Rhetoric of Quotes,' *College English*, XVII (1956), 293–297.

suggested in the Preface to *The Princess Casamassima*, where James deals with the problem of maintaining a balance between the intelligence a character must have to be interesting, and the bewilderment which is nevertheless an essential condition of the novel's having surprise, development, and tension: 'It seems probable that if we were never bewildered there would never be a story to tell about us.'

In the first paragraph of *The Ambassadors* James apprises us both of his hero's supreme qualities and of his associated limitations. Strether's delicate critical intelligence is often blinkered by a highly vulnerable mixture of moral generosity towards others combined with an obsessive sense of personal inadequacy; we see the tension in relation to Waymarsh, as later we are to see it in relation to all his other friends; and we understand, long before Strether, how deeply it bewilders him; most poignantly about the true nature of Chad, Madame de Vionnet—and himself.

This counterpoint of intelligence and bewilderment is, of course, another reason for the split narrative point of view we've already noted: we and the narrator are inside Strether's mind, and yet we are also outside it, knowing more about Strether than he knows about himself. This is the classic posture of irony. Yet I think that to insist too exclusively on the ironic function of James's narrative point of view would be mistaken.

Irony has lately been enshrined as the supreme deity in the critical pantheon: but, I wonder, is there really anything so wonderful about being distant and objective? Who wants to see life only or mainly in intellectual terms? In art as in life we no doubt can have need of intellectual distance as well as of emotional commitment; but the uninvolvement of the artist surely doesn't go very far without the total involvement of the person; or, at least, without a deeper human involvement than irony customarily establishes. One could, I suppose, call the aesthetically perfect balance between distance and involvement, open or positive irony: but I'm not sure that humour isn't a better word, especially when the final balance is tipped in favour of involvement, of ultimate commitment to the characters; and I hope that our next critical movement will be the New Gelastics.

At all events, although the first paragraph alone doesn't allow the point to be established fully here, it seems to me that James's attitude to Strether is better described as humorous than ironical; we must learn, like Maria Gostrey, to see him 'at last all comically, all tragically'. James's later novels in general are most intellectual; but they are also, surely, his most compassionate: and in this particular paragraph Strether's dilemma is developed in such a way that we feel for him even more than we smile at him. This balance of intention, I think, probably explains why James keeps his irony so quiet in tone: we must be aware of Strether's 'secret' ambivalence towards Waymarsh, but not to the point that his unawareness of it would verge on fatuity; and our controlling sympathy for the causes of Strether's ambivalence turns what might have been irony into something closer to what Constance Rourke characterises as James's typical 'low-keyed humor of defeat' (*American Humor*, 1931).

That James's final attitude is humorous rather than ironic is further suggested by the likeness of the basic structural technique of the paragraph to that of the funny story—the incremental involvement in an endemic human perplexity which can only be resolved by laughter's final acceptance of contradiction and absurdity. We don't, in the end, see Strether's probing hesitations mainly as an ironic indication by James of mankind's general muddlement; we find it, increasingly, a touching example of how, despite all their inevitable incongruities and shortcomings, human ties remain only, but still, human.

Here it is perhaps James's very slowness and deliberation throughout the narrative which gives us our best supporting evidence: greater love hath no man than hearing his friend out patiently.

III

The function of an introductory paragraph in a novel is presumably to introduce: and this paragraph surely has the distinction of being a supremely complex and inclusive introduction to a novel. It introduces the hero, of course, and one of his companions; also the time; the place; something of what's gone before. But James has carefully avoided giving up the usual retrospective beginning, that pile of details which he scornfully termed a 'mere seated mass of information'. All the details are scrupulously presented as reflections from the novel's essential centre— the narrator's patterning of the ideas going forwards and backwards in Strether's mind. Of course, this initially makes the novel more difficult, because what we probably think of as primary—event and its setting— is subordinated to what James thinks is—the mental drama of the hero's consciousness, which, of course, is not told but shown: scenically dramatised. At the same time, by selecting thoughts and events which are representative of the book as a whole, and narrating them with an abstractness which suggests their larger import, James introduces the most general themes of the novel.

James, we saw, carefully arranged to make 'Strether's first question' the first three words; and, of course, throughout the novel, Strether is to go on asking questions—and getting increasingly dusty answers. This, it may be added, is stressed by the apparent aposiopesis: for a 'first' question when no second is mentioned, is surely an intimation that more are—in a way unknown to us or to Strether—yet to come. The later dislocations of normal word-order already noted above emphasise other major themes; the 'secret principle' in Strether's mind, and the antithesis Waymarsh-Europe, for instance.

The extent to which these processes were conscious on James's part cannot, of course, be resolved; but it is significant that the meeting with Maria Gostrey was interposed before the meeting with Waymarsh, which James had originally planned as his beginning in the long (20,000) word scenario of the plot which he prepared for *Harper's*. The unexpected meeting had many advantages; not least that James could repeat the first paragraph's pattern of delayed clarification in the structure of the first chapter as a whole. On Strether's mind we get a momentously clear judgment at the end of the second paragraph: 'there was detachment in his zeal, and curiosity in his indifference'; but then the meeting with Maria Gostrey, and its gay opportunities for a much fuller presentation of Strether's mind, intervene before Waymarsh himself finally appears at the end of the chapter; only then is the joke behind Strether's uneasy hesitations in the first paragraph brought to its hilariously blunt climax: 'It was already upon him even at that distance—Mr. Waymarsh was for *his* part joyless'.

One way of evaluating James's achievement in this paragraph, I suppose, would be to compare the opening of James's other novels, and with those of previous writers: but it would take too long to do more than sketch the possibilities of this approach. James's early openings certainly have some of the banality of the 'mere seated mass of information': in *Roderick Hudson* (1876), for example: 'Rowland Mallet had made his arrangements to sail for Europe on the 5th of September, and having in the interval a fortnight to spare, he determined to spend it with his cousin Cecilia, the widow of a nephew of his father. . . .' Later, James showed a much more comprehensive notion of what the introductory paragraph should attempt: even in the relatively simple and concrete opening of *The Wings of the Dove* (1902): 'She waited, Kate Croy, for her father to come in, but he kept her unconscionably, and there were moments at which she showed herself, in the glass over the mantle, a face positively pale with irritation that had brought her to the point of going away without sight of him. . . .' 'She waited, Kate Croy'—an odd parenthetic apposition artfully contrived to prefigure her role throughout the novel—to wait.

One could, I suppose, find this sort of symbolic prefiguring in the work of earlier novelists; but never, I imagine, in association with all the other levels of introductory function that James manages to combine in a single paragraph. Jane Austen has her famous thematic irony in the opening of *Pride and Prejudice* (1813): 'It is a truth universally acknowledged, that a single man in possession of a good fortune must be in want of a wife'; but pride and prejudice must come later. Dickens can hurl us overpoweringly into *Bleak House* (1852–3), into its time and place and general theme; but characters and opening action have to wait. * * * In Dickens, characteristically, we get a loud note that sets the tone, rather than a polyphonic series of chords that contain all the later melodic developments, as in James. And either the Dickens method, or the 'mere seated mass of information', seem to be commonest kinds of opening in nineteenth-century novels. For openings that suggest something of James's ambitious attempt to achieve a prologue that is a synchronic introduction of all the main aspects of the narrative, I think that Conrad is his closest rival. But Conrad, whether in expository or dramatic vein, tends to an arresting initial vigour that has dangers which James's more muted tones avoid. * * *

It is not for me to assess how far I have succeeded in carrying out the general intentions with which I began, or how far similar methods of analysis would be applicable to other kinds of prose. As regards the explication of the passage itself, the main argument must by now be sufficiently clear, although a full demonstration would require a much wider sampling both of other novels and of other passages in *The Ambassadors*.[6] The most obvious and demonstrable features of James's prose style, its vocabulary and syntax, are direct reflections of his attitude to life and his conception of the novel; and these features, like the relation of the paragraph to the rest of the novel, and to other novels, make clear that the notorious idiosyncrasies of Jamesian prose are directly related to the imperatives which led him to develop a narrative texture as richly complicated and as highly organised as that of poetry.

No wonder James scorned translation and rejoiced, as he so engagingly confessed to his French translator, Auguste Monod, that his later words were 'locked fast in the golden cage of the *intraduisible*'. Translation could hardly do justice to a paragraph in which so many levels of meaning and implication are kept in continuous operation; in which the usual introductory exposition of time, place, character, and previous action are rendered through an immediate immersion in the processes of the hero's mind as he's involved in perplexities which are characteristic of the novel as a whole and which are articulated in a mode of comic development which is essentially that, not only of the following chapter, but of the total structure. To have done all that is to have gone far towards demonstrating the contention which James announced at the end of the Preface to *The Ambassadors*, that 'the Novel remains still, under the right persuasion, the most independent, most elastic, most prodigious of literary forms'; and the variety and complexity of the functions carried out in the book's quite short first paragraph also suggest that, contrary to some notions, the demonstration is, as James claimed, made with 'a splendid particular economy'.

6. A similar analysis of eight other paragraphs selected at fifty page intervals revealed that, as would be expected, there is much variation: the tendency to use non-transitive verbs, and abstract nouns as subjects, for instance, seems to be strong throughout the novel, though especially so in analytic rather than narrative passages; but the frequent use of 'that' and of negative forms of statement does not recur significantly.

SALLIE SEARS (1968)

[Negative Imagination and *The Ambassadors*]†

Like Paris, the great "jewel" that is its setting, *The Ambassadors* has a rare iridescence, luminosity of surface, and wealth of association. Though milder and more muted than *The Wings of the Dove* or *The Golden Bowl*, it is the most elaborate and richly textured of James's dramas of moral consciousness. It is unique too among the late works in its focus upon middle age (the "afternoon," the "twilight of life") rather than youth, for though the theme of youth is a predominant one in the book, our center of attention is a character far past that period in his life. In these respects—and perhaps in others—*The Ambassadors* has a certain spiritual kinship with *The Tempest*. Like Prospero, Strether is exiled temporarily from his native ground into a place of enchantment:

> In the garden of the Tuileries he had lingered, on two or three spots, to look; it was as if the wonderful Paris spring had stayed him as he roamed. The prompt Paris morning struck its cheerful notes—in a soft breeze and a sprinkled smell, in the light flit, over the garden-floor, of bareheaded girls. . . . The air had a taste as of something mixed with art, something that presented nature as a white-capped master-chef. [58–59]

All three of the late novels make deliberate use of the fairy-tale mode: motifs of enchantment, spells, figurative or real princesses and princes, sorcerers, and fairy godmothers. But in none of the three is this mode used in so sustained and at the same time so quiet a way as in *The Ambassadors*, where it is an important yet unobtrusive element affecting the tone and texture of the entire novel. The air is "charged," "infectious": "Poor Strether had . . . to recognise the truth that wherever one paused in Paris the imagination reacted before one could stop it" [69]. And the texture woven by the imagination in this novel is elaborate, complex, and lustrous. "I dare say . . . , [remarks Maria] that I do, that we all do here, run too much to mere eye. But how can it be helped? We're all looking at each other—and in the light of Paris one sees what things resemble. That's what the light of Paris seems always to show. It's the fault of the light of Paris—dear old light!" [126] Part of the complexity, the richness of *The Ambassadors* is in fact directly due to the conscious utilization of the principle of "resemblance," the yoking together of heterogeneous associations and areas of

† Reprinted from *The Negative Imagination: Form and Perspective in the Novels of Henry James* by Sallie Sears (Ithaca, N.Y.: Cornell University Press, 1968), 101–51. Copyright (©) 1968 by Cornell University. Used by permission of the publisher. The chapter has been abridged. Page references in brackets are to this Norton Critical Edition.

experience through the unifying medium of Strether's consciousness. Everything that Strether sees is a kind of haunt, a presence that suggests or evokes the quality of another presence, usually one that is gone irretrievably, or even one that was never there but only yearned for. In England, his first taste of "Europe," he strolls and pauses "here and there for a dismantled gate or a bridged gap, with rises and drops, steps up and steps down, queer twists, queer contacts, peeps . . . under the brows of gables," and his reaction is one of intense pleasure coupled with immediate evocation of the past: "Too deep almost for words was the delight of these things to Strether; yet as deeply mixed with it were certain images of his inward picture. He had trod this walk in the far-off time, at twenty-five" [24]. And what in turn had been the feelings that accompanied him then, in his first and youthful sojourn: the need and yearning to utilize the experience as a creative foundation for his future life. This reaction "consecrated"—declared sacred—the significance of that early pilgrimage, and took the form of a "private pledge of his own to treat the occasion as a relation formed with the higher culture and see that, as they said at Woollett, it should bear a good harvest." But the pledge remained unfulfilled, so that the color of his *present* experience becomes a bleak sense of all "the promises to himself that he had after his other visit never kept" [62], "mere sallow paint on the door of the temple of taste that he had dreamed of raising up" [63].

This coupling of immediate, vivid sensory detail with the sense of the significance it might have had but didn't and now never can—of present unobtainable riches and past irrevocable bankruptcy—is the characteristic mode of perception in *The Ambassadors*. Strether defines it in himself as a tendency to "uncontrolled perceptions," by which he means not that his mind is a jungle watering-ground, but that his sense of personal privation is irrepressible and that he would be happier if it weren't. So he sits with Maria Gostrey in England at a small table with rose-colored shades on the lighted candles and recalls that he had been "to the theatre, even to the opera, in Boston, with Mrs. Newsome . . . but there had been no little confronted dinner, no pink lights, no whiff of vague sweetness, as a preliminary" [42]. Maria's dress, low at bosom and shoulders, and her throat circled with a broad red velvet band do not serve—directly—as an incentive to lust but rather as a "rueful" recollection that "Mrs. Newsome's dress was never in any degree 'cut down,' and she never wore round her throat a broad red velvet band." He then begins to think what that lady *did* wear (an Elizabethan ruche), conscious of his own mental processes yet helpless to control them. Every immediate impression of any intensity that Strether has, serves, like the red band, "as a starting-point for fresh backward, fresh forward, fresh lateral flights" [42].

What Strether's consciousness both depicts and exemplifies here is the metaphoric imagination, the consistent presentation of which is largely responsible for the rich texture and thematic complexity of the novel. In addition, the statement the figures repeatedly make—"this is a symbol of all that I never had and never will"—determines the book's tone of bemused melancholy and passive yearning. We know that James wanted his protagonist to be "*fine,* clever, literary almost" [375] and that he considered but rejected making him a novelist (both on the grounds that that would be too much like William Dean Howells, whose impassioned plea to a mutual friend to "live" provided James the theme of *The Ambassadors,* and on the grounds that such a hero generally would be too improbable). James also rejected the possibility of making him an artist, because an artist, like a journalist, lawyer, or doctor "WOULD in a manner have 'lived' " [375]. But these considerations of a creative "type," though waived, are significant, and his hero eventually was to be, in spite of his personal shortcomings and his failure to achieve an identity through work, a man of imagination.

And the paradox of his character—the man of imagination who is at the same time a New England puritan—is a central paradox, of which the European-American antithesis is but one symbolic projection. Strether, we are warned at the outset, is burdened "with the oddity of a double consciousness. There was detachment in his zeal and curiosity in his indifference" [18]. In the immediate context, this refers to his ambivalence at the prospect of meeting Waymarsh, whose presence he wishes for yet whose absence he enjoys "extremely." But the broader context is the significance this meeting has for Strether, for Waymarsh is the true American representative, who is second only to the unseen yet ubiquitous Mrs. Newsome. He is an original specimen of the most typical New World genus: "a truly majestic aboriginal," the Great Father, the "American statesman . . . trained in 'Congressional halls,' of an elder day" [29]. The delay in their meeting means for Strether "such a consciousness of personal freedom as he had n't known for years," freedom to give over "his afternoon and evening to the immediate and the sensible" [18].

It is of course because Waymarsh is the externalization of one of Strether's inward voices that he dreads meeting him. If Strether did not have susceptibilities of conscience against his own delight in the "immediate and the sensible," he would feel no alarm. Not only does he have them, however, but they increase in intensity with the amount of pleasure he feels, so that strolling in the early morning of Paris, which hangs before him "the vast bright Babylon, like some huge iridescent object, a jewel brilliant and hard . . . twinkled and trembled and melted together . . . all surface one moment . . . all depth the next" [64], he is tormented with a kind of moral uneasiness. It takes the form of a rhetorical problem: "Was it at all possible . . . to like Paris enough without liking it too much?" [65] The implicit accusation of course is that *any* liking is, by definition, "too much"—and Strether does like it.

This war between the sense of rectitude and the sense of beauty is the basic conflict of the novel, as it is the basic conflict of Strether's character; indeed the former is simply an extension of elaboration of the latter. The book is not about Europe and America, or even about Europeans and Americans. It is about the significance that each place and its inhabitants have for a man burdened with "a double consciousness." What we are given is a complex study not in twofold but in fourfold reactions, for Strether is ambivalent to *both* of the great civilizations that are the symbolic terrain of his own internal struggle. It is by no means just Europe to which his responses are divided, though that continent is the actual setting of the events of the novel and is indeed Babylon to his feelings: place of iniquity, home of whores, yet precious beyond words, a temple, like Maria Gostrey's nest, to "the lust of the eyes and the pride of life" [80].

Though James typically is concerned with the *relation* of consciousness to the external human scene, finding in aspects of the latter analogues for the former (or items of special significance to it), the nature of that scene becomes progressively more abstract in each of the last three novels. * * *

In *The Ambassadors* (completed before but published after *The Wings of the Dove*), however, the "setting"—though as we have indicated it stands in analogic relation to conflicting aspects of Strether's consciousness—*is* projected in its three-dimensionality and detailed concreteness. The drama of the hero's sensibility takes place in a context of intensely vivid social realities—attitudes, customs, modes of thought and behavior, American speech and dress, Parisian gardens, streets, interior landscapes—which have *both* an extrinsic and an intrinsic relation to that sensibility.

In the novel we are given an extended ironic characterization of middle-class American and upper-class Parisian culture, "a comic work" as it has been observed, "in the general tradition of Molière and Jane Austen."[1] At the same time, however, its scope is far broader, its range of tone more complex than the typical "novel of manners." The effectiveness of Jane Austen's work, for example, largely depends upon the unquestioned acceptance of a fixed social and ethical code of behavior, deviations from which can be examined with minute exactness. But *The Ambassadors* has for its framework not one but two such codes, in radical opposition, neither of which in the final analysis completely triumphs or is completely defeated. It is in the study of half-victories and partial defeats of two world views as they relate to the personal history of Lambert Strether that the significance of the novel lies, for whatever its context, it is first and last his story. The lives of the other characters, as well as

---

1. Richard Chase, "James' *Ambassadors*," *Twelve Original Essays on Great American Novels*, ed. Charles Shapiro (Detroit, 1958), p. 129.

the cultural settings in which they take place, have meaning for us only as they have meaning for Strether, whose feelings, responses, perceptions, and reactions constitute the subject matter of the book.

So that the pertinent question is the nature of the relationship between the European-American dichotomy in the novel and the private life of Lambert Strether, the "ambassador" on a temporary mission from Woollett, Massachusetts, to Paris, France. * * *

Upon * * * two simple shifts in Strether's attitude hangs a tale half comic, half tragic, certainly pathetic, of the struggle of a complex and somewhat befuddled psyche to find, before it is too late, some meaning, significance, and beauty in life. One might say that the book is about how he almost finds it: almost, but not quite.

Europe and America each offers to Strether its own *modus vivendi*, its own elaborately articulated set of possibilities and philosophy of existence. That the basic assumptions of each are violently antithetical is something that Strether at first accepts as a matter of course, then in his hopeful delusion about "virtuous attachments" discards, then comes again painfully to recognize. But by that time a strange and complex interaction of the two styles of life has taken place within Strether, with the result that each has operated upon the other with something of the effect of a slow poison. He is left in the end with a lingering distaste—coupled with a nostalgia for the beauty that was almost truth too—for both places, a permanent spiritual exile, in possession only of the rather pathetic consolation that he had "not, out of the whole affair" [346], got anything for himself and has therefore, in some obscure but honorable way, been "right."

The great values upheld and cherished by Woollett are conformity, which passes as "equality," and rectitude. There are but two "types" in Woollett, the male and the female, and on any subject whatsoever but "two or three" opinions. One of Strether's first impressions of Europe is his sense of the multifold discriminations, rankings, and categories that, by contrast, are indulged in there. Miss Gostrey, he recognizes, was "the mistress of a hundred cases or categories, receptacles of the mind, subdivisions for convenience, in which, from a full experience, she pigeon-holed her fellow mortals with a hand as free as that of a compositor scattering type. She was as equipped in this particular as Strether was the reverse" [21]. This concept of "personal types" becomes the keynote of Europe for Strether, part of whose growth of experience consists in his increasing ability to recognize them when he sees them. But the significant thing is the concept itself, the very notion of a hierarchical ordering of values, rather than the degree of skill he shows in its practical application. It is a concept regarded with the profoundest mistrust and abhorrence by the sister communities and companions-at-arms, Milrose, Connecticut, and Woollett, Massachusetts, for it reeks of political and spiritual decádence, the old order, and the old, castoff world. Its great emblem is the Catholic Church: "The Catholic Church, for Waymarsh—that was to say the enemy, the monster of bulging eyes and far-reaching quivering groping tentacles—was exactly society, exactly the multiplication of shibboleths, exactly the discrimination of types and tones, exactly the wicked old Rows of Chester, rank with feudalism; exactly in short Europe" [38].

But what does it mean for the errant Strether? The chain of his association that leads to this perception of what Europe means to Waymarsh is significant here. The two of them, with Miss Gostrey, are strolling and gazing into shop windows, Waymarsh maintaining "an ambiguous dumbness that might have represented either the growth of a perception or the despair of one" [37] and looking "guilty and furtive" when his eye happens to be caught by some object of minor interest. Strether, however, is utterly entranced and apologizes for his rapture on the grounds of previous deprivation: "Do what he might . . . his previous virtue was still there, and it seemed fairly to stare at him out of the windows of shops that were not as the shops of Woollett, fairly to make him want things that he should n't know what to do with. It was by the oddest, the least admissible of laws demoralising him now; and the way it boldly took was to make him want more wants" [37]. He and Miss Gostrey find themselves disposed to talk as "society" talks, and discuss clothing, passers-by, faces, types: "Was what was happening to himself then . . . really that a woman of fashion was floating him into society and that an old friend deserted on the brink was watching the force of the current?" She allows him to buy a pair of gloves, and it is then that he realizes that for Waymarsh "mere discriminations about a pair of gloves" is emblematic of the fundamental wantonness of Europe and that Strether for indulging in such discriminations is like a "Jesuit in petticoats, a representative of the recruiting interests of the Catholic Church" [38].

What we have here is a complex set of associations and significances, all stemming from the single concept of "type," and having implications of a very broad range indeed. One of the most pertinent of these implications is the connection between that aspect of experience involving the making of "discriminations" and the phenomenon of taste. For a hierarchical ordering of values is a necessary condition of the latter: without it a sense of what is fitting, harmonious, or beautiful is impossible. That Strether applies it at the moment to a pair of gloves instead of, say, a painting is beside the point. What matters is the phenomenon itself: it is one of the possibilities of life that Europe offers and that America denies him.

Closely connected to the notion of taste—indeed an intricate part of it—is the whole realm of fluid, sensuous experience, of "sensible impressions and agreeable sensations," of strolls "where the low-browed galleries were darkest, the opposite gables queerest, the solicitations of every kind densest" [37]. It was the delight of such that was "too deep almost for words" [24] for Strether as he wandered earlier with Miss Gostrey, just as it is Waymarsh's present source of guilt and furtiveness when in spite of himself his eye happens to linger upon some interesting object. But if Strether's reaction had been merely delight, we would have a different novel; in fact, he shares with his fellow New Englander the pain of a stricken conscience, the inability wholly to give himself over to the flux of immediate experience. With Miss Gostrey he feels "as if this were wrong"; he labels the feeling "the terror. . . . I'm always considering something else; something else, I mean, than the thing of the moment. The obsession of the other thing is the terror" [26]. At the same time, he longs "unspeakably" to escape the obsession, goes so far as to beg her to help him do so.

Now this "failure to enjoy" is a "general" failure [25], as Strether tells Maria: it is not a personal flaw in either himself or Waymarsh, but rather an habitual trait of the New England conscience whose responses are dictated by the moral imperatives of "ought" and "ought not" (Woollett "isn't sure it ought to enjoy. If it were it would"). Woollett of course is in no such state of uncertainty as Strether pretends with respect to the lust of the eyes. Woollett is perfectly sure it ought not to enjoy: after all it is the New Testament, not the Old, that requests us to pluck out our right eye if it offends us. The direct Biblical connection is with the sin of adultery, as it is reinterpreted by Christ to involve desire as well as action: "But I say unto you, That whosoever looketh on a woman to lust after her hath committed adultery with her already in his heart" (*Matthew* V, 28). But the Sermon on the Mount mentions the eye in another connection too: with respect to its yearning for mammon and the treasures of the earth, which "moths and rust doth corrupt." The use of wealth specifically for food, drink, and clothing is condemned: "And why take ye thought for raiment? Consider the lilies of the field. . . . Even Solomon in all his glory was not arrayed like one of these." Poor Strether and his pair of gloves; no wonder he is painfully aware that Waymarsh considers him not only "sophisticated" and "worldly" but also "wicked," the three indeed being, to the New England conscience, synonymous. Later this is made explicit as it comes to Strether "somehow to and fro that what poor Waymarsh meant was 'I told you so—that you'd lose your immortal soul!' " [108]

So one of the dilemmas Strether is in as a man of taste burdened with puritan leanings is that the very things which most gratify his sensibility are the ones which most distress his conscience. Though he does not think (except ironically) in orthodox theological terms, he has internalized the trappings of Protestantism to the extent that his consciousness of the agreeable is continually marred by his consciousness of sin. Hence, he never has an unambiguous reaction to the delights of Paris: making a "frantic friend" [80] of little Bilham, finding himself moved and pleased by, if not envious of, the latter's tranquillity, he still thinks: "It was by little Bilham's amazing serenity that he had at first been affected, but he had inevitably, in his circumspection, felt it as the trail of the serpent, the corruption, as he might conveniently have said, of Europe" [83]. At the same time, Paris continually seduces him: it makes him "want more wants," it gives him a taste of "personal freedom" [17] such as he has not known for years, accompanied by "the full sweetness of the taste of leisure" [37], fills him with "that apprehension of the interesting" [67] totally unavailable in Woollett, Massachusetts, offers to him the "delicate and appetising" [67] effects of tone and tint. The effect of this split response is that as his exposure to Paris deepens, both sides of his conflict intensify. The purity, the rectitude, the reliability of the American character become something he yearns more and more to find in its European counterpart, while the flatness, the Philistinism, the inflexibility of the former grow increasingly distasteful to him, just as his suspicion of the Parisian serpent enlarges as its seductive powers more and more envelop him. He is becoming at one and the same time more alienated from and more involved with both civilizations.

The focus of this conflict is the relationship between Chad and Madame de Vionnet and the nature of Strether's own role with respect to it. Whatever his other inward inconsistencies, Strether is consistent in always living by his sense of duty. In the beginning, this sense is identical with Woollett's, but what happens in the book is a great swing from a public to a private conscience, from an established, predetermined, black-and-white, fixed code of conduct to a personal, flexible, more relativist code in which each case is judged by its own merits. This shift is foreshadowed early in the novel, in a conversation with Maria:

> "You've accepted the mission of separating him from the wicked woman. Are you quite sure she's very bad for him?"
> Something in his manner showed it as quite pulling him up. "Of course we are. Wouldn't *you* be?"
> "Oh, I don't know. One never does—does one?—beforehand. One can only judge on the facts. Yours are quite new to me." [44–45]

Madame de Vionet's "case" in Woollett's eyes is precisely that of a violator of a general code. Woollett's reasoning is syllogistic, deductive: all fornicators (they don't yet know that she is an adulteress) are immoral, Madame de Vionnet is a fornicator, therefore she is immoral. Strether, confronted with the example in the flesh and also by this time deeply involved in his own conflicting responses to Europe, is forced to reexamine his premises and ultimately to reason inductively. But it happens in a queer, roundabout way: in his attempt to reconcile the irreconcilable, he denies the *second* premise, not the first, until the bitter end. In so doing, he is able for a while to cling to the ethical system (absolute right and wrong, which are knowable) upon which he was reared, and thus to find the goodness that is America in the very heart of the charm that is Europe. What is at stake is considerably more than the possibility of an error of judgment about the nature of a given relationship: it is a whole way of life, an entire system of thought, belief, and behavior, a set of assumptions about the nature and significance of existence. He abandons the assumption of absolute right and wrong only when he is forced to, and comes finally to equate "virtue" with concepts other than celibacy; but it is a private equation he arrives at, a lonely one, one that Woollett would never accept in a thousand years. Madame de Vionnet always remains charming to him, but her virtue does not consist in her charm (at least not to his moral, though admittedly to his aesthetic, sense). It consists rather in her personal sacrifice to Chad: the devotion and love she has poured on him, the assistance she has rendered him, the man she has more or less made out of unpromising raw materials. It is not that Woollett would not recognize these as desirable attributes in a wife; but in a mistress they are merely further symptoms of wantonness.

Strether's personal moral history with respect to his attitude toward Madame de Vionnet is a re-enactment of a change in American cultural patterns that took place in the nineteenth century; the breakdown of the old puritanical code of conscience and the establishment of a new, freer, more relativistic code. The change in each case was for much the same reason: the old canon did not fit all situations, was too harsh, tended to ignore human considerations and distort the truth. So James writes, "*The* false position, for our belated man of the world . . . was obviously to have presented himself at the gate of that boundless menagerie primed with a moral scheme of the most approved pattern which was yet framed to break down on any approach to vivid facts; that is to any at all liberal appreciation of them" [7].

What then is the difference between Strether and Chad, whose moral transportations may be said to be similar, at least up to a point? The difference is significant in its intuition of two divergent trends in American culture, both of which are connected with the breakdown of the puritan standard of ethics. Chad's relativism leads him directly into opportunism, manipulation, and exploitation: it is he who is the advertising man of the future. Strether's relativism on the other hand leads him to a struggle for a code of honor outside any system, to some private ideal of selflessness and personal allegiance, the significance of human ties, of intimacy, passion, and pain. The New England conscience had its strengths as well as its weaknesses, and one of its strengths was the sanctioning of the idea of behavior based upon responsibility toward one's fellows. This Strether preserves all the way through, though its form, significance, and finality have altered for him by the time the events have run their course.

But there are other differences between Strether and Chad too, not the least of which is that Chad is "the young man marked out by women" [98]. Once again, Strether's associations in connection with this perception are pertinent, as they link different areas of experience that together form part of the significance of his European adventure. Chad, he recognizes in their first conversation, not only is handsomer than he remembers him, but also is completely made over. His manners are "formed," he is a gentleman and man of the world, in other words "a man to whom things had happened and were variously known" [97]. Like a work of art, he has "a form and a surface," a design, tone, accent. His "identity so rounded off" and his "massive young manhood" hint at "some self-respect." It occurs then to Strether that the proper designation for this young man marked out by women is that of an "irreducible young Pagan." The qualities of Chad's Parisian sea change thus are sophistication, worldliness, taste, youth, and potency: a sensuous, polished surface and a sexual, pagan nature.

And in spite of Strether's sense of duty, his insistence that the only way he can be "right" is to get nothing out of the whole affair for himself, he does have a personal investment in the lives of Chad Newsome and Madame de Vionnet. They represent for him his last chance to "live," through vicarious participation in their experiences. His capitulation to and defense of them (and therefore, by extension, of Europe) is, he confesses to Maria, his "surrender," his "tribute" to youth: "It has to come in somewhere, if only out of the lives, the conditions, the feelings of other persons. . . . The point is that they're mine. Yes, they're my youth; since somehow at the right time nothing else ever was" [199].

Strether thus joins the long list of characters in James, those who achieve their strongest emotional satisfactions by observing and sometimes manipulating the lives of others.   *   *   *

The Ambassadors has been objected to precisely on the grounds of Strether's passivity and the vicarious quality of his experience, with critics remarking that these attributes are responsible for a certain attenuated quality about the novel that persists in spite of its obvious charm. Richard Chase writes that the "general lack of masculine reciprocation, especially in Strether himself, accounts in part for the somewhat tenuous quality—the softness at the center—of life as depicted in James' novel . . . despite the wealth of reported observation,"[2] and then goes on to compare (a comparison he acknowledges is invidious) the novel unfavorably with *Antony and Cleopatra.* And Matthiessen writes,

> The burden of *The Ambassadors* is that Strether has awakened to a wholly new sense of life. Yet he does nothing at all to fulfill that sense. Therefore, fond as James is of him, we cannot help feeling his relative emptiness. At times, even . . . it is forced upon us that, despite James' humorous awareness of the inadequacy of his hero's

2. *Twelve Original Essays,* p. 136.

adventures, neither Strether nor his creator escape a certain soft
fussiness. [437]

Such remarks come down to a moral—not aesthetic—demand that
a novelist conceive of his characters in terms of the most dubious ban-
alities: unexamined cultural stereotypes having to do with "masculinity,"
aggressiveness, and so forth. Behind this in turn lies a conception of art
based on standards lifted without examination from realistic fiction: art
should directly engage and passionately move the spectator by its imitation of the texture of daily life, its representation of "real" (in this case
sexually vigorous) three-dimensional people.

James himself of course repeatedly insists upon the intimate connection between art and life. * * * In the Preface to *The Ambassadors*,
he writes, "Art deals with what we see, it must first contribute full-
handed that ingredient; it plucks its material . . . in the garden of life
—which material elsewhere grown is stale and uneatable" [4]. But
the amount of "felt life" evoked comes down ultimately to "the artist's
prime sensibility," the "quality and capacity" of which represent the
work's "projected morality." This attribute itself is finally viewed by James
as "some mark made on the intelligence." In other words, the measure
of "life" in a work of art for James turns out to be the intensity and
complexity of the consciousness that is operating upon the material it
receives from the external world. From this vantage point, notions like
"masculine reciprocity" are not only irrelevant but needlessly confusing:
they tell us nothing about James's art for better or for worse, and ask us
to bring to bear upon that art standards that obscure, not clarify, its
nature.

In the case of Strether, James determined to make his a drama of
consciousness rather than of action in part because of

> the dreadful little old tradition, one of the platitudes of the human
> comedy, that people's moral scheme *does* break down in Paris.
> . . . [and to avoid the platitude James decided] The revolution
> performed by Strether under the influence of the most interesting
> of great cities was to have nothing to do with any *bêtise* of the
> imputably "tempted" state; he was to be thrown forward, rather,
> thrown quite with violence, upon his lifelong trick of intense re-
> flexion. [7–8]

Moreover, while it is true enough in a sense that "the burden" of the
novel is that its hero "has awakened to a wholly new sense of life," the
fact that he does not fulfill himself is not a lapse on James's part but is,
on the contrary, deliberate. Speaking of Strether's cry to little Bilham
to "live"—which is both the "germ" of the novel and an "independent
particle" lurking "in [its] mass"—[1] James writes,

He has accordingly missed too much, though perhaps after all constitutionally qualified for a much better part, and he wakes up to it in conditions that press the spring of a terrible question. *Would* there yet perhaps be time for reparation?—reparation, that is, for the injury done his character; for the affront, he is quite ready to say, so stupidly put upon it and in which he has even himself had so clumsy a hand? The answer to which is that he now at all events *sees*; so that the business of my tale and the march of my action, not to say the precious moral of everything, is just my demonstration of this process of vision. [1– 2]

James answers obliquely the question whether Strether would have enough time to make up for all he has missed, and the answer is negative: there isn't enough time, but at least Strether sees—what he has missed and that it is too late for reparation. Like his creator, he "was to go without many things, ever so many—as all persons do in whom contemplation takes so much the place of action."[3] The excruciation of the novel, its intensity, is precisely *due to* the contrast between Strether's awakened sense of what might have been and what is—or, to put it another way, his awareness that what might have been and what can never be are one and the same. The blow to him is total: the past is undone, the future without promise, the present both a reminder and a measure of both. * * *

* * * *The Ambassadors* is especially interesting in this respect, for it is the only novel that explicitly articulates the masculine-feminine opposition into contrasting social structures. * * *

Strether summarizes the role of the male in [his] woman-bound society as one that exemplifies, simply, "failure of type," which really means failure of individuality, not of generality or typicality. "Small and fat and constantly facetious, straw-coloured and destitute of marks, [Jim] would have been practically indistinguishable had n't his constant preference for light-grey clothes, for white hats, for very big cigars and very little stories, done what it could for his identity" [213–14].

The problem of self, the search for personal significance, is at the very center of Strether's story: the novel has to be seen in part as a comic quest for identity, and primarily sexual identity, even though the quest is obscured under a number of layers of mist and is articulated only indirectly in the book. * * *

* * * *The Ambassadors* also contain[s] a pastoral element, a contrast between innocence and corruption, a critique of "court" life. They are stories, too, of sexual initiation, the *rite de passage* into manhood.

The limits and the possibilities of Strether's quest are symbolized, as

3. Henry James, *Autobiography: A Small Boy and Others; Notes of a Son and Brother; The Middle Years*, ed. F. W. Dupee (New York, 1956), p. 17.

we have suggested, by the alternatives offered by the two contrasting civilizations and their respective styles of life and attitudes toward life, even their social and political structure. The book works toward two elaborate definitions of the significance that each culture has for Strether. What does he seek, what is his quest *for*? The whole book is a definition or articulation of this, through an intricate process of observation, perception, experience, and association on the part of the searcher, who is a man of divided inclinations.

To be a male in the America of Mrs. Newsome's Woollett, Massachusetts—at least a married male—is to be the second sex; to lack respect, responsibility, authority, and power; to be used for breeding and escort purposes but little else, in short, to lack personal identity. To be a male is to be "out of it," is to be not a type but rather, and precisely, a "failure of type."

Whereas the central phenomenon of Strether's European adventure is the very concept itself of "types," the hierarchical ordering of experience. Everything important that happens to him, everything that has any significance at all for him in Europe, is a function of some concrete embodiment of this concept or of something closely associated with it. As we have seen, it is intimate to the notion of taste, or an attitude toward *things* that is selective and qualitative, and to the experience itself of sensuous delight in those things that the imagination selects as worthy of delight. And who is best equipped to exercise the faculty of taste? Who but that type who most compels Strether's fancy, the man of the world. And what is the object best suited to delight his taste? What but that other great work of European art, the *femme du monde*. She, the woman who can look graceful with her elbows on the table, is the central image of desire in the novel, just as Mrs. Newsome (all "cold thought," all "moral pressure") is the central image of the repudiation of desire. Madame de Vionnet moves in a medium of privacy, peace, dignity, and style: the "ancient Paris" that Strether was always looking for and finds objectified by her surroundings. * * *

Her image is explicitly connected with the phenomena of artistry, aristocracy, patriarchy, and these in turn with her compelling sexuality: "At bottom of it all for him was the sense of her rare unlikeness to the women he had known. . . . Everything in fine made her immeasurably new, and nothing so new as the old house and the old objects" [146]. Strether's Europe presents him, in other words, with diverse realms of experience whose boundaries merge into one another in phantasmagoric fashion, through the process of association, to form a complex symbolic pattern. There is a dreamlike progression from the central concept of "type" through the related concept of taste to the phenomenon of sensuous relish in the immediate flux of experience, which in turn becomes associated in Strether's mind with a kind of golden sensuality, paganism, and uncorrupted sexuality. The last is of course his ardent puritan delusion, his wishful belief in the "virtuous" nature of the attachment between Chad and Madame de Vionnet: Strether wants to make a Paradise of his Paris. His New England conscience is destined to be overthrown twice, once when the delusion is shattered, again when he is forced to acknowledge that virtue is not necessarily equatable with chastity.

In the interim, however, the delusion serves its temporary function of reconciling irreconcilable worlds, of removing the taint of sin from the promise of masculinity. We have said earlier that all of Strether's needs, wishes, and ambivalent response to both civilizations are focused upon Madame de Vionnet and Chad, and more than anything else it is Chad's casual male dominance that attracts and compels Strether. And here again, in the series of revolving mirrors and shifting images by means of which Strether looks at Chad, we find the same progression from one realm of experience to another. Chad is "a gentleman," which is to say "a man of the world," "a young man marked out by women," "an irreducible young Pagan" [99]. There is no "failure of type" here, but a kind of lush abundance of alternative yet equivalent categories of identity in which being a gentleman is somehow the same as being a pagan. Chad is Strether's noble savage, his prefallen Adam; it is above all Chad's "romantic privilege" that he envies him, the privilege of having been young and happy in the charged air of Paris among the "delicate and appetising" effects of tone and tint, of having "the common, unattainable art of taking things as they come," of demonstrating in his person "some sense of power . . . something latent and beyond access, ominous and perhaps enviable" [99].

And the society that has made this possible is a society in which prerogatives and authority are vested in the male. Madame de Vionnet's marriage was arranged for her; she had no option, no recourse. In turn, Chad arranges the marriage of her daughter—at the very time when Woollett wishes him home not only for reasons of business but, more important, to "marry him off," and when Mrs. Newsome has taken the first steps in selecting his mate for him by sending Mamie Pocock along.[4] Indeed, the striking contrast between the young girls produced by each culture is illuminating in this respect: Jeanne de Vionnet, *jeune fille*, delicate, charming, passive, perfectly obedient, and Mamie Pocock, already portly, mature, standing perpetually in the receiving line.

The great symbol of the male prerogative in this European civilization is the Catholic Church, that most organized of patriarchies. We have already seen that for Waymarsh the Church is emblematic of the intrinsic treachery of Europe: the "enemy," the "monster," the "multiplication of shibboleths . . . rank with feudalism," whose hierarchical ordering of the universe represents the grossest dangers to the free democratic

---

4. Further, it is Mamie who decides she doesn't want Chad, not the other way around.

spirit. The Church means "society" to Waymarsh and the "discrimination of types." We have seen the intricate associations that led from "mere discriminations about a pair of gloves" on Strether's part to fear of the "loss of his immortal soul": associations proceeding, once again, from the concept of "type" to that of taste, to enjoyment of sensuous particularity, from there to the hidden serpent lust buried in Europe's bosom; the American equation of sophistication with wickedness.

It is significant therefore to look at Strether's associations when he meets the great artist Gloriani in the company of ladies and gentlemen "in whose liberty to be as they were [Strether] was aware that he positively rejoiced." The scene, in a spacious garden attached to old noble houses with delicate and rare decorations, speaks to Strether "of survival, transmission, association, a strong indifferent persistent order" [119]. The open air in these conditions seems "a chamber of state," and he presently has "the sense of a great convent, a convent of missions, famous for he scarce knew what, a nursery of young priests, of scattered shade, of straight alleys and chapel-bells, that spread its mass in one quarter; he had the sense of names in the air, of ghosts at the windows, of signs and tokens, a whole range of expression, all about him, too thick for prompt discrimination" [120].

Gloriani, Chad, Waymarsh, and little Bilham each in his way represents success to Strether, and each functions in the role of alter ego for him, but none so intensely as the great sculptor, "with his genius in his eyes, his manners on his lips, his long career behind him and his honours all round." During their brief encounter, with the sculptor's eyes holding his, Strether experiences a revelation about Gloriani that is at the same time a profound self-exposure; he is at a loss to know whether he has been told something or asked something. In fact, both things have occurred: each man has taken the measure of the other. The difficulty for poor Strether is his consciousness of how little there is in himself to be measured, either successful personal relationships or achievement in the affairs of men. But Gloriani represents both. Where Strether had dreamed in his youth of forming a relation with the higher culture and raising up the "temple of taste," Gloriani's accomplishments are realities, not broken dreams; with that "most special flare, unequalled, supreme, of the aesthetic torch, lighting that wondrous world for ever" [121], he is "a dazzling prodigy of type" [120], the great artist. And where "it was absolutely true" of Strether that "even after the close of the period of conscious detachment occupying the centre of his life, the grey middle desert of the two deaths, that of his wife and that, ten years later, of his boy—he had never taken any one anywhere" [43], Gloriani is surrounded by *femmes du monde*; there is "deep human expertness in [his] charming smile—of, the terrible life behind it!" [121]; he is "the glossy male tiger, magnificently marked" [133].

This vision of Gloriani is the apotheosis of Strether's European adventure. The artist is the exalted image of the complex set of personal possibilities—ones, however, that only *might* have been, represented by Europe for Strether, who is reduced to murmuring helplessly after their encounter, "Oh, if everything had been different!" The whole novel, as has been mentioned, is an elaborate definition of what constitutes that "everything," but all the intricate associations making up the definition are condensed and fused in the figure of Gloriani: Strether's longing for release from both avoidance and caution (which is his definition of personal freedom) so that he might enjoy the thing of the moment, take things as they come, satiate his appetite for beautiful things, even smoke with a woman. The latter of course is a thinly disguised version of the male tiger's activities: one must always with Strether's remarks about himself read behind the obscuring veil dropped by his New England conscience. But no matter what the devious routes, mazes and metaphors, elaborate veneers of civilization, all the paths in this novel lead finally to the jungle (Strether's word). * * * With whatever overlays of ambivalence, the ordeal of sexuality is *the* major theme of *The Ambassadors*.

This ambivalence is of course conscious, intentional: we are warned at the outset of the oddity of Strether's double nature; he is intended to be the embodiment of the reluctant puritan, hating his own "odious ascetic suspicion of any form of beauty," labeling with the word "failure" the general inability to enjoy that is one of Woollett's main characteristics, recognizing with an inward chill that Mrs. Newsome is "all cold thought" or "all moral pressure." The drama of the novel is meant to be a drama of self-division. Strether dips his toe, so to speak, in the unholy waters of Babylon but remains shivering, and peeping, on the bank while others take the plunge for him. This insistent yet somewhat shady, or voyeuristic, timorousness is typical of James's sensitive male protagonists and here is superbly faithful to the novel's study of the New England conscience and the American puritan temperament, one characteristic of which is precisely the combination of rectitude of behavior and lasciviousness of thought. It is a diabolic twosome, as Hawthorne knows, and shows so well in "The Minister's Black Veil," where the man of God imagines sin where none exists and himself becomes the profound emblem of righteous dirty-mindedness. Similarly, when in their initial interview, Chad denies that he is or ever was "entangled," Strether asks,

> "Then what are you here for? What has kept you? . . . if you *have* been able to leave?"
> It made Chad, after a stare, throw himself back. "Do you think one's kept only by women?" His surprise and his verbal emphasis rang out so clear in the still street that Strether winced till he remembered the safety of their English speech. "Is that," the young

man demanded, "what they think at Woollett?" At the good faith in the question Strether had changed colour, feeling that, as he would have said, he had put his foot in it. He had appeared stupidly to misrepresent what they thought at Woollett; but before he had time to rectify Chad again was upon him. "I must say then you show a low mind." [101]

It is of course what they think at Woollett, and there has been no misrepresentation except as Strether would feel, in the spirit of the thing: Woollett is after all indignant, not acquiescent, and the filth isn't their own imagining (he imagines): Chad *is* being kept by a woman. As indeed he is; Strether's ethical re-education in Europe eventually leads him to the point where he ceases to make the automatic equation between sex and sin, at least for others. But for himself the two sides of the dialectic remain unsynthesized, and the real end result of his adventures is to render America and Europe both unfit abodes for his soul. Furthermore, such an outcome is absolutely characteristic of James. It is intrinsic to his imaginative vision of things to see the world as rent asunder, with half its goods on the left hand of God, half on the right, and no passage in between. * * *

* * * The basic pattern * * * is the same; it consists of the gradual undeception of protagonist and antagonist alike, but always after irrevocable harm has been done. The same painful lessons are learned too late again and again by both camps on the battlefield. * * * Madame de Vionnet's final interview with Strether wrings from her the admission that she has made a change in his life:

"I've upset everything in your mind as well; in your sense of—what shall I call it?—all the decencies and possibilities. It gives me a kind of detestation . . . of everything, of life. . . .

What I hate is myself—when I think that one has to take so much, to be happy, out of the lives of others, and that one is n't happy even then. One does it to cheat one's self and to stop one's mouth—but that's only at the best for a little. The wretched self is always there, always making one somehow a fresh anxiety. What it comes to is that it's not, that it's never, a happiness, any happiness at all, to *take*. The only safe thing is to give. It's what plays you least false." [323]

But if there is never any happiness in taking, neither is there in the determined pretense that takers are absent from the world. James's victims share the burden of responsibility with their victimizers, and the events of the novels must be seen as a kind of cooperative venture in pain. The "guilt" of Isabel, Milly, Strether, and Maggie is a wilful blindness, a staggering self-deception based upon wishful thinking. The victims in each case wish to believe in the appearance put forth by those who practice upon them; their cases are complementary, and the responsibility is divided. James's finest talent in a way is for seeing what will not work. He is the most unsentimental of our great romanticists.

NICOLA BRADBURY (1979)

'The Still Point': Perspective in The Ambassadors†

'FRANKLY, QUITE the best, "all round", of my productions' was James's estimate of *The Ambassadors*. The rounded 'medallions' of the twelve books chime with this judgement. *The Ambassadors* is James's most finished work. Yet it is the true precursor of the last novels in being open-ended. Duality, rather than roundness, is the characteristic of *The Ambassadors*, and the 'detachment in his zeal and curiosity in his indifference' which James attributes to Strether are encouraged in the reader too, through the author's own poise. Through this novel we can learn how to read late James.

The germ of *The Ambassadors*, Strether's 'Live all you can' speech to little Bilham at Gloriani's garden party, has frequently been read as the author's own expression of faith. But the *Notebook* entries and later New York Preface to *The Ambassadors* reveal the Master analysing a latent ambivalence in the cry, and creating for it the context in which it could be 'led up to' with 'seemingly inevitable' complexity. James immediately recognized in the 'beautiful outbreak' the 'ironic' accent of a 'false position'. His approach to the narrative fuses process and effect as, avoiding 'the mere muffled majesty of irresponsible authorship', he aims at an 'ambiguity of appearance that is not by the same stroke, and all helplessly, an ambiguity of sense'.

The minutiae of stylistic technique in *The Ambassadors* are, therefore, both decorative and functional, stimulating imaginative identification and detached discrimination too. As the Preface points out, 'Art deals with what we see . . . But it has no sooner done this than it has to take account of a *process.*' James had already written: 'The business of my tale, and the moral of my action, not to say the precious moral of everything, is just my demonstration of this process of vision.'

James's terminology reflects an interest in the visual arts which persisted throughout his career. In 'The Art of Fiction' he had written, 'The analogy between the art of the painter and the art of the novelist is, so far as I am able to see, complete.' To him 'A psychological reason is

---

† From *Henry James: The Later Novels* (Oxford: Oxford University Press, 1979), 36–71. Copyright (©) Nicola Bradbury 1979. Reprinted from *Henry James: The Later Novels* by Nicola Bradbury (1979) by permission of the author and Oxford University Press. The chapter has been slightly abridged, and the page references to criticism and to the first English edition of *The Ambassadors* have been omitted.

. . . an object adorably pictorial; to catch the tint of its complexion—
I feel as if that idea might inspire one to Titianesque efforts. Yet the
picture, like the novel, has its compositional laws. The artist is confronted with a radical duality of substance and form, which may sometimes be related and sometimes distinguished, in order to combine
economy and clarity of perspective:

> To give the image and the sense of certain things while still keeping
> them subordinate to his plan . . . to give all the sense, in a word,
> without all the substance or all the surface, and so to summarise
> and foreshorten, so to make values both rich and sharp, that the
> mere procession of items and profiles is not only, for the occasion,
> superseded, but is, for essential quality, almost 'compromised'—
> such a case of delicacy proposes itself at every turn to the painter
> of life . . .

In this context, 'formality', or the code of laws governing artistic expression, becomes more than a condition of expression: it offers a potential
metaphor for the subject itself.

The discriminating appreciation required from the reader in this process mirrors that developing in James's protagonist within the novel. As
Dorothy Van Ghent recognizes, since 'in James's world the highest
affirmation of life is the development of the subtlest and most various
consciousness', therefore, 'James was able to use the bafflements and
illusions of ignorance for his "complications", as he was able to use,
more consistently than any other novelist, "recognitions" for his crises'
(*The English Novel: Form and Function*). In *The Ambassadors*, as in a
late Shakespeare romance, the 'recognition scene' crisis is a turning-
point: a stage in the action at which the intellectual and the moral
consciousness of the observer come together in imaginative understanding.

The aesthetic of this fusion of discrimination and synthesizing imagination is formulated by the art critic and psychologist Rudolph Arnheim,
in the notion that 'all perceiving is also thinking, all reasoning is also
intuition, all observation is also invention' (*Art and Visual Perception:
A Psychology of the Creative Eye*). Such a complex situation does not
lead to confusion because 'The situations we face have their own characteristics, which demand to be perceived "correctly". . . . This objective
element in experience justifies attempts to distinguish between adequate
and inadequate conceptions of reality.' Thus, in *The Ambassadors*, the
growth of consciousness in Strether enables him to achieve a more
'adequate' conception of 'reality', as he understands what is behind the
forms of social behaviour which he sees. Yet Strether's understanding
is not limited to the placing of his experience. Pursuing the art metaphor
further, the end of *The Ambassadors* can be likened to the 'vanishing-
point' of a picture composed according to central perspective. Instead

of a rigid two-dimensional structure of meaning, the ambiguity of simple irony, the drama is a three-dimensional development, leading towards a pointed but not limiting conclusion, which transcends the imagination that conceives it. In Arnheim's terms:

> In central perspective, infinity paradoxically assumes a precise location within finite space itself . . . It is within reach and unreachable at the same time. . . . Finally it should be observed that central perspective locates infinity in a specific direction. This makes space appear as a pointed flow, entering the picture from the nearsides and converging towards a mouth at the distance. The result is a transformation of the simultaneity of space into a happening in time—that is, an irreversible sequence of events. The traditional world of being is redefined as a process of happening.

The stress on the temporal links the pictorial metaphor with James's other major analogy: the drama. Although the drama is distinguished from the picture by its dynamism, it is similar to it in being governed by rules of composition which prevent 'confusion' and the 'stultification of values'. This linking thread runs through the alternating sequence of picture and scene in *The Ambassadors*, just as Strether's development of consciousness does; for it is in his appreciation of the structures of meaning, whether in fine art, the drama, or the social code, that Strether's understanding is demonstrated or ironically qualified. Through 'double consciousness', the reader is allowed an ironic apprehension of the fact which Strether does not at first see. 'Form', whether artistic, dramatic, or social, is used in the setting up of a situation which appears different to the reader who knows, and to Strether who does not know, 'the rules'; but form is later seen as a mere location for something beyond these conflicting views. After measuring and 'going behind' appearances, in the Jamesian phrase, there is the going beyond.

James's formal devices may be followed one after another as they appear in *The Ambassadors*, through the analysis of stylistic idiom, location, and action. Strether apprehends experience in this way, through time; and every reading of a novel is sequential. Yet there is also a 'spatial' or synchronic apprehension, essential to irony. The pattern built up by comparison and contrast (for example between the 'case' of Chad and that of Strether) is revealed, as we shall see, not only through the 'formal device', but the 'scene', or dramatic unit of composition.

The dynamic tension of dualism is encapsulated in the scenic method. James saw this in terms of its links with both picture and drama. He notes 'the odd inveteracy with which picture, at almost any turn, is jealous of drama, and drama . . . suspicious of picture'. But this conflict helps define the subject: 'Between them, no doubt, they do much for the theme; yet each baffles insidiously the other's ideal.' Out of this contention is created 'the discriminated occasion—that aspect of the subject which we have our choice of treating either as a picture or scenically . . . Beautiful exceedingly, for that matter, those occasions . . . when the boundary line between picture and scene bears a little the weight of the double pressure.'

Recognizing the 'discriminated occasion' as a basic structural unit in *The Ambassadors* emphasizes the solidity of the various formal devices which James uses both to create and to resolve ambiguity. The verbal metaphor exemplifies only one extreme of a series of devices functioning 'metaphorically', or sometimes with the full weight of symbols. Whole scenes may do this, as well as single figures of speech, and deeds as well as words may carry symbolic significance. The action of *The Ambassadors* is 'framed' by Strether's voyage to Europe and his prospective return, and on a different level the novel is punctuated by figures of speech concerned with water and boats. The theme builds to a superbly economical climax when the 'figure' is realized dramatically as Strether watches two people in the boat of his Lambinet scene, and perceives the true nature of the relationship between them.

The precise context of a perception is all-important. In Arnheim's pictorial terms: 'The frame of a painting creates . . . an enclosure. It is a fence that to some extent protects the play of forces in the picture from the fettering influence of the environment', yet 'a visual pattern cannot be considered without regard to the structure of its spatial surroundings . . . ambiguity can result from a contradiction between form pattern and location pattern.' In *The Ambassadors*, Strether's misunderstandings arise from his attempt to 'place' the Parisian situation in a New England framework of moral judgement, and to interpret the behaviour of those in Paris according to the patterns of New England custom and prejudice. On his first evening at the theatre with Maria Gostrey, Strether fails to appreciate the framing effect of the proscenium arch, and in his cultural *naïveté* thinks, 'It was an evening, it was a world of types, and this was a connection, above all, in which the figures and faces in the stalls were interchangeable with those on the stage.' In the Lambinet episode he commits the opposite fault, in drawing a fanciful frame around a dramatic scene, and thus mistaking the 'formal context' of the phenomena he witnesses. It is a recognition which marks Strether's full consciousness: not new experience, but the placing of his perceptions in perspective, within the right frame.

The frame, implied through the details of style, is accessible to the reader before Strether becomes aware of it. On every level of expressive diction, from that of sound to the syntactic, the imagistic to the scenic, two kinds of stimulus are offered: one encouraging a 'substantiating' imaginative identification, the other developing detached discrimination, or 'placing'. Before noticing these techniques in context, as a reader does, it may be helpful to group them critically, according to their effect. 'Substantiating' devices include James's use of clichés, his play upon recurring thematic words, the literalization of figurative expressions, and the concrete rendering of abstracts. Larger structural devices, such as thematic imagery on the interlocking verbal and scenic levels, also enhance the 'solidity of specification' of the novel world. In contrast to these devices, a group of 'dissociative' techniques encourage intellectual, rather than imaginative, attention. 'Poetic' effects such as alliteration, inversion, and incremental repetition are formal and exaggerated in the novel; and excess also characterizes James's comic hyperbole, and, in a different way, the heavily stressed formalism of the recurring art and drama metaphors. Somewhere between the 'substantiating' and 'dissociative' groups come certain idiosyncratic Jamesian techniques which both require imaginative involvement and encourage detachment. The quasi-surrealistic technique of focusing attention on parts of the body, which endows seemingly independent 'eyes' or 'elbows' with intense life, has this dual effect: one T. S. Eliot was to exploit as a satirical device in his early poetry. James also uses a series of 'paired' words,[1] which effectively draw together the sympathetic and discriminatory visions at the same time as pointing the contrast between them.

'Paired' words are used to present the contrasted Woollett and Paris versions of Strether's experience; but that they may do more is hinted at the outset. The paradox of his 'double consciousness' places Strether outside the rigour of the mutually exclusive categories of Woollett and Paris alike: the first glimpse of a transcendent consciousness which will free him from both worlds.

The simple opposition of terms early in the novel—'failure/successes', 'wicked/charming', 'divine/impossible', 'brutalized/refined'—becomes less and less straightforward. Amidst the hesitations of 'advance and retreat . . . his impulse to plunge and . . . his impulse to wait', Strether considers an opposition which is one of concepts, but not of balanced vocabulary: here the contrasted terms are two forms of the same verb: 'These were instants at which he could ask whether, since there had been fundamentally so little question of his keeping anything, the fate after all decreed for him hadn't been only to *be* kept' [James's italics].

Another complication is suggested when Strether is overwhelmed by Paris. Though his confusion is unequivocally stated, and 'what seemed all surface one moment seemed all depth the next', the two terms used for the city, 'the vast bright Babylon' and a 'glittering jewel', are scarcely paired opposites. The variation on a pattern indicates how Strether's judgement is swayed under the impression of Paris.

A different variation is the nice play on words in the comical interchange between Strether and Waymarsh after Strether has seen Chad's apartment:

---

1. Professor R. Ellmann first drew my attention to these 'pairs' in a lecture at Oxford, 1973.

'I saw, in fine; and—I don't know what to call it—I sniffed. It's
a detail, but it's as if there were something—something very good
—*to* sniff.'
. . . 'Do you mean a smell? What of?'
'A charming scent. But I don't know.'
Waymarsh gave an inferential grunt. 'Does he live there with a
woman?'
. . . 'I don't know.'

One is reminded of Lear's Fool: 'All that follow their noses are led by
their eyes but blind men.' Waymarsh, with his almost animal 'grunt',
indeed sees the implications Strether misses here; yet Strether's 'charmed'
sense is nearer the truth which he ultimately accepts, of the value of
the relationship he comes out to destroy but stays, unsuccessfully, to
preserve.

The technical figure of paired contrasting words is the basis for the
most important riddling phrase of *The Ambassadors*: the 'virtuous attachment'. Little Bilham's quibble salves his conscience without *quite*
misleading the reader. Like the description of Madame de Vionnet as
'dressed in black, but in black that struck him [Strether] as light and
transparent; she was exceedingly fair', or the paradox, 'if she were worse
she would be better for our purpose', the phrase becomes more than a
pun. These riddles are not simply ambiguous and ironic: they rise beyond
the constrictions of an 'either—or' meaning, just as Strether's understanding is to do. The 'bliss and bale' are inextricable, and, as Marie
de Vionnet despairingly asserts, success is only in failure: 'It's never, a
happiness . . . to *take*. The only safe thing is to give. It's what plays
you least false.' Her restatement of the ancient Christian paradox is
noticeably opportunist, in keeping with her Parisian morality; but
Strether himself demonstrates that 'to give', though far from safe, is his
'only logic. Not, out of the whole affair, to have got anything for myself.'

The comparison and contrast of two points of view is more economical
in James's use of cliché. In a novel which links the development of
consciousness with that of *savoir-faire*, the cliché, at once a meaningless
social token of communication and a potentially valuable unit of expression, is an important stylistic device. Through a kind of double bluff,
the mere pattern of words can become a daringly overt statement of the
'subtext'. Yet colloquialism also provides a 'bridge' between dialogue
and the thoughts of Strether, and thus furnishes a flexible medium of
narration.

The significant clichés of *The Ambassadors* are numerous, and have
been noticed by many critics. The central moral concern, for example,
is pointed by the repetition of such clusters as 'a good woman', 'excellent',
'better', and in the catch phrases 'all right', 'awfully good' and 'If she
were worse she would be better for our purpose'. At the other extreme

is Maria Gostrey's deliberately oversimplified phrase, 'the wicked woman', and her 'bad for him'.

The theme of 'knowledge', Strether's quest in two senses, also recurs frequently. Maria 'knew her theatre, she knew her play, as she had known triumphantly, for three days, everything'. Strether laughs, 'I *don't* really want to know!' In conversation with Waymarsh in Paris, the words are insistent in their repetition:

> 'I don't know. . . .'
> 'Then what the devil *do* you know?'
> 'Well,' said Strether almost gaily. 'I guess I don't know anything!'

Later, with Waymarsh,

> 'Doesn't he know what *she* is?' he went on.
> 'I don't know. I didn't ask him. I couldn't. . . . Besides I didn't want to . . . You can't make out over here what people do know.'
> . . . . . .
> 'Oh,' Strether laughed, 'You're not one of *them*! I do know what *you* know!'

'Knowledge' acquires almost biblical overtones, or perhaps half-echoes of *Paradise Lost*: the clichés of 'the feeling . . . had borne fruit almost faster than he could taste it', and 'the fruit of experience' extend the image of European 'corruption', 'the trail of the serpent'. The Old Testament flavour of Woollett righteousness is hinted too in the cliché of 'sacrifice'. Strether's uneasy conscience is vividly exaggerated: 'I want . . . to have been . . . expiatory. I've been sacrificing so to strange gods . . . I feel as if my hands were embrued with the blood of monstrous alien altars.' The 'sacrifice' theme intersects disturbingly with the materialist ethic as the phrase 'sacrifice mothers and sisters' links with 'give people away', 'give . . . up', or 'give over to'. Miss Barrace's comment that Marie de Vionnet 'has too much at stake' hovers uneasily between the primitive motif of sacrifice and the sophisticated decadence of the gambling theme.

This last is worded in two ways. One set of phrases, based on 'play', makes a verbal connection with the acting theme, while another, centred on the dead metaphor 'plunge', obliquely reflects the water imagery of *The Ambassadors*. Thus the phrases 'playing . . . any game', 'play fair' and the 'play of innuendo' may be linked with the social 'trick' and 'on the cards', besides the sense of 'plunging' and 'Strether took the plunge'.

The social game is largely pretence, 'acting . . . on instructions', or having 'acted his part'. Madame de Vionnet creates a 'drama' not far removed from the London theatre or the Comédie Française; Strether feels the lack of 'the power of any act of his own' when Madame de Vionnet is 'a part of the situation'.

Strether, however, learns to distinguish acting from action. 'I see',

'see for myself', 'he saw now', relate sight and understanding. Miss Barrace's 'see about' and Maria Gostrey's 'see you through', on the other hand, betray an opportunist ethic, common to both Woollett and Paris, which Strether eventually leaves behind.

The conditions of perception arise from the scene. 'In the light of Paris one sees what things resemble', but not necessarily what they *are*. Strether is 'in the dark'; and even when it seems 'at present . . . there was light', it is liable to be the delusory 'light of Paris', the social glitter, like that of Marie de Vionnet, whose very blackness strikes Strether as 'light and transparent', or Chad's, who 'was excellently free and light about their encounter'.

It is at these points that Strether must 'judge' on the 'evidence', the 'facts', not be misled by the 'charming' or by 'glamour'. The approach of the strict enquirer conflicts with that of the romancer again and again, and whenever they occur, these words act as warning signs that Strether is liable to be mistaken.

The 'realization' of images through setting also promotes a dual awareness in the reader. Strether's situation lends itself to James's extended puns: he 'pays' for his experience in cash as he does in suffering, and the social gambles of Marie de Vionnet and Maria Gostrey too are equally concretely rewarded. Strether comes to Europe by boat, literally, finds himself 'in the same boat' as Madame de Vionnet and Chad, metaphorically, and finally sees them literally sharing one boat in the 'midstream' of the Lambinet scene. Strether is 'launched' and 'at sea'; little Bilham has suffered 'shipwreck'; Strether decides to 'burn his ships', but hopes 'it may be plain sailing yet'.

This sort of punning invites 'substantiating' imaginative involvement, but also draws attention to its own artifice, and promotes an intellectual, detached response: a surrealistic awareness. Strether's view had 'taken a bound'; he had 'taken hold', 'got his job . . . in hand'. Maria Gostrey proves adept in 'bustling traffic' in 'the exchange of such values as were not for him to handle'. Madame de Vionnet 'by a turn of the hand' makes an encounter into a relation. Chad is expert in manipulation: 'One doesn't know quite what you mean by being in women's "hands". It's all so vague. One is when one isn't. One isn't when one is. And then one can't quite give people away'.

The jaded sensibilities of those familiar with social form are roused, or thrown into relief, by means of a slightly distorted view, and James's technique hovers between comedy and the grotesque. Strether is happy to find himself 'face to face' with Maria Gostrey, but disturbed to find he must 'look his behaviour in the face'. He admires the ease with which Chad and Madame de Vionnet sit, 'elbows on the table', but winces with the Pococks at 'a play of innuendo as vague as a nursery rhyme, yet as aggressive as an elbow in his side'. Encounters 'face to face' and 'meeting his eyes' are commonplace; but the repetition heightens our apprehension of the parts of the body so that an ordinary phrase becomes charged with meaning, and there is a poetic intensity about Strether's having 'by this time struck himself as living almost disgracefully from hand to mouth', while Sarah Pocock's plight is positively grotesque as 'she felt the fixed eyes of their admirable absent mother fairly screw themselves into the flat of her back'.

Not only the 'visual' devices for emphasis, but the verbal 'poetic effects' which James uses in *The Ambassadors* are generally dissociative rather than sympathetic. At the outset, both the richness and confusion of Strether's imagination are revealed in his mixed metaphors, as he relishes 'such a deep taste of change' and hopes 'to colour his adventure with cool success'. Strether's romantic tendencies have a certain literary quality, which is rendered rather than stated. There is a conscious poeticism about the inversion: 'deep and beautiful, on this, her smile came back', or, 'strange and beautiful to him was her quiet, soft acuteness'. The editor of the green review formulates his experience in such terms; but Strether comes to recognize artificialities of diction, and to be conscious of his form of expression.

As Strether is initiated into the deceptions of Parisian *savoir-faire*, a double negative further negated betrays his confusion as well as his inexpert duplicity: '*He* knew, more or less, what she meant, but the fact was not a reason for her not pretending to Waymarsh that he didn't.' An over-used comparative provides another syntactic signal of confusion. In Gloriani's garden, there is a nice irony in Strether's relishing 'what was presently clear . . . what was clearer still . . . what was clearest of all'. On the same occasion, a similar point is made through Strether's string of adjectives (unpunctuated in the New York edition): 'bright, gentle, shy, happy, wonderful'; and the irony is completed with the alliterative claim, 'All vagueness vanished', and the Woollett security of the declaration: 'He saw the truth'.

Stylistic devices make a dual appeal to the reader's fancy and judgement, and we enter into Strether's experience while preserving sufficient detachment to avoid his mistake; syntactic ambiguity is perhaps more stringent. Strether learns, however, that it is 'the proportions', the very 'conditions of perception', the 'terms of thought' that must be adjusted according to situation, and this is what we too are required to attempt, in order to read irony correctly. Ambiguity is particularly evident in conversation, and often turns on the use of pronouns. In an early interchange with Maria, Strether's talk of his career is mistaken for a more personal confession: a revealing error:

> 'I *never* made a good thing!' he at once returned.
> She just waited. 'Don't you call it a good thing to be loved?'
> 'Oh we're not loved. We're not even hated. We're only just sweetly ignored.'

The 'we' transposes the subject from Strether's relations with Mrs. New-some to his relations with the world through the green review which Mrs. Newsome finances. Maria, comically and tellingly, assumes that this is a brilliant sidestepping of the personal issue:

> She had another pause. 'You don't trust me!' she once more re-peated.

This interchange provides a clue to Maria's interest in Strether, and a warning as to her motivation in Paris. Whilst she appears to be helping Strether arrive at the truth, her efforts are qualified by the need to protect him both from a shock which would precipitate him into the arms of Mrs. Newsome, and from a suspicion of his confidante which might turn him towards Marie de Vionnet.

When Madame de Vionnet meets Strether, her first impulse is an outspoken honesty appropriate to her own estimation of her feelings for Chad and of the evident good she has done him. In Paris, she might be regarded with respect. But to Woollett prejudice, such openness could only be grounded on conscious innocence: a purely Platonic relation-ship. Seeing this, Madame de Vionnet is forced to abandon her first brave honesty, and to adopt the very subterfuge which Woollett would expect of a 'fallen woman'. Thus, when to her 'Tell her [Mrs Newsome], fully and clearly, about *us*', Strether stares: 'You and your daughter?' Madame de Vionnet climbs down, to accept the assumption he has made about the antecedents of her pronoun: not Chad, but, 'Yes—little Jeanne and me.'

Miss Barrace is less adept at following or anticipating the changes of subject made over unspoken assumptions than the main characters, who are all remarkably quick to catch an allusion. The very clumsiness of her interchange with Strether at Chad's dinner draws the reader's atten-tion to the way in which this kind of formal ambiguity works:

> 'At all events' he roundly brought out, 'the attachment's an in-nocent one.'
> 'Mine and his? Ah,' she laughed, 'don't rob it of *all* romance!'
> 'I mean our friend's here—to the lady we've been speaking of.'

Strether, Waymarsh, Miss Barrace, Chad, and Madame de Vionnet are in turn referred to, either through pronouns or through nouns of general applicability: 'our friend', 'the lady'. Miss Barrace does not understand; and her hesitation engenders a comical excess of speculation in Strether:

> Mystified by his abrupt declaration, she had glanced over at Gloriani as the unnamed subject of his allusion, but the next moment she had understood; though indeed not before Strether had noticed her momentary mistake and wondered what might possibly be behind that too. He already knew that the sculptor admired Madame de Vionnet; but did this admiration also represent an attachment of

which the innocence was discussable? He was moving verily in a strange air and on ground not of the firmest.

One final example is in a sense the development of our first: an interchange between Strether and Maria Gostrey whose unspoken subtext is a concern for the relationship between them. Strether has now grown beyond the mere aptitude with guessed meanings; his curiosity for the truth is tempered with an understanding of what is better not expressed, since silence is less hurtful than denial. Maria can only ruefully concur, retiring with a good grace:

> 'No. Tell her [Madame de Vionnet] nothing.'
> 'Very well then.' To which, in the next breath, Miss Gostrey added 'Poor dear thing!'
> Her friend [Strether] wondered; then with raised eyebrows: 'Me?'
> 'Oh no. Marie.'
> He accepted the correction, but he wondered still.
> 'Are you so sorry for her as that?'
> It made her think a moment—made her even speak with a smile. But she didn't really retract.
> 'I'm sorry for us all!'

The Ambassadors is a dense, though not a heavy book. James's style exacts the kind of attention we cannot here afford; nor is there room to trace 'the process and the effect' of each 'discriminated occasion' in relation to the whole. We shall have to concentrate on a few scenes and sequences. It is important, however, to remember and acknowledge that any selective appreciation omits details James considered necessary, for 'everything in [The Ambassadors] that is not scene . . . is discriminated preparation, is the fusion and synthesis of picture' (Preface). Close reading shows not only how we are led and Strether misled, but also how preparations are made for an eventual reversal of this misapprehension.

Strether's first meeting with Chad exemplifies this clearly. The whole of the third book of The Ambassadors is used to delay their confrontation in narrative terms, as Chad does through his social manoeuvres. When the encounter finally takes place, it is in contrast with the kinetic tension of the preparatory movement, with its series of other, less important, interviews, that this, with its curiously static quality, stands out. The theatrical setting recalls Strether's evening with Maria in England, and in turn prepares for the drama of the Lambinet scene. Standing out against the 'framed' quality of 'the waxed and gilded vista' in the Louvre, this episode at the Française also trains the reader, while it marks a stage in the development of Strether, in distinguishing picture and drama.

Within the 'discriminated occasion' itself, James uses various 'formal codes' to reveal exactly what is happening. On a social level, Chad's late entrance demonstrates his expertise: Strether knows he could not have managed this so easily. Strether's New England unsophistication is obliquely reinforced in literary terms through a series of verbal echoes of Henry Thoreau, famous for his straightforward and markedly 'unsocial' thinking. The textual parallel with Thoreau's *Walden* ironically implies a similar renunciation by Strether of social artifice and temporizing: activities which flourish in Paris. And, of course, in the novel: James's manipulation of the New Englander's ideas plays masterfully with this threat to his own complex and devious form, subordinating it to his design whilst extracting from it both aspects of an interest distinctly ambiguous. Thus, Strether echoes Thoreau in wanting to keep 'the sky of life' clear of 'clouds of explanation', and to preserve instead 'a grand idea of the lucid'. What begins as a faint literary echo turns into full pastiche. Yet, while teasing, James's account of bluff New England honesty provides a startling challenge to Parisian intrigue—

> A personal relation was a relation only so long as people either perfectly understood or, better still, didn't care if they didn't. From the moment they cared if they didn't it was living by the sweat of one's brow; and the sweat of one's brow was just what one might buy one's self off from by keeping the ground free of the wild weed of delusion. It easily grew too fast, and the Atlantic cable now alone could race with it.

* * * Postponed by such digressive, but ironically apt, considerations, the interview between Chad and Strether really begins some ten pages after Chad's entrance: although Strether attacks immediately, the edge has already been taken off what he has to say, and Chad's is the managing hand. As Stephen Spender explains, James

> revolutionizes the method of presentation in the novel; altering the emphasis from the scene to that intellectual and imaginative activity which leads to the scene, so that his scenes are always symptoms, not causes; always anti-climaxes, not climaxes, in the sense that any explosion, any break-down of nervously accumulating forces is anti-climactic. (*The Destructive Element*)

When Strether speaks, verbal ambiguity is brought into play, as his announcement has the double force of the charged cliché. 'I've come, you know, to . . . take you straight home' could mean 'home immediately' or 'honourably'. The note is ironically taken up again with Strether's 'If you'll promise me—here on the spot and giving me your word of honour—to break straight off, you'll make the future the real right thing for all of us alike'. Only later does Strether come to realize that the two meanings are in conflict with each other, and the 'straight' thing is for Chad to stay.

Although the encounter appears to be seen through Strether's eyes, social 'language' as well as the diction of the narrative helps us understand more than he does. When Chad leans forward with his elbows on the table, Strether perceives how 'at bottom, and in spite of the shade of shyness that really cost him nothing, he had from the first been easy about everything.' The cliché is significant in this materialist world; but equally so is the gesture of ease.

Strether finds a formula for Chad's appearance: 'that of a man of the world'; he sees that the younger man is 'brown and thick and strong'. This is reported directly, but from the oblique diction of the ensuing description the reader cannot tell how much Strether himself sees, and how far his perceptions are refined by the narrator. The effect is unobtrusively to improve on Strether's understanding: starting with Strether's impressions, we have a deeper apprehension of what they imply. To us, it is clear that Chad's good appearance is essentially of the surface: it is described in artistic terms, which indirectly recall Titian's 'overwhelming' 'young man with a glove' in the Louvre. Chad's development has 'retouched his features, drawn them with a cleaner line . . . cleared his eyes and settled his colour and polished his fine square teeth—the main ornament of his face; and at the same time it had given him a form and a surface, almost a design'. We are alerted by the ambiguous force of the word 'design', and the 'improvement' is suspect. Chad's shining teeth, in particular, seem a feature of ambivalent significance. Maria Gostrey warned Strether in England that two things might have happened to Chad: 'One is that he may have got brutalized. The other is that he may have got refined.' These teeth, curiously and confusingly, strike both notes, and the prepared categories of judgement are thrown into disarray.

Strether himself is lost in wonder at Chad's changed appearance, so that he fails to read the signs correctly. His acceptance—'What were such marked matters all but the notes of his freedom?'—smacks to us of licence here as well as liberty. It is not until Strether meets Maria again that what he has missed is spelt out. We, if not Strether, must be alerted by her exclamation: 'I've known nothing but what I've seen, and I wonder . . . that you didn't see as much. It was enough to be with him there'. For Maria, it is enough to see that 'the fact itself *is* the woman' to guess the nature of their relationship. But Strether, bringing the moral standards of Woollett to judge a lady, does not understand her 'good' or 'excellent' qualities in the way that Paris does. Despite Maria's hint that 'You must forgive him if it isn't quite outspoken. In Paris such debts are tacit', the narrator continues, in complicity with the reader, 'Strether could imagine;—but still——!'

It is at Gloriani's garden party that Strether first meets Marie de Vionnet and has an opportunity to see her with Chad; and the occasion necessarily obscures the intimacy of their relationship with the formality of normal social decorum. The episode reveals more about the Parisian *monde* than about the 'attachment' itself; but it introduces Strether, and us, to the Parisian 'conditions of perception' in a way which marks a deepening of his involvement in the situation, while allowing us a certain detachment.

The scene is remarkable for the balance of economy and an impression of fullness. 'The expectation of something special' is rapidly built up; yet there is in the very diction a warning that the reader is not to be wholly caught up in Strether's excitement. Critical tension is established between hyperbolical excess, which demands reduction, and an insistent repetition of words and phrases recurring throughout the scene, and importantly used elsewhere in the book. We are likely to ignore the warning in a phrase which seems obliquely to express Strether's own hyperbole: 'He had by this time . . . let himself recklessly go'; but the same sentence carries a threat in its developed insistence: 'cherishing the sense that whatever the young man showed him, he was showing at least himself.' The 'show' is converted in the ironic dimension of meaning from a revelation to a spectacle, which entertains by artifice and illusion; Chad becomes a 'cicerone', Strether is 'smothered in flowers', and the 'panem et circenses' smack of decadence and corruption, so that Strether's conscious hyperbole becomes for the reader an accurate indication of the ironic truth.

The ambiguous extremes of appearance and reality are clearly marked for us, though Strether himself is unable to recognize the significance of Chad's 'game, his plan, his deep diplomacy' as long as he persists in the 'almost angry inference that this was only because of his [Strether's] odious inbred suspicion of any form of beauty'. We recall a whole body of 'play' images, connecting 'acting' with 'gambling', and indicating the undercurrents of social intercourse within which Chad is able to manipulate the 'ambassador' through a 'deep diplomacy' which the older man will only recognize in 'touching bottom'. Meanwhile, Gloriani's garden, like Paris on Strether's first impression, 'twinkled and trembled and melted together, and what seemed all surface one moment seemed all depth the next'.

The unwittingly ironical diction of Strether's thoughts maintains an equilibrium for the reader, who is not required to condemn Strether's blindness, but merely to perceive more than Strether yet does. While Strether sees 'reluctance to pry' as 'consecrated', we are warned by the phrase 'judged in the light of that talk' that vigilance must be maintained. The 'silence' 'offered . . . as a reserve' by Chad may be a gift, like the 'panem et circenses' and the smothering flowers, designed only to distract the observer.

Such hesitations are abandoned by Strether, but not by us, once the observer is 'launched' into the mood induced by the powerful but vague and confusing influence of the place. The 'medium of the scene' retains an element of deliberately illusionary artifice, which overwhelms only the culturally unsophisticated New Englander. For him, 'the place itself was a great impression . . . sweeping away, as by a last brave brush, his usual landmarks and terms'. Strether is not only launched, but adrift.

Syntax as well as thematic vocabulary conveys the effect of this scene upon Strether. Parallel phrases are juxtaposed without conjunctions, like the brush-strokes of the impressionist painting, which conveys the perception of the observer with sensory immediacy, without the disciplined interpretative 'perspective' of formal, classical rules of line and outline. Strether 'had the sense of names in the air, of ghosts at the windows, of signs and tokens, a whole range of expression all about him, too thick for prompt discrimination'. There is a clear distinction between the impressionist rendering of experience which Strether enjoys here, and James's own concern with 'Expression, the literal squeezing out, of value.'

The precise nature of Strether's inability to appreciate the 'assault of images' is further defined when he meets Gloriani the sculptor. It is not art itself that is illusionist and deceptive, but the confusion of forms in imprecise apprehension. Strether finds Gloriani 'almost formidable', and invests the artist with 'the light, the romance, of glory'. He realizes his own *naïveté*, 'quite aware he couldn't have spoken without appearing to talk nonsense'. Yet he is sufficiently conscious to realize that he has 'positively been on trial', and although he describes Gloriani's smile, with a vague romanticism, as 'charming', Strether sees the 'terrible life behind it', and sees too that it 'was flashed upon him as a test of his stuff'. Both judgement and depth of vision are evidently within Strether's capabilities, even if they are not exercised upon this occasion.

When little Bilham approaches, Strether gives way to the impression, rather than exercising the faculties, of visionary inspiration: the romantic 'fit was on him'. Though the encounter with 'reality' dramatized in the meeting of eyes with Gloriani is analytically conveyed in this conversation, Bilham warns Strether that he is 'not a person to whom it is easy to tell things you don't want to know'. The young man does not insist; 'What more than a vain appearance does the wisest of us know? You'll see for yourself. One does see.' Whatever their specific context, such reverberating phrases are read in relation to the moral drama in which Strether is only partly aware of his involvement. They have more than the simple irony of a double meaning: the one Strether sees and the one he does not. The paradox of the 'vain appearance' remains, like that of the 'virtuous attachment', which both is and is not virtuous, to the extent that it remains an attachment, and which at the same time can be either the link of a real affection or a constricting bond.

The next 'relation' within the scene, Strether's meeting with Miss Barrace, lightens the pressure of moral significance, yet does not wholly relax the ironic tension which has been built up. 'Seeing', the abstract perception, becomes in this context a pragmatic 'seeing about'; Miss Barrace has 'given it up', and merely admires those who 'face' 'these things'. Although her words find a place in the structure of recurrent phrases, their moral weight is barely stressed here. While Miss Barrace, unlike Strether, can see 'in the light of Paris . . . what things resemble', her appreciation of appearances does not penetrate what lies beyond. Strether is right to reflect, 'You've all of you here so much visual sense that you've somehow all "run" to it. There are moments when it strikes one that you haven't any other.' 'Any moral', as little Bilham explains. Miss Barrace's 'resemblance' foreshadows Madame de Vionnet's ambiguous remark upon the *'invraisemblance'* of the occasion in the country, Strether's Lambinet scene. The gallicism of both ladies' expressions 'places' them in the context of a society which uses appearances; but this may also make the point for the discriminating reader 'that every like is not the same'.

Meanwhile the impressionist scene in the garden develops dramatically: Chad is 'again at hand', and the reader, like Strether, is swept into the supreme 'connexion' with Madame de Vionnet. The interplay of narrative voice and reported speech and thought allows for a simultaneous apprehension of Strether's feelings on the occasion and his subsequent analysis; and this creates an impression of growing awareness which is a development rather than a mere sequence. Though Strether is sufficiently aware to feel 'estimated . . . handed over and delivered; absolutely, as he would have said, made a present of, given away', Chad controls the scene. Yet half-recognized or unattached apprehensions gather for Strether: 'There were precautions, he seemed indeed to see, only when there were really dangers'. There is an advance towards his reading of the 'evidence', and 'the thing really unmistakable was that it rolled over him as a wave that he had been, in conditions incalculable and unknowable, a subject of discussion'. The impressionist figures give way to judicial and analytical terms, as the 'motives behind' are sensed. The encounter is interrupted, however, by 'a trick played with a social art of which Strether . . . felt himself no master's; again, deception is linked with gambling in the 'play' motif, and Chad's hand is discovered for the reader behind apparent accident.

The recognition of this manipulation does not come yet, however. Strether's central 'Live all you can' speech to little Bilham is the first outcome of his supposition that 'if at the worst he had been overturned at all, he had been overturned into the upper air, the sublimer element with which he had an affinity and in which he might be trusted awhile to float'. James is again invoking the echo of Thoreau, for whom Heaven was 'under our feet as well as over our heads' in Walden pond. But the transcendentalist paradox goes beyond ironic ambiguity, and rises above Strether's limitations as a judge of appearances. It is impossible to say precisely how far the undermining effect of a knowledge of Strether's delusion at the garden party destroys his statement of faith to little Bilham. Comic ambiguity in the social drama of manners gives way to near-tragic irony in a different perspective:

'I see it now. . . . and now I'm too old . . . for what I see.
. . . One lives in fine as one can. Still, one has the illusion of
freedom; therefore don't be, like me, without the memory of that
illusion.'

This address, which might be taken as a concluding statement, has
a dual force which is established and maintained by the ambiguous
quality of the scene in which it occurs. The 'false note' is sounded
particularly in the phrase 'the illusion of freedom'. Yet far from ending
the illusion, Strether's speech suggests recognition of the unreality only
to give way to the fancy again, and this is heightened rather than un-
dermined.

The resumed pattern of encounters re-echoes that of the 'first half'
of the scene, but with Jeanne de Vionnet now being introduced to
Strether. Strether's 'full picture' is ironically shown to exceed both logical
and artistic decorum, as it has 'another impression . . . superimposed';
and the contradiction of reality in Strether's interpretation of appearances
is embodied in the disjunction of form and content in the expression of
his thoughts.

Chad sweeps little Jeanne off to rejoin her mother, with a proprietorial
air that Strether mistakes for that of the accepted suitor: 'There was the
whole of a story in his tone to his companion, and he spoke indeed as
if already of the family'. Strether's romantic fancy creates the 'story': 'It
made Strether guess the more quickly . . .'. But little Bilham has gone:
there is no one to tell his thoughts to, and no one to point out his
mistake.

When Miss Gostrey joins Strether, the reader is enlightened more
than Strether himself as to Madame de Vionnet's position. Labouring
under the delusion of an attachment between Chad and little Jeanne,
Strether is not prepared to read between the lines of what Maria Gostrey
says. Both of them consider the truth so obvious as to be understood
without being plainly stated, but they have different ideas of what it is.
The non-communication between them is so gross that the only thing
plain to the reader is the fact of a misunderstanding. When Strether
exclaims, 'It's the child!'—a statement hardly so explicit as to stand
without further elaboration—Miss Gostrey's response is seen from
Strether's point of view: 'And though her direct response was for some
time delayed he could feel in her meanwhile the working of this truth.'
There is no indication here that this interpretation is wrong: that this is
the speechlessness of incomprehension, rather than assent. Not until
the metaphors in the next sentence recall Strether's fanciful impressions
earlier in the scene is there any hint, building on that cumulative irony,
that his extravagance is wrong again. The indirect diction used for Strether's thoughts and for the objective narrative alike blurs distinctions even
here between supposition and reality. It is left for the imagery of flood,

the gallicism of 'ces dames', and the sheer difficulty of the syntactic and logical sequence of the sentence to reveal to the reader that nothing exists but confusion worse confounded by the illusion of clarity. It is a situation not reported or analysed, but rendered through the very diction of the narrative:

> It might have been simply, as she waited, that they were now in presence, altogether, of truth spreading like a flood and not, for the moment, to be offered in the mere cupful . . .

The 'simply' is quietly ironic; the sentence grows increasingly involved:

> inasmuch as who should ces dames prove to be but persons about whom—once thus face to face with them—she found she might from the first have told him almost everything?

There is a subtle shift in the middle of this sentence from 'the narrator-taking-Strether's-point-of-view' to 'the narrator-reporting-Maria's-thoughts'. The voice of the narrator is a constant factor; but this glosses over the confrontation of two misdirected presuppositions of an 'understanding' which does not exist.

The irony of misunderstanding, which all but the most alert reader will have failed quite to grasp, as it is mimed in the sentence with the shifting point of view, is made increasingly plain throughout the interchange between Miss Gostrey and Strether. There is both direct and oblique warning in the text itself:

> There could be no better example—and she appeared to note it with high amusement—than the way, making things out already so much for himself, he was at last throwing precautions to the winds.

There is also simple irony:

> It was a relief, Miss Gostrey hinted, to feel herself no longer groping . . .

Amidst such clear short sentences of spoken or reported speech, Strether's continuing misapprehension is obliquely revealed, not in the sense, but in the 'poetic style' of his thoughts. There is alliteration, grandiose diction, limitless imagery, in this conception, entirely at variance with the true state of affairs:

> The waste of wonder might be proscribed; but Strether, characteristically, was even by this time quite in the air.

The vision of the soaring intelligence of the observer is nicely put between two precise locations: Miss Gostrey's clarity—'She's coming to see me —that's for you . . . but I don't require it to know where I am'—and

Strether's security of ignorance: 'By which you mean that you know where *she* is?'

The word-games are set aside, however, once Maria Gostrey translates these theoretical, even metaphysical, abstractions into the terms of social intercourse. In social language, her sentence is unequivocal: 'I mean that if she comes to see me I shall . . . not be at home'.

The mounting delusion of the garden scene 'explains' Strether's stance here, while on the other hand the blatant irony here 'reads back' to confirm the ironic distance of truth from appearance throughout the preceding scene. Miss Gostrey's admonitions and repeated rephrasing of her stance would be excessive in this context, were they not also setting right in retrospect the fantastical romanticism of the preceding scene. 'I shall . . . not be at home. . . . Don't be so literal. I wash my hands of her. . . . *I'm* impossible. It's impossible. Everything's impossible'. For Strether to respond to this with a sublimely unaware, 'I see where you're coming out. Everything's possible', is a stroke of irony made possible only in the context of a delusion stretching both before and after this. Thus it is that Maria's outburst can warn the reader almost directly of the secret hitherto revealed indirectly through the use of ambiguous formalities in the garden scene, yet Strether can remain unaware of the truth so plainly put, without appearing stupid in his blindness. It is a question of process as much as of effect, for reading the novel is more than a series of discrete perceptions.

The conversation with Maria Gostrey 'concludes' this 'occasion' by confirming the delusion which Chad has artfully created, and the romantic Strether elaborated for himself. The interchange also acts, however, as a transition to the next move and further confirmation of the mistaken view of Chad and Madame de Vionnet. There is no perceptible break between the scene at Gloriani's house and the sequence of further meetings, first with Chad, then with Madame de Vionnet, and finally at Chad's dinner party, where the two of them are present, acting as host and hostess.

The visit to Madame de Vionnet's house illustrates James's conception of the 'organic form' of the novel, in which everything is 'all one and continuous'. The scene is economical yet densely allusive, full of the 'solidity of specification' which realizes setting, and rich in ambiguous dialogue; it is an education in imaginative appreciation. Both description and conversation form part of a developing sequence. Besides the series of interviews beginning at Gloriani's garden party and leading towards Chad's dinner, this meeting contributes to the pattern formed by Strether's encounters with Marie de Vionnet alone. This carries the reference back to the garden party, and forward to the encounter at Notre Dame and the intimate luncheon by the Seine. Most importantly, the visit provides a pattern of 'the habit of privacy, the peace of intervals, the dignity of distances and approaches', which will stand in contrast to the climactic last meeting between Strether and Marie, set amidst the same surroundings, but quite different in tone.

The visit is formally set in a social context, even the time, 'quite by half-past five', establishing the situation. Besides the referential value of the hour it has various social connotations: the time after tea and before dinner, when only acquaintances of a certain degree of intimacy are received. There is also a *trompe l'œil* narrative effect, fitting this scene between the garden party and the dinner without apparent interruption: in this telescoped sequence, the pace of events meets the imaginative pressure of Strether's experience.

It is through the setting that Madame de Vionnet's 'credentials' are given. Far more than any explanatory apologies from Chad or Maria Gostrey, this scene 'justifies' Strether's misplaced confidence in Marie's tone. The 'hereditary, cherished, charming' furnishings, described in one long leisurely sentence, represent a sense of age, value, and an assured taste. The contrast with Chad's house and Maria's 'little museum of bargains' is felt; but Strether is clearly not yet able to evaluate its significance. In the later interview with Marie in these rooms, he will be able to perceive her as distinct from her setting, to appreciate how much she gains from it, and correspondingly, what her personal stature is. At this first interview, however, Strether is represented as artistically perceptive but culturally naïve, unable to communicate on equal terms with a woman for whom he has an imaginative, but untutored, sympathy. We see the limitations of Strether's understanding without losing sympathy for his attempts at clearer perception, while we ourselves are being prepared to make the finer distinctions of the concluding scene.

The greater the charm of Madame de Vionnet, the better we can understand Strether's reaction to her 'very presence, look, voice, the mere contemporaneous *fact* of whom, from the moment it was at all presented, made a relation of mere recognition'. This is the beginning of a development which imaginatively justifies Strether's turning away from both Mrs. Newsome and Maria Gostrey. That he does not, in the end, turn from them to Marie de Vionnet will be gradually and sub-stantially accounted for as her relation with Chad is revealed; but, for the moment, 'at the back of his head, behind everything, was the sense that she was—there before him, close to him, in vivid imperative form—one of the rare women he had so often heard of, read of, thought of, but never met . . .'. There is a direct, unequivocal comparison: 'That was not the kind of woman he had ever found Mrs. Newsome, a con-temporaneous fact who had been distinctly slow to establish herself; and at present confronted with Madame de Vionnet, he felt the simplicity of his original impressions of Miss Gostrey. She certainly had been a fact of rapid growth; but the world was wide, each day was more and more a new lesson.' 'Fact', as applied to Mrs. Newsome and Maria Gostrey, has a bathetic vulgarity which is quite absent in connection with Marie de Vionnet. Here it has an almost existential weight, enhanced by the positioning of the verb 'was' before the syntactic break of the parenthesis. Like Cleopatra, Madame de Vionnet is a 'rare' being.

Through the sequence of 'discriminated occasions' representing Strether's encounter with Chad, Madame de Vionnet, and the Parisian *monde*, James interrelates the minutiae of style and tone within each scene and between the various occasions. Ironic ambiguity points Strether's misapprehensions for the reader; but we, like Strether, are carried along by the pace and flow of the narrative, sharing his experience. James uses the social situations and draws on pictorial dramatic and literary allusions too, not only to 'place' Strether, the New Englander in Paris, but to prepare for the eventual movement through this perspective towards an 'infinity' paradoxically located but not contained by it. We may smile at Strether's *naïveté* now, but we shall be ready to respect his judgement and his feelings in the end.

The temptation to pursue an analysis of 'the process and the effect of representation' through the discriminated occasions of *The Ambassadors* is increased both by their individual power and by the 'architectural' strength with which they support each other. To take less than the whole is to do the novel an injury. But in our limited space for close reading, I shall concentrate not on the Lambinet scene, which has been extensively and sensitively explicated,[2] but on the sequence of encounters at the conclusion of the novel: in a sense, these scenes balance those we have already noticed.

The closing movement cannot be utterly divorced from its context. The comicality of the Pocock embassage is as important in preparing for the end as the earlier 'romance' of the garden party, the encounter at Notre Dame, the luncheon *à deux* by the Seine. When fresh ambassadors arrive from New England and Strether's alignment with the Parisians is confirmed, there is an opportunity to count the cost to him of the abandonment of his old protectress. He will not have to stoop to such considerations at the end.

The Lambinet episode too clarifies the position. Before the end, Strether's disillusionment, the disgust at 'the quantity of make-believe involved, and so vividly exemplified, that most disagreed with his spiritual stomach' has already been digested. Within a page of that nadir, Strether has 'found himself supposing everything'—emended in the New York text to 'innumerable and wonderful things'.

The last book of *The Ambassadors* comes after both illusion and disillusionment. Neither condemnatory nor condoning moral failing, it shows Strether, now 'seeing' clearly, coming to terms with human beings as they are, but not accepting their condition as the best conceivable.

2. Notably by David Lodge in 'Strether by the River', *Language of Fiction* (1966).

The isolation of the perceiver, confronted with experience but not one with it, is now reflected both in themes and style. The familiar motifs of fantasy and artifice recur, but there is a greater explicitness in the interpretation of symbols and the statement of conclusions. The protagonist's vision has come to equal that of the narrator, and although he remains a romancer, Strether is distanced enough to recognize the extent of his fancies. In the *Postes et Télégraphes* office, Strether sees with comic clarity what his position now is, amidst 'the influence of the types, the performers concocting their messages; the little prompt Paris women, arranging, pretexting, goodness knew what . . . He was mixed up in the typical tale of Paris, and so were they, poor things . . .'. This is Strether looking over his own shoulder, and acknowledging with colloquial forthrightness: 'They were no worse than he, in short, and he no worse than they—if, queerly enough, no better; and at all events he had settled his hash.'

When the final interview begins, Strether still sees Madame de Vionnet in artistic terms, but these are explicitly voiced: 'the picture that, each time, squared itself, large and high and clear, around her: every occasion of seeing it was a pleasure of a different shade'. Strether is critically discriminating: an interesting adjective qualifies the noun in his reiterative image: 'He was moving in these days, as in a gallery, from clever canvas to clever canvas'. While he accepts the conditions of perception, he does so consciously, and with an appreciation that has no hint of delusion: 'The light in her beautiful, formal room was dim, though it would do, as everything would always do'. Strether's vision of Madame de Vionnet as a tragic heroine, an aristocratic victim of the Revolution, is fanciful, but not inappropriate. It is warranted both by its intensity and because it elucidates the situation. The 'historic sense' befits the Parisian drama, and Madame de Vionnet has a 'tragic rôle' in that context, whatever the limitations of her stature seen in a different perspective.

Strether is not impervious to the old impressions which he has learnt to appreciate, but he knows that 'whatever he should find he had come for, it wouldn't be for an impression that had previously failed him'. He is aware both of the local value of all that Marie de Vionnet embodies, and of how far this value is localized, rather than infinite. The knowledge that 'he should soon be going to where such things were not' progresses beyond his recognition in the Lambinet scene that 'in *these* places such things were'. When there is repetition in Strether's account, its effect is not to alert the reader to excess, but to suggest how Strether himself recognizes the movements of his imagination: 'He knew in advance he should look back on the perception actually sharpest with him as on the view of something old, old, old, the oldest thing he had ever personally touched'. He distinguishes between the 'facts' of place and setting, and the temporary expedients of artifice, recognizing the value of each:

> She might intend whatever she would, but this was beyond anything she could intend, with things from far back—tyrannies of history, facts of type, values, as the painters said, of expression—all working for her, and giving her the supreme chance, the chance of the happy, the really luxurious few, the chance, on a great occasion, to be natural and simple.

There is an ironic contrast between this and the thrice-repeated, hollow, 'charming chance' of the recent Lambinet scene.

The sense of proportion and appreciation is insistent throughout the interview, even while Marie becomes increasingly emotional. Strether responds to her oblique, coquettish appeal—'He was not to mind if she bored him a little: she had behaved, after all,—hadn't she?—so awfully, awfully, well'—with an impatience, not at the delivery, but at the appeal itself: he could be relied on now to take such preliminaries for granted. He is 'the more prepared of the two' and knows it. Though Marie runs through every pose from self-abasement—'Selfish and vulgar—that's what I must seem to you'—to proud appeal—'How can I be indifferent . . . to how I appear to you?'—her self-interest is as clear to Strether as it is to the reader. Even Marie's recognition of Strether's 'dislocation' is bound up for her with the selfish desire to have him stay in Paris to 'consecrate' her liaison with Chad. Her insight is not wholly vitiated by her interest, however. Her words place Strether at least negatively—as infinity, though it cannot be pinned down, can be indicated by the lines of perspective in a picture. This is the positive implication of her question:

> 'Where *is* your "home", moreover, now—what has become of it? I've made a change in your life, I know I have; I've upset everything in your mind as well; in your sense of—what shall I call it?—all the decencies and possibilities.'

Marie's declaration of the need to 'give' is equally pertinent to Strether's vision, and equally inverted. Against the selfishness of her recognition that 'it's not, that it's never, a happiness, any happiness at all, to *take*. The only safe thing is to give. It's what plays you least false', Strether's true generosity will eventually stand out in his disinterested avowal that 'not, out of the whole affair, to have got anything for myself' is the only way 'to be right'.

Madame de Vionnet does not recognize the privileges of Strether's 'displaced' position. He can see, as she cannot, Chad's limitations, and the limitations of her work on him, which, despite the 'consecration' of Strether's interest, remains 'of the strict human order'. Unlike Strether, 'she had but made Chad what he was—so why could she think she had made him infinite?'. As the lady weeps, Cleopatra-like, descending to the level of that maid-servant, 'vulgarly troubled', that Jeanne de Vionnet never became, there is a certain theatricality in her collapse: ' "It's how you see me, it's how you see me"—she caught her breath with it— "and it's as I *am*" '. Strether remains outside the storm of emotion, detached, though not unsympathetic. Though 'serving her to the end', he is quite conscious of 'some vague inward irony in the presence of such a fine free range of bliss and bale.' So far has his understanding risen above the half-truths and histrionics of Paris that though he pities Marie de Vionnet, he does not find his moral categories compromised by this response. While she is pathetic, Strether attains to the dignity of tragic understanding, unflawed by self-pity. He is a little remote: 'It was actually, moreover, as if he didn't think of her at all, as if he could think of nothing but the passion, mature, abysmal, pitiful, she represented, and the possibilities she betrayed'. There is a quiet irony in Strether's ambiguous parting words, of which the most certain thing is the finality of the past tense: 'Ah, but you've *had* me'. He has loved Marie, and she has used him; but he will not be used again.

After the finality of this parting, Strether's isolation grows, with an inevitability compounded of collusion amongst his erstwhile 'friends' and the distancing within himself of clearer perception. This isolation is not in space only, though at the end of the book it will be imaged in geographical terms, but in time as well: when Strether thinks of Waymarsh, it is, 'Waymarsh who already, somehow, seemed long ago'.

Though Strether at first waits to be summoned by Madame de Vionnet and by Chad, his passivity is based on patient understanding: he remains in control of his own conduct.

> Strether assumed, he became aware, on this reasoning, that the interesting parties to the arrangement [Chad and Madame de Vionnet] would have met betimes, and that the more interesting of the two—as she was after all—would have communicated to the other the issue of her appeal.

The fact that Strether is able to pause in the midst of this formulation for a parenthetical appreciation of Madame de Vionnet shows how far he is from the blindness of close involvement with the situation he is shortly to leave behind; but it demonstrates also that Strether's detachment does not decrease his imaginative appreciation of the qualities which his experience during the course of the novel has taught him to value.

The pause between the interview with Marie de Vionnet and that with Chad is taken up with a quieter interlude with Maria Gostrey. Though she is another woman whose as yet unvoiced claims will eventually have to be made explicit and met, there is no real doubt as to the settlement of the account; and Strether's 'using' Maria to fill this time rests on generous confidence in her understanding rather than a blind or cruel misleading of the confidante. James makes it clear in the New

York Preface that he supposed the 'redundancy' of Maria at the conclusion of the novel self-evident, and was mainly concerned that it should
not be too obtrusive. The inevitability of the final parting is shown
obliquely in the penultimate encounter and more directly in the last
scene. Strether's taking Maria shopping, his showing her the penny
steamboats and the *bateaux mouches*, are more than indulgence in the
romantic delights of 'Kubla Khan', destined to end at the dreadful 'reckoning'. These activities, while the reckoning is postponed, are calculated
to demonstrate how far Strether has come through the novel, since the
time when Maria guided him around the shops and he watched Chad
and Marie de Vionnet in a boat on a river. Strether has now no practical
need of Marie or Maria: he can indeed, as Maria once prematurely put
it, 'toddle alone'.

The necessity of separation is not solely based upon redundancy,
however. It is not simply that Maria has outlived her usefulness, but
that she, like all the other women in Strether's experience (except the
young ladies: Jeanne suffering in silence, and Mamie, 'disinterestedly
tender'), has betrayed his trust, putting her own desire for him above
his need for the truth. This realization has been gradual for Strether,
and on a careless reading we too may miss the signs of the confidante's
betrayal. Yet the recognition lurks near the surface before it is made
explicit; Strether 'knew, that is, in a manner—knew roughly and
resignedly—what he himself was hatching; whereas he had to take the
chance of what he called to himself Maria's calculations'. His indifference to Maria's motives here is not callous, but shows a proper regard
for the rightness first of all of his own actions. Strether's moral fineness
is exhibited in a 'supreme scruple' which can have reference only to his
own motives, and not to those of the people surrounding him:

> He wished not to do anything because he had missed something
> else, because he was sore or sorry or impoverished, because he was
> maltreated or desperate; he wished to do everything because he was
> lucid and quiet, just the same for himself on all essential points as
> he had ever been.

The 'sameness' of Strether's need 'to be right' is not stasis, but 'infinity':
an affirmation that certain values transcend the limitations of time and
space. In the 'vanishing-point' of the novel, Strether is not transformed,
in the sense that he becomes superhuman or inhuman; but his humanity
moves into the freedom of absolute imaginative morality, away from
the constrictions of formal decorum inevitable in social intercourse.
When Maria Gostrey tells Strether 'You're magnificent', he replies,
'You're too much struck with everything' (in the New York edition,
James revised the terms to 'You're complete' and 'You're always too
personal').

The movement beyond Paris is one Strether must make alone. Marie de Vionnet, who was once 'his youth', is left behind: 'She was older for him tonight, visibly less exempt from the touch of time'. Maria Gostrey has long since been outdistanced, though it is only now that Strether realizes why. He becomes 'even sure that she was in possession of things he himself couldn't have told; for the consciousness of them was now all in her face and accompanied there with a shade of sadness that marked in her the close of all uncertainties'. Maria has been biding her time; but having 'played strictly fair' is not enough. She would still be willing to take what the situation 'might furnish forth to her advantage'. With the close of all uncertainties, it becomes clear that for Strether to bind himself to Maria would be to sell the freedom of his imaginative experience, to exchange 'infinity' for a fixed location.

The settlement of accounts with Chad is different in tone from that with the two women, although the thematic pattern is similar. Strether has already grown away from Chad, recognizing that he has 'other qualities. But no imagination, don't you see? at all', and that Marie de Vionnet, the more interesting of the couple, 'had but made Chad what he was—so why could she think she had made him infinite? . . . he was none the less only Chad'. The situation now is simple for Strether: 'he must see Chad, but he must go. The more he thought of the former of these duties the more he felt himself making a subject of insistence of the latter'.

This interview, like those with Marie and Maria, is in a familiar setting: a fact which has imaginative force as well as narrative shapeliness; for there is a sense of foreknowledge of the end, rather than any uncertainty. Strether himself recognizes the 'completed' quality of this experience, as he approaches Chad's rooms:

> Present enough always was the small circumstance that had originally pressed for him the spring of so big a difference—the accident of little Bilham's appearance on the balcony . . . at the moment of his first visit, and the effect of it on his curiosity. He recalled his watch, his wait, and the recognition on the young stranger's part that . . . had brought him up—things that had so smoothed the way for his first step.

There is a brief concession to be made to the present situation before Strether can be freed of Chad, and of all local ties. This is expressed in Strether's acknowledgement that Chad's presence on the balcony represents 'clearly a conscious surrender', whilst his own concern demonstrates that he is 'still practically committed—he had perhaps never yet so much known it'. In fulfilling the undertaking he made to Marie de Vionnet—the counterpart to his original mission for Mrs. Newsome—Strether will finally free himself of all obligations; though he will also renounce his 'youth':

> If he had just thought of himself as old, Chad, at sight of him, was thinking of him as older; he wanted to put him up for the night just because he was ancient and weary.

Chad, like Marie, would be prepared to keep Strether 'indefinitely'; but there is hardly any wavering over this. The interview is not to settle Strether's fate, but Chad's and Marie's. 'He had come to say goodbye —yet that was only a part; so that from the moment Chad accepted his farewell the question of a more ideal affirmation gave way to something else'. It is the way Chad treats the question of his relations with Madame de Vionnet as being of interest to Strether rather than absolute in themselves, that betrays him. Just as Chad would once have returned to Woollett at his mother's summons, so now he treats his faithfulness as a tribute to Strether: a gesture. Strether understands 'that he would abound for him, to the end [the ironic ambiguity of this phrase is nicely unstressed], in conscientious assurances'. The 'conscientious' is the restrictive note of Woollett; but Strether is moving amidst the greater truths of absolute right and wrong: the morality which distinguishes humanity rather than society. He warns Chad, 'You'll be a brute, you know— you'll be guilty of the last infamy—if you ever forsake her'. Restated, this becomes even more clearly a question of right, not of reputation or appearances: ' "It's not a question of advising you not to go," Strether said, "but of absolutely preventing you, if possible, from so much as thinking of it. Let me accordingly appeal to you by all you hold sacred".' In the New York edition there is a third admonition, after the appeal of humanity and of the sacred, sinking to the terms of mere legality: 'You'd not only be, as I say, a brute; you'd be . . . a criminal of the deepest dye.' It is to this warning that Chad responds, with a 'sharper look', and the disturbing protest, 'I don't know what should make you think I'm tired of her.'

The fusion of Strether's understanding with the omniscience of the narrator, the guiding intelligence of the author himself, is nowhere clearer than here, where no colloquialism is needed to indicate that the implications of the situation are perceived by Strether, though apparently presented through the narrator. Abstraction, the use of the verb 'to be', neologism, an unusual word-order, and the use of imagery, all mark Strether's intelligence, though the attribution of his thought-processes is oblique: 'there was none the less for him [Strether], in the very manner of his host's allusion to satiety as a thinkable motive, a slight breath of the ominous'.

By comparison with Strether's insight and feeling, Chad's words sound vulgar and unimaginative. He is the colloquial speaker—'An awful ass, wasn't I?'—the crassly commercial—'If one *should* wish to live on one's accumulations?'—the complacent egotist—'And he scrupulously went further. "She has never been anything whatever that I could call a burden." ' The inadequacy of Chad's imagination is epitomized, in 'Jamesian shorthand', when he calls advertising, a commercial manipulation of the aesthetic, 'an art like another, and infinite like all the arts': an allegation to which Strether responds with dry precision: 'Advertising *is* clearly, at this time of day, the secret of trade. It's quite possible it would be open to you—giving the whole of your mind to it—to make the whole place hum with you'.

The isolation of Strether in this scene is clearly a positive move, though negatively revealed through the exposure of Chad's baseness. To be free of such relations, the 'relations involved in staying', is shown to be a good thing; and the presentation of this fact throws stress on what Strether escapes rather than on what he is now to do: a difficult question, but not one which the conclusion allows us to dwell on.

The final scene with Maria comes as a sort of coda after the series of three interviews. It is introduced as 'another separation to face', and the issue is never in doubt. But James uses the facts of setting to substantiate this certainty. The 'little Dutch-looking dining room' of Maria's apartment, the 'retreat' he could find with her, is scarcely inviting: 'at the back of the house, with a view of a scrap of old garden that had been saved from modern ravage'. The ironic imagery of setting is meticulously detailed and pointed: 'To sit there was, as he had told her before, to see life reflected for the time in ideally kept pewter.' The shift of tenses here into the pluperfect, and the suggestion of a short-lived future too, perfectly exemplifies James's minute narrative tact. Details such as this acquit the scene of any charge of raw sarcasm, and contribute to an extended ironical appreciation of true and of transient values.

Strether is now 'out, in truth, as far as it was possible to be', and although there is a question of 'getting in again', the movement must be unencumbered by gain. Maria's offer of a haven 'might well have tempted. It built him softly round, it roofed him warmly over, it rested, all so firm, on selection. And what ruled selection was beauty and knowledge'. Yet even these things, which Strether's experience has taught him to appreciate, are now an unnecessary constriction. Beauty and truth, in this sense, are ways and means for vision, not a goal. Strether recognizes that they are not of the order of the eternal: 'so far as they made his opportunity, they made it only for a moment'.

The final movement for Strether must be onwards and alone, not because he has been deserted, nor because he has abandoned his fellows, but because in his near-tragic stature, he has no fellows: there is no one else in the novel who 'can't do anything else' but acknowledge and be ruled by what is 'dreadfully right'. In his final words, there is no uncertainty, but a reassurance to Maria, an approval, an almost existential acceptance of the order of things: 'Then there we are.'

Coming out of the development of the novel, comprehensible only within the terms set up there, and in return, lending direction to the flow of the whole, Strether's last words carry the two qualities of stillness and movement, that characterize the vanishing-point. The 'negative capability' lacking in *The Sacred Fount* is achieved here: an end without finality. As Eliot puts it:

> 'Except for the point, the still point,
> There would be no dance, and there is only the dance.

MAUD ELLMANN

"The Intimate Difference": Power and Representation in *The Ambassadors*†

When good Americans die, they go to Paris.
—Oscar Wilde, A *Woman of No Importance*

1

There was once a famous contest in which two painters known as Zeuxis and Parrhasios challenged one other to produce the most deceptive illusion. The younger contestant, Zeuxis, painted grapes that looked so real that the birds swooped down to peck them off the vine. It seemed that victory was his; but then he asked Parrhasios to draw aside the curtain draped over the latter's picture, only to discover that the curtain had been painted by Parrhasios himself, so that there was nothing hidden underneath its folds. Zeuxis confessed himself defeated. The story seems to hint that verisimilitude is for the birds; if you want to fool a man, you must elicit his desire to see beyond appearances, to penetrate the nothingness behind the veil.[1]

The Ambassadors also explores the enticements of illusion; specifically, the way in which appearances arouse the desire for a truth whose power depends upon its hiddenness. Representation, in the many meanings of the term, forms the kernel of the novel's action: representation in the political sense, whereby ambassadors are sent abroad to represent the interests of their country; and representation in the aesthetic sense, whereby the work of art is thought to represent a prior and exterior reality. What *The Ambassadors* reveals is that the nature of reality depends upon the way one represents it to oneself. Henry James said he was concerned with the "process of vision"; and the novel demonstrates that vision *is* a process rather than an instantaneous epiphany, a process

---

† Originally published in *Henry James: Fiction as History*, ed. Ian F. A. Bell (London: Vision Press, 1984), 98–113. The essay has been rewritten for this Norton Critical Edition. © 1993 by Maud Ellmann. Reprinted by permission of the author.
1. Lacan discusses this story in *The Four Fundamental Concepts of Psycho-Analysis*, tr. Alan Sheridan (London: Hogarth, 1977), 112.

fraught with decoys, blind spots, and evasions, in which the drive to truth capitulates to the seductions of illusion (2).[2] The hero of the novel, Lambert Strether, sees what he desires, not what is; his mind draws a picture frame around reality, which excludes as much as it encompasses. In the end, however, his enchantment with "phantasmagoria" is shown to be wiser than the realism of a Zeuxis who would strip away the veil, abolishing appearance for the nothingness of truth.

If the novel takes representation as its central theme, James also represented *The Ambassadors* itself in a multitude of postscripts and prefigurements. His Preface, for example, written several years after the novel proper, is one of his most anthologised critical works. Previously he had sent his publishers a 20,000-word "Project," the size of a novella in itself, outlining Lambert Strether's earlier New England life: "a good many earnest and anxious experiments—professional, practical, intellectual, moral, personal," yet deprived of "any very proportionate sense of acknowledged or achieved success" (378). In a conventional sense, this Project is more novelistic than the novel, for it contains more story than the finished work, more moral and explanatory intervention by the novelist. The novel seems to have evolved out of a process of purgation, eliminating action, character, and author to focus more intensively on the interiority of consciousness. According to James's Notebook, the germ of *The Ambassadors* arose out of a conversation with Jonathan Sturges about the novelist William Dean Howells, who had spent some days in Paris visiting his "domiciled and initiated son," and had confronted in the young man's life the many pleasures he had spurned or avoided in his own. Anguished by this revelation, Howells had urged Sturges to "live all you can: it's a mistake not to. . . . I haven't done so—and now I'm old. It's too late. It has gone past me—I've lost it. You have time. You are young. Live!" (374)

In his Preface, James describes *The Ambassadors* as a "*supplement* of situation" added to this passionate defense of life, which Strether redelivers—with improvements—at a Paris garden party (3). If the novel represents a "supplement" to Howells's belated recognition of his loss, the Preface, the Notebook, and the Project supplement this supplement; and all these afterwords and prolegomena revolve around an emptiness described as "life" and yet defined by its unlivability. James says of Strether, "The main truth of everything was . . . that everything represented the substance of his loss" (283): in other words, everything is representation, and everything bespeaks the absence of the represented —the loss of the original experience and the desertion of the object of desire.

In *The Ambassadors*, this loss becomes contagious, insinuating itself

---

2. All page numbers in the text refer to this Norton Critical Edition.

into all forms of representation. The most important of these absences is Mrs. Newsome, who never enters the narrative directly; yet it is from the central void betokened by her name that messages and messengers proliferate. James writes in the Project for the novel:

> lively element as she is in the action, we deal with her presence and personality as an affirmed influence, only in their deputed, represented form; and nothing, of course, can be more artistically interesting than such a little problem as to make her always out of it, yet always *of* it, always absent, yet always felt. (380)

The *deus absconditus* of the narrative, Mrs. Newsome only manifests herself through scripture: through the telegrams and letters she showers on her missionaries in the vain attempt to keep them harnessed to her cause. These letters, too, are only known in their "deputed, represented form"; the novel tells us less about their contents than about their material trajectories, as they "reckon with the Atlantic Ocean, the General Post Office, and the extravagant curve of the globe" (110). By the same token, the ambassadors that Mrs. Newsome sends across this ocean could be seen as human letters—texts incarnate—words made flesh. Commissioned to extend her presence, her delegates instead disseminate the absence of which they are the ghostly representatives, an absence that weaves itself into the texture of the prose through the repetition of the word "nothing" and its equivalents.

Mrs. Newsome sends forth two embassies to Paris, for it is part of the "strange logic" of this text that major episodes repeat or re-present themselves (60). First, Strether is dispatched with Waymarsh to rescue Mrs. Newsome's son, the wayward Chad, who has become embroiled with a French adulteress. Chad has ignored his mother's orders to return to Woollett, Massachusetts, and to take over the family business: "the manufacture of some small, convenient, homely" article of domestic use, too vulgar to be named (380). Frequently invoked but never defined, this "nameless article" becomes the most hilarious of the lacunae scattered through the text to taunt the reader with the promise of an ultimate unveiling. On his way to Paris, Strether stops in Chester, where he meets Miss Gostrey, an "agent for repatriation" whose self-appointed task is to save Americans for America. "I'm a general guide—to 'Europe,' don't you know?" she says. "I wait for people—I put them through. I pick them up—I set them down. I'm a sort of superior 'courier-maid' " (26). Miss Gostrey questions Strether about his mission, puzzled as to what he stands to gain; it emerges that the payoff, should he succeed in saving Chad, is marriage to Mrs. Newsome, with all the perks. So the novel could be seen as a middle-aged fairy tale: the suitor has to undertake a dangerous journey and fulfill a task imposed upon him by the princess so that he may win her hand in marriage. But the trouble with this suitor is that he takes so much pleasure in the journey that he gradually forgets about the prize; the lure of "life," experienced by proxy in the form of Chad, extinguishes the lure of profit.

Once in Paris, Strether meets the representatives of Chad some time before he catches up with the original. For instance, when he first attempts to visit Chad, he encounters an ambassador instead, the enigmatic little Bilham, and the two spies scrutinise each other, the younger "amused by an elderly watcher" and "curious even to see what the elderly watcher would do on finding himself watched" (69). Standing on the balcony, little Bilham blocks the window into Chad's domain, as if to intimate that representation has supplanted presence, precluding access to the real. From the reader's point of view, the whole encounter is elided, because the second book comes abruptly to a close as soon as Strether is across the *porte-cochère*. After a hiatus, the incident is represented in the tranquillity of Strether's chronically belated consciousness (70).

When he finally sets eyes on Chad, Strether is astonished by the transformation: all the crassness of the Woollett youth has been been refined into Parisian suavity. The artist responsible for this transformation is the mysterious Madame de Vionnet, whose friendship with Chad is described by little Bilham as a "virtuous attachment" (112). It is the ambiguity of this locution that enables Strether to maintain a willful blindness to the sexuality of the relationship. He procrastinates, unwilling to' tear Chad away from such improving influences; and Mrs. Newsome, exasperated by his indecision, launches a second delegation, consisting of her daughter Sarah, who endorses all her mother's moral stringencies, and Sarah's husband Jim Pocock, who thinks Paris is a great place to spend a weekend and cannot understand the fuss. Sarah, having no imagination, is not deceived by any talk of virtuous attachments: as far as she can see, Chad has been debauched, and Strether, too, has been corrupted by the enemy. As Miss Barrace, a minor character, tells Strether at a Paris party, "You come over to convert the savages, and the savages simply convert you!" (125).

The double deputation in the novel stands for two conflicting styles of interpretation. Sarah champions the principle of single meaning: as Strether tells her, she shuts her eyes to each side of the matter, "in order, whichever side comes up, to get rid of the other" (281). But Strether falls in love with "difference": what Chad is, or what Chad was, intrigues the hero less than Chad's capacity for change and transformation. James insisted that "difference" was both the theme and the aesthetic of the text: "Difference—difference from what he expected, difference in Chad, difference in everything; and the Difference, I also again say, is what I give" (390). Difference, for Strether, is the lotus flower that diverts him from his course and tempts him to forget his homeland. As soon as he arrives in Paris, he senses "the plenitude of his consciousness of difference"; and difference has the last word in the novel, too, when Strether tells Miss Gostrey he must leave her to return to "a great difference"—and nothing more (60, 346). In his "acceptance" of Paris, Strether gives his "authority away" (64): he surrenders Mrs. Newsome and her world of things, identities, and facts for a world of differences without positive terms.

Sarah Pocock, on the other hand, can only understand Chad's difference as treachery: in her eyes, her brother has betrayed the values he should represent, and therefore the economy of representation demands his realignment with his mother as urgently as the economy of Woollett does. To save Chad would be to save mimesis and to reunite the signifier with the signified. Strether, for his part, conceives of Chad as a text admitting many possibilities of meaning, and revised by the subtlest of editors: "the new edition of an old book that one has been fond of— revised and amended, brought up to date," in little Bilham's words (111).

Strether's mission, imposed by Mrs. Newsome, is to read between the lines that Madame de Vionnet has superscribed in order to restore the single meaning of Chad's character. But instead of saving meaning, Strether saves the principle of endless reading, symbolised by the fact that the only booty he takes home from his adventure is the complete works of Victor Hugo. Thus Strether's "only logic" is the logic of loss: "Not, out of the whole affair, to have got anything for myself" (346). He sacrifices all the women offering themselves to him—Mrs. Newsome, Miss Gostrey, and Madame de Vionnet—for the sake of "a little super-sensual hour in the vicarious freedom of another" (376). What Strether wants is not a woman, and not even perhaps a man, in spite of his infatuation with the "secret" world of Chad; what he desires is the desire of the other; he yearns to represent, in his own being, the ashes of another life, a borrowed love.

This is why he is a reader, for he prefers his life, as he prefers his literature, secondhand; and he finds it more appealing to peruse the book of Chad than to surrender to the young man's nameless pleasures. If Chad is a book, however, Strether's whole identity is intertextual. His first name Lambert comes from Balzac's Louis Lambert, and his reputation in the world depends upon the Woollett magazine that bears his name:

> His name on the green cover, where he had put it for Mrs. Newsome, expressed him doubtless just enough to make the world— the world as distinguished, both for more and for less, from Woollett—ask who he was. . . . He was Lambert Strether because he was on the cover, whereas it should have been, for anything like glory, that he was on the cover because he was Lambert Strether. (62)

Thus Strether is the phantom of the text he edits, on which his name has been enshrined in green. His role as editor, moreover, aligns him with Madame de Vionnet, for both these characters emend the Chad they read, enlisting "memory and fancy" to their aid, unlike Sarah Pocock, who disdains their editorial revisions (320). Sarah stands for semantic, as well as moral, absolutism; in her conception of the world, there is one law, one meaning, and one truth, dictated by one monarch, Mrs. Newsome. By identifying knowledge with power, Sarah finds corroboration in the English language, in that many words for knowledge also mean possession, violation, or constraint: we "grasp" or "seize" or "apprehend" the things we know, much as we might apprehend a fugitive from justice. *The Ambassadors* pursues another form of truth, heterodox and volatile, to which James gives the name of "Paris."

What is Paris? Not so much a geographical as a discursive space, an energy within the text that dissipates identities and definitions. Although it designates a place, it is inwardly displaced by the transatlantic vacillations of its denizens. A site of transformation, Paris is most itself when it is least itself and passing into other modes of being:

> It hung before [Strether] this morning, the vast bright Babylon, like some huge iridescent object, a jewel brilliant and hard, in which parts were not to be discriminated nor differences comfortably marked. It twinkled and trembled and melted together, and what seemed all surface one moment seemed all depth the next. (64)

This passage quivers like the city it describes, with "signs and tokens . . . too thick for prompt discrimination" (120). For Paris, among its many meanings, designates the iridescent surface of the prose, the "residuum of difference" in the text itself that eludes the wariest Pocock (21). "In the light of Paris," little Bilham says, "one sees what things resemble. That's what the light of Paris always seems to show" (126). Not what things *are*—leave that to the Pococks—but the metaphoric possibilities of things. Madame de Vionnet, as representative of Paris, embodies "the big Difference": under her influence, binary oppositions twinkle and tremble and melt together, abandoned to the flux of negativity. Strether sees her as "Cleopatra in the play, indeed various and multifold. She had aspects, characters, days, nights. . . . she was an obscure person, a muffled person one day, and a showy person, an uncovered person the next" (160). All surface one moment and all depth the next, her power lies in her ability to differ from herself, and to alter everyone who falls under her spell. She even manages to bring out the Mark Antony in Chad, the epicurean hidden in the ruffian.

Mrs. Newsome, on the contrary, repudiates the world of difference. The "ruff" she wears around her neck, which Strether associates with Queen Elizabeth, seems to represent her strangulating certainties; as opposed to the red ribbon round Miss Gostrey's neck, which represents the principle of difference, insofar as it transforms "the value of every other item" of her dress (42).[3] It is Mrs. Newsome's "fixed intensity" that Strether gradually learns to dread (250). "She doesn't admit surprises," he complains to Miss Gostrey:

> "there's no room left; no margin, as it were for any alteration. She's filled as full, packed as tight, as she'll hold, and if you wish to get anything more or different either out or in—"
> "You've got to make over altogether the woman herself?"
> "What it comes to," said Strether, "is that you've got morally and intellectually to get rid of her." (300)

Packed with positivities, the text of Mrs. Newsome prohibits all revision, emendation, marginalia: "She's the same," says Strether. "She's more than ever the same" (345). No prefaces or afterwords for her: they take too long. In her eyes, Chad's difference can only mean one vile and unmentionable thing; for Woollett, like its queen, must have its meanings fast—as fast as it produces nameless articles. But Strether learns that difference entails deferral, "perpetual postponement" (391); to read a text like Paris, one must be prepared to wait for the charm of difference to emerge. The first paragraph of *The Ambassadors* hints of a "secret principle" that enables Strether to "wait without disappointment" (17); and he explains to Sarah Pocock that waiting is a strategy of reading. Chad's "obscure," he declares, "and that's why I'm waiting" (194). The novel grows as dilatory as the hero: it practices what Roland Barthes would call "the infinite deferment of the signified."[4] James himself advised an early reader to loiter through his novel in the same way that Strether dawdles through his pilgrimage:

> Take, meanwhile pray, *The Ambassadors* very easily and gently: read five pages a day—be even as deliberate as that. . . . keep along with it step by step—and then the full charm will come out. . . . I find that the very most difficult thing in the art of the novelist is to give the impression of the *real lapse of time, the quantity* of time, represented by our few poor phrases and pages, and all the drawing-out the reader can contribute helps a little perhaps the production of that spell. (408–9)[5]

The Pococks and the Newsomes could never cope with late James. One can almost hear them muttering with Leavis that "the energy of the 'doing' (and the energy required for the reader)" are "disproportionate to the issues" of the text; no doubt they would agree with Arnold Bennett

---

3. The fact that French aristocrats after the Terror wore red ribbons round their necks to commemorate the guillotine contributes to the theme of the collapse of sovereignty, discussed below.
4. Roland Barthes, *Image—Music—Text*, ed. Stephen Heath (Glasgow: Fontana, 1977), 158.
5. Letter to the Duchess of Sutherland, 23 December 1903 (408).

that "the book was not *quite* worth the great trouble of reading it" (439).[6] It is telling that attacks on *The Ambassadors* tend to frame themselves in economic terms, with critics complaining that the story is not "worth" the words expended on it. For James's prose refuses to *save* meaning; instead, it lavishes and wastes its words, as if, in the textual economy, there were never any bills to pay. Its complexities are wildly gratuitous: rather than delivering their meaning wholesale, like assembly lines producing nameless articles, they prolong the process whereby meanings twinkle, tremble, and melt together in the incessant play of difference upon difference.

By identifying Woollett with industrial capitalism, James hints that bourgeois readings mimic bourgeois economics to extort the highest profit from the text. Mrs. Newsome's "interest" lies in meaning, and she concerns herself only with the most efficient way to manufacture and recuperate it. Strether, more aristocratically, resists the avarice of meaning: he squanders time and sense away to lose himself in someone else's *jouissance*. Difference is "only repeatable as difference"; and Strether finds that to interpret the difference in Chad is to relive each lingering moment of his transformation.[7]

The Pococks must have answers. But *The Ambassadors* begins with a question, and the narrative runs on questions as an engine runs on fuel. Strether soon surrenders his "resolve to simplify," and learns instead to draw a warm circle in which every question "would live . . . as nowhere else" (162, 80). The "most difficult of the questions" has to do with the nature of the "virtuous attachment," and this is the only question that cannot be asked (102). The answer, in Pockockian terms, is sex, the open secret that disseminates itself throughout the text in gaps and blanks, such as Miss Barrace's "Oh, oh, oh!" or little Bilham's "Ah, ah, ah!" (124, 156–57, 160, 165). Sarah Pocock, like Zeuxis, tries to strip away this veil of reticence in order to expose Chad's secret shame; but Strether prefers the appearance to the truth, knowing that Chad's outward show has triumphed over the dullest of realities. It is "tact" that prevents Strether from denuding this reality; tact sustains his questions, deferring recognition of the knowledge that would speed desire to its nemesis.

"Tact" is James's term for a discourse that avoids the vulgar truth, but also circumvents the vulgar falsehood. Madame de Vionnet's apartments are the architectural embodiment of tact; for James's buildings, like his "house of fiction," often represent linguistic strategies: "large and open, full of revelations, for our friend, of the habit of privacy, the peace of intervals, the dignity of distances and approaches" (145). Private and open, distant and revealed, veiled and unveiled at the same time,

6. For Bennett, see *Henry James: The Critical Heritage*, ed. Roger Gard (London: Routledge and Kegan Paul; New York: Barnes and Noble, 1968), 373.

7. Barthes, *Image—Music—Text*, 159.

this is a world in which the depth can no longer be distinguished from the surface, nor secrecy from candour. As Chad says, "I have no secret, though I may have secrets!" (142). The expression "virtuous attachment" epitomises tact, since its apparent falsehood conceals a deeper truth: that is, the virtue of the education of the senses.

2

The Pococks have no tact, for they believe that words should represent their meanings unequivocally, just as ambassadors should represent the interests of their nation. *The Ambassadors* reveals, however, that in language as in politics, the representative extends the presence of the represented, but also undermines the latter's self-sufficiency; because the represented *needs* the representative: the source is powerless without the supplement, the dictator without the deputy, the referent without the sign. Yet as soon as there is representation there is treason, because it is impossible to overcome the "difference" that opens up, like the Atlantic in the text, between the origin and its derivatives. Thus it is significant that terms like "members" or "detachments," which are synonyms for representatives, imply the amputation or castration of their origins. Mrs. Newsome's detachments, her suitor and her son, betray her cause and mock mimesis. Their waywardness suggests that monarchism can no longer delimit the effects of a decentralised and transferential form of power. Set loose from Mrs. Newsome, all the characters become ambassadors to one another; and power circulates among them, centreless and empty of intention. They think, act, speak, desire on behalf of one another, relaying messages, instructions, and requests, so that information buzzes round like power, destitute of origin.

In this way *The Ambassadors* anticipates Foucault's explosion of the myth of sovereignty, in which he argues that the sovereign is "a fantastic personage, at once archaic and monstrous" (like Mrs. Newsome, the phantom origin of *The Ambassadors*).[8] Nonetheless, the paradigm of sovereignty still haunts our thought, concealing the pervasive influence of power. According to Foucault, power in the modern world no longer oppresses from above but surges from below, implemented by the very forces that resist its "capillary" infiltration. In place of "the unique form of a great power," contemporary power takes the form of mutual surveillance, in which every subject is compelled to keep an eye on every other, because there is no final point of view to which these prying gazes are referred.[9] Shaky as political theory, Foucault's concept of surveillance nonetheless provides a useful insight into *The Ambassadors*, where Mrs.

8. Michel Foucault, "Prison Talk," in *Power/Knowledge: Selected Interviews and Other Writings, 1972–1977*, ed. Colin Gordon (Brighton: Harvester, 1980), 39.
9. See Foucault, *The History of Sexuality: An Introduction*, tr. Robert Hurley (London: Allen Lane, 1978), especially 88–98.

Newsome's sovereignty grows "thin and vague," her omniscience weakening with each of her detachments (250). Meanwhile her emissaries scrutinise one another constantly: Chad's ambassadors spy on Strether at the same time that he attempts to spy on them, while the Pococks spy upon the spies.

The roles of watched and watcher oscillate throughout the text: Strether first meets Chad, for instance, in the theatre, the space of spectatorship *par excellence*; yet we are told that "the figures and the faces of the stalls were interchangeable with those on the stage" (43). Thenceforth Strether tries to penetrate Chad's "private stage" in the hope of discovering a primal scene, but he is borne along instead by the compulsion to repeat it. Similarly, the reader only witnesses Chad's love affair by proxy, through the medium of Strether's reenactment, his "super-sensual hour in the vicarious freedom of another." At the end of the novel, when Strether switches his allegiance to Madame de Vionnet, while Chad is deserting her for Woollett, it is as if the latecomer has usurped the forerunner, and representation has unseated presence.

In this world, the only person who sees nothing is Mrs. Newsome, the sovereign presumed to see it all: even though she instigates the circulation of the gaze, she never comes into the picture, either as the seer or the seen. Thus the seat of power is the place of blindness rather than omniscience. Deprived of any ultimate spectator, gazes cross and interweave, enmeshing every subject in their unseen eyebeams. It is in the scene of Strether's last awakening, when he discovers that Madame de Vionnet and Chad were lovers after all, that his vision of the world collapses in the face of the "loss" it was constructed to conceal: the absence hollowed out by sexuality.

This scene occurs in Book Eleventh, when Strether takes a trip into the countryside, following an "artless impulse" to refresh his memory of art, specifically of "a certain small Lambinet that had charmed him, long years before, at a Boston dealer's and that he had quite absurdly never forgotten" (303). In a curious inversion of the order of mimesis, he perceives the real French landscape as a representation of its own representation; that is, of the painting he could never own, since it was priced "beyond a dream of possibility." Thus Strether's experience represents "the substance of his loss," in this case the loss of Lambinet; in his "belated vision," the present scene is marked by absence, mourning, repetition, since the *real* landscape stands for the *represented* landscape that "he *would* have bought," but now relinquishes to nature (303, 313). The novel intimates, however, that Strether is himself imposing a picture frame around reality: "the oblong gilt frame disposed its enclosing lines; the poplars and willows, the reeds and river . . . fell into a composition, full of felicity." (304). Yet this episode reveals that Strether, by keeping sex out of the picture, has been framed by his own frame, entrammeled by his own representations.

The narrative abounds with references to art, including painting, writing, drama, and even cooking, which James refuses to disparage as a lesser art, presenting it instead as the summation of them all: when Strether meets the landlady of his hotel, "the *picture* and the *play* seemed supremely to melt together in the good woman's *broad sketch* of what she could do for her visitor's appetite" (308; my emphases). The countryside is described as "the nursery of letters," rather than a nursery of trees, and its painterly enchantments coalesce with those of "fiction," "fable," and "performance" to create a semiotic landscape, or a language in green: "not a breath of the evening that wasn't somehow a syllable of the text" (303, 311, 313, 308). As he wanders through this picture, drama, text, or feast, Strether begins to think about his growing intimacy with Madame de Vionnet, and by doing so he opens up a gap within the picture, since she is absent from its frame. He is also meditating on the gap between them—that is, on the uncertainty of their relationship—and he reflects that "it was amazing what could still come up without reference to what was going on between them" (306). An algebra of pronouns and prepositions, this sentence quivers with innuendo: what *is* going on between them, and what, for that matter, is "coming up"? Does "them" refer to Strether and Madame de Vionnet, or rather to Madame de Vionnet and Chad? The syntax implicates the former pairing in the latter, suggesting Strether's wish to take Chad's place, and creating a hallucinatory subtext in which his fantasies may be fulfilled.

This use of pronouns typifies James's later style. In *The Golden Bowl*, Maggie's struggle to preserve her marriage with the Prince is constantly subverted by the pronouns, which contaminate both spouses with their rivals: Adam Verver (excessively devoted to his daughter Maggie) and his wife Charlotte (secretly embroiled with the Prince). By leaving pronouns unspecified, James entices the reader to supply the missing names and thereby to participate in the transgressions of desire. The adultery and incest which never literally take place are constantly anticipated at the level of grammar. In *The Ambassadors*, the pronouns also make the characters conspirators to one another's passions, conscripting everyone into the transference of power and desire.

Returning to the French countryside, however, we are told that Strether "really continue[s] in the picture," in spite of his yearning for Madame de Vionnet, until he reaches the auberge where he is informed that two unexpected guests have just arrived "in a boat of their own" (307, 308). These "figures," floating down the river as if to ornament the scene, resemble the tiny human figures in French landscape painting, known as *parerga* or *staffage*, which Kant regarded as redundant to the composition as a whole.[10] Strether, on the contrary, realises that

10. Jacques Derrida discusses Kant's attitude to *parerga* in *La vérité en peinture* (Paris: Flammarion, 1978), especially Ch. 2.

"these figures, or something like them, had been *wanted* in the picture" all along (309; my emphasis); and the pun on "wanted," meaning lacking and coveted, identifies the absence in the picture as the locus of desire. At the moment that these figures break into Strether's vision, they also break through his illusions, and even the chapter breaks to mark the rupture of the picture frame:

> While he leaned against a post and continued to look out he saw something that gave him a sharper arrest.
> What he saw was exactly the right thing—a boat advancing round the bend and containing a man who held the paddles and a lady, at the stern, with a pink parasol. (309)

Shortly afterwards, this lady recognises Strether with a start, before he can identify her as Madame de Vionnet, and before he recognises her companion, "the coatless hero of the idyll," as the "expert" and initiated Chad (310, 309). In this "sharp fantastic crisis" (310), Strether realises that his mental picture has always masked a gap, and that he must have "scotomised" his own perception of the love affair.[11] "There is something whose absence can always be observed in a picture," Lacan writes; what bursts through Strether's picture frame at last, like the return of the repressed, are the unbidden figures of sexuality.[12]

It is in another picture that Lacan unveils the lack in vision, but it is also known as "The Ambassadors," the famous painting by Hans Holbein. On either side of Holbein's canvas, two ambassadors gaze out symmetrically, answering the gaze of the spectator, and surrounded by Renaissance images of vanity, which seem to emphasise the narcissism of this headlong form of vision. However, in the foreground of the painting, a jutting object catches the spectator's eye. Hidden by a trick of perspective, this object turns out to be a death's head, but it can only be identified from an oblique position, when the spectator leaves the painting's circle of enchantment. This memento mori opens a perspective from which the viewer may be overlooked, thus disrupting the relationship between the subject and the object of the gaze. Suddenly, the painting is revealed for what it is—a tracery of brushstrokes, rather than a window to another world. The skull implies that there is nothing underneath this system of appearances but death. Far from seeing the whole picture, the subject is confronted with his own extinction: "Holbein makes visible to us something which is simply the subject as annihilated," Lacan declares.[13]

---

11. For "scotomisation," or the process of visual erasure, see Freud, "Fetishism," in *On Sexuality* (Harmondsworth: Penguin, 1977), 353.
12. Lacan, *The Four Fundamental Concepts*, p. 108.
13. Lacan, *The Four Fundamental Concepts*, p. 88.

James's *Ambassadors* reveals the lack in vision as the space of the desire of the other, for the figures "wanted in the picture" are those of someone else's sexuality. Similarly, the phallicism of the skull in Holbein's painting portends castration, as does Strether's reaction to the lovers who disrupt his representations: "the violence of their having 'cut' him, out there in the eye of nature, on the assumption that he wouldn't know it" (311). And just as Holbein's painting brandishes its artifice, so James's novel underlines its own contrivances, for a scopic skepticism overtakes the narrative: artfulness displaces art; and words like "fiction," "fable," and "performance" come to signify the stratagems of guile rather than the visions of imagination. When Strether leaves Paris for his country jaunt he still believes that a picture represents reality; by the time he returns, however, he has realised that a picture is a trap to catch desire. Like the veil of Parrhasios, the fascination of the picture lies in what it "wants," and not in what it shows. In the realm of desire, everyone is framed and no one sees the whole: even Strether's eye can never take all pictures in at once, for the lack in vision drives him "from clever canvas to clever canvas" (318), since every picture represents "the substance of his loss." Rather than comforting the subject with a mirror of his unity and mastery, the picture opens up the "want" where death inscribes its "intimate difference" (395).

As we have seen, *The Ambassadors* reveals that representation is founded on the loss of origin. In the realm of politics, the sovereign is disempowered by her own ambassadors; in the realm of language, the play of difference unbinds the signifier from the despotism of the signified. "With a deep audible gasp," Mrs. Newsome's moral and semantic fixities grow "thin and vague" (248); and the authority of the original dissolves in a phantasmagoria of difference. However, the convulsions of the old regime bring forth a stranger form of power, too inhuman to be lodged in the figure of the sovereign. This power infiltrates through pleasure, rather than oppression, and interpellates the subject in the circulation of desire. In this world (as James's shifty pronouns intimate), all experience becomes vicarious, all passion transferential, all thought telepathic.

Thus Strether can only experience his "life" in a "deputed, represented form"; he is the good American, of Wilde's famous quip, who goes to Paris when he dies, so that he can live Chad's afterlife. He does not want an object; what he wants is to identify with someone else's want; his desire is mimetic, substitutional, ambassadorial. Indeed, his mission in the narrative is to reveal the delegative nature of desire, which yearns not for the possession of an object so much as for identification with another subject: a "supersensual hour in the vicarious freedom of another." Strether's deepest wish—which he achieves—is to get rid of every object in order to be *other to himself.* "Yes," writes James, "he goes back other, and to other things" (405).

MILLICENT BELL (1991)

[Meaning in *The Ambassadors*]†

The Ambassadors is James's greatest study of a character whose life has seemingly failed to contain a degree of doing to match his intensity of being. Unlike Isabel Archer, Lambert Strether thinks it too late to find an adequate plot for himself, but engages himself in the effort to discover—and even to rewrite—the story of another man. The novel is a history of his education in the traps and delusions inherent in such an undertaking; it figures his adventure, his search, his creative effort, but becomes at the same time an exploration into his own latencies of being, his own renewal of doing, despite his conviction that the time for this is past. This double process produces James's most elaborated exhibition of the way a work of fiction may be a contest enacted from page to page among different possibilities of story, rather than *a* story proceeding with undeviating determinism from the opening page to the last. The opening paragraph, as Ian Watt has shown, does, in a sense, predict the whole of the book with its syntactical emphasis upon deferral of interpretation—its impressionism. But in saying this we say that it announces at once that no straight line will lead to disclosure and closure at the end. Yet surviving in this demolition of the idea of plot is the older view that personal being, if it is intense enough, needs no other expression than its own recognitions.

The "germ" of *The Ambassadors* is well known—the declaration of an older man to a younger that he has failed to "live." Howells, who said something of the sort to a young friend of James, probably meant he had missed a particular kind of sensuous and cultural experience, more available in Europe than in America, a sense carried into Lambert Strether's confession in Gloriani's garden. But the failure to live has also a more absolute sense in James's novel; it is the condition of the richly endowed character who has been denied a sufficient plot, the quality of being which has found no adequate doing. James had actually conceived of something like—though not precisely the same as—this idea at least two years before October, 1895, when he recorded hearing about

† For permission to photocopy this selection, please contact Harvard University Press. Reprinted by permission of the publishers from *Meaning in Henry James* by Millicent Bell (Cambridge, Mass.: Harvard University Press, 1991), 324–77. Copyright (c) 1991 by the President and Fellows of Harvard College. The chapter has been slightly abridged. Page references in brackets are to this Norton Critical Edition.

Howell's outburst—and it is possible to suspect that his real start for the
novel was a more personal feeling than his interest in a friend's
experience. * * *

* * * James saw, as he looked again at *The Ambassadors*, that even
the finished text of the novel, "critically viewed, is touchingly full of
. . . disguised and repaired losses [of its original intention], these insidious
recoveries, these intensely redemptive consistencies" [14]. James's revision of himself in the New York Edition, along with the still further
revising prefaces, is at once an artistic act of rewriting and a revision of
personal self. He is now that "passionate corrector and fingerer of style"
who does find a "second chance" in this way, and above all, by the
acquisition * * * of better readers who will revise their own earlier
understanding of him.

The story the novel undertakes to tell is that of a man who embraces
the same opportunity as the author—in life rather than art—to revise
and to revise again, to rewrite his personal plot. And nothing could be
more appropriate to such a story than the self-revising method of the
text itself, which builds upon occasions each corrective of the last,
proposes to the reader one after another development, aborting expectations while preserving possibilities. It is this process which is enacted
both by the hero and by the reader, making for the novel's remarkable
thematic integrity. The sense of loss and gain, destruction and repair
which James felt as he reread his novel is what the reader will also
experience without sharing precisely the author's own recognitions and
regrets; the reader, too, will experience the "might haves" of the novel
at each unfolding moment. As Strether moves from one attitude to
another, from one view to its correction, he finds himself, as James
describes in his scenario for the novel, "sinking . . . up to his middle
in the Difference—difference from what he expected, difference in
Chad, difference in everything; and the Difference . . . is what I give."
It is tempting, though not at all necessary, to give "difference" in this
statement a deconstructive sense James could not have intended, as a
pun upon deferral indefinitely prolonged.

James felt, rightly, that it was necessary to read the novel slowly,
responding to its oscillations, and we should heed the advice he gave a
reader,

> Take, meanwhile, pray, *The Ambassadors* very easily and gently:
> read five pages a day—be even as deliberate as that . . . Keep along
> with it step by step—and then the full charm will come out . . .
> I find that the very most difficult thing in the art of the novelist is
> to give the impression of the *real lapse of time, the quantity* of
> time, represented by our few poor phrases and pages, and all the
> drawing-out the reader can contribute helps a little perhaps the
> production of that spell. [408–9]

James's Strether is not only a man who has had a too limited measure and kind of experience. The structure of presentation which gives him to us at the outset of the novel suggests absence of a more extreme order by its virtual omission of appropriate beginning. As in earlier instances, James's "international situation" inserts an oceanic separation between the hero's past and that moment when we see him just landed on an alien shore where everything will be different. But the past from which this present differs is out of our view. The novel implies a missing first chapter in the America from which the hero has come. Woollett has sent Strether to Paris; in Woollett waits the strong princess whose ambassador he is and whom he will marry if his mission succeeds. But we are never shown, even in retrospect, this starting ground. James does not allow the narrative to turn back for the briefest direct vision of it, as he did in the few pages that permit us to glance at Isabel Archer in Albany. * * *

Strether's subsequent life has contained enough event to bring him to the point of being ready to marry again. But Mrs. Newsome, a widow with grown children, does not have a first name either—and though others speak for her, we never hear her own voice or see her. She is supposed to be a source of imperial power, exercising authority in distant lands, but her power instantly begins to be ineffectual upon Strether's arrival in Europe; long before he renounces his embassy he begins to betray it. Mrs. Newsome, who proposed to write a story for Strether, is bound to fail by the very act of making him her ambassador; by the expectation that her desires will be fulfilled by someone else, she has incurred a failure inherent in delegation in a world in which only the immediate, the present, is going to count.

In Europe Strether seems newborn. His freshness of apprehension, his moral "innocence," while features of his character and even his nationality, are also the consequence of this suppression of the past. James thought he had made up for this suppression by explanations offered in Strether's early conversation with Maria Gostrey: "Thanks to it we have treated scenically, and scenically alone, the whole lumpish question of Strether's 'past' " [13], he says in his preface. But it is not Woollett that is really made "scenic" in this conversation; Maria, the mere *ficelle*, has already become an interest in herself, a representative of Strether's new life. She is the visible lady in the red velvet neck-ribbon who supersedes Mrs. Newsome in her Elizabethan "ruche," glimpsed only in a passing comparison. The *in*visible lady's identification even as one term of a comparison has already been lost when Strether, wondering at his immediate ease with Maria, reflects, "Well, she's more thoroughly civilized—!" The narrator, underlining his omission, adds, "If 'More thoroughly than *whom*?' would not have been for him a sequel to this remark, that was just by reason of his deep consciousness of the bearing of his comparison" [21].

James appears to have surprised himself by the way Maria became "a prime idea" when she was intended only as a convenience, and the way she did so causes him to observe what this novel will illustrate—more richly, perhaps, than anything he ever wrote—how narrative development permits unexpected turns and surprises, provokes us to consider variant possibilities. The emergence of Maria in his story, he says, "shows us afresh how many quite incalculable but none the less clear sources of enjoyment for the infatuated artist, how many copious springs of our never-to-be-slighted 'fun' for the reader and critic susceptible of contagion, may sound their incidental plash as soon as an artistic process begins to enjoy free development" [13]. So, the unanticipated history of a relationship with the hero amounting to a plot of her own, which ensues for Maria, will contest for its presence in the novel with the main story of Strether's search for a vision of Chad, and with the companion story of his personal rediscovery. But Maria, it must be admitted, though she is present, still fails to have a manifest life of her own; she suffers from that insufficiency of both the hero's and the author's interest which inheres in her functionary role.

We may see, eventually, that she has her own mute story, nonetheless. She is still another of James's precariously surviving female figures, who requires some closure of personal destiny—marriage, most obviously— which she cannot achieve. * * * She is someone who makes herself useful to more fortunate friends who help her to get by; she helps bewildered fellow Americans negotiate the European scene. But for these friends—and Strether is one of them—she will not ever be sufficiently regarded for herself; she will be a convenience, a *ficelle*, as she is for the author. * * * It seems Maria met his friend Waymarsh in Milrose, Connecticut—a place as remote from their own encounter in Chester as Woollett—and she thinks he must know *her* friends, the Munsters. But these connections produce no recollection in Strether. Without a start "their attitude remained, none the less, that of not forsaking the board; and the effect of this in turn was to give them the appearance of having accepted each other with an absence of preliminaries practically complete" [19].

* * * It is Maria who helps Strether to begin a story which can dispense with a narrative start in Woollett. "Nothing could have been odder than Strether's sense of himself as at that moment launched in something of which the sense would be quite disconnected from the sense of his past and which was literally beginning there and then" [20], he reflects as he prepares to see Chester with this new acquaintance.

If Strether already is felt to be the man who has not lived—or whose past is not worth remembering—his character has managed just the same to prevail against his fate, and he has remained "a man of imagination . . . of thickened motive and accumulated character" [3], of potentiality. The "deep human expertness" of the artist, Gloriani, seeing as James himself sees, flashes upon him during the garden party in book 5 "a test of his stuff" which concedes "possibilities . . . if everything had been different" [121]. James himself had wondered on behalf of his hero, "*Would* there yet perhaps be time for reparation?—reparation, that is, for injury done his character; for the affront, he is quite ready to say, so stupidly put upon it?" [1]. Can the ellipsis of experience be filled by the future? Already it is evident even to Strether that though he may not have "lived" in the usual sense, "it [is] nothing new to him that a man might have—at all events such a man as he—an amount of experience out of any proportion to his adventures" [137]. And at this very moment the adventure Strether despairs of is beginning. * * *

Such a confidence in the fertility of perception and of response to the immediate may be called impressionism—and it is opposed not only to traditional conceptions of plot but particularly to the philosophy and aesthetic of naturalism, which, as we have already seen, challenged James's imagination in a crucial way. Strether's moment of crisis in Gloriani's garden contains his own admission of naturalist inevitability. To Little Bilham, he cries desperately, "Live," but he is more aware than James has permitted the reader to be of all the initial and determining influences in his American life—his probably Puritan upbringing, his materially and spiritually straitened American circumstances: "The affair—I mean the affair of life—couldn't, no doubt, have been different for me; for it's at the best a tin mould, either fluted and embossed, with ornamental excrescences, or else smooth and dreadfully plain, into which, a helpless jelly, one's consciousness is poured—so that one 'takes' the form, as the great cook says, and is more or less compactly held by it: one lives in fine as one can." Yet, having offered this perfect naturalist metaphor for the determined fate, he draws back to assert the value of the belief in freedom. "Still, one has the illusion of freedom; therefore don't be, like me, without the memory of that illusion. I was either, at the right time, too stupid or too intelligent to have it; I don't quite know which. Of course at present I'm a case of reaction against the mistake; and the voice of reaction should, no doubt, always be taken with an allowance. But that doesn't affect the point that the right time is now yours. The right time is *any* time that one is still lucky as to have" [132].

The desire for an adventure adequate to his own character—in that time he is lucky still to have—is implied in the impulse which prompts Strether to delay his encounter with Waymarsh at the very moment of his landing in Liverpool. "His business would be a trifle bungled should he simply arrange for this countenance to present itself to the nearing steamer as the first 'note' of Europe" [17]. What is this "business"? It is not Woollett's commission—which would hardly be deflected by encounter with this reminder of New England. Rather, it is a private undertaking of new experience, implied by language which makes the character the writer who deliberates the opening "note" of his own novel, just as James must have done in writing *The Ambassadors*. The appropriate note Strether requires is "such a consciousness of personal freedom as he hadn't known for years, such a deep taste of change and of having above all for the moment nobody and nothing to consider, as promised already, if headlong hope were not too foolish, to colour his adventure with cool success." The cool success and the "adventure" implied are not to be achieved by the fulfillment of his assignment from Mrs. Newsome. Already, instead of consorting with some of his fellow voyagers, reminders of home, he had "given his afternoon and evening to the immediate and the sensible," though this might be only "a qualified draught of Europe, an afternoon and evening on the banks of the Mersey" [18].

The surrender to the "immediate and the sensible" is an impressionistic surrender of narrative preconceptions and a program not only for the hero but for the reader. Such a statement should not be confused with the idea that there is specific evidence in *The Ambassadors* of James's descriptive imitation of Impressionist paintings. Certain scenes in the novel can be said to remind one of those works, and Charles Anderson has even argued that particular paintings were in James's mind. There is the scene of Strether in the Luxembourg Gardens, when "terraces, alleys, vistas, fountains, little trees in green tubs, little women in white caps and shrill little girls at play all sunnily 'composed' together" [59], which seems to Anderson to be copied from Pissarro's *Jardin des Tuileries* (1899). Or the scene of Chad and Madame de Vionnet as Strether sees them in their boat in the country, which is, Anderson is convinced, a transcription of Monet's *La Seine à Vétheuil* (1880) or else a "fabulous coincidence."[1] My view of James's impressionism is not based on these analogies but rather on his way of making his novel a succession of moments, visually scenic or otherwise. It is James's most developed experiment in the mode of a narrative that submits itself flagrantly to successions of interpretation based on instant states.

The method of the novel is the hero's method of personal continuity. For Strether, impressionism is a personal program of perception implying an openness to chance and to a multitude of personal "impressions" as they come, to a multitude of possible responses. Paris, the scene of his adventure, will come to seem a "jewel . . . in which parts were not to be discriminated nor differences comfortably marked." He will find that "it twinkled and trembled and melted together and what seemed all surface one moment seemed all depth the next" [64]. But James tests

---

1. Charles R. Anderson, *Person, Place and Thing in the Novels of Henry James* (Durham, N.C., Duke University Press, 1977), pp. 239, 273–284.

the Paterian impressionistic outlook by Strether's prompt suspension of his mission, his willing subjection to the effects of each moment immediately upon his landing in Europe. As he prepares for the inevitable encounter with Waymarsh at Chester, Maria arrives to encourage this project, to protect him from restriction to the story begun for him in Woollett. One of the first things he admires in her—and contrasts with Mrs. Newsome's unwavering sense of an ending—is her ability to respond to "the advantage snatched from lucky chances" [21]. As time goes on, she promotes her new friend's project of living for the immediate occasion instead of "always considering something else" [26]. It is a "plunge"—the first of several he will feel himself making, by which he divests himself of the past and abandons that double vision which keeps him always from thinking of "the thing of the moment." Strether confesses that his lingering "obsession of the other thing"—particularly the dictates of the past—is "the terror." By the end of book I he knows that his new program will cost him his past "in one great lump" [40].

Maria is ready to prepare him to think of life in a wide variety of narrative ways. It is for this reason that she is a repository of fictional concepts, narrative alternatives, "mistress of a hundred cases or categories, receptacles of the mind, subdivisions for convenience, in which, from a full experience, she pigeon-holed her fellow mortals with a hand as free as that of a compositor scattering type" [21]—a sentence which, as I have observed, identifies her with the novelistic imagination itself and puns on the word "type." In the informed epistemic awareness she possesses, in the range of her knowledge of alternatives, in her breadth of taxonomic categories of the human species, she offers Strether a certain liberation from prescribed story, though it is a liberation that Strether himself will go beyond, dispensing even with her generous choice of conceptions.

James, as though both providing for and imitating his character, writes in *The Ambassadors* a novel which considers the "receptacles of the mind" and brings them into question. In the end, its own method is more indifferent to conventional narrative linearity and makes consistency of character more problematic than it is in any of his previous fictions. James's narrative method in *The Ambassadors* has been compared to the modernist technique called "stream-of-consciousness"—which it does not closely resemble; it is too clearly structured by the continuity of logical thought governed by the narrator's analytic comment. But there is a sense in which the narrative does submit itself to merely temporary conditions of the mind of its central character, a process which can be compared to the experiments of Woolf or Joyce or Faulkner. James's determination to center his story undeviatingly upon this one mind—more consistently than in any other long work he ever wrote—maximizes the relativism of the restricted point of view. Without intervention from another source, the narrative becomes an accretion of moments kept free of final interpretation and the sense of origin and end.

So, Strether, unlike a Winterbourne [in *Daisy Miller*], submits himself to his impressions; he will float on their stream. Inescapably, he is tempted to use those "receptacles" of character—some, at the outset, very much like Winterbourne's—by which he can seize mental hold of Chad Newsome and his new European associations. He will struggle to contain in one or another narrative preconception what he observes. But he will not be "stiff" like Winterbourne; he will surrender to the effects of new impressions, and he will do this again and again, till it seems evident that there can be no absolute and rigid conclusion about these matters. When he urges Little Bilham to "live," his conviction of wasted time is made acute by his appreciation of Chad Newsome's fulfillment. That occasion also seems to represent the end of his inquiry into the secret history of this other man. Seeing Chad and young Jeanne de Vionnet together, "was the click of a spring—he saw the truth" [133]. But this very "truth" is only another in a series of hypotheses later to be rejected by Strether and the reader. Moments earlier, Little Bilham had warned him, "What more than a vain appearance does the wisest of us know? I commend you the vain appearance" [124]. The gap of ignorance concerning Chad has not really been repaired, his story is still obscure. At the same time, another narrative repair has, all unconsciously to Strether, been set into motion—by the cultivation of his appreciation of the "vain appearance." His own unlived life, which he so deplores, is about to acquire what has been bypassed; his own history will be supplied with the missing element of passion. *The Ambassadors* will continue its braiding of two plots whose motive is the search for story itself.

When Maria declares that she likes Strether for not being a vulgar American success, for not having fulfilled the compulsory American male plot, which consists of a career of moneymaking, she contrasts him with such a man as his friend Waymarsh, who has done just that. She praises him for being a "failure"—"anything else is too hideous" —and notes her own twinship to him, for she also has failed to live the right story (which would be to marry someone with money) and Strether acknowledges, "You too are out of it" [40]. But he is not yet quite out of it. His Woollett-instructed mission is, curiously, a version of the female plot of marriage, but this Cinderella is male. And this banal, self-suppressing self-interest must give way also to true self-realization even at the expense of the surrender of plot. Maria asks him what he stands to lose by failing in his mission, and he says, first, "nothing," then admits, "everything" [56]. Waymarsh, the businessman, correctly understands the venture upon which Strether has been launched: if Chad returns to the family business as a result of Strether's efforts, the family interest in the business will "boom," and Mrs. Newsome and the man she marries will be richer. "You'll marry—you personally—more money." So Strether is "fierce for the boom" [75].

But it is Waymarsh who sees that the "rescue" of Chad is the wrong plot for Strether's character. "You're being used for a thing you ain't fit for" [74], he tells his friend—and Strether himself pauses from time to time to wonder whether, indeed, his ambassadorial role "might pass for interested" [113]. Only by embracing failure in Woollett's terms does he, paradoxically, gain. His final resolution, "not, out of the whole affair to have got anything for myself," rejects any gain at all of visible kind—even the consolation offered by Maria ("the offer of exquisite service, of lightened care, for the rest of his days" [346]—in a recoil of severest consistency from Woollett's calculus of profit making, from the idea of getting something or somewhere "in the end." It is a refusal of futurity matching the novel's early disengagement from the past—a seeming defect of visible closure—just as his vacant past was signified by the suppression of narrative beginning. But by this foregoing of a marriage-plot "reward" Strether has been left free for an unforeseen compensation. His "making up" will be the belated height of feeling reached by his imagination and sympathy—an augmentation of his rich potentiality, which remains available for whatever still comes.

In his effort to understand at the start what has happened to Chad, Strether has brought with him from Woollett trite narrative preconceptions of the young man's likely entrapment and degeneration in Paris, conceptions compounded of Puritan prejudice and Victorian cliché. These preconceptions of plot James saw as a danger for the writer, who might himself think in this fashion, or for the reader, for that matter, with his own triggered response to the idea of Parisian temptations for the unwary Anglo-Saxon—"the dreadful little old tradition, one of the platitudes of the human comedy, that people's moral scheme *does* break down in Paris; that nothing is more frequently observed; that hundreds of thousands of more or less hypocritical or more or less cynical persons annually visit the place for the sake of the probable catastrophe, and that I came late in the day to work myself up about it." The effect of Paris upon Strether himself was to be, James insisted, of a different kind of "revolution"—"he was to be thrown forward, rather, thrown quite with violence, upon his lifelong trick of intense reflexion," which was "to bring him out . . . *in* Paris, but with the surrounding scene itself a minor matter, a mere symbol for more things than had been dreamt of in the philosophy of Woollett" [8]. But this does not mean that Strether does not initially embrace the "dreadful little old tradition" in his anticipations of Chad's story.

It is appropriate that he should offer this scenario to Maria during an evening at the theater in London, where melodrama on the stage accompanies his description of Chad's suppositious female attachment as "base, venal, of the streets." Maria, however, suggests that there are *two* possible stories—"one is that he may have got brutalized. The other is that he may have got refined" [45, 53]. It is the second which emerges from Strether's first view of Chad's flat in the Boulevard Malesherbes. Yet in the contest of plots which continues in the text the first hypothesis, crass as it is, is never entirely forgotten and will even have a certain renewal.

Meanwhile, Strether is finding himself "in the presence of new measures, other standards, a different scale of relations" [77]. Before Chad appears in the box at the *Comédie* it already seems likely that Paris has refined rather than coarsened the heir to the Newsome fortune. Strether even finds himself charged by Chad with having a "low mind" for thinking that a woman of any sort has kept him from returning home: "Don't you know how much I like Paris . . . Do you think one's kept only by women?" [100–1]. Strether can imagine Woollett's skepticism about a plot *sans femme*. "He fairly caught himself shooting rueful glances, shy looks of pursuit, toward the embodied influence, the definite adversary, who had by a stroke of her own failed him and on a fond theory of whose palpable presence he had, under Mrs. Newsome's inspiration, altogether proceeded" [104]. Yet if there is a woman in the story, how shall the accustomed storyteller or reader classify her? If it still seems likely that a woman does hold Chad back, she is a woman "too good to admit" rather than the "wretch" imagined by a low mind. This would explain the fine changes in Chad—only such a woman could be responsible. But such an influence might imply something inadmissible by the very exhibition of its "unnatural goodness"—a suggestion so unsettling to Strether that he can only say, crudely, "Ah then you're speaking now of people who are *not* nice." To which Maria, the adept at classification, responds, with a certain impatience, "I delight in your classifications. But do you want me to give you in the matter, on this ground, the wisest advice I'm capable of? Don't consider her, don't judge her at all in herself. Consider her and judge her only in Chad" [107]. On the other hand, Chad's "disavowal" may not be gallantry: "It's the effort to sink her," Maria proposes. He wants to "shake her off." To which Strether objects indignantly, "after all she has done for him?" and Maria responds ruefully, "He's not as good as you think!" [108].

Here, before we have even reached the halfway mark of the novel, are a dozen different contending potentialities, which will thrust against one another till the end. The theory of the superior woman who had done so much for Chad and the theory of Chad as a person marvelously improved and "good" will reemerge when Strether is ready to accept the idea of his young friend's "virtuous attachment" to Madame de Vionnet. The view that theirs is just a passing "affair" and that she is a mistress whom he is ready to discard is justified later, yet it does not rout its alternative; she is still the wonderful friend who has done so much for him and to whom he is grateful. Strether's partisanship, even on these latest terms, for the woman abandoned, is the ripest of his realizations, yet so early as this he has shown himself ready to betray Woollett's commission for her sake.

The constant generation of new plots for Chad derives, technically, from the central obscurity in the presentation of the story of Chad and Marie de Vionnet. What he *is* and what she *is* are never cleared up in the unfolding of Strether's impressions, which have no exterior verifiability. We will never see Madame de Vionnet and Chad as they are when out of the sight of this one bemused witness. We will never see them alone with each other, and never know positively how they feel about each other; we see things only from Strether's limited view, to which the narrator refrains from adding further insight. We cannot fill this hermeneutic gap except, as Strether does, by an excess of imagination. The abandonment of one romantic plot elicits another, its opposite. "It seemed somehow as if [Chad] couldn't *but* be as good [as Strether had thought] from the moment he wasn't as bad" [108]. Mildness and charm mark every encounter with Chad and his circle and so frustrate Strether's expectations of "violence" that "he might almost have passed as wondering how to provoke it" [109].

For Little Bilham, the new "improved" Chad is also a text he reads with contending feelings, confessing to a preference for "the well-rubbed, old fashioned volume" he had once known; the revised Chad is "like the new edition of an old book that one has been fond of—revised and amended, brought up to date, but not quite the thing one knew and loved." Chad, by this favorite Jamesian image of man as a book, becomes a fiction ordered by plot concepts or character concepts old or new. And, continuing the image, Strether asks who the "editor" is who has revised the old novel to read as a new story [111].

Little Bilham, this "intense American" who cannot be supposed to lie, offers Strether a reading. He says that Chad really wants to go back and take up his Woollett future, a career which "will improve and enlarge him still more," as one improves or expands a text in still another way—another example of James's way of comparing persons to books and a reference to that revisionary process in both which is the central subject of this novel. Little Bilham explains that Chad isn't happy— despite appearances—because he's not "used . . . to being so good," and being good means that he isn't free to go home because the attachment in Paris is "virtuous" [111–12]. So, Strether's speculations—communicated to Maria—ensue. What narrative suppositions can be based on this fact of a "virtuous attachment" along with the news that Chad's greatest friends are a mother and a daughter whom he is anxious to introduce to his mother's emissary? The attachment may be virtuous because it is to two women rather than one, or because he has not yet made up his mind between them. The attachment must be to the daughter, considering his age; she may be old enough for marriage. But then, why doesn't he say so? Perhaps because the girl doesn't like him. Or maybe she can't face Woollett. Or maybe he's really "on terms" with the mother. If the girl's of the right age can the mother be? But maybe the girl's only a little girl. Is the mother a widow? If she isn't, maybe that's what makes the relation "virtuous." Finally, Maria refuses to say that she believes in the "virtuous attachment," anyhow. "Everything's possible. We must see" [117], she says, leaving the reader and Strether standing at a crossroads from which one might journey down a dozen divergent paths of expectation, as though the writer himself has stopped to consider every alternative story.

At this point what we have been given, again, is a bewildering review of a variety of potentialities. Some will continue to reverberate. The mother turns out to be still marvelously young and pretty, though of a respectability so distinct that she reminds Strether of the women of his Puritan Woollett. But she is not a widow—and so it may follow that Chad is in love with the daughter, who is just old enough, lovely, and plainly fond of their friend. Miss Barrace observes that "in the light of Paris" one always sees "what things resemble," a relativity of definition quite different from the one demanded by the man from America, who insists on knowing "what they really are." "Oh I like your Boston 'reallys,' " this sophisticated lady exclaims. When Strether persists in wanting to know whether Madame de Vionnet "really show[s] for what she is," he still gets no answer beyond, "She's charming. She's perfect" [127].

To his own mind, the exquisite lady shows for what she is. Strether is sure that all she wants of *him* is help in working things out for her daughter. But when he asks her, "Do you want [Chad] to marry your daughter?" she answers, "He likes her too much" [151]—and Strether is again thrown into confusion. Likes her too much to do what? To take her to America where she won't be happy, perhaps? Or to use her as a cover for the other relationship? He realizes very soon that little Jeanne isn't Chad's attachment. It *is* Madame de Vionnet, even though there is no possibility that she can divorce her husband to marry him. Pressed, Chad, for his part, says that for him she is "too good a friend" to leave summarily. He "owes [her] too much"—and Strether is convinced that this declaration itself places the lady above reproach. Her irreproach-ableness, anyhow, is what Chad himself insists on—and we are in no position, at the end of book 5, to consider that he lies. Nevertheless, the reader is likely to have become sensitized to contrary possibilities by all the previous play of speculation. Portentously, Maria Gostrey inex-plicably washes her hands of her old school friend.

Already, Strether's sympathies have caused him to forget his promise to achieve Chad's return. He tells Madame de Vionnet, "I'll save you if I can" [152]—thought a little later he confesses that he is still trying to discover what his own words mean [162]. More and more he is convinced that the "high fine friendship" which has done so much for Chad is worth the sacrifice, even, of Chad's American chances. He arrives at a chiasmus, as has been often noted, in the novel's exact center at the end of the first volume, passing over from being Woollett's ambassador to the side of Madame de Vionnet and the view that Chad should remain. "Let them face the future together! . . . I mean that if he gives her up . . . he ought to be ashamed of himself!" [170].

But it is less generally observed that the real crossover of plots is that it is Strether who is ready to offer Madame de Vionnet such devotion and such sacrifice. Chad, on the other hand, wants to take up the plot of Woollett, to marry a Woollett woman and make the business "boom," endings that are fast fading out of Strether's future. Strether feels still that he has no life of his own, only "a life . . . for other people" [127]. In a sense this will continue to be true. But Strether's response to Madame de Vionnet begins to deserve the name of passion. Most readers of the novel continue to see him as the man who has missed his hour irrecoverably. But from the sixth book onward the text begins to express Strether's instead of Chad's love—along with Strether's acceptance of the sacrifice of gain Chad refuses to make. "What was their relation moreover—though light and brief enough in form as yet—but whatever she might choose to make it? Nothing could prevent her—certainly he couldn't—from making it pleasant. At the back of his head, behind everything, was the sense that she was—there, before him, close to him, in vivid imperative form—one of the rare women he had so often heard of, read of, thought of, but never met, whose very presence, look, voice, the mere contemporaneous *fact* of whom, from the moment it was all presented, made a relation of mere recognition" [150]. That had not been the case with Mrs. Newsome; it was not the case even with Miss Gostrey. Strether's recognition of Chad's *femme du monde* has become adoration, expressed in a supreme poetic reverie. * * * To create this image of absolute femininity James has invoked the highest associations of myth and poetry—she is a goddess or nymph, like Venus emerging from the sea foam, like some divinity on a classic coin—and like Shakespeare's unparalleled Cleopatra. [160]

His relationship with her begins on a new basis after a chance meeting in Notre-Dame when he sees her first, without recognition, as "some fine firm concentrated heroine of an old story, something he had heard, read, something that, had he had a hand for drama, he might himself have written." He had recently purchased seventy volumes of Victor Hugo, and in the great cathedral, one of Hugo's subjects, wondered "where, among packed accumulations," this "fruit of his mission" might find a place. This is more than a digressive association and a reference to his thoughts of return and the literal problems of the tourist's baggage.

Where, indeed, in his remainder of life, will Strether find place for the romantic kind of story Hugo wrote? He feels that his purchase is "out of proportion . . . for any other plunge," he tells Madame de Vionnet. Yet, "even as he spoke how at that instant he was plunging," for Madame de Vionnet "was romantic for him far beyond what she could have guessed." He is writing the old romantic play or story after all. During their *déjeuner* he feels that "in the matter of letting himself go, of diving deep . . . he ha[s] touched bottom" [178].

He has, indeed, "travelled far since that evening in London, before the theatre, when his dinner with Maria Gostrey, between the pink-shaded candles, had struck him as requiring so many explanations." He now neither seeks or requires such explanations as Woollett or even Maria would have expected—but gives himself to the "reasons" of sensation which precede "lucidity," as these might have been captured in an Impressionist painting—a moment of color and light that shimmers beyond "explanation" as they dine on the Left Bank with a view of the Seine from their window table. [178] * * * He has written to Woollett to report Chad's transformation and its cause. He receives in response the ultimatum to bring Chad back immediately—or, if he cannot do so, to return himself. Chad is ready to go, but—the chiasmus of plot completing itself—Strether insists that he wait, and will not heed his own recall. He will risk the Pococks, who will be sent in his place, hoping that they will appreciate the "new facts," refusing to heed Chad's warning that his replacement by Mrs. Newsome's daughter "bears upon—well, you know what" [191]. For if he loses his futurity in Woollett he gains back, now, his lost past, the youth he never had, the beginning so summarily dealt with by the narrative structure of the novel. [199] * * * But at [the] moment of reparation, the predicted future that promises *no* true recovery of a lost past erupts into the present. The eighth book, culminating in the wonderfully comic scene between Sarah Pocock and Madame de Vionnet, provides a shocking prevision for Strether of his American potentiality and rereads his present in Woollett's terms. The great question, of course, is whether the Pococks will see how Chad has changed. As they give no evidence of seeing it, Strether is brought to wonder whether he has not been deluded—along with Maria, Madame de Vionnet, and Chad himself. "Did he live in a false world, a world that had grown simply to suit him, and was his present slight irritation . . . but the alarm of the vain thing menaced by the touch of the real? Was this contribution of the real possibly the mission of the Pococks?—had they come to make the work of observation, as *he* had practiced observation, crack and crumble, and to reduce Chad to the plain terms in which honest minds could deal with him?" [214]. The relativity to which restricted subjective narration reduces ideas of the "real" is brought to the fore, and shakes our own as well as Strether's confidence in his personal vision.

His Woollett future—the plot he had once embraced—is exhibited in Jim Pocock, James's satiric type-portrait of the American Businessman who leaves a "whole side of life"—social relations, even "culture," presumably—to his women. Strether asks himself if *his* exclusion from this side, "had he married ten years before [would] have become now the same as Pocock's? Might it even become the same should he marry in a few months?" American society, Strether reflects on behalf of James, is "a society of women"—and Pocock knows this as he warns Strether, "Don't go home!" and thinks Chad ought to stay where he is. Strether then asks himself "if what Sally wanted her brother to go back for was to become like her husband" [215–16]. Strether and Madame de Vionnet hope Jim will provide Chad with "a warning" of Woollett's idea of "redemption" from his present state [235]. In fact, he is a more-than-likely anticipation of a plot outcome for Chad which is to be glimpsed beyond the last gateposts of the novel.

Sarah (Sally) Pocock may be seen as a belated restoration to the plot of its initial omission of Mrs. Newsome. When Maria suggests, a bit later, that Chad ought to go home for a visit to his mother, Strether observes "his mother has paid *him* a visit. Mrs. Newsome has been with him, this month, with an intensity that I'm sure he has thoroughly felt; he has lavishly entertained her, and she has let him have her thanks" [298]. Despite some differentiation, Sarah is so much the same type as her mother as to forecast what Strether's Woollett spouse would be. But her intrusion, now, is too late to modify the truncation from the past that Strether's European adventure has effected. At their meeting, Madame de Vionnet's intimations of intimacy with him can only be read in one way by Sally, in terms of the discarded trite plot of Paris. Stories depend upon their readers, and Strether is appalled to discover that "it would be exactly *like* the way things always turned out for him that he should affect Mrs. Pocock and Waymarsh as launched in a relation in which he had really never been launched at all" [221]. Strether himself momentarily goes back to such an interpretation when he mentally says to the woman he has thought of as the goddess of love, "After all, what *is* between us when I've been so tremendously on my guard and have seen you but half a dozen times?" [221].

But, immediately, he dismisses his fear of Woollett's inferences and recaptures his own version of things. "He had quite the consciousness now that not to meet [Madame de Vionnet] at any point more than halfway would be odiously, basely to abandon her. Yes, he was *with* her, and opposed even in this covert, this semi-safe fashion to those who were not, he felt, strangely and confusedly, but excitedly, inspiringly, how much and how far. It was as if he had positively waited in suspense for something from her that would let him in deeper, so that he might show her how he could take it" [224]. He goes willingly into Madame de Vionnet's "boat," we are told in an image that anticipates the literal later scene of Chad and the same woman on the river in the country, in book II; by this fusion of images he anticipates his replacement of Chad. "It rocked beneath him, but he settled himself in his place. He took up an oar and, since he was to have the credit of pulling, pulled" [222]. The image, of passive submission to the flow of things, exactly fits his own version of his experience. Later, in their scene of final confrontation and rupture, Sarah will accuse him of "sacrific[ing] mothers and sisters to [Madame de Vionnet] without a blush, and . . . mak[ing] them cross the ocean on purpose to feel the more, and take from [him] the straighter how [he does] it"—but "purpose," the sense of narrative *telos*, is foreign to Strether's impressionistic receptivity. He can only respond to her, "Everything has come as a sort of indistinguishable part of everything else. Your coming out belonged closely to my having come before you, and my having come was a result of our general state of mind. Our general state of mind had proceeded, on its side, from our queer ignorance, our queer misconceptions and confusions—from which, since then, an inexorable tide of light seems to have floated us into our perhaps still queerer knowledge" [279].

The Pococks and Waymarsh comically demonstrate how their own plots reverse themselves, even as Strether's own is doing—and refute the very conception of design and consistency they have seemed to uphold. Mamie, who was destined to marry Chad, turns out to prefer Little Bilham. Intelligent Mamie has had the mission, like Strether's own, of saving Chad, and she has rejected it because, alone of her family, she has seen that he is already improved—and, besides, she doesn't even like Chad! Mamie provides one of those surprises for which Strether's own surrender of prejudice makes him ready when he finds her alone in the Pocock hotel suite and discovers her difference from his preconceptions, her possession of "something . . . that touched him to a point not to have been reckoned beforehand" [249].

Not only does Jim form a certain alliance with Madame de Vionnet—whom he continues to see as a wicked, fascinating woman—but Mrs. Pocock, the representative of Woollett propriety, has her Paris escapade with Waymarsh. And Waymarsh, who once hated Europe and urged Strether to abandon his embassy, is entrained in Woollett's service. At the same time, this same Waymarsh is having the time of his life, a Paris fling, a romantic "adventure." Strether envies him, and thinks himself, by comparison, still stuck after all, in that condition of "too late" he had bewailed to Little Bilham. And he feels this—with a backtracking swing of the story—despite the liberation he has felt with Maria Gostrey, despite his recent commitment to Madame de Vionnet: "It came to him in the current of thought, as things so oddly did come, that *he* had never risen with the lark to attend a brilliant woman to the Marché aux Fleurs; this could be fastened on him in connexion neither with Miss Gostrey nor with Madame de Vionnet; the practice of getting up early for adventures could indeed in no manner be fastened on him. It came to him in fact that just here was his usual case: he was for ever missing things through his general genius for missing them" [271].

But such mild ironies over the meaning of "adventure" give place, at the end of the tenth book, to the absolute clash of Strether's and Woollett's reading of the story of Chad and Paris. The woman Strether calls "charming and beneficent" Sarah refuses to consider "even an apology for a decent woman" [279–80]; she finds Chad's development under Madame de Vionnet's influence, not "fortunate," as Strether urges, but "hideous," their life together not "a thing one can even *speak* of." Strether's despairing exclamation, "Oh, if you think *that*—" is finished for him by Sarah with "Then all's at an end" and her own "I do think that," after which "resolute rupture" she charges off. It *is* an ending to the tale of ambassadorship and reward. "It probably all *was* at an end" [282].

There follow two chapters of postmortem—the first with Chad and the second with Maria. Chad remonstrates that Strether is giving up so much—"dished," as far as his prospects with Mrs. Newsome; an "assured future" and "a good deal of money" gone [287, 288–89]. "What I don't for the life of me make out is what you *gain* by it" [292], the young man says—missing the sense of forward movement toward some discernible end in Strether's behavior. To Maria, Strether admits that he does "lose everything," but though he might still recover the Woollett story by releasing Chad from his promise not to return, he seems not to mind the loss of the "opulent future" represented by Mrs. Newsome, and even of Mrs. Newsome herself.

For she has shown no interest in surprises, while he has, from the first, been ready for the unexpected effect of new impressions; as Maria notes, he "came over more or less for surprises." And they have come —his surprise at his renewed view of Chad, his surprise in his discovery of Madame de Vionnet, most of all, but many others stimulated by new circumstance and by the very experience of Paris. For Mrs. Newsome there can be only one narrative.

> That's just her difficulty—that she doesn't admit surprises. It's a fact that, I think, describes and represents her; and it falls in with what I tell you—that's she's all, as I've called it, fine cold thought. She had, to her own mind, worked the whole thing out in advance, and worked it out for me as well as for herself. Whenever she has done that, you see, there's no room left; no margin, as it were, for any alteration. She's filled as full, packed as tight, as she'll hold,

and if you wish to get anything more or different either out or in
. . . what it comes to . . . is that you've got morally and intellectually
to get rid of her. [299–300]

Chad asks him what he stands to gain for his sacrifice—to which
Strether responds that Chad has "no imagination," and Chad in turn
declares that Strether has "rather too much." It is by imagination that
Strether will "gain," while the future captain of industry has admitted,
even in his concern for Strether, only his own definition of profit [302].
In one sense, of course, Mrs. Newsome has had plenty of imagination
for the conventional "horrors" she expected him to find. "I was booked,
by her vision—extraordinarily intense, after all," he observes, "to find
them; and that I didn't, that I couldn't, that, as she evidently felt, I
wouldn't—this evidently didn't at all, as they say, 'suit' her book" [301].
What he now does want he has "ceased to measure or even to understand," but his own "book" is like James's, full of impressionistic fertility.

As he gazes out into the Paris night from Chad's balcony, Strether
hangs over that kind of impressionistic window view which appears in
so many paintings—in Monet's "Boulevard des Capucines," for
example—in which the street below becomes a vague, poetic implication
of sight and sound, and the window frame suggests that the drama, the
subject, is the perception of these things. From the same balcony Strether
had seen, more than three months earlier, a multitude of signs that
reminded him of the "youth he had long ago missed," but signs also
that what he had missed, what Paris represents, is "an affair of the
senses" [284]. The senses—rather than the analytic mind, of course—
are the gateways of "impressions"; this is the reason that visual experience
seems so insistently to represent Strether's immediate reception, before
intellection, of what stands outside him.[2]

But the reader, if not Strether, is also being prepared for the famous
moment in the eleventh book when, out for a day in the country, Strether
unexpectedly encounters his friends. He realizes, seeing them so obviously prepared for a clandestine night, that the idea of the "virtuous
attachment" is a blind. Theirs has been "an affair of the senses." The
episode is also a culmination of the meaning of the novel because it is
concerned with the characters' relation to the plots that have obsessed
them and us. The disclosure of their enacted sexual connection is a
refutation, by Strether's beloved pair, of the plot which they have encouraged him to believe in—that they, like himself, have willingly
maintained a gap of nondoing in *their* "affair of life." Their sexual

---

2. More negatively, Tony Tanner has noted these balcony scenes and interpreted them to signify
Strether's preference for a "perched privacy" by which he takes "visual possession from above"
and contemplates life without being reached by it. "The Watcher from the Balcony: *The
Ambassadors*," *Critical Quarterly* 8, no. I (Spring 1966), pp. 35–52. If, on the other hand,
they suggest Strether's impressionistic receptivity, they signify his openness to life, his refusal
to exercise discriminatory judgments that would reduce perception to preconception.

"doing" refutes Strether's conception that mere being what they are has been enough for them. It refutes the idea that Chad's character has gained simply by association with a charming woman, excluding what is properly called the sexual "act." Strether has to concede that "intimacy at such a point, was *like* that—and what in the world else would one have wished it to be like?" [315].[3]

He has come to this moment in a mood of holiday and a return of that readiness, felt so thrillingly in Chester, to take things as they come. Appropriately, he receives his new understanding of his friends as though viewing an Impressionist painting. First, he sees the river, then a boat, then two persons in it, one a woman with a pink parasol; *then*, he identifies the human figures, *then* he understands the nature of their relation. It is the progression made by the viewer who, stepping back from the confusion of color and light on a canvas comes to the naming of persons, the analysis of situation not first but last. Identity, significance, literary plot, have followed as mental afterthought the impact of sensation. The remembering and anticipating mind corrects the eye. Not so much the visual similarity of the scene to a painting as the process of such viewing is impressionist and a correlative for the way we pass from the sensation of the moment to understanding.

Strether's excursion had begun with a preimpressionist idea of landscape, the viewpoint of the Barbizon school represented by a Lambinet he had admired long before in a Tremont Street gallery. The remembered painting causes him to expect a scene as it might be located within "the oblong window of the picture frame," a "land of fancy . . . the background of fiction, the medium of art, the nursery of letters, practically as distant as Greece"—romance rather than reality. The Lambinet is a symbol, too, of the life-that-might-have-been that Strether wished he had had; it is, after all, the picture he "would have bought" if he could have afforded it, in his youth. He walks into a space of poplars and willows, reeds and river, "a river of which he didn't know, and didn't want to know, the name," till what he sees falls "into a composition, full of felicity," like the Lambinet—"the sky was silver and turquoise and varnish; the village on the left was white and the church on the right was grey." Yet his impressionistic susceptibility already expresses itself in the way he takes a train and dismounts at a station selected "almost at random." Free of his Woollett mission—of any sense of

---

3. Negatively, also, Philip Sicker has found Strether's blindness and his behavior with women throughout the book a symptom of "the perfect condition of psychosexual androgyny." *Love and the Quest for Identity in the Fiction of Henry James* (Princeton, N.J., Princeton University Press, 1980). And Maxwell Geismer has diagnosed Strether's as a case of suppressed homosexuality. *Henry James and the Jacobites* (Boston, Mass., Houghton Mifflin Co., 1963), p. 277. James's text does not forbid such filling in of psychological gaps in his portraits, but such gaps also encourage us to read Strether's adventure of perception more philosophically, as a willed suspension of judgment, a willingness to entertain even improbabilities, a reluctance to "conclude."

"mission" or "end" at all—his "idleness" seems sweet as "he walked and walked as if to show how little he had now to do; he had nothing to do but turn off to some hillside where he might stretch himself and hear the poplars rustle." He has brought a book along, but it stays in his pocket, though the Seine region reminds him of Maupassant as once Notre-Dame had reminded him of Hugo—with different effect, his expectations now being as different from that earlier moment as Maupassant's mode of story-telling might be from Hugo's [303–4].

Nothing has been better proof of his freedom from former obsessions than his latest meetings with Madame de Vionnet. There had been no more "tiresome" talk between them, Chad's name had not even come up, it was as if he had been calling on her for the first time. He felt himself acting as if he told her aloud, "Don't like me, if it's a question of liking me, for anything obvious and clumsy that I've, as they call it, 'done' for you . . . don't be for me simply the person I've come to know through my awkward connexion with Chad." They had escaped the plot of Chad and begun another by simply doing nothing as time "slipped along so smoothly, mild but not slow, and melting, liquifying, into his happy illusion of idleness" [307]. Maria has asked him, "Are you really in love with her?" and he has answered, "It's of no importance I should know" [293]. He needs only to submit to his impressions without titling his feelings by an obvious term.

But the old story-making compulsion returns upon the encounter at the river. The narrative now insistently resorts to the language of literary forms. "It was as queer as fiction, as farce" [310] that their meeting should occur. The whole incident appears like a flagrant literary use of coincidence in "the general *invraisemblance* of the occasion" [311]. But Madame de Vionnet makes the chance meeting a happy element in a tale contrived on the spot; her remark, "*comme cela se trouve!*" [311] is the complacent observation of the successful storyteller. "Fiction and fable *were* inevitably in the air," as everything fell with "a marked drop into innocent friendly Bohemia" [313], a light tale, that is, of *la vie bohème.*

Madame de Vionnet herself reverts to convention, no longer the incalculable beloved of his recent view. Her nervous chattering in her own French has the effect of "veiling her identity, shifting her back into a mere voluble class or race" [312]—she becomes a familiar "type," for which Winterbourne would have had a ready name. The tale of her relationship with Chad relapses almost to its earliest formulation before Strether had met her—it *is*, after all, "a typical tale of Paris," in which, perhaps, they were all "floating together on the silver stream of impunity" [317]. When he sees her again in her apartment full of historic memorabilia she reminds him of Madame Roland, ready for execution, and he is not sure to which story, farcical or tragic, he should assign her. In the end he realizes that she is both type and unfathomable individuality, unexpressed in either conventional story: "the finest and subtlest creature, the happiest apparition, it had been given him in all his years, to meet"—"vulgarly troubled . . . as a maidservant crying for her young man" [325].

Chad is likewise again a "type" rather than the mysterious personality developed under her influence. Strether realizes that though Chad has been made "better," he has not been made "infinite" [324]. Can he live up to the sublimity Strether had imagined for him? "You'll be a brute, you know—you'll be guilty of the last infamy—if you ever forsake her," Strether tells him, and Chad denies any intention of the sort. But what he says is, "I don't know what should make you think I'm tired of her." For us, as for Strether, there must be "in the allusion to satiety as a thinkable motive a slight breath of the ominous . . . he spoke of being 'tired' of her almost as he might have spoken of being tired of roast mutton for dinner" [336–37, 339]. Here, surely, is the closure of the story of sexual adventure. Can we not say that we know the end without the further suspicion, admitted by Strether in his last conversation with Maria, that there is "some other woman in London" [346]?

It would almost seem, by this, that Strether's policy of impressionistic receptivity has been refuted, for, in the end, one does name and interpret; mere impressions must be corrected by knowledge. In interpreting the story of Chad and Marie de Vionnet, Strether has suspended judgment to the point of imbecility in the eyes of a great many readers, whose reaction seems anticipated in Maria Gostrey's mocking, "What on earth—that's what I want to know now—had you then supposed?" He recognizes that "he had really been trying all along to suppose nothing" [315]. He has cultivated ignorance as he long before persuaded Maria to do concerning the domestic article manufactured in the Newsome factory, a "vulgar" actuality which he never got around to naming.

His cultivation of ignorance has also made him indifferent to the romantic momentum of the plot initiated in Chester with Maria Gostrey, and now he is unready for its closure. His obliging *ficelle* has waited and watched with him, helped him to interpret the story of others—and quite possibly loved him. But she has come to realize, after his commitment to Marie de Vionnet, that his relationship with her was "no longer quite the same. . . . The time seemed already far off when he had held out his small thirsty cup to the spout of her pail. Her pail was scarce touched now, and other fountains flowed for him; she fell into her place as but one of his tributaries, and there was a strange sweetness—a melancholy mildness that touched him—in her acceptance of the altered order" [198]. Her final offer to him—an alternative to his unpromising return to Woollett—is refused, though she tells him "There's nothing, you know, I wouldn't do for you" [346]. * * * In a sense, too, he has duplicated Chad's own casting off of the woman who

has done so much for the man she has loved, educated, and refined—
and he is no less a "brute."

He has, of course, never been so exaltedly in love with his good friend
Maria as he has been with her namesake Marie de Vionnet; one can
guess that he is too much in love with love to accept the consolation
she offers. This is not, however, what James's hero himself says. What
he says, rather, is that the only way he knows of being "right" is "not,
out of the whole affair to have got anything for myself" [346]—rejecting
all possibility of gain as a result of the mission that had begun with the
expectation of gain—rejecting any "end." Maria's answer is profound:
"But with your wonderful impressions you'll have got a good deal." The
supreme impressionist has gained after all. He has mended the ellipsis
of his lost youth by an adventure of the generous imagination. If so,
James's story ends optimistically with the restoration of narrative deficiency. The past can be recovered; his bright illusions, though passing,
have been his experience of what he had missed. Chad and Marie de
Vionnet have been, for *him*, as he had told Maria earlier, his lost youth,
whether or not they are their own best and brightest selves.

Yet this is not, despite such restoration, an ending that satisfies the
appetite for final closure. The story of Chad and Madame de Vionnet,
once an enigma whose solution is withheld, is now told, in one sense
—though we must reflect that we are never to know positively what each
is and feels. More blatantly, Strether's own plot, the detective's own
story, remains unconcluded. Many readers have felt that James makes
his hero simply eccentric—or unnatural—when he refuses Maria, his
breach with Mrs. Newsome being "past mending." But his future must
remain open since he is the representative of the potentiality of character
which cannot be exhausted by plot. It is completely appropriate to this
novel that its structure, its very style—those sentences which delay exact
significance till the end and even leave it problematic then, casting the
reader upon his impressions like a boat surrendered to a stream—should
reflect the hero's experience.

James observed in his preface to the novel, "One's bag of adventures,
conceived or conceivable, has been only half-emptied by the mere telling
of one's story. It depends so on what one means by that equivocal
quantity. There is the story of one's hero, and then, thanks to the intimate
connexion of things, the story of one's story itself" [5]. The telling of
The Ambassadors "empties," as we have seen, only certain of Strether's
possible adventures from out the bag of what might be imagined for
him—yet our sense of his potentiality allows us to see what these alternatives might be, to see them latent in the narrative. Intimately connected with this is the story of James's story, its own advances and retreats
of self-making, its very method of seeming to refrain from conclusion,
of being blind to the obvious way to go on or to unravel its knot, and

then of saving or solving itself after all, while, to the last, being ready
to admit that other courses are possible. The hero's adventure and the
novel's adventure are the same.

PHILIP FISHER (1992)

["One of the Master Texts of a Whole Generation"]†

* * * One of the master texts of a whole generation of American
study was Henry James's *The Ambassadors*, perhaps from an academic
point of view the most perfect book ever written by an American. James's
hero Strether creates a myth of Paris, a myth of his charge, Chad, a
myth of Chad's relation to Mme. de Vionnet. Each myth is betrayed
by fact, stained by the complexity of the real world. An entire academic
generation saw its own love of criticism, observation, nuance, disappointment, myth, and defeat in James's novel.

As the great academic popularity of James's novel made clear, if there
has been one history lovingly traced by intellectuals over the past fifty
years, it has been the history of intellectuals themselves. * * *

† †From *Redrawing the Boundaries: The Transformation of English and American Literary
Studies*, ed. Stephen Greenblatt and Giles Gunn (New York: Modern Language Association,
1992), 235. Reprinted by permission of the author and the Modern Language Association.

Henry James Chronology

1843	Born April 15 in New York City, the second of five children of Henry James, Sr., and Mary Walsh. William James is his older brother, Alice James his younger sister.
1843–45	Family travels in France and England.
1845–55	Childhood spent in New York City and Albany, New York.
1855–58	At schools in Switzerland, England, and France.
1858	At school in Newport, Rhode Island, where the James family settles.
1859–60	Returns to Europe and studies in Switzerland and Germany.
1860–62	Back in school at Newport. Back injury.
1862–63	Enters Harvard Law School for a term. Starts sending stories to magazines. Younger brother wounded in the Civil War.
1864	First anonymous story published. Writing stories and reviews.
1865	First signed story in the *Atlantic Monthly*. Writing anonymous reviews.
1869–70	Traveling in Europe. Cousin Minnie Temple dies of tuberculosis at twenty-three. Meets various English literary figures, including George Eliot.
1870–71	Living in Cambridge, Massachusetts. First novel published. Friendship with William Dean Howells.
1872–74	In Europe with sister and aunt. Doing newspaper travel sketches. Living in Paris and Rome.
1875	*Roderick Hudson, A Passionate Pilgrim and Other Tales*, and *Transatlantic Sketches* (travel writings). Tries living in New York City. Returns to Europe.
1875–76	Settles in Paris. Friends with Ivan Turgenev; meets various French literary figures, including Gustave Flaubert, Emile Zola, and Guy de Maupassant.
1877	Settles in London. *The American*.
1878	Story "Daisy Miller" attracts wide attention. *French Poets and Novelists*.
1879	*The Europeans, Confidence, Hawthorne*. Active in London literary society. Friendships with Robert Louis Stevenson, Edmund Gosse, and Henry Adams.

1880–81   *Washington Square*. In Florence, writes *The Portrait of a Lady*, which is serialized in both England and the United States.

1881   Revisits the United States.

1882   Mother and Father die. Joins the Athenaeum Club.

1883   Macmillan publishes Collective Edition of James's works in fourteen volumes. *The Siege of London* (stories) and *Portraits of Places*.

1884   Alice James, now an invalid, comes to live in England. *A Little Tour of France, Tales of Three Cities*, and "The Art of Fiction."

1886   *The Bostonians* and *The Princess Casamassima*.

1887   Extended visit to Italy. Friendship with Constance Fenimore Woolson.

1888   *Partial Portraits* (essays) as well as *The Reverberator, The Aspern Papers*.

1889   *A London Life* (stories).

1890   *The Tragic Muse*. Begins writing for the theater.

1892   Death of Alice James in London.

1893   Writing plays unsuccessfully until 1895. *Essays in London and Elsewhere*.

1895   *Guy Domville* play booed. Abandons play-writing. Begins writing scenarios for his novels. *Terminations* (stories).

1896   *Embarrassments* (stories) and *The Other House*. Starts dictating his work.

1897   *The Spoils of Poynton* and *What Maisie Knew*.

1898   "The Turn of the Screw" serialized. Leases Lamb House, Rye, Sussex, which he later buys. Friendship with Jonathan Sturges.

1899   *The Awkward Age*. Employs James B. Pinker as his literary agent.

1900   *The Soft Side* (stories). Begins *The Ambassadors*.

1901   *The Sacred Fount* published. Completes *The Ambassadors* and begins *The Wings of the Dove*. Takes rooms at the Athenaeum.

1902   *The Wings of the Dove*.

1903   *The Ambassadors* and the biography *William Wetmore Story and His Friends*. Friendship with Jocelyn Persse.

1904   *The Golden Bowl*, James's last major novel.

1905   Returns to the United States for a tour. Lectures on American speech and Balzac published in *The Question of Our Speech*. *English Hours* (essays).

1906   Begins revising and writing prefaces for the collected New York Edition of his works.

1907   *The American Scene* (observations on America).

1907–9   The financially unsuccessful New York Edition of James's works in twenty-four volumes.

1909   *Italian Hours* (travel writings).

1910   James ill. *The Finer Grain* (stories). Returns to the United States with the failing William James, who dies.

1911   Honorary degree from Harvard. Returns to England. *The Outcry*, James's last completed novel.

1912   Honorary degree from Oxford. Friendship with Edith Wharton. Leases a London flat.

1913   *A Small Boy and Others*, the first volume of James's autobiography. Friends celebrate James's seventieth birthday with a portrait by John Singer Sargent.

1914   *Notes of a Son and Brother*, the second volume of autobiography, and *Notes on Novelists*.

1915   Engages in war relief work. Becomes a British subject. His writing is criticized by H. G. Wells.

1916   Awarded the Order of Merit. Dies February 28.

1917   Unfinished novels *The Ivory Tower* and *The Sense of the Past* as well as his unfinished autobiography *The Middle Years*.

1919   *Within the Rim* (late essays).

1920   *The Letters of Henry James*.

Selected Bibliography

For editions of *The Ambassadors* published in James's lifetime, see p. 348.

BIBLIOGRAPHIES AND CHECKLISTS

Bradbury, Nicola. *An Annotated Critical Bibliography of Henry James*. Brighton, Sussex: Harvester, 1987.

Budd, John. *Henry James: A Bibliography of Criticism, 1975–1981*. Westport, Conn.: Greenwood Press, 1983.

Edel, Leon, Dan H. Laurence, and James Rambeau. *A Bibliography of Henry James*. 3rd ed. Oxford: Oxford University Press, 1982.

Funston, Judith E. *Henry James, A Reference Guide: 1975–1987*. Boston: G. K. Hall, 1991.

McColgan, Kristin Pruitt. *Henry James, 1917–1959: A Reference Guide*. Boston: G. K. Hall, 1979.

Ricks, Beatrice. *Henry James: A Bibliography of Secondary Works*. Metuchen, N.J.: Scarecrow Press, 1975.

Scura, Dorothy McInnis. *Henry James, 1960–1974: A Reference Guide*. Boston: G. K. Hall, 1979.

Taylor, Linda J. *Henry James, 1866–1916: A Reference Guide*. Boston: G. K. Hall, 1982.

BIOGRAPHIES, NOTEBOOKS, LETTERS

Edel, Leon. *Henry James. The Master: 1901–1916*. Philadelphia: J. B. Lippincott, 1972.

James, Henry. *The Complete Notebooks*. Edited by Leon Edel and Lyall H. Powers. New York: Oxford University Press, 1987.

———. *The Letters of Henry James*. Edited by Percy Lubbock. 2 vols. New York: Oxford University Press, 1920.

———. *Letters: 1895–1916*. Edited by Leon Edel. Vol. 4. Cambridge, Mass.: Harvard University Press, 1984.

———. *The Notebooks*. Edited by F. O. Matthiessen and Kenneth B. Murdock. New York: Oxford University Press, 1947.

Kaplan, Fred. *Henry James: The Imagination of Genius*. New York: Morrow, 1992.

Lewis, R. W. B. *The Jameses: A Family Narrative*. New York: Farrar, Straus and Giroux, 1991.

Matthiessen, F. O. *The James Family*. New York: Oxford University Press, 1947.

ADDITIONAL SELECTED CRITICISM OF *THE AMBASSADORS*

Anderson, Quentin. *The American Henry James*, 207–31. New Brunswick, N.J.: Rutgers University Press, 1957.

Armstrong, Paul B. *The Challenge of Bewilderment: Understanding and Representation in James, Conrad, and Ford*, 63–109. Ithaca, N.Y.: Cornell University Press, 1987.

Barrett, Louise K. "Speech in *The Ambassadors*: Woollett and Paris as Linguistic Communities." *Novel* 16 (1983): 215–29.

Bellringer, Alan W. *The Ambassadors*. London: Allen and Unwin, 1984.

Berland, Alwyn. *Culture and Conduct in the Novels of Henry James*, 185–227. Cambridge, Eng.: Cambridge University Press, 1981.

Bloom, Harold, ed. *Henry James's "The Ambassadors": Modern Critical Interpretations*. New York: Chelsea House Press, 1988.

Chase, Richard. "James's Ambassadors." In *Twelve Original Essays on Great American Novels*, edited by Charles Shapiro, 124–47. Detroit: Wayne State University Press, 1958.

Crews, Frederick C. *The Tragedy of Manners*, 30–56. New Haven, Conn.: Yale University Press, 1957.

Cross, Mary. "Style as Plot in *The Ambassadors*." *Language and Style* 18 (1985): 46–63.

Dooley, D. J. "The Hourglass Pattern in *The Ambassadors*." *New England Quarterly* 41 (1968): 237–81.

Dunn, Albert A. "The Articulation of Time in *The Ambassadors.*" *Criticism* 14 (1972): 137–50.

Dupee, F. W. *Henry James*, 207–16. New York: Doubleday, 1956.

Fogel, Daniel Mark. *A Companion to Henry James Studies*. Westport, Conn.: Greenwood Press, 1993.

———. *Henry James and the Structure of the Romantic Imagination*, 20–48. Baton Rouge: Louisiana State University Press, 1981.

Fussell, Edwin Sill. *The French Side of Henry James*, 177–214. New York: Columbia University Press, 1990.

Gargano, James W. "*The Ambassadors* and *Louis Lambert.*" *Modern Language Notes* 75 (1960): 211–13.

Gibson, William M. "Metaphor in the Plot of *The Ambassadors.*" *New England Quarterly* 24 (1951): 291–305.

Greenslade, William. "The Power of Advertising: Chad Newsome and the Meaning of Paris in *The Ambassadors.*" *ELH* 49 (1982): 99–122.

Griffin, Susan M. "The Selfish Eye: Strether's Principles of Psychology." *American Literature* 56 (1984): 396–409.

Holland, Laurence Bedwell. *The Expense of Vision: Essays on the Craft of Henry James*, 228–82. Princeton, N.J.: Princeton University Press, 1964.

Johnson, Courtney, Jr. *Henry James and the Evolution of Consciousness: A Study of "The Ambassadors"*. East Lansing: Michigan State University Press, 1987.

Kaston, Carren. *Imagination and Desire in the Novels of Henry James*, 82–108. New Brunswick, N.J.: Rutgers University Press, 1984.

Knoepflmacher, U. C. " 'O Rare for Strether!' *Antony and Cleopatra* and *The Ambassadors.*" *Nineteenth Century Fiction* 19 (1965): 333–44.

Lodge, David. "Strether by the River." *Language of Fiction*, 189–213. London: Routledge and Kegan Paul, 1966, 1984.

Macnaughton, William R. *Henry James: The Later Novels*, 57–79. Boston: Twayne Publishers, 1987.

McKee, Patricia. "Making Do: The Art of Appreciation in *The Ambassadors.*" *South Atlantic Quarterly* 87 (1988): 253–309.

McWhirter, David. *Desire and Love in Henry James: A Study of the Late Novels*, 13–82. New York: Cambridge University Press, 1989.

Paterson, John. "The Language of 'Adventure' in Henry James." *American Literature* 32 (1960): 291–301.

Poirier, Richard. *A World Elsewhere: The Place of Style in American Literature*, 124–43. New York: Oxford University Press, 1966.

Posnock, Ross. *The Trial of Curiosity: Henry James, William James, and the Challenge of Modernity*, 221–49. New York: Oxford University Press, 1991.

Rivkin, Julie. "The Logic of Delegation in *The Ambassadors.*" *PMLA* 101 (1986): 819–31.

Samuels, Charles Thomas. *The Ambiguity of Henry James*, 194–209. Urbana: University of Illinois Press, 1971.

Seidel, Michael. *Exile and the Narrative Imagination*, 131–63. New Haven, Conn.: Yale University Press, 1986.

Sharp, M. Corona. *The Confidante in Henry James*, 150–80. Notre Dame, Ind.: University of Notre Dame Press, 1963.

Smith, George E., III. "James, Degas, and the Modern View." *Novel* 21 (1987): 56–72.

Smith, Peter. *Public and Private Value: Studies in the Nineteenth-Century Novel*, 147–81. New York: Cambridge University Press, 1984.

Stallman, R. W. " 'The Sacred Rage': The Time-Theme in *The Ambassadors.*" *Modern Fiction Studies* 3 (1957): 41–56.

Stone, Alfred E., Jr., ed. *Twentieth-Century Interpretations of "The Ambassadors": A Collection of Critical Essays*. Englewood Cliffs, N.J.: Prentice Hall, 1969.

Tanner, Tony. "The Watcher from the Balcony: Henry James's *The Ambassadors.*" *Critical Quarterly* 8 (1966): 35–52.

Thurber, James, Mark Van Doren, and Lyman Bryson. "*The Ambassadors.*" *Invitation to Learning* 1 (1951–52): 364–71.

Tintner, Adeline R. *The Museum World of Henry James*. Ann Arbor, Mich.: UMI Research Press, 1986.

Wallace, Ronald. *Henry James and the Comic Form*, 119–36. Ann Arbor: University of Michigan Press, 1975.

Walton, Priscilla L. *The Disruption of the Feminine in Henry James*, 101–19. Toronto: University of Toronto Press, 1992.

Ward, J. A. *The Imagination of Disaster: Evil in the Fiction of Henry James*, 110–26. Lincoln: University of Nebraska Press, 1961.

Warren, Austin. "The New England Conscience, Henry James, and Ambassador Strether." *The Minnesota Review* 2 (1962): 149–61.

Wegelin, Christof. *The Image of Europe in Henry James*, 86–105. Dallas: Southern Methodist University Press, 1958.

Weinstein, Philip M. *Henry James and the Requirements of the Imagination*, 121–64. Cambridge, Mass.: Harvard University Press, 1971.

Wilt, Judith. "A Right Issue from the Tight Place." *Journal of Narrative Technique* 6 (1976): 77–91.

Woolf, Judith. *Henry James: The Major Novels*, 83–102. Cambridge, Eng. Cambridge University Press, 1991.

NORTON CRITICAL EDITIONS

NORTON CRITICAL EDITIONS